Adolescent Psychology Around the World

Edited by Jeffrey Jensen Arnett, Ph.D.
Clark University, Worcester, MA

Ψ Psychology Press
Taylor & Francis Group

NEW YORK AND LONDON

Published in 2012
by Psychology Press
117 Third Avenue
New York, NY 10017
www.psypress.com

Published in Great Britain
by Psychology Press
27 Church Road
Hove, East Sussex BN3 2FA

Psychology Press is an imprint of Taylor & Francis Group, an Informa business

Typeset in Times by RefineCatch Limited, Bungay, Suffolk, UK
Printed and bound by Sheridan Books, Inc. in the USA on acid-free paper

10 9 8 7 6 5 4 3 2 1

Library of Congress Cataloging-in-Publication Data
Adolescent psychology around the world / Jeffrey Jensen Arnett, editor.
    p. cm.
Includes bibliographical references and index.
ISBN 978–1–84872–888–2 — ISBN 978–1–84872–889–9   1. Adolescence—Cross-cultural studies.   2. Adolescent psychology—Cross-cultural studies.   3. Teenagers—Cross-cultural studies.
I. Arnett, Jeffrey Jensen.
HQ796.A3344 2012
155.509—dc22   2011015707

ISBN: 978–1–84872–888–2 (hbk)
ISBN: 978–1–84872–889–9 (pbk)
ISBN: 978–0–203–80912–9 (ebk)

Adolescent Psychology Around the World

Contents

Preface

This book paints a portrait of adolescent psychology in four major regions: Africa/the Middle East, Asia, the Americas, and Europe. It is intended to address the imbalance between where most scholarship on adolescence is concentrated and how the vast majority of the world's adolescents actually live. The publication of the book comes at a propitious time. Growing attention to the phenomenon of globalization has reached the field of adolescent research, and scholars in the West today are increasingly aware of the necessity of expanding their awareness of the cultural context of adolescent development. Among the general public, too, awareness of globalization has led to increasing interest in understanding how people in different cultures live.

This book is an abridged and updated version of the two-volume *International Encyclopedia of Adolescence* published by Routledge in 2007. Although it contains fewer chapters than the encyclopedia, the international scope of this book is broad. Most of the chapters are on non-Western countries. The lives of the adolescents in these countries provide an especially sharp contrast to the lives of adolescents in the West. For example, although in industrialized countries adolescence is typically associated with attending secondary school, the reader of this book will find many countries where attending school beyond the early teens is the exception rather than the rule, especially for girls. By that age many adolescents in developing countries have left school to assist their parents on the family farm or to go to work in a factory in order to contribute to their family's income.

Alas, not all regions of the world are equally represented. Finding authors for the countries of Africa and the Middle East proved to be the most difficult challenge. Many of these countries have a limited tradition of social science research. Nevertheless, we were able to include several chapters from countries in this region, including Cameroon, Nigeria, Morocco, and Sudan.

The book is intended for courses in adolescent psychology, lifespan development, and/or cultural (cross-cultural) psychology taught in departments of psychology, human development and family studies, sociology, and education. It will also appeal to researchers and clinicians who study or work with adolescents.

The Content of the Chapters

The introductory chapter explains why the countries were selected and introduces the book's common themes. The section on *Africa and the Middle East* introduces students to teen life in Cameroon, one of the few places left where adolescents go through formal puberty rituals. In addition, readers learn about adolescent life in Ethiopia, Israel, Morocco, Nigeria, and Sudan. Next we travel to Asia—China, India, Indonesia, and the Philippines. Here readers see how India's growth is creating opportunities for young people whereas despite China's growing global economic impact, its political system limits opportunities for change. In *The Americas*, readers are introduced to life in Argentina, Canada, Chile, Mexico, Peru, and the United States. The book concludes with adolescent life in Europe including the Czech Republic, France, Germany, Italy, The Netherlands, Russia, Sweden, and the UK.

Nearly all authors of the chapters were indigenous to the country on which they were writing, and this enabled them to write as informed observers and interpreters of the research evidence available. The authors of each chapter were given a template to follow, so that all chapters would contain information on the same topics, to allow readers to find specific information and to make it easy to compare countries on a given topic. Consequently, all chapters include sections on *Background Information*, *Period of Adolescence*, *Beliefs*, *Gender*, *The Self*, *Family Relationships*, *Friends and Peers/Youth Culture*, *Love and Sexuality*, *Health Risk Behavior*, *Education*, *Work*, *Media*, *Politics and Military*, and *Unique Issues*.

A map is provided at the beginning of each chapter so the reader can see where the country is located and what countries border it. The end of each chapter contains a list of **References and Further Reading**, which includes sources used by the author as well as additional sources that may be of interest. A complete **index** is provided to assist the reader in finding information on a topic that may not be obviously part of a specific chapter section.

Most of the authors of the chapters are psychologists, but contributors also include sociologists, educators, economists, and demographers. Although the majority of them were writing in a language that is not their first language, they wrote with exceptional clarity, and their chapters are a pleasure to read. Together, the authors of the chapters have provided an extraordinary panorama of adolescent life that is compelling and engaging in its diversity.

Acknowledgments

I would like to thank each of the authors who contributed to the chapters in the book. Most of them I have never met and perhaps never will, but I admire the work they have done here. I thank them for what they have taught me in these chapters about adolescence in their countries, and I am delighted for the opportunity to share their chapters with other readers who are eager to learn more about how adolescents around the world experience this dramatic, fascinating, rapidly changing time of life.

I would also like to thank the reviewers, Larry J. Nelson of Brigham Young University, Phillip L. Hammack of the University of California, Santa Cruz, Ramaswami Mahalingham of the University of Michigan, and Lisa Cramer Whitfield of Santa Clara University.

Jeffrey Jensen Arnett
Clark University
Worcester, Massachusetts, USA

Introduction

Adolescence as a field of scholarship is widely viewed as having begun about a century ago with the publication of G. Stanley Hall's two-volume magnum opus in 1904. Hall was an American, and he drew mostly from American and European sources in his description of adolescence.

A century later, the study of adolescence remains a predominantly American enterprise. The Society for Research on Adolescence (SRA) is to a large extent a society for research on American adolescents. At SRA's biennial conferences over 90% of the presentations are by American scholars on American adolescents, and SRA's Journal of Research on Adolescence publishes papers that are almost entirely by American scholars, with an occasional European. The other major adolescent journals are similarly dominated by American and European scholarship.

The dominance of Western scholarship in the field of adolescence is not surprising, given the abundant research resources in Western countries and their relatively long scholarly traditions. "The rich get researched," one might say. However, this dominance is oddly incongruent with the realities of life as experienced by adolescents around the world. Of the world's nearly seven billion people, only about 10% of them live in the West. Furthermore, that proportion is shrinking daily. By the year 2050, the world's population is projected to surpass nine billion, and virtually all of the growth will come from non-Western countries.

This book is intended to address this imbalance between where most scholarship on adolescence is concentrated and how the vast majority of the world's adolescents actually live. The publication of the book comes at a propitious time. Growing attention to the phenomenon of globalization has reached the field of adolescent research, and scholars in the West today are increasingly aware of the necessity of expanding their awareness of the cultural context of adolescent development. In the general public, too, awareness of globalization has led to increasing interest in understanding how people in different cultures live.

The international scope of this book is broad. Most of the chapters are on non-Western countries. The lives of the adolescents in these countries provide an especially sharp contrast to the lives of adolescents in the West. For example, although in industrialized countries adolescence is typically associated with attending secondary school, the reader of this book will find many countries where attending school beyond the early teens is the exception rather than the rule, especially for girls. By that age many adolescents in developing countries have left school to assist their parents on the family farm or to go to work in a factory in order to contribute to their family's income.

Alas, not all regions of the world are equally represented. Finding authors for the countries of Africa and the Middle East proved to be the most difficult challenge. Many of these countries have a limited tradition of social science research. Nevertheless, we were able to include several chapters from countries in this region, including Cameroon, Nigeria, Morocco, and Sudan.

The Content of the Chapters

"Adolescence" is widely recognized by scholars as a socially—and culturally—constructed period of the life course, so it is important in an international volume on adolescence to be clear about how I defined it and why. In view of the vast range of cultures to be included in the book, I wanted to be as inclusive as possible in how adolescence was defined, to accommodate the entire range of perspectives likely to exist across cultures. Consequently, I simply asked authors to cover development during the age range from 10 to 25. Scholars view adolescence as beginning with puberty, and age 10 is when the first outward signs of puberty occur for most girls in industrialized countries (boys usually begin about 2 years later). In recent decades this age has become typical in developing countries as well, as nutrition and access to medical care in these countries has improved.

Setting the upper age boundary of adolescence is more difficult and more subject to cultural variability. Scholars generally view adolescence as ending when adulthood begins, which sounds simple enough—until one tries to answer that question of when adulthood begins. If we use marriage as the quintessential marker, the way anthropologists and sociologists have in the past, then the end of adolescence varies worldwide from the early teens for girls in places such as rural India and northern Africa, to about age 30 for young people in Western Europe. Furthermore, it is highly questionable that marriage is any more the quintessential marker of adulthood around the world, given research showing that young people in industrialized countries no longer regard it as such, preferring psychological markers such as accepting personal responsibility and making independent decisions.

Age 25 was chosen as the upper boundary of adolescence for this book partly for practical reasons. Many international organizations such as the United Nations and the World Health Organization use age ranges up to 24 or 25 years old in the information they collect on "youth" around the world, and those organizations are rich sources of statistics that pertain to many of the topics in the book. However, the question of the age boundaries of adolescence was also explicitly addressed in the chapters. Each chapter contains a "Period of Adolescence" section in which the authors indicate whether adolescence is recognized as a distinct life stage in their country, and if so when it is considered to begin and end.

Age 10 to 25 is a wide age range, and in every culture the typical 10 year-old is vastly different than the typical 25 year-old. For this reason, I also asked authors to describe differences between the early and the later part of this age range. Specifically, I asked authors to address the question of whether a period of "emerging adulthood" exists in their country, that is, a period that takes place after adolescence but prior to full adulthood, during which young people are more independent of their parents but are not yet committed to adult roles (e.g., marriage, parenthood). This period is now widely recognized as a new life stage in industrialized societies, reflecting the later age of entering adulthood in those societies compared to past generations, but it also exists among the urban elite in many developing countries. Emerging adulthood is generally viewed as lasting from about age 18–25, so this was another reason for making 25 the upper age boundary in the book.

Nearly all authors of the chapters were indigenous to the country on which they were writing, and this enabled them to write as informed observers and interpreters of the research evidence available. The authors of each chapter were given a template to follow, so that all chapters would contain information on the same topics, to allow readers to find specific information and to make it easy to compare different countries on a given topic. Consequently, all chapters include the following sections:

Background Information. A brief overview of the nation including topics such as age distribution, ethnic groups, economics, political system, geography, and major historical events.

Period of Adolescence. Addresses whether adolescence exists or not as a recognized life stage; if so, how long it has been recognized as a separate stage of life; when it begins and ends (i.e., age when changes of puberty are first evident and age when full adult status is attained). Also includes topics such as changes in the length of adolescence in recent decades and rites of passage recognizing that puberty has been reached or that adulthood has been attained. If relevant, may address the question, is there a period of "emerging adulthood," that is, a period that takes place after adolescence but prior to full adulthood, during which young people are more independent of their parents but are not yet committed to adult roles (e.g., marriage, parenthood)? If so, does emerging adulthood exist for most young people or only for the elite?

Beliefs. Discusses whether the country tends toward individualism or collectivism, and how these values are taught and whether they are currently changing. Also describes the main religious beliefs and how they are transmitted to adolescents.

Gender. Discusses gender role expectations, including gender-specific preparation for adult work roles, gender-specific physical ideals, and any gender and body image issues that are especially important in adolescence (for example, eating disorders, male or female circumcision).

The Self. Describes the development of personal and cultural identity, including ethnic identity formation among immigrants and ethnic groups. Also issues such as self-esteem and self-concept.

Family Relationships. Topics such as common parenting practices, amount of time spent with various family members, and amount and sources of conflict with parents. Also relationships with siblings, grandparents, and other kin. May include rates and effects of divorce and remarriage.

Friends and Peers. Discusses how much time adolescents spend with peers compared to time with family or alone. If relevant, may describe main peer crowds (defined by common interests in sports, music, devotion to school, or other activities). Includes a description of youth organizations (if they exist) and what the focus of their activity is—sports, social activities, political activities, etc.

Love and Sexuality. May include dating, cohabitation, marriage, sexual experimentation, birth control, pregnancy, sexually transmitted diseases, parental attitudes toward adolescent sexuality, sex education, and homosexuality.

Health Risk Behavior. Discusses the extent to which adolescents have problems such as drug and alcohol use, crime, car accidents, suicide, and depression.

Education. Includes literacy rates, characteristics of secondary schools, participation rates in secondary schools, and gender differences in access to education, as well as performance on international tests of achievement.

Work. Describes work contributed to family and common types of adolescent employment. Also addresses working conditions (e.g., sweatshops, sexual exploitation, slavery). May include apprenticeships and other job training programs, unemployment.

Media. Describes rates of media use by adolescents (including television, recorded music, computer games, mobile phones, Internet, magazines, movies).

Politics and Military. Discusses whether adolescents are involved in politics and in what ways. Also addresses the extent to which adolescents participate in military activities, and volunteer work/community service if common.

Unique Issues. Issues pertaining to adolescents that are especially important in the country but have not been covered by the other entries.

Most of the authors of the chapters are psychologists, but contributors also include sociologists, educators, economists, and demographers. Although the majority of them were writing in a language that is not their first language, they wrote with exceptional clarity, and their chapters are a pleasure to read. Together, the authors of the chapters have provided an extraordinary panorama of adolescent life that is compelling and engaging in its diversity.

SECTION I
Africa and the Middle East

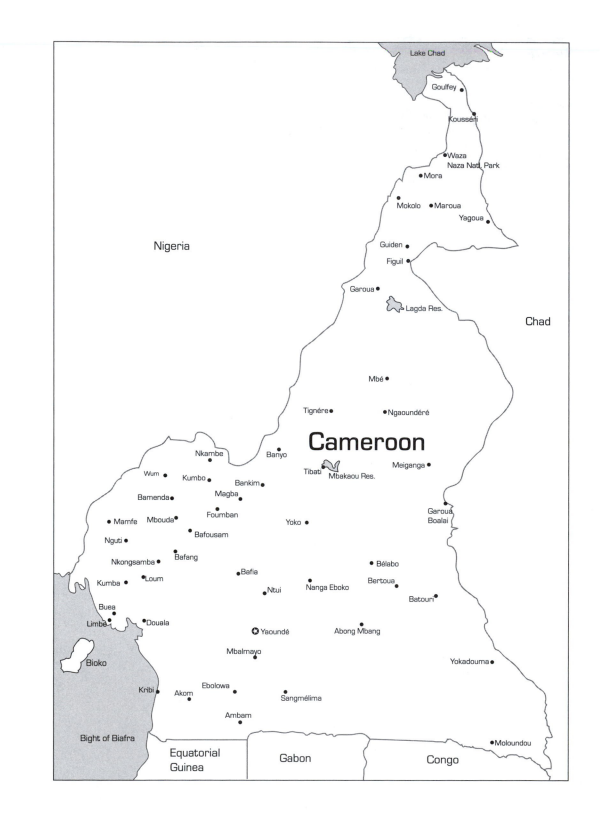

Chapter 1
Cameroon
Therese Mungah Shalo Tchombe and
Josephah Lo-oh

Background Information

Cameroon's population of 16 million is 71% Francophone and 29% Anglophone, with about 279 ethnic groups. About 230 African languages are spoken in Cameroon. Cameroon has abundant natural resources and favorable agricultural conditions. The main exports are cocoa, coffee, rubber, cotton, bananas, petrol, timber, and aluminum. The political system of Cameroon is multiparty, with a democratically elected government.

The geography of Cameroon is characterized by plateaux and mountain chains, with the highest being the volcanic Mount Cameroon. Types of terrain are savannah, humid grassland, rich volcanic soil, and equatorial forest. Climatic features are equatorial and tropical with two major seasons, dry and wet.

Major historical events include the granting of the independence of French Cameroon on January 1, 1960, and the reunification of the British and French colonies on February 11, 1961 (Carte Scolaire du Cameroun Annuaire Statistique, 2003–2004).

Period of Adolescence

Biologically, pubertal changes are generally first evident between the ages of 10 and 14. Puberty is a period marked by sensitization to appropriate gender identity and roles. Among many ethnic groups in Cameroon, adolescence is ushered in by puberty rites of initiation. The Bamileke ethnic group of the western region, for example, terms 6- to 12-year-olds *mooh-goh* ("girl child") and *mooh seup* ("boy child"). The 12- to 15-year-olds are known as *tchieu-goh* ("young girl") and *tchieu-seup* ("young boy"). They can participate in ceremonies and rituals. The age period 12–15 is marked by retreat and isolation in gender groups in preparation for the transition to adulthood. Boys are given instructions about their roles as men and girls are trained to be good wives and mothers.

During their period of isolation, adolescents are told stories about the culture, the strengths and weaknesses of their ethnic group and the values they should emulate. They are instructed on the tribal wars fought and the outcomes. Narratives are presented on land issues and intermarriages with other tribes with whom there have been disputes. Major activities are initiation into farming, trading, construction, production of traditional tools, and solidifying age-group membership.

The 15- to 20-year-olds are known as *goh* ("girl") and *seup* ("boy") They are at the age of marriage, with total submission to parents, elders, social laws, and regulations. During this stage, young people visualize themselves as proto-adults who have just completed training in adult roles and are currently practicing what it means to live acceptably in the adult community. The social internship is designed to cultivate virtuous character and instill values of cooperation and generosity. Puberty rites mark the point at which adolescent boys and girls begin to take their place in cultural affairs of society, first as their parents' representatives and later in their own right, particularly for boys.

Typically, the initiation of adolescent boys includes circumcision, a collective affair performed before the community. For adolescent girls initiation is subtler and less public as it focuses on training for proficiency in housekeeping and reproduction, accompanied by rites concerned with fertility. Among the Kom, the girl child may be subjected to a "family bath" or "public bath" ritual to ensure fertility. This ritual requires that the eldest of the family, such as the mother, grandmother, or a community notable or herbalist, bathes the girl child in cold fresh water and gives her some to drink. The bathing is believed to clean the womb of all forms of dirt, including any previous irresponsible sexual activities that might have contaminated the womb.

Full adulthood status requires being married with one's own property (Nsamenang, 1992).

The socialization of some Cameroonian youth is changing, being affected by prolonged schooling as well as by urbanization and commercialization (Nsamenang, 2002). A longer adolescence, and a form of emerging adulthood, exists for the minority of individuals going on to tertiary education and lacking financial autonomy (Durkin 1995).

Beliefs

African values are essentially relational and interdependent, not individualistic and independent (Turnbull, 1979). In Cameroon, ties between individuals are collective because each person is expected to work for the common good of society. From birth children are educated and initiated into cohesive ingroups where a strong notion of interdependence is felt and practiced throughout life. The adolescent period is more complicated today because of the conflicting values from more individualistic cultures due to globalization. Nevertheless, the various strands of Cameroon's rich cultural values continue to promote the development of a sense of responsibility to care for others.

Religious beliefs are central in the lives of Africans. About half (40%) of the Cameroonian population practices traditional African cult worship (World Guide 1997–1998). Christians are a majority in the south (40%), while Islam (20%) predominates in the north (Carte Scolaire du Cameroun Annuaire Statistique, 2003–2004). These traditional religious practices vary in expression among different ethnic groups. For example, with the Kom the cornflour sacrifice by the girl adolescents coincides with goat sacrifice by the boys. Both sacrifices are intended to recognize the fact that the individual has come of age and can now provide food to their kin and ancestors. With the cornflour sacrifice, usually heavily attended by elderly women, the girl provides large quantities of corn (maize), a staple food of the Kom people, filled in a huge basket to the brim. The maize is shared among participants and as they eat it and carry some home, the girl who offered the sacrifice is believed to have fed her female kin and ancestors.

The goat sacrifice by the boy carries the same understanding as the cornflour sacrifice. It requires the provision of fowls and a goat by the boy, which are slaughtered and shared among elderly men. This is offered at the death of a biological father or each maternal aunt. Unless these sacrifices are performed, it is believed the adolescent will remain stagnant and may never succeed in life. As the adolescent boy approaches adulthood, he is expected to offer a goat sacrifice for a maternal aunt or uncle and also for his father.

Gender

Gender role expectations are embedded in the socialization process, with a focus on the reproductive role functions of females and the productive role functions of males. Orientation to specific gender roles is necessary in order to prepare adolescents for the gendered work they will take on as adults. This orientation is led by the same-sex parent, older siblings, and extended family members living with the family. They model appropriate gender roles for adolescents. Observation and participation in the apprenticeship model prevails.

At the age of seven, gender differential preparations begin in earnest. Mothers in Cameroon inculcate gender-specific skills in the girl child, including how to care for children, how to cook, basic hygiene, and female ethics concerning good morals and habits. In some tribes, skills for attracting the attention of potential husbands are taught. In the Kom these may include good cooking habits, respect, obedience, hard work, housekeeping, home management, sibling care, and cleanliness.

It is feared that when girls explore, they may easily get hurt. They are also restricted from extensive explorations of their immediate environment for fear of impeding their ability to get married and have children. The dream of parents in the Kom is to successfully have their girls married. Exploring may put them to risks of getting sexually involved and this may lead to loss of virginity or unwanted pregnancies, which may reduce their possibility of finding a husband. Meanwhile boys are oriented more toward activities that encourage explorations of the wider community, whereby more knowledge of the environment is acquired, given their future roles in the family and society as a whole. By exploring their environment, boys learn skills such as hunting, masquerade dancing, farming, and community labor with which they are able to live independently and support their families.

In a longitudinal study on the psychological value of education in preparing the adolescent for living in Cameroon, findings showed that parents engaged more adolescent boys than girls in family work (Tchombe & Nsamenang, 1999). There is a prevalent belief that employing boys ensures continuity, as girls will eventually belong to another family through marriage. In rural more than urban settings, boys hunt and fish with their parents. In agricultural settings, adolescents (both males and females) work on farms. Parents insist on these orientations to build self-reliant skills in their adolescents and to encourage them to appreciate manual work and nature. In a country whose main economic activity is agricultural, parents help their adolescents to build up a gender schema through gender-linked activities. Gender division in agricultural skills of adolescents is visible in the Kom. Boys get into the more muscular skills of hunting, clearing of farms, felling of trees, and transporting crops from farm to home. They are also responsible for providing wood for the drying of maize. The girls on their part do hoeing, weeding, and harvesting. They have to care for the crops until they are ready for harvest.

Both boys and girls copy adolescent modes of other cultures in terms of weight-watching and hair styles. They also pierce their ears and noses and wear rings or earrings. Body tattoos are done to beautify the body and as a group membership symbol, mainly around the arms and palms of the hands.

Male and female circumcision is prevalent in Cameroon. Adolescence is marked by initiation rites, with male circumcisions taking place in traditional settings, although today most families would circumcise their male child immediately after birth. Ninety-three percent of males are circumcised according to 2004 statistics. Lower rates of male circumcision are prevalent among males in the far north (62%), the rural areas (87%), and the nonreligious (77%).

Female circumcision, also known as female genital mutilation (FGM), is a traditional practice that is performed primarily on children and adolescents and also on some adult women. Circumcision is undertaken during a special ceremony after which the circumcised are taught how to dance. However, currently only 1.4% of women are circumcised (Institut National de la Statistique (INS) et ORC Macro, 2004). It is more common for women between the ages of 20 and 24 to be circumcised among rural populations (2.1%) and populations living in the far north (5.4%), the north (2.2%), and the southwest (2.4%). Uneducated women (4.7%) and Muslim women (5.8%) also engage more in this practice. The prevalence of FGM has dropped over the years with international campaigns against FGM. There has been a lot of education and sensitization that has brought these practices to an insignificant level. Cameroon's legal system has also stood against these practices.

While some women think FGM violates the physical and mental rights of the girl and woman, others say it protects the integrity of the woman and is a valuable cultural heritage. It is also seen as having aesthetic, medicinal, and socioeconomic benefits while maintaining the sexual purity of the woman before marriage.

The Self

Formation of identity in the Cameroonian context is nurtured in shared roles. Accordingly, a balanced sense of self and one's emerging identity is circumscribed by a sense of place within an extended family that is perceived as part of the community. The values implied in social processes override personal identity, thus reducing crises of self-identity among Cameroonian adolescents. Although the independent self is a prevailing construct in Western cultures, in Cameroon the self is characterized by a fundamental connectedness of persons to each other (Oerter, Oerter, Agostiani, Kim, & Wibowo, 1996).

In the Cameroonian setting, the interdependent self is viewed not as separated from the social context but as more connected and less differentiated from others. Accordingly, personal identity can be defined within a social group structure. For example, among the Fulanis, a Muslim ethnic group, cultural identity is characterized by dress code and praying models. Their dressing and attitude to prayer is supposed to respect the prescriptions of the Holy Koran. For Bakwerians, cultural identity entails excellence in activities such as hunting, fishing, preparation of traditional food, and the enhancement of physical beauty. Among the Kom, cultural identity can be measured by the ability to speak the traditional language, prepare local food and show respect for elders.

Of necessity, adolescents construct and modify their social identities through successive interpersonal encounters and experiences making up their individual history. In response to societal expectations, adolescents construct gender and ethnic identities consistent with cultural scripts and gender demands of their worldviews and economic obligations (Nsamenang, 2002). Girls are socialized to see marriage, good wifehood, and raising children as self-defining. Getting married becomes the ultimate ambition for most female adolescents. Adolescent boys already begin to see themselves as future family heads.

Adolescents have little time to be alone. Most often adolescents are either with parents at home or on the farms, in the family compound with siblings and extended family members, with peers at schools and universities, or in the neighborhood.

Family Relationships

Adolescents are socialized to consider the family as comprising people beyond the nuclear family unit. Parents generally require obedience, yet with much care and love. For various reasons such as poverty, death, problem children, and distance from schools, many children are not brought up by their biological parents but by uncles, aunts, cousins, grandparents, or elder siblings. These family members take care of the children as they would their own biological children. This communal spirit is a hallmark of family solidarity in children's upbringing.

Incidence of conflict between parents and adolescents is visibly connected with problems of participation in family chores, appropriate dress code, and personal hygiene. Related more to late adolescents are conflicts about dating, cohabiting, late nights, alcohol use, and smoking. More intense conflict with girls is about matters related to sex and choice of friends. A major source of conflict is not only the amount of financial allowance allocated but the demand by parents for accountability on how the money has been used.

Siblings constitute the basis for establishing relationships and practicing social values. Usually adolescents are left with the responsibility for directing and caring for younger siblings. These inter-sibling activities are characterized by helping with homework, bathing, and preparing evening dinners. An emerging sense of interdependence among siblings develops skills for interpersonal relationships and understanding.

In most households there are what we call "house helps" or "fictive kin." These are usually employed into the household as domestic servants; however, usually without any prearranged financial package. They live as members of that household and also receive benefits such as educational and apprenticeship opportunities. Some of them would have been with the family from the time most of the adolescents were born. The house helps see to the hygiene and welfare of the adolescents and are very caring and protective. Others found in the household would be extended family members (such as cousins, grandparents, uncles or aunts, and friends' children). Each one of these persons significantly influences the lives of the adolescents as a source of information and counseling.

The divorce rate, especially among adolescents in the Muslim community, is high and remarriage is very common, though not approved of by society. However, there are no specific statistics to demonstrate this observation. Remarriage is more common for men than for women.

It is uncommon to find arranged marriages in Cameroon today. However, marriage is a family affair and there are three stages that are usually followed. The first step is the traditional marriage with two levels, beginning with the introductory phase to establish family contact. At this phase the girl's family gives orientations on the conduct of the traditional marriage process. After the fulfillment of all traditional rites, such as payment of dowry for those who request it and giving presents, the girl becomes the wife of the said family. The second step is the civil marriage in court. The third is the religious marriage for those who respect this tradition. At each stage there are celebrations financed by both families, even though the intending husband and his family play a greater role in most sub cultures.

Friends and Peers/Youth Culture

Cameroon is known for its sporting activities, especially football (soccer). Peer group affiliation is sometimes a function of love for the same football team. Other sporting activities with peer crowds are basketball and table tennis. Many youth organizations exist, based around sports or religious, social, or political activities.

Peer groups are also defined by an involvement in songs and dance, as is the case with those who can dance the *fumban* (female dance) and the *ilung* (male dance) of Kom, also known as ballet. Kom ballet dance is not the conventional Western style of ballet. Kom ballet is characterized by graceful and dignified body movements performed during very special traditional celebrations. Females dress differently from males and dance using a rhythm that is soft, gentle, and elegant. The females dance apart from the males. The dressing and rituals that accompany the dance are very rich and colorful.

Other peer groups are bound by their interest in academic excellence. Their main activities center on educational activities such as study groups; they search for information and continue discussions on school assignments.

Peer groups that meet and hang out in the streets also exist. Some focus on business; others on crime. Three categories can be applied to Cameroon (as have been applied to Mexican street children by Peralta, 1995): (1) Independent street workers; some of these attend school. They work to help their families and to earn enough money to be able to continue their education. (2) Family street workers; the children in this group work with other family members selling food and other things. These children are part of a family unit working in the street. (3) The most troubled group are the children who are homeless. Adolescents in this group are more likely to admit involvement in illegal work, gang membership or drug abuse, and serve time in institutions.

There is a distinct youth culture, in both urban and rural communities, that is marked off from adult culture by dress, hairstyle, tattooing/piercing, music, and slang. Adolescents are interested in new modes of style and self-expression. Their dress code, music, sports, and other ideals are all the latest fashions of the Euro-American cultures, though they will always return to their own cultural modes, especially during traditional festivals. Tattooing and piercing seem to be coming back into fashion. This is as much a traditional African cultural practice as a Euro-American one.

Love and Sexuality

Traditional beliefs in Cameroon restrict sexuality to procreating, with both boys and girls encouraged to delay sexual activity until they can assume more productive responsibilities and become emotionally mature (Nsamenang, 2002). Nevertheless, about 40% of adolescents attending school are sexually active. Rwenge (2000) stated that the average age at first intercourse was 15.6 years for males and 15.8 for females. The main reason given for initiating sexual activity was curiosity (53% of males and 42% of females). Some 37% of females and 30% of males, however, said their first sexual experience had not been voluntary. According to a UNAIDS (2008) report, more girls (26%) than boys (18%) have had sexual intercourse before the age of 15, but more males (31%) than females (6%) reported having had sex with more than one partner in the past 12 months.

Although physical attraction is the main reason for most romantic relationships among adolescents, the desire for material and/or financial gain closely follows as a motivation for sexual relationships (Temin et al., 1999). In some major city centers in Cameroon, one can find commercial sex workers, some of them school drop-out adolescent girls.

Marriage is a family issue because in the African traditional context you marry into a family, not to an individual. Early marriage during adolescence, i.e., before age 15, is encouraged only by some ethnic groups (such as Muslim families and girls in rural areas). Early marriages ensure girls' virginity, attract a dowry, allow early entry into the roles of wife and mother, and avoid the fear of the HIV/AIDS scourge that results from engaging in multiple partnerships and increasing sexual experimentation.

Sex education was, and in some cases still is, handled through initiation rites, chaperones, folklore, and the orientation of adolescents to acceptable sexual behaviors by grandparents through oral tradition (Tchombe 1998). In schools, sex education is taught as an integrated topic through other disciplines.

Birth control is not an open topic for discussion, as parents see this as encouraging adolescents' promiscuity, though some adolescents are already using condoms and pills. For some adolescents condom usage is problematic because it signifies lack of trust and undermines emotional relations. However, a variety of folk remedies (quinine tablets, whisky, and traditional herbs) are used in an effort to prevent pregnancy or induce menstrual flow among adolescents (Njikam, 1998; Tchombe 1998).

A report of UNAIDS (2008) on Cameroon revealed that at the national level the prevalence of HIV/AIDS among those aged 15–49 years in 2007 was 5%. This report stated that young people aged 15–24 years were the highest affected group, at 5.5%. There are more women (4.3%) with HIV/AIDS than men (1.2%). There is marked evidence of a general downturn in HIV/AIDS infection in Cameroon in the late 1990s and early 2000s.

Parental attitudes towards adolescents' sexuality are closed, since sex is sacred and a taboo subject that must not be handled outside marriage. A way of checking in traditional settings to see if an adolescent girl has had intercourse is through the use of an egg (Njikam 1998). When a daughter is suspected of being promiscuous, the mother takes an egg with the rounded end facing her and places the pointed end in the opening of the vagina with the girl lying on her back. Passage will be difficult if the girl has never had intercourse, but not if she has.

Health Risk Behavior

Although there are no specific studies on rates of substance use among Cameroonian youth, it is normal to observe adolescents in secondary schools in towns such as Yaounde in groups smoking or drinking alcohol during school hours. Drinking is a highly social activity during adolescence and is expected in a peer context, as their social life is organized around drinking sites.

Adolescents may engage in delinquent acts such as robbery, fights, and use of guns and knives. If they are caught for these infractions, they are taken to the courts as minors. Some are sent to reformatory schools.

The desire to be slim is a phenomenon of almost all urban adolescents and can lead to anxiety, eating disorders, and depression. But in traditional African settings, an aspect of initiation rites for girls is to fatten them up. Among the Kom and most of the ethnic groups in the grass fields of Cameroon, young girls, especially those that are engaged for marriage, are put on a special diet of food rich in fats and oil. The intention is partly to fatten and freshen them up and also to improve on their beauty. Specifically in the Kom, these girls are made to eat a lot of meat (dry meat in particular) mixed with much palm oil.

Education

The literacy rate in Cameroon is increasing. The adult literacy rate is 63%, and about 70% of adolescents are literate and 80% of children in Cameroon attend primary school. Education in Cameroon is generally Eurocentric in its content and approach because it was established in colonial times. Consequently, it is not adequately suited to the African thought system and its processes. Traditional education expects that through engagement in everyday activities within the family, the child by the period of adolescence would have completed his or her education, addressing physical, social, intellectual, and practical skills.

Cameroon's educational system has two subsystems (English and French), each with its own programs and examination practices following its colonial heritage. Secondary education is offered by the government as well as lay-private and religious groups. The schools are coeducational or single-sexed, with boarding and day facilities offered in varying degrees. Secondary education, which is not compulsory, is a seven-year program for first and second cycles, with five years for the first cycle. Each cycle ends with public examinations.

About 50% of adolescents attend secondary education and 20% attend higher education. Although with no specific statistics, we find that boys outnumber girls in gaining access to school, but girls are more likely to pass the exams at the end of the cycles than the boys. The closing of the gender gap in terms of access to education is notable, particularly with the increasing awareness of the importance given to girls' education on the international scene. This new trend has had a positive effect on the attitudes of Cameroonian parents towards the education of their daughters. Today, there seem to be more girls than boys attending higher education in Cameroon.

Work

Families in Cameroon expect adolescents to participate in household chores and other family engagements as their contribution to the family. For example, adolescent boys and girls from the Fulani tribes take cattle to the field for grazing as early as 8 a.m. until 2 p.m. daily. This contribution enables them to own their herds of cattle by the age of 17 years. Even though girls stay at home and take care of younger siblings, clean the compound, and wash dishes, they are expected to milk the cows and sell the milk. In the absence of brothers and fathers, girls are also expected to take the cattle for grazing. Even adolescent street workers share their proceeds by paying their fees and those of younger siblings for buying food and medications.

Although this may be the case for working-class adolescents in rural towns, in middle-class families other types of engagement are insisted upon. These homes have paid house helps, but parents insist that their adolescents should not leave all the house chores to the house help. They should also clean and wash. So, in the Cameroonian family tradition, each family member, according to his or her ability, contributes to the welfare of the family to varying degrees. Yet striking a balance between academic demands and domestic work puts a lot of stress on the adolescents.

Adolescents are engaged in income-generating activities through jobs such as driver, mechanic, car washer, hairdresser, and clerical worker. They also work as domestic servants and gardeners. There are elements of exploitation, which adolescents tolerate because they need money. In some cases the conditions are good in terms of payment, working hours, and even access to resources for health problems.

Unemployment is a source of social ills, leading to increasing numbers of delinquent adolescents. The current youth unemployment rate is 9%. With increasing school enrollment and more youths making the effort to qualify, the urgent challenge facing the Cameroonian government is to create job opportunities for those with more education.

Media

Adolescents spend some of their leisure time on watching TV, playing computer games, and participating in video clubs. They also spend time at cybercafés, exploring the Internet through chatting and watching pornographic films. Since the reading culture is low, only 1% of adolescents read newspapers, but they read magazines that have love and beauty information. In the case of music, they tune to both foreign and national music channels and are seen carrying radios around.

Cameroon's indigenous culture is threatened by the culture of other countries as brought in by television and the computer revolution. Endangered aspects include music, manners of dressing and expression, arts and crafts, as well as cinema. For example, music from Congo or the USA eclipses Cameroonian music. The rate of media use by adolescents is higher in urban areas in Cameroon than in rural areas because practically all homes in towns have TV. With TV in public places such as bars and restaurants, many adolescents with no TV at home stay out late to watch TV, particularly during World Cup football games.

Politics and Military

Adolescents in Cameroon are involved in politics, serving more as pressure groups than as political mechanisms. They have served different political parties. The ruling Cameroon People's Democratic Movement (CPDM) has a youth wing for young people aged between 18 and 29. They participate greatly in party political activities and rallies when they are organized. The voting age is 18, and many of the youths fulfill this civic duty. However, it is difficult to determine exactly the percentage of 18–24 year-olds who effectively vote.

In the first decade of the twenty-first century, more adolescents were being recruited into the army and other such services with a brief training period. Youth are recruited into the army through competitive examinations and interviews.

Adolescents engage in volunteer work, community services, and with NGOs helping HIV/ AIDS patients, orphanages, and the poor. They offer services by working in areas such as the botanical gardens and in research activities with development objectives. These free community services have created openings for employment and scholarships for further studies for some youths.

Unique Issues

Today Cameroonian adolescents are growing up in rather difficult times, marked by a lack of resources. Many of them go to school or university but do not have the required basic textbooks to facilitate learning. Furthermore, many youths who obtain educational credentials are unable to find jobs afterwards. Increased rural-to-urban migration in search of jobs, with no assurance of improved life conditions, only increases adolescents' problems. The reverse is sometimes also the case, with urban-to-rural migration due to recession in urban settings.

References and Further Reading

Aptekar, L. (1994). Research on street children: Some conceptual and methodological issues. *International Society for the Study of Behavioural Development Newsletter, 1*(25), 1–2.

Barthelemy, K. D. 1998. Emerging patterns in adolescent sexuality, fertility and reproductive health in Africa. In K. D. Barthelemy (Ed.), *Sexuality and reproductive health during adolescence in Africa* (pp. 15–35). Ottawa, Canada: University of Ottawa Press.

Cameroon National Institute of Statistics (2002). *Principal indicators of the world of work in Cameroon.* Yaounde, Cameroon: CNIS.

Carte Scolaire du Cameroun Annuaire Statistique. (2003–2004). *Central Bureau of Census and Population Studies. 2004. Statistics of Employment in Cameroon. Country Guide. 2001.* Yaounde, Cameroon: Dominique Auzias and Associates.

Drama changes attitudes towards genital mutilation. (2002). Retrieved from http://news.bbc.co.uk/2/hi/africa/2412231.stm

Durkin, K. (1995). *Developmental social psychology: From infancy to old age.* Cambridge, MA: Blackwell.

Enquête Démographiques et Sanitaires. (1994–1999). *Enquête Démographique et de Santé. 2004. Rapport Preliminaire, National Commission for the fight against HIV/AIDS and the Ministry of Health.* Yaounde, Cameroon: Institute National de la Statistique.

Institut National de la Statistique (INS) and ORC Macro (2004). *Enquête Démographique et de Santé du Cameroun 2004.* Calverton, MD: INS and ORC Macro.

Larson, R. W., Wilson, S., Brown, B. B., Furstenberg, F. F., Jr., & Verma, S. (2002). Changes in adolescents' interpersonal experiences: Are they being prepared for adult relationships in the twenty-first century? In R. W. Larson, B. B. Brown, & J. T. Mortimer (Eds.), *Adolescents' preparation for the future: Perils and promise. A report of the study group on adolescence in the twenty-first century.* Ann Arbor, MI: Society for Research on Adolescence.

Larson, R. W., Wilson, S., & Mortimer, J. T. (2002). Conclusion: Adolescents' preparation for the future. In R. W. Larson, B. B. Brown, & J. T. Mortimer (Eds.), *Adolescents' preparation for the future: Perils and promise. A report of the study group on adolescence in the twenty-first century.* Ann Arbor, MI: Society for Research on Adolescence.

Ministry of Higher Education. (2002). *Statistical year book of higher education.* Yaounde, Cameroon: Ministry of Higher Education.

Ngam, F. C. (2002). *The culture, traditions and customs of the Kom people: The last words of an elderly prince of Kom.* Bamenda, Cameroon: Neba Publishers.

Njikam, O. M. (1998). Adolescents' beliefs and perceptions toward sexuality in urban Cameroon. In K. D. Barthelemy (Ed.), *Sexuality and reproductive health during adolescence in Africa*. (pp. 77–90). Ottawa, Canada: University of Ottawa Press.

Nsamenang, A. B. (1992). *Human development in cultural context: A Third World perspective*. London, UK: Sage.

Nsamenang, A. B. (2002). Adolescence in sub-Saharan Africa: An image constructed from Africa's triple inheritance. In B. Bradford Brown et al. (Eds.), The world's youth: adolescence in eight regions of the globe. (pp. 261–304). Cambridge, UK: Cambridge University Press.

Oerter, R., Oerter, R., Agostiani, H., Kim, H.-O., & Wibowo, S. (1996). The concept of human nature in East Asia: Etic and emic characteristics. *Journal of Culture & Psychology, 2*, 9–51.

Peralta, F. (1995). Status report on street children in Mexico City after the 1994 financial crisis. In N. Tello (Ed.), *Rediseñando el futuro: Retos que exigen nuevas respuestas* (pp. 75–87). Mexico City, Mexico: D.R. Plaza & Valdés, UNAM.

Rwenge, M. (2000) Sexual risk behaviors among young people in Bamenda, Cameroon. *International Family Planning Perspectives, 26*(3), 118–123, 130.

Songwe, Omer (2002). Cameroon princess fights mutilation. Retrieved from http://news.bbc.co.uk/2/hi/africa/2547503.stm

Tchombe, T. M. (1998). School-based approach to adolescent sexuality and reproductive health. In K. D. Barthelemy (Ed.), *Sexuality and reproductive health during adolescence in Africa* (pp. 301–319). Ottawa, Canada: University of Ottawa Press.

Tchombe, T. M., & Nsamenang, A. B. (1999). *The psychological value of education in preparing the adolescent for living in Cameroon*. An unpublished longitudinal study funded by the Jacobs Foundation, Zurich, Switzerland.

Temin, M. J., Okonofua, F. E., Omorodion, F. O., Renne, E. P., Coplan, P., Heggenhougen, H. K., et al. (1999). Perceptions of sexual behaviour and knowledge about sexually transmitted diseases among adolescents in Benin City, Nigeria. *International Family Planning Perspectives, 25*, 186–190, 195.

Turnbull, M. C. (1979). *Man in Africa*. London, UK: Pelican Books.

UNAIDS. (2008). HIV/AIDS in Cameroon. *Report on the global HIV/AIDS epidemic*. San Francisco, CA: University of California San Francisco School of Medicine.

UNAIDS/WHO. (2008). *A fact sheet for HIV/AIDS in Cameroon*. Geneva, Switzerland: World Health Organization.

World Guide (1997–1998). Cameroon country profile. Oxford, UK: New Internationalist.

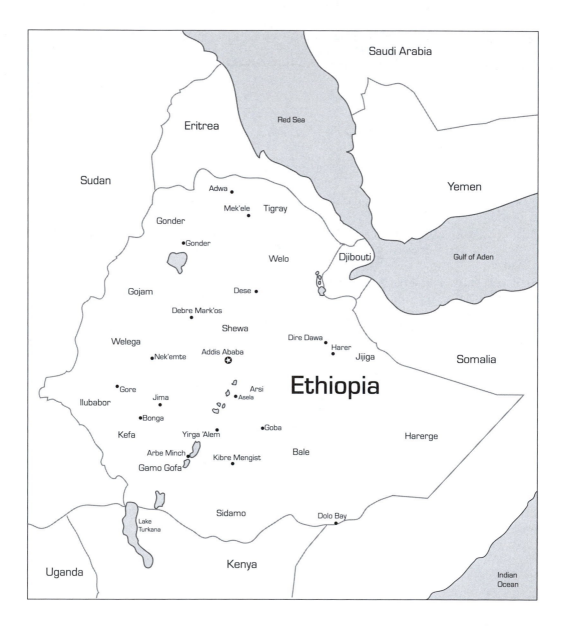

Chapter 2
Ethiopia
Getnet Tadele and Woldekidan Kifle

Background Information

Ethiopia is located in the Horn of Africa and is bordered by Djibouti, Eritrea, Sudan, Kenya, and Somalia. Ethiopia's topography varies from the highest peak at Mount Ras Dashen, which is 4,550 m above sea level, down to the Afar Depression at 110 m below sea level. The climatic conditions differ along with the topography, with temperatures as high as 47°C in the Affar Depression and as low as 10°C in the highlands.

Ethiopia's total population was estimated at about 80 million in 2010. The population is predominantly rural, and urban dwellers account for only 16% of the total population. Persons below the age of 15 account for 45% of the population. Ethiopia is inhabited by over 80 ethnic groups, with the greatest diversity in the southwest, where around 70 languages are spoken. The Oromos, Amharas, Somalis, and Tigrians comprise the largest ethnic groups (35%, 27%, 6%, and 6% of the population, respectively) (FDRE in Ethiopian Society of Population Studies, 2008). In the political and cultural arena of the country, of all ethnic groups, the Amharas and Tigrians have been the most influential historically.

Ethiopia is one of the poorest countries in the world. The average annual income per person is USD220. Agriculture accounts for the highest proportion of GDP, 46%. This is followed by the service sector, which makes up 40% of GDP and records the highest growth. Industry and manufacturing are distant third and fourth contributors to GDP, at 13% and 5%, respectively (World Bank, 2008).

Following favorable changes in the policy environment, there has been a boom in the private sector. This has been characterized by a growing affluent class, especially in Addis Ababa, who are engaged in the importing of manufactured goods and agricultural inputs, the exporting of agricultural products, real estate development, and provision of various services. The telecommunication sector is still a government monopoly, and the financial sector is off limits to foreign investors.

Ethiopia has maintained its independence despite the brief Italian occupation between 1936 and 1941. A military government came into power in 1974, overthrowing Emperor Haile Selassie, but was deposed in 1991 by the Ethiopian People's Revolutionary Democratic Front (EPRDF). The country experienced its first seemingly multiparty election in 1995 (CIA, 2005). As outlined in the 1995 constitution of the country, a parliamentary form of government and an administration based on an ethnic-based federal system of nine regional states and two special city administrations prevail in the country (Library of Congress, 2005).

Period of Adolescence

Considering the wide range of ethnic groups and specific cultures, it is not possible to make generalizations regarding a distinct period of adolescence applicable to all these cultures. In rural societies, the period of adolescence starts earlier than in urban areas, in the sense that children in rural areas are expected to assume responsibilities earlier. Rural adolescents (particularly those who do not attend school) are subject to strict control by their parents while a permissive approach prevails in urban areas.

Different cultural and traditional beliefs and practices result in the period of childhood as well as adolescence being cut short for many, following the expectation to assume and execute adult roles. As a case in point, it is not uncommon for adolescents to get married before they reach the age of 10. This is especially true in rural settings where, despite these acts being proscribed by law, the society is very loyal to its age-old cultural norms. Conversely, in urban settings there is a growing recognition of adolescence as a distinct period in its own right because of the waning influence of traditional cultural values.

Except in some ethnic groups, there is no formal ceremony recognizing the transition from childhood to adolescence or from adolescence to adulthood. The transition from one stage to another is a series of informal processes through which the person accepts increased responsibilities and societal values and norms proper to his or her sex. Marriage and begetting a child mark the transition to adult status. Menstruation is an important defining moment that signals the girl's transition from childhood to puberty (Levine, 1972).

Beliefs

Religion plays a significant role in the lives of Ethiopians. Most people explain both minor events in life and significant events such as disasters (famine, HIV/AIDS, despotic rulers) with reference to God. There is a widespread conception that things happen for a reason and are expressions of God's will.

The most prominent religions in the country are Orthodox Christianity and Islam. Orthodox Christianity came to Ethiopia from the Byzantine world around 340 AD. Islam began a few centuries later after being introduced by merchants from Arabia (Library of Congress, 2005). Adherents of Orthodox Christianity make up 44% and followers of Islam account for 34% of the population. Protestants comprise about 19% of the population. Religions with smaller proportions of followers include traditional beliefs (3%), Catholic (1%), and others (1%) (FDRE Population Census Commission, 2008).

Children and adolescents are oriented and initiated to observe certain religious practices. Most of the orientation takes place in the religious places such as churches or mosques. Parents often take their children to these religious places for this purpose. As the children grow into adolescence, they start practicing the religion on their own, although with implicit observation/supervision by parents, who try to make sure that the adolescents do not go "astray" or become alienated from the rules and regulations of a given religion.

Consequently, adolescents typically take up the religion of their parents. However, conversion is not uncommon, especially to Protestantism, which was introduced very recently compared to the other two main religions, and seems appealing to many youth. During conversion, though, an individual is likely to face fracture of relationships with other family members and relatives, who often put pressure on the person to return. The pressure will be stronger if the converts happen to be adolescents, because of their dependent status in the family.

Collectivism has been the predominant value across the country in all ethnic groups, especially among the vast proportion of rural dwellers, who still live by traditional norms and values. In urban areas, away from one's roots and with the declining presence of the extended families and kin, people tend to adopt individualism.

Overall, it seems that religion and religiosity are reviving in the country after having been relegated to the background during the 17 years of the Marxist regime, and there is a strengthening commitment to fundamental religious identities among Christian and Muslim adolescents and young people these days.

Gender

With the vast majority of the population living in rural areas and often adhering to traditional ways of life, there is widespread inequality and discrimination in favor of men, despite the immense contribution of women to the household economy. Generally, the participation of women is confined to the informal sector and their accomplishments are little acknowledged. Most Ethiopian women spend about eight to 16 hours every day engaged in varied tasks.

The subordinate status of women is something that is reinforced through socialization, where the differential treatment of the sexes is observed consciously and unconsciously. The attitude of the majority of parents is discriminatory against female children. Girls are encouraged to be shy. They start helping parents with challenging tasks about two years earlier than their male counterparts. Educationally, boys are considered more astute than girls (CYO and Italian Cooperation 1995). The government has been implementing affirmative action measures to improve participation of girls and women in higher educational institutions. One such measure is setting the cumulative grade point average (GPA) required for girls to join higher institutions lower than for boys.

A range of body images that are specific to females or males are prompted or condoned in different cultures. The most pervasive of these practices is female genital cutting (FGC). It is practiced for cultural and hygienic reasons. Such interrelated factors that serve as a justification and reinforce the practice include the need to suppress girls' sexual urges and the high importance placed on maintaining virginity until marriage (Alasebu 1985, in Almaz 1997).

The period during which FGC takes place differs among different ethnic groups and cultures. In the southeastern part of the country among members of the Adere and the Oromo ethnic groups, the girl is circumcised between the age of four and puberty. Among ethnic groups in the northern part of the country, circumcision takes place on the eighth day after birth (Missailidis and Gebre-Medhin, 2000). A national baseline survey in 2003 stated that about 90% of women undergo one of four forms of FGC. The first type is incision and refers to "making cuts in the clitoris, cutting free the clitoral prepuce, but also relates to incisions made in the vaginal wall and to incision of the perineum and the symphysis". The second type is clitoridectomy and refers to "partial or total removal of the clitoris". The third type is known as excision and includes "the removal of the clitoris and partial or total removal of the labia minora. The amount of tissue that is removed varies widely from community to community". The fourth type is "removal of the clitoris, partial or total removal of the labia minora and stitching together of the labia majora" (UNFPA 2011).

There is widespread support for female circumcision among Ethiopian women. Women's perception and experience of FGC, though, has gradually been changing. The proportion of women endorsing FGC declined from 60% in 2000 to 31% in 2005, and the proportion of women who experienced FGM was down to 56% in 2007 (Ringheim et al. 2009). A range of beliefs and perceptions perpetuate FGC, including that it eases childbirth, increases fertility, helps control the sexuality of girls, promotes cleanliness, and suppresses the rebellious characters of girls,

A gender-specific bodily alteration popular among the Suri culture, one of the peoples living in southwestern Ethiopia, is the insertion of a circular plate made of wood or clay in the girl's lower lip. The practice is an expression of the girl's attractiveness. The bigger the plate, the more attractive the girl is considered. The plate brings to girls a sense of achievement, and the practice is sustained over time by the high regard that community members have toward the act, and the subsequent exclusion nonconformity entails (Almaz, 1997). The practice is extremely painful and involves the extraction of lower incisors, and piercing and stretching the lower lips to fit the plates in. Scarifications are another popular practice among Suri girls, whereby the girls cut their skin with blades to leave permanent scars on their body. The scars carry specific meanings (BBC, 2008).

Other common gender-specific differentiations toward adolescents include the practice of letting boys come and go from home at any time, with or without parental permission. Women's presence in public space is often sexualized and, except for schooling, church, work, and other accepted reasons, adolescent girls are restricted from going out of the home and occupying public space. As in many other societies, girls tend to be closely supervised and are prevented from spending time with boys/men, as a high premium is placed on the virginity of girls at the time of marriage. Particularly in the era of HIV/AIDS, parents' strict control of girls is inevitable (Tadele, 2005).

A gender double standard has always been in place in Ethiopia and can be attributed to the prevailing inferior social, political, and economic status of women and the imbalance of power in interpersonal relations. Household chores are the exclusive domain of women, and men are not expected to do domestic/kitchen work. In most cases, premarital sex for boys is considered an ordinary course of nature, whereas girls are told that virginity is a prize to be kept for their future husbands.

The Self

Ethiopia is known for peaceful ethnic coexistence. Since the EPRDF assumed power, Ethiopia has been a federal republic composed of a number of seemingly self-governing regions mainly based on ethnicity. In recent years there has been a strengthening of commitment and identity to one's own ethnic group. As a result, minor and major ethnic conflicts have been observed in some parts of the country.

Family Relationships

In Ethiopian society, parents and children are normally not vocal about expressing their affection toward one another. It is uncommon for parents to express their affection through hugging or kissing. There are, though, occasions when parents become very outspoken when they think the child deserves/requires special praise or admonition. If ever appreciation is to be expressed, it is not done one-on-one, but to a third party (Aptekar & Heinonen, 2003; Heinonen, 1996).

Children are supposed to unquestioningly live up to the expectations of their parents. Children are socialized to appreciate the need for giving due respect to parents in particular and adults in general through constant appraisal, which is accompanied by physical punishment, reprimand, and advice. The expression of respect toward others is considered vital to ensure the child's place in the society (Aptekar & Heinonen, 2003; Heinonen, 1996). In rural communities, members of the extended family and neighbors in the village play an important role in the rearing of the child. The role of these groups in urban areas, however, is minimal (Heinonen, 1996).

There are differences in childrearing practices among different ethnic groups and across different socioeconomic classes (Heinonen, 1996). Despite differences in expression, the widespread pattern of childrearing in Ethiopia is authoritarian. In the past two decades there has been evidence of a gradual transition, among educated families or those living in urban areas, to a child-centered type of childrearing (Seleshi & Sentayehu, 1998).

The childhood period in Ethiopia is characterized by little communication between children and parents in the family. There is a general belief that children are subordinate to adults, and hence should express unconditional respect. Failure to live in accordance with these social norms might entail disciplinary measures (Seleshi & Sentayehu, 1998). Fear is also incited by parents as a way of getting children to live up to expectations.

Recent massive socioeconomic and technological changes in Ethiopian society spurred by globalization and modernization have created a gap between young people and their parents. Despite social and economic circumstances that have changed earlier patterns of relationships between parents and children, parents usually refer back to the way they were brought up, and do not seem willing to consider the wide generation gap between themselves and their children in terms of behavior, attitudes, and values. Many parents have difficulty understanding that the world of adolescents today is very different from that of their generation, with many new influences on behavior, including mass communication, the Internet, TV, and radio. Thus, the main causes of disagreement between children and parents include children's reluctance to live by the words of their parents (CYAO & Italian Cooperation, 1995).

Other behaviors traditionally considered appropriate for children and adolescents include not being vocal, not delving into adults' discussion, and not being confrontational with parents. Likewise, parents are not supposed to respond to seemingly "personal questions," or admit mistakes to children (Seleshi & Sentayehu, 1998). Traditionally, whenever parents feel that their children have done wrong one way or another, the most popular measures taken include insulting/cursing, advising, and whipping (CYAO & Italian Cooperation, 1995).

Friends and Peers/Youth Culture

In rural societies, the period of childhood is brief and children are expected to assume different tasks early in their lives. More often than not, they have little playing time. Conversely, in urban settings, adolescents go to video houses, which are ubiquitous, to watch Hollywood movies and listen to popular American music. Such video houses, which are illegal, are found in the capital as well as in towns in the regions. The Ethiopian Television (ETV) network also shows Hollywood movies and music from America. There is a trend of identifying with African American artists in music and film. Adolescents wearing T-shirts bearing pictures of American rap performers are a common sight in the capital and other towns.

Football (soccer) is the most popular sport in the country. Male adolescents are very much into soccer, and watching the Premier League (the top English football league) on television is the most popular weekend pastime for many in the capital and towns.

Ethiopia is characterized by tolerant relationships among adherents of different religions, and it is common for a friendship group to be composed of individuals from different religions.

Cross-sex fraternal friendship, however, tends to be restricted, though it is not completely forbidden in urban areas.

Clubs of various types are often set up in schools. Some of the common forms are anti-HIV/AIDS clubs, children's rights clubs, environment clubs, and girls clubs. Such clubs are often established with the support and initiation of government and NGOs. Other kinds of clubs include music, drama, literature, and sports clubs.

Love and Sexuality

Public dating is tolerated in urban areas, and it is common for unmarried couples to be seen in public. In rural areas a different form of romance prevails, whereby adolescents meet and share intimate moments clandestinely. It is not acceptable in rural areas for unmarried couples to engage in public dating, and sexual intercourse before marriage is strongly prohibited, as a huge value is placed on the virginity of the girl until marriage.

There is a growing tolerance of cohabitation in urban areas. Due to the popularity of this arrangement, the Family Law introduced in 2000 recognizes and provides legal status to such a relationship.

Despite being illegal, abduction is one way of concluding marriage in certain Ethiopian cultures. Every day, on average, eight girls are estimated to be abducted with the intention of marriage. The girls are often captured when they are on their way to/from school or running errands. They are often caught by a group of men including the husband-to-be and his accomplices. The man, via his family and community leaders, will negotiate a bride price (dowry) and make peace with the girl's family, and they will be recognized as a married couple in their community. Lately, the Ethiopian government has taken a strong stand against this cultural practice, The Penal Code revised in 2005 states that abduction is punishable by 10 years of imprisonment, and sexual abuse against minors entails 10 to 15 years' incarceration. All the same, there are strong cultural pressures that discourage the girl's family from reporting abduction. Parents often do not want to go to the police for fear that defying local arbitration, and the publicity of the case, would bring shame to the family. Besides, since the girl has lost her virginity, her chances of marrying another person are slim.

The most common form of marital arrangement, particularly among Christians, is monogamous. Polygamy, though, is commonplace among Muslims and in the southern part of the country. In rural societies, the marriage arrangement is made by parents or clans without the knowledge and consent of the bride. Although the parents have the final say, the groom is involved to some extent. There is a growing practice whereby the groom would inform his parents of the girl of his choice.

A national behavioral surveillance survey identified 16 years as the average age for sexual initiation among the unmarried in-school youth (15- to 19-year-olds). One-tenth of these youths reported sexual experience, with the figures significantly different across gender (15% male, 5% female). Close to three-fifths of sexually active youth admitted not using condoms consistently. A significant proportion of females (15%) reported that they were coerced when they had their first sex (MOH, 2005). The national Demographic Health Survey in 2000 also found that 27% of males and 58% of females aged 15 to 24 were married. The proportion of females married before they reach the age of 15 was higher than that of males (28% and 1%, respectively) (CSA, 2006).

In Ethiopia, homosexuality is so strongly disapproved of that it is virtually impossible to talk about it or come across the topic being discussed. It is not only perceived as a sin or as deviant behavior, but is also illegal. When homosexual acts take place, it is clandestinely, since such acts entail prison sentences ranging from three months to five years. Though not common, some recent studies highlight that homosexuality seems an emerging sexual orientation in the country, especially among the youth. According to an explorative study in the capital city, homosexuality is widely prevalent underground, characterized by gay spaces and symbols. Homosexuals have a diverse profile and include professionals, students in higher institutions, and unemployed youth. Because of the strong stigma attached to the behavior and the legal implications, many disguise their homosexuality by being in a heterosexual relationship and complying with social expectations. The effort against HIV/AIDS seems to disregard homosexuality, and there are few prevention and care services targeting this group (Tadele, 2010; Tadele, 2011).

Health Risk Behavior

Socioeconomic stagnation, poor governance, and war, intensified by recurrent drought and famine, severely affect adolescents and young people and rob them of any vision of a bright future. Many young people end up as street vendors or simply hang around in the town. They are under great economic stress, the precursor of helplessness, depression, self-hatred, and involvement in activities that are commonly known as deviant behaviors (such as the sale of sexual labor; use of drugs such as chat; use of alcohol; theft; rape).

These days, many adolescents are willing to risk their lives in order to get out of Ethiopia. Reports indicate that suicide rates are increasing among young people who succumb to the overwhelming frustration that results from joblessness and failure in educational achievement.

Involvement in crime is another challenge facing adolescents. In some cases, young people organize themselves into gangs which clash with each other. Because of a lack of personnel and facilities, youth are often treated the same way as adults, despite the law specifying a special treatment. There has been a change in this regard with the establishment of Child Protection Units, comprising police officers and social workers, in police stations that tend to the special needs of young offenders and victim children. The involvement of youth in crime is attributed, among other things, to economic deprivation and lack of support (MYSC, 2004).

A study on beggary in Addis Ababa found that about 60% of the beggars in the city were below the age of 30 (MYCS, 2004). For many adolescents and young people street activities such as begging, petty theft, prostitution, and involvement in other deviant and criminal activities have increasingly become the only alternatives for survival, or just part of their daily routine.

Problems of a sexual nature are also widespread and affect a significant proportion of adolescents, particularly females. These include prostitution, abduction, early marriage, and sexual harassment. School girls, especially those who have to travel a long distance between home and school, are exposed to various forms of sexual abuse and exploitation including rape, abduction, and physical abuse. These girls are pushed to quit school. Some live in rented houses in the inner city, away from their families, for fear of being abducted or raped on their way to and from school. What is more, girl students experience various violations on the street, which are committed against them with sexual motives, including name calling, snatching property such as exercise books, threatening, stalking, and persistent requests/advances for sexual favors/relationships. It seems that lack of opportunities, hopelessness and an inability to fulfill customary economic roles and obligations to win the hearts of women has led young men to harass girls and commit sexual violence to boost their masculinity and self-esteem.

A 1992 study on sex workers in 124 towns found that of the 44,707 sex workers, over half (58%) were between the ages of 15 and 24. Widespread poverty, rural-to-urban exodus, early marriage, HIV/AIDS and sexually transmitted diseases, and limited educational and job opportunities exposed adolescents to commercial sexual exploitation (US Department of State, 2005).

HIV/AIDS poses less of a problem for adolescents and youth in Ethiopia than in many other countries in Africa. Prevalence of the virus among males between the age of 15 to 24 ranges between

0.2% and 0.7%. The prevalence rate is higher among females in the same age group (1.1% to 1.9%) (UNAIDS/WHO, 2008), due to early sexual initiation of girls with older men.

Education

The average literacy rate among youth for the period 2003–2007 was 50%. There was a significant difference between male and female youth, with far more males (62%) literate than females (39%). The net primary school enrollment ratio is 74% for male primary-school-age children and 69% for female (UNICEF, 2010).

Despite being exempted from tuition fees, families find it challenging to pay for uniforms and other "hidden costs" of so-called free education. The majority of Ethiopians have little or no education, with females being much less educated than males. In urban areas 46% of adolescents 15 to 19 years old are enrolled in secondary schools, while only 2% of rural adolescents in the same age group are enrolled (DHS, 2000). Literacy levels vary widely among regions, from a high of 68% among women in Addis Ababa to a low of 9% of women in the Somali region. Literacy among men ranges from a high of 87% in Addis Ababa to a low of 16% in the Somali region (CSA, 2006).

The overcrowded schools accommodate, on average, more than 60 students per class (mixed or same sex). Two and sometimes three students sit on logs jammed up close to each other and share a table. In most cases, public and government schools are dilapidated; the desks, chairs, and blackboards are worn out. The level of qualification of the teachers is far from satisfactory. Some of the high-school teachers do not even have an undergraduate degree from a university, and there are no trained teachers for some subjects. Aware of the dwindling remuneration and the ebbing of social respect for teachers, most young people who have succeeded in entering colleges and universities all over the country do not want to be teachers, and many of those who are forced to teach by involuntary placement do not want to continue in this profession. The upshot is that many teachers leave the profession when they find other employment opportunities with NGOs and government organizations.

Because of the scarcity of teachers and the shortage of classrooms and other essential facilities, students attend classes in two or three shifts and have plenty of free time on their hands. About 43% of primary and 70% of secondary schools were functioning in two shifts in 2003. In a society where access to proper recreational facilities are scarce, a shift system presented ample time for some school pupils to indulge in chewing chat and visiting pornographic video houses.

Work

Owing to widespread family poverty, adolescents have to contribute to the household economy to support their families or sustain themselves. This engagement by adolescent members of the family is imperative, considering the complete absence of a social welfare system in the country.

In rural areas, adolescents are expected to be involved in farming, bringing water, gathering firewood, and other household chores. In urban settings, high proportions of adolescents are engaged in various income-generating activities such as petty trade, daily laboring, domestic service, shoe shining, and street peddling such as selling local roasted grain, lottery tickets, newspapers, and the like (Tadele, 2005). Unemployment and underemployment are rampant in both rural and urban settings. With agriculture being the major sector of the economy, education does not guarantee employment.

A common practice across the country, particularly in urban areas such as Addis Ababa, is the migration of adolescent girls to the Gulf countries, including Lebanon, Saudi Arabia, Bahrain,

Yemen, and the United Arab Emirates, to work as domestic servants. Most of them live under appalling working conditions, and there are widespread reports of physical and sexual abuse by employers. There are a few cases of girls committing suicide or retaliating against their abusive employers. Cases in point are the four Ethiopian girls who were reported to have committed suicide in Lebanon in 2009, and an Ethiopian housemaid who allegedly killed her employer in Kuwait in 2008.

Another source of employment for adolescent girls is commercial sex work, which is pervasive in urban and semi-urban cities in Ethiopia. The vulnerability of adolescents to commercial sex work is reinforced by the increasing demand for young sex workers due to the belief that because of their young age, the girls will be less experienced and less prone to HIV.

Media

Radio and TV, which are the most prominent mass media in the country, are controlled by the state. People's access to the media (newspaper, radio, and TV) is generally low. Among those aged 15 to 24, 83% of women and 70% of men have no media access (CSA, 2006).

Ethiopia has one of the lowest mobile phone and Internet penetrations in sub-Saharan Africa. Many contend that the ownership and structuring of the ICT sector are to blame for the dismal state of ICT access in the country. The ICT sector in Ethiopia is under the exclusive control of a public operator, the Ethiopian Telecommunication Corporation. Despite paying lip service to involving private actors in the sector, the government has steadfastly resisted any influence from international development organizations to liberalize the sector. The government holds that public ownership of the sector is in the interest of the general public (Lishan & Woldekidan, 2005).

The media are predominantly indigenous, as local issues constitute much of the content. The potential of media in terms of influencing adolescents is very much recognized. Fairly recently, in urban settings, there has been a public outcry to crack down on illegal video houses, as they are thought to contribute to loss of moral restraint, and involvement in drugs and risky sexual behavior among adolescents. Due to their relative accessibility—mainly cost-wise—these video houses are frequented by adolescents who cannot afford to go to cinemas. The public perceives that porno-graphic films shown in video houses erode the culture and traditions of the society and expose youths to HIV/AIDS and related problems. These days, the common public discourse in Ethiopia is that young people are perceived as a spoiled or morally corrupted generation, rough and bold. They are perceived to be disrespectful of their culture, and more attracted to the Western culture they see on videos and in cinemas.

Politics and Military

The youth were very active in the country's politics about 30 years ago, just before the 1974 revolution that led to the overthrow of the emperor. The military regime that came to power after the revolution used excessive measures to quell the youth from opposing its administration. There was gross torture and killings of several thousand youth, especially in the government measure referred to as the Red Terror. The persecution also resulted in the exodus of adolescents to neighboring countries.

The legacy of that period forced the general public and the youth in particular to shun anything that was considered political. More recently, there was a resurgence in youth participation in politics prior to and after the May 2005 election. There was a huge turnout of youth on voting day, and during political demonstrations for and against the government. Most of those who perished or were detained in various parts of the country during the June and November 2005 election-related unrest and violence were young.

Youth comprise the vast majority of the military, in part because they are driven to the military due to unemployment. Forcibly or with their own consent, many young people found themselves deployed in the civil war that lasted almost two decades during the Marxist regime (1974–1990) and in the two-year border war with Eritrea under the current regime (1998–2000) These wars claimed the lives of many young people.

Unique Issues

The situation of those adolescents living on the street in Ethiopia deserves special attention. According to NGOs operating to address the issue of street children, there are between 500,000 and 700,000 such children in Ethiopia. Addis Ababa, the country's capital, has the largest proportion of the street children population. According to UNICEF (2004), there are approximately 150,000 children working and living on the streets there, devoid of care and support. Females are estimated to constitute one-fourth of the total street children population.

The majority of these children live in conditions of severe deprivation, suffering from inadequate nutrition, exacerbated by exposure to adverse weather and physical abuse while on the streets, which imperils their physical, mental, and social development. They do not have the social, economic, and cultural capital to negotiate life successfully. Their needs are not addressed adequately by either the government or civil society, and they are left to fend for themselves at an early age.

In their own society, they seem to have been marginalized as strangers. They do not have an opportunity to hear from parents and other adults that they are loved, valued, and are important as individuals. They have internalized feelings of neglect and worthlessness, and their lives are characterized by low self-esteem and frequent exposure to substance abuse, poverty, and violence. Too many of them believe that neither the present nor the future offers any promise. Drugs are often used as a way of self-medication to soothe their anger or frustration.

With respect to love and sexuality among street children, although the motives in play are vague, female adolescents on the street, who comprise only a fourth of the street population, often have boyfriends either as a coping strategy to fend off abuse by other male street children or as an expression of a romantic relationship. There is competition for girls among street boys, and it is often older and aggressive boys who seem to have "wives." It is not uncommon for female street adolescents to be forced to embrace commercial sex work as a survival strategy.

Another unique issue is the border conflict between Ethiopia and Eritrea, which has strong negative implications on the welfare of adolescents. This border conflict resulted in massive rural–urban migration and displacement, forcing many adolescents to become street children in urban areas. The conflict between the two countries escalated into full-scale war between May 1998 and June 2000, and resulted in large-scale displacement, expulsion/deportation, and the death of hundreds of thousands of people from both countries. The exact number of casualties of the Ethio-Eritrean war is not known. The governments of both countries have played down the casualties on their side while overstating the losses on the other side.

The two countries agreed to a comprehensive peace agreement and binding arbitration of their disputes under the Algiers Agreement in 2000. Since the early 2000s, tension has increased and there are allegations that the governments of both countries are using this growing tension to distract and suppress internal instability. There is increasing confrontation between the two countries and with the international community that it is feared will escalate into war. The border dispute has not yet been resolved. However, despite the sporadic war of words, there is relative peace at present.

References and Further Reading

Almaz, E. (1997). Issues of gender and sexuality in the context of cross-cultural dynamics of Ethiopia—
    Challenging traditional perspectives. In K. Fukul, E. Kurimoto, & S. M. Kyoto (Eds.), *Ethiopia in broader*

perspective: Volume III, papers of the XIIIth International Conference of Ethiopian Studies. Kyoto, Japan: Shokado Book Sellers.

BBC. (2008). *Tribe: The Suri.* London, UK: BBC. Retrieved from www.bbc.co.uk/tribe/tribes/suri/index.shtml

BBC. (2010). *Ethiopia country profile.* London, UK: BBC. Retrieved from http://news.bbc.co.uk/2/hi/europe/country_profiles/1072164.stm

CIA. (2005). *The world factbook: Ethiopia.* Langley, VA: CIA. Retrieved from www.cia. gov/cia

CSA. (2006). *Ethiopia demographic and health survey 2005.* Addis Ababa, Ethiopia: CSA.

CYAO (Children and Youth Affairs Organization) and Italian Cooperation. (1995). *Research report on child abuse and neglect in selected parts of Ethiopia.* Addis Ababa, Ethiopia: CYAO and Italian Cooperation.

Ethiopian Society of Population Studies. (2008). *Gender inequality and women's empowerment: In-depth analysis of the Ethiopian Demographic and Health Survey 2005.* Addis Ababa, Ethiopia: Ethiopian Society of Population Studies.

FHI/USAID. (2004). *Assessment of youth reproductive health programs in Ethiopia.* Durham, NC: Family Health International. Retrieved from www.fhi.org

Heinonen, P. (1996). *Some aspects of child rearing practices in the urban setting of Addis Ababa (with special reference to street children).* Stockholm, Sweden: Save the Children Sweden.

Hosken, F. P. (1989). *Female genital mutilation: Strategies for eradication.* Presented at The First International Symposium on Circumcision, Anaheim, CA, March 1–2, 1989. Retrieved from www.nocirc.org/symposia/first/hosken.html

Levine, D. N. (1972), *Wax and gold: Tradition and innovation in Ethiopian culture* (5th ed.). Chicago, IL: University of Chicago Press.

Library of Congress—Federal Research Division. (2005). *Country profile: Ethiopia.* Washington, DC: Library of Congress. http://lcweb2.loc.gov/frd/cs/ profiles/Ethiopia.pdf

Lishan, A., & Woldekidan, K. (2005). Ethiopia. In A. Gillwald (Ed.), *Towards an African e-index: Household and individual ICT access and usage across 10 African countries.* Cape Town, South Africa: Research ICT Africa

Lvova, E. (1997). Forms of marriage and the status of women in Ethiopia. In K. Fukul, E. Kurimoto, & S. M. Kyoto (Eds.), *Ethiopia in broader perspective: Volume III, papers of the XIIIth International Conference of Ethiopian Studies.* Kyoto, Japan: Shokado Book Sellers.

Ministry of Foreign Affairs. (2005). *General profile.* Addis Ababa, Ethiopia: MFA. Retrieved from www.mfa. gov.et

MOH. (2005). *HIV/AIDS behavioral surveillance survey. Ethiopia. Round two.* Addis Ababa, Ethiopia: National AIDS Resource Center. Retrieved from www.etharc.org

Missailidis, K., & Gebre-Medhin, M. (2000). Female genital mutilation in eastern Ethiopia. *The Lancet, 356,* 137–138.

Muleta, M. (2004). Socio-demographic profile and obstetric experience of fistula patients managed at the Addis Ababa Fistula Hospital. *Ethiopian Medical Journal, 42,* 9–16.

MYSC. (2004). *National youth policy (2004).* Addis Ababa, Ethiopia: Ministry of Youth, Sport and Culture.

Seleshi, Z., & Sentayehu, T. (1998). *Parenting style differences among selected ethnic groups in Ethiopia.* Addis Ababa, Ethiopia: Forum on Street Children – Ethiopia (FSCE) in cooperation with Save the Children Sweden.

Tadele, G. (2005). *Bleak prospects: Young men, sexuality and HIV/AIDS in an Ethiopian town.* Leiden, The Netherlands: African Studies Centre.

Tadesse, E., & Nigussie, S. (2000). Adolescent pregnancies in Addis Ababa. *East African Medical Journal, 77,* 431–434.

Terefe, H. (1997). Gender and cross-cultural dynamics in Ethiopia with particular reference to property rights, and the role and social status of women. In K. Fukul, E. Kurimoto, & S. M. Kyoto (Eds.), *Ethiopia in broader perspective: Volume III, papers of the XIIIth International Conference of Ethiopian Studies*. Kyoto, Japan: Shokado Book Sellers.

UNAIDS/WHO. (2008). Epidemiological fact sheet on HIV and AIDS: Core data on epidemiology and response: Ethiopia. Geneva, Switzerland: WHO.

UNICEF. (2004). *The state of the world's children 2005 – Childhood under threat*. New York: UNICEF.

UNICEF. (2010). *Ethiopia: Statistics*. New York: UNICEF.

US Department of State: Bureau of Democracy, Human Rights, and Labor. (2005). Ethiopia: Country reports on human rights practices: 2004. Washington, DC: US Department of State.

Voice of America. (2005). Ethiopia–Eritrea stalemate could spark renewed war. 31 March.

World Bank. (2008). *Ethiopia at a glance*. Washington, DC: World Bank. Retrieved from http://devdata. worldbank.org/AAG/eth_aag.pdf

Chapter 3
Israel
Rachel Seginer and Shirli Shoyer

Background Information

Israel was established as a state in 1948, following a 1947 UN resolution to establish a Jewish state in parts of Palestine. At that time, the local population consisted of 640,000 Jews and 1,300,000 Arabs. However, the war that broke out following the UN resolution and the establishment of the State of Israel, as well as the massive immigration of Jews to Israel, led to drastic demographic changes. In 2008, the Israeli population consisted of about 5.5 million Jews, about 1.5 Arabs and Druzes, and about 300,000 non-Jews who were either non-Arab Christian or unclassified individuals (Israel Central Statistical Bureau, 2009). Among the non-Jewish population, 68% are Muslims, 9% are Christians, 7% are Druzes, and 16% are non-Arab Christians or individuals of unclassified religion.

Geographically, Israel is part of the Middle East. Politically, economically, educationally, and culturally it is in line with modern, Western, industrial countries. The establishment of Israel as a democratic Jewish nation state, the Declaration of Independence promising full social and political equality to all its citizens, and the Israeli "Law of Return" granting citizenship to almost every Jew created many inner tensions. Thus, Arabs and Druzes have been citizens participating in democratic life but have not had equal access to educational and economic resources.

Period of Adolescence

Adolescence is a marked developmental period in all sections of the Israeli population. Legally, its end is marked by the minimum age of marriage: 17 years for girls and 18 for boys. While the biological indicator of puberty is individual, entrance into junior high school at age 13 (seventh grade) may be regarded as a collective marker of the beginning of adolescence.

The trend of an extended adolescence and the emergence of the new developmental period referred to as emerging adulthood (Arnett, 2000) that characterizes the Western world has also been prevalent in Israel. One clear indicator is mean age of marriage, which from 1970 to 2009 rose for all major religious–cultural groups (Table 3.1). As entrance to adulthood has been gradually delayed in recent decades, economic, political, and military advancement is slower and army soldiers (aged 18 to 21) are often referred to as "children."

Table 3.1 Mean age of marriage of major Israeli religious–cultural groups in two periods: 1970 and 2007

Religious–cultural group	1970		2007	
	Women	Men	Women	Men
Jewish	22	25	26	28y
Muslim	20	24	21	26
Christian	22	28	24	29
Druze	19	23	21	26

Beliefs

Israel is a multiethnic, multicultural society. As such, it is not possible to describe it as guided by a single value orientation. Instead, some sectors of Israeli society endorse collectivistic orientations and some hold more individualistic orientations. This division overlaps with ethnicity and religious beliefs. Ethnic minorities in Israel, and particularly the Arabs and the Druzes, tend to endorse more collectivistic value orientations than do Jewish Israelis (Seginer, Shoyer, Hossessi, & Tannous, 2007; Seginer & Vermulst, 2002). However, within Israeli Jewish society, orthodox Jews endorse more collectivistic value orientations than do traditional and nonreligious Jewish Israelis.

Israeli Jews celebrate the Bar Mitzvah of their sons (at age 13) and the Bat Mitzvah of their daughters (at age 12). In the majority of families, including families who do not practice religion in everyday life, the Bar Mitzvah celebration also involves a symbolic religious ceremony that takes place in the synagogue and for which the boy prepares himself for several months. Nevertheless, for nonreligious adolescents and their families, the Bar Mitzvah celebration is a family rather than a religious event, and its tone is that of a grand birthday party.

Similarly, for religious girls the Bat Mitzvah marks the beginning of the obligation to follow religious rules (*mitzvoth*), whereas for the nonreligious it is mainly a large-scale birthday party and a big family celebration. A religious Bat Mitzvah ceremony, comparable to that of Bar Mitzvah boys, can be practiced only in Reformist synagogues where women participate in religious ceremonies.

In the seventh grade—the grade in which the majority of children reach their thirteenth birthday—students (girls and boys) work on a family history project devoted to studying and recording their family roots. The children are instructed to trace back the biographical story of their grandparents, underscoring events that have not only family but also national meaning, such as the Holocaust and the survival of the Jewish people and their immigration to Israel. In many schools this assignment is considered a Bar Mitzvah project.

Among the Muslim Arabs and Bedouin tribes in the northern and southern parts of the country no comparable ceremonies take place. Among Christian Arabs, Catholics hold the Confirmation ceremony.

Gender

Israel's Declaration of Independence, announced on May 15, 1948, guarantees "full social and political equality of all its citizens, without distinction of race, creed or sex." Thus, legally, Israeli women of all ethnic groups enjoy equal rights and equal opportunities for education, career, and political participation. In practice, the extent to which legal rights for equality are materialized is specific to both ethnicity and domain. Overall, Jewish women are more emancipated and experience greater equality of the sexes than do Arab, Druze, and Bedouin women. However, given that all matters of marriage and divorce are governed by religious rather than by civil law, women in all groups often suffer greater inequality in these than in other everyday matters.

Globalization of the mass media has led to the rapid transmission of information and values in general and for youth in particular. Consequently, a body image based on the notion that "slim is beautiful" has been adopted by Israeli girls, except for the ultra-orthodox Jewish and traditional Muslim girls. Surveys conducted in 1994 and 1998 (Harel, Kani, & Rahav, 2002) showed that the number of girls describing themselves as overweight was 40% and stayed stable over the years. However, a second survey of the eating habits of Israeli adolescents in the 11 to 15 age group (Harel, Molcho, & Tilinger 2004) showed that although the majority (70%) of Israeli youths think they look good, 24% of 11-year-old girls and 36% of 15-year-old girls think they are overweight. Moreover, although only 10% of 13-year-old girls and 7% of 15-year-old girls suffer from being overweight, 27% of these girls engage in weight-losing diets (Harel et al., 2004). Recent findings concerning 14- to 18-year-old Israeli Jewish adolescents indicate that 20%–30% of girls and 5%–10% of boys are diagnosed with disordered eating, which may develop into full-blown eating disorder syndrome (Latzer, 2004; Latzer, Witztum, & Stein, 2008).

The Self

Israel, as noted previously, is a multiethnic, multicultural society. Hence, issues of personal and cultural identity should be analyzed in their sociocultural context. Among the Israeli Jewish population, the main cultural groups are: the secular Israeli-born, the national-religious (modern orthodox), the ultra-orthodox, immigrants from former Soviet Union countries, and immigrants from Ethiopia. Among the non-Jewish population, the main groups are Muslim and Christian Arabs, Druzes, and Bedouins. For reasons of access and researchers' interests, data on issues pertinent to personal and cultural identity are inconsistent, and cultural identity has been studied especially among the non-Jewish and Jewish new immigrants.

Analysis of self indicators of new immigrants from the former Soviet Union and of veteran Israeli adolescents (Ullman & Tatar, 1999, 2001) showed that while the multiple changes new immigrant adolescents experience did not affect their global self-esteem, adolescents who recently immigrated (less than five years since immigration) were more engaged in self-exploration, as a precondition for forging an Israeli identity and developing a sense of integration and belongingness.

The hegemonic Israeli society in place since the pre-state era has traditionally consisted mainly of East European Jews and their descendants, and the expectation for new immigrants has been to be "absorbed" into this society and adopt its values and norms (Eisenstadt, 1952). Thus, research on new immigrants in general and on recent new immigrants from the former Soviet Union and Ethiopia in particular has been mainly concerned with acculturation patterns. These studies showed that, despite cultural differences, adolescents who immigrated from both the former Soviet Union and Ethiopia were more inclined to balance their established cultural identity and their new Israeli identity than to reject one at the expense of the other (Orr, Mana, & Mana, 2003). Several studies (e.g., Mirsky & Prawer, 1992; Toren-Kaplan, 1995) of adolescents who immigrated from the former Soviet Union during the 1990s showed that only a minority (8% to 27%) considered themselves Israelis, whereas the majority considered themselves either Jews or Russians. Toward the end of their high school education—when Israeli youths start their military service—30% of the former

Soviet Union adolescent immigrants did not want to serve in the army (in comparison to 10% of other adolescents) (Tatar, Kfir, Sever, Adler, & Regev, 1994).

Family Relationships

The majority of Israeli children—46% of the Jewish children and 71% of Arab and Druze children and youth (ages 0 to 17)—grow up in two-parent biological families. The rate of divorce for the Jewish population is almost twice as high as that of the Muslim population (Israel Central Statistical Bureau, 2009).

As in other Western countries, as children grow up and enter adolescence relatively more of their time is spent with unrelated peers than with family members. However, this pattern is somewhat different for Arab and Druze adolescents, for in their culture there is more overlap between family and peer relationships, so that one's social circle consists mainly of kin (Seginer, 1992).

Spending more time with peers does not affect the sense of closeness Jewish adolescents feel with their parents. Several studies conducted in the past two decades indicate that Israeli Jewish adolescents experience warm relationships with their parents. Specifically, in a survey of a random-systematic sample of 13- to 18-year-old Israeli Jewish adolescents, two-thirds of the respondents felt close to their parents, thought their parents readily listened to their problems, and got along well with them (Sherer, Karnieli-Miller, Eizikovitz, and Fishman, 2000). This pattern was also found in an earlier study (Seginer and Flum, 1987) of Israeli Jewish adolescents (aged 14 to 18) where the majority (75%) described themselves as having good relationships with their parents, and over half of them took part in family decision making, felt their parents were proud of them, accepted parents' authority, and would like their future families to be similar to their own families. Overall, the family relationships score of the Israeli Jewish adolescents was higher than that of the American adolescents' norm group.

Adolescent–sibling relationships have been studied in the Jewish, Arab, and Druze communities. These studies (Seginer, 1992, 1998; Seginer et al., 2007) showed that, when asked to relate to the one sibling they considered closest to them, eleventh-graders of all three ethnic groups described relationships with this sibling as consisting of high warmth (indicated by such indices as friendship, intimacy, and admiration) and low negative relationships (indicated by such indices as rivalry, jealousy, and antagonism). However, the meaning of sibling relationships among the three ethnic groups differs. This is particularly reflected in the role of the older sister, considered in the Arab but not in the Jewish families as the "mother deputy" (Seginer, 1992), whose responsibilities change with siblings' age. Whereas at a younger age her responsibilities are mainly in helping her mother with household chores and care of her younger siblings, as the family grows older and the younger sisters (but never any of the brothers) share with her the household chores, the responsibilities of the older sister shift to the interpersonal realm, counseling her younger sisters about issues ranging from school matters to relationships with boys that their mother—leading a more traditional life—is unfamiliar with.

Friends and Peers/Youth Culture

Two surveys (Harel, Ellenbogen-Frankovits, Molcho, Abu-Asba, & Habib, 2002; Sherer et al., 2000) examined peer relationships, focusing on the frequency of spending time with peers after school and on attitudes to friends. Their findings show that of the Jewish respondents, 87% strongly agreed and only 2% disagreed with the statement "it is important for me to spend time with friends" (Sherer et al., 2000). The majority (75% to 80%) of these respondents also reported having close friends for many years who were willing to listen to their problems (66% endorsed the "strongly agree" category).

Moreover, as adolescents move from young (age 13 to 14) to late adolescence (age 17 to 18) they feel closer to their friends, get along with them, and feel friends willingly listen to their problems. In a similar vein, less than 10% reported having only one or no friends (Harel et al., 2002). Separate analyses for Arabs and Jews showed that more Arab than Jewish adolescents (25% and 6%, respectively) reported having only one or no friends. However, the larger number of siblings and greater proximity to extended family among Arabs may explain this difference.

Friendship patterns notwithstanding, time spent with friends is similar for Jewish and Arab adolescents. Specifically, 41% of the Jewish adolescents and 38% of the Arab adolescents spend four or five afternoons each week with their friends, and 19% of both Jewish and Arab adolescents spend five or more evenings per week with friends. Gender differences in number of evenings spent with friends were found only among Arab adolescents. Given that surveillance over girls' conduct is stricter than over boys (Booth, 2002), fewer girls (14%) than boys (25%) spend five or more evenings with friends (Harel et al., 2002).

Historically, in the pre-state era and the early years of the State of Israel known as the Golden Period of intensive nation building, youth movements played an important role in the social life and personal, political, and ideological socialization of Jewish adolescents, and balanced individual and collective goals. Consequently, youth movements contributed to nation building and social development of the Israeli Jewish society (Kahane, 1997). Ideology varied from centrist (Scouts) to moderate socialist (the Working and Studying Youth), leftist socialists (Young Guards), and national religious (Bnei Akiva), but regardless of ideology all Israeli youth movements were characterized by an informal structure (Kahane, 1997).

After the establishment of the State of Israel and the gradual value shift from collectivistic to individualistic orientations, youth movements lost their meaning as the center of peer activities particularly serving as a transitional setting, as well as their role as agents of ideological–political socialization and consequently their public image (Kahane, 1997). The exception has been the national religious Bnei Akiva youth movement, which "has moved in the direction of parochialism, slowly assuming the form of a religious sect ... [Thus] members of the movement tend to express their religious commitment in extra-institutional activities, such as settlement in disputed territories" (Kahane, 1997, p. 94).

As indicated by rate of participation, youth movements attract early rather than late adolescents. Specifically, 26% of Jewish and 23% of Arab ninth-graders but only 15% of the Jewish and 18% of the Arab eleventh-graders belong to a youth movement (Harel et al., 2002). Moreover, youth movements appeal more to Jewish girls than boys and more to Arab boys than girls. The age-related decline in youth movement participation suggests change in the nature of youth movement activities.

Over the years, youth movements have retained the form of their activities: Members convene twice a week (on a weekday and on Saturday) for a structured afternoon or early evening activity, and for more extended activities such as hiking trips or camp activities during school holidays. Altogether, members of Israeli youth movements engage in seven major activities: hiking trips and excursions, camping, political activities, cultural activities, sports, intellectual discussions, and games (Kahane, 1997). However, the underlying messages conveyed by these activities vary with the ideological coloring of each youth movement, age of members, and time. For middle adolescents, youth movement membership also offers an opportunity for personal growth and development provided by acting as youth leaders for groups of younger adolescents.

Love and Sexuality

The prevalence of romantic relationships among Israeli adolescents increases with age. In one study (Shulman & Scharf, 2000) of 168 14-, 16-, and 19-year-old Israeli Jewish adolescents, the number of those reported to be currently involved in romantic relationships rose from 15% to 45% to 51%, respectively. Girls of all age groups were involved in romantic relationships for a longer duration and with greater emotional intensity than boys. With the exception of one large-scale study (Antonovsky 1980), research on sexual behavior among Israeli youths has been limited to a few small-scale studies (Harel et al., 2002).

Although legal, homosexuality is still not socially acceptable in Israel and homosexual and lesbian individuals may suffer discrimination and harassment. According to data published by the Israeli Homosexual, Lesbian, Bisexual and Transgender Association, of the 3,000 individuals asking for help via the Association stress line, 40% were under 22 years of age (Yachad, 2002). The Israeli Gay Youth organization is currently operating 15 branches, offering gay youths both help and a place for social activities. The organization is supported by voluntary and professional organizations as well as by the Ministry of Education, and its activities are led by psychologists, social workers, and professionals in the arts (e.g., theater and creative writing) (Israeli Gay Youth, 2011). It is important to note, however, that both the adult and the youth organizations serve mainly the Jewish secular population. At present, no parallel activities and organizations exist in the Jewish ultra-orthodox, Arab, and Druze sectors.

Health Risk Behavior

Most Israeli adolescents are not frequent drinkers of alcohol. However, comparison of surveys conducted in 1998 (Harel et al., 2002) and in 2009 (Bar-Hamburger, 2009), shows a drastic increase among Jewish adolescents. Thus, whereas in 1998 close to 70% of Jewish adolescents and 80% of Arab adolescents did not drink at all in the 30 days before responding to the questionnaire, in 2009 the rate of abstention among Jewish adolescents was 40%. Among Arab adolescents the rate of abstention was up to 87%. Among both Jewish and Arab adolescents more boys than girls drink at least once a month (37% of the Jewish boys and 22% of the Jewish girls, and 31% of the Arab boys and 10% of the Arab girls) (Harel et al., 2002). The rate of drinking increases with age, so that by tenth grade 39% of the Jewish adolescents (49% of the boys and 28% of the girls) and 18% of the Arab adolescents (31% of the boys and 9% of the girls) drink at least once a month. Incidents of getting drunk were reported by fewer Arab (12%) than Jewish (20%) adolescents.

Data on the smoking habits and attitudes of Israeli adolescents were collected as part of the third international survey on social welfare, health, and risk-taking behaviors in international perspective (HBSC) (Israeli Committee on Disease control (ICDC), 2009). This report shows that the average age of cigarette smoking initiation is 13 and that by the time Israeli adolescents reach tenth grade, 12% of the Jewish boys and 8% of the Arab boys smoke at least one cigarette per day. Recent surveys of the Israeli Ministry of Health (2009) among the 13- to 14-year-old age group show that whereas overall the number of smokers is relatively small, it is higher for Jewish (5% smoke occasionally and 1.6% smoke daily) than for Arab adolescents (3% smoke occasionally and 1.1% smoke daily). Among both groups, smoking is more frequent for boys than for girls.

The Harel et al. (2002) report also indicated that Nargila (hookah) smoking is a popular social pastime among Israeli adolescents: 48% and 37% of the Jewish tenth-grade boys and girls, respectively, and 33% and 5% of the Arab tenth-grade boys and girls reported Nargila smoking with friends (Israeli Ministry of Health, 2003).

Israeli police official information (2004) shows that in the age groups of 17 to 18 and 19 to 29, the percentage of drivers involved in car accidents is higher than their percentage in the drivers' population. Thus, although 2.7% of the total population is 17 to 18 years old, 4.1% of this age group were involved in car accidents. In a similar vein, 14.9% of the total population is 19 to 29 years old, but they were involved in 20.8% of the car accidents. Moreover, for both age groups, involvement in car accidents is caused more by self (as driver) than by others: Of the total number of drivers involved in car accidents, 36.5% are from the 17 to 18 age group and 24% from the 19 to 29 age group.

The HBSC (Health Behaviors in School-Aged Children) surveys of Israeli adolescents for 1994 and 1998 (Harel et al., 2002) included a set of items regarding the prevalence of physical and emotional symptoms. Physical symptoms pertained to headache, stomachache, backache, and dizziness. Emotional symptoms pertained to anger, nervousness, or bad mood. Responses indicated that overall, Arab adolescents reported a higher rate of symptoms than did Jewish adolescents. Thus, 51% of Arab adolescents and 37% of Jewish adolescents reported having physical symptoms at least once a week or more often and 34% of the Arab adolescents and 14% of Jewish adolescents experienced emotional symptoms almost daily. Only 9% of Arab adolescents but 32% of Jewish adolescents reported they feel tired on the way to school at least four times a week. However, twice as many Arab (35%) as Jewish adolescents (17%) find it difficult to fall asleep at night (Harel et al., 2002).

Education

Each Jewish school is under the supervision of one of three systems: state, state-religious, or ultra-orthodox. Eighty-one percent of junior high school and 66% of senior high school students attend state schools; 19% and 17% of junior and senior high school students respectively attend the state-religious schools; and 1% and 18% of junior and senior high school students respectively attend the ultra-orthodox schools. Within each sector a student may attend one of three tracks: general-academic, vocational, or agricultural. Arab high school education has only two tracks: general-academic and vocational.

In recent years Israel participated in several international achievement studies. The earliest was the TIMSS 1995 for mathematics and science. Israeli Jewish eighth graders ranked 21st in mathematics and 23rd in science out of 41 countries. In the TIMSS 1999 for mathematics, Israeli eighth graders ranked 28th out of 38 and below the international average on all subjects (e.g., fractions and number concepts, algebra, geometry). The 1999 study further showed that Israel was one of the few countries with gender-related differences (girls had lower grades than boys) and ethnicity-related differences (non-Jewish students had a lower achievement than Jewish students) (Zozovsky 2000).

Among ultra-orthodox Jewish families, poverty, early marriage, childbearing, and growing up in ultra-orthodox families lower girls' chances of entering higher education and pursuing a career. Regarding ultra-orthodox girls, in recent years a growing number of girls have continued education beyond high school in teachers' colleges or other occupational training programs.

Arab high school girls—particularly those growing up in traditional Muslim families—are in a quandary. Although they believe that "education is a weapon in women's hands" (Seginer & Mahajna, 2003) and aspire to university education, the prospects that their families will allow them to travel to the city and enroll in an Israeli university are slim. Instead, they stay home and commute to a Muslim or Jewish teachers' college in their area. The alternative is that they become engaged to be married while still at high school and get married as soon as the law permits (age 17 for girls).

Higher education is still more prevalent among the Jewish then the Arab population, although in recent years the difference between the two groups has narrowed. Data pertaining to the 18–24 age group show that 28% of the Jewish and 22% of the Arab women and men completed 13 to 15 years of education. Of this age group, 4% and 6% of the Jewish and Arab groups completed 16 or more years of education (Israel Central Statistical Bureau, 2009). Because for Jewish adolescents (girls and boys) and for Druze boys military service is compulsory and relatively long (two and three years for girls and boys, respectively), the majority enter higher education as young adults. Their residence and much of their social life are outside the university.

Work

The 1953 law on adolescent work maintains that the minimum age for work is 15 for a regular job and 14 for summer jobs (Israel Ministry of Industry, Commerce and Employment 2004). The law also states that adolescents' work should not exceed 8 hours per day and 40 hours per week. Adolescents who have reached age 16 may work more than 8 hours per day provided they do not exceed 40 weekly hours. Adolescents should not be employed on their religious free day (i.e., Friday for Muslims, Saturday for Jews, and Sunday for Christians).

Despite the clarity of the law, information on adolescents' work is scarce. Recent official statistics report that 8% of the total number of 15- to 17-year-olds and 6% of Arab youth hold a paid job (Israel Central Statistical Bureau, 2009). Altogether, information about the number, work conditions, and wages of working underage adolescents (below age 15) is lacking.

Media

A survey of TV viewing among a representative sample of 1,000 Israeli Jewish youths aged 12 to 17 showed that 64% of the youths had a TV set in their room (Midgam, 2004). During weekdays, adolescents watch TV more than adults do (3.5 and 2.9 daily hours, respectively).

Nevertheless, a study carried out as part of a multicultural project (Lemish & Liebes, 1999) showed that Israeli adolescents watched TV less than adolescents in Western European countries (e.g., Denmark, France, Germany, UK), with the exception of Switzerland. However, data on time spent TV watching varies by data source. Thus, while the Cohen and Weimann (2000) ninth to twelfth graders spend 3.4 hours per day during weekdays and the Midgam (2004) 12- to 17-year-olds spend 3.9 hours, according to Lemish and Liebes (1999), among those watching TV, young adolescents (age 12 to 13) watch 129 minutes per day and middle adolescents (age 15 to 16) watch 99 minutes per day. By comparison, Danish young and middle adolescents watch 158 and 168 minutes per day, respectively, and British young and middle adolescents watch 164 and 171 minutes per day, respectively. Analysis of favored genres (Cohen & Weimann, 2000) showed that on average, the most frequently watched genres have been movies ($M = 3.88$ daily hours, SD = 0.973), comedies ($M = 3.60$, SD = 1.28), MTV ($M = 3.30$, SD = 1.37), horror and mystery series ($M = 3.30$, SD = 1.26), and news ($M = 3.17$, SD = 1.03).

Israeli Jewish adolescents use computers slightly more than adolescents from European countries, with the exception of Dutch computer users who use them more (48 and 41 minutes per day for Israeli young and middle adolescents and 50 and 74 minutes per day for Dutch young and middle adolescents). In a similar vein, Israeli adolescents who use the Internet use it more than adolescents from European countries, with the exception of Dutch Internet users (30 and 32 minutes per day for Israeli young and middle adolescents and 49 and 42 minutes per day for Dutch young and middle adolescents). Israeli adolescents use the telephone considerably more than adolescents from European countries (43 and 73 minutes per day by young and middle adolescents, respectively, and 21 and 25 minutes per day for Finnish adolescents) (Lemish & Liebes, 1999). The rate of computer users decreases in emerging adulthood: 45% for the 18- to 21-year-olds and 41% for the 22- to 24-year-olds. Thus, it is plausible that schools prompt computer usage; it is also possible that at least for some adolescents computers are available only at school.

Politics and Military

Adolescents' political involvement has two major aspects. One is related to the endorsement of political parties and the other pertains to Jewish–Palestinian relationships. The views of political parties are most clearly expressed in general elections. Although the voting age in Israel is 18 and the majority of Israeli youths are not commonly involved in politics, during the election period political issues become more salient, leading larger numbers of adolescents to be politically interested and active in informal political debates and endorsement of political parties and their campaigns. Some of these activities take place in high schools, supported by the school educational staff. Particularly known are trial elections in several high schools whose voting patterns resemble the official election results, and thus unofficially are considered as their predictors.

Exceptions to Israeli youth's low interest in politics have been two groups holding extreme political attitudes: Arab students identifying with the Communist Party and Jewish national religious Bnei Akiva youths identifying with messianic parochialism, which has led some of them to active resistance and violent behavior in disputed territories settlements (Kahane, 1997).

A small group of ultra-orthodox youths holding extreme messianic nationalistic attitudes operates in the West Bank. The informal name of this group is the Hills Youth (Noar Hagvaot). The group consists of unemployed Yeshiva dropouts who direct their violent behavior toward the Palestinian inhabitants and toward the Israeli security forces engaged in the evacuation of illegal Jewish posts in the West Bank. Prior to the August 2005 disengagement many of them moved to the Gaza Strip Jewish settlements, training themselves to resist by force the anticipated evacuation of the Jewish settlements (Harel & Hasson, 2005).

The Israeli law of mandatory military service requires Jewish boys and girls and Druze boys to serve in the army. However, whereas boys serve for three years, girls serve for only two years. Moreover, women declaring a religious background and orthodox men enrolled in religious studies (Yeshiva) are granted exemption from military service. Altogether, 23% of the Jewish men and 40% of the Jewish women are exempted from military service. Among women, the main reason for exemption is religious background; among men, 10% are exempted for religious studies reasons and 13% for medical and mental health, low intellectual ability, and criminal record reasons (Schtrasler, 2005). In response to public protest against granting orthodox men exemption from military service, in recent years a growing number of them, especially those not studying in the Yeshiva, have been conscripted.

Several surveys of the motivation of potential conscripts to serve in the Israeli army (e.g., Ezrahi & Gal, 1995; Gal, 1986) showed that the majority are highly motivated to serve in the army and view it as fulfilling a personal duty. As noted by Gal, military service has become "an integral phase in the life of any Israeli youth" (1986, p. 59) and should be understood in terms of the cultural heritage of voluntary participation in self-defense organizations since the beginning of Jewish immigration to Palestine at the turn of the twentieth century (Seginer, 1999). Until recently, dissidence has been limited to a relatively small number of reservists who opposed military action during the Lebanon war and the first Intifada (Linn, 1996) as well as the al Aksa Intifada (started in October 2000), and an even smaller number of mandatory service soldiers who refused service for conscientious objection reasons.

Developmental studies of the military recruits focused on two issues: the effect of military service on the recruits' sense of personal growth and the interdependence of adolescent–parent relationships and adjustment to military service. Both lines of research showed the positive effect of military service. Specifically, military service has a positive effect on a sense of personal growth (Lieblich & Perlow, 1988) and particularly on the development of future orientation (Seginer & Ablin, 2005), a growing sense of such attributes as independence, self-confidence, social sensitivity, and ability for intimate relationships (Dar & Kimhi, 2001), as well as improved adolescent–parent relationships (Mayseless and Hai, 1998). Moreover, a sense of parental autonomy granting had a positive effect on adjustment to military service (Mayseless & Hai, 1998; Mayseless, Scharf, & Scholt, 2003).

Unique Issues

This section is devoted to new immigrant adolescents, particularly focusing on new immigrants from the former Soviet Union and Ethiopia who immigrated to Israel during the 1990s. The immigration of former Soviet Union Jews was much larger and the background of the immigrants much more diverse. The number of former Soviet Union children and adolescents immigrating to Israel during the 1989 to 1995 period was over 150,000. They came from small families (57% of them were only children) and their likelihood of growing up in single-parent families (20%) was three times as high as that of children growing up in veteran Jewish families. About 6,000 of them immigrated without their parents and were placed in Youth Alia boarding schools and kibbutz schools (Horowitz, 1998).

The extent to which adolescent new immigrants forge an Israeli identity varies by study and relates to such factors as immigrating with their families and taking part in the decision to immigrate to Israel (Mirsky, 1994; Rapoport & Lomsky-Feder, 2002), experiencing low psychological distress, developing social relationships outside the new immigrant community, and mastering the Hebrew language (Mirsky, 1994).

Although immigration of Ethiopian Jews started in the 1970s and still continues, the majority of Ethiopian Jews arrived in Israel in one of two immigration waves known as the Moses Operation (Mivzah Moshe) in 1984–1985 and the Salomon Operation (Mivzah Shlomo) in 1991. The majority of the Ethiopian adolescents (85% to 90%), altogether over 10,000 girls and boys, were educated in Youth Alia boarding schools (Amir, 1997). It is important to note that the majority of Ethiopian Jews resided in remote rural areas and therefore were detached from Orthodox Jewry and unaffected by the modernity brought by the Italian occupation prior to the Second World War and the reforms of the Marxist revolution in the 1970s (Adler, Toker, Manor, Feuerstein, & Feldman, 1997).

The majority of Ethiopian Jews (90%) were illiterate. Among the adolescents admitted to the Youth Alia schools, 22% were one to two years below the achievement level of their age group in Youth Alia. The rest were further behind (three to four years below their age group achievement or unable to take the tests). The educational gap, cultural differences, and dark complexion led to the phenomena of school dropout, alienation from the Israeli society, and identification with Black culture (Sawicki, 1994), and lower motivation to serve in the army, interpreted as an expression of the disillusionment of Ethiopian-born army graduates who encountered difficulties finding jobs.

Nevertheless, within a 10-year period, the percentage of Ethiopian immigrant students completing high school education rose from 1.5% in 1985 to 16% in 1995 (Adler et al., 1997). Given that military service is considered an important marker of adjustment to Israeli society, Ethiopian youths have been known for their overall high motivation and good adjustment to military service, and the number of officers among them rose from five in 1991 to 15 in 1994 and 30 in 1996 (Adler et al., 1997).

References and Further Reading

Adler, H., Toker, D., Manor, Y., Feuerstein, R., & Feldman, M. (1997). Absorption of Ethiopian youth in Youth Alia, 1985–1995. In E. Amir, A. Zehavi, & R. Pragayi (Eds.), *One root, many branches: The story of the absorption of young immigrants from Ethiopia in Youth Alia* (pp. 255–303). Jerusalem, Israel: The Magnes Press.

Amir, E. (1997). Introduction. In E. Amir, A. Zehavi, & R. Pragayi (Eds.), *One root, many branches: The story of the absorption of young immigrants from Ethiopia in Youth Alia* (p. 8). Jerusalem, Israel: The Magnes Press.

Antonovsky, H. F. (1980). *Adolescent sexuality: A study of attitudes and behavior.* Lexington, MA: Lexington Books.

Arnett, J. J. (2000). Emerging adulthood: A theory of development from the late teens through the twenties. *American Psychologist, 55,* 469–480.

Aviezer, O., Sagi, A., Resnick, G., & Gini, M. (2002). School competence in young adolescence: Links to early attachment relationships beyond concurrent self-perceived competence and representations of relationships. *International Journal of Behavioral Development, 26,* 397–409.

Bar-Hamburger, R. (2000). *Drug use among new immigrants in the State of Israel.* Jerusalem, Israel: The Anti-Drug Authority.

Bar-Hamburger, R. (2009). *Alcohol use among Israeli residents: Epidemiological survey findings.* Jerusalem, Israel: The Anti-Drug Authority.

Bar-Tal, D. (2004). Nature, rationale, and effectiveness of education for co-existence. *Journal of Social Issues, 60*, 253–271.

Baron-Epel, O., & Haviv-Messika, A. (2004). Factors associated with age of smoking initiation in adult populations from different ethnic backgrounds. *European Journal of Public Health, 14*, 301–305.

Bendes-Yakov, O., & Friedman, Y. (2000). *NALEH: Youth immigrating to Israel without their parents.* Jerusalem, Israel: The Henrieta Szold Institute.

Ben Tzvi-Mayer, S., Hertz-Lazarovitz, R., & Safir, M. (1989). Teachers' selection of boys and girls as prominent pupils. *Sex Roles, 21*, 231–246.

Ben-Zur, H. (2003). Happy adolescents: The link between subjective well-being, internal resources, and parental factors. *Journal of Youth and Adolescence, 32*, 67–79.

Booth, M. (2002). Arab adolescents facing the future. In B. B. Brown, R. W. Larson, & T. S. Saraswathi (Eds.), *The world's youth: Adolescents in eight regions of the globe* (pp. 207–242). Cambridge, UK: Cambridge University Press.

Brook, U., & Tepper, A. (2002). Consumption, knowledge and attitudes of high school pupils towards alcohol and alcoholism: The Israeli experience. *Patient Education and Counseling, 47*, 115–119.

Cohen, J., & Weimann, G. (2000). Cultivation revisited: Some genres have some effects on some viewers. *Communication Reports, 13*, 99–114.

Dar, Y., & Kimhi, S. (2001). Military service and self-perceived maturation among Israeli youths. *Journal of Youth and Adolescence, 30*, 427–448.

Dror, Y. (2004). The educational system as an agent of Jewish patriotism in the State of Israel: From "pioneering Zionism" to "balanced Israeliness." In A. Ben-Amos & D. Bar-Tal (Eds.), *Patriotism: Homeland love* (pp. 137–173). Tel Aviv, Israel: Hakibutz Hameuchad (in Hebrew).

Eisenstadt, S. N. (1952). *The process of absorption of new immigrants in Israel.* London, UK: Tavistock.

Eisikovits, R.A. (1995). "I'll tell you what school should do for us": How immigrant youth from FSU view their high school experience in Israel. *Youth and Society, 27*, 230–255.

Eisikovits, R.A. (2006). Intercultural learning among Russian recruits in the Israeli army. *Armed Forces and Society, 32*, 292–306.

Epstein, S. (1983). *The mother–father–peer scale.* Unpublished manuscript. Amherst, MA: University of Massachusetts.

Eshel, Y., & Rosenthal-Sokolov, M. (2000). Acculturation attitudes and sociocultural adjustment of sojourner youth in Israel. *Journal of Social Psychology, 140*, 677–691.

Ezrahi, Y., & Gal, R. (1995). *World views and attitudes of high school students toward social, security and peace issues.* Zichron Ya'akov, Israel: Carmel Institute for Social Studies.

Farbstein, I., Dycian, A., Gothelf, D., King, R. A., Cohen, D. J., Kron, S., et al. (2002). A follow-up study of adolescent attempted suicide in Israel. *Journal of the American Academy of Child & Adolescent Psychiatry, 41*, 1342–1349.

Gal, R. (1986). *A portrait of the Israeli soldier.* New York, NY: Greenwood Press.

Grusec, J. E. (2002). Parenting socialization and children's acquisition of values. In M. H. Bornstein (Ed.), *Handbook of parenting: Vol. 5: Practical issues in parenting* (2nd ed., pp. 143–167). Mahwah, NJ: Lawrence Erlbaum Associates.

Habib, J. (1998). Groups at risk among the new immigrants. In M. Sicron & E. Leshem (Eds.), *Profile of an immigration wave: The absorption process of immigrants from the former Soviet Union, 1990–1995* (pp. 409–441). Jerusalem, Israel: The Magnes Press (In Hebrew, with English abstract).

Harel, A., & Hason, N. (2005, January 2). The Hills' Youths moved to Gaza and began training to undo the disengagement. *Haaretz* Newspaper (Hebrew & English).

Harel, Y., Ellenbogen-Frankovitz, S., Molcho, M., Abu-Asba, K., & Habib, J. (2002). Health behaviors in school-aged children (HBSC): A World Health Organization cross-national study. Jerusalem, Israel: The Center for Children and Youth JDC–Brookdale Institute and Ramat Gan, Israel: Department of Sociology and Anthropology, Bar Ilan University.

Harel, Y., Molcho, M., & Tilinger, A. (2004). *Youth in Israel: Health, psychological and social well-being and patterns of risk taking behavior*. Ramat Gan, Israel: Bar Ilan University (in Hebrew).

Helman, S. (1993). *Conscientious objection to military service as an attempt to redefine the contents of citizenship*. Unpublished doctoral dissertation, Hebrew University of Jerusalem, Israel.

Horowitz, T. (1998). Immigrant children and adolescents in the educational system. In M. Sicron & E. Leshem (Eds.), *Profile of an immigration wave: The absorption process of immigrants from the former Soviet Union, 1990–1995* (pp. 368–408). Jerusalem, Israel: The Magnes Press (in Hebrew, with English abstract).

Ichilov, O. (1985). Family politicization and adolescents' citizenship orientation. *Political Psychology, 9*, 431–444.

Israel Central Statistical Bureau. (2004a). *Israel statistical yearbook*. Jerusalem, Israel: Central Bureau of Statistics.

Israel Central Statistical Bureau. (2004b). *Pupils in grades VII–XII: Staying on vs. dropping out, 2001/2*. Jerusalem, Israel: Central Bureau of Statistics.

Israel Central Statistical Bureau. (2009). *Israel statistical yearbook 2008*. Jerusalem, Israel: Central Bureau of Statistics.

Israel Knesset Research and Information Center. (2003). *Drug use among Israeli youths*. Jerusalem, Israel: Knesset.

Israel Ministry of Education. (2004a). Gifted students programs. Jerusalem, Israel: Israel Ministry of Education. Retrieved from www.education.gov.il/gifted/misgarot.htm (in Hebrew).

Israel Ministry of Education. (2004b). *The law of special education*. Jerusalem, Israel: Israel Ministry of Education. Retrieved from http://cms.education.gov.il (in Hebrew).

Israel Ministry of Education. (2004c). *Number of classrooms and students in special education programs 2004*. Jerusalem, Israel: Israel Ministry of Education. Retrieved from http:// cms.education.gov.il (in Hebrew).

Israel Ministry of Health. (2009). *Minister of Health smoking report 2007–2008*. Jerusalem, Israel: Israel Ministry of Health. Retrieved from www.health.gov.il/smoke 2007-2008 (in Hebrew).

Israel Ministry of Health. (2010). *Minister of Health smoking report 2009*. Retrieved from www.cancer.org.il/smoking (in Hebrew).

Israelashvili, M., & Taubman, O. (1997). Adolescents' preparation for military enlistment in Israel: A preliminary evaluation. *Megamot, 38*, 408–420 (in Hebrew).

Israeli Gay Youth. (2011). *About Israeli Gay Youth*. Retrieved from www.igy.org.il/content/about (in Hebrew).

Israeli Committee on Disease Control (ICDC). (2009). Smoking among youth in Israel. In Israel Ministry of Health, *Minister of Health smoking report 2007–2008* (pp. 29–32). Jerusalem, Israel: Israel Ministry of Health.

Israeli Ministry of Industry, Commerce and Employment. (2004). *Youth work act 1953: Summary*. Jerusalem, Israel: Israeli Ministry of Industry, Commerce and Employment.

Kahane, R. (1997). *The origins of postmodern youth: Informal youth movements in a comparative perspective.* Berlin, Germany: Walter de Gruyter.

Knafo, A., & Schwartz, S. H. (2003). Parenting and adolescents' accuracy in perceiving parental values. *Child Development, 74,* 595–611.

Kurman, J. (2003). The role of perceived specificity level of failure events in self-enhancement and in constructive self-criticism. *Personality and Social Psychology Bulletin, 29,* 285–94.

Larson, R. W., Richards, M. H., Moneta, G., & Holmbeck, G. (1996). Changes in adolescents' daily interactions with their families from ages 10 to 18: Disengagement and transformation. *Developmental Psychology, 32,* 744–754.

Latzer, Y. (2004). Disordered eating behaviors and attitudes in diverse groups in Israel. In M. R. Giovanni (Ed.), *Eating disorders in the Mediterranean area: An exploration in transcultural psychology.* Huntington, NY: Nova Science.

Latzer, Y., & Gilat, I. (2000). Calls to the Israeli hotline from individuals who suffer from eating disorders: An epidemiological study. *Eating Disorders, 8,* 31–42.

Latzer, Y., Witztum, E., & Stein, D. (2008). Eating disorders and disordered eating in Israel: An updated review. *European Eating Disorders Review, 16,* 361–374.

Lemish, D., & Liebes, T. (1999). *Children and youth in the changing media environment in Israel.* Jerusalem, Israel: The Hebrew University, School of Education, the NCJW Research Institute for Innovation in Education (in Hebrew).

Levinson, D. J. (1978). *The seasons of a man's life.* New York, NY: Ballantine.

Lieblich, A., & Perlow, M. (1988). Transition to adulthood during military service. *The Jerusalem Quarterly, 47,* Summer, 40–78.

Lifshitz, C., & Noam, G. (1994). *A survey of young Ethiopian immigrants: Interim report.* Jerusalem, Israel: JDC-Brookdale Institute.

Linn, R. (1996). When the individual soldier says "no" to war: A look at selective refusal during the Intifada. *Journal of Peace Research, 33,* 421–431.

Mahajna, S. (2005). *Future orientation: Its nature and meaning for adolescent females growing up in different Israeli Arab sectors.* Unpublished PhD dissertation, University of Haifa, Israel.

Maoz, I. (2004). Coexistence in the eye of the beholder: Evaluating intergroup encounter interventions between Jews and Arabs in Israel. *Journal of Social Issues, 60,* 437–452.

Maoz, I., & Ellis, D. (2001). Going to ground: Argument in Israeli–Jewish and Palestinian encounter groups. *Research on Language and Social Interaction, 34,* 399–419.

Margieh, I. (2011). *Future orientation in social context: The case of Israeli Palestinian university and college students.* Unpublished master's thesis, University of Haifa, Haifa, Israel.

Mayseless, O., & Hai, I. (1998). Leaving home transition in Israel: Changes in parent–adolescent relationships and adolescents' adaptation to military service. *International Journal of Behavioral Development, 22,* 589–609.

Mayseless, O., Scharf, M., & Sholt, M. (2003). From authoritative parenting to an authoritarian context: Exploring the person–environment fit. *Journal of Research on Adolescence, 13,* 427–456.

Mesch, G. S. (2001). Social relationships and Internet use among adolescents in Israel. *Social Science Quarterly, 82,* 329–339.

Midgam. (2004). *Adolescent attitudes to advertising and programs on Channels 2 and 10.* Tel Aviv, Israel: Midgam Yeutz Umechkar (in Hebrew).

Mirsky, J. (1994, November 21). *Adjustment patterns of new immigrant university students.* Paper presented at the Identity and Transition Culture conference. Jerusalem: The Hebrew University.

Mirsky, J., & Prawer, L. (1992). *To immigrate as an adolescent: Immigrant youth from the former Soviet Union to Israel.* Jerusalem, Israel: ELKA and the Van Leer Institute.

Mitrany, E., Lubin, F., Chetrit, A., & Modan, B. (1995). Eating disorders among Jewish female adolescents in Israel: A 5-year study. *Journal of Adolescent Health, 6*, 454–457.

Orr, E., Mana, A., & Mana, Y. (2003). Immigrant identity of Israeli adolescents from Ethiopia and the former USSR: Culture specific principles of organization. *European Journal of Social Psychology, 33*, 71–92.

Rapoport, T., & Lomsky-Feder, E. (2002). "Intelligentsia" as an ethnic habitus: The inculcation and restructuring of intelligentsia among Russian Jews. *British Journal of Sociology of Education, 23*, 233–248.

Safir, M., Hertz-Lazarovitz, R., Ben Tzvi-Mayer, S., & Kupermintz, H. (1992). Prominence of girls and boys in the classroom: Schoolchildren's perceptions. *Sex Roles, 27*, 439–453.

Salomon, G. (2004). Does peace education make a difference in the context of an intractable conflict? *Peace and Conflict, 10*, 257–274.

Sawicki, T. (1994). Dancing to an African beat. *Jerusalem Report, 53*, 22–24.

Scharf, M., & Mayseless, O. (2001). The capacity for romantic intimacy: Exploring the contribution of best friend and marital and parental relationships. *Journal of Adolescence, 24*, 379–399.

Scheinberg, Z., Bleich, A., & Kolovsky, M. (1992). Prevalence of eating disorders among female Israel Defense Force recruits. *Harefuah, 123*, 73–78 (in Hebrew).

Schtrasler, N. (2005, January 6). How lovely is 'civilian service'. *Haaretz* newspaper.

Seginer, R. (1992). Sibling relationships in early adolescence: A study of Israeli Arab sisters. *Journal of Early Adolescence, 12*, 96–110.

Seginer, R. (1998). Adolescent sibling relationships in the context of other close relationships. *Journal of Research on Adolescence, 8*, 287–308.

Seginer, R. (1999). Beyond the call of duty: The service of Israeli youth in military and civic contexts. In M. Yates & J. Youniss (Eds.), *Roots of civic identity: International perspectives on community service and activism in youth* (pp. 205–224). New York, NY: Cambridge University Press.

Seginer, R. (2000, July). Adolescent–sibling relationships in the context of adolescent–parents relationships: Congruence is not enough. In R. Seginer, A. Vermulst, & J. Gerris (conveners), *Family congruence and adolescent well-being*, Symposium conducted at the 16th biennial meeting of the International Society of Behavioral Development, Beijing, China.

Seginer, R. (2001). Young people chart their path into adulthood: The future orientation of Israeli Druze, Arab and Jewish adolescents. Special Issue: The child in Israel (C. Greenbaum and I. Levin, Eds.), *Megamot, 41*, 97–112 (in Hebrew).

Seginer, R. (2005). Adolescent future orientation: Intergenerational transmission and intertwining tactics in culture and family settings. In W. Friedelmeier, P. Chakkarath, & B. Schwarz (Eds.), Culture and human development: The importance of cross-cultural research to the social sciences (pp. 231–251). Hove, UK: Psychology Press.

Seginer, R., & Ablin, E. (2005). *Can military service enhance the future orientation of emerging adults? A short-term longitudinal analysis.* Unpublished manuscript. Haifa, Israel: University of Haifa.

Seginer, R., Dan, O., & Naor-Ram, A. (1994). *Do schools need consultants? Screening candidates for the Mabar special project for advancing low S.E.S. senior high school students.* First interim report to the Israeli Ministry of Education and Culture (in Hebrew).

Seginer, R., Dan, O., & Naor-Ram, A. (1995). *Expert intervention programs in classes of the Mabar special educational project for advancing low S.E.S. senior high school students.* Second interim report to the Israeli Ministry of Education and Culture (in Hebrew).

Seginer, R., Dan, O., Naor-Ram, A., Schlesinger, R., & Somech, A. (1997). *The operation of Mabar special educational project in high schools: From screening to teaching, learning, and plans for the future.* Final report to the Israeli Ministry of Education and Culture (in Hebrew).

Seginer, R., & Flum, H. (1987). Israeli adolescents' self image profile. *Journal of Youth and Adolescence, 16,* 455–472.

Seginer, R., Karayanni, M., & Mar'i, M. (1990). Adolescents' attitudes towards women's roles: A comparison between Israeli Jews and Arabs. *Psychology of Women Quarterly,* 14, 119–133.

Seginer, R., & Mahajna, S. (2003). "Education is a weapon in women's hands": How Israeli Arab girls construe their future. *Journal for Sociology of Education and Socialization,* 23, 200–214.

Seginer, R., & Mahajna, S. (2004). How the future orientation of traditional Israeli Palestinian girls links beliefs about women's roles and academic achievement. *Psychology of Women Quarterly, 28,* 122–135.

Seginer, R., Shoyer, S., Hossessi, R., & Tannous, H. (2007). Adolescent family and peer relationships: Does culture matter? In B. B. Brown & N. S. Mounts (Eds.), *Linking parents and family to adolescent peer relations: Ethnic and cultural considerations* (pp. 83–99). San Francisco, CA: Jossey-Bass.

Seginer, R., & Somech, A. (2001). In the eyes of the beholder: How adolescents, teachers and school counselors construct adolescent images. *Social Psychology of Education,* 4, 139–157.

Seginer, R., & Vermulst, A. (2002). Family environment, educational aspirations, and academic achievement in two cultural settings. *Journal of Cross-cultural Psychology, 33,* 540–558.

Seginer, R., Vermulst, A., & Shoyer, S. (2004). The indirect link between perceived parenting and adolescent future orientation: A multi-step model. *International Journal of Behavioral Development, 28,* 365–378.

Sherer, M., Karnieli-Miller, O., Eizikovitz, Z., & Fishman, G. (2000). *Attitudes of Israeli Jewish adolescents 2000.* Haifa, Israel: The Minerva Center for Youth Studies, University of Haifa (in Hebrew).

Shulman, S., & Ben Artzi, E. (2003). Age related differences in the transition from adolescence to adulthood and links with family relationships. *Journal of Adult Development, 10,* 217–226.

Shulman, S., & Scharf, M. (2000). Adolescent romantic behaviors and perceptions: Age- and gender-related differences, and links with family and peer relationships. *Journal of Research on Adolescence, 10,* 99–118.

Stein, D., Luria, O., Tarrasch, R., Yoeli, N., Glick, D., Elizur, A., et al. 1999. Partial eating disorders in newly drafted Israeli servicewomen. *Archives of Women's Mental Health, 2,* 107–116.

Stein, D., Meged, S., Bar-Hanin, T., Blank, S., Elizur, A., & Weizman, A. (1997). Partial eating disorders in a community sample of female adolescents. *Journal of the American Academy of Child and Adolescent Psychiatry, 36,* 1116–1123.

Suleiman, M. A. (2001). *Parental style and Arab adolescents' future orientation.* Unpublished master's thesis, University of Haifa, Haifa, Israel (in Hebrew).

Tal, D. (2005). *Special needs adolescents and curricula developed for them.* Jerusalem, Israel: Israeli Ministry of Education.

Tatar, M., Kfir, D., Sever, R., Adler, C., & Regev, C. (1994). *Integration of immigrant students into Israeli elementary and secondary schools.* Jerusalem, Israel: NCJW Research Institute for Innovation in Education (in Hebrew).

Toren-Kaplan, N. (1995). *Adolescent future orientation in the context of immigration and absorption: The case of former-USSR immigrants to Israel.* Unpublished master's thesis, University of Haifa, Haifa, Israel (in Hebrew).

Ullman, H., & Tatar, M. (1999). *Self definition, self esteem, and life satisfaction among veteran Israeli and former Soviet Union new immigrant adolescents.* Jerusalem: The Hebrew University, School of Education, the NCJW Research Institute for Innovation in Education (in Hebrew).

Ullman, C., & Tatar, M. (2001). Psychological adjustment among Israeli adolescent immigrants: A report on life satisfaction, self-concept, and self-esteem. *Journal of Youth and Adolescence, 30*, 449–63.

Weiss, S. (1995). How do Israeli adolescents of four religions obtain alcoholic beverages and where? *Journal of Child and Adolescent Substance Abuse, 4*, 79–87.

Yachad. (2002). *The condition of homosexuals and lesbians in Israel.* Retrieved from http://yachad.snunit.k12.il (in Hebrew).

Zozovsky, R. (2000). *The international study in mathematics and science (TIMSS) 1999.* Jerusalem, Israel: Office of the Chief Scientist, Israel Ministry of Education.

Spain

Mediterranean Sea

Tangier

Melilla (Spain)

Chechaouene
Ouezzane

Al Hoceima
Nador

Oujda

Taounate

Taourint

Kenitra

Taza

Rabat
Salè

Fès
Meknès

Casablanca

Khemisset

Ben Slimane

Azrou

El Jadida

Settat

Oued Zem
Khenifra

Khouribga

Midlelt

Bou Arfa

Beni Mallal

Figuig

Safi

Azilal

Atlantic Ocean

Essaouira

Marrakech

Morocco

Ouarzazate

Agadir
Taroudaut

Tiznit

Tata

Algeria

Sidi Ifni

Tan-Tan

Tarfaya

Western Sahara

Mauritania

Chapter 4
Morocco
Douglas A. Davis and Susan Schaefer Davis

Background Information

Morocco is located in the northwest corner of Africa and is marked by mountains, desert, and temperate zones. The economy is based on agriculture, much of it subsistence, with citrus, phosphate, and textiles the major exports. Tourism and remissions from Moroccans working in Europe are other major sources of revenue. In 2005, Morocco was a nation of roughly 32 million people, with one third under the age of 15. Major languages are Moroccan Arabic, Berber/Amazigh, and French. Morocco was held by France and Spain as a colony from 1912 to 1956. It is now a constitutional monarchy, where King Mohammed VI has ruled since the death in 1999 of his father, Hassan II.

Morocco is well over 99% Muslim, with an estimated Jewish population of about 4,000 and a Christian population of 1,000. Politically, Morocco has been closely linked to the European Union—where millions of Moroccans work and live—and friendly to the United States. Since about 2000, the increasing readiness to address human rights concerns and the abuses of the previous regime, plus the 2004 liberalization of Muslim family law, are major positive signs. However, very high unemployment, even among educated youth, is considered a major problem. Islamist critiques of the regime are outspoken, but most Moroccans appear optimistic that increased participation in a globalized economy and a strong identity as a Muslim nation are compatible.

Period of Adolescence

The literary Arabic term for adolescence, *as-sinn al-murahaqa*, is used only by educated individuals, and there was no generally recognized term for this period of life in rural Morocco 30 years ago. This is changing and a period of adolescence is becoming more widely recognized in the early twenty-first century. Moroccans often describe the teenage years coinciding with high school education as a time both of irresponsible, impulsive (*taish*) behavior, and of increasing *'aql,* a term referring to reasonableness, responsibility, and a sense of the social context of one's acts. In general, females are recognized to develop *'aql* sooner than males, whether they went to school or not. Both adults and youth readily give examples of the emotionality and recklessness of youth: drug use, fighting, unemployment. On the other hand, Moroccan youth living with their families continue for the most part to show a great deal of respect to older relatives and older siblings, and often take responsibility for the wellbeing of younger brothers and sisters.

In the early 1980s, adolescence began with puberty in the mid-teens for both sexes in semirural towns and extended to the early twenties or marriage, whichever came first, for females (Davis & Davis, 1989). If a young woman had not married by her early or mid-twenties, she still developed the *'aql* or social responsibility that marks adults. For males, adolescent behavior continued until marriage, even if that was at age 35; i.e., they often continued activities such as drinking, gambling, and promiscuity until they married and settled down.

The physical changes of puberty are accompanied, for girls, by increasing expectations of modesty in social settings and by observance of the Ramadan fast. Every year during Ramadan, adult Muslims do not eat or drink from before sunrise to sunset for a lunar month. Children around 9 or 10 may practice for a couple of days, but with menarche, girls are expected to fast. Boys, too, start to fast around puberty, but because the physical changes are less marked than for females, the timing of beginning to fast is more flexible.

From the point of view of sociocultural adulthood, a prolonged adolescent phase characterized by years of education or apprenticeship for adult roles without the economic means to become an independent adult seems to be the norm, especially for males; this pattern holds for much of the Arab world (Gregg, 2005). Marriage marks the end of adolescence for both sexes. Before this, young people who attend university away from home have the opportunity for more freedom or "emerging adulthood" than do less educated peers who remain in the household. In the latter group, males will usually be away from the house most of the day, working or with friends, while females will spend more time at home or with neighbors doing household tasks. Moroccan marriages are occurring at a later age for both sexes, mainly because it is more difficult to get a job and accumulate the means necessary to marry, especially to establish an independent household. In 1960, the average age at marriage was a little over 17 for both urban and rural girls, but it has risen sharply, and in 2004 it was about 25 for rural and 27 for urban young women. For males, the ages were 29 and 32 (Royaume du Maroc, 2004).

Morocco is rapidly urbanizing, and urban youth appear to have more and earlier experiences of conflicts over values, more opportunities for sexual liaisons, and more exposure to some alien media than their rural cousins.

Beliefs

Morocco is typically described in Western academic accounts as displaying both strongly individualistic and strikingly collectivistic tendencies (Gregg, 2005). Moroccan life stories often contain accounts of how the individual overcame great obstacles related to poverty, loss of parents, or failed romance, by virtue of personal forbearance, courage, or piety. On the other hand, individuals are typically well aware of family, social class, and linguistic/ethnic (Arab/Berber) group memberships, which they expect will shape their identities and their successful assimilation into adult Moroccan society. While this suggests a collective rather than an individual focus, individuals within the same family experience greatly varied success in school and career and are respected for their personal qualities of intellect and morality.

The focus on honor, applied to an entire family, is striking. Honor most often refers to proper sexual comportment, e.g., not mixing with the opposite sex when single for females. Males have much more liberty without dishonoring the whole family. Adolescence is a time of increasing sexual interest for both sexes, but the risk of sexual exploration is much greater for females, who could dishonor the whole family by frequent open dating and certainly by getting pregnant outside marriage (Davis, 1993). This is still one of the main reasons for encouraging female marriage at an early age, even though recent reforms have raised the legal age to 18 for both sexes.

On the other hand, the rapidly growing consumer culture has been accompanied by conspicuous displays of house, car, and personal appliances as tokens of success. Moroccan humor and films often belittle and critique such displays, revealing the current tension between collective and individual orientations.

Islamic beliefs in Morocco vary widely. In the 1980s and before, "folk Islam" was most prevalent in rural areas. This included non-orthodox practices such as traveling to local saints' tombs in search of blessings (*baraka*) and employing healing groups to cure physical and psychological distress. Since the early 1980s, youth have been routinely exposed in school to modernist and "scientific" views, as well as to more orthodox (and sometimes radical) Islam. High school teachers often provide critical perspectives on parents' practices. Youth may struggle to reconcile the values and acts of their uneducated parents with their own aspirations for white-collar careers and "modern" marriages. In the semirural community studied by Davis and Davis (1989), these apparent contradictions did not usually lead to stress or conflict between the generations.

Religious observance has become more important in recent decades. In the 1960s, most rural Moroccans prayed at the mosque only on major holidays or in old age, and males were much more visibly observant than females. By the early 1980s, more people of all ages and both sexes were praying at the mosque, especially at the major Friday prayer, and more adults prayed the required five times daily regularly at home. Youth probably still pray less than older adults, but a much larger proportion participates in prayer now than in the past. Even as the traditional Moroccan veil over the lower face has largely disappeared, the Muslim headscarf (*hijab*) has become common. The prevalence of bearded and *hijab*ed young people is the most vivid indication of increased consciousness of oneself as a Muslim.

Gender

Gender role differentiation begins almost at birth. Moroccan families usually host a public ceremony at the end of the first week of an infant's life (the *usbu'a*), and this was traditionally more elaborate for males (Davis, 1983). Males were usually circumcised at about five years of age, and this was the occasion for the family to host another gathering in the boy's honor. However, in the early twenty-first century, educated parents often have the circumcision done in the hospital at birth. Morocco has no tradition of female circumcision.

Gender role expectations are sharply different for female and male children after infancy, as girls—whether in school or not—early take on family responsibilities helping with housework and the care of younger children, activities expected of them as adults. Traditionally, young women were competent in these roles by about age 15, but this is less true as they become more educated. Boys have more time on their own, and as they get older they are expected to make some attempt to bring in income from outside the family.

In addition to both sexes helping the family in adolescence, males gain more freedom of movement at this time, while females are more restrained by the modesty expected of them. Males may drink alcohol and smoke cigarettes as mild forms of rebellion, but females rarely do, except occasionally in an elite urban context. In all but the most isolated rural areas, females are more apt now than a generation or two ago to meet males surreptitiously for flirtation and sometimes sexual activity (Davis, 1993). While overt dating is still taboo, except among the urban elite, the sexes may get together to study, and young people often meet at weddings and other large social occasions. A strong double standard still prevails when rumors of sexual activity reach the ears of family and friends. For males, such behavior is often expected and may be admired by peers, but for females reported sexual activity is usually condemned and likely to be punished if discovered.

Modesty for girls after physical adolescence is still a striking feature of Moroccan society. If girls decide to wear *hijab*, or modest Muslim dress with head, arms, and legs covered, they often begin during their teens and after menarche. This trend has increased since the mid-1980s, and one-fourth to one-half of urban young single women may dress in this way. There is no parallel change in dress for males at this age, but they may grow a beard to show their respect for religion as they reach college age. Adult male life stories often feature a period of youthful wildness and then a gradual settling down, while for a female wild behavior is avoided, as it may disqualify her for marriage.

Both sexes are visibly concerned with physical attractiveness and become more concerned with clothing and style in their late teens. Many boys take bodybuilding or martial arts classes. A few girls jog, but in general they are much less likely to participate in sports outside classes. A light complexion is seen as attractive in both sexes. Traditionally, plump girls were seen as more attractive than thin ones, although this is changing, especially in urban settings.

The Self

Like youth across the Middle East and North African region (Gregg, 2005), young people in Morocco aspire to remain "Moroccan" while partaking of the economic and intellectual resources of a modern global economy and preserving a sense of themselves as Muslims. Urban–rural divisions are quite distinct in Morocco, and the population has gone from 80% rural to more than 50% urban in the lifetime of older adults at the turn of the century. The notion of being a "country bumpkin" is at the root of many jokes, so some teens try to deny rural roots or at least appear sophisticated, but on the other hand, rural simplicity and morality are often admired. Arab/Berber is a difference that is more often articulated since 2000, with radio and TV news available in Berber dialects and some schools being taught in Berber. While Berbers often note a pride in their heritage, there does not seem to be antagonism between the groups.

The increased interest in Islam and wearing of Islamic dress is often a manifestation of cultural identity in a country where French language and manners are still a mark of the elite. Morocco is visibly bicultural, with billboards, films, and social events such as weddings conducted in Arabic as well as French and with an increased awareness of the country's Berber roots. Youth are exposed to political arguments and cultural materials from Europe, the Middle East, and Africa, and many expect to move in a global culture and economy as adults.

Family Relationships

Most families in Morocco now are nuclear in form, with the couple and children sometimes adding a grandparent or a rural cousin who needs access to better schools. Most live near to grandparents, aunts, and uncles so they have wider family networks, and most social gatherings are family-based. While families have been nuclear for several decades, sometimes newlyweds live with the male's parents for a few years to save money for a home of their own. There is usually stress between the mother-in-law and daughter-in-law in this situation, due to competition for the young man's affection and resources. Moroccan families are decreasing in size, with the estimated average fertility of Moroccan women declining from 4.8 children in 1987 to 2.4 in 2007 (World Bank, 2009b).

Traditionally, children and youth spend much more time with mothers than with fathers, since mothers are the main caretakers and fathers usually work away from the home. In their teens, young men are out of the household more and are socialized more by the "street" than are their sisters. Young women learn adult female roles from their mothers and older sisters. Young men now seldom work with their fathers, except perhaps in agricultural communities. Fathers often spend a good deal of time at their jobs and in cafés; it is not considered manly to spend too much time at home. Adolescents are very close to their mothers, especially females, and both sexes often feel distant from their fathers (Davis & Davis, 1989). Fathers' main role in childrearing is as disciplinarian, and mothers use them as a threat. Although this is infrequent, either parent may strike a child, and fathers are the ones who deal with older children, usually boys, and administer more severe punishment.

In the semirural community of Zawiya, which the authors studied in the 1980s, there was relatively little overt conflict with parents, despite the fact that most children had been to school and almost all parents were illiterate. The conflicts observed were often related to control issues (denial of permission to go out) or to parents not providing something (such as enough money for a new outfit). Youth-related conflict is now more widely discussed in all parts of Moroccan society, and there appears to be increasing evidence of youthful crime, drug use, and opposition to adult attempts at control. These tensions are most visible in Moroccan cities.

Sibling relations are close and affectionate, although older brothers often irritate sisters with attempts to control their behavior in the name of preserving family honor. Children are sometimes raised by extended family members, such as grandparents or aunts and uncles, when a parent is not available or suitable by reason of illness or bad character. Some youth board with relatives closer to school, especially after primary school. Youth know their actual relation to each person, but may call both an aunt by whom they have been raised and their biological mother "mother."

Divorce statistics are hard to locate, but in the authors' small survey of Zawiya (Davis & Davis, 1989), it was found that roughly 50% of marriages ended in divorce. This figure is close to what Maher (1974) found a decade earlier for a town in southeastern Morocco. Nearly all divorced men remarry, as do many divorced women. When children are involved, it is typically expected that the new wife will favor her own children and will mistreat those of her husband, and young people try to leave such households as soon as they are able.

Street children are a relatively recent phenomenon in Morocco. From observation, such children seem to be nearly all male and in their early to mid-teens. Girls may be sent to relatives or acquaintances to work as "small maids," a child labor problem that Morocco is attempting to eliminate (Human Rights Watch, 2005).

Friends and Peers/Youth Culture

Moroccan adolescents have significantly less free time than has been reported in studies of the wealthier Westernized societies. Thus, school exerts a heavy influence on the friendships and aspirations of those youth who are still enrolled, although upper-school girls, especially, may still spend time with family or with neighbor girls who are not in school.

Moroccan parents have strong concerns about their children's friends and classmates as influences on behavior, and we heard of some who did not send their daughters to high school because they feared both the influence of some of the girls there and their daughters talking to young men on the long daily walk to and from the school in a nearby town. Often high schools are not in one's hometown, and this distance and the lack of supervision with peers are among the reasons many rural girls do not go to high school, despite many government and foreign aid programs to improve girls' education.

Peers are nearly always the same sex in rural areas, while upper-class urban youth may get together in mixed groups. Among other activities, such urban groups often go to films or discos together. Most males are involved in groups for sports, formally or informally, with football (soccer) as the most popular sport. There is no comparable sports outlet for girls. Government-sponsored youth clubs in towns and cities are open to both sexes and offer activities such as chess, sports, and theater productions, but more males than females attend.

Girls, especially those who have left school, may attend a government-sponsored center to learn skills such as knitting, sewing, and embroidery, and to visit with peers outside the neighborhood in a respectable setting. They may gather informally in homes with neighbor girls for the same activities. Girls are interested in learning these skills, which are the traditional marks of a well-brought-up young woman, and also enjoy the conversation about marriage, neighborhood events, and popular TV programs that accompanies them.

Love and Sexuality

Images of dating, romantic attraction, and sexual experimentation are readily available and appealing to Moroccan youth via satellite TV, imported films, and the Internet. On the other hand, Moroccan families attempt to keep their girls from becoming sexually active before marriage, and young people often complain that it is difficult to find opportunities to be alone together and to explore the kinds of relationships they desire. Traditional communities and neighborhoods strongly sanction open displays of affection, and a girl's reputation as sexually available is still a widespread source of shame. Parents are fearful of female adolescent sexual activity, since it can ruin a girl's chances of marriage with a suitable young man. While some people say that an unmarried girl who gets pregnant can be beaten or killed by her male relatives, no such examples were found in extensive inquiries in a semirural town in the 1980s (Davis & Davis, 1989). Such statements appear to be made mainly to frighten teenage girls.

While imported images of romance are readily available, sexual attraction and experimentation are not limited to Western influences. In-depth interviewing in a semirural town in the 1980s revealed that some parents and grandparents of the current generation had had premarital sexual experiences, as did a different study of older women in highly urban Casablanca (Naamane-Guessous, 1992). Although dating is taboo, except in some upper-class urban families, youth in most areas do get together surreptitiously. Larger towns and the enrollment of more girls in school have facilitated this, since it is more difficult to observe and control the activities of all girls, and many have school as a valid excuse to be outside the home. Meetings may involve flirtation, some physical contact, or intercourse—sometimes leading to pregnancy and/or marriage (Davis, 1993).

While birth control is widely available over the counter (contraceptive prevalence was reported at 63% among women aged 15 to 49 in 2004; World Bank 2009a), unmarried young women are embarrassed to purchase contraceptives (or to ask a mother or sister to do so), and young men are mostly disinclined to use them. Abortion is religiously forbidden but available from some doctors, and prices for a secret abortion are quite generally known to youth.

Since virginity is prized in a bride, and its lack can lead to repudiation, some young women have surgery to repair the hymen if it has been damaged. The traditional practice of displaying sheets stained with hymeneal blood at weddings is now criticized and on the decline, but for brides still facing this ordeal there are ruses involving their own blood or a substitute.

Sexual education is very limited. High school science classes contain some information on sexual physiology and reproduction, but that is all. Most parents do not discuss sexuality with their children, as it is a taboo topic between generations. The authors found that several girls in a semirural town had been frightened by their first menstrual periods because no one had explained it to them, and as a "shameful" occurrence, they were hidden from observation by siblings. For girls, their main sexual education is eavesdropping on the discussions of mothers and their friends, and for boys it may be discussions with peers and sometimes a visit to a prostitute. Sexual images and text are now readily available on the Internet, and males in particular may accumulate a great deal of erotic material.

Sexually transmitted diseases are known to exist but do not seem to be important deterrents of sexual behavior. While AIDS was largely denied as a problem in Morocco for years, the NGO Association pour la Lutte Contra Sida (ALCS) now gives young people at risk information on HIV prevention and testing; in 2009 there were billboards with a hotline number.

While large urban settings have some open male homosexuality, most Moroccans believe a homosexual lifestyle to be incompatible with Islam, and most youthful homoerotic behaviors do not continue to adulthood. Males in Zawiya in the 1980s frequently reported homoerotic play, but there was shame associated with the passive role and the colloquial word *zamel*, referring to a passive homosexual, was frequently seen as graffiti on school walls. Females did not report sexual play with other girls, and most did not seem to have imagined adult female homosexuality. Male masturbation was associated with great shame and seldom discussed. Males were more ready to discuss anal than oral sexual activity, while females did not mention either (Davis & Davis, 1989).

Mate selection was traditionally done by parents, resulting in arranged marriages. This is still largely true in many rural areas but less so in cities. Today, most young Moroccans have at least imagined a romance-based marriage like those portrayed in films and popular music. Since the 1980s, even small-town adolescents are meeting potential spouses and suggesting them to parents, usually the mother. Family approval is still important and almost always sought in both rural and urban areas. Marriage is the largest ceremonial event for both sexes, and the most obvious marker of entry into adulthood.

Health Risk Behavior

The main sources of adolescents' problems are seen as stresses coming from failure at school or finding a job, from "bad" behavior linked to drug or alcohol use among males, or to promiscuity among females. Parents and teachers frequently blame peers for promoting delinquency. Some boys in urban settings are now visibly involved in street crime as burglars, pickpockets, and drug dealers. Unfortunately, statistics are not systematically collected on these topics, so the following is based mainly on observation in Morocco during frequent visits and longer stays over the period 1965–2010.

Youthful drug and alcohol use was rare in smaller communities in the 1980s but appears to be more common in the twenty-first century, particularly for males. Morocco is a significant source of hashish for the European market and a trans-shipper of Asian heroin and Latin American cocaine, and methamphetamine and ecstasy are known in sophisticated urban settings. Thus drugs of various sorts are becoming easier for Moroccan youth to obtain, and most communities now acknowledge some problem of youthful drug abuse. Drug use can lead to crime and violence, even in small towns. In impoverished neighborhoods, addiction to glue is also a significant problem, and one of the most widely discussed Moroccan films of recent years, *Ali Zaoua* (2000), concerns a group of glue-addicted street boys in Casablanca. Drug and alcohol abuse is rare among young females but sometimes occurs in very Westernized settings.

Alcohol is forbidden by Islam, but many young men experiment with it as a form of mild rebellion. Alcohol is not legally sold in small rural towns, but may be purchased in bars and grocery stores in large cities. One sees long lines of working-class young men in their twenties in such stores on Friday evenings, stocking up for an evening's intoxication with friends. Much youthful male drinking in Morocco entails bingeing accompanied by day-after boasts about the absurd behavior of one's friends. Since drinking is forbidden, there are few adult models of responsible or social drinking.

Since the mid-1980s, there have been increased reports of "psychological crises" during youth. Such psychological tensions are in fact increasing, but widespread access to modern media also adds to the sense that such social problems are pervasive. Both males and females sometimes have psychological problems in their teens or early twenties related to their gender roles. These are called *crise* ("crisis") in French, or *'aqd nefsani* ("psychological blockage") in Arabic. Males are more likely than females to become unable to function when facing or failing an important exam, such as the baccalaureate at the end of high school. Some males even threaten or commit suicide. Females may be very fearful of exams too, but appear to be less often totally in crisis. Instead, problems with romance or marriage are more likely to disable them. Some female eating disorders are reported in urban areas, but this does not appear to be a large problem.

HIV/AIDs is now recognized as present in Morocco, but there is little public discussion. Sexually active youth may fear infection, but the reported HIV prevalence was only 0.1% for ages 15–49 in 2007, with drug users, homosexual males, and sex workers the main victims (World Bank, 2009b).

Education

Before Moroccan independence in 1956, there were very few public schools and almost all of the rural population was illiterate beyond basic tutoring in the Koran. Morocco has devoted a relatively high percentage of its national budget to public education since independence. While a few sex-segregated public schools exist in Morocco, most schools from the primary level through university have the sexes studying together.

While primary school attendance in urban areas is about equal for males and females and virtually all children are initially enrolled, in rural areas girls are less apt to attend school than boys, especially at higher grade levels. Nationally, by 2007, 79.2% of girls and 87.4% of boys were completing primary school (World Bank 2009a). Illiteracy in the over-15 population was reported to be 34.3% among males and 60.4% among females in 2003 (World Bank, 2008). Government programs, NGOs, and international aid projects have targeted female illiteracy in recent years, and figures show the effect, especially for the young: In 2004, the literacy rate for ages 15–24 was 80.8% for males and 60.5% for females (Royaume du Maroc, 2004).

Although the situation is changing, there are many reasons for gender differences in school attendance. Boys are more expected than girls to have jobs that require education as adults; only about 18% of women had paid employment in 2004 (Royaume du Maroc, 2004). While state education is free, the costs of books, supplies, and appropriate clothing may keep poor families from sending all children to school, and males are usually given priority. Some families worry about the security of adolescent girls walking to and from distant schools, and some rural girls cite lack of school toilet facilities after they reach menarche. Finally, girls are much more helpful around the house, and sometimes practice crafts such as weaving that can add to the family income.

In the early 1980s, Morocco began to Arabize the mainly Francophone system inherited from the French colonial period. Many Moroccans felt by 2000 that this had led to lower standards of both French and Arabic, as Modern Standard Arabic's highly complex grammar was poorly taught and not widely employed in daily social interaction. French now begins as a foreign language in year three of public primary school, and the math and science curriculum was fully changed from French to Arabic in high school in the 1990s. A program of basic training in Tamazight, the most common Berber language, was initiated in 2003 in some public schools, including those in mostly Arabophone areas.

Yet many university professors continue to teach in French, most library materials are in French, and students are expected to read and write exams in French, a language in which they are not fully trained; they often attribute their failure to lack of language skill and appropriate written texts. Classes are often huge and library resources are minimal, with many public universities holding less than two catalogued books per enrolled student.

Those who are able send their children to private schools, with the urban elite attending schools supported by the *Alliance Française* or private schools with an American curriculum and instruction in English. There is a widespread sense that educational opportunity has not kept up with an exploding population, and that even many years of successful education does not ensure a career (World Bank, 2008). As disillusionment with employment opportunities after completion of a public education increased during the 1990s, private schools promising more useful skills in the technology or business sector have become widespread. Most highly talented students specialize in either a business or science/engineering track deemed likely to lead to good jobs or to admission to a graduate program abroad.

Work

Moroccan youth traditionally feel a responsibility toward their families, providing a portion of income (or even of government-provided college scholarships) to the household budget. In the poorest communities Moroccan girls are often employed as maids, sometimes by more wealthy urban relatives who house them and use their labor in return for a little remuneration. Poor boys often sell sweets, gum, and cigarettes on the street or work as apprentices, and some teens become involved in petty crime. A report on child labor in Morocco by Human Rights Watch in 2005 reported that 18% of children of ages 12 through 14 worked, and 19% of rural children of ages 7 through 14 worked, mainly on farms.

Well-off urban youth devote their time to school and rarely have jobs. Most others try to help their families with a variety of jobs, usually in the informal sector. This is usually after they have left school, but males sometimes do manual labor in the summer if they can find it. Full-time jobs are rare. Some girls embroider trousseau items such as tablecloths to sell in the summers, and those who have left school may do this or work as seamstresses full time. This handwork is usually done at home or while visiting with friends, although a few work in urban factories. The same is true for weaving rugs, a skill passed from mother to daughter that can provide a better income than embroidery; and some rural southern villages survive more on women's weaving than on men's agricultural income. A less desirable job for females is field laborer, although female laborers may be preferred over males for their docility and lower pay rates. Adolescent males who have left school may apprentice in a trade such as plumbing, mechanical, or electrical work, and females may apprentice in government-run weaving cooperatives. Apprentices are usually minimally paid.

The government has a variety of technical training programs in the trades for adolescents who have completed the basic eight years of education, including a few technical high schools, and also training in agriculture, preschool and handicraft teaching, and computer use. More qualified adolescents who have finished high school may attend a private technical training school instead of university.

While males were traditionally expected to contribute their income to the family both before and after marriage, females were not. There was evidence of this expectation changing in the early 1980s, when mothers remarked that their adolescent daughters gave them part of the pittance they earned from embroidery, while their sons not only gave no money but requested money to buy cigarettes. One could expect this to lead mothers to be more supportive of their daughters staying in school so they could eventually earn—and share—a decent income. Indeed, young women with a regular job are now more desirable as marriage candidates.

The difficulty of finding regular work is a major factor that leads Moroccan youth, especially males, to consider emigration, legal or illegal, to Spain or other EU countries. In an interview study of 100 young people of both sexes between the ages of 24 and 32 who were looking for a job, 60% of them had considered leaving Morocco to find one, and 80% of that group, or 48% of the total, had taken some action to do so (Bennani-Chraibi, 2000). The colloquial Moroccan word for illegal emigration is *herraga*, suggesting to burn one's papers or past; it is frequently employed in Moroccan popular media (Graiouid, 2005).

Media

There has been a dramatic change in the media in Morocco since the middle 1990s, with rapidly accelerated introduction of new communications devices. At independence in the mid-1950s, radios were uncommon, and TV came to semirural areas only in the late 1960s. Movies were also available in urban areas and much attended by young men, but hardly ever by females. In the 1970s there was one government TV channel, with programs in French and Modern Standard Arabic that were unintelligible to the less-educated Moroccan Arabic and Berber-speaking population.

In the early 1980s, Morocco began to screen Egyptian TV films and soap operas, and these were hugely popular. Some adolescents began to affect Egyptian accents, and attitudes toward family, gender, and romance were influenced by Cairo soap operas or the singing of popular Egyptian performers. In the 1990s, the arrival of satellite TV dishes, along with code-breaking devices to allow access to hundreds of European and Middle Eastern channels, transformed public taste. Elite neighborhoods, impoverished urban shantytowns, and rural communities with electric generators all display satellite dishes. Moroccan TV and radio now broadcast films and programs in colloquial Arabic and Berber along with Standard Arabic, French, and a bit of English. Adolescents usually watch TV with their families, and parents censor "shameful" programs, i.e., those with obscene language or representation of sexual activity.

The explosive spread of mobile phone technology, from almost none in 1999 to 20 million Moroccan users (or about two-thirds of the population) in 2007 (ANRT, 2007), is perhaps the most striking feature of new information and communication technology in Morocco. Youth routinely communicate privately with peers and prospective romantic partners by voice and text message. Even the illiterate now "beep" to show they are thinking of each other, and converse on a daily basis.

Moroccan Internet access began in late 1995, reached technical universities in early 1996, and became readily available through home dial-up and cybercafé access in the late 1990s. Personal computer prevalence was 3.4% by 2008 (OpenNet, 2009), still very low by world standards, but access to the Internet in cybercafés has become a striking feature of youthful Moroccan experience for both sexes. Thanks largely to "*cybers*," Moroccan Internet access increased from 0.7% in 2001 to 33% of the population in 2008 (World Bank, 2009b). Adolescents of both sexes now use computers in cybercafés. While initially more males than females were patrons, many *cybers* are respectable places for young women to spend time. Some are even supervised by young women, who handle payment and problem-solving.

In addition to exploring social roles and political and religious values not otherwise available in Morocco, young people use these new technologies to build identities they hope will sustain them in a modernized world. Many young people look on the Internet for employment or marriage opportunities outside Morocco, and educated Moroccan youth are now beginning to chat on Instant Messenger and Skype, to discuss coursework on school websites, and to create their own blogs. Both female and male students at such institutions as Al Akhawayn University, where an American curriculum is taught in English, use new social networking tools such as Facebook. Both religious authorities and educators complain that Moroccan youth are becoming alienated from the values of a traditional Muslim society as a result of Western media, and there is widespread adult concern (and youthful fascination) with the pornographic and political possibilities of the Internet. On the other hand, pious youth use the Net to learn more about Islam and have access to a wide range of theological argument.

Politics and Military

Military service is voluntary and has often been a path to a better life for poor, rural male youth in Morocco, providing employment and further education for those with the ability. With Morocco's involvement in a war over control of the former Spanish Sahara in the late 1970s and 1980s, the Moroccan military was expanded and many young men (and some young women) enlisted. Soon after 2000, young women were accepted as police officers, and around 2004 the numbers and types of police were expanded to provide much-needed jobs for youth.

The widespread ignorance of or cynicism toward the Moroccan political process that characterized youth in the 1980s has somewhat given way to increased interest in political parties, as more transparent elections have placed new political figures in the Moroccan parliament, and Morocco's voting age was lowered to 18 in 2002. Some young people have joined organizations involved specifically with Muslim values and with the role of Islam in politics. The percentage of politically active Moroccan youth is still very small, but public discussions of human rights and the abuses of the previous regime now engage educated youth.

One expression of youth involvement in politics is rather superficial but dramatic: political demonstrations. Before 2000, the government reacted harshly to limit political demonstrations related to Moroccan (as opposed to international) issues, and police fired on university demonstrators protesting price hikes and the lack of educational and employment opportunities, but protests have become safer and more open. Morocco's Union of Unemployed University Graduates held months of demonstrations in front of Parliament in Rabat in the late 1990s, and human rights groups have demonstrated for changes in Muslim family law. There have been numerous political challenges to government attempts to monitor and censor personal web pages.

Another avenue for civic expression is NGOs (non-governmental organizations). They were very restricted due to fear of political activities until the mid-1980s, but the former King Hassan II allowed them to expand, and his son Mohamed VI has followed suit. Many young people in their twenties join these groups, whether to support women's rights, improve education or the environment, or for other causes. Sometimes this voluntary work can lead to a paid job with the organization—another reason for their popularity with young people.

Unique Issues

Morocco is, if not unique, at least unusual in the way that traditional religious and cultural values survive and accommodate in the age of the Internet. One area where this is true is changing gender relations: The sexes are not supposed to mix, yet Moroccan youth have ideas and ideals of romantic love. They meet on the Internet, yet ask parental approval to marry. Women often work outside the home; sometimes their husbands help at home—but not when their relatives might see them.

Another area is media. They are visibly both more immersed in non-Moroccan media than their parents could have imagined *and* more ready to interest themselves in global cultural and religious politics. Moroccan young people, whether in school or not, have largely given up on reading literature or science and have settled for quick conversations on the cell phone, SMS tweaks of each other's attention, and the occasional cyber romance. They listen to a heady sampling of the world's most engaging music, with a healthy mix of colloquial Moroccan hip-hop. They have friends who have tried to make a living online and found themselves in a world of scams (the Moroccan dirham does not convert to hard currency), and everybody knows someone who married their true love after a courtship conducted between cybercafé patrons—but also approved by parents. These youth are, by conventional standards, poorly and inappropriately educated for a 21st-century life (World Bank, 2008). They are, however, surprisingly "wired," and ready to make their way into a global information economy, if they can find an economic and cultural home there. You'll find them on YouTube producing mash-ups of American with Moroccan audiovisuals that attract hundreds of thousands of viewers and thousands of public comments. They are the next generation of Moroccans.

References and Further Reading

Agence Nationale de Réglementation des Télécommunications (ANRT). (2007). *Le rapport annuel 2007*. Rabat, Morocco: ANRT. Retrieved from www.anrt.ma

Ali Zaoua, prince de la rue. (2000). A film by Nabil Ayouch. See www.imdb.com/title/tt0260688

Bennani-Chraibi, M. (2000). Youth in Morocco: An indicator of a changing society. In R. Meijer (Ed.), *Alienation or integration of Arab youth*. Richmond, UK: Curzon.

Davis, S. S. (1983). *Patience and power: Women's lives in a Moroccan village*. Rochester, VT: Schenkman.

Davis, S. S. (1993). Self and sexuality: Changing gender relations in a Moroccan town. In J. Tucker (Ed.), *Women and Arab society: Old boundaries, new frontiers*. Indianapolis, IN: University of Indiana Press.

Davis, S. S., & Davis, D. A. (1989). *Adolescence in a Moroccan town: Making social sense*. New Brunswick, NJ: Rutgers University Press.

Graiouid, S. (2005). Social exile and virtual *hrig*: Computer-mediated interaction and cybercafé culture in Morocco. In M. Wiberg (Ed.), *The interaction society: Practice, theories and supportive technologies*. Hershey, PA: Information Science Publishing.

Gregg, G. S. (2005). *The Middle East: A cultural psychology*. Oxford, UK: Oxford University Press.

Human Rights Watch. (2005). Morocco: Inside the home, outside the law: Abuse of child domestic workers in Morocco. New York: Human Rights Watch. Retrieved from www.hrw.org

Maher, V. (1974). *Women and property in Morocco: Their changing relation to the process of social stratification in the Middle Atlas*. New York, NY: Cambridge University Press.

Naamane-Guessous, S. (1992). *Au-delà de toute pudeur: La sexualité féminine au Maroc*. Casablanca, Morocco: Soden.

OpenNet Initiative. (2009). *Morocco*. Retrieved from http://opennet.net/research/profiles/morocco

Royaume du Maroc. (2004). *Haut Commissariat au Plan. Recensement Général de la Population et de l'Habitat. Caractéristiques démographiques et Socio-économiques de la Population*. Rabat: Royaume du Maroc. Retrieved from www.hcp.ma

World Bank. (2008). *The road not traveled: Education reform in the Middle East and North Africa*. MENA Development Report. New York: World Bank. Retrieved from http://web.worldbank.org

World Bank. (2009a). *Genderstats*. New York: World Bank. Retrieved from http://web.worldbank.org

World Bank. (2009b). *World development indicators database*. New York: World Bank. Retrieved from http://ddp-ext.worldbank.org

Chapter 5
Nigeria
Peace N. Ibeagha

Background Information

Nigeria is bordered to the north by the Republic of Niger, to the east by Cameroon and the Republic of Chad, and to the west by the Republic of Benin. About 800 km of the Atlantic Ocean coastline forms the southern border. Nigeria came into being in 1914, when the former British Colony and Protectorate of Southern Nigeria was amalgamated with the Protectorate of Northern Nigeria. Nigeria is the tenth largest country in Africa, and the most populous, with about 140 million people (FOS, 2006).

The river Niger-Benue (after which the country is named) divides the country into three major physical blocks, which roughly correspond to the former political regions of Northern, Eastern, and Western Nigeria. The climate is influenced mainly by the rain-bearing southwest winds from the ocean and the dry, dusty northwest winds from the Sahara Desert.

Nigeria has abundant supplies of underground minerals, forest, water resources, fossil fuels, and metallic, nonmetallic, and radioactive minerals. Some of the known minerals are petroleum, coal, lignite, columbite, gold, and iron ore. Others are uranium, limestone, marble, tin, gravel, and feldspar. Hardwood is the chief product obtained from Nigeria's forest. It is widely exploited throughout the country as timber poles, scaffolding planks, and stakes, and as fuel wood. Some forest and savanna trees produce useful fruits, nuts, and seeds. These forests and savanna are also used as game reserves. Hunting is an important traditional occupation in Nigeria.

Administratively, most of the ethno-linguistic groups that make up Nigeria previously existed as separate and autonomous political entities before they became part of the British Colonial Empire. The people lived in kingdoms and emirates with sophisticated systems of government.

The affairs of the colonial administration were conducted by the British until 1914, when a few Nigerians for the first time were appointed as nonofficial members of the executive council. From this point there was increased political awareness. In 1946, Nigeria was formally divided into three regions (Northern, Eastern, and Western) and each had a regional assembly consisting of persons selected by the Native Authority. In 1963, Nigeria became a Republic, severing all political links with the British Crown yet retaining membership of the British Commonwealth of independent nations.

In January 1966 the first administration of the first Republic was toppled in a military coup and replaced by a military administration. Nigeria came back to democratic administration in May 1999. The age structure of the Nigerian population is a young one, with about 45% being under 15 years of age and only 3.5% aged 65 years and above.

Period of Adolescence

Female adolescents have their first menstruation during their early teens. The *Nigerian Institute of Social and Economic Research* (1998) reported that 45% had menarche by their thirteenth birthday and 68% had it by age 14.

Many Nigerian communities have ceremonial rites or rites of passage that are arranged to support adolescents in their transition to adulthood. Rites of passage have been intensified as socialization strategies that provide a structured, formalized, and holistic process through which adolescents develop competencies that empower them to cope with the many challenges they will encounter as they enter adulthood. Some of these traditional rites of passage are the Ovia-Osesa festival of the Ogori people, a three-month festival to mark puberty, during which there is confirmation about a girl's chastity and the forecast of her future by the oracle of the community. The celebration includes presentation of gifts. The fear of what the oracle might say motivates girls to strive to maintain their chastity (Awe, 1986).

Other rites include clitoridectomy by the Ijaw people in the Niger Delta. Clitoridectomy is the removal of the clitoris and is believed to prevent difficult labor during childbirth. Some of the rites for boys also entail harsh physical trials. The Fulani culture engages in Shadi, a festival of flogging the adolescent male, to prove his maturity and braveness.

In other groups, rites focus more on adult roles than on physical trials. Among the Igbos, adolescents at puberty are initiated into the social age group where they hold meetings and discuss growing up and preparedness for marriage. The adolescent girls, who in most cases are already betrothed, are given out to marriage and assume adult roles according to their age grade. Most of the celebrations for rites of passage are designed to prepare the adolescent for handling the adult rites associated with marriage and future responsibilities. The Kalapesi/ereso, a passage rite for boys in the Riverine part of Nigeria, trains boys to participate in communal rituals, which will supply manpower during communal works. Males at this stage are called upon to dig graves, and girls to cook for visitors during funerals. In other ethnic groups when a boy successfully cuts down his first bunch of palm fruits it is an indication that he has attained "young adulthood."

In Nigerian tradition, adolescence has a relatively short history as a recognized stage in the life span of girls and boys. The interval between puberty and marriage lasted longer for boys than for girls in the traditional Nigerian society. Males generally need time to acquire resources before setting up a marital household and therefore do not marry until they are older, compared with the point at which the females marry. Traditionally, many girls had no period of maidenhood, defined as the interval between menarche and marriage. Girls were married soon after menarche and sometimes moved into their husband's family residence even before reaching puberty. Thus girls of those days had no visible adolescence (Makinwa et al., 1998). Circumstances are changing for girls in the present Nigerian society where education is becoming widespread, age at marriage is increasing, age at menarche is declining, and the interval between puberty and marriage is lengthening. As a result, girls are facing a prolonged risk of premarital pregnancy and reproductive health problems prior to marriage.

Beliefs

There are three major religious groups in Nigeria: Christianity, Islam, and the traditional indigenous religion. Religious diversity has been a complicated issue resulting in frequent conflict in Nigeria. Currently, Muslims account for 50% of the population, Christians 40%, and followers of indigenous religions 10%. There is a larger Muslim population in the northern states and a larger Christian population in the southern states (National Population Commission (NPC), 2000).

Indigenous theology includes obligations to dead ancestors, whose spirits demand adherence to the moral rules governing all human actions. The belief about supernatural residents of the land applies to spirits of places such as trees, rock outcrops, rivers, and of snakes or other animals and objects. Thus such trees will never be cut down; snakes will not be killed even if they are found in the house. These spirits are believed to ensure continual fertility of both land and people, and protection against misfortune. They are also believed to punish personal or communal immorality through sickness, drought, fires, and other catastrophes. There are special practitioners who are believed to be in control of supernatural forces to heal illnesses and counter evil intentions by others. Many young Nigerians have been socialized to arm themselves with charms and medicinal products purchased from the practitioners. These charms are believed to protect against peer rivalries, cult clashes and killings among adolescents, political rivalries, sickness, and misfortune.

The Muslim parts of Nigeria have grown more conservative in recent years. From 1999 to 2000 several northern states moved to institute Sharia law, a strict form of Islamic law based on the Koran (Gupta, Busa, and Mehdi, 2004). At present 12 of the 36 states in Nigeria are seeking to institute or have instituted some form of Sharia law. These moves have led to widespread rioting and violence by non-Muslim residents of these states.

Gender

Nigerian society is very patriarchal. This originates in the family system in which male power over women and children derives from the social role of fatherhood and is supported by a political economy in which the family unit retains a significant productive role. This patriarchal relationship is found to be changing as a result of education, employment, and income.

With regard to adolescents, Karanja (1992) noted that girls above age 10 or 12 help their mothers with cooking, fetching of water, minding children, washing clothes, serving fathers lunch or dinner, collecting farm produce, and purchasing commodities in other cities or markets. Boys do less because while they may help their parents with family business, they are not as involved in domestic work as the girls. Thus gender division of labor at this stage will no doubt have serious implications on school and the general life chances of the girl child. In addition, the issue of girl child marriage which is still being practiced by some communities jeopardizes the continued education of the girl.

The Self

Traditional education during the evenings involves folktales that teach several morals on the value of different human traits, informally told by people of the older generation to the younger ones within the community. This promotes intergenerational rapport and transmission of the language and culture. The informal atmosphere of folktales allows for the asking of questions, feedback of different sorts, and other types of informal interaction that encourage the development of identity and solidarity with the community essence (Eya, 2003).

One-third of adolescents in cities are migrants from rural areas. When these migrants come to the cities, their world changes drastically. Their identity changes from one dominated by traditional values to one reflecting a version of Western values, one which is neither genuinely Western nor, any longer, based on Nigerian traditional values. The language is neither correct English nor correct ethnic language. Away from the watchful eyes and traditional values of their families and communities, these adolescents get involved with the language, values, and culture that belong to the town they migrate to, and forget their roots and tradition.

The changing trends in identity development among the migrant adolescents indicate that they lack basic knowledge of their parent communities and traditions. Violations of their parent values and norms are no longer a taboo. They do not see anything wrong with premarital sex, night parties, and induced abortion where marriage could not be arranged. They dress differently—more like the ethnic group to which they have migrated. However, there is this culture and language that is neither Western nor Nigerian, which has its own language and way of dressing. Being together at school without the family is the source of influence of the peer group and its consequences.

Family Relationships

Traditionally, everybody living in the community where a child is born is a parent to that child. When greetings are said, inquiries are made about "our children"—that is, identifying with a child from the other family. For most young adolescents the feeling of belonging to the extended family that offers mutual aid and a sense of common purpose and belongingness has been seriously compromised in recent years. Ties to family and community are becoming less and less important as families become smaller and workers become mobile and independent of the families.

Nevertheless, the kinship system in today's changing world still operates with the same mechanisms as it did before, and primary loyalties are given to members of the family. Individuals know that as long as their behavior is within the expected bounds, someone will feed, clothe, and school them, and they expect to be called on to do the same for others. There is security in the knowledge that these relationships will never be broken and also in knowing clearly what is expected.

The tradition of polygamy in Nigeria supports this value of interdependence. In the traditional society, all the wives live together and rear the children communally. In the past polygamy was tolerated, though occasionally the wives were suspicious of one another over the security of their children. Ibeagha, Onocha, Adedimeji, & Jonathan-Ibeagha's (1998) report on their adolescent study showed that 67% of the respondents had fathers married to only one wife, but 23% of the fathers had two wives, and 6% had three wives or more.

In most of Nigeria adolescents do not separate into a distinct group with its own identity and values. They live with their families and participate in adult activities to a comparable extent. For example, they assume responsibilities in the running of the household at an early age, and grow into handling adult responsibilities. These activities formally initiate the child into adult society. At the age of adolescence the child is already aware of the role he/she is to play in the society as an adult male or female and has been groomed to assume such roles, which have been clearly defined by the same society. There is therefore no conflict or confusion and no peer pressure that conflicts with parental pressure.

When Nigerian adolescents and parents experience conflict it is most often due to differences in the judgments of parental authority on making rules that concern adolescent friendship, demands on their rights, and music and clothing (Ibeagha, 2003). Adolescents' conception of the parenting role obligation regarding their person is limited to morals. Thus when parents make rules on these other issues they instigate conflict between themselves and their adolescents.

Parents are deemed ultimately responsible for the behavior of their children when the parents teach and model interaction among members of the household. Parents send children on errands as a method of training their cognitive development and assumption of responsibilities. Adults believe that children are the products of the family environment in which they are raised. If the child is errant, it is the parents' responsibility for failing to instill the proper social values. This obsession with family honor results in parents exerting as much control as possible over offspring.

Relationships with parents are marked by autonomy and are very affectionate even though emotions are not always expressed verbally. Parents tell the children what they should do, but more in terms of suggestions. Children keep the close link to their parents even after they move out of the house, and they continue to care for parents. Today, schooling and the predominance of English have produced a generation gap where the young ones know more than the adults, but they respect the adult knowledge of traditional ways and the gap is not a problem.

Friends and Peers/Youth Culture

Nigerian adolescent boys are initiated into social age groups where they learn to be men. These groups have dance festivals during which spectators are entertained, and some festivals serve as a source for spouses. Other leisure activities adolescents are involved in include going to parties, smoking, and drinking.

Music (Juju, religious, etc.) and sports such as football have occupied increasingly important positions in the lives and outlook of Nigerian adolescents. Personal and collective immersion in music and sports has, more than ever before, become both a coping mechanism in the face of local and global adversity and an empowerment strategy for dealing with poverty. Some adolescents use music and sports to liberate themselves from this era of widespread disillusionment and alienation. The emergence of global TV and its round-the-clock music and sports programming with the Internet has facilitated the growth of these leisure strategies.

Football (soccer) is a major leisure game for the boys. Dance involving traditional and Western styles is a major leisure activity that stretches across ethnic, religious, male, and female groups. The girls who usually are not allowed to go out indulge in indoor games such as ludo and cards.

Visits to friends of the same sex are a favorite pastime. However, there is growing interest in visits to friends of the other sex. These visits are not usually direct; they may be indirect, using some adult-acceptable passage such as religious gatherings, sports, and student gatherings. In the northern part of Nigeria, the Islamic religious way of life does not permit free interaction between unmarried teenagers of different genders. Despite the restriction, the adolescents still find a way to interact with members of the other sex at hidden places.

Some groups of adolescent friends cause disruptions to others. "Area boys" are a type of juvenile gang mainly found in Lagos as youths who contribute to contemporary urban violence (Omitogun, 1994). The area boy phase is a dangerous one in the degeneration of youths who previously played a positive role in their communities into social miscreants and hoodlums perpetrating all kinds of terror on the streets of Lagos.

Love and Sexuality

Traditional preliterate Nigerian society did not allow unguarded socializing among boys and girls in their teens. There were strict codes of behavior and penalties prescribed for transgressors. As a result of these cultural values, boys and girls were to be educated in separate institutions supervised by teachers of the appropriate sex. In recent years, not only are many of the existing institutions mixed, but also premarital chastity is no longer cherished.

Today, boyfriend/girlfriend relationships are common in Nigeria except where religious prohibitions inhibit them. The context of sexual and social relationships among adolescents is influenced by love or lust and the desire to experiment. This has led to conflicts between traditional and modern sexual values. Young men will attempt to have sexual relationships with their age-mates, but may decide not to marry a girl who has given in to them. They are also extremely protective of their sisters. This leads to some mistrust in the relations between the sexes.

Traditionally, the wedding festivities would culminate in the bride's and groom's retreat to a bedroom, and briefly afterwards, a female member of the family would bring out blood-stained bed sheets for display to the crowds. Today, many young couples have in fact had sexual relations before the wedding, so the display of bed sheets can be a problem. The custom is being abandoned in middle-class families, who may even resort to a civil marriage only.

Makinwa-Adebusoye (1991) reported that most young persons in a survey considered that 18 years, which is the age when young persons attain voting and other rights in Nigeria, is the ideal age when boys and girls can date in groups and also when a boy may begin to go out alone with a girl. However, 19 years was considered the ideal age for a girl to go out alone with a boy.

A focus group discussion among adolescent schoolboys and schoolgirls in Ibadan revealed that not only are many of them initiated early in sexual activities but some delight in keeping many sexual partners even at their age (Adejumo, 2001). Knowledge of STDs is fairly widespread, and one out of every four females and one out of every three males stated that they considered STDs a common problem. Responses to further probing revealed that 75% of females and 81% of males had heard about AIDS. Gonorrhea was well known from advertisements on billboards advertising cures for gonorrhea by traditional herbalists. Two percent of females and 13% of males stated that they had been infected by an STD.

Thirty-six percent of female respondents and 33% of male respondents reported that the ideal age for a girl or a boy to have first intercourse is when the girl or boy is married. Other respondents favored age 18 or 20 for boys and age 18 for girls. The Nigerian Demographic Health Survey (NDHS) (1999) showed a median age at first intercourse in 1990 of 16 compared with 18 in 1999. The majority of young persons appear to favor premarital sexual relations when there is the prospect of eventual marriage to the sexual partners.

The NDHS reported that on a national scale, there has been a slight shift from marrying during the midteen years to the later teen years. The median age of marriage has shifted slightly to 18 for females and 25 for males. There is a slight decrease from 18 in the rural community compared to the urban.

Groups of young females stand on the streets of big cities such as Lagos, Ibadan, and Port Harcourt at night to look out for customers to whom they will prostitute themselves. The average age range of these young women is between 15 and 27 years. These young prostitutes assume some respectability for the trade, and they call it "doing business." They take customers as they get them, but the special attraction is Western migrant workers who have dollars or pounds sterling. Some practice this trade as a part-time job, such as college students, university undergraduates, and office workers. It also has export dimensions, known as "plucking tomatoes." The "tomatoes" are young women uprooted from their native soil for overseas use. Most girls are lured deceitfully, but some willingly participate in the trade.

Health Risk Behavior

Adolescents living in Nigeria are 10 times more likely to die from road traffic accidents than are their counterparts living in the developed Western world (Adejumo, 2004). However, drug abuse is relatively low among adolescents in Nigeria. Hamzat, Okeze, and Olaleye (2004) reported that among youth 12 to 25 years old, 6% smoke cigarettes, 10% drink alcohol, 24% drink coffee, and 11% chew kolanut, a mild stimulant that eases hunger and fatigue.

As a result of social problems as well as uncertainties and frustration, some youth in their desperate bid to survive in the society join gang groups that provide a sense of belonging, achievement, and peer support. Gang involvement may include engaging in illegal or improper extortion of money from motorists, passers-by, and market men and women. The boys who join these gangs often possess few or no skills and therefore cannot take on urban jobs. They occupy the slums and other unplanned areas of the city. Most youths in these groups usually engage in menial jobs and sometimes beg, pilfer, and indulge in street fighting. However, some of these youth organizations assume security responsibilities in city motor parks and garages, and control traffic on the roads in eastern Nigeria and also in Lagos. It should be noted that the youth who join these organizations are caught up in the rapid economic and political changes and disintegration of traditional family structures which tend to produce a large number of children or youth who go uncared for.

Education

According to Fafunwa (2003), the Nigerian educational system is shaped by three forces: traditional, Islamic, and Western. From the very beginning, as a people Nigerians have had indigenous traditional education. Traditional education is the type that goes on in the home and in the farms, streets, clans, and shrines, and includes the "moonlight stories" and their interpretations, proverbs, and idioms of the various communities. This education cares about the way a person looks, laughs, and even the way a person cries. The growing child interacts with the tradition and learns.

Sule-Kano (2000) reported on how traditional Koranic scholarship was made an integral part of the socioeconomic, political, and cultural way of life of the predominantly Islamic social formation in Northern Nigeria. Beginning from 1804, a vigorous campaign to eradicate illiteracy and develop the youth was launched by the leadership of the Caliphate. Qualified teachers were sent to urban and rural areas for what was then referred to as the intellectual upliftment of the people. The tutors instructed the students in the area of religious studies; five different languages; philosophy; arithmetic; history; and theological sciences. Scholarship flourished and many parents sent their children—both boys and girls—to these schools.

Later the colonial state in Nigeria engineered policies that undermined the traditional Koranic school system and it was rendered irrelevant in the dispensation of knowledge. It was left to its own devices, the outcome being deprivation, poverty, and destitution. There was virtually no more community support. Parents were left to make individual contributions to the institution whenever they so wished. Most parents would prefer to shed the burden of their children to the traditional schools.

Today, the relatively low literacy rate of 65% is one of the problems facing adolescents. According to the data from the National Population Commission, one adolescent out of four cannot read or write. The high cost of education to already impoverished parents causes an alarming rate of educational wastage (dropout and repetition) as reported among adolescents. The problem is so acute that UNICEF is currently engaged in arresting the tide of the high rate of educational wastage among male youths in several states in southeastern Nigeria.

Girls are more likely than boys to have received no education, and the percentage of boys enrolled in secondary and tertiary institutions is higher than for girls. Early marriage has been identified as a factor that curtails schooling in girls in Northern Nigeria. There is no free basic education even from primary to Junior Secondary School. In many states, recent decrees/edicts have legalized

payment of one form of educational levy or another, to the extent that the quality of education a child receives in Nigeria depends on the amount of money his or her parents are willing to pay for it.

Economic hardship has forced many families to withdraw their youths from school and put them to work as apprentices, hawkers, and artisans. Other parents have withdrawn their youths because the public school system has become unreliable as it presents an uninteresting, secularized, and outdated curriculum leading to acquisition of inadequate and irrelevant skills and knowledge.

Work

Adolescents and children are involved in economic activities. Some simultaneously attend schools and work. Oloko (1998) reported that the proportion of students in Lagos who admitted that they engaged in street vending after school hours increased from one out of four in 1979 to two out of four in 1988 and two out of three in 1997. The proportion of young vendors who worked all day without respite was 21% in 1998. Adeagbo (1997) reported that 58% of street traders in southwest Nigeria are young adolescents and youth. They sell items ranging from lamps and clocks to biscuits and fruit juices on major roads, particularly during traffic jams. These are familiar sights in many cities in the southern states.

Apart from street vending, other work that adolescents are involved in includes begging, car-washing, shoe-shining, and scavenging. In the formal sector, adolescents are involved as apprentices, mechanics, vulcanizers, iron/metal and wood workers, bus conductors, cloth weavers/tailors, hairdressers, and workers in hotel catering. Many Nigerian adolescents go through the tradition of being recruited as domestic servants, called "house helps." These house helps are integrated into the new family. They may benefit in some way from the family, but in most cases these children are exploited, doing too much work for long hours.

According to Okojie (1994), while a majority of youth from middle and high socioeconomic backgrounds enter tertiary institutions, most poor youth drop out of the educational system and end up in vocational training as apprentices. Girls take up sewing and hairdressing while boys engage in carpentry, welding, plumbing, block making, and motor mechanics.

For urban adolescents who are out of school there is an opportunity to engage in some income-generating activities. These include helping parents at home, farming, engaging in odd jobs, and religious activities. Some stay at home with nothing to do. Urbanization provides job opportunities for many unskilled migrant youths who go back to their village homes during festive periods to display their success.

Media

Nigerian adolescents have access to some electronic media. Over 90% of adolescents in rural areas listen to radio compared to 85% in urban areas. TV viewing is also common. For example, Eigbado and Ibeagha (2003) reported that over half of adolescents watched TV for about four to seven hours per day. The easy access to the media has positively influenced the literacy level of the adolescents, who have learned a lot of positive activities such as cookery, sports, games, and education courses through the media. The media also influence their experimentation with drugs and use of fashion.

There is some cultural conflict from the influx of Western films into Nigeria. The Western styles of clothing, awkward facial expressions, and grotesque eye makeup—all attributable to film influence of American, European, and Asian origin—conflict with the Nigerian dressing norms, thereby causing conflict between some adolescents and their parents.

Many adolescents—about one-fourth—preoccupy themselves with pornographic films, not in their homes but on the Internet. Despite repeated warning against this preoccupation by the government, educators, and school authorities, an increasing number of youths still go to cybercafés to see the pictures of nude men and women.

Politics and Military

Nigerian adolescents are allowed to vote for the political leader at the age of 18 years. In a study by Ibeagha (2003) on Nigeria's democratic process and adolescent/youth opinion, the findings showed that 35% of the participants disagreed with the democratic setup currently in place, while 63% of the participants saw the elections as not being free and fair. The youth groups in Nigeria are of the opinion that the lawmakers are not truly representing the interest of the masses but rather are in government to fulfill their selfish desires, forgetting the needs of those that elected them. As a result, the youth are easily manipulated by political and religious fanatics who foment eruptions of violence.

Youth/adolescent campus politics is an avenue for interested youth to get involved and express their political desires in the student leadership within the universities. Such student leaders are expected to end up as the future leaders in Nigeria.

Children aged 15 or older are eligible for recruitment into any of the armed forces. Paramilitary organizations, road safety, intelligence, and police networks do not recruit people below 18 years of age. However, in war situations such as the Nigerian Biafran war (1967–70), there was compulsory recruitment of adolescents into the army by the Biafrans and into other paramilitary forces such as the Militia, the Red Cross, the Boys and Girls Brigade, and the Boy Scouts. These groups were used as vigilantes for the communities to detect the infiltration of enemies, provision of first-aid to the injured, and maintenance of peace within the community.

Unique Issues

Adolescents in Nigeria enjoy repetition of words, such that they seem to have formed their own language which is peculiar to them and is understood mostly by them. They express themselves in duplicate words, for example: *cry cry* (cry often), *chop chop* (eating), *lie lie* (liar), *chooku chooku* (thorny), *fry fry* (you fry a lot), *jaga jaga, nyama nyama* (untidy), *thief thief* (a suspect for stealing), *yori yori, lekpe lekpe* (weak), *play play* (you play a lot), *waka waka* (restless), *notin notin* (hopeless), *holy holy* (purity), *copy copy* (imitation).

Another unique thing about language development among the Nigerian adolescents is their formation of words and phrases with part western and part Nigerian language. Thus they form language that is understood by themselves. These include: *na bend down* (second-hand product), *shay* (you understand), *no wahala* (I am fine), *spirikoko* (acts spiritual), *fife & six* (we are close in relationship), *over sabi* (inquisitive), *I de ha* (I am hungry), *level don change* (promotion), *tear rubber* (new car). When an adolescent sees someone she is not expecting, in excitement she will exclaim, *na lie, na lie*. If an adult is near such an adolescent, the adult will not understand whom the adolescent is referring to. The unique adolescent language has grown to the point that it is used in song. They sing songs that many adults cannot understand because of the word combination for example, *Na you bu chim o o*.

References and Further Reading

Adeagbo, D. (1997). *Physical and socio-economic impact of street trading: Case study of Ibadan*. Monograph 10. Ibadan, Nigeria: NISER.

Adejumo, O. (2004). *Influence of psychosocial factors on HIV sexual risk behaviour among adolescents in Ibadan, Nigeria*. Poster Exhibition: The 3rd IAS Conference on HIV Pathogenesis and Treatment, Rio de Janeiro, Brazil: Abstract no. MoPe9.5C09.

Awe, B. (1986). *The place of cultural festival in national development. A case of Ovia–Osese festival, Ovia festival digest* (Proceedings of the First National Seminar, an Ovia–Osese festival).

Eigbado, G., & Ibeagha, P. N. (2003). *Adolescents and the media*. Paper presented at Conference on Nigeria and Democracy, Univesity of Ibadan, Nigeria.

Eya, R. N. (2003). *Child psychology*. Enugu, Nigeria: Auto-Century Publishing.

Fafunwa, B. A. (2003). Education in Nigeria: First Foundation Annual Lecture. E. Yoloye and A. Osiyale (Eds.).

Gupta, S., Busa, T., & Mehdi, A. (2004). *School education and religious communal tensions in India, and possible analogues with Nigeria: Legislation, policy and curriculum*. Workshop on Globalisation, Identity Politics and Social Conflict: Ethnic, Literary and Sociolinguistic Perspectives, Lagos, Nigeria.

Hamzat, T. K., Okpeze, C. N., & Olaleye, O. A. (2004). Health related behaviour of students of Federal College of Agriculture, Animal Health and Production Technology. *Contemporary Issues and Researches on Adolescents*. Ibadan, Nigeria: Royal People (Nigeria).

Ibeagha, P. N. (2003). Parenting factors influencing parent–adolescent conflict in Ibadan. *Nigerian Journal of Clinical and Counselling Psychology*, 9(1).

Ibeagha, P. N., Onocha, C. O., Adedimeji, B., & Jonathan-Ibeagha, E. (1998). *An assessment of the adolescent in Oyo State*. Commissioned by the John D. and Catherine T. MacArthur Foundation, Chicago, IL.

Makinwa-Adebusoye, P. K., Onadeko, M., Afolayan, A. A., Ibeagha, R. P. N., & Jegede, D. (1995). *The situation analysis of women and the girlchild in Nigeria*. Lagos, Nigeria: WORDOC/UNICEF.

National Population Commission. (2000).

Nigerian Institute of Social and Economic Research. (1998). *Adolescent sexual behaviour, Reproductive health and fertility in Nigeria*. Lagos, Nigeria: Population Research Fund Management Unit, NISER.

Okojie, C. E. (1994). Poor housing and the integration and employment of youth in Nigeria. In J. Albert et al. (Eds.), *Urban management and urban violence in Africa* (Vol. 12, pp. 179–190). I. Proceedings of International Symposium on Urban Violence in Africa, Ibadan, Nigeria, 7–11 November, sponsored by French Institute for Research in Africa (IFRA).

Oloko, S. B. A. (1998). Protection and violation of child rights in Nigeria: An overview. *Child Protection in Nigeria* (Vol. 4). New York, NY: UNICEF.

Omitogun, W. (1994). The area boys of Lagos. A study of organized street violence. In J. Albert et al. (Eds.), *Urban management and urban violence in Africa* (Vol. 12, pp. 179–190). Proceedings of International Symposium on Urban Violence in Africa, Ibadan, Nigeria, 7–11 November, sponsored by French Institute for Research in Africa (IFRA).

Sule-Kano, A. (2000). *The Nigerian youth and the Nigerian state*. Positive Leadership Monograph Series no. 4. Center for Social Science Research Development.

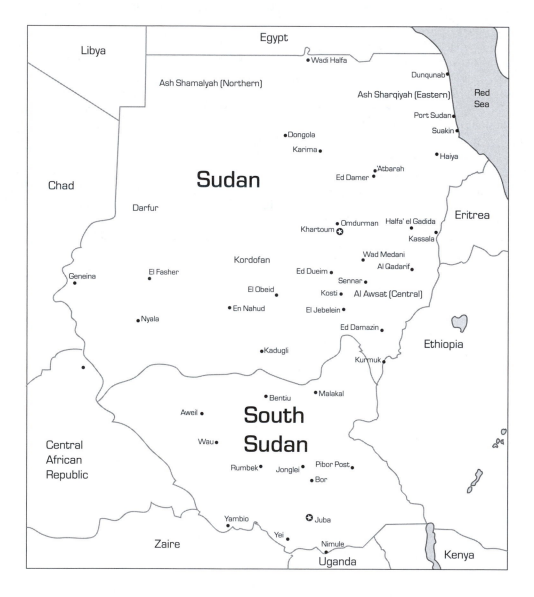

Chapter 6
Sudan
Abdelbagi Dafalla Ahmed

Background Information

Sudan lies in the northern part of Africa, bordering the Red Sea, between Egypt and Eritrea. The Nile River and its tributaries dominate its landscape. With an area of over 2.5 million square kilometers, it is the largest country on the continent. The terrain is generally marked by flat plains, although there are mountains in the east and west. The climate is tropical in the south. Arid desert conditions prevail in the north, with a rainy season lasting from June to October. Soil erosion and desertification are observable environmental problems.

In ancient times, Kushite kingdoms ruled over most of the land that constitutes the present Sudan. These kingdoms influenced and were in turn influenced by Pharaonic Egypt. Most of the inhabitants of Nubia were converted to Coptic Christianity in the sixth century, and by the eighth century three states flourished in the area. These states long resisted invasions from Egypt, which came under Muslim rule around 640. However, from the thirteenth to the fifteenth centuries, the region was increasingly infiltrated by people from the north, and Nubia gradually became Muslim. The southern part of modern Sudan continued to adhere to traditional African beliefs (Mahdi, 1965).

In 2009, the population was estimated at about 39 million. The annual growth rate is 3.6%. Half of the population is under 16 years of age. According to the 2009 census, the majority of the population lives in rural areas (69%), and 28% live in urban areas, while 3% are nomads (Central Bureau of Statistics report, 2009).

The people of Sudan can be divided into three main ethnic groups. The largest ethnic group is the Arabs, but this category is internally split by regional and tribal loyalties and affiliation to various Muslim politico-religious groups. The major Muslim-but-non-Arab groups are the Nubians in the far north, the nomadic Beja in the northeast, and the Fur in the west. Southern non-Muslim groups include the Dinka (more than 10% of total population and 40% in south), the Nuer, and numerous smaller ethnic groups. The total number of ethnic groups is 246. There are about 115 spoken dialects, but Arabic is the primary and official language of the country. English is the common second language in the south.

Sudan has turned around a struggling economy with sound economic policies and infrastructure investments, but it still faces formidable economic problems, stemming from its low level of per capita output. Since 1997, Sudan has been implementing International Monetary Fund (IMF) macroeconomic reforms. In 1999, Sudan began exporting crude oil, and in the last quarter of 1999 recorded its first trade surplus, which, along with monetary policy, has stabilized the exchange rate. Increased oil production, revived light industry, and expanded export processing zones helped sustain gross domestic product (GDP) growth at 6.4% in 2005. Until the second half of 2008, Sudan's economy boomed on the back of increases in oil production, high oil prices, and large inflows of foreign direct investment. GDP growth registered more than 10% per year in 2006 and 2007. Agriculture remains Sudan's most important sector, employing 80% of the workforce and contributing 39% of the GDP, but most farms remain dependent on rain and susceptible to drought. The major crops are cotton, peanuts, sorghum, millet, wheat, sugarcane, mangos, papaya, bananas, sweet potatoes, and sesame (Sudan Economy, 2010).

The nature of the government changed from a military ruling junta (1989) to a presidential republic when an election was held in 1996 resulting in a National Assembly (parliament). Southern Sudan was led by a group of Dinka soldiers who believed that the southerners were underestimated in governing their region and Sudan as a whole, so they led the longest internal war in the nation's recent history (1983–2005). This war greatly influenced southerners' access to education, health, and general stability. A new peace treaty was signed in January 2005, granting autonomy to the southern rebels. A referendum took place in Southern Sudan from 9 to 15 January 2011, on whether the region should remain a part of Sudan or become independent. The referendum was one of the consequences of the 2005 Naivasha Agreement between the Khartoum central government and the Sudan People's Liberation Army/Movement (SPLA/M).

On 7 February 2011, the referendum commission published the final results, with 98.83% voting in favor of independence. The predetermined date for the creation of an independent state is 9 July 2011.

In 2003, conflict erupted in the Darfur region, resulting in the death and displacement of thousands, if not millions. Presidential and parliamentary elections were held in April 2010 to elect the President of Sudan and the National Assembly of Sudan. The election brings to an end the transitional period which began when the decades-long Second Sudanese Civil War ended in 2005.

Period of Adolescence

The time preceding adulthood is not traditionally seen as a separate stage, but it is recognized as the beginning of sexual maturation, which will culminate in sexual engagement. The concept of adolescence is usually applied when criticizing adolescents' misbehavior. It is the stage when secondary signs of puberty start to appear. Puberty and adolescence denote only a sexual concept. The term used for puberty in Arabic is *bilooq*, which means reaching sexual maturity. Adolescence is also labeled in Arabic as *murahagah*, which means suffering in controlling sexual urges and behaving as a mature person. The term *bilooq* is used at the beginning of sexual development, while *murahagah* is applied when the child is functioning as a sexually mature individual.

Secondary signs of puberty start to appear at the age of 11 for girls and at 13–14 for boys. In remote rural areas, these signs may lead the father to prevent his daughter from going to school because he might think she would be sexually assaulted; the school may be located far away, perhaps 5 km or so. Consequently, she might remain in the house helping her mother in domestic work, and if she is physically developed, she might get married at the age of 14 or 15. This rarely happens among females in urban centers.

The modern system of schooling for the economic elite in urban, semi-urban, and even in most rural centers prolongs the time of dependence on family resources until graduation from university, which generally occurs between the ages of 21 and 25. Many females get married while doing their university studies, or within two years after graduation. Females marry earlier than males, who may go abroad (often to Gulf countries) to prepare themselves financially for marriage. Staying abroad for work may last 20 years. Some adults may marry during education and live with their rich extended families. Those who did not complete their education may either marry at 21 years of age or go abroad to assist their families in facing everyday demands.

Beliefs

The Sudanese people are sociable, easygoing, and conservative in their social interaction. Traditionally, Sudanese society has been organized as a patriarchal system in which power rests with elders, particularly males. To confirm this, there is a famous Sudanese proverb that says "Those who have no elder must search for one." Older males are socialized to take care of their younger brothers, so the system emphasizes the family over the individual. Older sisters usually follow after the role of their mothers, especially in domestic matters such as washing the clothes of all family members, preparing food, and cleaning the house. Young males, meanwhile, usually assist their fathers in their work or work independently. Older females and males are socialized to feel lifelong responsibility for younger brothers. All offspring are socialized to be responsible for and take care of their parents as they get old. The collective method of living widely practiced in Sudan is unlikely to change drastically in the foreseeable future, as it is a well-established system rooted in religious and traditional culture.

The main religious beliefs practiced depend on whether the adolescent is Muslim or Christian. These beliefs are transmitted through different institutions and means of socialization. For example, it is compulsory to study religious courses throughout all classes in primary and secondary education. It is also compulsory to study a religious course in the first year of university, regardless of one's field of study. In addition to the effort of parents in advising their children as to the right religious teaching, there is the local method of Koranic centers, found in north Sudan (Khalwa), where students of all ages study and memorize the Koran.

Parents traditionally attended mosque or church with their children, and taught them how to say or to do prayers. Muslim families are keen to take their children with them to attend and do at least Friday prayers. In general, members of the older generations are very keen to maintain their religious practices; the majority of adolescents learns their prayers from their older relatives, and attend to them faithfully. Families encourage teenagers to train themselves for an hour or a day or two days to prepare for the 30-day fast of Ramadan, the holiest month in the Muslim year. But when he must fast at Ramadan the adolescent usually gets used to it, and he will break the fast with elders as a sign of social and religious maturation.

Gender

Each sex is expected to refrain from socializing with the other sex during adolescence. Moreover, female adolescents are expected to dress decently. The issue of female dress may differ according to religion. Christian females often dress in Western styles, leaving their hair uncovered. Muslim women, however, wear *alzay-alislami* (Islamic dress), in which either the female covers her entire face and wears gloves, or covers her body with a wide and thin dress and her head with a piece of cloth (called *hijab,* which means "the protector"). Other Muslim women may choose to wear Western-style clothing, but wear the hijab over their heads.

Traditionally, when girls reach adolescence, especially in rural areas, they wear the Sudanese *toub*, a long piece of cloth that covers all of the body and head, whereas the traditional male adolescent wears a Sudanese dress named the *jalabyyia* with a long piece of cloth ringed over the head, or a casual outfit like the jalabyyia called the araaqi, which is shorter, with a long under-dress. Today most adolescents in urban and semi-urban areas wear a shirt and pants, which may be rejected by most rural adolescents. Nowadays most female adolescents quit wearing the Sudanese toub for *ibaaya*, a famous Gulf-countries female dress, or dressing in a long skirt with a long-sleeved blouse and putting hijab on their heads.

Females may be prohibited from walking outdoors unaccompanied, especially at night. Males have more freedom, and can generally move as they wish out of doors. Moreover, females are expected to avoid talking loudly or laughing in public areas, or interacting with the opposite sex. These behaviors are considered unacceptable in almost all Sudanese communities, and the young woman who does not follow this code of conduct is generally considered not suitable for marriage.

Female adolescents are prepared during their overall socialization process to be successful household wives. Women are not barred from finding a job outside the home, although the majority of working married women work in education, because this field has a significant amount of vacation time and the work day is shorter than that of many other fields. This allows time for housework. Adolescent males are prepared to be good fathers who care for their children and respect their wives, and to have a good and respectable source of income. They are also prepared to take care of younger brothers and sisters.

The distinction between males and females is very important in the shaping and sharing of values in Dinka society (Deng, 1971). While the woman is not a slave, she is considered inferior to the man. However, women occupy a very important role in shaping children's sense of self and personality. In Nuer society, females of 12 or 13 begin to observe established traditional gender customs. For instance, from this point on, a female must never eat before a male of her own age or older. Furthermore, she must never see him eat if there is any possibility that he may be a suitor for her hand. If the female for any reason falls ill, the family quickly seeks medical help to guarantee the cattle they will acquire when she gets married. It is important to mention here that many traditions and customs of these tribes are changing because of modernization and the move toward living in urban centers.

A slim body is preferred today by both male and female adolescents in urban areas, especially among secondary school students. Traditionally, a heavier, well-built adolescent girl was preferred, and when a female was being prepared for marriage she would spend more than two months sitting in her home just eating and whitening her skin to look attractive on her wedding day. This is still the case in almost all of Sudan.

The Sunni type of female circumcision, which involves cutting the tip of the clitoris, is widely practiced in almost all of northern Sudan. Many NGOs have attempted to put an end to this practice. Pharaonic circumcision, in which the clitoris and labia minora are removed and the labia majora are sewn closed, leaving only a small opening for urination and menstruation, is still practiced in some remote rural areas, but there are many urban families who do not circumcise their daughters at all. The custom is gradually diminishing in almost all urban centers and in some semiurban centers.

The Self

Sudan traditionally may be divided into three major groups: Arabs, African origin tribes, and the minority Coptic Christians. Each group considers itself the superior and some tribal conflict may stem from these beliefs.

Many institutions contribute to shaping adolescent identity. The most important one is the extended family. Socialization in Sudanese communities emphasizes the family over the individual. Moreover, each individual's actions also affect all of the individual's relatives, no matter how distant the relationship may be. This fact checks individuals to some extent in their misdeeds, for any infringement of Nuer law affects not only them, but all their people as well (Johnson, 1997). The community or village is also an important component of the self. In Nuer society, for example, the Nuer person does not live for self but is a part of a particular village.

The extended family system is followed in all parts of Sudan (Muslim or Christian). Therefore, most males prefer to get married during early adulthood, sharing the big house with other members of the extended family. Females leave the household at marriage to live with their husband's family.

Coptic Christian parents exert strong control over their females, and do not allow them to marry outside the Christian community. Although it is permissible for a Muslim man to marry a Christian woman, the opposite is not permitted. This may put a great burden on the Coptic Christian adolescent to avoid Muslims and to avoid the temptation to join a Muslim society or convert. Some Coptic female adolescents may refuse to attend university, given that they do not think it appropriate to be in a coeducational setting.

Family Relationships

Family organization varies according to its type, whether nuclear, fraternal joint, or extended joint family. The senior male—usually the father or grandfather, or the oldest brother—is the head of the household and theoretically the final judge in all matters. He allots the money for household expenses. The finances may be rigorously controlled by the senior male; other members of the family must appeal to the master of the house for any money required. A senior woman—usually the grandmother—also generally assumes a superior position, giving frequent orders to others (especially women), looking after children, and telling them folkloric stories and tales (Cloudsley, 1983).

The professed ideal within the Sudanese family is that everyone should live to an equal standard and no one goes without necessities. However, some people in rural areas still regard females as inferior, which may affect this ideal. Children are the responsibility of everyone living in the village or the compound. Adolescents are permitted to contribute their opinions on family problems but are not fully-fledged decision-makers.

In Dinka society and in most Nilotic tribes a rich man may marry several women, and a chief may have over 100 wives. When there are many wives there are many houses, and each one includes a senior wife, her children, junior wives, and their children. In Islam, a man can marry many women, but he must not exceed four women simultaneously. Therefore, polygamy is quite acceptable in traditional Sudanese culture (Deng, 1971). It is still quite common to find four wives or more with their children living in the same household compound, children of different wives playing together. Some conflict may arise if the father is not firm and fair enough with his wives.

Adolescents across all these groups are expected to hold the standards and traditions of their tribes and religious teachings, and to be responsible for their younger siblings. They may quarrel often with their older or younger brothers. Adolescents are socialized to be obedient to their parents and other older persons in the family, so conflict between adolescents and parents is usually infrequent. Adolescents are socialized to show deference to parental authority, and to demonstrate love and respect toward their parents and siblings.

It is important to mention that drought, desertification, and war in the south and in Darfur led to the movement of a large number of persons to large cities and left hundreds of nuclear families uprooted from their traditions and social support. As a result, thousands of children were pushed to the streets.

There is a Sudanese proverb: "When your son grows up, make him your brother." This proverb has only one meaning: that a father must stop beating adolescents when they make a mistake; instead, they have to sit and negotiate with them when they commit a fault or when trying to take a decision concerning the whole family.

Recently parents have become more permissive with their adolescents, letting them voice their opinions, especially on issues of concern. Traditionally, adolescents, especially female, have not had the right to speak their opinions, even in matters such as their own wedding. Today, even in remote rural areas females have begun to speak out at least on issues of high importance.

Friends and Peers/Youth Culture

Parents are always monitoring the companions of their adolescents, especially in urban centers. During early adolescence, peers have traditionally been mostly relatives or neighborhood children, simply because such individuals are familiar and therefore their behavior is well known. Parents encourage this type of relationship, for females in particular, as long as these are same-gender friendships. Some Nilotic tribes' adolescents, especially those educated and living in urban centers, and some Arabs who are influenced by Western styles of living, may engage in male and female friendship, likely without their parents' knowledge.

Friendship is greatly valued in Sudanese culture, because it is a religious teaching. However, parents warn their adolescents, especially males, against companionship with wicked males who are regarded as a "bad influence" because adolescents imitate each other, share their adventurous experiences, and play the role of psychological supporter—especially when they get in trouble with parents or other peers.

There is only one big shopping mall in Khartoum, which opened in 2004 (many new big malls will open soon). Many adolescents, mainly males, use it as a social meeting place, wearing Western-style clothes and hair. This phenomenon is completely new to Sudanese culture. The majority of these adolescents are sons of expatriates, coming to spend their vacations with relatives in the homeland. Some adolescents in Khartoum also meet in fast-food restaurants, clubs, Internet cafés, and sometimes in an empty apartment exchanging talk, watching films on video, and smoking cigarettes. Adolescents of rural areas usually meet in big yards that lie in front of or behind their village, especially on moonlit nights, where they chat, play, or tell stories.

Love and Sexuality

One of the most sensitive issues in a Sudanese community is relationships between unmarried members of opposite sexes. Adolescents are not supposed to have much interaction—certainly not sexual interaction—with nonrelatives of the opposite sex. However, these taboo relations are becoming more flexible in urban and suburban centers, despite growing religious conservatism.

During group discussion among many adolescents about love and dating, they agreed that it is quite common to have a love relationship with the opposite sex, and the criteria for this love are admiration, ethnic group, and the possibility of frequent meeting (i.e., relatives or someone in the neighborhood) (Abdelbagi, 2006). The most common means applied by today's adolescents for chatting and dating are the telephone and mobile telephone. An unusual yet increasingly popular phenomenon is "mobile phone sex," in which two adolescents of the opposite sex imagine sexual intercourse through talking. This is clearly an urban phenomenon. An example of a mobile telephone message, taken with permission from a female adolescent's phone, is as follows: "In my life I learned how2 love, how2 smile, how2 work, how2 be happy, and how2 be strong, but I did not learned how2 stop missing you." Another message was written as follows: "I hope that I can kiss you 999 kisses, and I make a mistake in counting, so, I restart counting." A third example of these messages is: "with my 1 heart, 2 eyes, 5 liters blood, 206 bones. 1.2 million red cells, 60 trillion D.N.A.s, all are telling you happy New Year." This is very difficult to say for a teenage female, though it can be written easily, and become a point of a dialogue later.

In rural areas, love relationships are restricted to exchanging of smiles and glances. If it goes further, they may sit with others and chat all together. When reaching puberty, adolescent lovers may declare themselves engaged, and this is known among other villagers as a serious relationship, which usually ends with marriage. A male adolescent's sister (a third person) usually arranges dating for her brother with his girl, or a daughter of his relatives arranges the meeting between the two lovers. This is because it is permissible for a girl to enter the house and talk with her friend. Telecommunication now makes it possible to bypass the role played by a third person.

An adolescent female from the Barri tribe who resides in Juba Town stated (in a group discussion, 2010) that it is quite normal to practice sex with the lover, and that this is just a style of expressing their love to each other. It is very important to mention that this is completely an urban phenomenon. Traditionally, it is completely prohibited to practice premarital sex. If this happens, the female's brothers may kill both adolescents. It is believed that this adolescent has dishonored the family and broken traditional and heavenly laws. In case of pregnancy among adolescents, it would be *fadiiha* (shame), and the female would be compelled to break off all ties with her village relatives, remaining forever in a distant place, never daring to face a relative again for fear of her life. She may lead the life of a prostitute (Cloudsley, 1983).

Sexuality issues are rarely discussed with parents; concepts of it are usually shared with peers of the same age, or through reading about it from specialized books or magazines. WHO reports noted that AIDS and other forms of devastating sexually transmitted diseases are rare among Sudanese adolescents (Fellmeth, 2008). Nevertheless, every day newspapers and declarations of the ministry of health stated that AIDS was spreading in southern regions and the national capital. The national program of AIDS in Sudan carries out continuous lectures and publicity informing secondary and university students about this disease. Statistics about the exact number of infected adolescents are not available.

Homosexuality is not an openly common practice among adolescents. In fact, the role of the passive homosexual is disgraceful in traditional Sudanese culture. *Lawtti*, the name for such individuals, is a strong term of abuse in the Sudanese community. In rural areas, male adolescents often practice sex with donkeys, goats, and cows, and rarely with the opposite sex (Brown & Saraswathi, 2003).

Health Risk Behavior

Drug use and abuse is considered an expensive habit, which the majority of Sudanese adolescents cannot afford. Nevertheless, adolescents of rich families may use drugs, but it is not very common. The most practiced habit among Sudanese in general and adolescents in particular is a kind of tobacco applied inside the lower lip, which is named *sawoot*. The majority of adolescents have not seen alcohol and have no knowledge of its types because it is not sold legally in Sudan. In many rural areas some male adolescents may drink a famous local type of alcohol made of dura (*mareesa*), and a strong alcoholic drink made of dates (*arakie*). Drinking alcohol is not widespread among adolescents.

The drugs most widely used by Sudanese are hashish and bango. Adolescents may smoke them with other peers or alone. It is worth mentioning here that it is male adolescents that use these drugs generally; few females do.

Education

In governmental and private secondary school education, students generally attend sex-segregated schools, but they join together in university education. Secondary schools include programs of academic study, technical tracks (industrial or agricultural), and vocational courses, in addition to study in hundreds of private schools. Despite being in separate schools, males and females study the same books and follow the same curriculum.

Estimates from 2009 indicate that 46% of the population over age 15 can read and write (58% of males, 35% of females). These estimates did not classify the literacy percentages of each age category (i.e., adolescents, adults, etc.). The estimates also indicate that the illiteracy rate is very high (66%) among females over 15 years of age. Although the illiteracy rate among females is higher, the number of females enrolled in university is now higher than for males.

The younger generation enjoys a much higher literacy rate than do their mothers and grand-mothers—thus, the overall percentage of female literacy may change radically in the coming 10 years. However, both structural adjustment policies and civil war have decreased resources available for learning. In addition, the circumstances in rural areas often are not in favor of females remaining in education through secondary school, either because there is no school in the village or because females are not permitted to walk a long distance to attend schooling. Instead, they help their mothers in domestic matters.

Work

Traditionally speaking, adolescents are not responsible for securing money for the family to meet everyday expenses. The majority of adolescents are supposed to be enrolled in education. Nevertheless, to understand the pattern of division of labor among the Sudanese community, it is necessary to refer to the symbolic content of tasks. Male tasks relate to the public sphere of societal decision-making, cooperation and defense, and the herding of cattle. Female work represents an extension of the nursing and sheltering implied by the maternal role, although many Sudanese women now occupy important positions that were traditionally men's jobs.

Female adolescents help their mothers in domestic work. They learn how to cook, and how to prepare a tray with different kinds of foods. They clean the yard and the rooms of the house, collect wood for cooking, bring water from a well or a canal, and milk goats. The amount of this work depends to a large extent on whether the adolescent lives in a rural or urban center, has a rich or poor family, and is attending school or not. An exception to this gendered division of labor is among the Beja tribe in eastern Sudan, who consider that milking is taboo for women; this is because a cultural linkage of milk and semen justifies a taboo in which symbolically man is the essential provider of food.

Male adolescents usually assist their fathers in their work, in addition to caring for the flocks of sheep and goats pastured at a distance from the house. They may also do everyday shopping, bring prepared trays of food to the father, wash guests' hands before and after eating, and do any kind of work that needs strong muscles.

There are no accurate statistical data about adolescent employment. Nevertheless, there are many professions held by adolescents during vacations or as a permanent job, such as car-washing, car maintenance, building labor, money collector in general transportation, handcrafting, telephone operator, server in a restaurant, seller or cashier in a mall, shepherd, and farmer. It is important to state that a large number of urban adolescents may not do any of this work, because their families do not need their income. Instead, they just play football in the evening, go to Internet cafés at night, and so on.

Hundreds of female high school or college graduates now work in Gulf countries as school-teachers or university lecturers, with marriage not necessarily a top priority. Females' contribution to the overall family income has eradicated the traditional idea that females are of no use in helping their parents financially.

Media

The most favored media among adolescents are TV, radio, recorded tapes, and magazines respectively. All these media are available in both urban and rural areas. Adolescents do not favor indigenous media, especially regarding TV. They are fascinated with satellite channels. A satellite dish is found in almost every house in rural and semirural areas. The variety of issues and fields broadcast by them meet adolescents' interests. The favored channels are those of music videos, sports, and movies.

Most parents view media as corrupting to the moral standards of the Sudanese community, and this corrupting effect may be clearly viewed in dress design, hair combing, and many tempting pictures that do not relate to Sudanese customs. One of the things that parents reject in imported

TV channels is the frequent viewing of high levels of sexual content and low levels of portrayal of responsible sexual conduct (i.e., not showing the consequences of sexual behavior such as diseases and pregnancy). Parents try to control their adolescents by advising them to watch respectable channels, but adolescents like to watch channels that satisfy their interests.

Politics and Military

Adolescents in Sudan are considered one of the greatest resources for political parties, especially Islamic-affiliated parties, because the parties offer both services and hope that adolescents need. Traditionally, secondary schools and universities used to fuel leftist movements with young members. Today, there is little enthusiasm for leftist movements and more attraction to Islamist movements. Islamists motivate youth to be better Muslims, and give youth an opportunity to contribute in one way or another to the welfare of humanity, which is part of Islamic teaching. Therefore, youth have a great opportunity to participate in politics and policy-making, although the legal voting age for Sudanese is 18 years.

Underage children have been drafted as soldiers in tribal militias, although this clearly violates Sudanese law, which provides that only men of 18 years of age and older may be conscripted. The Sudan People's Liberation Army (SPLA) has long had a policy of separating males from their homes and families for military training (and some education). Thousands of males went to the Ethiopian refugee camps hoping for an education and received mostly military training. The SPLA inducted males as young as 11 into its ranks. Youth have been involved in the long war in the south, and in tribal conflicts that frequently occur in different parts of Sudan.

Voluntary work carried out by adolescents is usually in school activities. They often clean main streets, plant trees, build a room for a poor family, or collect cotton in harvest season.

Unique Issues

The most distinctive aspects of Sudanese adolescents can be summarized in the following points.

1. Most adolescents have not seen alcoholic drinks in bars, they do not even differentiate types of such drinks, and they do not deal with alcohol in general, because it is banned by the state in general places and hotels. This does not mean that adolescents do not drink local alcohol.
2. There are no places of prostitution that could be visited to meet adolescent sexual desires, because professional prostitution is also banned by the state. Rich adolescents might rent an apartment to invite their friends of both sexes, and there can practice sex, drink alcohol, smoke cigarettes, and have drugs. But this is not a rule for all rich adolescents.
3. Many adolescents put a certain type of tobacco (snuff) under their lower lips or in other areas inside the mouth. This type of snuff is used extensively all over Sudan by a virtually nonsmoking/nondrinking population. This Sudanese snuff contains inordinately high levels of the tobacco-specific toxins. These are considered to be major contributors to the induction of cancers of the digestive tract in tobacco chewers, snuff dippers, and smokers.
4. Many rural male adolescents are allowed to sleep outside their houses. They group together in a big host house belonging to one of them; usually in an isolated big room inside the yard of the house. This is considered a sign of becoming independent. Some rural girls might do the same, but with close relatives. Sleeping outside the house might permit adolescents to commit some bad deeds far away from parents' control.

5. The ongoing war in Darfur and clashes in some parts of the South have forced many teenagers to leave school and take part in these wars, which have had enduring effects on their lives.

References and Further Reading

Abdelbagi, D. (2006). *Adolescents' knowledge, attitudes, and behavior towards risk sexual practices*. Unpublished paper.

Ahmed, A. D. (2006). *Adolescent knowledge, attitudes, and behavior towards risk sexual practices*. Unpublished paper.

Brown, L., & Saraswathi, S. (2003). *The world's youth*. Cambridge, UK: Cambridge University Press.

Central Bureau of Statistics report (2009). Khartoum, Sudan: Central Bureau of Statistics. Retrieved from www.cbs.gov.sd

Cloudsley, A. (1983). *Women of Omdurman: Life, love and the cult of virginity*. New York: St Martin's Press.

Deng, F. M. (1971). *Tradition and modernization: A challenge for law among the Dinka of the Sudan*. New Haven, CT: Yale University Press.

Fellmeth, A. X. (2008). State regulation of sexuality in international human rights law and theory. William and Mary Law Review, 50(3). 797–936.

Johnson, D. H. (1997). Nuer prophets: A history of prophecy from the Upper Nile in the nineteenth and twentieth centuries. New York, NY: Oxford University Press.

Mahdi, M. (1965). *A short history of the Sudan*. London, UK: Oxford University Press.

Ministry of Interior Annual Report (2008). A report on the situation and statistics of crime in the whole country, published annually by the information unit of the Ministry of Interior, Khartoum, Sudan.

Sudan Economy (2010). Source: 2010 *CIA World Factbook*. Retrieved from www.theodora.com/wfbcurrent/sudan/sudan_economy.html

SECTION II
Asia

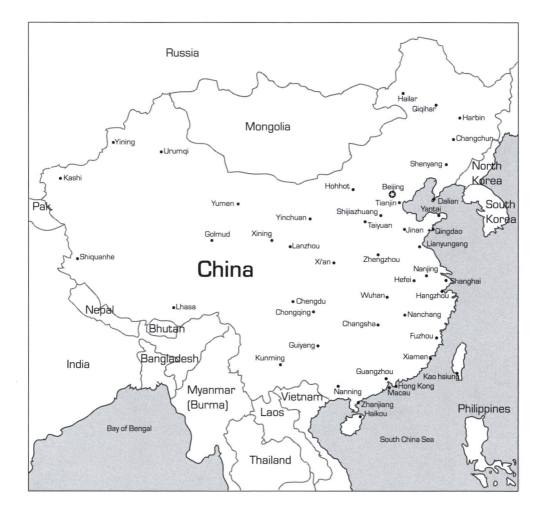

Chapter 7
China, People's Republic of
Xinyin Chen and Lei Chang

Background Information

China has a total population of approximately 1.3 billion people, the largest in the world. Most of the population (58%) lives in rural areas. According to a document of the All-China Youth Federation (China Youth Policy and Youth Work, 2005), there are approximately 200 million youth aged between 15 to 24, accounting for 16% of the total population. There are 56 ethnic groups in China, with the Han nationality representing about 92% of the population of the country.

Mainland China established a socialist political system with the creation of the People's Republic in 1949. Since the late twentieth century, however, China has carried out a full-scale reform toward a market economy that allows for the adoption of many aspects of capitalism. The centrally planned command economy has rapidly been transformed, which has led to major changes in economic and social structures. As a result, the living standard in most parts of China has improved significantly. According to China state statistics (*Bulletin of China's Economic and Social Development in 2009*, 2010), the annual per capita income was 5,153 yuan (approximately $736 USD) for rural residents and 17,175 yuan (approximately $2,435 USD) for urban residents in 2009.

Period of Adolescence

Adolescence is generally recognized as a period ranging from 11 or 12 until 18 to 19 years. The major event associated with the beginning of adolescence is the completion of primary school (first to sixth grades) and entry into middle school. The end of adolescence is often represented by the entrance to a college or university or the job market after the completion of middle school (twelfth grade). There are no particular formal rites to mark puberty or transition into adulthood. Some high school students start to celebrate the transition into adulthood on their eighteenth birthday. Many of these celebrations are organized by schools.

The improvement in living standards, including improved nutrition, control of infectious diseases, and provision of health care, has had significant impact on the physical growth and development of Chinese adolescents (Ye, 1995). For example, the onset of the adolescent growth spurt, such as sudden change in height, was brought forward from ages 12.9 and 11.7 years in the 1950s to ages 12.1 and 11.2 years in the 1990s, for boys and for girls, respectively (Ye, 1995).

Whereas adolescence in many Western cultures is often characterized by heightened stress and social and emotional problems such as juvenile delinquency, pregnancy, identity crisis, conflict with parents, and mental disorders (Powers, Hauser, & Kilner, 1989), Chinese adolescents appear to be less troubled by these issues and experiences. This may be due in part to the consistent social and cultural norms, customs, and expectations in Chinese society that serve to guide young people in their decision-making and choice of goals. It is also possible that continuous monitoring and support from family members, including parents and grandparents, serve a protective function that buffers against psycho-emotional problems.

There is an "emerging adulthood," mainly in urban areas, in which young people study or work after finishing secondary school but often live at home with their parents. During this period, parents may gradually become less involved in their children's social lives such as their relationships with friends and peers.

Since the 1990s, an increased number of adolescents and youth in rural areas have left their families and gone to cities to seek opportunities for economic advancement. For these young people, it is critical to learn to be independent more quickly because they need to be responsible for their own lives, and in many cases, to provide financial support to their families in rural villages.

Beliefs

Chinese society is relatively homogeneous in its cultural background, with Confucian collectivism serving as a predominant ideological guideline for group and individual functioning. In addition to Confucian philosophy, Taoism, an indigenous religious belief system in Chinese culture, has significantly influenced the values and lifestyles of the Chinese people, especially among people with low social and educational status.

A major feature of Chinese culture is that individual behaviors are often interpreted and evaluated in a broad context, in terms of their connections and interactions with social relationships, group norms, and ecological factors. This holistic view is reflected in Taoist concern about how one lives in relation to one's natural conditions (such as climate, food, and resources) and in Confucian notions about how one lives in the social environment. Achieving and maintaining harmonious family functioning and social relationships is particularly emphasized in Confucian doctrines. Consistent with the holistic perspective, the Chinese collectivistic orientation is highly attentive to the order and stability of society. According to the collectivistic principles, the interests of the individual are considered to be subordinated to those of the collective. Selfishness, including seeking individual benefits at the expense of group interests and indifference to group interests, is regarded as a cardinal evil (King & Bond, 1985).

The emphasis on collective wellbeing and group achievement in Chinese culture is reflected in socialization goals and expectations. In Western individualistic societies, children are socialized to develop social and cognitive competencies that are required for personal adaptation and achievement. Accordingly, acquiring personal social status and maintaining positive self-perceptions and feelings are major indexes of developmental accomplishment. In contrast, the primary task of socialization in Chinese culture is to help children and adolescents learn how to control individualistic acts, develop collectivistic ideologies and cooperative skills and behaviors, and finally to become a part of the group and to make contributions to the wellbeing of the collective (Chen, 2000).

The socialization goals have a strong impact on school education including various political, social, and academic activities in China. Students in Chinese schools are required to attend regular political–moral classes in which collectivistic principles and requirements are systematically illustrated. Students are also encouraged to participate in extensive extracurricular group activities that are organized by formal organizations such as the Young Pioneers and the Youth League. It is believed that during these activities, students can learn cooperation with each other and develop positive relationships in the peer group. Moreover, they are expected to learn values that are conducive to group functioning such as obedience, conformity, and interdependence.

As Chinese society has been undergoing dramatic changes toward a market economy, Western individualistic values and ideologies such as liberty, individual freedom, and independence have been introduced into the country along with advanced technologies. Many schools have expanded the goals of education to include helping children develop social and behavioral qualities that are required for adaptation in competitive society. Children are encouraged to develop social skills such as expression of personal opinions, self-direction, and self-confidence, which have traditionally been discouraged in Chinese culture. The macro-level social and cultural changes may have exerted extensive influence on adolescent beliefs, attitudes, and value systems, resulting in the so-called Westernization or Americanization of youth and adolescents in behaviors and lifestyles, particularly in urban regions of China.

Gender

Traditional Chinese families are authoritarian and hierarchical, with men generally the dominant gender (Lang, 1968). The hierarchy in the family is backed by legal and moral rules, such as the "three rules of obedience" for women (an unmarried girl obeys her father, a married woman obeys her husband, and a widow obeys her son). Men are responsible for maintaining and enhancing the status and reputation of the family (Ho, 1987).

In the feudal times of Chinese society, social contacts for girls from early adolescence onward were limited to family members (parents, siblings, husband, and children). Some of the stereotypical gender values and ideologies may still exist in contemporary China. For example, girls are often more likely than boys to be expected to help parents with household chores (Chen, Dong, & Zhou, 1997).

However, this account of gender conceptions has to be weaved into the tapestry of contemporary society. Gender-related ideologies in China have been affected by the major social, political, and economic events of the past century (Chang, 1999). The first gender equality movement coincided with the early Communist emphasis on the emancipation of the suppressed and exploited people. Enforced from the central government, a gender equality policy swept the nation overnight with the founding of the People's Republic. Women were regarded as among the suppressed, and the improvement of their social and political status was an important goal of the Communist cause. Such gender equality appeared to take effect initially on the surface, as shown by the fact that wives do not take husbands' surnames, but eventually has had a substantial and long-term impact on women's status in society. In most regions, for example, girls and women now have virtually the same opportunities as boys and men to receive education in elementary and high schools as well as colleges and universities. Women work outside the home in professions that have traditionally been mainly reserved for men, such as government, army, education, and science and technology (Chen & He, 2004).

The gender equality issue is related to family socialization and school education. Due to the one-child policy, urban adolescents in the early twenty-first century are almost all only children. Consequently, whether having a daughter or a son, parents usually encourage their only child to do well in school and in society. In schools girls clearly outperform boys throughout middle school and even in college (Chen, Cen, Li, & He, 2005). Ding and Yue (2004) called this a "strong female, weak male" phenomenon. Indeed, girls do better than boys in academic achievement as well as social and psychological areas (Chang et al., 2005; Chen et al., 2005).

The Self

Given the distinctive features of collectivistic Chinese culture, researchers have been interested in whether Chinese adolescents differ from their Western counterparts in self-concept (Chan, 1997). It has consistently been found that Chinese adolescents have lower scores on self-perceptions of competence than their Western counterparts. In a cross-cultural study of self-perceptions of social and scholastic competence and general self-worth, for example, Chen et al. (2004c) found that compared with their Canadian counterparts, Chinese adolescents had lower self-perceptions of their scholastic competence although they tended to perform better. Chinese adolescents also had lower scores on perceived general self-worth than their Canadian counterparts. The relatively low self-perceptions and self-esteem in Chinese children may be due to the endorsement of modesty in self-evaluation, high social standards of achievement, and great pressure to improve and conform with the group in Chinese culture (Chen, 2000).

What are the factors that may affect the development of self-concept in Chinese adolescents? Are self-perceptions of competence relevant to performance in Chinese culture? In a longitudinal study, Chen, He, Li, and Li (2004a) found that perceived self-worth and school competence each contributed to the prediction of the other. The mutual contributions indicate that general self-attitudes may be determined in part by school competence and, at the same time, self-perceptions of self-worth may affect school performance.

Chinese society is relatively homogeneous, and there are virtually no immigrants. As a result, ethnic identity is not a salient issue in most of China. Cultural or ethnic identity among most adolescents is often associated with nationalist values such as the "Chinese people being the descendants of the Dragon" or the "children and grandchildren of the common ancestors Yian and Huang." Although there are 56 ethnic minority nationalities in the country, it is largely unknown whether and how adolescents in these groups develop culturally distinct identities, due to the lack of research in this area.

Family Relationships

Unlike Western cultures, Chinese culture views the family, rather than the individual, as the basic social unit. Maintaining family harmony and wellbeing is considered a major goal in human lives. This is often achieved based on the hierarchical structure of the family (Lang, 1968). The hierarchy may be reflected in the social and moral rules such as filial piety for children. According to the doctrine of filial piety (Xiao, 2001), children must obey their parents, and parents in turn are responsible for governing or disciplining their children (Ho, 1986). To facilitate the socialization process, parents are encouraged to use high-power strategies such as restrictive and controlling childrearing practices (Chao, 1994; Ho, 1986). Moreover, to maintain parental authority, the culture endorses parents' control of their emotional and affective reactions in parent–child interactions. Filial piety is regarded as the "root of all virtues" and serves as a philosophical and moral basis for family organization (Ho, 1986).

Findings from several research programs appear to support the arguments about the hierarchical nature of parent–child relationships in Chinese families. Compared with Western parents, Chinese parents are more controlling and power assertive and less responsive to their children (Chao, 1994; Chen et al., 1998; Dornbusch, Ritter, Leiderman, Roberts, & Fraleigh, 1987). For example, Chinese parents are highly concerned with children's behavioral control. They are less likely to use reasoning and induction and appear more authoritarian than Western parents. Chinese parents are also less likely to encourage their children to be independent and exploratory. Finally, it has been found that Chinese parents are less affectionate toward their children and more punishment-oriented than North American parents (Chen et al., 1998).

An important question about Chinese parenting is how parental affection and power assertion are associated with child behaviors. Researchers have argued that parenting styles such as parental warmth and parental authoritarianism, which are initially developed based on Western cultures (Baumrind, 1971), may have limited relevance to social, cognitive, and emotional functioning in Chinese children (Chao 1994). Inconsistent with this argument, however, recent studies have clearly demonstrated that these fundamental parenting dimensions are associated with child adjustment "outcomes" in a virtually identical fashion in Chinese and Western cultures (Chang, Lansford, Schwartz, & Farver, 2004; Chen, Dong, and Zhou, 1997; Chang, Schwartz, Dodge, & McBride-Chang, 2003; Chen, Liu, & Li, 2000). Specifically, it has been found that parental affection and inductive reasoning are likely to contribute to the development of social and cognitive competence and psychological wellbeing. In contrast, parental rejection and power assertion, which figure in the authoritarian style, are associated with behavioral problems and maladaptation (Chang et al., 2003; Chen et al., 1997; Chen, Liu, & Li, 2000).

In Chinese families, fathers and mothers differ, both quantitatively and qualitatively, in child-care, childrearing, and parent–child interactions. Like their Western counterparts (Parke & Buriel, 2006), Chinese mothers are regarded as important for providing care and affection to the child (Ho, 1987). Unlike Western fathers, who often interact with their child like a playmate (Lamb, 1987; Parke & Buriel, 2006), Chinese fathers engage in little play activity with children (Ho, 1987). The role of the father in the family is mainly to help children achieve in academic areas, learn societal values, and develop appropriate behaviors (Ho, 1986).

In a study concerning parent–child conflict in Chinese families, Yau and Smetana (2003) compared samples of adolescents in Hong Kong and a city in mainland China, Shenzhen, on their disagreements with parents over daily issues. The results indicated that adolescents in both places reported conflicts on choice of activities, schoolwork, interpersonal relationships, and chores. However, the conflicts were generally few in number, moderate in frequency, and mild in intensity. The intensity of the conflicts appeared to decline with increasing age from early adolescence (11 to 12 years) to late adolescence (17 to 18 years). According to adolescents' self-reports, most conflicts were resolved by giving in to parents.

Due to social and economic factors (such as limited housing in the cities), large, or joint, families have decreased in number, and small nuclear families have increased in number in China. There are still many "medium-size" families in which three generations (parents of husband or wife, husband and wife, and children—or usually only one child) live together. About a third of families consist of three generations (Chen & He, 2004).

The divorce rate is generally low, but it is growing (Liu, 1998). Particularly among the younger generations with high educational levels, divorce is no longer regarded as shameful. The divorce rate has risen rapidly since 1980 (below 5% in 1980, 11% in 1995, and 13% in 1997; Ni, 2000). In 2007, the national divorce rate was 21%, with divorced males outnumbering divorced females by 28% (National Statistics Bureau of China, 2008). It is higher in major cities such as Shanghai and Beijing than in the countryside. Li (2008) found that the divorce rate was 39% in Shanghai in 2007, and Zhang (2008) estimated the divorce rate to be 35% in Beijing in 2005. Accordingly, the number of single-parent families has increased considerably in urban areas.

Since the late 1970s, China has implemented the one-child-per-family policy. This policy has apparently been highly successful, especially in urban areas. The birth rate has declined dramatically (Achievement of the family planning program in China, 2000). As a result, most children in the urban areas (98% and 96% in Beijing and Shanghai in 2008) are only children (Shanghai Municipal Population and Family Planning Commission, 2009). Although the only-child policy has not been so successful in rural areas (less than 5% in some remote regions; Nie & Wang, 2007), most families do not have as many children as traditional families used to have in the past.

An important issue concerning the impact of the one-child program is how it affects parental behavior, which in turn affects children and adolescents' social and behavioral development. Many parents and educators in China are concerned about whether only children are "spoiled" in the family (Jiao, Ji, and Jing, 1980; Tao & Chiu, 1985). Early reports from China tended to suggest that only children might have more negative behavioral qualities and social and school problems such as impulsiveness, aggressiveness, selfishness, poor peer relationships, and high demand for immediate satisfaction (Jiao et al., 1980). Later studies, however, have indicated that as a group, only children and adolescents may not differ significantly from, or may even show certain advantages over, sibling children (Chen, Rubin, & Li, 1994; Tao et al., 1999). According to Falbo and Poston (1993), where differences are present, only children are taller and weigh more than sibling children, and only children have better verbal abilities. Similar findings have been reported by others (Rosenberg & Jing, 1996).

Friends and Peers/Youth Culture

In Chinese culture, friendship has often been regarded as akin to sibling relationships. "Having a true friendship" is regarded as highly important by contemporary Chinese children and adolescents in their value systems (Sun, Chen, & Peterson 1989). In a study using the criterion of reciprocity in friendship nominations, Tse, DeSouza, and Chen (2001) found that approximately 66% of male and 79% of female adolescents in Chinese schools had mutual friendships. While almost all adolescents reported having close friends in class, approximately 80% of them indicated that they had friends outside of the class or school. Length of friendship in the class typically ranged from two years to five years.

Like Western adolescents, Chinese adolescents consider companionship and intimacy the primary functions of friendship. There are clear gender differences: Whereas females emphasize the functions of intimacy and mutual understanding, males place greater value on companionship and assistance. Unlike North American adolescents who perceive self-validation or enhancement of self-worth ("My friend makes me feel important and special") as important in friendship, Chinese adolescents pay little attention to this aspect of friendship. In contrast, they tend to emphasize "instrumental" assistance and guidance ("My friends teach me how to do things that I don't know") and mutual understanding ("My friend really understands me") (Chen, Kaspar, Zhang, Wang, & Zheng, 2004b).

There are various formal or institutionalized groups and organizations in Chinese schools (groups in class, the Young Pioneers, science and technology interest groups, sport teams). For example, each class typically consists of four to five groups with 10 to 15 members in each group. These groups are the basic units of the school for social activities, and are largely similar in structure. Every student belongs to a group, and group membership is determined by the teacher. In general, students are not allowed to change from one group to another, and they are encouraged to develop a sense of belonging and loyalty to the group. Children are required to participate in regular group activities such as meetings in which they discuss various social, academic, and other issues. Children also discuss group achievement and problems and evaluate each member's school performance on a regular basis. Finally, children may participate in intergroup activities organized at the higher level, such as the class committee and the school student association.

There are other groups in Chinese schools, such as the Young Pioneers and the Youth League, that consist of selected members. These groups are hierarchical in structure, from class level to school, to municipal, and even to national levels. Group leaders are responsible, under the guidance of the teacher, not only for planning and directing group activities but also for monitoring other students' behavior. Students who violate the rules of the group or organization may receive different types of penalty, such as warning and expulsion, which is recorded in the student's file and forwarded to the new school or work place in the future. In contrast to formal or institutionalized groups, children and adolescents are generally discouraged from participating in informal cliques or crowds. This may be related to the general cultural background in Chinese society, which emphasizes united and uniform social actions under the direct control of the authority.

Love and Sexuality

Marriage has traditionally been arranged by parents in Chinese society. Soon after the Communists took power in China, the first State Marriage Law decreed that the convention of parental arrangement of marriage must be abolished. Men and women should be allowed to choose their own marriage partners. Arranged marriage is no longer accepted because it is regarded as the old fashion. Although the decision on a marriage may still involve the whole family, parents usually accept children's choices.

The minimum legal age for marriage is 20 years for a woman and 22 years for a man. From the early 1970s, however, the government has been encouraging late marriage and childbearing to reduce the population pressure, and many municipal governments have established local policies that do not support marriage until the late twenties. Although people may marry before their late twenties by law, they may be deprived of certain basic and privileged opportunities and rights, such as career promotion and child welfare, that are controlled by the local governments.

Adolescents in China have few opportunities to date and engage in premarital sexuality. This is largely due to the high control of adults on children's behaviors and the requirement of concentrating on academic achievement. Not long ago, adolescents who were found to date or engage in intimate activities such as kissing or hugging a member of the opposite sex in school or another public place might have received "political education" and some type of punishment. Young people often started to date and engage in serious relationships only after they had a secure job or graduated from a college. Accordingly, cohabitation, birth control, pregnancy, and sexually transmitted diseases are not major concerns for Chinese adolescents.

However, it has been found that adolescent attitudes toward premarital sexuality have changed since the 1990s. Increased numbers of high school students believe that premarital sexual behaviors are acceptable and should be tolerated (Long, 2003). Although there are still many restrictions on dating in high school, dating and premarital sexuality have been more common in recent years among students in colleges and universities as the educational authorities start to accommodate students' demands for greater independence. The government and educational institutions are facing new problems such as birth control and pregnancy of students.

Sex education still has not been included in the school curriculum, although some schools offer sex education classes and many teachers may discuss the topic in human biology classes. However, attitudes to sex education are changing as sexual diseases become increasingly threatening in the country. Discussions about sex-related topics, particularly HIV/AIDS, among students are encouraged at many universities and colleges. And more books, magazines, and videos involving sexual and reproductive knowledge are now available to adolescents.

Health Risk Behavior

Serious health risk behaviors such as illegal drug use, stealing, killing, and robberies are generally low in Chinese adolescents. Violent or delinquent behaviors in the form of large groups or gangs are also rare. In addition, since few adolescents possess cars, car accidents are not a concern at this time.

In a cross-cultural study (Chen, Greenberger, Lester, Dong, & Guo, 1998), it was found that Chinese adolescents did not differ from American adolescents in most areas of misconduct such as getting into a fight or smoking cigarettes. However, whereas many American adolescents were involved in delinquent behaviors such as smoking illegal drugs, carrying weapons, and gang fighting, few Chinese adolescents engaged in these activities. The generally low frequencies of delinquency and crime in Chinese adolescents are largely due to the fact that they are prohibited with the many sociopolitical constraints imposed by Chinese society. Indeed, illegal drugs, guns, and other materials that can be used in crimes and delinquent behaviors are better controlled in China than in countries such as the United States and are generally unavailable to adolescents.

Cigarette smoking and drinking are relatively common in Chinese adolescents, particularly male adolescents. Xu and Luo (2003) found that 37% of male adolescents at ages 15 to 19 years were smokers; this rate was 1% for female adolescents. About 38% of male adolescents and 9% of female adolescents were alcohol drinkers.

Another health-related problem in Chinese adolescents is emotional disturbances such as depression. Adolescents in China, both male and female, may experience an equal or greater number of emotional problems of an internalizing nature compared with their North American counterparts (Chen, Rubin, & Li, 1995; Dong, Yang, & Ollendick, 1994). However, individual emotional problems have not received as much attention from professionals and the public in Chinese culture as in Western cultures because they are directed toward the self, rather than the collective (Kleinman, 1986). This may be the case particularly in Chinese children and adolescents because they are expected to concentrate on their social and school performance (Ho, 1986).

A particular type of stress for adolescents in China is related to academic achievement. The limited opportunities in tertiary education in China together with a tradition that emphasizes social stratification through schooling creates a social context in which children and their parents engage in an indefatigable and ceaseless competition from kindergarten into high school. High schools and middle schools are streamed into academically elitist to poor schools. This "through train" system sometimes links good high schools to elitist primary schools and even kindergartens. The constant academic competition and the anxiety over the college entrance examination at the end of high school constitute substantial stress and distress for Chinese adolescents (Lou & Chi, 2000).

Education

China is working toward nine-year compulsory education. By the end of 2004, the program had covered approximately 94% of school-aged children in the country. The enrollment rate was 99% at the primary school level and 93% at the middle school level (China sees progress in six aspects of education, 2005). The latest data show that 8% of the population aged 15 years and over are illiterate, with a wide range from 3% in Beijing to 19% in Gansu province (*Bulletin of China's Economic and Social Development in 2009*, 2010). Among young adults, the illiteracy rate had been reduced to less than 5%. The college and university entrance rate was 19%.

Almost all schools from kindergarten to university are public schools in China. However, private schools have been increasing in number at all levels in recent years. Many universities have developed gifted programs for bright students. The number of gifted programs, however, is declining due to controversies over their effects. Researchers and educators have argued that although the gifted programs may benefit the intellectual development of students, the social environment that the programs create, such as the lack of social interactions with same-age peers, may have negative effects on the learning of social skills such as self-control and responsibility. In contrast to gifted programs, schools for special education for disabled children have been growing steadily (China sees progress in six aspects of education, 2005).

Since the mid-1980s, academic achievement in Chinese children has received substantial attention from developmental and educational researchers. It has been consistently found that Chinese children outperform their counterparts in the United States and many other countries in academic areas and that the differences persist throughout the elementary and high school years (McKnight et al., 1987; Stevenson, Chen, & Lee, 1993). Academic excellence in Chinese children may be related to traditional values on achievement in the Chinese culture (Ho, 1986). Success in school achievement is directly associated with attainment of a high level of education, which in turn leads to high social and occupational status.

However, due to limited opportunities to receive higher education in China, there is strong academic competition in elementary and high schools. As a result, children are pressured constantly by parents and teachers to perform optimally on academic work. The pressure is particularly high in the final years of junior and senior high schools, because acceptance to senior high schools and colleges and universities is based on scores in examinations. Almost all high school graduates participate in the three-day nationwide college entrance examinations in June or July each year on major subjects such as Chinese language and mathematics. Whether they have the opportunity to enter a college or a university completely depends on whether their scores from these examinations reach the standard. Given this background, it is understandable that the high pressure that students experience is a major factor in academic achievement in Chinese children. Without this pressure, students might not work so diligently or pay so much attention to guidance and assistance from teachers and parents.

The high achievement of Chinese children and adolescents may also be associated with effective strategies of classroom instruction and positive family influences such as parental involvement (Stevenson et al., 1990). Chinese students, for example, spend most of their time in school and most of their school time on academic work. Most of them continue their academic work after school. High school students attend school full-time from 8:00 a.m. to 5:00 p.m. Most schools are open for additional self-learning or tutorial sessions either in the morning from 6:00 a.m. or in the evening, when students may return to school after dinner and stay until 10:00 or 11:00 p.m. It is also a common practice that to save time for study, students in graduating classes take up residence in the school for an extensive period, during which they bring blankets and sleep in the classroom at night.

There is a designated head teacher in each class who stays with the class, often for multiple years. The head teacher usually teaches a main subject such as Chinese language or mathematics. In addition, the head teacher is responsible for all the social, political, academic, and other affairs in the class. The head teacher keeps in close contact with students' families. The head teacher system in China allows the school and teachers to be involved extensively in children's and adolescents' activities that are organized to facilitate academic achievement (Chang 2003, 2004; Chang et al., 2004).

Work

Under Chinese, law all children under the age of 16 must go to school and are not allowed to hold full-time jobs. In rural areas, however, it is common that children and adolescents help parents on the farm after school. Moreover, in some rural areas poverty, may have driven a large number of adolescents out of the classroom and into lives of labor. Since the mid-1990s, many adolescents from rural areas have gone to cities, such as Beijing, Shanghai, and some in southern China's coastal regions, to work for privately owned industrial or commercial firms (Ying & Lu, 2003). Due to their lack of job skills, these adolescents usually work under poor conditions and earn low wages.

The situation is quite different in relatively wealthy cities in China. Most families do not need adolescents to work for extra income. Some adolescents may even have few opportunities to do housework. One of the reasons for their low contribution to work inside and outside of the family is that given the high pressure on academic achievement, adolescents are often required to spend as much time as possible on their school assignments and in academic programs during evenings, weekends, and holidays.

According to the Survey Report on Youth Employment conducted in some major cities (Youth unemployment rate remains high, 2005), the majority of the youth indicated that the ideal work units for them included government departments and state-run enterprises. About 20% of the youth would like to set up their own businesses. The unemployment rate for youth between ages 15 and 29 was 9%, higher than the 6% overall unemployment rate. Most unemployed youth have been jobless for a long period. The survey also indicated that the quality of employment for youth was relatively low; most of the youth had no security of tenure, long working hours, and low income.

Community service is advocated mainly as a part of school moral education in China. In 1993, the government initiated a program—Youth Volunteer Activities—to promote volunteer work among adolescents on a large scale. The program was continued and extended to most regions of the country, and numerous adolescents are involved in it each year.

Media

TV is common in both rural and urban areas in China. Adolescents spend a considerable amount of their leisure time watching TV programs. According to a survey conducted in 31 provinces (Extra-curricular activities among elementary and high school students, 2003), over 80% of high school students spent most of their after-school time watching TV programs. In addition to watching TV, the survey indicated that over 60% of high school students reported listening to music, and about 30% reported reading books and magazines that were not directly related to school work.

Internet use and playing computer games are increasingly popular among adolescents in cities and towns. In Beijing, for example, over 70% of families possess a computer, and adolescents are the main users because many parents are unable to use a computer or the Internet (Computer use in elementary and high school students, 2003). Indeed, the rate of high school students using the Internet or playing computer games is above 80% in Beijing. According to one survey (Li, 2003), the majority of adolescents (67%) reported that they used the Internet mainly to obtain information. Other main uses of the Internet included chatting (53%), playing games (46%), reading news (42%), and receiving and sending emails (27%). Most computer games that adolescents like to play are related to violence and competition such as shooting and fighting, adventure, and car racing (Yi & Yu, 2003).

Parents and educators in China are seriously concerned about excessive adolescent use of computers and the Internet, although adults and adolescents agree that they can be beneficial for learning if used properly (Li, 2003). The results of several studies among university students in China indicate that time spent on the Internet is positively associated with social dissatisfaction and feelings of social isolation and negatively associated with interpersonal trust and self-esteem (Yi & Yu, 2003). Teachers, parents, and professionals have been urging the government to set regulations to curb commercial Internet activities that target youths and adolescents. The Beijing municipal government has issued a law that prohibits people under 18 from visiting Internet cafés. However, the law is mostly ignored.

A phenomenon that is related to media is celebrity worship or idolization among adolescents. Yue and his colleagues (Yue & Cheung, 2000) conducted a series of studies over six years to compare idolization of media celebrities between mainland Chinese and Hong Kong Chinese adolescents. The findings indicate that idolizing pop stars, movie stars, and sports stars is common among Chinese young people, particularly in Hong Kong. In comparison to Hong Kong adolescents, mainland adolescents were more likely to worship luminary idols, intellectuals, and historical figures, and less likely to endorse entertainment and sports celebrities. In both places girls are more likely to idolize entertainment stars than boys.

Unique Issues

Over the past two decades, the Chinese government has relaxed the enforcement of migration restriction and allowed cities to absorb surplus rural labor. As a result, many rural people, mostly young adults, have moved to cities, which constitutes "the largest migration in human history" (Zhang, 2004). Rural migrant people often stay in the city for years while maintaining links to their villages of origin (e.g., Shen, 2006; Wang, 2004). Under the *hukou* system of household registration, migrant people do not have an urban registration and thus do not have the same privileges as urban residents (e.g., greater employment opportunities, subsidized housing, medical care, and old-age pensions). As a result, almost all migrant workers work in such sectors as manual labor (e.g., manufacturing, cleaning streets, transporting goods), construction, and commerce (e.g., street peddlers, small vendors) (e.g., Survey Center of the National Bureau of Statistics of China, 2006).

Cumulative evidence has indicated that rural migrant people tend to experience more social and psychological problems than their urban counterparts. Chen, Wang, and Wang (2009) found that compared with urban youth, migrant youth reported significantly higher levels of depression in China. Similar results were found in other studies (e.g., Shen, 2006). The higher levels of depression in rural migrant youth are likely to be related to the difficulties they face in the new environment. For example, rural migrant adolescents may experience prejudice and discrimination in the city during their interactions with urban residents (e.g., Sun, 2006). The adverse life conditions and the exposure to negative social feedback about personal and group status may facilitate the emergence of a negative self-image and the development of depressed feelings among rural migrant youth.

It has been argued that adverse conditions do not necessarily have a negative impact on the adjustment of migrants, especially those who are resilient and have social support systems (e.g., Fuligni, 1998). Moreover, according to the constructivist perspective (e.g., Garcia Coll et al., 1996), diverse family and social experiences can serve as resources for individuals to learn different values and skills that are beneficial for the development of social competence. It will be interesting to investigate in the future how rural migrant youth in China integrate various social expectations and values and use them in adjustment.

References and Further Reading

Achievement of the family planning program in China (2000, November 7). *The People's Daily (Overseas Edition)*, p. 1.

Baumrind, D. (1971). Current patterns of parental authority. *Developmental Psychology Monograph, 4* (1, Part 2).

Bulletin of China's Economic and Social Development in 2009 (2010, February 25). Beijing, China: Xin Hua She.

Chan, D. W. (1997). Self-concept domains and global self-worth among Chinese adolescents in Hong Kong. *Personality and Individual Differences, 22,* 511–520.

Chang, L. (1999). Gender role egalitarian attitudes in Beijing, Hong Kong, Florida, and Michigan. *Journal of Cross-Cultural Psychology, 30,* 722–741.

Chang, L. (2003). Variable effects of children's aggression, social withdrawal, and prosocial leadership as functions of teacher beliefs and behaviors. *Child Development, 74,* 535–548.

Chang, L. (2004). The role of classrooms in contextualizing the relations of children's social behaviors to peer acceptance. *Developmental Psychology, 40,* 691–702.

Chang, L., Lansford, J. E., Schwartz, D., & Farver, J. M. (2004). Martial quality, maternal depressed affect, harsh parenting, and child externalizing in Hong Kong Chinese families. *International Journal of Behavioral Development, 28,* 311–318.

Chang, L., Li, L., Li, K. K., Lui, H., Guo, B., Wang, Y., et al. (2005). Peer acceptance and self-perceptions of verbal and behavioral aggression and social withdrawal. *International Journal of Behavioral Development, 29,* 48–57.

Chang, L., Schwartz, D., Dodge, K. A., & McBride-Chang, C. (2003). Harsh parenting in relation to child emotion regulation and aggression. *Journal of Family Psychology*, *17*, 598–606.

Chao, R. K. (1994). Beyond parental control and authoritarian parenting style: Understanding Chinese parenting through the cultural notion of training. *Child Development*, *65*, 1111–1119.

Chen, C., Greenberger, E., Lester, J., Dong, Q., & Guo, M. S. (1998). A cross-cultural study of family and peer correlates of adolescent misconduct. *Developmental Psychology*, *34*, 770–781.

Chen, X. (2000). Social and emotional development in Chinese children and adolescents: A contextual cross-cultural perspective. In F. Columbus (Ed.), *Advances in psychology research*, (Vol. I, pp. 229–251). Huntington, NY: Nova Science Publishers.

Chen, X., Cen, G., Li, D., & He, Y. (2005). Social functioning and adjustment in Chinese children: The imprint of historical time. *Child Development*, *76*, 182–195.

Chen, X., Dong, Q., & Zhou, H. (1997). Authoritative and authoritarian parenting practices and social and school adjustment. *International Journal of Behavioral Development*, *20*, 855–873.

Chen, X., Hastings, P., Rubin, K. H., Chen, H., Cen, G., & Stewart, S. L. (1998). Childrearing attitudes and behavioral inhibition in Chinese and Canadian toddlers: A cross-cultural study. *Developmental Psychology*, *34*, 677–686.

Chen, X., & He, H. (2004). The family in mainland China: Structure, organization, and significance for child development. In J. L. Roopnarine & U. P. Gielen (Eds.), *Families in global perspective* (pp. 51–62). Boston, MA: Allyn and Bacon.

Chen, X., He, Y., Li, D., & Li, B. (2004a). Self-perceptions of social competence and self-worth in Chinese children: Relations with social and school performance. *Social Development*, *13*, 570–589.

Chen, X., Kaspar, V., Zhang, Y., Wang, L., and Zheng, S. (2004b). Peer relationships among Chinese and North American boys: A cross-cultural perspective. In N. Way & J. Chu (Eds.), *Adolescent boys in context* (pp. 197–218). New York, NY: New York University Press.

Chen, X., Liu, M., & Li, D. (2000). Parental warmth, control and indulgence and their relations to adjustment in Chinese children: A longitudinal study. *Journal of Family Psychology*, *14*, 401–419.

Chen, X., Rubin, K. H., & Li. B. (1994). Only children and sibling children in urban China: A re-examination. *International Journal of Behavioral Development*, *17*, 413–421.

Chen, X., Rubin, K. H., & Li, B. (1995). Social and school adjustment of shy and aggressive children in China. *Development and Psychopathology*, *7*, 337–349.

Chen, X., Wang, L., & Wang, Z. (2009). Shyness–sensitivity and social, school, and psychological adjustment in rural migrant and urban children in China. *Child Development*, *80*, 1499–1513.

Chen, X., Zappulla, C., Alida, L. C., Schneider, B., Kaspar, V., Oliveira, A. M. D., et al. (2004c). Self-perceptions of competence in Brazilian, Canadian, Chinese and Italian children: Relations with social and school adjustment. *International Journal of Behavioral Development*, *28*, 129–138.

China Youth Policy and Youth Work (2005). All-China Youth Federation Documents. Beijing, China: CYPYW.

China sees progress in six aspects of education (2005). *China Education and Research Network: Education in China, News and Events*, March, p. 3.

Computer use in elementary and high school students (2003). *China Youth Study*, *7*, 92–93.

Ding, G., & Yue, L. (2004). Educational equality in the campus environment: Investigation and consideration of the male students' inferior positions. In G. Ding (Ed.), *China's education: Research and review* (Vol. 6). Beijing, China: Education and Science Press.

Dong, Q., Yang, B., & Ollendick, T. H. (1994). Fears in Chinese children and adolescents and their relations to anxiety and depression. *Journal of Child Psychology and Psychiatry*, *35*, 351–363.

Dornbusch, S., Ritter, P., Leiderman, R., Roberts, D., & Fraleigh, M. (1987). The relation of parenting style to adolescent school performance. *Child Development, 58*, 1244–1257.

Extra-curricular activities among elementary and high school students (2003). *China Youth Study, 12*, 89–90.

Falbo, T., & Poston, D. L. (1993). The academic, personality, and physical outcomes of only children in China. *Child Development, 64*, 18–35.

Fuligni, A. J. (1998). The adjustment of children from immigrant families. *Current Directions in Psychological Science, 7*, 99–103.

Garcia Coll, C., Crnic, K., Lamberty, G., Wasik, B. H., Jenkins, R., Garcia, H. V., et al. (1996). An integrative model for the study of development competencies in minority children. *Child Development, 67*, 1891–1914.

Ho, D. Y. F. (1986). Chinese patterns of socialization: A critical review. In M. H. Bond (Ed.), *The psychology of the Chinese people* (pp. 1–37). New York, NY: Oxford University Press.

Ho, D. Y. F. (1987). Fatherhood in Chinese culture. In M. E. Lamb (Ed.), *The father's role: Cross-cultural perspectives* (pp. 227–245). Hillsdale, NJ: Lawrence Erlbaum Associates.

Jiao, S., Ji, G., & Jing, Q. (Ching, C. C.). (1986). Comparative study of behavioural qualities of only children and sibling children. *Child Development, 57*, 357–361.

King, A. Y. C., & Bond, M. H. (1985). The Confucian paradigm of man: A sociological view. In W. S. Tseng & D. Y. H. Wu (Eds.), *Chinese culture and mental health* (pp. 29–45). New York, NY: Academic Press.

Kleinman, A. (1986). *Social origins of distress and disease.* New Haven, CT: Yale University Press.

Lamb, M. E. (1987). *The father's role: Cross-cultural perspective.* Hillsdale, NJ: Lawrence Erlbaum Associates.

Lang, O. (1968). *Chinese family and society.* New Haven, CT: Yale University Press.

Li, A. (2003). The public media and the development of adolescents: A report of the current status on adolescent contact with the media. *Journal of Shanxi Youth Management College, 16*, 5–19.

Li, M. (2008). A survey of high divorce rate in China. *Government and Law, 14*, 34–36.

Liu, D. (1998). *Changes of Chinese marriage and family.* Beijing, China: China Social Sciences Publisher.

Long, R. (2003). Teenager's premarital sexual behavior: Its current situation and countermeasures. *Journal of Guangxi Youth Leaders College, 13*, 15–17.

Lou, W., & Chi, I. (2000). The stressors and psychological well-being of senior secondary school students. *Psychological Science (China), 23*, 156–159.

McKnight, C. C., Crosswhite, F. J., Dossey, J. A., Kifer, E., Swafford, J. O., Travers, K. J., et al. (1987). *The underachieving curriculum: Assessing U.S. school mathematics from an international perspective.* Champaign, IL: Stipes.

National Population and Family Planning Commission of P. R. China (2007). *Statistical communiqué of sample survey on population and family planning in 2006.* Beijing: NPFPCPRC. Retrieved from www.chinapop.gov.cn

National Statistics Bureau of China (2008). *China Statistical Yearbook 2008.* Beijing, China: China Statistics Press.

Ni, S. (2000, November 3). How should we revise the Marriage Law? *The People's Daily (Overseas Edition)*, p. 5.

Nie, P., & Wang, Z. (2007). The study of family wealth transfer between two generations in rural areas: A Hebei village as an example. *Northwest Population, 28*, 62–68.

Parke, R. D., & Buriel, R. (2006). Socialization in the family: Ethnic and ecological perspectives. In N. Eisenberg, W. Damon, & R. M. Lerner (Eds.), *Handbook of child psychology: Vol. 3, Social, emotional, and personality development* (6th ed., pp. 429–504). Hoboken, NJ: Wiley.

Powers, S. I., Hauser, S. T., & Kilner, L. A. (1989). Adolescent mental health. *American Psychologist, 44*, 200–208.

Rosenberg, B. G., & Jing, Q. (1996). A revolution in family life: The political and social structural impact of China's one child policy. *Journal of Social Issues, 52*, 51–69.

Shanghai Municipal Population and Family Planning Commission (2009). *The 2008 annual report on family planning in Shanghai*. Shanghai: SMPFPC. Retrieved from http://rkjsw.sh.gov.cn

Shen, R. (2006). Problems and solutions for child education for migrant rural worker families. *Journal of China Agricultural University (Social Science Edition), 64*, 96–100.

Stevenson, H. W., Chen, C., & Lee, S. (1993). Mathematics achievement of Chinese, Japanese, and American children: Ten years later. *Science, 259*, 53–58.

Stevenson, H. W., Lee, S., Chen, C., Stigler, J. W., Hsu, C., & Kitamura, S. (1990). Contexts of achievement. *Monographs of the Society for Research in Child Development, 55* (Serial no. 221).

Sun, H. (2006). About the social adaptation of children of migrant workers in the city. *Reports of the China Youth and Children Research Center*, December, 2.

Sun, Y., Chen, X., & Peterson, C. (1989). A survey on value systems of contemporary Chinese adolescents. *Youth Study, 1*, 58–61.

Survey Center of the National Bureau of Statistics of China (2006). Life quality of migrant workers. *The National Bureau of Statistics of China*. October 19. Retrieved from www.stats.gov.cn

Tao, G., Qiu, J., Li, B., Zeng, W., Xu, J., & Goebert, D. (1999). A longitudinal study of psychological development of only and non-only children and families: A 10-year follow-up study in Nanjing. *Chinese Mental Health Journal, 13*, 210–212.

Tao, K., & Chiu, J. (1985). The one-child-per-family policy: A psychological perspective. In W. Tseng & D. Y. H. Wu (Eds.), *Chinese culture and mental health* (pp. 153–165). New York, NY: Academic Press.

Tse, H., DeSouza, A., & Chen, X. (2001, April). *Friendship and social and psychological adjustment in four cultures*. Presented at the Biennial Conference of the Society for Research in Child Development (SRCD), Minneapolis, MN.

Wang, D. (2004). A survey of educational problems among children of migrant workers. *Chinese Population Science, 4*, 58–64.

Xiao, Q. (2001). *Filial piety and Chinese culture*. Beijing, China: The People's Press.

Xu, J., & Luo, M. (2003). A study of adolescent cigarette smoking and alcohol drinking. *China Youth Study, 5*, 60–63.

Yau, J., & Smetana, J. (2003). Adolescent–parent conflict in Hong Kong and Shenzhen: A comparison of youth in two cultural contexts. *International Journal of Behavioral Development, 27*, 201–211.

Ye, G. J. (1995). The nutrient intakes of Chinese children and adolescents and their impact on growth and development. *Asia Pacific Journal of Clinical Nutrition, 4*, Suppl. 1, 13–18.

Yi, X., & Yu, G. (2003). A review on adolescent internet addiction. *China Youth Study, 12*, 60–63.

Ying, M., & Lu, Y. (2003). A perspective on the phenomenon of child labor in our country. *Labor and Protection, 6*, 50–53.

Youth unemployment rate remains high (2005, May 25). *The Voice of China,*. Retrieved from www.chinanews.cn

Yue, X. D., & Cheung, K. C. (2000). Selection of favorite idols and models among Chinese young people: A comparative study in Hong Kong and Nanjing. *International Journal of Behavioral Development, 24*(1), 91–98.

Zhang, J. (2004). *The adaptation to the city*. Beijing, China: The Commercial Press.

Zhang, Y. (2008). The marital situation and its changing tendency in China today. *Heibei Academic Journal, 28*, 6–12.

Chapter 8
India
Nandita Chaudhary and Neerja Sharma

Background Information

Historically known for exotic spices and rich textiles, India is now recognized as one of the largest consumer societies in the world, with a population of over one billion. Although mostly poor, in absolute numbers Indians form one of the largest pools of technically qualified personnel anywhere in the world. This paradox is the reality of India, where diversity in every sphere of life is more the norm than the exception. There are a total of 1,652 languages spoken in the country (Ramanujan, 1994), of which 22 are registered as official languages. In terms of religious diversity, the populations of religious groups often outnumber total populations of countries. For instance, outside of Indonesia, India has the largest number of Muslims in any single country.

India became independent from British rule in 1947, through a long struggle led by leaders such as Gandhi and Nehru. Today, despite significant poverty, illiteracy, and many other difficulties, natural and man-made, India has become an important contender in the global market. In recent decades, achievements in trade, commerce, and technology have been remarkable (Central Statistical Organization, 2005).

The diversity of India could easily be described as characteristic of all domains of culture and nature: geographical, ecological, climatic, ethnic, economic, architectural, linguistic, culinary, and spiritual, to name a few. Diversity and plurality are thus fundamental features of the country, making it, perhaps, more like a continent than a nation. Despite this pluralism, the "idea" of India is an old one, and one that has sustained each historical phase of the country.

Period of Adolescence

In Indian thought and writing, the idea of adolescence *per se* is rather ambiguous. On one hand we have texts suggesting that the interpersonal distance away from adults is not experienced in India, where young people spend more time with than away from their family (Verma & Larson, 1999). There is a correspondence of interests, activities, and presence of children of all ages in most social settings. On the other hand, in the Hindu view, the idea of *kishoreawastha* places the pubescent child (particularly the male child) away from the family for a period of learning, dedication, and service. *Kishoreawastha*, the phase of being the equivalent of an adolescent, appears within the following sequence: *balavastha* (childhood), *kishoreawashtha* (adolescence), *yuvawastha* (youth), *prodawastha* (middle age), and *vridhawastha* (old age).

Contemporary positions on adolescence are different for different domains of activity. Legally a person is not an adult until 18 years of age. Men can marry at 21 years whereas women can legally marry at 18 years. However, the legal, social, cultural, and conventional markers of adolescence in contemporary India are without consensus. According to a report of the UNFPA (2000), at the macro level, Indians have a basic "resistance to the idea of adolescence," attributing this resistance to a delay in the onset of puberty due to malnutrition and prevalence of early marriages, leaving little or no period between the beginning of puberty and the entry to adult roles and responsibilities for a large majority. This is supplemented by the fact that the distance between the different generations is not so wide, although, the report says, the patterns are changing, particularly for urban, educated youth. Within the family, adolescence remains, especially for women, a closely guarded period of life for the large majority.

For the Indian urban adolescent, however, the distance between childhood and adulthood has begun to extend, especially in upper-class families. Correspondingly, discourse of adolescence and its problems has also begun to find attention. Largely, one could say that financial progress, modernity and change of outlook have affected some areas more than others. The first domains to be affected are women's employment, fertility rates, and educational status. In contrast, family obligations and residential patterns are still guided by tradition in most Indian homes. Of course, there are pockets of Indian elite society that live like their counterparts anywhere else in the world, but that is only a small, albeit significant, minority.

Puberty is reached earlier now than in the past, perhaps on account of the improvements in nutritional and health status. In consonance with data from other sources, around 68% of girls achieved menarche between 12 and 14 years of age (Bagga & Kulkarni, 2000). Some evidence for late menarche has been reported among specific populations, on account of either lower nutritional intake (specifically protein) (Bagga & Kulkarni, 2000; Padmavati, Poosha, & Busi, 1984), or higher sporting activity (Sidhu & Grewal, 1980). Typically, among both boys and girls, the growth spurt tends to occur more slowly and over a longer period of time than among populations of developed countries (Elizabeth, 2001).

Among the critical issues facing India is the fact that many children and adolescents grow up in very difficult circumstances due to poverty, destitution, disease, and disability. Many of our poor live on the streets of urban areas and their needs for livelihood, health care, nourishment, and education are not being met. Many live and earn on the streets from a young age. Unfortunately, India's vast population and expanse interfere with the appropriate delivery of programs, whether government-run or voluntary. This makes youth from poor clusters a very vulnerable group. Poor youth face hunger, malnutrition, illiteracy, disability, destitution, prostitution, and crime on the street and in the neighborhood. These problems are exacerbated when the family is absent or dysfunctional due to death, substance abuse, gambling, or criminal activity. In such instances, the basic protection of the young person from the harsh environment is lost. Due to strong family traditions, the state often leaves much of the care of the growing child to the family. State intervention is far from satisfactory and systems for child protection are still at a nascent stage. On account of this, the adolescent living outside of the family is particularly at risk.

Beliefs

Regarding the issue of individualism versus collectivism, it can be proposed that the Indian sense of self is highly committed to family values (Roland, 1988) and displays a combination of agency/autonomy and interpersonal relatedness (Kagitcibasi, 2002) that has been encountered in other modernizing populations with a strong tradition of family closeness. Children grow up among others and are often cared for by other people within the family rather than exclusively by their mothers or parents (Kurtz, 1992; Trawick, 2003). This develops an early sense of "belongingness" that lasts a lifetime, making the identity of the Indian adolescent deeply connected with the social relationships within which he or she is growing up. There is an intense commitment to family values demanded by adults (Chaudhary & Kaura, 2001) but children, adolescents, and youth are also actively encouraged by the family to have simultaneous and situation-related autonomy and competitiveness with the outside world.

Within Hindu ideology, the fundamental purpose of an individual soul is to gain gradual but effective separation from worldly experiences. Participation in religious activity is difficult to estimate, although it would not be wrong to say that children and adolescents form an integrated part of the collective religious activity at the time of festivals, rituals, and family and community functions. There is no segregation of children, except perhaps for occasions such as death ceremonies and last rites. During religious festivals, young men and women take to the streets to actively participate in the community song and dance festivities. This active participation characterizes all religious groups and is in fact intensified in the case of minority communities such as the Muslim community (Sriram & Vaid, 2009).

Among Hindus and indeed in all connected religions in India, social stratification is an important divide. Indians are deeply conscious of social status, socialized within the family to engage differently with people who are seen as different. Social discourse, even the style of language used (forms of address and other markers) are deeply sensitive to social status. It is sometimes said that in encounters with unfamiliar people, Indians tend to first evaluate the relative social standing of the other person (Roland, 1988; Sen, 2005; Varma, 2005). The caste system was originally based on stratification by occupation. Today it remains as a vestige of the former classification, but is still an important element of the Hindu identity.

More recent efforts of the Government in terms of affirmative action for lower caste groups has in many ways intensified caste identities and sustained divisions between caste groups, although the objective was social upliftment. Nonetheless, there has been tremendous impact of social policy on caste, and the present Constitution of India declares that caste is not officially recognized as a feature of an individual for social standing. The secular policy of the government declares the all religions and caste groups are equal, rather than saying that these do not exist as far as the state is concerned. This feature of the Constitution is perhaps based on the tacit understanding that caste remains very important for individual and group identity and social practices such as marriage, friendship and community living (Government of India, 2008).

Gender

Gender equality is a major concern for India. Social activists have reported disadvantage to the girl from the day she is born, which is even being expressed in the form of female feticide and infanticide (Visaria & Visaria, 2003). The expectations for fertility and domestic work place tremendous pressures on young women, especially (although not exclusively) among the poor (Chaudhary & Mehta, 2004). Among the urban middle class, however, increasing attention to gender issues has led to positive responses toward gender equity, and girls enjoy near-equal status (Datar, 1995; Saraswathi & Pai, 1997). For the middle and upper classes education and career for women are often as important as for men. Increasingly, young men (even among the urban and rural poor) are seeking out partners who are educated, arguing that an educated woman is an asset to the family (World Bank, 2004).

Gender as a variable has been of significance in the study of socialization of children in the predominantly patriarchal communities in India. For the study of adolescence, it is of particular importance. Discrimination against the female child is well documented in psychological, sociological, and developmental research (e.g., *Girl Child in India*, 1995), especially among poor communities. However, most such research draws a generic profile of a girl victimized by her status and circumstances. A longitudinal study of the developmental journey of the girl from childhood to adolescence and later is largely lacking. With all the obvious and subtle forms of discrimination, what forms the core of the adolescent girl's identity, and what gives her the resilience to negotiate the vicissitudes she is surrounded with, is little known in psychological literature.

Probing the identity of the adolescent girl among 150 girls in the age range 16 to 19 years, Sharma (1996) found that gender identity was the primary feature of the female adolescent's sense of self. Although formal education generated certain questioning about self-worth and future aspirations, it did not seem to overwhelm her sense of identification with her gender role. The emphasis on her role as a future homemaker is never lowered, even at the highest level of education.

Women in India are worshiped, revered, feared, and victimized. This conflicting dynamics is difficult to understand and explain. An important fact is that it is not so much the person, but her role in any given situation that defines people's attitude to her. In the role of a mother, she is respected and even worshiped as a selfless sustainer of the family. As a young girl she may be loved, ignored, or feared as her conduct is considered to determine the family's honor. When we look at the collective statistics on women, we find much to be ashamed of in this day and age; and yet, India has been the home to many firsts as far as women are concerned. The Nobel Prize winning economist Amartya Sen (2005) wrote of his experiences with women in higher education, stating that as he moved from Calcutta to London to the United States, the number of women colleagues in his place of work reduced as he travelled westwards.

The Self

As discussed in the preceding section, gender is a strong feature of an Indian person's sense of self. Additionally, social status is determined by age and relative position in the network of relationships within the group, family, or community. Together, age and gender become the key features for determining the life chances within the constraints of the social situation.

A specific cultural setting will evoke particular images of the self that necessarily deviate from those in other locations. In some places, the idea of an independent "self" or a separate identity is not easily communicated in the native vocabulary and may even evoke laughter or incredulity (Chaudhary & Sriram, 2001). The interdependence with the context and others in the environment is now accepted as an important point of departure from the Western sense of self. In India, parents often find it uncomfortable to detach themselves from the lives and loves of their children. It is "connectivity" and not "separation" that characterizes group relations and self-orientations (Seymour, 1999). Relationships within the family, including relationships with siblings, form an integral part of the self of the Indian person (Roland, 1988; Sriram, Chaudhary, & Ralhan, 2002).

Within the physical limits of this life–world, the sense of self among Indians is believed to be constantly changing, evolving partly because the context is given primacy. Bodies are considered to be relatively "porous," "permeable," and predicated on the different life circumstances and relationships (Menon, 2003, pp. 431, 433). The transformations possible will be determined by the social and biological state of being woman or man, pregnant or young, and so on.

Family Relationships

There are several accounts of the family being at the center of adolescent lives in India, a feature not unusual in a society where relationships are based on interdependence. For example, in a detailed cross-cultural study, 100 Indian middle-class adolescents, both girls and boys (mean age 13.2 years), were compared with 220 middle-class European and American youths (Larson, Verma, & Dworkin, 2003). Indian adolescents were found to spend much more time with families than their American counterparts and to feel positive in doing so most of the time. Very few of them reported any signs of conflict with their parents and there was no attempt at breaking away. When together, Indian families were usually at home and involved in routine activities such as watching TV, talking, or doing homework (for school). The authors concluded that close relations with parents were beneficial to Indian adolescents.

The intergenerational continuity that is suggested in this study is also encountered in other research. While investigating interpersonal disagreements between adolescents and their parents in middle-class urban families, Kapadia and Miller (2005) found that there was very little disagreement and a favorable attitude to compromise between the two generations in the resolution of hypothetical issues related to marriage. The basic understanding between the two parties is that parents have the best interests of their offspring in mind. This belief leads to the fundamental acceptance of the intentions behind parents' actions. In a recent study of sleeping arrangements in the homes of college-going women (Chaudhary & Gilsdorf, 2010) it was found that out of a total of 46 (18–20 year old) women surveyed, 23 continued to sleep with parents, siblings, or grandparents in the same bed, while many others preferred to return to their mother's beds on occasions when they wanted proximity. Although these patterns may have been guided by situational constraints of space and other resources, the young women attributed them to the desire for warmth and closeness and to sometimes coping with fear and loneliness by sleeping with others.

Children are believed to require specific themes in care at different ages (Krishnan, 1998). The child under five years of age should receive affection, which is followed by discipline for the next 10 years. At 16, the child is believed to be like a friend and should be treated as such by the family, with respect for girls and regard for male children as responsible for the family line. The daughter is regarded as an essential but temporary member of her natal family because she will eventually marry and move away to live with her husband's family, although evidence has pointed to a greater intimacy between daughters and mothers subsequent to their marriage (Sharma, 1996).

It is not unusual for older siblings to be expected to "take care of" younger ones (Mascolo & Bhatia, 2002), and also for brothers to be protective of their sisters. The early network of relationships "predisposes children to develop not simply some kind of a homogenous group self, but rather a socially embedded, relational self that includes affective identifications and representations of multiple caregivers" (Sharma, 1999, p. 39).

On the whole, the single most significant leitmotif that characterizes Indian adolescents is their constant pull toward the family ethos that encourages them to place individual needs secondary to family needs, and subjugate their decisions to those made by the family to maintain cohesiveness. However, it is essential to understand that earlier interpretations of Indian collectivity were rather misplaced since there was no realization of the deep openness to debate (Sen, 2005) and negotiability

(Kapadia & Miller, 2005) in relationships and perspectives within the Indian family, depending on context. The dominant misunderstanding has been that Indian society is deeply hierarchical and authority-bound, always subordinating the self to the group; this position is mistaken (Miller, 2002).

Friends and Peers/Youth Culture

In contrast to the West, engagement with friends and peers is not perceived to be a crucial expectation from adolescents in India (Saraswathi & Ganapathy, 2002). In the process of making decisions, Indian adolescents continue to look to the family rather than to peers for important choices such as career and family (Ramu, 1988; Uplaonkar, 1995). Although not much is written about peer influence and the young adolescent, one study finds that Indian adolescents spend most of their time with their family rather than with friends, but whatever time is spent with friends is evaluated as very positive in terms of emotional affect (Larson et al., 2003).

The prevalence and continued importance of the large family network, in both reality and ideology (Uberoi, 2003), limit the role of friends and peers in the lives of Indian adolescents. However, there is evidence to support the increasing incidence of what may be termed "peer culture" among middle- and upper-class urban youth (Verma & Saraswathi, 2002) as affluence, mobility, and consumption become common. The extent to which these features will actually impact the primacy of the family as a socialization agent is yet to be discerned (Schlegel, 2003).

A feature of Indian society with important implications for peer relations is the early age of marriage for a majority of young men and women. Thus, peer contact is significantly truncated due to the fact that many youth are already married by their mid-teens. Peer contact for boys remains much higher than for girls, primarily due to the greater mobility that boys are allowed. In this regard, acceptance by peers and social standing were found to be far more critical for boys than for girls (Singhal & Rao, 2004).

Love and Sexuality

In India, 50% of girls between 15 and 19 are already married (UNFPA, 2000), although one finds a gradual rise in the age at marriage over the past century or so: from 13 years in 1901 to 16 in 1951 (Agarwala, 1962, p. 238), then rising to 20 in 1991, with slightly higher ages for urban areas (21) in comparison to rural areas (19). The most recent figures for average age at first marriage (2008) are 25 for men and 21 for women.

Since the idea of adolescence is Western in origin, the concept of adolescent sexuality is also largely based on the behavior of unmarried sexually active adolescents, as most adolescents in the West are unmarried. This position stands challenged in most developing nations, and issues of fertility replace those of sexuality, making it essential to address policy and programs related to delay of marriage. In one estimate, 55% of girls under 19 are already married (Singhal & Rao, 2004, p. 17), whether or not they have had the formal departure to the husband's home. Delay of marriage beyond puberty is considered a risk in many communities, placing pressure on parents to get daughters married early. Even if departure to the husband's home may be delayed for some years, marriages are usually fixed and solemnized before or soon after puberty.

Attending school has significantly delayed marriage. However, there is no denying that once maturity is reached, parents in a majority of Indian homes display latent or overt signs of eagerness for the daughter to find a home outside of her natal one. The unmarried daughter/sister is seen as a threat to the dynamics of a community, especially a rural community—a fact that is repeatedly seen in cultural content such as myth, folktales, and film (Kurtz, 1992). Parents feel forced to marry off their daughters at a young age due to concerns for reproductive health (Bruce, 2003), fears of sexual exploitation, and greater choice in finding a spouse.

Regarding arranged marriages in India in contrast with love marriages, it is difficult to estimate the proportions of each, for several reasons (Mathur, 2006). First, there are very few examples of "pure" forms of either marriage—young people who may find romantic love often choose to work through the known system of introductions through parents to keep respect for the system. In arranged marriages as well, some freedom is given to young couples to make choices of whom they would like to marry by encouraging some interaction before finalizing matters. Traditionally, there has always been a precedence of family over individual with reference to marriage choices. Appropriateness and social characteristics were always more important than romantic love. Love was believed to start after marriage was entered (Mathur, 2006). It remains true for many rural communities that early marriages of men and women are encouraged to prevent young people from making their own choices regarding a spouse. Among urban, educated populations, however, the delay in marriage and the increased contact between young people that is typical of an urban environment have led to an increase in the frequency and tolerance of marriages of choice.

A recent trend has been the introduction of websites that display captions such as "Arrange your own love marriage," "Meet your match online." Although no accurate data are available, there is much anecdotal evidence of young people and families increasingly using Internet encounters for both arranged and dating choices, but with marriage as the objective.

Living with a heterosexual partner without being married is restricted to a small section of the upper-class elite society. Similarly, homosexuality is only now becoming a matter of public opinion. Despite the fact that ancient Indian art, architecture, and literature demonstrate a great variety in sexual expressions of men and women, over the years this variety seems to have become suppressed for the common person.

There is no doubt that being married and having children is viewed as the ideal outcome of an individual's youth. Parents believe that they have not fulfilled their duty if their child has not married or not had any children. The pressure for getting and staying married and also having children has clear manifestations in the fertility figures and lower divorce rates for India among all religious and ethnic communities. These patterns are slowly changing and only time will tell whether the vibrancy of familial relationships, marriage, and childhood is able to sustain the pressures of modernity (Trawick, 2003).

Although primarily understood as an unromantic system dominated by family, arranged marriages and vows exchanged between partners at the time of the ceremony display a somewhat different flavor. In a Hindu marriage ceremony, the following vows are exchanged during the seven steps that a couple takes around the sacred fire (Badrinath, 2003, p. 136):

> With these seven steps, become my friend. I seek your friendship. May we never deviate from this friendship. May we walk together. May we resolve together. May we love each other and enhance each other. May our vows be congruent and our desires shared.

Dating as a concept is still quite unfamiliar to most Indians. It is a phenomenon that is viewed from the outside on the several Western television channels available. And yet, this is not meant to imply that romance for the young person is not experienced. The dense social environment and encounters with family and friends on the many social occasions that a person usually participates in provide young men and women with opportunities for romantic encounters. This, however, would be hidden from the public view and considered as transgression by most elders. More recently, urban spaces and Internet access provide young men and women with plenty of opportunity to interact with members of the opposite sex, at school, college, the workplace or on the Internet.

With international funding for AIDS awareness, sex education has become an important concern and several nongovernmental organizations, both national and international, are engaged in social action for sex education, which is largely avoided within the conventional spaces of the family. However, many young women and men receive indirect information from conversations of others. The recent explosion in access to the Internet would impact on this area as well.

Health Risk Behavior

Regarding concerns about health, in a study of over 25,000 adolescents from government and private schools (Singhal & Rao, 2004) it was found that around 30% emerged as having health concerns. Although this study was done only on school-going adolescents, there was a fair representation of family income groups. Health concerns included appearance, frequent aches and pains, inability to eat regularly, frequent illnesses, and weakness. There were no noticeable income-level differences in the problems identified by the respondents. Regarding appearance, boys outnumbered girls by 7 to 1 in assessing themselves as weaker than similar others (p. 164). Thus, although reproductive health remains a critical issue during adolescence, other matters linked with nutrition, body image, and peer pressure are important concerns of adolescents in India.

Youth on the street, particularly boys, remain vulnerable to substance abuse and petty crime in areas such as bus stands and railway stations. The participation of youth in gang warfare and group violence seems marginal, although they may be inducted by criminals for participation in crime. Exclusively youth gangs are not common. Among women, early induction into prostitution and labor seems to be the main concern for children of the poor. Rural and small city communities are close-knit and more organized. Most types of crime are more common in big cities such as Delhi and Mumbai.

An interesting observation about bulimia and anorexia, common ailments among Western adolescents, particularly women, is that these are very rare in the Indian community. Despite recent changes in body image in favor of the fashion model look, intense importance is placed on food as a source of love and nourishment within the family. Any rejection of food is considered a rejection of the person who has prepared the food, and in our more than 25 years of experience of teaching at a women's college in the University of Delhi, we have not yet encountered a single case of either of these difficulties among the young women we teach. Perhaps in a country where hunger is a persistent problem, eating disorders are likely to be fewer. Adolescent deaths are mostly still on account of infectious diseases and malnutrition (UNICEF, 2008).

Education

The educational system in postcolonial India is a collaborative reconstruction of missionary efforts, British rule, and the increasing importance given to indigenous ideologies (Srivastava, 2003). This reconstruction has had several important impacts on the way schooling is understood today. Several important indigenous movements such as the Arya Samaj, which attempted to return education to the glorious past of the Vedic period, have made significant contributions to the cause of education at all levels, especially education for girls. India has made progress in education in recent decades. However, despite legislation and planning, access to schools remains elusive for many communities. Nevertheless, the motivation for and the belief in schooling as a key to individual and family progress are encountered even among the poorest of the poor.

Repeated evaluations have suggested that no longer can the blame be placed solely on parents for not sending children to school; it is far more significantly a result of poor distribution of schooling facilities, especially at the primary level. If one compares educational achievement between India and China, India is both lower and more unequal (Dre'ze & Loh, 1995).

Girls' participation in education is growing and becoming more equal to that of boys. In higher education, we find that in 1951 only 10% of girls were being enrolled in education beyond high school; that figure had risen to 40% in 2000–2001 (Selected Educational Statistics, 2000–2001).

Regarding national government expenditure on education, we find a concerted effort at an increase in budgetary allocations at the state level. The number of higher educational institutions that adolescents can enter is increasing by the day. Although these are still a long way away from providing occupational, technical, and professional training for all interested youth, there has been a substantial jump in the gross number of youth with higher education. The educational status of youth in India is certainly rising. Increasing numbers of adolescents are attending and successfully completing school. Although boys still outnumber girls, there is a tremendous improvement in the literacy rates for young women. Recent years have seen the emergence of a very large population of technically qualified youth in India. Increasingly, this trend is gaining international attention, and India is accessing more jobs for its youth today than ever before.

For families from middle and upper classes, education-related issues are the top priority for adolescents. Parents declare that much of the scheduling of family time is negotiated around children's academic commitments (Verma et al., 2002). Despite national and state action and personal motivation, schooling remains elusive for the very poor. In most instances, reasons that keep children out of school are linked with responsibilities for work in the home (especially so for the firstborn child, male or female), such as care of younger children while the parents are out to work, lack of accessibility to school, frequent migration of families for work, harsh attitudes of teachers, and the absence of positive role models within the community (Chaudhary & Sharma, 2005). According to a World Bank study (2004), when children who do reach school against the odds it is for reasons including the following: they are later-born children (so an older child can take on household responsibility), a member of the family is keen to send them to school, school is accessible, there is encouragement from teachers, and the children are male. Education remains largely problematic, and with the absence of serious commitment from the state to provide schools in every neighborhood; to train teachers for commitment and positive attitudes to poor communities; and to provide infrastructure such as classrooms, toilets, and books, a large section of children of all ages (mostly girls) remain outside of school—keen to enroll but unable to do so.

For those upper- and middle-class children who do reach school and are potential members of the technically trained workforce of India, the major challenge is to face the deepening crisis of competing against large numbers of peers in education, training, and the job market. Academic matters have remained the largest factor contributing to stress among urban adolescents (Kaura, 2004). In a study of around 26,000 school-going children between 10 and 19 years of age (in and around Delhi) from different economic backgrounds attending both government and private schools, it was found that academic matters posed the most serious problem among 41% of children, both boys and girls. School tasks at this stage were found to be uniformly difficult across gender, social class, and type of school. Boys more frequently complained about "not liking" studies, and both sexes complained about classroom experiences, inability to comprehend, and examination fear (Singhal & Rao, 2004, p. 203).

Work

The law in India prohibits the employment of young children under the age of 14. However, due to economic difficulty, children of all ages find themselves in jobs, either with family or outside the family. A UNICEF report indicates that as many as 12% of children in India participate in the workforce, either as employees or within the family (UNICEF, 2008). Other estimates are even higher (UNFPA, 2000, p. 21). The participation of older adolescents (15 to 19 years), particularly boys, was as high as 50% according to one estimate (Singhal & Rao, 2004, p. 18). It is also important to note that estimates of employment among children and youth are very difficult to ascertain, especially for situations such as domestic, construction, and agricultural labor (Planning Commission, 2001; UNFPA, 2000). Most often children are employed in factories, small-time hotels, car repair shops, and domestic labor. In the last of these there is a greater prevalence of girls.

Media

The Indian media show clear preferences for urban, Westernized youth. Images of fashion models, Bollywood actresses and actors with light eyes, and svelte images of scantily clad women adorn glossies and dailies in the Indian market. In this sense, the Indian media are far more Westernized than the general population is.

The most recent media advance has been in the mobile phone industry, and the Indian market is booming. A total of just over 63 million mobile phone users and 500,000 Internet users have been identified (Bhatnagar, 2005). This unprecedented expansion in the communication sector is bound to impact the lives of young people in significant ways. It remains to be seen how these changes will become absorbed into the existing social and personal lives of Indian families in general and adolescents in particular.

Verma and Sharma (2003) examined adolescents' use of free time and found gender differences in free-time activities regarding content, duration, frequency, and quality. Leisure for girls was primarily home-based, such as watching TV, reading, cooking, and embroidery, while boys reported more outside activities such as playing sports, going to movies, and hanging out with friends. The authors concluded that in urban areas media technology has had a mediating role in replacing traditional leisure-time activities among youth with a more Westernized pattern, although family time and community activities seem to enjoy an important place in these as well.

Politics and Military

Regarding political activity and youth, a common lament is the lack of motivation for political participation and voting among youth (Raedler, 1999), for which the country has a great need in order to benefit from the energy and enthusiasm of the young (Solomon, 2003). Young voters reported being more concerned about their careers than about political parties, as they believe politics to be riddled with corruption (Raedler, 1999; Solomon, 2003), something they would rather stay away from.

Militarily, India is an advanced country. The armed forces have always been an attractive career, especially for young men. This has been linked with the colonial period when the British deliberately encouraged people from the warrior castes in the north (particularly Punjab and Haryana), through positive associations of their masculinity with a career in the army, to serve as soldiers in the British Army (Chowdhury, 1994). The trick worked, and the states of Punjab and Haryana still carry a great deal of enthusiasm toward a career in the armed forces. The armed forces of the Army, Navy, and Air Force in India have an image and function way beyond the idea of war, although that thought is invariably present, and defense of the country is always in the background as a noble idea. The armed forces also provide administrative, social, and emergency assistance to the government.

Being in the army does not carry the stigma that it does in some other parts of the world, and it offers a lucrative career for young men and also young women now. The local belief is that a person becomes more disciplined after a few years in the army. The National Cadet Corps (NCC) Act was passed by Parliament in India in 1948 with the objective of instilling discipline and unity among youth to enhance their participation in the nation, the armed forces, and community living. With these objectives, the NCC has recruitment centers all over the country and encourages the enrollment of young men and women. There are over a million cadets enrolled in the NCC as per the latest records (Keshavan, 2005). The cadets are trained for social, community, and military activity in regularly held camps all over the country. Cadets are selected through the educational institutions in which they are studying. They can volunteer to join the NCC, after which they are trained and given uniforms and ranks. The NCC is one of the largest organized youth activities in India.

Unique Issues

From the preceding discussion on adolescence in India, several critical issues have come to the surface. It is essential to understand that the adolescent in India faces a situation that is quite different from that of his or her Western counterpart.

- Younger people will continue to live with their families until marriage or departure for work or study. Young men may stay on with families even after marriage. Living separately is not a common practice.

- Parents continue to be concerned with the everyday lives of youth (and even adult children) for the rest of their lives. This concern often translates into advice, assistance, and/or interference.
- The belief in lifelong commitment to the family makes the network of social relationships very enduring, and family cohesion is highly valued.
- Great value is placed on compromise rather than conflict in all relationships.
- Young adolescents in India spend much more time with their families than do their counterparts in other parts of the world.
- Adolescents truly believe that their parents have their best interests in mind.
- The social unit of the peer group, fraternity, or any other collective is almost always subordinate to the family.
- The family remains an ideal group even among the homeless, abandoned, and street-based children.
- The heterodoxy of Indian community living leads to several significant variations according to region, religion, caste, income, or language.
- There is no doubt that modern influences have led to a greater negotiability in life choices and individual preferences of young people.

These features of family life in India make the experience of adolescence quite distinctive from adolescence in other parts of the world. Therefore, any discussion of intergenerational dynamics in India must account for these aspects of social reality. Policy, planning, and action related to adolescence have to work within the framework of these patterns of social life.

References and Further Reading

Agarwala, S. N. (1962). *Age at marriage in India*. New Delhi, India: Kitab Mahal.

Anandalakshmy, S. (Ed.). (1994). *The girl child and the family: An action research study*. New Delhi, India: Department of Women and Child Development, Ministry of Human Resource Development, Government of India.

Arora, M., Sinha, P., & Khanna, P. (1996). A study of relationships between crowded residence in a group of adolescents and their mental health in living conditions. *Indian Journal of Psychological Issues*, *4*(1), 25–31.

Badrinath, C. (2003). The householder, *grhastha* in the Mahabharata. In M. Pernau, I. Ahmad, & H. Reifeld (Eds.), *Family and gender: Changing values in Germany and India* (pp. 113–139). New Delhi, India: Sage.

Bagga, A., & Kulkarni, S. (2000). Age at menarche and secular trend in Maharashtrian Indian girls. *Acta Biologica Szegediensis*, *44*(1–4), 53–58.

Bezbaruah, S., & Janeja, M. K. (2000). *Adolescents in India: A profile*. New Delhi, India: United Nations Population Fund.

Bhatnagar, S. (2005, September 8). *India's mobile base surges to 63 million in August*. Reuters, India. Retrieved from http://in.today.reuters.com/news

Bose, A. (2001). *Population of India: 2001 census results and methodology*. Delhi, India: B. R. Publishing House.

Bosma, H., & Gerlsma, C. (2003). From early attachment relations to the adolescent and adult organisation of the self. In J. Valsiner & K. J. Connolly (Eds.), *Handbook of developmental psychology* (pp. 450–490). London, UK: Sage.

Brown, B. B., Larson, R. W., & Saraswathi, T. S. (Eds.). (2002). *The world's youth: Adolescence in eight regions of the globe*. Cambridge, UK: Cambridge University Press.

Bruce, J. (2003). Married adolescent girls: Human rights, health, and developmental needs of a neglected majority. *Economic and Political Weekly, 38*(41), 4378–4380.

Central Statistical Organisation (CSO). (1998). *Youth in India.* New Delhi, India: CSO.

Central Statistical Organisation (CSO). (2005). *India in figures (2003).* New Delhi, India: CSO.

Chaudhary, N. (2004). *Listening to culture.* New Delhi, India: Sage.

Chaudhary, N., & Gilsdorf, N. (2010). *Sleeping arrangements of college going women in New Delhi, India.* Unpublished report of the Department of Human Development and Childhood Studies, Lady Irwin College, University of Delhi, New Delhi, India.

Chaudhary, N., & Kaura, I. (2001). Approaching privacy and selfhood through narratives. *Psychological Studies, 46*(3), 132–140.

Chaudhary, N., & Sharma, N. (2005). From home to school. *Seminar, 546,* 14–20.

Chaudhary, N., & Sriram, S. (2001). Dialogues of the self. *Culture and Psychology, 7*(3), 379–393.

Chaudhary, S., & Mehta, B. (2004). Adolescents and gender equality: A pedagogic concern. *Perspectives in Education, 20*(1), 28–49.

Chowdhury, P. (1994). *The veiled women: Shifting gender equations in rural Haryana.* New Delhi, India: Oxford University Press.

CIA. (2005). *The world factbook.* Langley, VA: CIA. Retrieved from www.cia.gov

Datar, C. (1995). Democratising the family. *Indian Journal of Social Work, 55*(1), 211–224.

Diniz, M. (2005, March 3). *Premarital sex among youth today.* Retrieved from http://in.rediff.com

Dre'ze, J. (2003). Patterns of literacy and their social context. In V. Das (Ed.), *The Oxford India companion to sociology and social anthropology* (Vol. 2, pp. 974–997). New York, NY: Oxford University Press.

Dre'ze, J., & Loh, J. (1995). Literacy in India and China. *Economic and Political Weekly, 30*(45), 2868–2878.

Elizabeth, K. E. (2001). A novel growth assessment chart for adolescents. *Indian Paediatrics, 38,* 1061–1064.

Girl Child in India. (1995). *Journal of Social Change* (special issue), *25*(2–3), 3–254.

Government of India. (2008). *Constitution of India.* Retrieved from http://indiacode.nic.in

International Labour Organisation. (1993). *World of work.* Geneva, Switzerland: ILO.

Kagitcibasi, C. (2002). Autonomy, embeddedness and adaptability in immigration contexts: A commentary. *Human Development, 20,* 1–6.

Kakar, S. (1981). *The inner world* (2nd ed.). Delhi, India: Oxford University Press.

Kapadia, S., & Miller, J. G. (2005). Parent–adolescent relationships in the context of interpersonal disagreements: View from a collectivist culture. *Psychology and Developing Societies, 17*(1), 33–50.

Kaura, I. (2004). *Stress and family environment: Adolescents' perception and experiences.* Unpublished doctoral dissertation, Department of Child Development, University of Delhi, India.

Kaura, I., & Chaudhary, N. (2003, July). *Continuity and change: Narratives of conflict from the lives of Indian adolescents.* Paper presented at the conference of the International Association for Cross-cultural Psychology, Budapest, Hungary.

Keshavan, S. P. (2005). National Cadet Corps. Retrieved from www.bharat-rakshak.com

Kitayama, S., & Markus, H. R. (1994). Culture and self: How cultures influence the way we view ourselves. In D. Matsumoto (Ed.), *People: Psychology from a cultural perspective* (pp. 17–37). Pacific Grove, CA: Brooks/Cole.

Krishnan, L. (1998). Child rearing: The Indian perspective. In A. K. Srivastava (Ed.), *Child development: The Indian perspective* (pp. 25–55). New Delhi, India: National Council for Educational Research and Training (NCERT).

Kumar, K. (1986). Growing up male. *Seminar, 318,* 21–23.

Kurtz, S. N. (1992). *All the mothers are one: Hindu India and the cultural reshaping of psychoanalysis*. New York, NY: Columbia University Press.

Larson, R. (2002). Globalisation, societal change and new technologies: What they mean for the future of adolescence. In R. Larson, B. Brown, & J. Mortimer (Eds.), *Adolescents' preparation for the future: Perils and promise* (pp. 1–30). Ann Arbor, MI: Society for Research on Adolescence.

Larson, R., Verma, S., & Dworkin, J. (2003). Adolescence without family disengagement: The daily family lives of Indian middle class teenagers. In T. S. Saraswathi (Ed.), *Cross-cultural perspectives in human development* (pp. 258–286). New Delhi, India: Sage.

Mandelbaum, D. G. (1970). *Society in India. Volume 1: Continuity and change*. Berkeley, CA: University of California Press.

Marriot, A. M. (1976). Hindu transactions: Diversity without dualism. In B. C. Kapforer (Ed.), *Transaction and meaning: Directions in the anthropology of exchange and symbolic behaviour* (pp. 109–142). Philadelphia, PA: Institute for the Study of Human Issues.

Mascolo, M. F., & Bhatia, S. (2002). Culture, self and social relations. *Psychology and Developing Studies, 14*(1), 55–91.

Mathur, I. (2006). *First comes marriage, then comes love*. Retrieved from www.garamchai.com/weddingservices1.htm

Menon, U. (2003). Morality and context: A study of Hindu understandings. In J. Valsiner & K. J. Connolly (Eds.), *Handbook of developmental psychology* (pp. 431–449). London, UK: Sage.

Miller, J. G. (2002). Bringing culture to basic psychological theory: Beyond individualism and collectivism. *Psychological Bulletin, 128*(1), 97–109.

Mines, M. (1988). Conceptualising the person: Hierarchical society and individual autonomy in India. *American Anthropologist, 90*, 568–579.

Ministry of Human Resource Development (MHRD). (2000). *National youth policy*. New Delhi, India: Department of Youth and Social Affairs, MHRD, Government of India.

Misra, G., Srivastava, A. K., & Gupta, S. (1999). The cultural construction of childhood in India: Some observations. *Indian Psychological Abstracts and Reviews, 6*(2), 191–218.

Nieuwenhuys, O. (2003). The paradox of child labour and anthropology. In V. Das (Ed.), *The Oxford India companion to sociology and social anthropology* (Vol. 2, pp. 936–938). New Delhi, India: Oxford University Press.

Padmavati, V., Poosha, D. V. R., & Busi, B. R. (1984). A note on the age at menarche and its relationship to diet, economic class, sibship size, and birth order in 300 Andhra girls. *Man in India, 2*(64), 175–180.

Pandey, J. (2001). *Psychology in India revisited* (Vols 1 & 2). New Delhi, India: Sage.

Patil, M. V., Gaonkar, V., & Katarki, P. A. (1994). Sex-role perception of adolescents as influenced by self concept and achievement motivation. *Psychological Studies, 39*(1), 37–39.

Planning Commission. (2001). *Report of the working group on adolescents for the tenth Five Year Plan (2002–2007)*. New Delhi, India: Planning Commission, Government of India.

Raedler, J. (1999). *India's dissatisfied youth stays away from polling booths*. Retrieved from http://edition.cnn.com

Ramanujan, A. K. (1994). *Folk tales from India*. New Delhi, India: Penguin.

Ramu, G. N. (1988). *Family structure and fertility*. New Delhi, India: Sage.

Roland, A. (1988). *In search of self in India and Japan: Towards a cross-cultural psychology*. Princeton, NJ: Princeton University Press.

Saibaba, A., Mohan Ram, M., Ramana Rao, G. V., Devi, U., & Syamala, T. S. (2002). Nutritional status of adolescent girls of urban slums and the impact of IEC on their nutritional knowledge and practices. *Indian Journal of Community Medicine, 27*(4), 151–157.

Saraswathi, T. S. (1999). Adult–child continuity in India: Is adolescence a myth or an emerging reality? In T. S. Saraswathi (Ed.), *Culture, socialization and human development* (pp. 213–232). New Delhi, India: Sage.

Saraswathi, T. S., & Ganapathy, H. (2002). Indian parents' ethnotheories as reflections of the Hindu scheme of child and human development. In H. Keller, Y. P. Poortinga, & A. Schlomerich (Eds.), Between culture and biology: Perspectives on ontogenetic development (pp. 79–88). Cambridge, UK: Cambridge University Press.

Saraswathi, T. S., & Pai, S. (1997). Socialisation in the Indian context. In H. S. R. Kao & D. Sinha (Eds.), *Asian perspectives on psychology* (pp. 74–92). New Delhi, India: Sage.

Sartor, C. E., & Youniss, J. (2002). The relationship between positive paternal involvement and identity achievement during adolescence. *Adolescence, 37*, 221–234.

Schlegel, A. (2003). Modernisation and changes in adolescent social life. In T. S. Saraswathi (Ed.), *Cross-cultural perspectives in human development: Theory, research and applications* (pp. 236–257). New Delhi, India: Sage.

Schlegel, A., & Barry, H. (1991). *Adolescence: An anthropological inquiry*. New York, NY: Free Press.

Selected Educational Statistics. (2000–2001). Bangalore, India: Azim Premji Foundation. Retrieved from www.azimpremjifoundation.org

Sen, A. (2005). *The argumentative Indian: Writings on Indian history, culture and identity*. London, UK: Penguin.

Seymour, S. (1999). Cooperation and competition: Some issues and problems in cross-cultural analysis. In R. H. Munroe, R. L. Munroe, & B. B. Whiting (Eds.), *Handbook of cross-cultural human development* (pp. 717–738). New York, NY: Garland Press.

Sharma, D. (2003). Introduction. In D. Sharma (Ed.), *Childhood, family and socio-cultural change in India: Reinterpreting the inner world* (pp. 1–12). New Delhi, India: Oxford University Press.

Sharma, N. (1996). *Identity of the adolescent girl*. New Delhi, India: Discovery.

Sharma, N. (1999). Understanding adolescence. New Delhi, India: National Book Trust.

Sharma, N., & Sharma, B. (1999). Children in difficult circumstances: Familial correlates of advantage while at risk. In T. S. Saraswathi (Ed.), *Culture, socialisation and human development* (pp. 398–418). New Delhi, India: Sage.

Sidhu, L. S., & Grewal, R. (1980). Age of menarche in various categories of Indian sportswomen. *British Journal of Sports Medicine, 14*(4), 199–203.

Singh, A. P. (1998). Sibling distance and feeling of isolation. *Perspectives in Psychological Research, 21*(1 and 2), 69–73.

Singhal, S., & Rao, U. N. B. (2004). *Adolescent concerns through own eyes*. New Delhi, India: Kanishka.

Solomon, P. (2003). Youth of India's lack of interest in politics. November 2003. Retrieved from www.prashantsolomon.com

Sriram, S., Chaudhary, N., & Ralhan, P. (2002, October). *The family and self in dialogue*. Paper presented at the Conference of the Dialogical Self, Ghent, Belgium.

Sriram, S., & Vaid, S. (2009, December). *Being Muslim: A study of Muslim Youth in Delhi*. Paper presented at the 8th Annual Conference of the Asian Association of Social Psychology, New Delhi.

Srivastava, S. (2003). Schooling, culture and modernity. In V. Das (Ed.), *The Oxford India companion to sociology and social anthropology* (Vol. 2, pp. 998–1031). New Delhi, India: Oxford University Press.

Times of India, The. (2005, November 25). Pre-marital sex: Papa preaches for Sania, p. 6.

Trawick, M. (2003). The person behind the family. In V. Das (Ed.), *The Oxford India companion to sociology and social anthropology* (Vol. 2, pp. 1158–1178). New Delhi, India: Oxford University Press.

Uberoi, P. (2003). The family in India: Beyond the nuclear versus joint debate. In V. Das (Ed.), *The Oxford India companion to sociology and social anthropology* (Vol. 2, pp. 1061–1103). New Delhi, India: Oxford University Press.

UNDP. (2005). *The Human Development Report, 2005*. New York: UNDP.

UNFPA. (2000). Adolescents in India: A profile. New Delhi, India: UNFPA.

UNICEF (2008). India: Statistics. New York: UNICEF. http://www.unicef.org/infobycountry/india_statistics.html

Uplaonkar, A. T. (1995). The emerging rural youth: A study of their changing values towards marriage. *Indian Journal of Social Work*, *56*(4), 415–423.

Varma, P. (2005). *The great Indian middle class*. New Delhi, India: Penguin.

Verma, S., & Larson, R. (1999). Are adolescents more emotional? A study of the daily emotions of middle class Indian adolescents. *Psychology and Developing Societies*, *11*(2), 179–194.

Verma, S., & Saraswathi, T. S. (2002). Adolescence in India: Street children or Silicon Valley millionaires. In B. B. Brown, R. W. Larson, & T. S. Saraswathi (Eds.), *The world's youth: Adolescence in eight regions of the globe* (pp. 105–140). Cambridge, UK: Cambridge University Press.

Verma, S., & Sharma, D. (2003). Cultural continuity amid social change: Adolescents' use of free time in India. In S. Verma & R. Larson (Eds.), *Examining adolescent leisure time across cultures* (pp. 37–41). San Francisco, CA: Jossey-Bass.

Verma, S., Sharma, D., & Larson, R. (2002). School stress in India: Effects on time and daily emotions. *International Journal of Behavioural Development*, *26*(6), 506–508.

Visaria, L. (1999). Deficit of women in India: Magnitude, trends, regional variations and determinants. In B. Ray & A. Basu (Eds.), From independence towards freedom: Indian women since 1947 (pp. 80–99). New Delhi, India: Oxford University Press.

Visaria, P., & Visaria, L. (2003). India's populations: Its growth and key characteristics. In V. Das (Ed.), *The Oxford India companion to sociology and social anthropology* (Vol. 1. pp. 184–218). New Delhi, India: Oxford University Press.

World Bank, The. (2004). *Snakes and ladders: Factors influencing successful primary school completion for children in poverty contexts*. Discussion paper series, report no. 6, South Asia Human Development Sector. New Delhi, India: The World Bank.

World Health Organization (WHO). (2001). *Child and adolescent health and development: Report on the inter-country meeting, Bali, Indonesia, 9–14 March, 2001*. New Delhi, India: WHO.

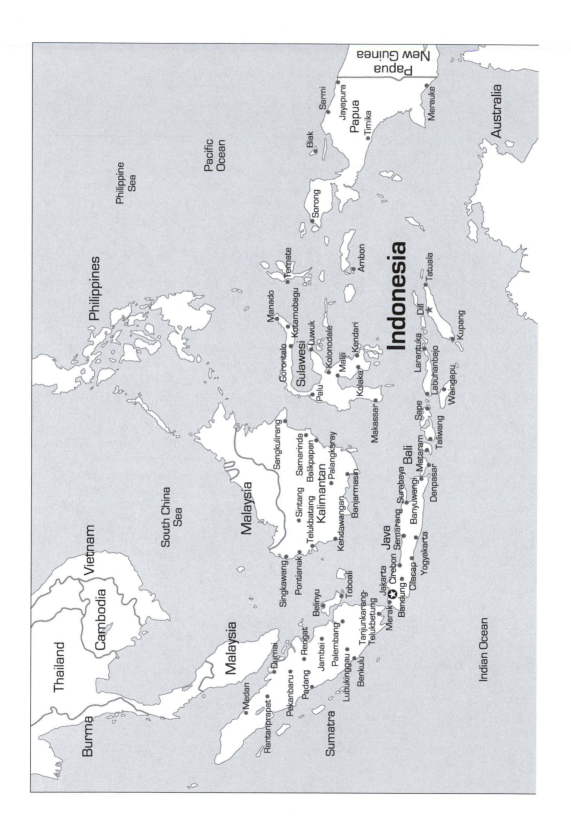

Chapter 9
Indonesia
Hera Lestari Mikarsa

Background Information

The Republic of Indonesia is an archipelago with 17,000 islands; some of the largest islands are Sumatra, Java, Kalimantan, Sulawesi, Papua, Bali, and Maluku. The most populated island is Java, which includes the capital, Jakarta. On August 17, 1945, Indonesia declared its independence after almost three and a half years of Japanese occupation.

There are about 300 distinct indigenous ethnic groups, with more than 500 local languages and dialects spoken. A national language, Bahasa Indonesia, functions as a unifying language. With such diversity, Indonesia has adopted the credo *Bhineka Tunggal Ika* or "Unity in Diversity," and the national philosophy is "Pancasila" or the five principles: (1) belief in God, (2) humanity, (3) unity of Indonesia, (4) deliberation and cooperation, and (5) social justice.

It was estimated that in 2009 the population of Indonesia was around 231 million (Central Statistics Bureau, www.bps.go.id/), and with 86% Muslims, Indonesia is the most populous Muslim country in the world. The rest of the population is Christian (Protestant and Catholic), Buddhist, Hindu, and other. At present the political system is a democracy, with a division of power between the president and parliament. In terms of the economy, Indonesia has an open-market policy.

Period of Adolescence

Taking the definition of adolescence from the World Health Organization (WHO), the Indonesian Ministry of Health considers unmarried people between the ages of 10 and 19 as adolescents (2002–2003 Indonesia Young Adult Reproductive Health Survey, IYARHS).

Rites of passage for life events in different ethnic groups include birth rituals among the Batak Toba ethnic group and the fishing community in Madura; rituals for mothers at the seventh month of pregnancy; the Javanese ritual that takes place the first time a baby steps onto the ground; and numerous wedding and death rituals. However, according to Koentjaraningrat (1985), in Indonesia there is no rite of passage marking adolescence. Some rituals that used to exist are no longer practiced. In the Papua Biak-Numfor culture, young males of 15 to 16 years of age once carried out the rite called *k'bor*. The meaning of *k'bor* is "to stab or cut the tip of something"—in this case, the tip of the penis (Mansoben 1994). *K'bor* is a ritual to affirm the change in someone's status from an ordinary member into a formal member in his society. This tradition became extinct when the Christian religion came to Biak-Numfor at the beginning of the twentieth century.

One common rite of passage for adolescent boys in Indonesia is *sunatan or khitan* (circumcision). *Sunatan* is regarded as a puberty rite, in which the boys' entrance into adulthood is being proclaimed. The sunatan ritual is an important Islamic practice, and one of the *sunnah* (things that are good, not an obligation but better done) encouraged by the Prophet Mohammed. *Sunatan* is a practice that is regarded as a *syariat* in Islam (*syariat* = rule), and, therefore, Muslim boys have to undergo it. Sunatan for girls is still a controversial issue, with some practicing it and others not.

In the more traditional cultures in Indonesia, circumcision is done when boys reach puberty (Putranti, Faturochman, Darwin, & Purwatiningsih, 2003). The more modern and educated families, however, opt to circumcise their sons when they are younger or even when they are still babies, and the circumcision is conducted by medical doctors. *Sunatan* for girls in Indonesia is usually carried out when the baby is newborn, performed by the midwife who helps with the delivery or the pediatrician in the hospital.

When Muslim boys and girls reach adulthood, they are required to do *sholat* (praying five times a day). Parents usually teach their children to do *sholat* and fasting at Ramadan (perhaps for a few hours or half a day) at a younger age; however, when they reach *akil baliq* or puberty, then *sholat* and fasting at Ramadhan become obligations.

Adolescents become young adults when they finish high school or university, and enter the world of work. In the eyes of the law, after the age of 21 one is no longer a child; thus, one acquires the rights that are bestowed on adults, such as the right to marry. Parents will probably not consider the young adult as having reached full adulthood until he or she marries and begins a family. Arnett (2004) calls this transitional period from adolescence into full adulthood "emerging adulthood," and this period is more common among the urban middle-class young people in Indonesia who further their study beyond the university's undergraduate level, to meet the demands of the job market.

Beliefs

Islam came to Indonesia centuries ago through Muslim traders. It spread throughout the archipelago and became the dominant religion. Hindu and Buddhist kingdoms used to exist in Java, but with the arrival of Islam the Hindu kingdom was forced to the island of Bali. The strong Hindu influence in Bali is expressed in the religious rituals and cultural manifestations that are an integral part of people's lives. *Ramayana* and *Mahabharata* are two famous Hindu epics still popular in Java. For more than 300 years the European influence (especially Dutch) was also present in Indonesia.

As the most populated island and the center for government, trade, and education, Javanese culture has a great influence on the nation overall. For the Javanese, cooperation and social attitudes are highly valued characteristics. Togetherness is a desirable way of life, as expressed by the Javanese saying *mangan ora mangan, asal kumpul*, which translates as "eating or not eating, as long as we are together." Deliberation and cooperation have been adopted by the country as the way to solve problems or conflicts, as shown by the idiom *musyawarah dan mupakat* (literal meaning: deliberation and cooperation to reach an agreement).

With this emphasis on cooperation, Indonesia tends to be more collectivist than individualist. The collectivist tradition is still prominent in the rural areas, and in small towns where kinship and neighborhood relationships are still close. However, the fast pace and hectic lifestyle in cities leave people with little time for social interaction. Collectivism, in the sense of encouraging cooperation, has faded, and exists in major urban centers as little more than a symbol of the ideal value of togetherness.

Religious teaching is a part of the school and university curricula. A study conducted by *Gatra* magazine in cooperation with the Political Science Laboratory and the Faculty of Social and Political Science of the University of Indonesia found that 95% of the 800 respondents, aged 15 and 22, believed that "religion is the guide for developing good morals and character."

Gender

The 1945 Constitution of Indonesia states that males and females have equal rights and obligations to support the country's development. Slightly over 50% of the Indonesian population is female, but their participation in the labor force is lower than that of men. For the age group 15–24 years, female's participation is about 44% (Hasoloan, n.d.). Differences in wages based on gender still exist; for similar work, female workers often are paid less than their male counterparts.

Discrimination based on gender can often be seen early in a child's life. In her study of Balinese school children, Parker (1997) discovered that school-age girls are expected to help with housework in their out-of-school time, thus they have to stay at home. Meanwhile, the boys are free to spend their time away from home, playing or socializing with friends. This gender role expectation is not only typical for Bali, but is also found in other subcultures in Indonesia.

The literacy rate in Indonesia is quite high; at the national level 99% of the age group 15–24 years can read and write (Global Education, 2010). There is no significant difference in the male and female literacy rate for this age group. However, if socioeconomic background is taken into account, then females in the poorest group have the lowest literacy rate.

Compared to males, duration of school attendance for females is shorter. School life expectancy from primary to tertiary level is 12 years for males and 11 years for females. Parents also usually put more value on education for boys than for girls, as the traditional role for males is as the breadwinner and for females it is as homemakers.

The educational system in Indonesia has changed in recent years; nine years' basic education (i.e. primary and junior secondary) is now compulsory for all children. At the senior secondary level (three years), young people can choose between general academic and vocational education. More females than males do not continue to secondary school (Suryadarma, Suryahadi, & Sumarto, 2006).

Male and female children are socialized to gender role expectations in the two villages studied by Tjitarsa (1995, in Saifuddin & Hidayana, 1999). Boys aged 11 to 12 years begin to assist their fathers in catching fish or working in the fishermen's boats, while girls help their mothers at home or work as babysitters or clothes-washers in other homes.

With globalization, the physical ideals of young people are also influenced by the celebrities they see in the media, especially on TV. Girls want to have bodies like famous singers or actresses, i.e., tall and slender. The same phenomenon is observed with male youth, but is not as extreme as among girls. Data about the number of young people suffering from eating disorders are not available. A small study conducted by Handayani (2005) with obese adolescent subjects (male and female) showed that although the subjects were overweight, they seemed to have a positive body image because they thought their obesity was caused by heredity.

The Self

The many subcultures existing in Indonesia have an impact on the cultural and personal identity of adolescents. In subcultures where tradition plays a major role, parents socialize their children according to the customs and beliefs practiced in their communities. Javanese children reared in a small traditional town in Central Java will develop a personal and ethnic identity that is distinctly Javanese, and stronger than that of Javanese children brought up in metropolitan Jakarta.

In her study of street children in Yogyakarta, Beazley (2003) emphasized the role of socialization in a subculture of street children in developing their collective identity. Beazley found that within the marginal urban niches where they live and earn money, the street boys construct their individual identity in interaction with the subculture's collective identity. The street boys created a doctrine for themselves that "it is great in the street," and "street life is better than conventional life." Over a long period, the street boys establish a new identity.

Except for communities in remote areas, a large proportion of young people in Indonesia have been exposed to a changing way of life, from the traditional to the more modern. Advanced technological information has opened up the world for adolescents. Globalization seems to be unavoidable, and affects tastes in clothing, music, food, and so forth. For young people living in the large cities, globalization and trends have shaped their social and collective identity. They dress in the same way as any other adolescents: t-shirts, jeans, and sneakers. Mobile phones seem to be the order of the day for adolescents.

Family Relationships

In a country populated by diverse ethnic groups, the parenting practices in Indonesia also reflect diversity. People continue to rely on tradition, while at the same time they try to adapt to modern developments. The extended family, which traditionally was the custom for family living, is now becoming rare. For the younger generation, especially those living in the cities, the nuclear family has become more predominant. However, many families have a housemaid, who after a long period of working becomes more like a family member.

The family is usually headed by a father who is usually authoritarian, and who in many cases acts as an emotionally distant figure who has to be respected (Mulder, 1999). However, family life is centered on mothers. Home is the mother's territory, while affairs in the outside world are the father's domain.

A cross-cultural study by Hoffman (1987; cited in Hadis, 1993) found that the value most desired by urban and rural Javanese and Sundanese parents was obedience from their children. In her study, Hadis (1993) also discovered that traditional parents wanted children who were obedient, honest, and diligent. More modern parents, however, generally preferred children who were independent, unspoiled, responsible, and had a sense of freedom. Parents were categorized as traditional or modern by their belief system. The traditional parents were usually females, living in rural and urban slum areas, with low educational and socioeconomic levels. This group perceived the mother as the person solely responsible for the upbringing of children. The modern parents consisted of couples living in urban areas who had high education and worked as professionals. They believed that fathers had to play a role and help mothers in raising children.

According to the Indonesian Religious Affairs Ministry, the rate of divorce is increasing (Asiafinest.com, 2009). Of 2 million couples that get married every year, more than 10% eventually get divorced. The most common reason mentioned in the religious court for divorce is polygamy, which incidentally is on the increase in Indonesia.

Friends and Peers/Youth Culture

The family and school obligations of Indonesian adolescents leave relatively little time for friends. Young people who are still at school or university spend about six to eight hours of their time each day in classes. For some, after-school activities will take up more of their time. Time is usually spent with family in the late afternoon or evening, if there are no other activities the young people have to do.

Nevertheless, friends are important to adolescents. A strong emotional attachment between friends is revealed in a study by Atmowiloto (1985), who found that more than 80% of senior high school students had been involved in fights because they wanted to show their solidarity with and support of their friends.

Time with friends comes mostly on weekends, at least in urban areas. With Saturdays free for some schools, the adolescents can spend their day in the shopping malls and other entertainment centers. A survey conducted by *Gatra* magazine concluded that Indonesia adolescents spend most of their time on *hura-hura* (i.e., leisure and pleasure) instead of doing more positive activities.

Cliques are established according to mutual interests. The Indonesian youth like music. Musical shows, whether they showcase underground music, heavy metal music, *dangdut* (a typical music popular in Indonesia), or another genre, are usually packed with young people. Youth organizations usually focus on sports, music, or religious or social activities.

According to Pickles (2000), "close-knit communities of young people sharing an interest in underground music have emerged throughout Indonesia, and punk is the most theatrical youth culture in Indonesia." The way these youth dress and style their hair proclaims their unique identity. Punk and other underground music may have originated in the West, but Indonesia's youth have indigenized these cultures and give them new meanings.

Love and Sexuality

Attitudes toward sex and adolescents' sexual behaviors have undergone remarkable changes in recent years. Formerly, sex was regarded as a taboo topic and censorship was applied to the media. Today, in the large cities adolescents enjoy more freedom in their personal conduct, and dating is more common than in rural areas.

According to Indonesian marriage law, girls can get married at 16 and boys at 19 years of age. Teenage girls' marriage usually occurs in areas where there is extensive poverty, or due to out-of-wedlock pregnancy.

It seems that young people are becoming more permissive and relaxed in their sexual behavior, as shown by a new survey by the Indonesian Child Protection Commission which claims that 32% of the 4,500 Indonesian urban teenagers sampled have had full sexual intercourse. If out-of-wedlock pregnancy occurs, either the couple are forced to marry or the girl seeks an illegal abortion, as abortion is prohibited by law. Cohabitation is regarded as an unacceptable and sinful behavior by society in general, and it is not commonly practiced.

Not all schools provide sex education. Some schools, usually private ones, provide sex education in the sixth grade of primary or junior high school. In the 2002–2003 IYARHS, about 50% of young people aged 15 to 24 mentioned that information about reproductive health was given at junior high school. Condoms are sold openly in drugstores, but young people's awareness of birth control is still limited. Only about half of the respondents in the 2002–2003 IYARHS had clear knowledge about the risk of pregnancy. Teenagers' unwanted pregnancies are usually caused by unplanned sexual intercourse and limited knowledge of human reproductive mechanisms. For social and religious reasons, providing a contraceptive service to unmarried adolescents is difficult in most Southeast Asian countries, including Indonesia (Brown, Larson, & Saraswathi 2002).

In the 2002–2003 IYARHS, about 87% of the respondents had heard about HIV/AIDS. Syphilis is another sexually transmitted disease with which the respondents were familiar. Education level attained and where they lived seemed to influence the respondents' knowledge of sexually transmitted disease. It is difficult to obtain data about sexually transmitted diseases among the adolescents, but with more permissive attitudes toward sexual relationships, it is assumed that the rate will increase. It was estimated in 2007 that HIV/AIDS prevalence among adult was 0.2%.

Only recently did homosexuality become an open topic for discussion; no figures can be found as to the number of teenagers who are homosexuals. Homosexual communities do exist in larger cities in Indonesia, albeit covertly; open homosexuality is still unacceptable.

There are many different ethnic and cultural groups in Indonesia, and they differ in their acceptance of open sexuality and sexual expression. Furthermore, with the geography of Indonesia at the intersection of Asia and Australia, and its policy of an open market, all kinds of cultural influences penetrate the daily lives of adolescents. Pornographic films, comics, magazines, and so on are sold on the street, cheaply. Therefore, even in areas that are known for their strict religious beliefs, parents are not always able to control their adolescents' sexuality.

Health Risk Behavior

Data from the Central Statistics Agency shows that 25% of Indonesian children aged 3–15 years have tried cigarettes, with 32% of those children being active smokers. Indonesia is the only country in Southeast Asia not to have signed The Framework Convention on Tobacco Control, and due to weak regulations, young people have become the target of promotions and advertisements by tobacco companies.

As noted above, the majority of the population is Muslim, and in general Islam forbids alcohol. However, in some areas of Indonesia local traditions make it possible to produce traditional alcoholic drinks. Moreover, modern alcoholic brews such as wine, whiskey, and vodka are sold legally in supermarkets or other establishments, or illegally in the little shops or *warung* that dot the cities. With the abundance of cafés, discotheques, pubs, and other entertainment venues, young urban affluent people are introduced to alcohol widely and repeatedly. Meanwhile, the less privileged consume cheap drinks that contain a dangerously high content of alcohol (illegally produced in home industries, or a mixture of different alcoholic drinks). Sometimes people die as a result of consuming these drinks.

In large cities such as Jakarta, motorcycle and car racing, usually at night, seems to be quite common. Motorcycle racing—popularly known in the lingua franca of young people as *trek-trekan*—usually involves several motorcycles. This kind of racing is illegal. Sometimes collisions between the racers and ordinary motorcyclists occur, with fatal consequences. During the fasting month of Ramadan, after the final meal and before dawn, young people come together on the streets, which are still very quiet, and race their motorcycles. Spectators often gather to boost the racers' spirit and enthusiasm.

Some young people have committed or attempted suicide because of their parents' poverty: They felt ashamed because the parents did not have the money to pay the school fees, final exam fees, or graduation ceremony fees. An example is a boy, a sixth-grader in a primary school in a small town in Java, who tried to kill himself because he could not pay for the extracurricular activity in his school. The amount he had to pay was Rp. 2,500, at that time the equivalent of around 30 US cents. Although this boy survived the ordeal, the effect of the traumatic event will be with him for life as he suffered brain damage and mental disruption.

Education

The national education system is divided into three main levels, i.e. basic education (general education of nine years, consisting of primary school of six years and junior secondary school of three years), secondary education (divided into general senior secondary school and vocational senior secondary school), and higher education (diploma program, and university undergraduate up to the doctorate program). Besides these general/academic and vocational training programs, there is also a type of school with more emphasis on Islamic religious teaching, from preschool up to the university level.

Children usually enter primary school between the ages of five and seven, and finish senior high school at around 18. Besides the general secondary school, there is also secondary vocational school, offering more specialized subjects such as tourism, food technology, hotel industry, and agriculture.

Compulsory education was implemented by the government decades ago, but in reality a number of children have to drop out of primary or junior high school due to economic hardship. The tsunami that hit the Aceh region in 2004 wreaked havoc on people's lives. As a result of the tsunami's devastation, children in that region have to be educated in makeshift schools, and a large number of high-school students failed final exams due to their disrupted daily lives.

A special education program for gifted children was started in 1983 as a pilot project of the Department of Education and Culture in some primary, junior high, and senior high schools. An enrichment program was provided for children and adolescents identified by psychologists and teachers as gifted. This pilot project lasted for three years; the project was then cancelled due to a lack of funding. A few years later, the gifted education program surfaced again, and at present, most schools that offer gifted education usually adopt the acceleration program. In general, education for gifted adolescents is conducted in schools where nongifted adolescents also study, either in a different class or mainstream with the gifted students. Educational programs for disabled adolescents are also available, in the forms of inclusive education or special schools for various disabilities. Special schools for adolescents with special needs existed long before gifted education started.

Work

As in other developing countries, the number of adolescents and young adults is growing rapidly in Indonesia. The increasing number of young people increases the problem of work and employment availability.

The economic crisis that hit Indonesia in 1997 severely affected the country's economy and the livelihood of the Indonesian people, including the young. After a few years of hardship, the economy seemed to have improved. However, rising oil prices and mismanagement of resources led to an economic downturn in the new millennium. In 2006, 90% of the labor force was employed; however, only 67% were fully employed (working 35 hours or more).

According to the Baseline Survey of Young Adult Reproductive Welfare in Indonesia (Demographic Institute, 1999), young people with a low educational level living in urban areas were especially hard hit by the economic crisis. This finding has been supported by data from the capital, Jakarta. About three out of ten members of the workforce aged between 15 and 24 are jobless. This youth group constitutes two-thirds of the unemployed (Ikhsan, 2006). The rate of unemployment for university-educated young people is only 4.9%.

Poverty has pushed many adolescents to work. More young people in the rural areas have to work than their counterparts in the urban areas, and more males than females work. As the majority of them live in the rural areas, they primarily work on farms.

In large cities, many young people work on the street, selling magazines, newspapers, candy, drinks, and cigarettes. Some of them will ply the trains and buses, playing guitar and singing for money. Young females from the rural areas come to the cities to work as housemaids. According to data from the 2001 Population Survey—Statistics Indonesia (in *Kompas* daily, 24 April 2005), 27% of house helpers registered in Indonesia are adolescent females. They usually live with the family they work for, with lodgings and food provided.

In its efforts to protect young people from work that is harmful and hazardous, the government has stated in the Labor Laws the five sectors of work that are forbidden for them. The government has also established a National Action Committee for the Prevention and Monitoring of Child Labor. However, some young people are still found working in hazardous places.

Apprenticeships are the traditional way of educating young people. However, this old tradition is probably more common in rural areas in the agricultural sector. More formal training programs are offered by various institutions or vocational schools.

Media

Television arrived in Indonesia in the early 1960s. Urban adolescents in the 2002–2003 IYARHS watched more TV (92%) than the rural adolescents (79%). The male and female urban and rural subjects in the IYARH Survey also enjoy listening to the radio.

A number of schools have provided computer facilities for their students, and the Internet can be accessed easily and cheaply in "Internet shops." With the availability of mobile phones that have Internet access, communication with the outside world becomes extremely easy. Young people also like to play computer games.

To a large extent, media in Indonesia are imported, with a strong Western flavor. Western media influence is very strong in Indonesia. Traditional music has lost much of its appeal for adolescents. With the development of information technology (TV, cable TV, CDs, etc.), Indonesia has become like a borderless country: Whatever is in fashion abroad will soon be on the market in Indonesia.

Complaints have been directed at media, especially magazines and TV, for their vulgar and graphic presentation of violent acts and sexual exploitation. Advertisements in newspapers, magazines, and TV have targeted children and adolescents as potential consumers. The advertisers use teenage models to make the advertised products appear closer to the "created needs" of the adolescents.

Politics and Military

Indonesian adolescents tend to be cynical toward politics, political parties, and the democratic process (National Democratic Institute for International Affairs 2002). Adolescents' participation in political activity is usually limited to voting in general elections. The legal voting age in Indonesia is 17 years.

In 2004 Indonesia held direct elections for the presidency and also for the members of Parliament and regional representatives. The election committee had encouraged a more "rational and educated" campaign, but sadly this kind of campaign was not very popular. The open forum type of campaign, with music and singers, attracted more people, including adolescents.

Military activities seem to be considered as adults' business. Compulsory service for young people does not exist in Indonesia, and armed combat is also an unfamiliar phenomenon. Paramilitary organizations are not known; however, there are some youth organizations that like to simulate the military in the way they dress.

At the level of the smaller community, young people organize themselves in a group called Karang Taruna Youth Centers. One of the activities of Karang Taruna is to "mobilize media to encourage involvement of youth in development" (in Brown, Larson, & Saraswathi, 2002, p. 202). Occasional voluntary or community work by adolescents does exist in Indonesia.

The world of entertainment is becoming the new main focus for young people; it promises glamour, fame, and wealth. Contests similar to *American Idol* or *Academia Fantasy* are very popular, and thousands of adolescents try their luck at these competitions. They know that if they succeed, then instant fame, recognition, and wealth will be theirs.

Unique Issues

Street fighting, commonly known as *tawuran*, between junior and more often senior high school students, mostly males, seems to be a common phenomenon of urban life in Indonesia. In Jakarta, for example, the Metropolitan Police Department noted that from year to year the level of street fighting has increased steadily, and the number of people who have been killed has also increased. *Tawuran* usually occurs between students from different schools that have a long history of hostility.

Casual observation of *tawuran* seems to show that it is seasonal (i.e., occurring more often at certain times). An Indonesian sociologist, Wirutomo (in Tambunan, 2001) has even said that *tawuran* is now functioning as a means of relief from the boredom of the daily routine. *Tawuran* seems to occur more often after mid-semester examinations, or after the results of exams have been announced. It seems that *tawuran* offers adolescents a means to reduce post-exam stress.

It has been said that high school students who fight on the streets come from vocational schools and from a low economic background. However, it is not easy to identify a single factor as the main cause for street fighting. It is true that a large proportion of the students involved in street fighting are from vocational schools (considered to be inferior to the general high schools). Social, economic, and psychological factors such as the density of the residential areas, lack of open space for sports and recreational activities, bad public transportation systems, and low motivation for academic achievement are intertwined.

Another interesting phenomenon is the appearance of Chinese youth in the political arena and entertainment world. Formerly, due to discrimination and other limiting factors, Chinese people focused their activities in trade and business. However, in recent years the political and social climate have become more open for anyone who wants to be involved in politics, the economy, the human rights movement, entertainment, and so forth. Young Chinese have stepped forward and become involved in a world that previously seemed to be taboo for them: politics and entertainment. With the mushrooming of political parties, people are free to choose the party that suits their ideology, and at present some Chinese sit in the House of Representatives.

References and Further Reading

Arnett, J. J. (2004). *Emerging adulthood: The winding road from late teens through the twenties.* Oxford, UK: Oxford University Press.

Atmowiloto, A. (1985). Hasil angket: Jangan Kaget. *Hai*, Nov. 26–Dec. 2.

Asiafinest.com (2009). *Indonesian divorce rate up 10 fold since reform era.* Retrieved from Asiafinest.com

Beazley, H. (2003). The construction and protection of individual and collective identities by street children and youth in Indonesia. *Children, Youth and Environments, 13*(1).

BPS–Statistics Indonesia (2002–2003). *Indonesia Young Adult Reproductive Health Survey*, funded by United States Agency for International Development, through ORC Macro, Jakarta, Indonesia.Brown, B. B., Larson, R. W., & Saraswathi, T. S. (2002). *The world's youth: Adolescence in eight regions of the globe.* Cambridge, UK: Cambridge University Press.

Demographic Institute. (1999). *Baseline survey of young adult reproductive welfare in Indonesia, 1988/1999* (six vols.). Jakarta, Indonesia: Demographic Institute, Faculty of Economics, University of Indonesia.

Global Education (2010). *Indonesia.* Dulwich, Australia: Global Education. Retrieved from www.globaleducation.edna.edu.au

Hadis, F. A. (1993). *Gagasan orang tua dan perkembangan anak.* Unpublished doctoral dissertation, Faculty of Psychology, University of Indonesia, Jakarta.

Handayani, P. (2005). *Gambaran citra tubuh dan penerimaan diri pada remaja akhir yang mengalami obesitas karena factor keturunan.* Unpublished undergraduate dissertation, Faculty of Psychology, University of Indonesia, Jakarta.

Hasoloan, M. A. (n.d.). *Country Report: The Indonesian labor market.* Presented at The OECD Forum on the restated OECD Jobs Strategy. New York: OECD.

Ikhsan, M. (2006). A flexible market will solve manpower issues. *Indonesia outlook 2005—Economic*, Jan. 6. Retrieved from www.thejakartapost.com

Indonesia Young Adult Reproductive Health Survey. (2002–2003). Jakarta, Indonesia: BPS-Statistics Indonesia and ORC Macro.

Koentjaraningrat. (1985). Ritus peralihan di Indonesia. Jakarta: PT Dian Rakyat. *Kompas*, 24 April 2005.

Mansoben. (1994). Ritus K'bor dalam masyarakat Biak-Numfor di Teluk Cenderawasih. In *Irian jaya: Membangun masyarakat majemuk.* D. K. K. Koentjaraningrat. Jakarta, Indonesia: Penerbit Jambatan.

Mulder, N. (1999). *Agama, hidup sehari-hari dan perubahan budaya. Jakarta, Indonesia: PT Gramedia Pustaka Utama* (original title: *Inside Southeast Asia: Thai, Javanese and Filipino interpretations of everyday life*).

National Democratic Institute for International Affairs. (2002). *Report on Penyelenggaraan Parlemen Remaja Indonesia (Indonesia Young People's Parliament).* A Pilot Project by Indonesia Child Welfare Foundation, and Directorate of Primary and Secondary Education, Ministry of National Education, Indonesia.

Parker, L. (1997). Engendering school children in Bali. *Journal of the Royal Anthropological Institute*, *3*(3), 497.

Pickles, J. (2000). Punks for peace. *Inside Indonesia*, Oct.– Dec. Retrieved from www.insideindonesia.org

Putranti, B. D., Faturochman, D., Darwin, M., & Purwatiningsih, S. (2003). *Male and female genital cutting, among Javanese and Madurese.* Yogyakarta, Indonesia: Center for Population and Policy Studies, Gadjah Mada University.

Saifuddin, A. F., & Hidayana, I. M. (1999). *Seksualitas Remaja.* Jakarta, Indonesia: Pustaka Sinar Harapan.

Suryadarma, D., Suryahadi, A., & Sumarto, S. (2006). *Causes of low secondary school enrollment in Indonesia.* Jakarta, Indonesia: Smeru Research Institute.

Tambunan, R. (2001). *Perkelahian pelajar.* Retrieved from www.e-psikologi.com

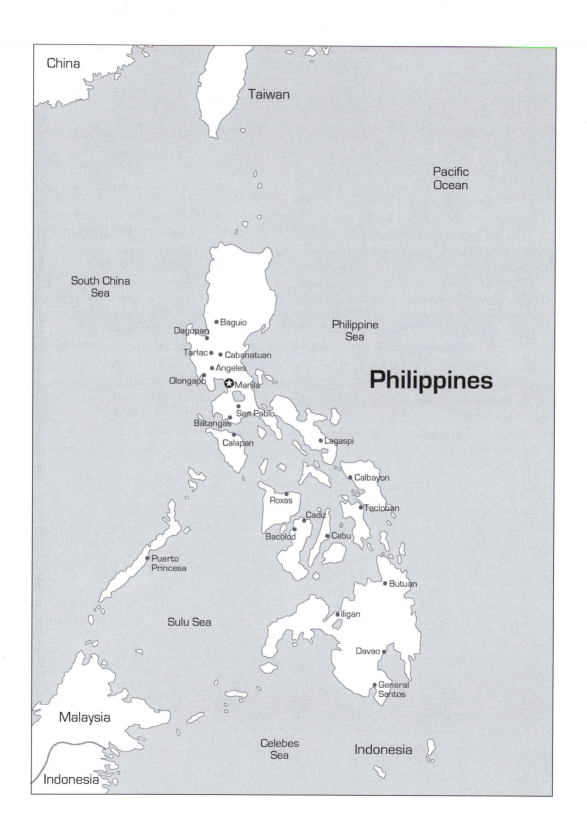

Chapter 10
The Philippines
Madelene Santa Maria

Background Information

The Philippine archipelago consists of 7,107 islands and is bounded to the south by Malaysia, to the west by Vietnam, and to the north by Taiwan. Located in the western part of the Pacific Ocean, the country is made up of three big island groups: Luzon to the north, Visayas at the center, and Mindanao to the south.

There are more than 98 dialects and languages (National Statistics Office (NSO), 2003b). The language most frequently spoken during early childhood is Tagalog. Colonizing cultures brought a variety of religions to the country. Spanish rule for 300 years brought the Roman Catholic religion. Protestantism developed as the Americans, who ruled the country for three decades, introduced the Baptist, Evangelical, Lutheran, and Methodist denominations. Islam had its foothold in the country long before the introduction of Christianity, and it continues to be a predominant religion in the southern part of the Philippines.

The country experienced erratic economic growth from the proclamation of martial law during the early 1970s until after its dismantling through a "People Power" revolt in the mid-1980s. Employment has not been able to expand to meet the demands of a steady increase of people entering the labor force each year (Philippine Social Science Council (PSSC), 2003). The 2007 census recorded the country's population at about 89 million, up from 77 million in 2000 (NSO, 2003a, 2010b). With an average household size of five people, more than half (56%) of the total population resided in Luzon, with 24% in Mindanao and 20% in Visayas (NSO, 2003b). In 2000, 48% of the population lived in cities and 52% in rural areas (NSO, 2010b).

Period of Adolescence

In many studies, the period of adolescence generally covers 10 to 24 years of age, with the process of achieving sexual maturity, independence, and adult psychological processes characterizing it (Gastardo-Conaco, Jimenez, and Billedo, 2003). Among females, the transition to adolescence is marked by the occurrence of menarche. At this time, the young girl receives instructions from the mother about proper hygiene and may be initiated to the rituals and beliefs to ward off negative consequences associated with having the monthly period. With the onset of menstruation, the young girl will begin to experience being treated differently as she will be required to be more careful and ladylike in her deportment and in her relations with the opposite sex. The social world will make the young girl more aware of the danger and abuse that may befall her in the outside world, and as a consequence she will develop fear and shame, especially toward males.

In the Philippines, the young person may be expected to remain close within the web of family obligations, especially when still unmarried, while maintaining a degree of economic independence. However, prolonged years of schooling and training are required of the youth before their entry into the world of work. Even as the young person can assume more mature roles by contributing more directly to the household income at about 16 to 20 years of age, marriage and becoming a parent for the first time tend to occur later, when the young person reaches the age of 24 or 25 (PSSC, 2003).

Laguna (2001) states that the phenomenon of leaving the home during adolescence usually happens when the young person needs to pursue higher education or to seek employment, often at the age of 16, after completing secondary school. The completion of education seems to be a central event that may signal the following events for the young person: the entrance to adulthood, marriage, entrance into the labor force, and perhaps one's departure from the parents' home.

Gastardo-Conaco and her associates (2003), through a series of focus group discussions with Filipino adolescents in the various age groups, from urban and rural areas, found how these youth were viewing the stage of life they were currently experiencing. From the perspective of the young respondents, adolescence was a time of many changes, a period of immaturity, a time to learn, and a time to be happy-go-lucky. For them, greater seriousness and independence marked the end of adolescence. They also believed that to prepare for adulthood, they needed to exhibit greater patience, control, and discipline.

Beliefs

The 2000 census of population and housing revealed that eight out of 10 Filipinos were Roman Catholics, while believers of Islam came second at 5%, followed by the Evangelicals at 3% (NSO, 2003b). A 1996 survey revealed that 86% of the Filipino youth respondents reported being brought up in deeply religious homes (PSSC, 2003). The survey also revealed that 82% of these respondents considered themselves to be "religious persons," and 68%of these respondents attended religious services at least once a week. Two-thirds of Filipino adolescents report that they pray regularly or sometimes together with their family (Cruz, Laguna, & Raymundo, 2002).

The PSSC (2003) report indicated that nearly all young Filipinos (99%) believe in the existence of a God, in the concept of sin (99%), in heaven (98%), that people have a soul (95%), and that there is life after death (91%). Filipino youth receive most of their religious instruction in their homes, which may be further sustained and strengthened within the school context. The PSSC report noted that surveys on the religiosity of the youth also revealed that female adolescents were more religious than their male counterparts, and that adolescent recipients of religious education possessed favorable attitudes to that instruction and found it to be relevant to their lives.

The survey done on Catholic youth revealed, however, that the youth minimally involved themselves in church activities outside of the regular religious services. Furthermore, the *Philippine Daily Inquirer* survey (cited in PSSC, 2003) found that the young people did not completely adhere to all the teachings of their religion, particularly on the issues of divorce, abortion, homosexuality, contraceptive use, and premarital sex. The youth were said to find the views of their church regarding these issues as outdated.

Gender

Role expectations that relate to gender are learned and played out in different contexts throughout the youth's life. Young Filipinos and Filipinas first imbibe the differences in gender roles and expectations in the family (PSSC, 2003). Ramirez (1988) observed that daughters usually maintain close relationships with their mothers, while sons perceive their fathers as emotionally distant. Sons are granted more freedom than are daughters, who usually experience more restrictions on their movements (Liwag, de la Cruz, & Macapagal, 1998). Females are more restricted because they need to be protected more than the males, who are expected to learn to defend themselves, as well as their family. Females should receive more protection because the Filipino culture accords greater value to female virginity than to male virginity, and the event of premarital pregnancy is likely to bring shame to a woman and her family (Cruz et al., 2002).

Liwag and her associates claim that studies in gender socialization in the Philippines show that this differential treatment given to boys and girls is more pronounced when they reach their adolescent years. The experience of adolescence for the Filipino/Filipina is likely to be most influenced by the manner in which gender is socialized in Philippine society and culture. That is, as the young adolescent female experiences more restraints within and outside the family, the young male adolescent will experience even more freedom and will generally be left to his own devices.

Gender differences are likewise to be found in the adolescents' responsibility training (Liwag et al., 1998). Girls are taught to assist with the housework. In poor families, the girls learn to help their mothers in the care of their younger siblings, thus serving as their mothers' and fathers' surrogates. They also participate at an early age in the income-earning activities of the family, assisting the mother in and out of the house. The young Filipina learns to be independent and is capable of taking care of herself at an early age. The boys are expected to assist in tasks that necessitate physical effort and strength, such as carrying heavy buckets of water into the house, or doing carpentry jobs. They generally play the role of being their father's assistants in the farm or in fishing. They may thus find themselves employed during adolescence. They may also be required to accomplish tasks usually assigned to the young girls, such as taking care of a younger sibling or washing clothes, when the female is not available for these tasks.

The differences in gender role expectations are also clearly seen in courtship. Gastardo-Conaco, Jimenez, and Billedo (2003) describe the behaviors expected of each gender during this process. Males are expected to play a more active role during courtship, make the first move, and show more direct expressions of affection. Females, on the other hand, should be able to show more control in their expressions. They are expected to be less verbal and more indirect. It is deemed desirable when the female is able to delay the courtship process. A female who actively initiates courtship or gives in immediately to a male's courting would be sanctioned with the most negative label of being "cheap" or "easy."

This double standard that exists between young males and females becomes even more apparent in their sexual socialization. Mothers do not usually play any role in the socialization of the females, while fathers and elder male family members may be active in assisting the young male's first sexual experience (Policy Project, 2003).

The Self

In all their activities, the Filipino youth are observed to be relatively well adjusted and integrated (PSSC, 2003). They also reported that they were happy with themselves, were more optimistic about the future than their parents' generation, and generally considered themselves to be in a good state of health. Compared to adolescents in lower-income families, those in middle-income families were found to have a more positive self-concept, better body image, and better nutritional status (Vasquez 1992, cited in Gastardo-Conaco et al., 2003).

Peña (1998) found the Filipino adolescent self to be consistent with the depictions of self in both so-called individualistic and collectivistic cultures. In line with the more Western (or individu-alistic) conceptualizations of the self, the Filipino adolescent self was found to be multifaceted and differentiated. At the same time, Filipino adolescents were found to conceptualize the self as rela-tional, role-related, and situation-bound—features that characterize a more collectivistic notion of the self. This phenomenon may be explained by the capacity of the Filipino youth to apply the norms and values of both cultural domains in various situations as they deem appropriate. A study on Filipinos' notions of self showed that both values of individual achievement and relationship-embeddedness were utilized for particular situational and relational demands (Santa Maria, 1999). It should be further emphasized that Filipino youth believe in asserting their independence and individuality (Go, 1994). We may attribute this to the amount of the Filipino youth's exposure to Western forms of media very early in life, which makes for an enhanced readiness to function within individualist-oriented norms and values, while continuing to adhere to collectivist values they are socialized into within the family.

Their capacity to flexibly adapt to the social and interpersonal demands of various situations has contributed to their general wellbeing. As a whole, studies show that Filipino adolescents are highly satisfied with their lives (Sandoval, Mangahas, & Guerrero, 1998). Their life satisfaction is based on gratifying social relationships and fulfilling communal commitments. More specifically, surveys are showing that they are satisfied with the way they get along with members of their social world—their parents, their neighbors, and all those they spend time with (Sandoval et al., 1998). They likewise claim that they are generally satisfied with themselves. They articulate experiencing fulfillment in their lives, their standard of living, their personal safety, and their jobs.

The goals of Filipino youth have consistently shown a veering away from more individualistic ones, and towards fulfilling social responsibilities, obligations, and commitments. These goals, as articulated by the youth, are, in descending order: (1) to help the family, (2) to help the needy and the poor, (3) to have a better standard of living, (4) to improve the community and country, and (5) to develop one's talents (Gomez, Pedro, Romero, Ruivivar, & Tee, 1986).

Family Relationships

In the Philippines, the adolescent grows up in a nuclear family as the basic form of household, con-sisting of the married couple and unmarried children (Shimizu, 1984). This nuclear form is not of the closed type, since frequent interactions may be observed with nearby families. Moreover, elderly grandparents or unmarried siblings may also be found living in the same household. Children may likewise continue living with their parents even after marriage until their own first or second child is born, which is a time when they would start building their own household, usually near the paren-tal home.

The young person forms mutually dependent and cooperative relationships with other mem-bers of the family—a condition that does not change throughout one's life (Shimizu, 1984). Ventura (1999) states that the first concept in the social development of the youth in Filipino families is that of *pakiramdam*, or the capacity for social sensitivity. The learning of "sociable–intimate" behavior patterns helps the young person maintain and manipulate various dyadic relations, while he or she skillfully downplays the expression of aggressive or rebellious attitudes. The young person learns, therefore, at a very young age that the maintenance of one's social world, primarily through *paki-ramdam*, is necessary for the realization of one's personal goals.

Parents generally set rules on adolescent activities, household chores, and responsibilities (Gastardo-Conaco et al., 2003). Mothers are reported to be the main rule setters, implementers, and enforcers. Adolescents claim that rules may be negotiated, but rules set by fathers are usually inflexible and less amenable to negotiation. It is therefore understandable that many adolescents view their fathers as stricter, while female adolescents are more likely to view both parents as strict, due to the stricter socialization the daughter receives in the family (Cruz et al., 2002).

The mother is regarded as a close confidante, while the father is seen as emotionally distant (PSSC, 2003). More than the father, the mother is seen to be accessible, approachable, and accommodating of the young person's needs (Gastardo-Conaco et al., 2003). Gastardo-Conaco and her associates report that female adolescents felt closest to the family, especially to its female members. They found that these adolescents would talk to their family members about their problems in school, their ambitions, and their studies, but they would find difficulty communicating to family members about sex and their love lives. Male adolescents also claimed to feel close to their parents and to some male members of the family, usually an older male sibling. The males find it more difficult to communicate with their parents because of embarrassment or a fear of being scolded or misunderstood.

Bennagen (2000) described the conflicts that occur between the adolescent and his or her parents. She found that these were mainly due to the differences in their self-perceptions and in their perceptions regarding the social categories of parents and of adolescents. The adolescents' relationship with their parents seemed to be better than with their siblings. The young Filipino would usually report a lack of closeness with their siblings (Gastardo-Conaco et al., 2003). The age disparity and the difference in their roles were common reasons for this lack of closeness, which contributed to their inability to exchange confidences with their siblings. They usually felt closest to the youngest sibling, whose age may range from five to 11 years old, and who they had to care for and look after as part of their duties within the family (Gastardo-Conaco et al., 2003).

Cruz and her associates (2002) mention survey data that show that 84% of adolescents have been raised under an intact family structure. This means that a considerable proportion of adolescents (16%) will not have experienced being brought up and guided by both parents. This phenomenon is said to be mainly due to increased incidences of single parenting and marital split-ups, as well as an increasing number of Filipinos going overseas for employment.

Parental support and supervision over the free time and leisure activities of the youth have also been jeopardized due to the increased incidences of both parents having to work full-time to keep the family economically afloat (PSSC, 2003). The decrease in parental supervision has caused increased TV viewing among the youth, which in turn adversely affects the youth's performance in school and in family relationships. Parents who now find themselves pressurized with time have allowed their children to make decisions on their own (McCann-Erickson, 1993).

Friends and Peers/Youth Culture

The peer group remains an important feature of adolescent life in the Philippines. Youth are able to express themselves more easily among their friends and peers than with their parents or other members of their family (PSSC, 2003). The topics and issues discussed more freely with their peers are those that have to do with their problems with their parents, as well as questions regarding sexual activities and relationships, their difficulties in school, and problems with their friends (PSSC, 2003). What the peers essentially do is to assist the young person in developing a sense of freedom and independence (Mendez & Jocano, 1979). This is accomplished in situations when youth, with their friends, try out new styles and engage in discussions of issues that currently confront them in their lives. The peer group becomes the main agent in the socialization of behaviors distinct from those exhibited in childhood (Lajom et al., in press).

The rising trend in parental absenteeism has caused youth to turn more to their friends not just for friendship and companionship, but also for nurturance, intimacy, security, and guidance. However, misunderstandings with friends are taken seriously by adolescents, making the peer group a source of their stress and conflicts (Gastardo-Conaco et al., 2003).

The clique or friendship group, or what Filipinos call the *barkada*, mostly comprises friends from high school or from college, as well as peers from church or community groups (Gastardo-Conaco et al., 2003). Of all these groups, Gastardo-Conaco and her associates found those formed from high school friendships are the most long-lasting, especially if these friends also happen to study in the same university later. Young Filipinos spend most of their free time in their *tambayan*, the place they choose to hang out. Otherwise, they go out together to the malls, movies, or parties. They also accompany one another to visit other friends for gossip and talk sessions, to court a love interest, or to provide the needed support or confidence (Mendez & Jocano, 1979; PSSC, 2003). The PSSC report in 2003 emphasized that the peer group is the most important source of information about sex-related matters. Most of the young men are initiated into sex activities through the guidance, support, and advice of their peer group.

The manner in which the *barkada* spends time while together differs according to the time of year (Gastardo-Conaco et al., 2003). During school year, the *barkada* would, of course, have fewer activities, its members having to spend most of their time at school. Their activities include having lunch together or hanging out together between classes. Summer vacation is a time when they have more time for their activities, which usually occur three times weekly. Sports, eating out, and music-related activities were found to be the most common youth pastimes, and by the 1990s the "malling" activity was added to the list (McCann-Erickson, 1993).

Youth organizations provide the venue for engaging in more productive activities together. Filipino youth, however, are not "joiners" (Sandoval et al., 1998). One in eight claims to be an active member of a sports and recreational group or church and religious organization, and only a tenth can be found joining youth organizations.

Peers are believed to influence the young person into behaviors and practices that society would label as negative. This happens, for example, when friends influence the young person to experiment with potentially addictive behaviors, such as smoking or drinking alcohol (PSSC, 2003). Peers also provide the youth with positive influences (Gastardo-Conaco et al., 2003). Adolescents claim that their peers help them develop more effective study habits and provide them with more positive attitudes to school and studying. Peers are also there to dissuade them from engaging in bad habits.

Love and Sexuality

In adolescence the courtship process will usually be initiated by the male by trying to get acquainted with the girl through her relatives or friends, attempting to communicate with her through various modes, and visiting her at her home (Gastardo-Conaco et al., 2003). Courtship usually happens after experiencing a crush, and most often precedes regular dating. Relationships among young Filipinos would typically proceed in the following sequence: crushes, courtships, romantic relationships, dating, and then sexual intercourse (Upadhay, Hindin & Guiltiano, 2006). In the study of Upadhay et al., respondents reported to have engaged in courting a few years after having crushes. They also reported dating and have romantic relationships at around the same time. They may engage in sexual intercourse, but only after a couple of years of dating. This observed sequence led Upadhay and his associates to conclude that adolescents in the Philippines tend to begin physically intimate relationships later than adolescents in other parts of the world.

Changes in the nature of relationships among the Filipino youth are happening over the years. The courtship period described above is shorter compared to the 1970s. A courtship arrangement emerging recently, for example, is called "MU" or "mutual understanding," where the relationship is somewhere between a purely platonic one and a romantic one (Francisco, Osabel, and Palafox, 1997). In this type of relationship, the couple have made known their liking for each other and thus can behave like a real couple, but there are no responsibilities regarding exclusivity with the partner.

The PSSC report (2003) points out that the peer group is the most important source of information regarding sex, because peers are less judgmental about one's views and activities than parents and older members of society. Aside from their peers, sex-related materials and literature as well as literature on gay and women's rights movements, which have become more accessible through media and the Internet, can influence the youth's views about sex and gender roles.

The youth also cited as sources of information their sex education classes in school or in community youth centers, as well as relatives of the same sex. A high proportion of the youth (over 80%) were found to be aware of family planning and methods of preventing pregnancy, sexually transmitted diseases, and the transmission of HIV/AIDS. This significant increase in awareness was attributed to the institution of sex education into the curriculum and in public health campaigns.

Cruz and her associates (2002) noted that sex discussions at home were likely to be held among siblings close to one's age and with family members of the same sex. Girls are likely to approach their mothers or sisters, while males would approach their older brothers. Fathers are rarely approached on matters that have to do with sexuality. Still, those most helpful in their current queries about sex are their friends of the same age. The youth in the Gastardo-Conaco et al. study (2003) still consider their parents as the most appropriate source of information about sexuality, but children are often too afraid or shy to ask them and therefore employ various ways to bring up the subject matter for discussion, such as through jokes. The reasons parents give when they refuse to talk about sex are that it is not the right time, that sex is a personal matter, or that they suspect the child is engaging in or is likely to engage in sex after their talk. During more serious conversations, parents usually advise their children to treasure their virginity or to finish their studies before engaging in sex with anyone.

The youth respondents also claim that they feel frustrated about not being able to get straight answers from their parents. They want to know more about the nature and process of sexual intercourse, prenatal development and birth, and how to control oneself from having sex. The youth are not content with the clinical information on sexuality that they often get in their sex education classes, but are more interested in the emotional and relational aspects of sexuality. The available sources of information, such as books, magazines, or the Internet, are inadequate. The youth still believe that talking to an adult will give them the knowledge they seek regarding their sexuality. Adults, too, could be the best source of information for that next stage in life, which is marked by a change in one's status in society, notably marriage.

Census data provided by the National Statistics Office (NSO, 2003a) for 2000 show that marriage occurs at around 27 years for males and 24 years for females. A tendency to marry earlier is found among adolescents in rural areas, where the tradition of prearranged marriages is still practiced.

The PSSC report (2003) provides a comprehensive picture of premarital sexual engagement among the youth in the Philippines. It points out that 3% of 15-year-old males and 1% of females of the same age say that they have engaged in premarital sex. If we look at the rates in the age period of 15 to 24 years, we see the proportion of males to be 25%, while that of females is lower than 10%. The increase in premarital sex with age is said to be an indication that premarital sexual activities among youth are related to their decision to marry later. That is, when they reach the age of 20 or 21, the young person may decide to postpone marriage but not necessarily the sexual activity that traditionally comes with it.

Gastardo-Conaco and her associates (2003) detail the meanings the youth attach to premarital sex. Gender differences in the way premarital sex is viewed may be observed. Females tend to connect premarital sex with love, while males see it as a pleasurable activity. Raymundo (1999) reports that premarital sex is accepted among the youth especially when love is experienced, when the relationship is secure, and when there is an intention to marry.

The increase in premarital sex among youth is not, however, accompanied by more responsible reproductive health practices. Gastardo-Conaco and her associates (2003) found that among their respondents, the use of contraceptives was unpopular because of the difficulty these bring to the sexual act and because of church prohibition. When contraceptives were used, the most popular form was the condom. The females were mainly responsible for the use of contraceptives, since they were the ones who faced the danger of pregnancy. Even though their attitudes to premarital sex may seem to be more relaxed, Filipino adolescents would still subscribe to the Filipino society's traditional way of solving a premarital pregnancy problem, that is, through marriage (Go, 1994).

The YAFSII nationwide survey in 1994 revealed the rising number of Filipino adolescents who were sexually active but largely ill equipped to handle the consequences of their sexual activities (Raymundo & Diaz, 1994). The survey revealed that most of the youth had heard of at least one method of family planning, but only 4% possessed knowledge about contraception. The number of sexually active youth who practiced contraception remained small. The 1994 YAFSII survey revealed that 74% of the respondents did not use any contraception even if they did not wish pregnancy to happen (Raymundo, 1994). The most popular forms of contraception were withdrawal and condom use with initial encounters, while the pill, the rhythm method, and IUDs were used in subsequent encounters. By 2000, the small proportion of males (14%) and females (30%) reporting to have had no sexual experience before marriage indicated more risk taking and changing norms among young Filipinos (Policy Project, 2003) In the third Young Adult Fertility Survey (YAFS 3) in 2003, 18% of the youth found cohabiting arrangements to be acceptable and 15% found nothing wrong with pregnancy without marriage (in Puyat, 2005).

Three types of premarital sexual experience were distinguished among Filipino adolescents by the Policy Project of the USAID in 2003: committed sex, commercial sex, and casual sex. Committed sex is characterized by having intercourse with someone who eventually becomes the marital partner. Approximately two-thirds of male and female adolescents fall under this category. Males usually have experienced the commercial sex category, which involves a one-time sexual experience or sex with multiple partners. Casual sex is normally engaged in by male and female adolescents with someone who will not subsequently become the marital partner.

Raymundo and Cruz (2003) observed an increase in contraceptive practice among the youth by 2002. These researchers note however that the conservative Catholic orientation in the country continues to influence the relatively low levels of reproductive health practices in the country. In 2002, only 19.2% of the youth respondents reported that they used protection during their first premarital sexual encounter (Raymundo & Cruz, 2003). The reasons given by adolescents for their low levels of contraceptive use are: They did not expect sex to happen and were therefore not prepared; they possessed little knowledge about contraception; their partners objected to the use of a method; they believed that the use of contraception was dangerous to one's health; they believed that the use of a method will decrease the fun one gets from the sexual activity; and they did not believe that pregnancy can happen with the first sexual encounter (Raymundo & Diaz, 1994).

Filipino adolescents have not done much to change their attitudes to marriage and virginity. An overwhelming number of youth continue to support the value of virginity before marriage (PSSC, 2003). The PSSC report further points out that Filipino youth are, in general, not in favor of abortion but are accepting of single motherhood, since they feel that being a single mother is generally accepted by friends and the family. The same conservative stance may be observed with regard to homosexuality. Ogena in 1991 reported that homosexual activity among Filipino youth was not as frequent as reports of homosexual attraction. The proportion of young Filipinos reporting having homosexual attractions is 9% to 10% (PSSC, 2003). Those who claim to be actively engaging in gay sex constitute a smaller proportion (3%), with more males than females claiming to be so engaged.

Health Risk Behavior

Filipino adolescents' health status is markedly determined by the adequacy of nutritional and medical care, which continues to be a problem, especially among those who live in conditions of economic distress. A 2000 survey conducted by the Food and Nutrition Research Institute–Department of Science and Technology (National Youth Summit, 2002) revealed that in the 11–19 age group, 33 out of 100 were found to be underweight. Diseases that can be prevented through the maintenance of cleaner environments continue to afflict young people. For example, pneumonia, chronic rheumatic heart disease, diarrhea, other gastrointestinal tract diseases and tuberculosis are the usual diseases that affect adolescents (National Youth Summit, 2002). The leading causes of death likewise suggest the environmental dangers present in youths' lives. The National Youth Summit in 2002 recorded that deaths in the 10–19 age group usually occur because of accidents and other forms of violence. However, Raymundo and Cruz (2003) note that incidences of death related to violence on the self (e.g., suicide), are low among the Filipino youth compared to such incidences worldwide.

Ages 16 and 17 are when many Filipino adolescents experiment with cigarettes, alcohol, and prohibited drugs (Domingo, 1994a). Smoking has remained common among male adolescents (40%), although rare (4%) among females (Domingo, 1994a). There are more youth alcohol drinkers than smokers. More than half of the youth in a large national survey reported trying drinking (Raymundo & Cruz, 2003). The study likewise revealed that there was a greater association of drinking with out-of-school youth and those who belong to the lowest educational strata (Raymundo & Cruz, 2003). Less common among the youth than smoking and drinking is the use of prohibited drugs—the incidence was found to be less than 3% in 2002 (Raymundo & Cruz, 2003).

Education

The Philippine educational system is closely patterned after the American system of formal education. Youth spend approximately 15 years in school: in the elementary level from six years of age, in high school from age 13, and in college at age 16. The young person would most likely have completed his or her degree at the age of 20 or 21. The types of higher education institutions the youth may enter after high school are the public or state-run university, the private university, college, or technical institute. Eighty-eight percent of higher education institutions are private, and 12% are public. Of the private schools, 66% are non-faith-based, while approximately 22% are faith-based (Commission on Higher Education, n.d.).

Ericta (2003) indicates that the youth have more access to education today than the older segments of the Philippine population had. In 2000, about 95% of the youth were found to be literate; that is, they were able to read and write and able to understand a simple message in a language or dialect. Government policies have resulted in 82% enrollment at the elementary, high school, and tertiary levels (Ericta, 2003). Unlike the trend in basic education, enrollment in tertiary education has been declining since 2004 in public schools and 2002 in private institutions (Virola, 2008).

The surge in enrollment in basic and secondary education has, however, strained government resources. The problem is manifesting itself in terms of the inadequacy in educational content and quality (PSSC, 2003). Education survival rates likewise do not necessarily provide a rosy picture of Philippine education: Only 42% of first-grade entrants are able to graduate from high school, and among those who succeed in finishing high school, only 17% pursue a college education (Cruz, Laguna, & Raymundo, 2002).

Youth who decide to drop out of school usually come from poor families. Poverty pushes the young person to search for work to augment family income. This is evidenced by lower participation rates in the country's poorer regions of Visayas and Mindanao (UNESS, 2009). Aside from financial constraints, the other reasons for leaving school were lack of interest in school, peer influence, and poor academic performance (PSSC, 2003). The PSSC report provides us with a profile of these youth: They live in the urban areas, and two-thirds of the urban out-of-school youth are females. Co and

Neame (2000) enumerate other factors associated with the existence and increasing number of out-of-school youth. Also mentioned were early marriage and parental separation or death. The traditional bias against women pursuing higher levels of learning, most prominently in the southern part of the country, also contributes to the number of the youth dropping out of school. The majority of youth who dropped out of school no longer have any plans to go back to school because of housekeeping duties or because they would rather go to work than stay in school (PSSC, 2003).

Technical and vocational training is also provided to young Filipinos. Data on the number of enrollees and the employability of graduates have not been encouraging. In 2006–2007, enrolment was 1,736,865 students, with a 60% employment rate of graduates during that school year (UNESS, 2009). The societal bias against technical and vocational education and the labor market demand–supply mismatch are among the challenges that prevent technical and vocational education from being popular among the Filipino youth (UNESS, 2009).

Work

Unemployment is relatively high among the young. For every 10 unemployed persons, five are in the age group 15–24 years (NSO, 2010a), while three are in the age group 25–34 (UNESS, 2009). High school graduates (33%) make up most of the unemployed (UNESS, 2009), while college graduates made up 19% of the young Filipinos who are not working (UNESS, 2009). The high percentage of unemployed college graduates highlights concerns about the demand–supply mismatch in Philippine higher education. A report by the Department of Labor and Employment (2003a) points out that despite the great number of youth who express interest in finding work, only about a third of them actually take steps to search for employment. This may be accounted for by the lack of qualifications these youth possess for jobs that are available in the labor market. These young people claimed that the types of job openings and conflicts with studies were the reasons for their non-interest in available job openings.

Gender and urban–rural differences are observable in the labor force characteristics of young Filipinos (Ericta, 2003). Young males have more work opportunities available to them in the formal labor market, while young females are likely to find employment in more informal work arrangements, such as housework. The labor characteristics of youth also show that in the urban areas more youth were not in the labor force than in the labor force, while in the rural areas the opposite was the case. This suggests that more work is available in the rural areas that requires youth labor. It may also be that the youth are expected to work at an earlier age in the rural areas than in urban areas. This may indeed be true, since most of the rural youth are found employed in agriculture, where the young person learns the tasks related to farming and fishing very early in life. Most of the young men and women in the urban areas are employed, on the other hand, in community and social services, manufacturing, and wholesale–retail trade (National Youth Commission (NYC), 1997).

Participation in the labor force also varies between the sexes. Males in the 15–24 age group make up 64% of the total population not in the labor force. Females, on the other hand, make up 38% of the population not in the labor force. There can be two explanations for this trend. The availability of more opportunities for employment for females may be one explanation. Another explanation may be found in the greater number of males in this age group seeking employment abroad compared to females (NSO, 2010b). There were indeed more males in the age category 15–24 working overseas, while there were more female overseas Filipina workers than males across all other age categories (NSO, 2010e).

Due to the scarcity of employment opportunities for the youth in the country, more and more youth are attempting to look for jobs overseas. The young overseas contract workers come mainly from the 20 to 24 age group, and are mostly females. The most popular job destination for them is Saudi Arabia, with Hong Kong, Japan, Taiwan, and the United Arab Emirates as other possible destinations (PSSC, 2003). Most of the young contract workers are found in domestic service, production jobs, and transport (PSSC, 2003).

According to the Department of Labor and Employment report (2003b), most youth aspire to set up their own business or to pursue careers in medicine, engineering, or education. However, most young Filipinos find themselves employed in agriculture (farming or fishing), and in services (community, social, and personal service jobs). The DOLE report also indicated that more than half of these youth collect salaries, most of them earning less than $100 per month. They do not enjoy any security in their jobs, since they are not covered by social security or work insurance. In view of the unfavorable employment rates among the Filipino youth, the Bureau of Labor and Employment and Statistics (BLES, 2003) recommend that interventions be undertaken in the form of skills training, improved on-the-job training programs, and apprenticeship programs before graduation.

Media

The Filipino Youth Study in 2001 (cited in PSSC, 2003) showed that the Filipino adolescent watches 10 to 14 hours of TV per week. Listening to music on the radio also takes a lot of the youth's time, ranging from eight to 10 hours per week. Popular among the programs young people watch on TV are local drama series that enable them to identify with story lines and characters.

Gastardo-Conaco and her associates (2003) note a growing appreciation of locally produced entertainment in media, even among youth in higher socioeconomic levels. Most appealing to the youth are comedy shows, variety shows, and romance or drama programs, and teenagers, females, single people, and urban residents are generally the biggest consumers of these forms of media (Cruz et al., 2002). Stories about the lives of their pop idols are followed closely in TV shows, as these provide them with guidelines as to how life should be lived.

The young person is the first to take advantage of progress in information technology. The PSSC report (2003) cited an AC Nielsen-Philippines study that showed that 70% of Internet users are young people. "Texting" using the ubiquitous cell phone is extremely popular among the youth and has become a very important communication medium for almost everyone in contemporary Philippine society. The Filipino Youth Study conducted in 2001 (cited in PSSC, 2003) specified that the Filipino youth "texted" messages almost five times a day. Interactive video games are also very popular, and youth are observed to prefer imported video games with violent content (PSSC, 2003).

Cruz and her associates (2002) point out that the exposure of the Filipino adolescent to reading materials such as newspapers, magazines, comics, or books has decreased in recent times. Readership is being confined to comics of the love story or romance variety and is particularly low among males, the married, and rural residents. News content in national newspapers is hardly read by young persons, indicating that they are not attuned to what may be going on nationally and internationally. New forms of technology, such as the Internet and the cell phone, are the media used by the youth in obtaining information about international and national events, as was observed in their involvement in political events in the country.

Politics and Military

The PSSC report in 2003 described the Filipino youth as generally socially conscious, aware of the issues of the day, and willing to act for the good of the country. A large majority (93%) of the youth were proud to be Filipinos and were not willing to alter their citizenship (Sandoval et al., 1998). They were also willing to fight for their country in case of war. They claimed that the strongest traits Filipinos have, and therefore they likewise possess, are industry, friendliness, charity, and hospitality.

This evident national pride cannot, however, be linked with their knowledge of historical facts, as seen in how little association the youth have with social and political realities (NFO-Trends, 2001). Young Filipinos in general are not very interested in government and its affairs, or in the country's political institutions. Gastardo-Conaco and her associates (2003) note the general perception that, in comparison to the young Filipino activists of the 1970s, the Filipino youth of the 2000s are more passive and are less willing to protest against prevailing conditions. The 1996 NYC-SWS survey (cited in Gastardo-Conaco et al., 2003), for example, revealed that a majority of youth were not interested in politics. Youth gave greater value to having a good marriage and family life, finding stable employment, and having a good education. This signifies that youth do not view political life as contributing to their growth or wellbeing.

Although responses concerning political institutions and processes revealed cynicism and negativity, the PSSC report (2003) revealed that the Filipino adolescent does not feel helpless or impotent to change society. There are, therefore, high feelings of political efficacy. Young Filipinos believe that when they choose to act, their actions will influence political processes.

Although Filipino youth are found to have limited participation in state-established political processes, they are known to participate in mass actions and rallies, as they did in two mass actions that led to the ousting of Presidents Marcos and Estrada (PSSC, 2003). Hundreds of thousands of Filipinos gathered at EDSA (Epifanio de los Santos Avenue) on two historically significant occasions, in 1996 and then in 2000, to oust these presidents. These mass actions are known worldwide as demonstrations of "People Power." There was huge participation of the youth in 2000. This led to speculation that there may be more politically active and involved youth now than in the past (Gastardo-Conaco et al., 2003).

The study of Santa Maria and Diestro (in press) revealed that Filipino adolescents are aware of their role in contributing change to society, but are hesitant to do so until they are prepared for political action. Focusing on their education is one such preparation. They view their present political participation in terms of engagement in community activities, participation in school civic activities, and performance of prosocial acts. The youth respondents of the study also mentioned that to be able to participate politically they need to trust or be confident about their capacities, to enhance their knowledge about society, and to be supported by their families and by others in the community. Preparation for political participation takes a different form for young Filipino activists. Diestro's (2009) investigation of these youth from a state university in Manila revealed that a readiness for political participation explicitly involves initial participation in activities where one is confronted with reconciling personal issues with those as viewed from the perspective of the community and its members.

Unique Issues

A unique issue for Filipino adolescents is the high number of their parents who are employed outside the country. The number of Overseas Filipino Workers (OFWs) during the period April to September 2009 was estimated at 1.9 million (NSO, 2010c). Studies on the effects of overseas employment on families are showing discrepant findings. The PSSC (2003) report, for example, claims no adverse consequences on the socialization of youth. Overseas employment has instead served to improve the socioeconomic conditions of families, thus giving the young members an opportunity to obtain for themselves good education, better health, and decent living conditions. The youth are appreciative of their parents' sacrifice to work abroad for the good of the family. Moreover, the youth with OCW parents have not been found to be more delinquent or unruly than their counterparts with fully present parents. There are disruptions in family life that result from parents working overseas, but these are rare and cannot, therefore, result in a generalized claim that parental absence resulting from overseas employment has negative consequences on the development of the young person.

The 2003 Children and Families Study (2004), on the other hand, reports that as the family gets used to the absence of a parent, the relationship with the migrant parent takes on a different dimension. That is, the child can find it difficult relating to a parent in the way a daughter or a son should. For example, the young person may now begin to treat his or her mother as an aunt or a distant relative.

Advanced communications technology has helped in bridging the gaps in relationships between parents and their children due to overseas work. The use of cell phones and other advanced technology, such as the webcam, allows parents and children to communicate more frequently with one another. The care and guidance provided by other family members, such as grandparents and aunts, is likewise allowing children to adjust well in the absence of their parents (Asis, 1995).

References and Further Reading

Asis, M. M. B. (1995). Overseas employment and social transformation in source communities: Findings from the Philippines. *Asia and Pacific Migration Journal, 4*, 327–346.

Balanca, F., Ong, M., Torre, B., Puzon, M., & Granada, I. (2007). *The impact of youth participation in the local government process: The Sangguniang Kabataan experience*. Manila, The Philippines: UNICEF.

Bureau of Labor and Employment and Statistics (BLES). (2003). *Measurements of Youth Unemployment, Labstat Updates* (Vol. 7, No. 20). Manila, The Philippines: Department of Labor and Employment.

Cabral, E. (2010). *Philippines: Statement*. Delivered at 43rd session of the Commission on Population and Development, United Nations, New York, April 1. Retrieved from www.un.org

Choe, M., & Raymundo, C. (2001). Initiation of smoking, drinking, and drug-use among Filipino youth. *Philippine Quarterly of Culture and Society, 29*, 105–132.

Commission on Higher Education. (n.d.) *Statistics index*. Manila, The Philippines: CHED. Retrieved from www.ched.gov.ph/statistics

Cruz, G., Laguna, E., & Raymundo, C. (2002). Family influences in the lifestyle of the Filipino youth. *Philippine Population Review, 1*, 39–63.

Department of Labor and Employment. (2003a). *Youth unemployment. Labstat Updates*. Manila, The Philippines: Bureau of Labor and Employment Statistics, Department of Labor and Employment.

Department of Labor and Employment. (2003b). *Supply and demand situation for nurses. Labstat Updates*. Manila, The Philippines: Bureau of Labor and Employment Statistics, Department of Labor and Employment.

Department of Labor and Employment. (2004). *The 2003 employment situation (The year in review). Labstat Updates*. Manila, The Philippines: Bureau of Labor and Employment Statistics, Department of Labor and Employment.

Diestro, J. M. A., Jr. (2009). Lessons beyond the classroom setting: Civic competencies in youth activist groups as antecedents to civic engagement. *Far Eastern University Psychological Review, 4*, 1–17.

Domingo, L. (1994a). Smoking, drinking and drugs: How prevalent among the youth? Young Adult Fertility and Sexuality Study (YAFSII). Quezon City, The Philippines: University of the Philippines Population Institute.

Domingo, L. (1994b). *Youth under threat of HIV/AIDS*. YAFSII Survey. Quezon City, The Philippines: University of the Philippines Population Institute.

Episcopal Commission on Youth–Catholic Bishops' Conference of the Philippines. (2003). *The national Filipino Catholic youth survey 2002*. Manila, The Philippines: Episcopal Commission on Youth–Catholic Bishops' Conference of the Philippines.

Ericta, C. N. (2003). *The Filipino youth: A statistical profile*. Quezon City, The Philippines: Philippine Social Science Center.

Gastardo-Conaco, M. C., Jimenez, M. C., & Billedo, C. J. (2003). *Filipino adolescents in changing times*. Quezon City, The Philippines: University Center for Women's Studies and Philippine Center for Population Development.

Go, S. (1994). The Filipino youth: Their views and values on marriage and family life. *Kaya Tao. 13*, 1–27.

Gomez, F., Pedro, A., Romero, R., Ruivivar, S., & Tee, E. (1986). *The Filipino youth: A sociological study*. Manila, The Philippines: University of Santo Tomas Research Center.

Laguna, E. (2001). *On their own: Effect of home- and school-leaving on Filipino adolescents; sexual initiation*. East–West Center Working Papers, Population Series no. 108–119. Honolulu, HI: East–West Center.

Lajom, J. A., Canoy, N., Amarnani, R., Parcon, A. M., & Valera, P. M. (in press). Barkadahan: A study of peer group norms and values among Filipino adolescents. *Philippine Journal of Psychology*.

Liwag, E. D., de la Cruz, A., & Macapagal, E. (1998). How we raise our daughters and sons: Child-rearing and gender socialization in the Philippines. *Philippine Journal of Psychology, 31*, 1–46.

National Statistics Office. (2003a). *Philippine yearbook*. Manila, The Philippines: Wellprint Graphics Centre, National Statistics Office.

National Statistics Office. (2003b). *2000 census of population and housing: Report no. 2, Volume 1: Demographic and housing characteristics*. Manila, The Philippines: Wellprint Graphics Centre.

National Statistics Office. (2010a). *Labor Force Survey in 2010*. Manila, The Philippines: NSO.

National Statistics Office. (2010b). *Philippines in figures*. Manila, The Philippines: NSO

National Statistics Office. (2010c). *2008 and 2009 Survey on overseas Filipino income and development*. Manila, The Philippines: Statistics Division, NSO.

National Youth Commission. (1997). *Situation of the youth in the Philippines*. Manila, The Philippines: National Youth Commission.

National Youth Summit. (2002). *PUNK 2001*. Manila, The Philippines: Department of Social Welfare and Development and the National Youth Commission.

NFO-Trends. (2001). *Youth study 2001*. Manila, The Philippines: Global Filipino Foundation, The Philippine Province of the Society of Jesus, the Grade 7 Parents Council 1998–1999 of the Ateneo de Manila Grade School and One Dream Foundation.

Philippine Social Science Council. (2003). *The Filipino youth: Some findings from research*. Quezon City, The Philippines: Philippine Social Science Center.

Policy Project. (2003). *Adolescent and youth reproductive health in the Philippines: Status, issues, policies and programs*. Manila, The Philippines: USAID.

Punzalan, L. (1981). Religious beliefs, attitudes and practice of the Filipino youth of today. *Life Today*, pp. 25–29.

Puyat, J. (2005). The Filipino youth today: Their strengths and the challenges they face. In F. Gale & S. Fahey (Eds.), The challenges of generational change in Asia. Proceedings of the 15th Biennial General Conference, Association of Asian Social Science Councils (pp. 191–205) Bangkok, Thailand: UNESCO

Ramos, M. 2002. Youth speak. *Intersect, 17*, 22–24.

Raymundo, C. (1994). *Youth's reproductive health: A public issue.* Young Adult Fertility and Sexuality Study (YAFSII). Quezon City, The Philippines: University of the Philippines Population Institute.

Raymundo, C. (1999). *Adolescent sexuality in the Philippines.* Quezon City, The Philippines: University of the Philippines Population Institute.

Raymundo, C., & Cruz, G. (2003). Dangerous connections: Substance abuse and sex among adolescents. *Philippine Population Review, 2*(1). Retrieved from www.childprotection.org.ph

Raymundo, C., & Diaz, G. (1994). 1.8M Filipino youth face risk of becoming teenage parents. *Young Adult Fertility and Sexuality Study (YAFSII).* Quezon City, The Philippines: University of the Philippines Population Institute.

Rimando, M. (1981). The changing morality of Filipino adolescents' sexuality and its effects on the family. *St. Louis University Research Journal, 12,* 321–338.

Sandoval, G., Mangahas, M., & Guerrero, L. (1998). *The situation of the Filipino youth: A national survey.* Paper presented at the 14th World Congress of Sociology, Montreal, Canada.

Santa Maria, M. (1999). Filipinos' representations for the self. *Philippine Journal of Psychology, 32,* 53–88.

Santa Maria, M., & Diestro, J. M. Jr. (in press). The youth speak: Political participation among the Filipino youth. *Philippine Journal of Psychology.*

Upadhay, U. D., Hindin, M. J., & Gultiano, S. (2006). Before first sex: Gender differences in emotional relationships among adolescents in the Philippines. *International Family Planning Perspectives, 32,* 110–119.

Varga, C., & Zosa-Feranil, I. (2003). *Adolescent reproductive health in the Philippines: Status, policies, programs, and issues.* Manilla, The Philippines: POLICY. Retrieved from www.policyproject.com

Ventura, E. (1999). Sikolohiya ng bata: Paghahambing ng mga pag-aaral noong 1966–1980 at 1980–1985 (Child psychology: A comparison of studies from 1966–1980 and 1980–1985). In E. Protacio-Marcelino & R. Pe-Pua (Eds.), *Unang dekada ng sikolohiyang Pilipino: Kaalaman, gamit at etika* (The first decade of Filipino psychology: Knowledge, application and ethics) (pp. 31–39). Quezon City, The Philippines: Pambansang Samahan sa Sikolohiyang Pilipino (National Association for Filipino Psychology).

Virola, R. A. (2008). Pinoy graduates: Whither thou goeth? Manila, The Philippines: National Statistical Coordination Board. Retrieved from www.nscb.gov.ph

Watkins, D. (1982). Causal attributions for achievement of Filipino barrio children. *Journal of Social Psychology, 118,* 149–156.

Xenos, P., Kabamalan, M., & Westley, S. (1999). *A look at Asia's changing youth population.* Honolulu, HI: Program on Population, East–West Center, Asia-Pacific Population and Policy.

Xenos, P., & Raymundo, C. (1999). The modern profile of Filipino youth. In C. Raymundo, P. Xenos, & L. Domingo (Eds.), *Adolescent sexuality in the Philippines* (pp. 6–18). Quezon City, The Philippines: University of the Philippines Population Institute.

SECTION III
The Americas

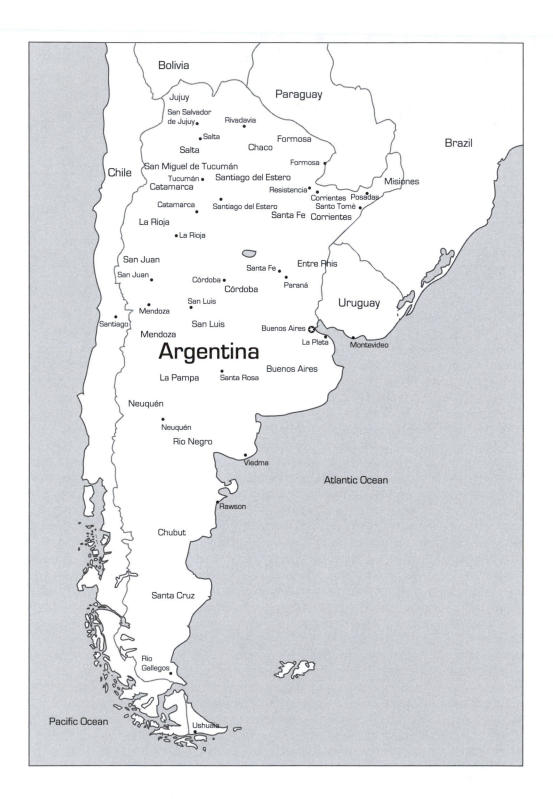

Chapter 11
Argentina
Alicia Facio and Santiago Resett

Background Information

Argentina, a vast nation located in the south of the American continent, had a population of about 40 million people (51% female) in 2009, with one-third living in the capital city, Buenos Aires, and its surrounding area. It is a developed country ranked 49th among the 182 nations of the world, according to the Human Development Index (HDI). This index is estimated by the United Nations Development Program, taking account of life expectancy at birth (75 years of age in Argentina), educational level (adult literacy is 98%), and average standard of living according to real gross domestic product per capita adjusted by purchase power (USD13,238 per year). Argentina is the second best positioned nation in Latin America on the HDI, surpassed only by Chile.

During the period between 1870 and 1930, millions of immigrants—mainly Italians and Spaniards—arrived in Argentina. This enormous wave of immigration turned Argentina into the most Europeanized country in Latin America, with less than 2% of the population claiming pure Native American status.

Research on normal adolescents in Argentina is scarce. Psychology is characterized by a strong predominance of psychoanalytic theory, little interest in quantitative research, and a bias toward psychopathological clinical cases. All of the information provided in this chapter, unless otherwise indicated, has been derived from the published and unpublished work of Facio and colleagues carried out in Paraná, a city with a population of 271,000. Two longitudinal random samples were studied. The first one was made up of 175 students surveyed for the first time in 1988, when they were 13 or 14, and again at ages 15 to 16, 17 to 18, and 25 to 26. The second one consisted of 698 students surveyed in 1998, when they were 13 to 16 years old, and again at ages 15 to 18 and 17 to 21; a randomly selected subgroup of 292 participants was examined for the fourth time at ages 21 to 25.

Period of Adolescence

Adolescence has been recognized as a life stage for a long time in Argentina. As early as 1918 Victor Mercante, an outstanding educator, authored the book *The Pubertal Crisis and Its Educational*

Consequences, where G. Stanley Hall was quoted and where adolescence was the stage ranging from 14 to 20 years old. Other historical literary milestones are *Adolescent Ambition and Anguish* and *Intimate Diary of an Adolescent Girl,* which were written by the medical doctor Anibal Ponce during the 1930s.

Between the ages of 12 and 13 years, menarche is present in more than 50% of females, and, before 14 years of age, in 85% to 90% of girls; at 13 to 14 years, 95% of boys reported having pubic hair, and 60% reported having undergone voice change.

Full legal adult status is acquired at 18, when complete labor and civil capacity are attained. Marriage is permitted at 16 for females and 18 years of age for males, and driving licenses may be acquired at age 18.

Emerging adulthood is a distinct period in the life course of many Argentinian people during their twenties. The percentage of those going through these years of exploration of a variety of life directions in love, work, and worldviews is similar to that of the United States, at least in the upper two-thirds of Argentineans who had received some high school education. Moreover, an over-whelming majority agreed with American young people in considering the individualistic criteria "accepting responsibility for one's self," "making independent decisions," and "becoming financially independent" as very important in defining adult status, just as in other industrialized countries (Arnett, 2006).

Beliefs

As regards individualistic or collectivistic values, Argentinians—like most people in Latin America—resemble European Americans in their level of individualism but differ from them in their higher level of collectivism. Familism—considered by some scholars as the essential core of collectivism—is very high in Argentina, a largely Latin and Catholic country of Italian and Spanish descent. Adolescents see their family as much more important than friends, country, religion, or political ideas. More than half of 17 to 18 year olds agreed that "family responsibilities should be more important than my career plans in the future" or that "despite opportunities in other areas of the country or outside the country, I should try to live near my parents in the future." Family, school, church, and mass media together convey the message of family preeminence.

The majority (89%) is nominally Catholic, but Argentina is a primarily secular society. Although only a small percentage do not believe in God, half of adolescents report being alienated from church activities or not belonging to church anymore. In Paraná, only 23% of 17 to 18 year olds attended services monthly or more frequently; this percentage is similar to that reported for the 15–29 age range across the country (World Values Survey Association, 2009).

Gender

In Argentina, the macho attitude in men has steadily decreased, and the gap between the genders in work, education, and political activity has been narrowing over the decades. Forty-five percent of 15–65-year-old women have a job (INDEC, 2001). Many traditionally masculine professions (medicine, law, chemistry, architecture) have similar percentages from both sexes today. As in other countries, fewer women than men reach the top management positions in private or public organizations, and females earn lower salaries on average (INDEC, 2001).

Where political involvement is concerned, due to a quota law passed in 1991, 34% of parliamentarians are female in both houses at both the national and provincial levels. There are women presiding over ministries and, as of 2004, there were female members of the Supreme Court of

Justice. Although few female governors or big city mayors have been elected, in 2007 the first female president was chosen through the people's vote to be in charge of the Executive.

Although women are highly regarded for their maternal role, young people of both genders considered "being capable of caring for children" as important for defining an adult man as it is for defining an adult woman. In addition, although females attached more importance to women being capable of supporting a family financially and of keeping it physically safe than men did, the majority of males also adhered to these statements. In spite of the fact that adolescent girls were more involved in domestic chores and less involved in jobs than boys, the majority of the latter (55%) had "sometimes" or "always" done housework during the past year.

When judging other-sex attractiveness, the criteria used by Argentinian adolescents are very similar to those endorsed by other Western youth. Regarding an adolescent boy's heterosexual appeal, boys equally underscored physical attractiveness, seduction, and kindness–maturity; girls, instead, ranked kindness–maturity, reliability, fidelity, tenderness, gentleness, and not being arrogant above physical appearance and seduction. The two genders shared the criteria for judging a girl's heterosexual allure: beauty tied with seduction and kindness, especially at the end of adolescence; virginity or affluence did not turn out to be requirements. Both boys and girls mentioned females' physical attractiveness to a greater extent than males' (75% versus 50%).

In different samples, 30% to 60% of females desired being slimmer despite only one out of seven being truly overweight according to body mass index. Girls struggled to get a lower-than-normal weight and the lower their weight, the more satisfied they felt, regardless of the risks involved (Vega, 2004). Twenty-three percent of girls and 5% of boys were involved in pathological diets, and 6% of females and 2% of males reported bulimic behaviors.

The Self

Research work on Argentinian adolescent identity development is almost nonexistent. When those entering college were requested to write a short essay about "I" (Wasser Diuk, 1997), most narratives included relationships with significant others, mainly family members, suggesting that they defined themselves mostly through their family relations. They focused their aspirations on carrying out present tasks rather than considering them as steps within a life project. Only a small percentage referred to future goals or to their plans after graduating from college, and only 15% mentioned expecting to achieve a sense of personal gratification through studying or, later on, practicing their profession.

When 14–24-year-olds from Greater Buenos Aires reported their most important life goals (Deutsche Bank, 1999), "to be happy" ranked first, at 86%, followed by "raising a family," "being a good parent," and "having a rich emotional life" (71%, 63%, and 59%, respectively). Only in fifth place (54%) did a goal referring to work appear: "developing a professional career." "Studying to be a scholar" was endorsed by 34% and "being a hard worker" by 31%. Almost half included "to care for and protect my parents," and 31% adhered to "helping those in need." Patriotism—"contributing to the country's welfare"—was espoused by 13%, and being an influential, prestigious person was chosen by only 7%. Small percentages adhered to "following the beliefs and moral standards enforced by my religious affiliation" (12%) and to "devoting an important part of my life to spirituality" (5%).

In spite of the serious difficulties that Argentina has undergone, its adolescents have been as optimistic about their personal futures as those in more prosperous and stable countries. Compared to 1992, the percentage of optimists was higher in 2002, when the economic and institutional context worsened. Furthermore, four years later—at age 23—they reported levels of life satisfaction comparable to those in Canada or the United States.

Family Relationships

Greater closeness to parents (especially mothers), siblings, and even members of the extended family over friends, as compared to North Americans and Northern Europeans, has been found in Argentinian adolescents. At 15 to 17 years old, when asked about the 10 people they loved most, 87% ranked their mothers and 64% ranked their fathers first or second.

The average Argentinian adolescent has parents with lower school attainment, lives within a two-parent family, and shares the household with non-nuclear relatives to a greater extent than the average adolescent studied by North American and Northern European researchers. In addition, the percentage of working mothers is lower (56% for the adolescents of Paraná).

Family relationship satisfaction is high among Argentinean adolescents. At ages 15 and 16, 64% reported the relationship with their mothers to be "very good"; 30% "good" and only 6% "fair" or worse; as regards feeling misunderstood, 64% stated that this happened "never" or "almost never," 29% "sometimes," and only 7% "almost always" or "always." The relationship with their fathers was slightly less satisfactory; at ages 15 and 16, 45% rated it as "very good," 35% "good," and 20% "fair" or worse; 53% felt misunderstood "never" or "almost never," 29% "sometimes," and 18% "almost always" or "always." At ages 15 and 16, approximately three out of four regarded the relationship with their siblings—excluding half and step siblings—as "very good" or "good" and the rest as "fair" or worse; "frequent" and "very frequent" quarrels with them were non-normative (26%) whereas 45% quarreled with them "sometimes" and 29% "almost never" or "never."

Whether adolescents would resort to parents or friends depends on the kinds of problems involved. Parents were overwhelmingly preferred when health, unwanted pregnancy, or alcohol or drug addiction was at issue, although the difference as to academic difficulties was narrow. Conversely, friends markedly surpassed parents as favorite confidants regarding problems with sexuality, romantic relationships, and friendship; in the case of these issues parents tied with friends during early adolescence, but friends prevailed during the middle and late teenage years. The vast majority preferred mothers to fathers as help providers. Siblings were the main support for a minority, and an even smaller group preferred romantic partners in this respect.

Concerning the degree of control parents exert, during middle adolescence the vast majority (around 80%) considered both parents to be interested in the child as much as he/she needed; only 10% perceived their fathers and 20% their mothers as overcontrolling and 10% their fathers and 1% their mothers as indifferent. The greater part reported that their parents "set some norms" (79% as regards fathers and 89% as regards mothers) whereas for the rest they "set too many norms" or "no norms" to be obeyed. Throughout adolescence, only 8% stated that parents were not interested in knowing their whereabouts.

At ages 17 and 18, the majority were satisfied with the degree of autonomy that both parents granted them: Parents allowed their children to choose their own friends (78%), their own dating partners (83%), their own career goals (79%), and so on, "without interfering too much." Girls considered themselves as autonomous as boys did with respect to their relationship with their mothers and fathers. Throughout adolescence, almost half stated that one or both parents yelled at them or insulted them when they did something wrong.

During middle adolescence school matters were the most recurrent area of conflict between children and their parents (more than one in four cases), followed by curfews and taking responsibility. Almost 20% affirmed that they were not criticized by their parents, and the same percentage said that there were no arguments with them. At ages 17 and 18, the highest degree of negative interchanges happened with siblings; mother and father held second place, romantic partners the third, and best friends the last rank. However, in none of these relationships did the average level of conflict and antagonism exceed the category "somewhat."

No national data are available concerning the divorce or separation rate in parents of adolescent children. In Paraná, at ages 13 to 15, 3.5% of students were born to single mothers, 12.5% of parents had divorced, and 4% of parents—mostly fathers—had died; when they were two years older, divorce had increased to 14% and deceased parents to 5%.

Twenty-one percent of Argentinian conjugal homes include a non-nuclear relative (INDEC, 2001). In Paraná, 16% of adolescents lived with one or more non-nuclear relatives in the household, such as grandparents, uncles, cousins, siblings-in-law, nephews, or nieces. Grandparents, who were present in 12% of the homes, were ranked fifth among the people adolescents loved most, whereas an uncle or an aunt occupied the sixth and a cousin the eighth place.

Friends and Peers/Youth Culture

In Paraná, when asked about the two leisure activities they preferred most, at ages 13 and 14, 57% chose being at home or going out with family, and 73% chose sharing time with friends, especially outings and going dancing. Almost 60% of those having a romantic partner preferred spending their leisure time with her or him. When they were four years older, at ages 17–18, 81% chose an activity shared with peers, and 38% preferred to spend leisure time with family, mainly at home. Among those having a romantic partner, 71% preferred spending leisure time with her or him. Only 11% mentioned solitary activities such as "watching TV" or "resting." In short, although the preference for being with friends and/or romantic partners increased throughout adolescence, spending time with family retained part of its attraction.

No barriers against different-gender friendships are prevalent in Argentina. In Paraná, throughout adolescence, over 80% of teenagers belonged to a group of friends who know each other well; in around two-thirds of the cases, these groups were mixed-sex. At 13 and 14 years old, among 76% of boys having a best friend, almost a third of the friends were girls; however, among 85% of females having a best friend, only 8% of the friends were males. At ages 17 and 18, 89% of both genders reported having a best friend; for 16% of males and 10% of females, this was a cross-gender friendship.

The vast majority of Argentinian teenagers do not suffer from restrictions to friendship caused by religious beliefs or ethnicity. Although all forms of discrimination—due to race, sex, religion, social class, or physical appearance—are illegal in Argentina, some degree of subtle discrimination due to social class is evident in everyday life. Adolescents prefer not socializing with either the *caretas*, as they call those belonging to a socioeconomic level higher than their own, who are viewed as arrogant, or with the *negros* or *villeros*, as the slang denominates those who have a lower status and who are ill mannered according to stereotypical conventions.

Forty-six percent of 14- to 17-year-olds in Greater Buenos Aires practice a sport in their leisure time (Deutsche Bank, 1999). In Paraná, at ages 13 and 14, 66% practiced a sport, whether at a club or at a more informal place; this percentage descended to 35% when the adolescents were four years older. Between the end of the 1980s and the beginning of the 1990s, a high increment in girls' participation in sports—mainly aerobic gym—was detected; however, for competitive sports, the gap between boys (46%) and girls (13%) widened. Small percentages of teenagers belong to youth organizations, whether religious, charitable, or political.

There is a distinct youth culture in Argentina that is marked off from adult culture by image (dress, hairstyle, tattooing/piercing), demeanor, argot, and mass-media consumption. It is so much influenced by American culture that vast sectors of Argentinian youth look very similar to their American counterparts. This happens to a lesser extent in rural and lower-socioeconomic-status urban environments; in the latter, a youth subculture prevails in which the hallmark is attending dancing places called *bailantas* in which the *cumbia villera*, an underground version of a kind of popular music that originated in Colombia, is preferred.

Love and Sexuality

In Paraná, the percentage of those having a romantic partner increased from 18% to 32% in boys and from 17% to 45% in girls across adolescence (from age 13 to 18). Small percentages of both genders (never higher than 10%) reported they were "just dating." The modal category, except in girls aged 17 to 18, was "I'm interested in someone but we are not dating."

With regard to sexual experimentation, despite Argentina being a Latin and Catholic country where restrictive attitudes to female premarital sex were held until the 1980s, men's average age of sexual debut is 16 and women's is 18. As is observed in diverse countries, in Argentina, females reported first coitus at a later age than males. The proportion of adolescent boys with sexual experience was equal to that of girls two years older. Boys now rarely resort to prostitutes as boys used to do.

The National Program for Sexual Health and Responsible Procreation, passed in 2002, provides for, among other objectives, preventing unwanted pregnancy and promoting adolescent sexual health. Authorizing the prescription and free supply of condoms and oral contraception in public hospitals even to minors has allowed the access of lower-economic-status adolescents to birth control. As laws change according to jurisdiction, in some places parents must authorize this type of medical consultation. The so-called morning-after pill and the intrauterine device are not usually permitted in public health institutions due to the pressure exerted by Catholic groups that consider them abortive. Abortion, a highly controversial issue, although illegal except when endangering the mother's life, is frequently practiced in Argentina: Among adolescent girls who reported having been pregnant (12%), half of them became mothers and the other half resorted to abortion (Kornblit, Mendes Diz, & Adaszko, 2006).

Fifteen percent of living newborns had mothers who were less than 20 years old (INDEC, 2001). Adolescent pregnancy is much higher among those who do not even enter secondary school. In a study of teenage mothers (Gogna 2005), only 41% lived with their partners; almost half had dropped out of school before getting pregnant, and, among the remainder, only four out of ten continued their education up to childbirth. Feeling ashamed of being pregnant or the fear of being discriminated against were the reasons for dropping out adduced by one-third of them.

AIDS prevention has been incorporated to the curricula at all levels of education. Young people were fairly conscious of the risk AIDS entailed for their health, and they knew very well how the infection could be caught. Kornblit et al. (2006) found that AIDS and unwanted pregnancy were the health issues that concerned adolescents the most (70% and 64%, respectively); although sexually active Argentinian adolescents reported using condoms (65%), contraceptive pills (13%), coitus interruptus (10%), or other protective measures (2%), 9% admitted not using any. Teachers (81%) and parents (71%) were the most important sex educators and 92% and 96% of adolescents, respectively, were satisfied with the instruction they provided.

At ages 13 and 14, parents were the favorite confidants regarding sexual concerns (42%). Two years later, friends and romantic partners held the first place (46%) and parents the second (34%); four years later, the preeminence of peers had increased even more (57%) versus parents (24%).

Argentinian society's tolerance toward homosexuality has been increasing in recent decades. In some jurisdictions, laws conceding some rights to homosexual cohabiting partners have been passed; in 2009 the legal marriage of two men was celebrated for the first time not only in Argentina but in Latin America. Forty-four percent of adolescents consider homosexuality a sexual choice rather than an illness (a belief espoused by 47%) or a vice (5%); besides, 3% report they would have sexual intercourse with a same-sex partner (Kornblit et al., 2006). In Greater Buenos Aires (Deutsche Bank, 1999), only 40% of young people would rent a room in their homes to a homosexual without any hesitation; the refusal was even higher when a union leader, a politician, a policeman, a military person, or an evangelist, among others, was under consideration. No research work is available on Argentinian gay and lesbian adolescents.

Health Risk Behavior

The use of licit drugs is widespread among Argentinian adolescents (SEDRONAR, 2001). Smoking cigarettes increases with age, from 22% having smoked at least once during the past year at ages 13 and 14 to 42% at ages 15 and 16 and to 53% at ages 17 and 18. In the oldest group, 31% had smoked six or seven days during the past week, and 20% had smoked five or more cigarettes daily. Only 15%, however, consider their tobacco use problematic. Girls are heavier consumers of cigarettes than boys.

Drinking alcohol increases with age as well, from 52% having drunk at least once during the past year at ages 13 to 14 to 77% at ages 15 to 16 and to 85% at ages 17 to 18. When reporting about the past week, the figures decrease to 23%, 42%, and 49% in the three successive age groups, respectively. One or more episodes of binge drinking during the past month were reported by 7% at ages 13 to 14, by 21% at ages 15 to 16, and by 36% at ages 17 to 18. Access is easy in Argentina, where the prohibition of selling tobacco and alcohol to minors is laxly enforced.

Use of illicit drugs is rare among adolescents. In Paraná, only 1% of adolescents reported using marijuana at least once during the past year at ages 13 to 14, although that rose to 4% at ages 15 to 16 and to 8% at ages 17 to 18. No other drug had prevalence in the past year above 5%, including cocaine, glue consumption, and tranquilizers. These figures are very similar to those reported by cross-sectional surveys covering the whole country (Kornblit et al., 2006).

Education

Since 1884, public education had been free, secular, and compulsory from the first to the seventh grade. In 1993, mandatory schooling was extended from kindergarten (for five-year-old children) through the ninth grade, and in 2006 through the twelfth grade. At present, primary school ranges from first to sixth grade and secondary school from seventh to twelfth. Whereas in the first three years of secondary school all the students learn the same subjects, different orientations (social sciences, natural sciences, business, arts, technology, etc.) are provided in the last three.

Ninety-nine percent of boys and 99% of girls attend primary school, 82% (79% boys and 85% girls) are in secondary school, and 39% (36% males and 41% females) attend higher-education institutions. These figures (INDEC, 2001) indicate that, regarding gender differences in access to education, a small bias favoring women exists in Argentina. Moreover, girls score higher in reading, mathematics, and scientific literacy in international achievement tests.

Significant problems relating to school performance afflict Argentinian secondary school students. Sixteen percent of students enter this level of education belatedly, 31% repeat one or more grades, and 16% drop out. These are the reasons why, at ages 18 to 24, only 43% have completed twelve years of schooling. Nevertheless, unlike other countries, nearly all who finish twelve-year schooling go into postsecondary education.

In the last decades of the twentieth century, the access of lower-economic-level adolescents to secondary school increased significantly. In 1980, 53% boys and 62% girls were enrolled as compared with 73% and 81%, respectively, in 2000. Another sign of this expansion of enrollment is that 81% of those 20 to 29 years old exceed their parents' educational attainment.

In Argentina, secondary schools can be public or private, large or small, for the poor or for the rich; they are of different types and administered by more than 20 different provincial governments. In spite of their diversity, the vast majority of them suffer from low budget, poor buildings, insufficient teaching resources, and meager salaries paid to their teachers, who divide their working hours among several secondary schools. Educators' pay is lower in Argentina than in Chile or Brazil. Teachers' absenteeism, turnover, and professional illnesses in addition to the numerous days they go on strike for better salaries bring about a lot of "vacant hours" during which students just socialize or are sent to their homes. Adolescents have 180 school days yearly in the United States and 220 in the United Kingdom; in Argentina, the 180 days required by law are not achieved for the abovementioned reasons. Although in 2002 only 2% of schools were equipped with computers with Internet access, in 2010 the federal government had implemented a two-year plan for providing portable computers for every student attending public secondary schools.

The majority of students attend classes 4.5 to 5 hours daily. Optional subjects are almost nonexistent. As the training in foreign languages, the use of computers, and music and the arts is insufficient in most schools, middle-class parents often send their children to private institutes devoted to these activities. Sports are mostly practiced at private clubs, which are affordable for ample sectors of the population. Neither dances nor other social meetings are held at schools.

On the Program for International Student Assessment tests (PISA), which evaluate the competencies of 15-year-old children in fifty-seven countries, Argentina ranked 51st in science competency, 52nd in mathematics and 53rd in reading, below other Latin American countries such as Chile, Uruguay, and Mexico (Organization for Economic Cooperation and Development, 2006).

Argentinian public universities, where the greater proportion of young people who decided to continue their postsecondary education enroll, are free, and in the majority of them no entrance examinations are required.

Work

Working is not a widespread activity among Argentinian adolescents. Child work is forbidden and adolescent work is protected by special restrictions. For youth aged 16 and 17, parents' authorization authenticated by the Ministry of Labor is required. Parental authority permits demanding that children aged 14 to 18 help with family work without being paid.

In Paraná, 12% of 13- and 14-year olds, 16% of 15- and 16-year olds, and 29% of 17- and 18-year olds had worked "always or almost always" during the past year, whether helping family members or neighbors in their jobs or being employed in a workshop, an office, a shop, or teaching private lessons or selling different merchandise by themselves, among other occupations. No gender difference in the proportion of working youth was found, although boys were employed for more hours per week.

Secondary-school students usually find a job through family members or friends. Generally, they are low-paying jobs in the informal economy that are carried out on school vacations or part-time during the school year, requiring minimum qualification. The majority of them last less than six months. Despite the precarious conditions, job satisfaction is high (80%). With regard to future work, the obstacles they anticipate are "lack of experience," "the scarcity of posts," and "lack of training," in order of importance (Aisenson and Research Team on Guidance Psychology, 2002).

Media

According to a study by Fundación Telefónica (2008), in which 1,970 10- to 18-year-old Argentinians were surveyed, 99% of adolescents' homes had at least one TV and 79% were connected to TV cable. The country has the most developed TV cable market in Latin America. On weekdays, more than half watched TV "more than two hours" daily, while the percentage decreased slightly on weekends. Almost half said they watched TV while doing homework assingments and 24% while studying; 16% admitted having watched programs parents did not allow them to. In Greater Buenos Aires (Deutsche Bank, 1999), the types of programs they preferred most were comedies (48%), sports (41%), popular music (41%), and youth programs (36%). TV was used to a lesser extent for informative purposes: 11% preference for newscasts, 7% for politics–economics–religion, 13% science and technology, 26% animals and environment, and 15% for arts and literature.

According to the Fundación Telefónica survey, 79% of adolescents' homes owned a personal computer, and 57% had an Internet connection. However, almost all adolescents were Internet users: Those not having access at home did so in public places (45%), available even in small villages in isolated areas. The percentage of those connected "more than 2 hours" daily was 40% on week-days and 50% on weekends. An overwhelming majority (84%) used the Internet for communication purposes (chatting, social networking) and only a minority for searching educational (20%) or cultural (17%) content. Almost half reported that their parents exerted no supervision at all on the contents they accessed.

Ninety-four percent of adolescents owned a mobile phone, 60% an MP3 player, and 92% a stereo.

In spite of globalization, the preference for Argentinian content was evident in both music and TV (UP and TNS Gallup, 2009): At ages 10 to 24, 72% listened most frequently to national musicians and 70% regularly watched Argentinian TV programs. The situation was quite different in the case of movies: 72% often watched foreign (mostly American) movies.

Adults in general think that modern media exert a negative influence on adolescents, so much so that many tried to explain the first Argentinian school shooting, of October 2004—when three students were murdered and another three seriously wounded—as due to the adolescent killer's admiration for a "Goth" singer. Adolescents are intensely targeted by the media and by advertisers, especially by beverage, beer, mobile phones, and candy campaigns.

Politics and Military

Compulsory military service was established in 1901 for all healthy males of 20 years of age—and later of 18 years of age—aiming at "public moralization" and the speeding up of the fusion of the diverse ethnic groups recently settled in the country. Beginning in 1995, conscripts were replaced by volunteers aged 18 to 24, of both genders.

Most Argentinian adolescents' political involvement is limited to voting. As of 18 years of age, they are legally required to participate in national elections. Although the payment of the fine for failing to do so is rarely demanded, the vast majority actually vote.

Adolescents' political involvement has been decreasing since the 1960s and the 1970s, when it reached its peak. The most dramatic consequence of teenagers' association with politics was the almost 250 13–18-year-old "missing" boys and girls who were abducted from their homes, from the streets, or when leaving their schools during the terrorism of state established by the military dictatorship, which ruled the country between 1976 and 1983. A paradigmatic case was "The Night of the Pencils." In La Plata city on September 16, 1976, seven secondary-school students who were fighting for a cheaper student bus fare were abducted from their homes while sleeping and tortured by the military; only one of them reappeared alive.

Student associations, which exist in almost every public secondary school, play a role of some importance in adolescent political socialization. The steering committee and the representatives of each grade are elected through the vote of students. In addition to discussing social problems, these associations devote themselves to other affairs, such as organizing parties and sports events, publishing the school magazine, or collaborating in the maintenance of the school building.

Young people between the ages of 15 and 29 do not differ from the adult population with regard to their trust in different state institutions. Trust in the executive (33%), the legislature (11%), the judiciary (19%), the police (15%), the military (27%), and the public administration (3%) are all markedly low. However, the percentage of those considering democracy as a "very good" or "good" political system for Argentina increased to 94% in recent years (World Values Survey Association, 2009).

Unique Issues

In 1853 Argentina became a representative, federal, and republican democracy, but its history is characterized by political instability and repeated economic crises that began around 1930. Since then, a series of military administrations that seized power through *coups d'état* have ruled, only to be replaced by constitutional governments elected by the people. The 1970s marked the end of the welfare state that, although never reaching the level of European countries, granted free education until leaving university, free health service, housing plans, and fair pensions.

In 1976, when the military forces seized power, state terrorism was installed. Thousands of "missing" citizens were abducted, tortured, and murdered. The national economy was destroyed with the indiscriminate opening of importation, and a large debt was contracted with international banks. Between 1982 and 1985, after the Malvinas war against the United Kingdom, the military dictatorship underwent such a crisis that it had to allow the return of democracy. After the initial euphoria, the Argentinian people discovered with great disappointment that this did not ensure the recovery of either the earlier living standard or the smooth functioning of institutions. The chronically high Argentinian inflationary rate reached an annual increase of almost 5,000% in 1989.

In 1992, the implementation of neoconservative policies generated, on one hand, the reduction of the inflationary rate to normal levels, but on the other, a severe impoverishment of the country: a high unemployment rate; job precariousness; the transformation of large sectors of middle-class and retired people into "the new poor," who were added to the structural poor; and the government's desertion of its leading role in securing social justice.

In December 2001, the political and institutional crisis intensified to such an extent that Argentina was front-page news in the world mass media. The federal administration took possession of all the savings that citizens had deposited in the banks. Popular riots forced the president to resign. Five successive presidents took office over the course of a fortnight. The Argentinian peso was devalued from 1 peso equaling 1 US dollar to a third of its rate. In 2002, Argentina was in its worst crisis in the past 100 years. The already high annual rate of unemployment rose to 22%, one of the highest in the world.

Although the new government, elected in 2003, generated hope initially, the upward mobility dream has been severely menaced. In 2010, around 30% of the population still lived below the poverty line, and one out of three of this group was extremely poor. The gap between the poorest and the richest remains wide. Having once been the most highly developed Latin American country— the land of hope for millions of European immigrants, the only Spanish-speaking nation with three Nobel Prizes in science—the present decadence is a cause of consternation for vast sectors of Argentinian people.

References and Further Reading

Aisenson, D., & Research Team on Guidance Psychology. (2002). *Después de la escuela* (After leaving school). Buenos Aires, Argentina: Eudeba.

Arnett, J. J. (2006). Emerging adulthood: Understanding the new way of coming of age. In J. J. Arnett & J. L. Tanner (Eds.), *Emerging adults in America*. Washington, DC: American Psychological Association.

Casullo, M. (1998). *Adolescentes en riesgo* [At-risk adolescents]. Buenos Aires, Argentina: Paidós.

Deutsche Bank. (1999). *Jóvenes hoy* [Youth today]. Buenos Aires, Argentina: Planeta.

Facio, A., & Batistuta, M. (1997). *Los adolescentes y sus padres. Una investigación argentina* [Adolescents and their parents. An Argentinian research paper]. Paraná, Argentina: National University of Entre Ríos Press.

Facio, A., & Batistuta, M. (1998). Latins, Catholics and from the far south: Argentinean adolescents and their parents. *Journal of Adolescence, 21*, 49–67.

Facio, A., & Batistuta, M. (2000). *La sexualidad de los adolescentes. Una investigación argentina* [Adolescent sexuality. An Argentinian research paper]. Paraná, Argentina: National University of Entre Ríos Press.

Facio, A., & Batistuta. M. (2001). What makes Argentinian girls unhappy? A cross-cultural contribution to understanding gender differences in depressed mood during adolescence. *Journal of Adolescence, 24*, 671–680.

Facio, A., & Micocci, F. (2003). Emerging adulthood in Argentina. *New Directions for Child and Adolescent Development*, 100, 21–31.

Facio, A., & Resett, S. (2006). Argentina. In J. J. Arnett (Ed.), *Routledge International Encyclopedia of Adolescence*. New York, NY: Routledge.

Facio, A., Resett, S., Mistrorigo, C., & Micocci, F. (2006). *Adolescentes Argentinos. Cómo piensan y sienten* [Argentinian adolescents. How they think and feel]. Buenos Aires, Argentina: Lugar.

Facio, A., Resett, S., Micocci, F., & Mistrorigo, C. (2007). Emerging adulthood in Argentina: An age of diversity and possibilities. *Child Development Perspectives*, *1*, 115–118.

Fundación Telefónica. (2008). *La generación interactiva en Iberoamérica* [The interactive generation in Ibero-America]. Barcelona, Spain: Ariel.

Gogna, M. (2005). *Embarazo y maternidad en la adolescencia* [Pregnancy and motherhood in adolescence]. Buenos Aires, Argentina: CEDES-UNICEF.

INDEC. (2001). *Censo nacional* [National Census]. Buenos Aires, Argentina: Ministerio de Economía.

Kornblit, A., Mendes Diz, A., & Adaszko, D. (2006). *Salud y enfermedad desde la perspectiva de los jóvenes* [Young people's perspectives on health and illness]. Buenos Aires, Argentina: Facultad de Ciencias Sociales Universidad de Buenos Aires.

Organization for Economic Cooperation and Development. (2006). *PISA 2006: Science competencies for tomorrow's world*. Paris, France: UNESCO.

SEDRONAR. (2001). *Encuesta nacional a estudiantes de enseñanza media* [National survey of secondary school students). Buenos Aires, Argentina: SEDRONAR. Retrieved from www.sedronar.gov.ar

UP & TNS Gallup. (2009). *Los adolescentes y su inserción en el mundo* [Adolescents' perception of the world]. Buenos Aires, Argentina: UP & TNS Gallup. Retrieved from www.palermo.edu

Vega, V. (2004). Epidemiología de los trastornos de la conducta alimentaria en población escolar adolescente [Epidemiology of eating disorders in adolescent students]. In *Memorias de las 11° jornadas de investigación*. Buenos Aires, Argentina: Facultad de Psicología de la Universidad de Buenos Aires Press.

Wasser Diuk, L. (1997). La evaluación del self mediante relatos escritos [Self-assessment through written essays). In M. Casullo (Ed.), *Evaluación psicológica en el campo socioeducativo*. Buenos Aires, Argentina: Paidós.

World Values Survey Association. (2009). *Official Data File v.2009090*. Stockholm, Sweden: WVSA. Retrieved from www.worldvaluessurvey.org

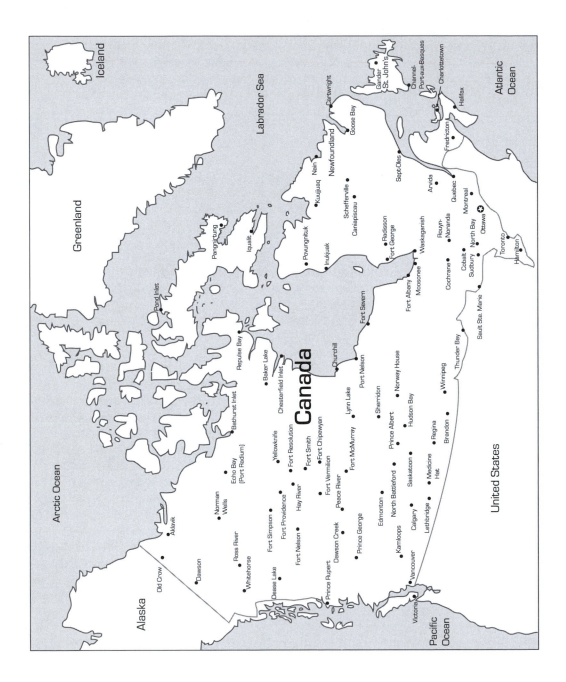

Chapter 12
Canada
Heather A. Sears

Background Information

Canada is located in North America, north of the United States, and borders the North Atlantic, North Pacific, and Arctic Oceans. It is the second largest country in the world, with an area of nearly 10 million square kilometers, and consists of 10 provinces and three territories. The capital city is Ottawa. In January 2010, the population was estimated at almost 34 million and was 50% male and 50% female. Based on the 2006 census, immigrants make up 20% of the total population (Chui, Tran, & Maheux, 2007). Canada's two official languages are English and French. Christianity is the dominant religion, with 43% of people identifying as Roman Catholic and 23% as Protestant (World Factbook, 2010). Canada has a parliamentary democratic government system. It obtained independence from the United Kingdom on July 1, 1867, but remains connected to the British crown. Canada Day is celebrated on July 1. Canada is a highly technological country that became mostly industrial and urban following growth in manufacturing, mining, and service sectors after the Second World War (World Factbook, 2010).

Period of Adolescence

The onset of adolescence may be marked by one's chronological age (typically 12 or 13 years) or physical and social changes, such as pubertal development (typically between 11 and 13 years) or the transition from elementary school to secondary school (often after Grade 5). Markers of the end of adolescence are less well defined, and may include a school-to-work transition, the attainment of legal adult status (age 18), or specific characteristics, such as accepting responsibility for one's actions (Cheah & Nelson, 2004; Tilton-Weaver, Vitunski, & Galambos, 2001). The existence of a period of emerging adulthood following adolescence is indicated in demographic trends, such as a longer period living with parents and a later age at completion of education, first marriage, and parenthood (Beaujot, 2004).

There are over 6.5 million youths in Canada between the ages of 10 and 24 years (49% girls, 51% boys) (Statistics Canada, 2009a). About 5% of them report an Aboriginal identity (Statistics

Canada, 2010a). Within the population of 15 to 24-year-olds, 13% are immigrants (Statistics Canada, 2010c). Approximately 64% of young people give their mother tongue as English, 20% give French, and 3% speak two languages (either both official languages or one official language and one non-official language) (Statistics Canada, 2010d).

Beliefs

Overall, youths are more individualist than collectivist in their values and views. They highly value having freedom and choices, and they believe that they have a key role in determining the course of their future. However, they also value connections to others, specifically friendship and being loved (Bibby, 2009). In terms of religious beliefs, the majority of adolescents (68%) report a religious affiliation, although many young people (62%) report infrequent or a significant decline in religious service attendance across Grades 9 to 12 (Bibby, 2009; Good, Willoughby, & Fritjers, 2009). Many adolescents (37%) who attend services infrequently are open to greater involvement with religious groups, and the majority of adolescents (85%) anticipate turning to religious groups for ceremonies when they encounter specific rites of passage (such as marriage). In addition, 68% of adolescents believe in God or a higher power and 75% believe in life after death (Bibby, 2009).

Gender

Girls and boys in Canada have equal access to fundamental resources that promote development, such as education and health care. However, markers of youths' internalization of their gender are evident, although they may be expressed to varying degrees and less in some contexts and more in others. Adoption of traditional gender roles is one marker that contributes to youths' self-perceptions and their interactions with others. For example, the traditional feminine ideal of thinness for young women is viewed as a key factor in the consistent gender difference in adolescents' dissatisfaction with their appearance, especially body weight. Research indicates that at least 40% of girls are dissatisfied with their weight, that more girls than boys are dissatisfied, and that girls' dissatisfaction increases with age (Barker & Galambos, 2003; Jones, Bennett, Olmsted, Lawson, & Rodin, 2001; McCreary Centre Society, 2009). In addition, more girls than boys act on their dissatisfaction and place their health at risk by dieting, binge eating, and purging (Jones et al., 2001; McCreary Centre Society, 2009). During the high school years, about 18% of adolescents show a problematic course of eating problems (chronic, high-decreasing, or increasing) (Aimé, Craig, Pepler, Jiang, & Connolly, 2008).

Adherence to traditional gender role norms is also seen in adolescents' interactions with peers. For example, boys who report more conformity to the masculine norm of emotional control are less willing to seek help from male friends and female friends, likely because they are more reluctant to share feelings or disclose problems (Sears, Graham, & Campbell, 2009). Boys who subscribe to the gender script that boys should initiate and pursue sexual involvement with girls may be more likely to use sexually coercive behavior with a romantic partner in the absence of concurrent psychological aggression (Sears, Byers, & Price, 2007). Similarly, girls who view sexual coercion as a normative part of romantic relationships may not be upset by experiences of sexual dating violence as other girls typically are (Sears & Byers, 2010). Pressure to conform to gender role norms can be strong, especially for boys, and they are more likely than girls to experience social sanctions from peers and adults when they violate these norms.

The Self

Canadian youths' self-concept has also been evaluated. For example, a two-year study of high school students found that boys reported higher scores on Harter's appearance and athletic competence domains, girls reported higher scores on the close friends and social acceptance domains, and boys and girls did not differ on the scholastic competence, job competence, and romantic relationships domains (Shapka & Keating, 2005). Adolescents' scores on most domains of self-concept increased with grade, although scholastic competence declined and athletic competence and appearance showed no change. Both girls and boys reported a positive level of self-worth, and girls' self-worth increased slightly over the two-year period whereas boys' self-worth decreased slightly. The appearance domain was the strongest predictor of general self-worth, across time and for girls and boys (Shapka & Keating, 2005).

Research also suggests that adolescents may use diverse processes to construct their sense of self and identity. One study revealed that young adolescents' conversations with their mothers may be used to jointly construct possible selves, and that the steps involved may occur concurrently and may vary by domain (e.g., personal characteristics versus adult work roles) (Marshall, Young, Domene, & Zaidman-Zait, 2008). Other studies have identified youths' use of a narrative approach. Adolescent boys' ability to incorporate their past experiences into their current and future sense of self showed an age-related increase, particularly during middle adolescence, and was also linked to a combination of higher autonomy and higher connectedness (McLean, Breen, & Fournier, 2010). Aboriginal youths preferred to use narrative strategies to think about personal persistence (i.e., a need to change *and* a need to stay the same within one's sense of self, and to tie together the past, present, and future), whereas non-Aboriginal youths preferred to use essentialist strategies. These preferences are strongly related to adolescents' culture of origin, and not to their age, gender, linguistic ability, or ethnic identification (Chandler, Lalonde, Sokol, & Hallett, 2003).

The cultural context in which identity development occurs is also important. Research indicates that young immigrant Chinese adolescents report moderate feelings of ethnic affirmation and belonging and ethnic identity achievement, with girls reporting slightly stronger feelings than boys (Su & Costigan, 2009). A stronger ethnic identity is shaped by mothers' but not fathers' expectations of family obligations and by positive parenting practices, and is related to more positive adjustment, such as higher self-esteem. It may also buffer the potentially negative effect of lower academic achievement (Costigan, Koryzma, Hua, & Chance, 2010; Su & Costigan, 2009). In addition, it appears that affiliations with the Canadian and the Chinese cultures develop independently. Among foreign-born youths, greater involvement in Canadian culture does not interfere with maintaining their ethnic identity and traditional values, and among Canadian-born youths, this involvement appears to encourage acceptance of ethnic identity and traditional values (Costigan & Su, 2004).

Family Relationships

Over 90% of youths 10 to 19 years of age are living with one or both parents. More than 75% of these adolescents reside in a two-parent family and about 22% are in a single-parent family (80% of which are headed by mothers). In contrast, 58% of 20–24-year-olds live with one or both parents (Statistics Canada, 2010b). Recent studies with younger (11 to 15 years) and older (15 to 19 years) adolescents indicate that most young people have a happy home life (Bibby, 2009; Boyce, King, & Roche, 2008). They report that their parents trust them, are important sources of influence and support, and they value what their parents think of them. However, some youths also feel that their parents expect too much of them, especially with respect to school (more boys than girls). In addition, adolescents view multiple extended family members as being significant in their lives—more often their maternal than paternal grandparents. Although they see these family members infrequently (on average, every two months), they regard them as teachers of values and look to them for affection and companionship (Claes, Lacourse, Bouchard, & Luckow, 2001; Pratt, Norris, Hebblethwaite, & Arnold, 2008).

Several studies of adolescents and their families have examined parent–adolescent conflict. One report showed an upward trend across Grade 6 (17%) to Grade 10 (27%) in the percentage of adolescents who have a lot of arguments with their parents (more girls than boys). Conflicts between adolescents and their parents were related to friends, money, television and telephone use, homework, and chores (Boyce et al., 2008). Research has also documented frequent, but low-intensity, disagreements between parents and young adolescents in immigrant Chinese families. Fathers report more intense conflicts with daughters, mothers report more intense conflicts with sons, and youths report similar levels of conflict intensity for their mothers and fathers. Greater discrepancies between parents and youths on traditional cultural values are linked to more areas of conflict with fathers and more intense conflicts with mothers (Dokis, Costigan, & Chia, 2002).

Sibling relationships have also received empirical attention. This research indicates that during early adolescence, youths disclose more frequently to their closest-in-age siblings than to friends or parents, and they are equally likely to discuss family, friendship, and academic issues (Howe, Aquan-Assee, Bukowski, Rinaldi, & Lehoux, 2000). In addition, disclosure to siblings is more likely when adolescents perceive their sibling relationships as warm, and less likely when they do not trust their siblings or do not expect to receive emotional support from them (Howe, Aquan-Assee, Bukowski, Lehoux, & Rinaldi, 2001; Howe et al., 2000). Negative issues of status and power between siblings are also more likely when young adolescents have a negative emotional response to their parents' divorce. Further, youths' perceptions of which parent is to blame for the divorce are related to their sibling relationships, with maternal blame linked to increased conflict between siblings and paternal blame linked to sibling rivalry (Jennings & Howe, 2001). However, the majority of older adolescents and emerging adults (17 to 24 years) who experienced their parents' divorce before age 15 report that the divorce brought them closer to their sibling; only 10% indicated that the divorce had a lasting negative impact on their sibling relationship (Bush & Ehrenberg, 2003).

Friends and Peers/Youth Culture

Friends play a central role in the lives of adolescents. Friendship tops the list of things that they value, and friends are their number one source of enjoyment as well as key sources of influence and support (Bibby, 2009). Over 80% of boys and girls have three or more close same-sex friends across adolescence, and over 60% of them have as many close other-sex friends (Bibby, 2009; Boyce et al., 2008). Longitudinal data show that while same-sex friendships predominate across Grades 6 to 10, the higher proportion of other-sex friends reported by girls in early adolescence also increases at a faster rate for girls than boys during these years. This increase is even more rapid for girls who mature early or are rated more popular by other girls (Poulin & Pedersen, 2007).

Adolescents' association with friends who are deviant has also been evaluated. During early adolescence, boys' and girls' involvement in deviant behavior may be enhanced by membership in peer groups, specifically those characterized by high visibility or low social acceptance (Ellis & Zarbatany, 2007). These different features suggest that multiple mechanisms underlie how peer groups socialize adolescents' behavior. Adolescents' attitudes toward delinquent behavior also play

a role, in that these attitudes predict stability/change in affiliations with delinquent and nondelinquent friends across time, which, in turn, predict subsequent delinquent behavior. Adolescents who
consistently affiliate with deviant friends over time and those who change from nondelinquent to
delinquent friends show the highest levels of delinquency one year later (Brendgen, Vitaro, &
Bukowski, 2000). Interestingly, parental behaviors may alter this trajectory. Parents' use of monitoring and of behavioral control reduces their adolescents' involvement with deviant friends and
delinquency, respectively (Brendgen et al., 2000; Galambos, Barker, & Almeida, 2003).

Peer relationships during adolescence may also involve experiencing and/or perpetrating
aggressive behavior, including bullying. About 32% of boys and 25% of girls in Grades 6 to 10
report that they have bullied others but have not been victimized (Boyce et al., 2008). In comparison, about 25% of boys and girls report having been victimized but not bullying others, and about
20% of boys and girls report having both bullied others and been victimized. More boys are teased
or physically victimized whereas more girls have rumors spread about them or experience cyber-
bullying (Boyce et al., 2008). Longitudinal research following adolescents from age 10 to 17 years
indicates that 10% of them are involved in consistently high levels of bullying, 35% in consistently

moderate levels of bullying, and 13% in a moderate level of bullying initially, then declining to almost no bullying by the end of high school. More boys than girls were among those who engaged in consistently high and consistently moderate levels of bullying (Pepler, Jiang, Craig, & Connolly, 2008). Canadian researchers and nongovernment organizations have partnered to establish PREVNet (Promoting Relationships and Eliminating Violence; www.prevnet.ca), a network whose goal is to stop bullying and to promote safe and healthy relationships for children and youths.

Love and Sexuality

About 20% of adolescents in Grades 5 to 8 report that they are currently in a romantic relationship (Connolly, Craig, Goldberg, & Pepler, 2004; Doyle, Brendgen, Markiewicz, & Kamkar, 2003). The transition to romantic involvement occurs as a sequential progression from same-sex friendships to mixed-sex friendships to romantic involvement with a partner. Boys and girls are similar in their romantic activities and in the sequencing of these activities. The relatively short duration of some adolescents' romantic relationships (e.g., two to six months; Connolly et al., 2004; Doyle et al., 2003) suggests that breakups are common. About 23% of adolescents in Grades 9 to 12 reported a breakup in the past six months, with 79% of girls and 61% of boys stating that they had initiated the breakup either on their own or jointly with their partner. The primary reason for a breakup from girls' and boys' perspective was that the relationship was not meeting the adolescent's romantic needs (Connolly & McIsaac, 2009).

Research has also examined adolescents' use and experience of psychologically, physically, and sexually aggressive behaviors in their romantic relationships. Results show that 43% of boys and 51% of girls in Grades 7, 9, and 11 have used at least one form of aggression with a romantic partner, and that some youths at each of these grade levels reported using all three forms of aggression (Sears et al., 2007). Further, 72% of boys and 67% of girls have experienced aggression from a romantic partner, and a majority of them have experienced two or three forms of aggression (Sears & Byers, 2010). Adolescents' individual characteristics, such as more accepting attitudes toward use of aggressive behavior, and contextual characteristics, such as fear of family violence and peer aggression, predict their use and experiences of aggression in a romantic relationship as well as recurrent aggression in a new relationship (Josephson & Proulx, 2008; Sears & Byers, 2010; Sears et al., 2007; Williams, Connolly, Pepler, Craig, & Laporte, 2008). Adolescents have indicated that they want specific skills to help them develop healthy relationships (Sears, Byers, Whelan, Saint-Pierre, & the Dating Violence Research Team, 2006), and teacher- and youth-led programs such as RISE (Respect in Schools Everywhere; www.riseaboveviolence.com) and The Fourth R (www.youthrelationships.org) have been developed to address this need.

Significant proportions of youths (and similar proportions of boys and girls) have engaged in preliminary sexual activities at least once. According to a national study of adolescents in Grades 7, 9, and 11, 66% of Grade 9 students and over 80% of Grade 11 students have participated in deep kissing, and 55% of Grade 9 students and 75% of Grade 11 students have engaged in touching below the waist (Boyce, Doherty, MacKinnon, & Fortin, 2003). Although fewer Grade 7 students report these behaviors, more boys than girls are having these experiences. About 30% of Grade 9 students and over 50% of Grade 11 students have had oral sex. Finally, about 20% of Grade 9 students and 43% of Grade 11 students have had vaginal sexual intercourse (Boyce et al., 2003). Rates of 32% and 53% for sexual intercourse have been reported elsewhere by Grade 10 and Grade 12 students, respectively (Hampton, Jeffery, Smith, & McWatters, 2001). The median age of first intercourse for both girls and boys is 17 years (Hampton et al., 2001; Maticka-Tyndale, 2008).

More sexually active adolescents are using contraceptive methods. Between 65% and 75% of these adolescents report using a condom the last time they had sexual intercourse (Boyce et al., 2008; McCreary Centre Society, 2009). While condoms are used more frequently at younger ages, as adolescents get older, the birth control pill becomes a preferred contraceptive method (Boyce et al., 2003; McCreary Centre Society, 2009). Given that approximately 25% of sexually active adolescents use either withdrawal or no birth control (Boyce et al., 2008; McCreary Centre Society, 2009), and that other adolescents do not use contraceptive methods consistently, it is not surprising that youths, especially girls, are at high risk for contracting STIs. Girls 15 to 24 years of age have higher rates of chlamydia than any other age group, and their rates are two to four times higher than those for boys. The highest rates of gonorrhea are found among girls of 15 to 24 years and boys of 20 to 24 years (Public Health Agency of Canada, 2009). As of December 2006, there were 729 cases of AIDS among youths 10 to 24 years of age, accounting for 3.5% of all AIDS cases (Public Health Agency of Canada, 2007). Sixty percent of the 104 cases in 10–19-year-olds were attributed to being recipients of blood/blood products whereas 51% of the 625 cases among 20–24-year-olds were attributed to men having sex with men, and another 21% to heterosexual contact. Pregnancy is of course another potential consequence of inconsistent or no use of contraception during intercourse. Approximately 7% of adolescents in school (Grades 7 to 12) have ever been pregnant or caused a pregnancy (Boyce et al., 2003; McCreary Centre Society, 2009). Girls 15 to 19 years of age accounted for 4% of all live births in 2007; the comparable figure for 20–24-year-olds was 16% (Statistics Canada, 2010f).

Because of the various negative consequences that can result from sexual activities, it is important for sexually active youths to have knowledge and skills to protect themselves and their partners and to promote their sexual health (Public Health Agency of Canada, 2008). School serves as an important source of sexual health information (Boyce et al., 2003). Although all Canadian provinces and territories mandate that schools provide sexual health education, the implementation of this directive is variable, even though failure to provide this information violates multiple articles of the United Nations Convention on the Rights of the Child which was ratified by the federal government in 1991 (Kennedy & Covell, 2009). Further, research with adolescents (Grades 6 to 12) and with parents and teachers has indicated that most are in favor of sexual health education, and the majority agree that parents and schools should share this responsibility. They also agree that sexual health education should cover a wide range of topics and that most topics should be covered by the end of Grade 8 (Byers et al., 2003a, 2003b; Cohen, Byers, Sears, & Weaver, 2004; Weaver, Byers, Sears, Cohen, & Randall, 2002).

Health Risk Behavior

Most young people have good physical and emotional health (Boyce et al., 2008; McCreary Centre Society, 2009). Nevertheless, a substantial proportion of youths engage in risk behaviors that have the potential to compromise their health. Accidents, the majority of which are motor vehicle, are the leading cause of death among youths 15 to 24 years of age. The death rate among young men is more than twice the rate for young women (Statistics Canada, 2009b).

Tobacco, alcohol, and marijuana are the three substances most commonly used by adolescents. Across Grades 7 to 12, about 23% of youths have smoked, although fewer smoke regularly. In comparison, about 55% of youths have tried alcohol, about 44% report binge drinking in the past month, and about 34% have used marijuana (Bibby, 2009; McCreary Centre Society, 2009; Willoughby, Chalmers, & Busseri, 2004). Similar proportions of girls and boys have smoked cigarettes, used alcohol, and engaged in binge drinking in the last month. Although girls and boys also use marijuana at similar rates, among those who have used, more boys are frequent users than girls (Bibby, 2009; McCreary Centre Society, 2009). Use of tobacco, alcohol, and marijuana each shows a linear increase across age. Fewer youths use harder drugs (Bibby, 2009; McCreary Centre Society, 2009; Willoughby et al., 2004).

Turning to delinquency, one study found that 59% of adolescents in Grades 9 to 12 participated in minor delinquency, such as shoplifting or joy riding, at least once in the previous year. In contrast, only 8% of youths were involved in major delinquency, such as carrying a gun or knife as a weapon (Willoughby et al., 2004). More boys than girls participate in delinquent behaviors, and, within types of offenses, boys and girls commit minor acts at similar rates whereas boys commit more serious acts than girls (Fitzgerald, 2003; Reitsma-Street & Artz, 2005). Girls and boys also differ in the timing and peaks of their involvement in early onset, late onset, or moderate patterns of delinquency across ages 10 to 17 years (Pepler, Jiang, Craig, & Connolly, 2010). Youths 12 to 17 years who commit illegal acts are adjudicated by the Youth Criminal Justice Act (available at http://laws-lois.justice.gc.ca). Currently, boys represent about 80% of convictions in youth court, and the most common sentence or disposition for girls and boys is probation (Reitsma-Street & Artz, 2005).

A significant minority of youths experience serious emotional distress during adolescence, and up to 10% have had an episode of clinical depression. Girls report higher rates of depressive symptoms and depressive disorders than boys (Bibby, 2009; Boyce et al., 2008; Galambos, Leadbeater, & Barker, 2004). Although the suicide rate among young people is lower than that of older age groups, suicide is the second leading cause of death among youths 15 to 24 years of age (Statistics Canada, 2009b). In one study, 12% of students in Grades 7 to 12 reported seriously considering suicide in the past year, and 5% had attempted suicide (McCreary Centre Society, 2009). While suicidal ideation and attempts are two to three times higher among girls, suicide completions are almost three times higher among boys, largely because boys use more lethal methods than girls. Suicide also occurs at a higher rate among Aboriginal youths, although cases are more common in specific Aboriginal communities that have not been able to preserve their culture (Chandler et al., 2003).

Education

The vast majority of Canadian children and adolescents attend public school full-time for approximately 13 years (kindergarten to Grade 12; from about five to 18 years of age). School attendance is compulsory in most jurisdictions until age 16. As a result, enrollment exceeds 90% until this age, and then drops to 75%–80% in the final years of high school. Because each province and territory establishes its own curriculum and general education structure, the availability of second-language immersion and alternative education programs varies across the country (Boyce, 2004). According to the 2006 Programme for International Student Assessment (PISA) for 15-year-olds, in comparison to 56 other countries, Canada ranked fourth in reading, fifth in mathematics, and third in science. While there were no gender differences in science results, girls outperformed boys in reading and boys outperformed girls in mathematics (Bussière, Knighton, & Pennock 2007). Canada's literacy rate is 99% (World Factbook, 2010).

Most provinces and the territories require two school transitions, one from elementary to middle school or junior high school (after Grade 5 or Grade 6) and one from middle/junior high school to high school (after Grade 8 or Grade 9). Given that about 50% of adolescents (more girls than boys) continue their education after graduating from high school by attending technical school, college, or university (Statistics Canada, 2007), many youths make another school transition during late adolescence. Students usually attend college for one to two years and graduate with a diploma or certificate, whereas they attend university for a minimum of three to four years and graduate with a degree. In 2005–2006, 44% of 22–24-year-olds had graduated from some form of post-secondary education program, and an additional 20% were still pursuing their education program (Statistics Canada, 2007).

Although a large majority of high school students plan to complete high school and go on to college or university (Bibby, 2009; McCreary Centre Society, 2009), some youths leave high school without a diploma. While the proportion of adolescents who drop out of school has decreased significantly, in 2003 8% of 19-year-olds had not completed high school. Boys and Aboriginal youths are more likely to leave school than girls and non-Aboriginal peers, respectively (Statistics Canada, 2007). Leaving school is related to a variety of factors, such as inattention, grade retention during elementary school, and unstable trajectories of school engagement for boys and for girls, and to family welfare dependence and lower parental supervision for boys only (Janosz, Archambault, Morizot, & Pagani, 2008; Pagani et al., 2008). About 38% of youths who leave high school return to some form of education by ages 22 to 24 years (Statistics Canada, 2007).

Work

At age 15, girls are more oriented toward professional careers than boys, a gender difference that persists after accounting for academic ability and home and school environments (Sikora & Saha, 2009). Although traditional gender differences in occupational expectations are still evident for specific occupations (e.g., hairdressing, interior design, carpentry, engineering), few differences are now observed for other occupations (e.g., medical doctors, lawyers). Interestingly, over 85% of high school students expect to be able to find the job they want after they graduate. Further, about 80% expect to be more financially comfortable than their parents, although only 43% think that they will have to work overtime to do it. These ideas are very similar for boys and girls and for immigrant and Canadian-born youths (Bibby, 2009).

Currently, more youths than ever before are participating in the labor force, in part because combining work and school is more common. During the 2004–2005 school year, 31% of full-time students ages 15 to 17 years and 46% of full-time students ages 18 to 24 years were employed. In comparison, 38% of students ages 15 to 17 years and 66% of students ages 18 to 24 years were employed during the summer (Usalcas & Bowlby, 2006). A larger proportion of girls than boys in these two age groups were working at both of these times. This trend is related to growth in retail and food service sectors, two areas in which girls are more likely to work. A majority of working students (60%) now work in these two sectors. While these jobs are more flexible than many, they generally do not require extensive education or experience and the pay is low. Students 15 to 17 years old worked an average of 13 hours per week during the school year and 19 hours per week in the summer; the comparable figures for students 18 to 24 years old are 16.5 hours and 29 hours per week, respectively (Usalcas & Bowlby, 2006). Despite more youths being employed, this segment of the population still has a high unemployment rate when compared to other age groups. In 2006, 15% of boys and 14% of girls 15 to 19 years old and 12% of boys and 11% of girls 20 to 24 years old were unemployed (Statistics Canada 2010e).

Media

Youths have access to and make extensive use of various forms of media (television, video games, music, the Internet). Almost all households in Canada have at least one television set, and at least 90% of adolescents watch television daily (Bibby, 2009; McCreary Centre Society, 2009). Television viewing appears to peak in early adolescence and then declines, likely in response to competing media and the demands of school and social activities. Although television can be a powerful teacher and offers opportunities to learn and be entertained, many programs communicate messages about risk behaviors in which youths engage (substance use, violence, sexual behavior) (Canadian Paediatric Society, 2003). While many adults have also expressed concern about the negative effects of exposure to video games, little is known about how these games, which range considerably in their content, affect various aspects of adolescents' development. About 60% of young people play video games on an average school day, with one half of boys and one third of girls playing for two hours or more (Boyce et al., 2008; McCreary Centre Society, 2009).

Music is another form of media that contributes to the lives of adolescents. Youths list music as their second highest source of enjoyment after friends, and the vast majority of them listen to music every day, accessing a wide variety of genres (Bibby, 2009). Finally, most adolescents now use a computer daily, with the proportion that spend two or more hours per day peaking at about 65% during the high school years (Bibby, 2009; Boyce et al., 2008). Youths indicate that the Internet is their third highest source of enjoyment. In terms of specific activities, more girls than boys access Facebook and use email whereas more boys than girls play computer games (Bibby, 2009).

Politics and Military

Youths are eligible to vote at age 18. However, about 70% of high school students have little interest in politics (Bibby, 2009). It is not surprising then that relatively few young people participate in politics by voting. Based on results from the January 2006 federal general election, the voter turnout rate was 44% for 18–24-year-olds. Although this rate of participation was an increase from 37% in the 2004 general election, it was still the lowest of all age groups and significantly below the estimated national average rate of 63% (Elections Canada, 2008).

Military service is not compulsory in Canada. Adolescents who are 17 years or older can enlist full-time in the Regular Force of the Canadian Forces in one of three elements (the army, the navy, or the air force) (Department of National Defence, 2010). Alternatively, youths aged 16 to 24 years can join the Reserve Force and pursue a part-time career. These individuals support the Regular Force while obtaining a variety of new skills and earning extra income; about 28% of them are students. Minors are required to have parental consent to join either Force. Through partnerships between the Canadian Forces and the Army Cadet League of Canada (www.armycadetleague.ca), the Navy League of Canada (www.navyleague.ca), and the Air Cadet League of Canada (www.aircadetleague.com), respectively, adolescents participate in local programs designed to develop the resourcefulness and leadership potential of young people through discipline and team building. Although these programs are based on a military structure and are staffed by members of the Reserves and regular or Reserve Force volunteers, the youths are civilians and have no commitment to serve in the military.

Unique Issues

About 5% of the youth population consists of a subgroup of young people who identify themselves as Aboriginal—either First Nations, Inuit, or Métis, three groups that have distinct histories, cultures, and languages. The development of these youths is unique in that they are confronted with the task of growing up in poorer socioeconomic circumstances than their peers (Statistics Canada, 2010a), circumstances that reflect a history of colonization, forced displacement, and discrimination. In what ways then are the attitudes and behaviors of Aboriginal youths similar to and different from those of their non-Aboriginal peers? Research shows that most Aboriginal adolescents 15 to 19 years hold the same core values, such as trust and honesty, as other youths. They also highly value family life, although they are less likely to live with both parents and are more likely to live with one parent or with extended family (Bibby, 2009; Statistics Canada, 2007). In addition, they are much more likely to have interracial friendships, 47% value Aboriginal spirituality and Christianity, and 25% report participating in religious services at least monthly (Bibby, 2009). The importance of family and religious beliefs also emerges in their criteria for reaching adulthood. In a university sample, Aboriginal students' higher identification with Aboriginal traditions was related to higher importance of specific criteria for adulthood, such as less alcohol use, earlier achievement of specific criteria for adulthood (such as having a family), and higher importance of religious beliefs and future obligations to parents. They were also more likely than European Canadian students to believe that they had reached adulthood (Cheah & Nelson, 2004).

During the high school years, Aboriginal youths have the same high hopes for the future as their peers, such as having a good family life, and getting a good education and a good job, although fewer expect to graduate from university (Bibby, 2009). In reality, many of their basic rights are not being met. Aboriginal young people 15 to 24 years are less likely to be attending school, to complete school, or to be employed (Zietsma, 2010). Instead, they are more likely to be living in poverty, to have health problems and inadequate health care, and to witness and experience violence. They also are more likely to be involved in risk behaviors, such as unprotected sexual intercourse and marijuana use, and they are overrepresented in both the child welfare and correctional services systems (Bennett, 2007; Bibby, 2009; Calverley, Cotter, & Halla, 2010; Maticka-Tyndale, 2008). According to Health Canada, rates of suicide among Aboriginal youths exceed the national rates by a factor of at least five. However, this statistic does not capture the variability found in specific Aboriginal communities. Over a 14-year period, the vast majority of youth suicides in one province (British Columbia) occurred in only a small proportion of the Aboriginal communities and more than half of them experienced no youth suicides at all (Chandler & Lalonde, 2008). Multiple markers of cultural continuity, such as attainment of self-government, control over educational and health services, and construction of cultural facilities, indicate that youth suicide rates are very high in First Nations communities that have not met various standards of self-determination. In contrast, substantially lower rates and even no cases are found in First Nations communities that are preserving and promoting their culture in these ways (Chandler & Lalonde, 2008). These results highlight the importance of considering adolescents' attitudes, beliefs, and behaviors within their social and cultural contexts instead of relying solely on demographic markers to capture their experiences.

References and Further Reading

Aimé, A., Craig, W., Pepler, D., Jiang, D., & Connolly, J. (2008). Developmental pathways of eating problems in adolescents. *International Journal of Eating Disorders, 41*, 686–696.

Barker, E., & Galambos, N. (2003). Body dissatisfaction of adolescent girls and boys: Risk and resource factors. *Journal of Early Adolescence, 23*, 141–165.

Beaujot, R. (2004). *Delayed life transitions: Trends and implications*. Ottawa, Canada: Vanier Institute of the Family.

Bennett, M. (2007). Aboriginal children's rights: Is Canada keeping its promise? In R. B. Howe & K. Covell (Eds.), *A question of commitment: Children's rights in Canada* (pp. 265–286). Waterloo, Canada: Wilfrid Laurier University Press.

Bibby, R. (2009). *The emerging millennials: How Canada's newest generation is responding to change and choice.* Lethbridge, Canada: Project Canada Books.

Boyce, W. (2004). *Young people in Canada: Their health and well-being.* Ottawa, Canada: Health Canada.

Boyce, W., Doherty, M., MacKinnon, D., & Fortin, C. (2003). *Canadian youth, sexual health and HIV/AIDS study: Factors influencing knowledge, attitudes and behaviours.* Toronto, Canada: Council of Ministers of Education, Canada.

Boyce, W., King, M. A., & Roche, J. (2008). *Healthy settings for young people in Canada.* Ottawa, Canada: Minister of Health. Retrieved from www.phac-aspc.gc.ca

Brendgen, M., Vitaro, F., & Bukowski, W. (2000). Stability and variability of adolescents' affiliation with delinquent friends: Predictors and consequences. *Social Development, 9,* 205–225.

Bush, J., & Ehrenberg, M. (2003). Young persons' perspectives on the influence of family transitions on sibling relationships: A qualitative exploration. *Journal of Divorce & Remarriage, 39,* 1–35.

Bussière, P., Knighton, T., & Pennock, D. (2007). *Measuring up: Canadian results of the OECD PISA study* (Statistics Canada catalog no. 81-590-XPE). Ottawa, Canada: Minister of Industry.

Byers, E. S., Sears, H., Voyer, S., Thurlow, J., Cohen, J., & Weaver, A. (2003a). An adolescent perspective on sexual health education at school and at home: I. High school students. *Canadian Journal of Human Sexuality, 12,* 1–17.

Byers, E. S., Sears, H., Voyer, S., Thurlow, J., Cohen, J., & Weaver, A. (2003b). An adolescent perspective on sexual health education at school and at home: II. Middle school students. *Canadian Journal of Human Sexuality, 12,* 19–33.

Calverley, D., Cotter, A., & Halla, E. (2010, Spring). Youth custody and community services in Canada, 2008/2009. *Juristat, 3*(1) (catalog no. 85-002-X). Ottawa, Canada: Statistics Canada.

Canadian Paediatric Society (2003). Impact of media use on children and youth. *Paediatric Child Health, 8,* 301–306.

Chandler, M., & Lalonde, C. (2008). Cultural continuity as a moderator of suicide risk among Canada's First Nations. In L. Kirmayer & G. Valaskakis (Eds.), *Healing traditions: The mental health of Aboriginal peoples in Canada* (pp. 221–248). Vancouver, Canada: University of British Columbia Press.

Chandler, M., Lalonde, C., Sokol, B., & Hallett, D. (2003). Personal persistence, identity development, and suicide: A study of native and non-native North American adolescents. *Monographs of the Society for Research in Child Development, 68*(2, serial no. 273).

Cheah, C., & Nelson, L. (2004). The role of acculturation in the emerging adulthood of Aboriginal college students. *International Journal of Behavioral Development, 28,* 495–507.

Chui, T., Tran, K., & Maheux, H. (2007). *Immigration in Canada: A portrait of the foreign-born population, 2006 census* (Statistics Canada catalog no. 97-557-XIE). Ottawa, Canada: Minister of Industry.

Claes, M., Lacourse, E., Bouchard, C., & Luckow, D. (2001). Adolescents' relationships with members of the extended family and non-related adults in four countries: Canada, France, Belgium, and Italy. *International Journal of Adolescence and Youth, 9,* 207–225.

Cohen, J., Byers, E. S., Sears, H., & Weaver, A. (2004). Sexual health education: Attitudes, knowledge, and comfort of teachers in New Brunswick schools. *Canadian Journal of Human Sexuality, 13,* 1–15.

Connolly, J., Craig, W., Goldberg, A., & Pepler, D. (2004). Mixed-gender groups, dating, and romantic relationships in early adolescence. *Journal of Research on Adolescence, 14,* 185–207.

Connolly, J., & McIsaac, C. (2009). Adolescents' explanations for romantic dissolutions: A developmental perspective. *Journal of Adolescence, 32,* 1209–1223.

Costigan, C., Koryzma, C., Hua, J., & Chance, L. (2010). Ethnic identity, achievement, and psychological adjustment: Examining risk and resilience among youth from immigrant Chinese families in Canada. *Cultural Diversity and Ethnic Minority Psychology, 16,* 264–273.

Costigan, C., & Su, T. (2004). Orthogonal versus linear models of acculturation among immigrant Chinese Canadians: A comparison of mothers, fathers, and children. *International Journal of Behavioral Development, 28*, 518–527.

Department of National Defence (2010). *Canadian forces recruiting.* Retrieved from www.forces.ca

Dokis, D., Costigan, C., & Chia, A. (2002, June). *Parent–adolescent conflict in immigrant Chinese families.* Poster presented at the Annual Meeting of the Canadian Psychological Association, Vancouver, Canada.

Doyle, A. B., Brendgen, M., Markiewicz, D., & Kamkar, K. (2003). Family relationships as moderators of the association between romantic relationships and adjustment in early adolescence. *Journal of Early Adolescence, 23*, 316–340.

Elections Canada (2008). *Estimation of voter turnout by age group at the 39th federal general election, January 23, 2006.* Retrieved from www.elections.ca

Ellis, W. E., & Zarbatany, L. (2007). Peer group status as a moderator of group influence on children's deviant, aggressive, and prosocial behavior. *Child Development, 78*, 1240–1254.

Fitzgerald, R. (2003). An examination of sex differences in delinquency. *Crime and Justice Research Paper Series* (catalog no. 85-561-MIE2003001). Ottawa, Canada: Canadian Centre for Justice Statistics.

Galambos, N., Barker, E., & Almeida, D. (2003). Parents *do* matter: Trajectories of change in externalizing and internalizing problems in early adolescence. *Child Development, 74*, 578–594.

Galambos, N., Leadbeater, B., & Barker, E. (2004). Gender differences in and risk factors for depression in adolescence: A 4-year longitudinal study. *International Journal of Behavioral Development, 28*, 16–25.

Good, M., Willoughby, T., & Fritjers, J. (2009). Just another club? The distinctiveness of the relation between religious service attendance and adolescent psychosocial adjustment. *Journal of Youth and Adolescence, 38*, 1153–1171.

Hampton, M., Jeffery, B., Smith, P., & McWatters, B. (2001). Sexual experience, contraception, and STI prevention among high school students: Results from a Canadian urban centre. *Canadian Journal of Human Sexuality, 10*, 111–126.

Howe, N., Aquan-Assee, J., Bukowski, W., Lehoux, P., & Rinaldi, C. (2001). Siblings as confidants: Emotional understanding, relationship warmth, and sibling self-disclosure. *Social Development, 10*, 439–454.

Howe, N., Aquan-Assee, J., Bukowski, W., Rinaldi, C., & Lehoux, P. (2000). Sibling self-disclosure in early adolescence. *Merrill-Palmer Quarterly, 46*, 653–671.

Janosz, M., Archambault, I., Morizot, J., & Pagani, L. (2008). School engagement trajectories and their differential predictive relations to dropout. *Journal of Social Issues, 64*, 21–40.

Jennings, M., & Howe, N. (2001). Siblings' perceptions of their parents' divorce. *Journal of Divorce & Remarriage, 35*, 91–106.

Jones, J., Bennett, S., Olmsted, M., Lawson, M., & Rodin, G. (2001). Disordered eating attitudes and behaviours in teenaged girls: A school-based study. *Canadian Medical Association Journal, 165*, 547–552.

Josephson, W. L., & Proulx, J. B. (2008). Violence in young adolescents' relationships: A path model. *Journal of Interpersonal Violence, 23*, 189–208.

Kennedy, C., & Covell, K. (2009). Violating the rights of the child through inadequate sexual health education. *International Journal of Children's Rights, 17*, 143–154.

Marshall, S., Young, R., Domene, J., & Zaidman-Zait, A. (2008). Adolescent possible selves as jointly constructed in parent–adolescent career conversations and related activities. *Identity, 8*, 185–204.

Maticka-Tyndale, E. (2008). Sexuality and sexual health of Canadian adolescents: Yesterday, today and tomorrow. *Canadian Journal of Human Sexuality, 17*, 85–95.

McCreary Centre Society (2009). *A picture of health: Highlights from the 2008 British Columbia Adolescent Health Survey.* Vancouver, Canada: McCreary Centre Society. Retrieved from www.mcs.bc.ca

McLean, K., Breen, A., & Fournier, M. (2010). Constructing the self in early, middle, and late adolescent boys: Narrative identity, individuation, and well-being. *Journal of Research on Adolescence, 20,* 166–187.

Pagani, L., Vitaro, F., Tremblay, R., McDuff, P., Japel, C., & Larose, S. (2008). When predictions fail: The case of unexpected pathways toward high school dropout. *Journal of Social Issues, 64,* 175–193.

Pepler, D., Jiang, D., Craig, W., & Connolly, J. (2008). Developmental trajectories of bullying and associated factors. *Child Development, 79,* 325–338.

Pepler, D., Jiang, D., Craig, W., & Connolly, J. (2010). Developmental trajectories of girls' and boys' delinquency and associated problems. *Journal of Abnormal Child Psychology, 38,* 1033–1044.

Poulin, F., & Pedersen, S. (2007). Developmental changes in gender composition of friendship networks in adolescent girls and boys. *Developmental Psychology, 43,* 1484–1496.

Pratt, M., Norris, J., Hebblethwaite, S., & Arnold, M. (2008). Intergenerational transmission of values: Family generativity and adolescents' narratives of parent and grandparent value teaching. *Journal of Personality, 76,* 171–198.

Public Health Agency of Canada (2007, November). *HIV/AIDS Epi Updates.* Ottawa, Canada: Public Health Agency of Canada. Retrieved from www.phac-aspc.gc.ca

Public Health Agency of Canada (2008). *Canadian guidelines for sexual health education* (catalog no. HP40-25/2008E). Ottawa, Canada: Public Health Agency of Canada. Retrieved from www.phac-aspc.gc.ca

Public Health Agency of Canada (2009). *Brief report on sexually transmitted infections in Canada: 2007* (catalog no. HP37-10/2007E-PDF). Ottawa: Canada: Public Health Agency of Canada. Retrieved from www.phac-aspc.gc.ca

Reitsma-Street, M. & Artz, S. (2005). Girls and crime. In J. Winterdyk (Ed.), *Issues and perspectives on young offenders* (3rd ed., pp. 57–82). Toronto, Canada: Thompson Nelson.

Sears, H., & Byers, E. S. (2010). Adolescent girls' and boys' experiences of psychologically, physically, and sexually aggressive behaviors in their dating relationships: Co-occurrence and emotional reaction. *Journal of Aggression, Maltreatment, and Trauma, 19,* 517–539.

Sears, H., Byers, E. S., & Price, E. L. (2007). The co-occurrence of adolescent boys' and girls' use of psychologically, physically, and sexually abusive behaviours in their dating relationships. *Journal of Adolescence, 30,* 487–504.

Sears, H., Byers, E. S., Whelan, J., Saint-Pierre, M., & the Dating Violence Research Team (2006). "If it hurts you, then it's not a joke": Adolescents' ideas about girls' and boys' use and experience of abusive behavior in dating relationships. *Journal of Interpersonal Violence, 21,* 1191–1207.

Sears, H., Graham, J., & Campbell, A. (2009). Adolescent boys' intentions of seeking help from male friends and female friends. *Journal of Applied Developmental Psychology, 30,* 738–748.

Shapka, J., & Keating, D. (2005). Structure and change in self-concept during adolescence. *Canadian Journal of Behavioural Science, 37,* 83–96.

Sikora, J., & Saha, L. (2009). Gender and professional career plans of high school students in comparative perspective. *Educational Research and Evaluation, 15,* 385–403.

Statistics Canada (2007). *Education indicators in Canada: Report of the Pan-Canadian education indicators program 2007* (catalog no. 81-582-XIE). Ottawa, Canada: Statistics Canada and Council of Ministers of Education, Canada.

Statistics Canada (2009a, November 27). Canada's population estimates: Age and sex. *The Daily.*

Statistics Canada (2009b). *Leading causes of death in Canada* (catalog no. 84-215-XWE). Ottawa ON: Statistics Canada.

Statistics Canada (2010a). Aboriginal peoples. *Canada Year Book 2009.* Ottawa, Canada: Statistics Canada.

Statistics Canada (2010b). *Age group of child (12), census family structure (7) and sex (3) for the children in census families in private households of Canada, 2006 census* (catalog no. 97-553-XCB2006011). Ottawa, Canada: Statistics Canada. Retrieved from www12.statcan.gc.ca

Statistics Canada (2010c). *Immigrant status and place of birth (38), sex (3) and age groups (10) for the population of Canada, 2006 census* (catalog no. 97-557-XCB2006013). Ottawa, Canada: Statistics Canada. Retrieved from www12.statcan.gc.ca

Statistics Canada (2010d). *Mother tongue (8), age groups (17A) and sex (3) for the population of Canada, 2006 census* (catalog no. 97-555-XCB2006020). Ottawa, Canada: Statistics Canada. Retrieved from www12.statcan.gc.ca

Statistics Canada (2010e). *Labour force activity (8), aboriginal identity (8B), age groups (13A), sex (3) and area of residence (6A) for the population 15 years and over of Canada, 2006 census* (catalog no. 97-559-XCB2006008). Ottawa, Canada: Statistics Canada. Retrieved from www12.statcan.gc.ca

Statistics Canada (2010f). *Live births, by age of mother, Canada, provinces and territories, annual, CANSIM* (Table 102-4503). Ottawa, Canada: Statistics Canada. Retrieved from www12.statcan.gc.ca

Su, T. & Costigan, C. (2009). The development of children's ethnic identity in immigrant Chinese families in Canada: The role of parenting practices and children's perceptions of parental family obligation expectations. *Journal of Early Adolescence, 29*, 638–663.

Tilton-Weaver, L., Vitunski, E., & Galambos, N. (2001). Five images of maturity in adolescence: What does "grown up" mean? *Journal of Adolescence, 24*, 143–158.

Usalcas, J. & Bowlby, G. (2006). Students in the labour market. *Education matters: Insights on education, learning and training in Canada, 3*(1) (catalogue no. 81-004-XIE). Ottawa, Canada: Statistics Canada.

Weaver, A., Byers, E. S., Sears, H., Cohen, J., & Randall, H. (2002). Sexual health education at school and at home: Attitudes and experiences of New Brunswick parents. *Canadian Journal of Human Sexuality, 11*, 19–31.

Williams, T. S., Connolly, J., Pepler, D., Craig, W., & Laporte, L. (2008). Risk models of dating aggression across different adolescent relationships: A developmental psychopathology approach. *Journal of Consulting and Clinical Psychology, 76*, 622–632.

Willoughby, T., Chalmers, H., & Busseri, M. (2004). Where is the syndrome? Examining co-occurrence among multiple problem behaviors in adolescence. *Journal of Consulting and Clinical Psychology, 72*, 1022–1037.

World Factbook (2010). *Canada.* Washington, DC: CIA. Retrieved from www.cia.gov

Zietsma, D. (2010). *Aboriginal people living off-reserve and the labour market: Estimates from the Labour Force Survey 2008–2009* (catalog no. 71-588-X, no. 2). Ottawa, Canada: Minister of Industry.

Chapter 13
Chile
M. Loreto Martínez and Patricio Cumsille

Background Information

Chile, located in the southwest of South America, has a population of about 16.5 million persons (Instituto Nacional de Estadísticas (INE), 2009). Economic development in recent decades has been characterized by high rates of growth in urban areas, where over 85% of the population lives. Life-expectancy rates have increased and fertility rates have decreased, thus changing the age distribution of the population. Chilean adolescents and emerging adults (15 to 29 years of age) represent approximately 25% of the country's population (4,082,396) (INE, 2009).

Youth exhibit the highest migration from rural to urban areas and concentrate in the latter (87% in 2007). Almost 19% of the adolescent population lives in poverty, and 5% in extreme poverty (Ministerio de Planificación y Cooperación Social (MIDEPLAN), 2006). Ethnically, the majority of Chileans are *mestizo*, an ethnic blend of Spanish and natives. Consequently, 90% of adolescents do not identify with any ethnic minorities. However, the percentage of natives in rural areas is double that of urban areas, and natives are concentrated in the southern provinces of the country. Ethnic minorities are overrepresented among low socioeconomic (SES) groups (Instituto Nacional de la Juventud (INJUV), 2009).

Chile proclaimed its independence from Spain in 1810. The military coup in 1973 and subsequent 17 years of authoritarian rule interrupted its long democratic tradition. Rapid economic growth and major sociopolitical changes (e.g., modernization of the state, educational system and health care reforms) since the reinstitution of democracy in 1990 have changed Chilean society's norms, values, cultural products, and symbols (Programa de Naciones Unidas para el Desarrollo (PNUD), 2003).

Period of Adolescence

Research on youth has shifted in focus to reflect the different historical and political circumstances that have shaped the experience of youth over time in Chile. The study of adolescence as a distinctive developmental phase began with studies in adolescent medicine and focused on physical growth and development (Muzzo & Burrows, 1986), public health, and the provision of health services to adolescents (Florenzano et al., 1988; Molina 1988). Subsequent studies examined adolescents' behaviors that pose risks to their health (Florenzano, Pino, & Marchandon 1993; Molina 1994).

Adolescence is recognized as a transitional developmental phase, and greater access to education and higher expectations for youth attainment have extended the duration of adolescence. Though publications provide different age ranges for the adolescent period, most concur that adolescence covers the second decade of life (Florenzano, 1997). For health policy and programs, adolescence extends from 10 to 19 years. For public policy purposes, "youth" includes the early twenties and characterizes diverse groups of young people (Instituto Nacional de la Juventud (INJUV), 1999, 2009). However, empirical studies of adolescence are still scarce in Chile.

Chilean youth view adolescence as a transitional phase in which youth assume more responsibility for their personal attainment and well-being (Soto, Matute and Peña 2003). Youth depict adolescence as a time to decide what to do with one's life (43%), to learn things that will be important to succeed in life (29%), and to have fun (17%) (INJUV, 2009). The decision-making is emphasized regardless of gender, age and SES. However, learning skills to succeed is less emphasized by low-SES youth. At the same time, younger adolescents more often think of youth as a time to have fun (INJUV, 2009).

Globalization and modernization have changed the transition to adulthood in Chile. Demographic trends suggest that the tasks and role transitions traditionally associated with adulthood (e.g., completing a career, getting a job, getting married, and having children) are no longer acknowledged by emerging adults as the single path to adulthood. Alternatively, diverse paths that place value on self-development are seen as markers of adulthood (Programa de Naciones Unidas para el Desarrollo, 2003). As the educational level and expectations for educational attainment have increased, economic independence and leaving home have been postponed. Similar trends are observed in expected ages for marriage and parenthood, particularly among high-SES groups (INJUV, 2004).

Beliefs

The Spanish colonization together with the strong imprint of the Catholic Church shaped Chile's religious and cultural beliefs. Though Chile's constitution proclaimed freedom of religious beliefs in 1925, Catholicism strongly influenced the organization of social life and values in society. Catholics have decreased and Protestants increased in numbers (INE, 2004), but the majority of the population continues to identify with the Catholic creed. Nonetheless, large numbers of people are not involved in church or religious activities.

For youth 15 to 29 years old, identification with the Catholic Church is reported to be around 50%, and identification with Protestant churches to be around 17% (INJUV, 2004). Interestingly, the percentage of adolescents and emerging adults 15 to 29 years of age who do not identify with any religious denomination went down from 31% in 2000 to 23% in 2003 (INJUV, 2004). At the same time, 29% of adolescents believe that "faith in God" is an important asset for personal success (INJUV, 2004), and the Catholic Church is one of the most trusted public institutions. While 96% of 16- to 18-year-old adolescents report believing in God, only 32% of them attend church on a weekly basis (INJUV, 2004).

Profound political and social changes in Chile over the past three decades transformed culture, values, and beliefs (Programa de Naciones Unidas para el Desarrollo (PNUD), 2002). The uniform view of one promoted by the military rule during the 1970s and 1980s evolved into a more diverse society with the advent of democracy. At the same time, economic development and the liberal market system promoted individualism, a more prevalent value orientation in Chilean youth (18- 21 years) rather than in older groups ((PNUD, 2003).

Youth's trust in institutions ranges from 31% for school and 32% for teachers to 27% for policemen and 30% for policewomen, 25% for churches, 18% for priests and 13% for media professionals. Judiciary systems and local governments are institutions trusted by around 10% of youth of 15–29 years, slightly above the least trusted Parliament, Congressmen and Congresswomen, political parties, and politicians (percentages under 3%). Youth express high interpersonal trust in family members, friends, work or study mates, teachers, and policemen.

Gender

Historically, the role of women in Chilean society has been contradictory. Though women gained important rights ahead of their counterparts in Latin America (first medical doctor graduated in 1886; women gained voting rights in municipal elections in 1934 voting in national elections in 1949), gender inequality remains a major issue in Chilean society, especially in regard to women's access to power and decision-making positions (Schkolnik, 2004). Women's participation in the labor force in Chile (39%) is one of the lowest in South America (Servicio Nacional de la Mujer (SERNAM), 2004). Chilean females have on average lower social status, less power, and fewer resources than males. Only 13% of the parliament lower-level chamber seats and government positions are held by women (SERNAM, 2003).

During the years of the military regime, a conservative image of women's roles (Mattelart, 1976) was promoted. Gender-equality issues were almost completely absent from official discourse, and women were minimally represented in government positions. As a consequence of the active participation of women in the transition to democracy, recent democratic governments have made concerted efforts to increase women's participation in the labor force and power positions (PNUD, 2002). During the first decade of this century, important signs of change were the appointment of women as Secretary of State and Secretary of Defense and the election of the first woman president in 2006.

In Chile, prevalent cultural standards of women as caregivers and men as providers operate early in the primary socialization contexts of families and schools (Schkolnik, 2004). Gender roles conform to the traditional pattern with fathers perceived as strong authority figures who set rules at home. Alternatively, mothers are perceived as more caring and involved with the family but are granted less authority (SERNAM, 2002a). Traditional family roles are also observed in that women take responsibility for larger proportions of household chores, such as cleaning, grocery shopping, and caring for children (PNUD, 2002). A similar division of labor is observed in the population 15 to 19 years of age, where girls' involvement in household chores is almost three times that of boys (SERNAM, 2004).

Clear gender differences are observed in beliefs and attitudes regarding women's roles. For example, 26% of men aged 18 to 24 consider that women should be most responsible for household chores, compared with only 13% of women in that age range (SERNAM, 2002a). In the same way, higher percentages of young men as compared to young women, consider that married women should not be involved in politics (26% versus 10%, respectively), and that a woman should not insist her point of view is correct over a man's view (26% versus 9%, respectively) (SERNAM, 2002a). These views and attitudes are highly influenced by SES, with low-SES respondents endorsing more traditional views of family roles. For example, 53% of men with elementary education or less believe women are mainly responsible for house chores, compared to only 10% of college-educated men (SERNAM, 2002a).

While boys and girls consider that both genders are equally talented, there is a tendency in males to consider themselves more talented in traditional areas such as math and sports (SERNAM,

2002b). Consistent with their attitudes and beliefs, a higher percentage of males aspire to professional careers requiring math as compared to females (43% versus 12% respectively) (SERNAM, 2002b). Further, a higher percentage of females than males (47% versus 28%) believe math is the most difficult subject in high school. On the other hand, higher percentages of women aspire to careers in the social sciences (33% versus 20%) and education (14% versus 2%). In terms of vocational expectations, women manifest a wider variety of professional preferences, while men concentrate in careers strong in math.

In terms of future work preparation, a higher percentage of girls (66%) aspire to pursue a college degree compared to boys (57%), and both groups feel supported by their parents to choose whatever they want to study. This signals a change in expectations compared with past generations (SERNAM, 2002b).

The Self

Chilean adolescents 15 to 18 years of age have positive self-concepts and high self-esteem. They describe themselves with positive attributes such as sociable (34%), easygoing (29%), and optimistic (25%) (INJUV, 2003). Negative attributes are not frequently selected in adolescents' self-descriptions.

Chilean adolescents report high future-oriented aspirations and expectations (INJUV, 2001; PNUD, 2003). However, Martinez, Cumsille, and Rivera (2004) found that adolescents' future-oriented aspirations and expectations decrease as adolescents grow older, a finding likely reflecting their enhanced capacity for self-evaluation. Changes in postsecondary educational aspirations have been more dramatic for girls (Martinez et al., 2004; Ministerio de Educación 2001), a finding related to changes in social-role expectations for women (PNUD, 2003). Aspirations and expectations of future educational attainment are also positively related to SES.

Physical appearance is highly valued by Chilean adolescents. In their view, adolescents should take care of their physical bodies (Soto et al., 2003). Because of prevalent beauty standards, weight is a common referent in adolescents' assessments of their physical identities. According to their body size, 59% of adolescents 12 to 18 years consider themselves as "normal," 15% thin, and 19% overweight. Seventy percent are satisfied with their physical appearance.

Family Relationships

In spite of rapid modernization and greater prevalence of individualistic values over recent decades, Chileans are highly positive in their assessments of the family as a social institution (PNUD, 2002) and manifest a strong family orientation. The two-parent nuclear family is the most prevalent family structure, though there has been an increase in single-parent families and a decrease in extended families since the 1990s. Nuclear families account for 57% of the homes in Chile, followed by 22% of extended families and 12% of single-parent families (INE, 2004).

Adolescents assign great importance to family relationships and expect to form their own families in the future. For example, in a 2003 national survey of adolescents and young adults 15 to 29 years (INJUV, 2004), 76% report their strongest commitment is to be with their family, and 34% believe that developing a family is the most important accomplishment for happiness in life. Close to 90% of adolescents 15 to 18 years of age consider the family as a central institution in society, and 73% report being highly committed to their families. In the same way, for 68% of adolescents marriage is part of their life plan, and an additional 15% expect to cohabit (SERNAM, 2002b). There are important socioeconomic differences in marital expectations, as 80% of high-SES compared to only 60% of low-SES adolescents expect to marry.

The commitment of adolescents to their families is partially based on a strong feeling of family as a caring institution. Over 96% of adolescents report liking their own family, and 77% of them consider their family home as a caring and loving place (INJUV, 2003). While both parents are positively evaluated in different areas, mothers are more highly evaluated than fathers. For example, on a scale from 1 to 7, with 7 the highest rating, the average rating of the overall quality of the relationship is 6.21 for the mother and 5.63 for the father. Among different aspects of the relationship assessed, communication with the mother receives the highest average rating (6.51) and time spent with father the lowest (5.27). Adolescents report their highest agreement with parents concerning future plans (88%), and their lowest agreement is political issues (47%). Finally, 58% of adolescents consider lack of time to spend with family to be a problem.

Friends and Peers/Youth Culture

Social bonds with peers are important relationships in the socialization of adolescents in Chile. Adolescents 15 to 19 years, 88% have a group of friends they see frequently (INJUV, 2004). Friendship networks become an important source of emotional support for young people by providing opportunities for adolescents to share their problems (29%), to talk about sexuality (60%) and interpersonal issues (56%), and by providing instrumental help to solve everyday issues (29%) (INJUV, 2003). Seventy percent of adolescents 15 to 18 years of age confide their personal problems to friends, and over 80% seek help from a friend when facing an important problem in life. Overall, friends appear to have a more prominent role in the lives of female, high-SES, and urban youth (INJUV, 2003).

Adolescent affiliation in organized youth groups is low. Twenty-one percent of 15- to 18-year-olds are involved in sports, 20% in religious groups, 17% in virtual groups, 16% in cultural groups, and 15% in hobby groups. Involvement in other youth activities such as volunteering, Scouts, or student councils does not elicit adolescents' interest. Spending time with friends in social gatherings and parties is the most frequent activity that adolescents engage in during weekends.

Greater access to postsecondary education in middle- and high-SES youth provides new opportunities for adolescents to extend and strengthen friendships. Almost 80% of emerging adults (19 to 24 years) have a group of close friends, and friends are their best confidants and help providers. Friendship networks consolidate in long-term bonds as they also influence mating, career opportunities, and business, thus enhancing the social capital of youth.

The emergence of urban tribes (and gangs) suggests that youth form distinct subcultures in Chile, including *flaites* (Chilean rappers), Goths, sharps, darks, punkies, and thrashers, among others. These groups differentiate from adults in their lifestyles, slang, dress, hairstyles, and music preferences. The formation of these crowds has been related to adolescents and emerging adults' need for affiliation and their efforts to cope with the anomie of living in an individualistic society (Ahumada, 2000).

Love and Sexuality

Romantic relationships are an important aspect of adolescents' social relationships in Chile. In 2001, 48% percent of adolescents 15 to 19 years of age were involved in romantic relationships. Of them, 44% reported going steady (INJUV, 2001). Subsequent figures for adolescents 15 to 18 years (INJUV, 2003) indicated that 23% were going steady, 11% were seeing someone, and 2% were cohabiting (INJUV, 2004).

Findings from a national survey indicate that the majority (53.1%) of Chilean adolescents 15 to 19 years of age are not sexually active (INJUV, 2009), but this number shows a decrease from previous surveys (66.9% in 2004; INJUV, 2004). For those sexually active, age of initiation is 16.7, with earlier initiation for males (16.4) than for females (17.1). Approximately 13% of adolescents 15 to 18 years report having sexual intercourse several times a week, and 19% at least once a week. At the same time, 37% report not having sexual relations in the past six months (INJUV, 2004).

Most of adolescents' sexual activity involves stable partners. For the sexually active (59%), boyfriends and girlfriends are the most frequent partners. In addition, 23% of youth report having sex with former romantic partners, and 10% with an occasional acquaintance (INJUV, 2004). The most frequent motivations for engaging in sexual activity that adolescents 15 to 19 years of age report are being in love (40%) and desire by both partners (38%) (INJUV, 2004).

Fernández et al. (2000) found that adolescents lack appropriate knowledge about sexuality. In adolescents' views, parents and teachers should be the main providers of sexual information starting at age 10 to 15 years.

Health Risk Behavior

Changes in Chilean society have brought about many of the social problems associated with modernization. Chilean adolescents present a high prevalence of behaviors that pose risks to their health, such as alcohol and drug use, antisocial behavior, and risky sexual behavior. A high prevalence of psychological problems has also been reported.

Several studies report that smoking is one of the most prevalent health risk behaviors in Chilean adolescents. For example, Valdivia et al. (2004) report a 47% lifetime prevalence of smoking in a high school population (14 to 18 years old). Prevalence rates were higher for females than for males (52% versus 42%), and for low-SES compared to middle- and high-SES (51%, 44%, and 47%, respectively). Furthermore, young Chilean adolescents 13 to 15 years rank highest in tobacco consumption in the international sample of the Global Youth Tobacco Survey (2003). Consistent with Valdivia et al. (2004), the Global Youth Tobacco Survey (2003) reports higher prevalence rates for girls (44% in Santiago) than boys (31% in Santiago). Interestingly, Chile is one of the few countries in this international sample in which prevalence rates of smoking are higher for girls than for boys.

Almost 56% of youth consider excessive alcohol and drug use to be the most serious problem youth face as a group, with consistent figures across gender, SES, and rural versus urban groups. Prevalence rate for alcohol use was 59% for adolescents 15 to 19 years old, and 77% for emerging adults (20–24 years) (INJUV, 2009). For those same ages, past year prevalence of marihuana was estimated at 15% and 22%, respectively. For both, alcohol and marijuana, higher SES youth report higher levels of use than lower SES (INJUV, 2009). A study of lifestyles conducted by the Chilean Secretary of Health showed that around 20% of adolescent males and 9% of females ages 15 to 19 could be considered problem drinkers according to their self-reported alcohol use (Ministerio de Salud (MINSAL), 2001). By far the most prevalent illegal drug used (lifetime prevalence) is marijuana (22%) followed by cocaine (6%) and crack (5%) (CONACE, 2003).

Teenage pregnancy has been reported at 6% for girls 15 to 17 years, and 22% for women 18 to 20 years old. About 16% of children born and registered in 2002 were born to mothers 19 years old or younger (MINSAL, 2002). Nevertheless, comparison of the 1992 and 2002 census data indicates a decrease in the percentage of children born to mothers 15 to 19 years old in the year before each census (SERNAM, 2002). It has also been reported (Ramirez & Cumsille, 1997) that in Santiago teenage pregnancy in low-SES adolescents is almost five times higher than in high-SES adolescents.

Education

Around 50% of youth (15–29 years) are students, with balanced percentages by gender. Almost 80% of adolescents 15–19 years of age are students compared to 45% of those 20–24 years and 20% of those 25–29 years. Youth from low SES and rural areas are overrepresented among the 50% of youth that is not studying. The most frequent reasons that youth claim for not studying include family economic need, looking for a job, and high school graduation.

Enrollment in secondary education reached 93% for the population 14 to 17 years of age in 2003 (MIDEPLAN, 2003). Substantive efforts and resources have been invested during the past decade in order to increase the quality of education in Chile. Findings from a national survey (MIDEPLAN, 2003) indicate that the educational duration of adolescents and emerging adults 15 to 24 years of age was raised from 10.2 years in 1990 to 11.2 years in 2004. Further, gains in education are most significant for youth from less privileged groups. On average youth from very low SES (the poorest 10% of homes) attained 1.5 years of education above that of their parents, and 2.5 years of education above that of their grandparents. Educational gains are also higher in rural youth. This group on average attained 1.6 years of education above that of their parents and 2.8 years of education above that of its grandparents (MIDEPLAN, 2003).

The Chilean educational system is highly segregated by SES and has a mixed administrative system. In 2002, 48% of the high school population attended public schools, 37% attended private subsidized schools, and 9% attended private schools. About a third of youth who graduate from high school continue to higher education at either a college institution (23%) or a professional or technical school (11%), but these figures vary greatly for rural and urban youth (INJUV, 2004). Overall, for youth 18 to 24 years of age, access to postsecondary education increased from 26% in

2000 to 33% in 2005, as reflected by freshmen enrollment in college institutions (MINEDUC, 2005). Access to postsecondary education varies greatly by SES. Almost 50% of high-SES youth enter college, compared to 18% of middle- and only 5% of low-SES youth (INJUV, 2003). Low-SES youth are selected into technical or vocational school.

Chilean youth's assessment of the quality of the educational process in their schools is fairly positive. On a scale ranging 1 to 7, 78% of adolescents 15 to 18 years of age believe their teachers' technical competence is fairly high (6.3), and 69% adolescents think their teachers' commitment and dedication are also high (6.12). Similarly, adolescents provide positive assessments of the extent to which their schools provide a good preparation for postsecondary studies (6.02), teach values (6.17), and guide them toward developing a personal life project (6.12). Despite these positive assessments, Chilean adolescents have not performed well in international tests of educational attainment. For example, in the 1999 Trends in International Mathematics and Science Study (TIMMS), 14-year-old Chileans performed below the international average and ranked 35 out of 38 countries (MINEDUC, 2000).

Work

Working is not a universal experience for Chilean adolescents. Over 45% of youth aged 15–29 years had their first working experience between 16 and 18 years, almost 25% at 15, and only 4% beyond 22 years. Rural youth start working at significantly earlier ages compared to their urban counterparts. Males start working earlier (16.3 years) than females (17.2 years) (INJUV, 2004).

Historically, youth unemployment in Chile is double that of adults (Fernández, 2004). Despite steady economic growth in the past 20 years, unemployment rose from 9% in 1994 to 16% in 2003 for the group aged 15 to 29 years (INJUV, 2003). The magnitude of youth unemployment and its consequences for the country's future development are a matter of concern in Chile. The latest data available, reporting unemployment for the first months of 2010, show that the unemployment rate for youth 15 to 24 years of age (20%) is more than double the rate for the general population (9%) (INE, 2010). Unemployment rates are higher for adolescents 15 to 19 years of age (23%) than for young adults 20 to 24 years of age (19%; INE 2010). These figures reflect structural features of the labor market (Tokman, 2004), as well as a mismatch between youth expectations and aspirations regarding salaries, jobs profiles, and the market supply. Seventy-six percent of youth perceive that the labor market discriminates against them in favor of more experienced workers.

Media

Access to new information and communication technologies has been growing steadily in Chile. Its effects are apparent in the processes of economic productivity as well as in the organization of social life. Daily use of a computer is reported by over 62% of youth 15 to 24 years of age, and use at least once a week by 20%. Percentages are significantly higher for high-SES youth, for middle-SES figures range between 78% and 42%, and are lower for youth from rural contexts (29%; INJUV, 2009). Additionally, 45% of youth aged 15 to 18 years own a cellular phone. The Internet activities most frequently described are obtaining information in males, sending and receiving emails as well as chatting, all reported in figures close to 50% of youth. Facebook use is high in females. Overall these practices indicate that youth are actors in the information society, though figures are significantly lower for rural youth.

Public policies aimed at reducing the digital gap between the most and least economically advantaged youth introduced communication and information technologies in the school system. The program Enlaces (Links) created digital networks connecting 90% of public schools and 100% of private subsidized high schools. Similarly, the Public Library Network links 368 libraries across the country and provides free access to the Internet, training, and opportunities for students to create their own websites. The Youth Information System provides public spaces with free access to the Internet.

In Chile 76% of the elementary school population has access to a computer (MIDEPLAN, 2003). Fifty-nine percent of poor youth and 80% of the poorest can only access a computer at school. Approximately 45% of adolescents aged 15 to 18 years master basic computer skills (INJUV, 2003), 30% have a medium-level skill, and 20% are not skilled in computer use (INJUV, 2003).

Zegers, Larrain, and Trapp (2004) examined the effects of Internet chatting on 124 young college freshman students. The average number of hours per week spent chatting was 4.4. However, 43% reported no involvement with chatting and 11% chatted more than eight hours per week. Significant gender differences were found in the extent that respondents used chatting as an active means to experiment with their personal identities. Males reported more involvement with multiple selves, masking and deceiving, and valued virtual interactions more positively than females. Similarly, a high percentage (over 88%) of Chilean high school students (14 to 18 years) have been reported to use chat, but for few hours a week (Altuzarra & Zegers, 2007).

Politics and Military

Military service has been mandatory for males 18 years old since 1900 (Maldonado, 1993). Legislation change has been proposed to render it voluntary (Maldonado, 2001). In reality only 20% of adolescents serve, the majority of whom are from low-SES groups. In 1980 almost 73% of those enrolled in military service had 11 years of education or less. Given that the expected age of high-school graduation is 17 to 18 years, this figure suggests that adolescents enrolled in the service were either behind or had dropped out of school.

How adolescents are faring as future citizens is an issue of renewed interest in Chile. Seventy-one percent of emerging adults 20 to 24 years of age were not registered to vote in 2000, as opposed to 48% in 1997. The percentage of adolescents 18 to 19 years who registered to vote decreased from 5% in 1988 to 2% in 2001. Similarly, youth manifest low levels of trust in political parties, government representatives, and public institutions (INJUV, 2000, 2004). The percentage of youth who identify with a political party has gone down from 68% in 1994 to 31% in 2000. Only 25% of youth (INJUV, 2002) participate in political and social organizations. Other surveys find that youths are not interested in electoral politics and manifest low support for democracy (PNUD, 2002).

Empirical findings (González, 2007; Martínez, Silva, and Hernández, 2010; Martínez, Silva, Carmona, Cumsille & Flanagan, under review) indicate that youth challenge the principles of a social order they consider unjust and advance proposals for social transformation reflecting their understanding of how the political system works. Youth value social, economic, and cultural rights, but voice unmet expectations for more active involvement as citizens. They advocate for reducing prejudice (e.g., youth as a problem to society), condemn discrimination (against youth and the less privileged), and aspire to advance social justice (e.g., social integration, equal rights in education).

Unique Issues

Chilean youth have played a significant role in social movements in Chile. University and high school students have been actors in social mobilizations at several moments of the 20th and current centuries. The student union of the largest public university in Chile has celebrated its centennial and documented its history of social action. During the 1960s university students' associations led a national movement towards changing the role of the university in society, from the ivory tower towards accomplishing its responsibility of giving back to society and commitment to solving urgent social problems. Mobilizations gained support form other universities' students' organizations and resulted in important reforms that modernized the university systems, teaching, and technology use.

In the mid-1960s the movement was well articulated and resulted in a major transformation of the university system in Chile, rendering it more progressive, accessible to a larger group of citizens, and democratic. Students' movement elicited support from large sectors of society, and were followed by the installation of a socialist government in 1970.

In 2006, high school students protested for free public transportation and changes in university admission procedures. This movement, labeled the "penguin revolution" (Domedel & Peña y Lillo, 2008) evolved towards a profound criticism of the educational reform and later to the foundations of the public educational system in Chile. This movement rallied vast sectors of Chilean society and placed equity of education on the national policy agenda in 2006.

References and Further Reading

Aceituno, R., Asún, R., Ruiz, S., Reinoso, A., Venegas, J., & Corbalán, F. (2009). Anomia y alienación en estudiantes secundarios de Santiago de Chile: Resultados iniciales de un estudio comparativo. *Psykhe, 18*, 3–18.

Ahumada, J. T. (2000). Urbanas en Chile: El ir y venir de una re-construcción identitaria. Retrieved from www.identidades.uchile.cl/Artículos

Almonte, C., Sepúlveda, G., Valenzuela, C., & Avendaño, A. (1990). Desarrollo psicosocial de adolescentes de 16 a 19 años. *Revista de Psiquiatría, 8*, 451–459.

Altuzarra, M. P., & Zegers, B. (2007). Modelo empírico, descriptivo y explicativo para el compromiso de identidad en el chat en adolescentes escolares chilenos. *Psykhe, 16*, 85–96.

Asún, D., Alfaro, J., & Morales, G. (1994). Análisis crítico de categorías y estrategias utilizadas para el estudio e intervención psicosocial con jóvenes en Chile. *Revista Chilena de Psicología, 15*, 5–14.

CONACE. (2000). *Estudio diagnóstico del consumo de drogas en población escolar de Chile a nivel comunal, año 1999*. Santiago, Chile: Gobierno de Chile.

CONACE. (2003). Quinto estudio nacional de drogas en población escolar de Chile, 2003, 8° básico a IV medio. Santiago, Chile: Gobierno de Chile.

Cummings, E., Wilson, J., and Shamir, H. (2003). Reactions of Chilean and U.S. children to marital discord. *International Journal of Behavioural Development, 27*, 437–444.

Cumsille, P., & Martínez, M. L. (1997). Síntomas de depresión en estudiantes de enseñanza media de Santiago. *Revista Chilena de Pediatría, 68*, 74–77.

Domedel, A., & Peña y Lillo, M. (2008). *El Mayo de los Pingüinos*. Santiago, Chile: Editorial Universidad de Chile.

Fernández, L., Bustos, L. González, L., Palma, D., Villagrán, J., & Muñoz, S. (2000). Creencias, actitudes y conocimientos en educación sexual. *Revista Médica de Chile, 128*, 574–583.

Fernández, P. (2004). *Flexibilidad laboral para los jóvenes chilenos*. Master's thesis, Universidad de Chile, Santiago, Chile.

Florenzano, R., Maddaleno, M., Bobadilla, E., Alvarez, G., et al. (1988). *La salud del adolescente en Chile*. Santiago, Chile: Corporación de Promoción Universitaria.

Florenzano, R., Pino, P., & Marchandón, A. (1993). Conductas de riesgo en adolescentes escolares de Santiago de Chile. *Revista Médica de Chile, 121*, 462–469.

Global Youth Tobacco Survey. (2003). *Differences in worldwide tobacco use by gender: Findings from the Global Youth Tobacco Survey*. Atlanta, GA: Centers for Disease Control and Prevention.

González, S. (2007). La noción de ciudadanía en jóvenes estudiantes secundarios y universitarios: Un análisis de estudios comparados de la nueva ciudadanía. In A. Zambrano et al. (Eds.), *Psicología comunitaria en Chile: Evolución, perspectivas y proyecciones* (pp. 335–372). Santiago, Chile: RIL Editores.

Instituto Nacional de Estadísticas. (n.d.). *Chile: Censo de población y vivienda 2002*. Santiago, Chile: INE. Retrieved from www.ine.cl

Instituto Nacional de Estadísticas. (2009). *Estadística vitales: Informe Anual 2007*. Santiago, Chile: INE. Retrieved from www.ine.cl

Instituto Nacional de Estadísticas. (2010). Mercado del trabajo cifras históricas hasta trimestre def 2010. Santiago, Chile: INE. Retrieved from www.ine.cl

Instituto Nacional de la Juventud. (1999). *Sociabilidad y Cultura Juvenil*. Santiago, Chile: Gobierno de Chile: Ministerio de Planificación y Cooperación.

Instituto Nacional de la Juventud. (2002). *La eventualidad de la inclusión. Jóvenes chilenos a comienzos del nuevo siglo. Tercera Encuesta Nacional de la Juventud*. Santiago, Chile: Gobierno de Chile: Ministerio de Planificación y Cooperación.

Instituto Nacional de la Juventud. (2004). *La integración social de los jóvenes en Chile 1994–2003*. Santiago, Chile: *Cuarta Encuesta Nacional de la Juventud*. Santiago, Chile: Gobierno de Chile: Ministerio de Planificación y Cooperación.

Instituto Nacional de la Juventud. (2009). *6ta Encuesta nacional de juventud. Principales resultados*. Santiago, Chile: Gobierno de Chile: Ministerio de Planificación y Cooperación.

Maldonado, C. (1993). La polémica del servicio militar obligatorio en Chile. In *Estudios Interdisciplinarios de América Latina y el Caribe*, Vol. 4. Tel Aviv, Israel: Tel Aviv University.

Maldonado, C. (2001. Estado de situación del servicio militar en Chile. *Security and Defense Studies Review, 1*, 84–92.

Martínez, M. L., & Cumsille, P. (1996). Bienestar psicológico de adolescentes urbanos: Su relación con niveles de competencia psicosocial, sistemas de apoyo social y calidad del tiempo libre. *Psykhe, 5*, 185–202.

Martínez, M. L., Cumsille, P. & Rivera, D. (2004). *Adolescents' future-oriented aspirations and goals: The role of family expectations and parental practices*. Paper presented at the 18th Biennial Meeting of the International Society for the Study of Behavioural Development, Ghent, Belgium.

Martínez, M. L., Silva, C., Carmona, M., Cumsille, P., & Flanagan, C. (under review). *Young Chileans' views of citizenship: Findings from the first post-Pinochet generation*.

Martínez, M. L., Silva, C., & Hernández, A. C. (2010). *¿En qué ciudadanía creen los jóvenes? Aspiraciones de ciudadanía en jóvenes líderes y sus motavaciones para la participatión social psukhé, 19*, 25–37.

Mattelart, A., & Mattelart, M. (1970). *Juventud chilena: Rebeldía y conformismo*. Santiago, Chile: Editorial Universitaria.

Mattelart, M. (1976). Chile: The feminine version of the coup d'etat. In J. Nash & H. I. Safa (Eds.), *Sex and class in Latin America*. New York, NY: Praeger.

Ministerio de Educación. (2000). *Resultados del TIMSS son un desafío para la educación chilena, Departamento de comunicaciones, 6/12/2000*. Santiago, Chile: Gobierno de Chile: MINEDUC.

Ministerio de Educación. (2002). *Indicadores de la Educación en Chile 2002*. Santiago, Chile: Gobierno de Chile: MINEDUC.

Ministerio de Educación. (2003a). *Educación cívica y el ejercicio de la ciudadanía*. Santiago, Chile: MINEDUC, Unidad de Currículum y Evaluación.

Ministerio de Educación. (2003b). *Nota Técnica: Factores que explican los resultados de Chile en PISA+*. Santiago, Chile: MINEDUC, Unidad de Currículum y Evaluación.

Ministerio de Educación. (2004). *Sistema educacional*. Santiago, Chile: Gobierno de Chile: MINEDUC.

Ministerio de Educación. (2005). *Educación superior*. Santiago, Chile: Gobierno de Chile: MINEDUC.

Ministerio de Planificación y Cooperación Social. (2003). *Encuesta de Caracterización Socioeconómica Nacional (CASEN)*. Santiago, Chile: Gobierno de Chile: MIDEPLAN.

Ministerio de Planificación y Cooperación Social. (2006). *Casen 2006*. Santiago, Chile: Gobierno de Chile: MIDEPLAN.

Ministerio de Salud. (n.d.). *Mortalidad de los adolescentes por servicio de salud y sexo, 2003*. Santiago, Chile: Gobierno de Chile: MINSAL.

Ministerio de Salud. (2001a). *Encuesta nacional de calidad de vida y salud*. Santiago, Chile: Gobierno de Chile: MINSAL.

Ministerio de Salud. (2001b). *Mortalidad adolescente y sus componentes por servicio de salud*. Santiago, Chile: Gobierno de Chile: MINSAL.

Ministerio de Salud. (2001c). *Encuesta nacional de calidad de vida y salud*. Santiago, Chile: Gobierno de Chile: MINSAL.

Ministerio de Salud. (2002). Nacidos vivos inscritos según edad de la madre por servicio de salud y comuna de residencia de la madre. Santiago, Chile: Gobierno de Chile: MINSAL.

Ministerio de Salud. (2003). *Mortalidad de los adolescentes por servicio de salud y sexo*. Santiago, Chile: Gobierno de Chile: MINSAL.

Molina, R. (1988). La salud del adolescente en Chile. In *Sistemas de Atención para Adolescentes Embarazadas* (Capítulo X, pp. 195–231). Santiago, Chile: Editorial CPU.

Molina, R. (1991). Medicina reproductiva del adolescente. *Revista de Pediatría Universidad de Chile, Facultad de Medicina, 34*, 105–111.

Molina, R. (1994). Conceptos de Riesgo en adolescentes embarazadas. *Revista Chilena de Obstetricia y Ginecología Infantil y de la Adolescencia, 1*, 77–78.

Muzzo, S., & Burrows, R. (1986). *El adolescente chileno: Características, problemas y soluciones*. Santiago, Chile: Editorial Universitaria.

Programa de Naciones Unidas para el Desarrollo. (2002). Santiago, Chile: PNUD. Retrieved from www.desarrollohumano.cl

Programa de Naciones Unidas para el Desarrollo. (2003). *Transformaciones culturales e identidad juvenil en Chile*. Santiago, Chile: PNUD. Retrieved from www.desarrollohumano.cl

Ramírez, V., & Cumsille, P. (1997). Evaluación de la eficiencia de un programa comunitario de apoyo a la maternidad adolescente. *Revista Latinoamericana de Psicología, 29*, 267–286.

Saiz, J. L., & Gempp, R. (2001). Estudios empíricos sobre la identidad nacional chilena: Revisión y nueva evidencia. In J. L. Salazar (Ed.), *Identidades nacionales en América Latina*. Caracas, Venezuela: Fondo Editorial de Humanidades y Educación, Universidad Central de Venezuela.

Schkolnik, M. (2004). ¿Por qué es tan increíblemente baja la tasa de participación de las mujeres en Chile? Retrieved from www.expansiva.cl

Schwartz, S. H. (2004). Mapping and interpreting cultural differences around the world. In H. Viken, J. Soeters, & P. Ester (Eds.), *Comparing cultures: Dimensions of culture in comparative perspective*. Leiden, The Netherlands: Brill.

Sepúlveda, G., Almonte, C., Valenzuela, C., & Avendaño, A. (1991). Estilos de socialización de los padres y desarrollo psicosocial en adolescentes de 16 a 19 años. *Revista Chilena de Pediatría, 62*, 396–403.

Servicio Nacional de la Mujer. (2002a). *Hombres y mujeres: Cómo ven hoy su rol en la sociedad y en la familia*. Documento de trabajo no. 78. Santiago, Chile: Gobierno de Chile: SERNAM. Retrieved from www.sernam.cl

Servicio Nacional de la Mujer. (2002b). *Análisis y detección de expectativas de vida y proyecto de vida en niños, niñas y adolescentes*. Documento de trabajo no. 80. Santiago, Chile: Gobierno de Chile: SERNAM. Retrieved from www.sernam.cl

Servicio Nacional de la Mujer. (2004). *Mujeres chilenas. Tendencias en la última década*. Santiago, Chile: Gobierno de Chile: SERNAM. Retrieved from www.sernam.cl

Soto, F., Matute, I., & Peña, C. (2003). *Cultura de la imagen y hábitos alimenticios de los jóvenes*. Santiago, Chile: Gobierno de Chile: Instituto Nacional de la Juventud.

Tokman, V. (2004). *Desempleo juvenil en el Cono Sur: Causas, consecuencias y políticas*. Serie Prosur. Santiago, Chile: Fundación Friedrich Ebert.

Torney-Purta, J., Amadeo, J., & Pilotti, F. (2004). *Fortalecimiento de la democracia en las Américas a través de la educación cívica*. Washington, DC: Organización de los Estados Americanos.

Valdivia, G., Simonetti, F., Cumsille, P., Ramírez, V., Hidalgo, C. G., Palma, B., & Carrasco, J. (2004). Consumo de tabaco en población menor de 18 años: Estudio de prevalencia en escolares chilenos. *Revista Médica Chile, 132*, 171–182.

Velásquez, E., Martínez, M. L., & Cumsille, P. (2004). Expectativas de autoeficacia y actitud prosocial asociadas a participación ciudadana en jóvenes. *Psykhé, 3*, 85–98.

Vicente, B., Rioseco, P., Saldivia, S., Kohn, R., & Torres, S. (2002). Estudio chileno de prevalencia de patología psiquiátrica (DSM-III-R/CIDI) (ECPP). *Revista Médica de Chile, 130*, 526–536.

Zegers, B., Larrain, M. E., & Trapp, A. (2004). El chat: ¿Medio de comunicación o laboratorio de experimentación de la identidad? *Psykhe, 13*, 53–69.

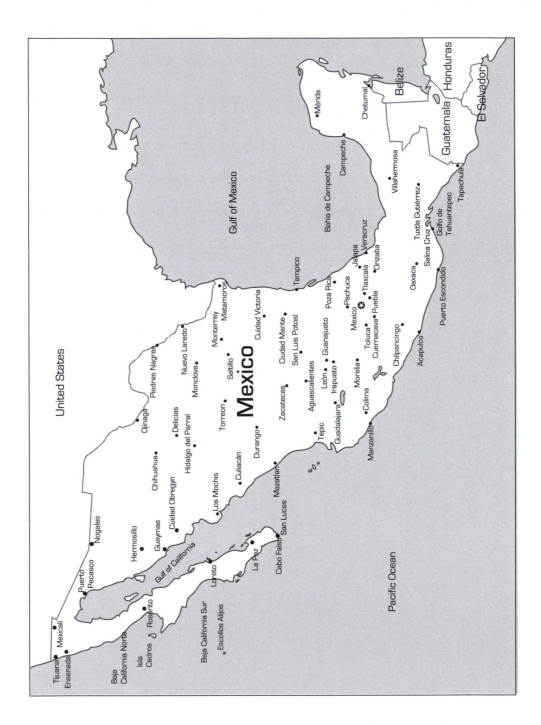

Chapter 14

Mexico

Rebeca Mejia-Arauz, Ruby Sheets, and
Martha Villaseñor

Background Information

Mexico is a federal republic situated in North America. Its official name is United Mexican States (Estados Unidos Mexicanos). It has a territory of nearly 2 million square kilometers and borders the United States of America in the north and Guatemala and Belize in the south. Across the country environmental conditions, habitats, microhabitats, climate, and geology vary widely, ranging from deserts to tropical rainforests to mountains, generating a great variety of vegetation and fauna.

The original inhabitants, indigenous societies, were conquered by the Spanish early in the sixteenth century. Over time the populations have mixed, causing the majority of its citizens to be considered *mestizo*. As a result of the colonization, Mexico's official language is Spanish and the majority of the population (92%) is Roman Catholic (INEGI, 2000).

Independence from Spain was achieved in 1810. One hundred years later, in 1910, the fight for land rights and democracy continued with the Mexican Revolution. Afterwards, indigenous groups occupied a more salient position, though they remain in disadvantaged socioeconomic conditions today.

In 2005, the total population reported was about 103 million, of which 24% lived in rural areas. Youth aged 12 to 29 make up 33% of the entire population (INEGI, 2005). The country's cultural and ethnic diversity is reflected in the number of native languages (80) (Bertely Busquets, 2003), and speakers of indigenous languages (over 6 million; 28% are between the ages of 15 and 29) (INEGI, 2005).

Period of Adolescence

A social conception of youth started to develop in Mexico at the beginning of the twentieth century, after a series of political and social transformations at the end of the previous century. In 1870, the constitution stated that citizens under the age of 21 needed to be protected from danger. The country followed the French model, which considered youth to end at age 21 and to begin at age 14 for males and age 12 for females (Necoechea, 2003; Urteaga, 2004). In 1968, the legal adult age changed from 21 to 18.

The idea of adolescence was not yet common at the beginning of the twentieth century. Work and marriage marked the transition from childhood to adulthood. By age 12, boys started apprenticeships. In rural communities, men usually married at 18 or 19 years of age and women at 16 or 17, whereas in cities, men married at around 23 and women at around 20 (Necoechea, 2003).

The primary source of information on Mexican youth today is the National Youth Survey conducted by the Mexican Institute of Youth (ENJ, 2002, 2006). It does not study adolescents specifically, having surveyed citizens between 12 and 29 years of age, though the results are divided into four age groups: 12 to 14, 15 to 19, 20 to 24, and 25 to 29. The large age range (12 to 29) reflects the fact that government institutions no longer consider the transition from adolescence to adulthood to follow traditional patterns of role sequences (family–school–work–social participation). Factors that have contributed to this change in perspective are: transformations in family dynamics and structure, especially the increased participation of women in the workplace; an increase in education levels and its inverse relation with access to employment and social mobility; and the diversification of the labor market and an increase in forms of participation in the informal economy (ENJ, 2002).

It is important to note that most scientific research on adolescence in Mexico focuses on health issues, sexuality, and risky behavior. Only recently has it begun to consider cultural and psychosocial aspects of adolescence. In addition, unlike the National Youth Survey, scientific research follows the definition of adolescence provided by the World Health Organization, considering youth to be between 10 and 19 years of age. Most adolescents consider adolescence to end not at a certain age but according to one's responsibilities and circumstances. For example, adolescence ends once one starts working, has children, formalizes a relationship with someone else, uses drugs, goes to jail, or dedicates oneself to prostitution (Villaseñor Farias, 2003).

Beliefs

The majority of Mexican adolescents claim to be Catholic, though few consider themselves to be practicing Catholics. Nonetheless, when asked what they believe in, they mention themes related to the Christian doctrine such as the soul, sin, miracles, and the Virgin of Guadalupe (similar to the Virgin Mary, this virgin has indigenous features and is central to Latin American culture, especially Mexican culture). Among those who claim to be Roman Catholic, only 20% feel that their religious beliefs influence their attitudes about sexuality (ENJ, 2002).

Most adolescents in Catholic families go through confirmation between the ages of 16 and 18. As in other Catholic celebrations in Mexico, confirmation is a social and religious hybrid event in which beliefs and celebration go together. In most cases the adolescent's confirmation is more a decision of the family than of the adolescent. In fact, since the mid-1990s there has been a growing tendency in adolescents to turn to other religious groups or to abandon their Catholic family practices, particularly after they reach the age of 18. Evangelical Protestant groups are growing in Mexico and it seems that their belief systems are of particular interest to Mexican adolescents.

An especially important ritual event for girls at 15 years of age is the *quinceañera*. This tradition involves a mass followed by a dance and big party to celebrate the fifteenth birthday of the young woman. The celebration was originally carried out with the intention of introducing the women to society and the adult world, serving to mark the period when they were permitted to start dating. The tradition has been preserved and continues to the present day, though it no longer has the same meaning of transitioning to the next stage of life. In modern times, adolescents look forward to these events more for the celebratory aspects of being with friends at the party than for any religious or ritualistic association.

Upon analyzing the National Youth Survey of 2000, Flores (2003) concluded that in Mexican society, youth between 12 and 29 years old are the social group with the highest tolerance of ethnic, religious, sexual, and political differences, among other issues. For example, compared to Mexican adults, this age group appears to be more open and respectful of AIDS victims.

Mexico has often been considered a collectivistic nation, but this is mostly because of the relevance of family ties throughout life and also because some indigenous and rural communities are organized in such a way that the community in some aspects and events seems to be prioritized over the individual. However, Mexico is a multicultural and very diverse country in terms of traditions and cultural practices. There are also very strong differences between urban and rural populations, with more individualistic lives led in urban areas. While it could be said that collaboration and social participation are characteristic of many social groups all over the country, it could also be said that more modern and industrialized urban centers have shifted to different ways of social organization.

Gender

Both young men and young women are very self-conscious about their bodies, creating various personal conflicts. Their references are stereotypes developed from commercial and universalistic beauty models. Young men are most concerned about their height (desiring to be tall), their physical condition and strength, the size of parts of their bodies (hands and feet), their faces, and their hair. Young women are most concerned about their weight (not wanting to be fat), their height (wishing to be tall), their faces, their hands, and the size of parts of their bodies (bust, hips, waist, and mouth) (Villaseñor Farias, 2003).

In tandem with the importance they give to their physical appearance, Mexican adolescents are very concerned about being fashionable (ENJ, 2002). In addition, young men value having a strong personality, taking initiative, dating actively, and being clean, active, friendly, decisive, and jealous. Beyond their particular interest in their physical appearance (such as having a good figure), young women value being attentive, complacent, docile, calm, clean, simple, homely, and faithful, but not jealous or demanding (Villaseñor Farias, 2003).

Adolescent males perceive themselves as participants in public environments such as the street, school, sports scenarios, and work. In contrast, adolescent females identify themselves according to their participation in the home and limited public environments, such as school. They have a more pronounced tendency toward low self-esteem and self-identification using negative attributes, though this can be found in both groups. In fact, most young women perceive themselves as less capable academically than young men. Their life trajectory is centered on marriage and having children. This changes with time, as women older than 20 appear to perceive their social and labor participation differently, with a less submissive slant (Villaseñor Farias, 2003; Villaseñor & Martinez, 2002).

The Self

Much like in any nation, it is difficult to generalize about the identity or the self of the country's youth because of their cultural variants and diverse ways of being. These differences are even more marked in Mexico than in other nations. Groups differ according to their location (urban or rural areas), their socioeconomic level (with a large divide between lower and upper classes), their heritage (indigenous, Spanish, mixed, or other), and their immigration status (especially migrants who travel to the United States).

When Mexican adolescents talk about adolescence in general, utilizing an academic discourse, they mention negative qualities that are related to the socially popular concept of adolescents, for example that they are rebels, non-collaborative, or tend to look for trouble. In contrast, when they talk about themselves as adolescents they highlight positive qualities, such as friendship, solidarity, sincerity, courage, and happiness despite adversity (Villaseñor Farias, 2003; Villaseñor & Martinez, 2002).

Family Relationships

Mexico is considered to be a traditional society, regimented by the authority of the family and characterized by authoritative and hierarchical forms of power and politics (Flores, 2003). The majority of youth live with both of their parents, while only 27% have left their parents' home between 18 and 20 years of age; however, this percentage increases by age 25 (ENJ, 2006). Activities in the home are distributed traditionally by gender. For example, domestic chores and caring for children and the elderly are generally tasks performed by mothers and daughters, while activities such as house repairs are more likely to be done by fathers and sons (ENJ, 2002, 2006).

Traditionally, Mexican families were large, with six to eight children, but in the last three decades of the twentieth century the size of the family decreased to an average of three children. Also, single-parent families increased from 7% in the 1970s to 9% in the 1990s (Flores, 2003) to 17% in 2000 (INEGI, 2001).

The National Youth Survey of 2000 revealed that most youth look to their families for solidarity and support and consider their family members to be responsible and hardworking. Youth spend most of their free time with their family. They spend between two and four hours per day with their parents and siblings, whether it is during the week, a weekend, or a holiday. After family, they spend the most time with friends or the person they are dating (ENJ, 2002).

Research on adolescents and their family relationships is scarce; however, recent research performed in several regions of the country, mostly urban, concurs that most Mexican adolescents are very close to their family members. They report themselves to be seriously affected by family problems such as infidelity, divorce, domestic violence, unemployment, and poverty (ENJ, 2002; Villaseñor Farias, 2003; Villaseñor Farias & Castañeda, 2002).

In households where extended families live, it is often the case that the caregivers are older siblings or grandparents while both parents go to work. Thus, often adolescents—male or female—take care of their younger siblings, attending to their needs from feeding, bathing, and dressing them to helping with the school homework and taking them to school. They are given the authority that this responsibility involves. For example, they can scold the children and decide for them in their best interest (Alcalá, Mejia-Arauz, & Rogoff, in preparation). In other households where grandparents live, the adolescents themselves may be cared for by the grandparents or, alternatively, adolescents may help in taking care of their grandparents. At all social levels, it is common to find that adolescents establish good emotional relationships with their grandparents, since often grandparents are more affectionate and indulgent than parents.

Research on Mexican adolescents indicates that although they are close to their parents emotionally, they consider the communication that they have with their parents to be poor, especially the communication with their fathers. Both young men and women generally communicate more with their mothers than with their fathers about all topics, whether they are related to their emotions or with general issues in their everyday lives. These latter conversations, however, are not very frequent. The most common topics discussed are work and studies, while sex and politics are mentioned the least. With their mothers, youth tend to discuss more about religion and their emotions in addition to work and school than with their fathers (ENJ, 2002). Results of other studies indicate that about 50% of adolescents reported communication with parents about topics related to sexuality to be poor (Díaz Loving, 1993; Pick, 2002).

Adolescents point out that the greatest obstacle to communicating well with their parents is that their parents do not know how to listen. They appreciate their parents' efforts but wish that they were more accepting of their tastes and way of life. They wish their parents created more flexible rules and that they demonstrated less aggression towards their children (Villaseñor Farias, 2003). Despite this lack of communication, adolescents agree with the idea that they have to respect their parents' authority (Flores, 2003).

Adolescents picture themselves creating a different family model when they become parents. They imagine an ideal family in which the men are affectionate, participate in household chores, are supportive of their partner, and are nonviolent. Young women accept the maternal roles they see in their families, even when they feel that they would give their daughters more freedom than they themselves had. They visualize various changes in their ideals as wives: They would be less submissive, more sexually active, and they would not tolerate violence.

Friends and Peers/Youth Culture

Mexican youth form a clearly distinguished group marked in particular by a kind of aesthetic definition that includes the way they dress, the use of certain accessories, tattooing and piercing, and certain kinds of music (ENJ, 2002). It is interesting to note that while the style of clothes and accessories are influenced by foreign countries, especially the United States, the music they prefer is of Mexican origin.

Overall, 69% of youth between 12 and 14 years of age and 65% of those between 15 and 19 years of age claim to spend between one and three hours of a regular day with friends (ENJ, 2002). There seem to be small differences between young men and young women in the extent to which they spend time doing particular activities, though it is clear that males spend more time with their friends than females and females spend more time with their families than males.

The participation of youth in social organizations is very low. Only 23% of youth between 12 and 29 years of age report themselves as participating in an organized sport or a student or religious organization.

For decades there has been a stable tendency in Mexico, especially among youth of low socioeconomic levels, to form groups known as *chavos banda*, somewhat like gangs. These groups identify themselves with a particular territory and develop diverse characteristics related to choices of music, their ways of dress, and their activities. In general, they are associated with the consumption of inhalants, alcohol, and illegal drugs. Some display violent behavior, especially when confronting other gangs. Recent research about such gangs has focused on these groups in terms of the search for a social identity and the reclaiming of a social space shared by youth living in disadvantaged sociocultural and economic conditions (Stern & Medina, 2000). This second perspective was reflected in the tragic aftermath of the 1985 earthquake in Mexico City, where due to the structure of the gangs, the *chavos banda* were able to organize themselves and made a great impact by rescuing a large number of victims.

Love and Sexuality

Early adolescent dating (14 to 17 years) appears to be a way by which youth can identify with a reference group and, thus, gain access to activities with their peers and friends of the same age. It is especially important for young women to be dating someone because their dating status is an indicator of their physical attractiveness, while for young men it is an indicator of their masculinity (Welti, 2003). The National Youth Survey of 2000 and 2005 data show that most young people start dating when they are between 15 and 18 years of age.

The National Youth Survey of 2005 also revealed that of the youth who have had sexual relations, 43% reported that the age when they initiated having sexual intercourse was between 15 and 17 years. During adolescence it is common for youth to be insecure about their own sexuality and how to express it. In Mexico this is especially related to a negative attitude and lack of communication that prevails among adults with respect to sexual activity among adolescents. This attitude contributes to the spread of myths, false information, and confusing messages about sexuality (Tello, 1998).

Research has found that the more youth are informed about gender and sexuality issues, the more likely they are to have positive attitudes about sexual relations. School tends to be their main source of information about sexuality, but often focuses on biological explanations, which make it less important for them than what they hear from their peers (Alfaro Martinez, 1992; Pick, 1997). The mass media is also a very important source of such information, though adolescents recognize that the information they learn at school helps them to understand what they see in movies and on TV (Stern, Fuentes-Zurita, Lozano-Trevinòo, & Reynoso, 2003). The National Youth Survey of 2000 revealed that in youth between 12 and 19 years of age, close to 50% of males never talk to either parent about sex, whereas almost 30% of girls do not discuss it with their mothers and 60% do not discuss it with their fathers.

A study conducted by UNAM (National Autonomous University of Mexico) in the states of Chiapas, Guerrero, Puebla, Guanajuato, and San Luis Potosi summarized youths' perspectives on this issue, which are consistent with local research in other states of the country. The sample included over 15,000 youth between 13 and 19 years of age, 58% female and 42% male (Menkes, Suárez, Núñez, & González, 2006). Seventy-three percent of men and 66% of women did not use contraceptives the first time they had sexual intercourse despite being aware of their benefits, because the event was not planned. Eighty percent of those surveyed confirmed being knowledge-able about condoms, but only 50% of those who were sexually active claimed to use them. Ninety percent of those surveyed knew about birth control pills, but only 15% knew how and when to use them. The emergency pill was only somewhat familiar to 28% of those surveyed. 21% of the males and 5.5% of the females claimed to be sexually active. When asked who they had their first sexual experience with, they answered: Males: 51% with their girlfriend, 27% with a friend, 7% with a prostitute, 1% with their spouse or partner. Females: 80% with their boyfriend, 9% with a friend, 2% with a family member, 1% with their spouse or partner, 0% with a prostitute. Fifty percent of males claimed to have resorted to abortion, as had 23% of females. Thirty-six percent of males claimed that women should be virgins when they marry, and 80% of females felt the same way.

Some of these results confirm that adolescent sexual practices have little to do with knowledge. In practice, despite knowing about risks and being educated in condom use and that of other contraceptives, condom use continues to be low. These results were similar to those reproduced in various local studies performed in large urban areas (for example in Guadalajara, by Tello, 1998, and Martinez Ramirez, Villaseñor, & Celis de la Rosa, 2002). This inconsistency between knowledge and sexual practices extends to university students. Adolescent men are reported to feel uncomfortable talking about prevention methods with their friends and girlfriends, and consequently they rarely use contraceptives (Stern, Fuentes-Zurita, Lozano-Trevinòo, & Reynoso, 2003). This is consistent with the results of the National Youth Survey in 2005, where 36% of the youth who have sexual relations stated that they do not use contraceptive methods (ENJ, 2006).

Peer pressure among adolescent men with respect to having sex is common, and those who have not had sex are labeled as gay, the worst of insults for a male Mexican adolescent. The only way to disprove the insult is to engage in physical violence or sexual activity with a female (Gutmann 1994, 2000). Though the dominance of the Catholic Church dictates a general intoler-ance of homosexuality, there is a growing acceptance. Paradoxically, gay men are more accepted than lesbian women.

In 2008, 18% of births were to women under 20 years of age (INEGI, 2009). The National Youth Survey of 2005 found that 30% of the women between 14 and 29 years of age have been pregnant, and of those, 27% said that their pregnancy was before they were 18 years of age. It has been widely documented that teenage mothers, especially those under 18 years of age, experience greater health risks (Casanueva, Soberanis, Ortis, & Bobadilla, 1991; Langer & Romero, 1996) and their children are more vulnerable than the children of mothers 20 years and older living in the same socioeconomic conditions (Buvinic, Valenzuela, Molina, & Gonzalez, 1998; Escobedo, Fletes, & Velasquez, 1995; Stern, Rodiguez, & Pick, 1994). Unwanted pregnancies are a major social risk for both mother and child.

Health Risk Behavior

Mexican adolescents make up the healthiest group of the population despite the fact that they are exposed to the greatest number of risk situations (Celis de la Rosa, 2003; Stern & Medina, 2000). There is growing national concern about adolescent drug addiction and unprotected sexual activity. The latter concern is as much related to sexually transmitted infections (STIs) as to the high incidence of adolescent pregnancies. Another severe problem is the high mortality rate from accidents and violence.

As for adolescent tobacco and alcohol consumption, the mean age of starting these is between 15 and 17 years (ENJ, 2006). The National Health Survey indicates that 9% of adolescents between 10 and 19 years old claim to smoke (having smoked at least 100 cigarettes in their lifetime), while 42% of adolescents in this age range claim never to have smoked (Celis de la Rosa, 2003). The rest have tried smoking but have not smoked more than 100 cigarettes. Regional research reports that adolescents start smoking with friends, and their reasons for smoking are curiosity and a search for social acceptance and a sense of security. In contrast, 11% of adolescents from the same age range claim to have consumed alcohol, whereas 83% report never to have done so. In both types of consumption, the percentages increase with age, especially after 16 years of age (ENSA, 2000; Celis de la Rosa, 2003).

Mexico's level of illegal drug consumption is low when compared internationally, though it is on the rise (Medina Mora et al., 2003). Consumption is greater in urban areas and in the northern border cities. Drugs are most commonly obtained through illegal sales in parks and on the street. The National Survey on Addictions (CONADIC, 2002) found that about 2% of the population are adolescents who have used drugs at some time. Only 1% of youth between 12 and 17 years of age consumed marijuana, 0.04% consumed hallucinogens, 0.22% consumed cocaine, and other drugs or amphetamines were consumed by 0.13%. Adolescents who feel that they are social failures are more likely to consume drugs.

Another serious problem prevalent in adolescence is obesity. The National Health Survey of 2000 reported that this problem is more common among adolescent girls than boys. In fact, one-third of young Mexicans over 16 years of age are overweight (Celis de la Rosa, 2003), yet many suffer from nutritional problems because of the low nutritional value of the food that they consume, such as sweets, junk food, and fast food.

Automobile and other motor vehicle accidents are the leading cause of death among young men. Homicide is another leading cause of death in young men between 15 and 19 years of age. In contrast, the leading causes of death for young women of the same age range are related to pregnancy complications, especially while giving birth.

Education

In Mexico basic education consists of nine grades grouped into two stages: elementary school (six years) and secondary school (three years). Originally, only elementary school was compulsory. It was not until 1993 that secondary school also became compulsory as a result of national educational policies created in an effort to draw more attention to the needs of adolescent development. As part of these efforts, the public education system strove to serve more students.

Secondary school is followed by three years of high school or technical school. The latter prepares students who cannot afford to continue their education at the university level with a technical profession. Following a regular course of study, adolescents finish elementary school (sixth grade) at age 12, secondary school at age 15, and high school or technical courses at age 18.

The National Youth Survey of 2005 reported that 93% of adolescents between 12 and 14 years of age and 41% of 16- to 19-year olds attend school, but 24% leave school by age 15 (ENJ, 2006; INEGI, 2001). Despite efforts to improve public education on a national level in the last part of the twentieth century, the country faced a crisis at the turn of the 21st century, particularly at the secondary and high school levels. The attendance rates for elementary and secondary school are far below the expectations established by the National Education System. Of youth between 12 and 15 years, 17% have never attended a formal educational institution, for economic or family reasons. More than 25% of adolescents between 12 and 14 years do not finish elementary school (INEGI,

2001). About 48% discontinue their studies after elementary school, and 13% drop out before finishing secondary school. Among the reasons for abandoning school, 25% of students claim not to like school, and 21% claim they cannot afford it (ENJ, 2002).

The international study performed by PISA PLUS revealed that less than 7% of Mexican students in grades seven through nine can be defined as good readers. Forty-four percent fall into the category of poor readers, while 49% are on an intermediate level. Results in other areas of academic achievement are similar (Castillo, 2004). Despite the educational crisis, there has been an important change in the levels of education reached. The last few generations have surpassed their parents' levels of education; in some cases the average years of study have doubled (Perez Islas & Valdez Gonzalez, 2003).

There are important differences in access to education in urban and rural contexts. Most adolescents have more educational opportunities if they live in urban centers. Adolescent boys in rural communities are expected to assist their parents as they work in the fields or contribute to the family income in another way, whereas adolescent girls are expected to help with household chores and other tasks in the home. Many youth opt for leaving school in order to be able to fulfill their obligations to help provide for their family. This is similar for adolescents of rural origins that have relocated to the cities. Often such adolescents between 13 and 17 years of age drop out as early as elementary school (INEGI, 2001). The percentage of illiteracy (49%) among indigenous youth older than 15 is four times higher than the national average (Ehrenfeld-Lenkiewicz, 2003).

Marked differences in opportunities and life conditions between youth of varying socioeconomic backgrounds affect whether those youth continue studying in secondary school and high school. Ninety percent of middle-class youth between 15 and 19 years of age are in school compared with only 18% of poor youth.

Work

By law, Mexican youth cannot be employed until they are 14 years of age. At that point their possibilities are limited to age-appropriate jobs that guarantee conditions of safety and wellness and that do not require them to work later than 10:00 p.m. In order to obtain employment, they must prove that they are enrolled as secondary students and that they have their parents' permission. Despite these restrictions, the National Youth Survey of 2005 reported that 36% of youth started to work before they were 16 years old. Although it is difficult to define the number of adolescent workers due to the large number of informal work situations, a significant number of children work in the street, especially compared with more developed countries.

According to a national survey, the average working youth works about six hours daily, five or six days a week (DIF-UNICEF-PNUFID, 1999). Most begin working when they are between 15 and 19 years of age, though a significant number of adolescents (30%) start working between 12 and 14 or even younger. Most find work through family contacts or friends.

Initially, working adolescents combine their studies and their work. Data from the National Youth Survey of 2000 indicated that 86% of working adolescents between 12 and 14 years old continue studying, while only 62% of those between 15 and 19 continue. Youth who start working at an early age are more likely to quit school, most with their parents' permission, without having finished secondary school. This is especially true for females and adolescents from families with limited resources.

The National Youth Survey of 2000 also reported that the majority of working youth (81%) are satisfied or pleased with their work, because they recognize it as an opportunity to learn, see it as a positive environment, or realize that they are gaining experience. Those that are not satisfied with their work situation (16%) complain primarily of their low pay.

While middle-class and lower-class families expect their children to work to contribute to the family income or at least to help with their personal expenses such as school supplies, upper-middle- and upper-class families encourage their children to dedicate themselves exclusively to their studies. Work is generally not valued for the experience attained as part of one's development or civic education but for the monetary contribution it brings or as a responsibility equivalent to that of the adults of the family, which explains why it is only common among adolescents with limited resources.

Although education levels have increased in recent generations in Mexico, there has not been a corresponding increase in opportunities in the job market (Perez Islas & Valdez Gonzalez, 2003). For most of the population, it is clear that more years of education do not result in greater socio-economic mobility. Even though the influences of globalization dictate a need for higher education levels, there still does not exist a direct and positive relation between educational level and employment, income, or standard of living.

Due to an employment crisis since the 1980s and the perception that high education levels do not necessarily correspond to better work opportunities, many parents feel that the sooner their children start to work, the better, even when the jobs pay little or offer few opportunities for advancement. In addition, it is looked positively upon to have children who help with the parents' work, especially when the boys help the father and the girls help the mother. From an early age (9 to 10 years old), parents occasionally bring their children to observe them or help them with their work in the evening or on Saturdays, especially fathers who have service jobs (such as carpenters and plumbers) or their own small business, but not fathers with white-collar jobs. This practice serves children to start learning a trade. It also serves to keep them off the streets and out of trouble.

Media

TV is a central part of each family's living space, especially among the lower classes, who are more likely to have it on in the background, whether or not anyone is watching it (Orozco Gomez, 2005). Youth in Mexico City watch an average of two hours of TV per day, and those in the rest of the country watch 1.5 hours per day. Near the northern border, the average level of TV viewing is higher than in Mexico City (three hours daily—comparable with the average in the United States) (Flores, 2003). A study in the border city of Tijuana showed that young men tend to watch TV alone in their rooms, choosing their own programs, whereas young women tend to watch shows directed towards younger children as they care for their siblings. Both groups were found to prefer the humor of US programming to that of Mexican programming (Gonzalez Hernandez, 2004).

Mexico is noted for its high production and readership of comic books. It is more common for someone to buy a comic book than to buy a newspaper. Some trace this attraction to drawn images back to the original indigenous communities found in Mexico before the Spanish arrived (Del Rio Garcia, 2004; Doñan, 2004). Carlos Monsivais (1982), one of the few researchers that study Mexican comic books, explained that a paradox exists in that the country consumes the most comic books per citizen yet produces the comic books of the worst quality in the world. The Secretary of Public Education (SEP) attempted to build on this attraction to the comic book and increase interest in reading by making Mexico the first and possibly only country to distribute nationally a series of history books in the form of comic books, throughout the national public school system (Del Rio Garcia, 1983).

The National Youth Survey of 2000 reported that 77% of youth between 12 and 29 years old receive their news information exclusively from TV, 23% from the radio, and 12% from newspapers. Twelve percent have personal computers, and only 6% have access to the Internet (ENJ,

2002). Though many have computer and Internet access through school, a large portion of the population does not, especially considering that not all schools have electricity (Orozco Gomez, 2005). Yet the presence of the Internet is very important because it has globalized the news and opinions available, removing a great deal of the control the government formerly had over information and knowledge of political events (Schmidt, 2003).

Politics and Military

The majority of youth feel it is important to have a society that enforces and respects laws (76%), a statistic that is consistent with other findings that young Mexicans do not believe in their national justice system and they distrust politicians and the government in general. Thirty-seven percent indicate that it is very important to have a society free of delinquency, and 26% wish for a more democratic society. These views are easily explained by considering that Mexico was governed by a single, authoritarian political party for over 70 years.

One of the most important political changes in Mexican history occurred in the year 2000. Although it was a democracy, a single party (PRI) was in power for over 70 years. It was in the year 2000 that the opposing party (PAN) won the presidential election, creating hope that a government of change was taking over. The authoritarian governing style of PRI created general apathy in regard to political participation, a sentiment shared by adolescent groups. This was due in great part to another important historical event: the massacre of Tlatelolco in 1968, in which hundreds of student protestors were killed or imprisoned. As a result, generations of young adults have lost civic interest, which has been reflected in their decreased participation in protests and other forms of political participation. This is somewhat paradoxical considering that it was following 1968 and due to the influence of the student protests of that time that the voting age was reduced from 21 years to 18, greatly increasing the number of young voters in the country.

Though the participation of youth in the 2000 elections was significant, with almost 49% of voters between 18 and 25 years of age voting for PAN, in general young people are disappointed by the government and think it lacks credibility. They display a strong degree of apathy in relation to the politics of the country. This lack of interest was documented in the National Youth Survey of 2000. Of the respondents between the ages of 12 and 29, 18% claimed to be interested in politics, 52% were a little interested, and 26% were not at all interested. However, 51% believed that citizens can greatly influence political decisions, 36% said they can only a little, and 12% said they cannot at all. While 60% of youth between 12 and 29 years old believed that political elections can lead to a better government, they did not trust political parties because they felt that political parties do not represent the interests of the majority (Flores, 2003). Fifty-eight percent of adolescents between 15 and 19 years of age considered the country's most relevant problem to be poverty, followed by unemployment, corruption, lack of education, and violence.

For many decades, civic education has not been addressed formally either in schools or in other scenarios with high adolescent participation. In the educational system, a few topics are addressed to teach aspects of citizenship and politics, but adolescents become aware of and learn about political issues through the media more than they do through formal education. Thirty-six percent of adolescents between 15 and 19 years of age reported learning about politics through the media, while 22% reported learning at school, and another 22% learned from conversations with parents. Also, 34% of adolescents 15 to 19 years old reported learning about human rights from their parents, and 39% learned about them from school (ENJ, 2002).

In Mexico, 18-year-old men serve in the military for one year. However, this service only involves receiving military training once a week for a year. During that time and for several subsequent years, they remain registered as available in case of extreme military action. There are no corresponding obligations for women. Young people that choose to join the national army tend to be from economically disadvantaged families with few educational and employment opportunities.

Unique Issues

Mexico had a mix of cultural traditions long before the arrival of Spanish colonists, as indigenous groups competed for cultural and material dominance. The Spanish arrival had a strong homogenizing effect, creating a traditional society with authoritative and hierarchical forms of power both in politics and in family structure. This societal structure experienced accelerating changes over the second half of the twentieth century, due in great part to globalization but also to Mexico's location and situation as a developing country sharing a border with a very powerful developed country, the United States.

Mexico is considered young in terms of modern services provided to its citizens. For example, in the 1940s, health and education levels were very low. Life expectancy was 39 years and illiteracy was as high as 58%. Thirty-five percent of the population lived in the cities, and 65% lived in rural areas. By 1960, life expectancy had increased to 59 years, but illiteracy was still high at 67%, while 51% of the population lived in urban areas (Flores, 2003). Though life expectancy has continued to rise and literacy rates have finally increased, illiteracy is still high and the number of people moving out of rural areas has increased astronomically, due in great part to an agricultural crisis.

These changes have created a great deal of mobility as primarily men leave the home in search of work either in urban areas or in the United States. The money sent home from Mexican immigrants in the United States makes up the second largest national source of revenue after petroleum. Though most migrants plan to return after a few years, with increased security after 9/11 and worsening conditions in Mexico, most remain far from their homes, leaving many small towns without men. This has a significant effect on the lives of Mexican adolescents. They are greatly influenced by what they learn about the north from migrants, the media, and tourists, or they migrate themselves. The influence is especially pronounced along the border.

Mexico is considered a developing country, yet it had the tenth highest Gross Domestic Product in the world in 2003 and the fifteenth highest in 2009. Though far behind its northern neighbor, with USD875 billion in 2009 compared to the United States's USD14 trillion, it is second in terms of Latin-American countries, with Brazil ahead of Mexico in ninth position. Disenfranchised families migrate north from Central America to Mexico in search of better opportunities, just as Mexicans migrate to the United States.

References and Further Reading

Alcalá, L., Rogoff, B., Mejía-Arauz, R., Coppens, A. D., & Roberts, A. (2011). *Children's contributions to family work: Cultural differences within Mexico*. Manuscript in preparation.

Alfaro Martinez, M. L. B. (1992). *Actitudes y conocimientos hacia la sexualidad y SIDA en estudiantes de preparatoria* (Vol. 4). Mexico City, Mexico: Asociación Mexicana de Psicología Social.

Andrade Palos, P., Pick de Weiss, S., & Alvarez Izazaga, M. (1990). Percepción que los hijos tienen de las actitudes de sus padres hacia su sexualidad y autoconcepto de adolescentes que han y no han tenido relaciones sexuales. *La psicología social en México* (Vol. 3). Mexico City, Mexico: Asociación Mexicana de Psicología.

Bertely Busquets, M. (Ed.). (2003). Educación, derechos sociales y equidad. In *La investigación educativa en México* (pp. 3–238). Mexico City, Mexico: COMIE.

Buvinic, M., Valenzuela, J. P., Molina, T., & Gonzalez, E. (1998). La suerte de las madres adolescentes y sus hijos: La transmisión de la pobreza en Santiago de Chile. In B. Schmukler (Ed.), *Familias y relaciones de genero en transformación* (pp. 451–492). Mexico City, Mexico: Population Council, Edamex.

Casanueva, E., Soberanis, T. Ortis, A., & Bobadilla, M. A. (1991). Cambios en la composición corporal en el periodo perinatal en un grupo de adolescentes. *Perinatologia y Reproducción Humana*, 5, 28–32.

Castillo, M. A. (2004). La crisis en secundaria. Una crisis de desarrollo social. Observatorio Ciudadano de la Educación. Mexico City, Mexico: OCE.

Celis de la Rosa, A. (2003). La salud de adolescentes en cifras. *Salud pública de Mexico*, 45, 153–166.

CONADIC. (2002). *Encuesta Nacional de Adicciones, 2002*. Mexico City, Mexico: Secretaria de Salud, Instituto Nacional de Psiquiatría, Consejo Nacional contra las Adicciones.

Del Rio Garcia, E. (1983). *La Vida de Cuadritos, Guía Incompleta de la historieta*. Mexico City, Mexico: Grijalbo.

Del Rio Garcia, E. (2004). *Los Moneros de México*. Mexico City, Mexico: Grijalbo.

Díaz-Loving, R. (1993). Personalidad: Hallazgos para una psicología cultural. *Revista de Psicología Social y Personalidad, IX, 2, 21-36*.

DIF-UNICEF-PNUFID. (1999). Informe ejecutivo del estudio de niñas, niños y adolescentes trabajadores en 100 ciudades. Mexico City, Mexico: DIF-UNICEF-PNUFID.

Doñan, J. J. (2004). Explosión monográfica. In *El Libro Monero, Crónica del birote y su arrimón a las letras*. Mexico City, Mexico: Universidad de Guadalajara/Editorial Universitaria, Instituto Tecnológico y de Estudios Superiores de Occidente, Secretaria de Cultura, Jalisco.

Ehrenfeld-Lenkiewicz, N. (2003). Los jóvenes y la familias. Encuentros y tensiones entre filiaciones e identidades. In J. A. Perez Islas et al. (Eds.), *Nuevas miradas sobre los jóvenes*. Mexico City, Mexico: INJ.

Encuesta Nacional de Juventud (ENJ). (2002). *2000 Resultados Generales*. Mexico City, Mexico: Secretaría de Educación Pública, Instituto Mexicano de la Juventud, Centro de Investigación y Estudios sobre Juventud.

Encuesta Nacional de Juventud (ENJ). (2006). *Encuesta Nacional de la Juventud 2005. Jóvenes Mexicanos Tomos I y II*. Mexico City, Mexico: Secretaría de Educación Pública, Instituto Mexicano de la Juventud, Centro de Investigación y Estudios sobre Juventud. Retrieved from http://cendoc.imjuventud.gob.mx

ENSA (Encuesta Nacional de Salud). (2000). Secretaria de Salud, Instituto Nacional de Salud Pública. Mexico. Retrieved from www.insp.mx

Escobedo, E., Fletes, J. & Velasquez, V. (1995). Embarazo en adolescentes: seguimiento de sus hijos durante el primer año de vida. *Boletín Médico Hospital Infantil de México*, 52, 415–419.

Flores, J. I. (2003). De apuestas, ganancias y pérdidas. Valores y creencias juveniles. In J. A. Perez Islas (Ed.), *Nuevas miradas sobre los jóvenes*. Mexico City, Mexico: INJ.

Gonzalez Hernandez, D. 2004. *El sueño americano en México: Televisión estadounidense y audiencias juveniles en Tijuana*. Master's thesis, ITESO, Guadalajara, Jalisco, Mexico.

Guía para el trabajo de menores en México. Retrieved from www.naalc.org

Gutmann, M. C. (1994). Los hijos de Lewis: La sensibilidad antropológica y el caso de los pobres machos. *Alteridades, 4*, 9–19.

Gutmann, M. C. (2000). *Ser Hombre de verdad en la Ciudad de México. Ni macho ni mandilón*. Mexico City, Mexico: El Colegio de México.

INEE. (2003). La calidad de la educación básica en México. Primer informe anual. Retrieved from http://capacitacion.ilce.edu.mx

INEGI. (2001). *XII Censo general de población y vivienda, 2000. Tabulados básicos. Aguascalientes, Ags*. Mexico Ciy, Mexico: INEGI.

INEGI. (2005). *Conteo de Población y vivienda 2005*. Mexico City, Mexico: INEGI.

INEGI. (2009). *Estadísticas demográficas 2008*. Mexico City, Mexico: Instituto Nacional de Estadística y Geografía.

Langer, A., & Romero, M. (Eds.). (1996). El embarazo, el parto y el puerperio. ¿Bajo qué condiciones se reproducen las mujeres en México? (pp. 13–39). Mexico City, Mexico: The Population Council.

Martinez Ramirez, M., Villaseñor Farías, M., & Celis de la Rosa, A. (2002). El condón masculino y su eficacia. Información y creencias en adolescentes escolares. *Revista Medica, IMSS, 40*, 35–41.

Medina Mora, M. E., Cravioto, P., Villatoro, J., Fleiz, C., Galvan Castillo, F., & Tapia Conyer, R. (2003). Consumo de drogas entre adolescentes: Resultados de la Encuesta Nacional de Adicciones. *Salud Pública de Mexico, 45*, 16–25.

Menkes, C., Suárez, L., Núñez, L., & González, S. (2006). *La salud reproductiva de los estudiantes de educación secundaria y media superior de Chiapas, Guanajuato, Guerrero, Puebla y San Luis Potosí*. Cuernavaca, Mexico: UNAM, Centro Regional de Investigaciones Multidisciplinarias.

Monsivais, C. (1982). *Y todo el mundo dijo "gulp". Notas en torno a los comics. El comic es algo serio*. Mexico City, Mexico: Eufesa.

Muñoz Izquierdo, C. (2001). Implicaciones de la escolaridad en la calidad del empleo. In E. Pieck (Ed.), *Los jóvenes y el trabajo. La educación frente a la exclusión social*. Mexico City, Mexico: Cinterfor. Retrieved from www.cinterfor.org

Necoechea, G. (2003). Los jóvenes a la vuelta del siglo. In J. A. Perez Islas et al. (Eds.), *Nuevas miradas sobre los jovenes*. Mexico City, Mexico: INJ.

Orozco Gomez, G. (2005). *Televisión, audiencias y educación*. Mexico City, Mexico: Norma.

Perez Islas, J. A., & Valdez Gonzalez, M. (2003). La juventud en México: Nomadismos en fuga. In J. A. Perez Islas et al. (Eds.), *Nuevas miradas sobre los jóvenes*. Mexico City, Mexico: INJ.

Pick, S. S. (1997). Los efectos indeseables de una educación autoritaria. *La Jornada*. Retrieved from www.jornada.unam.mx

Pick, S. S. (2002). *Educación Sexual, Educación para la Vida*. Conferencia impartida en la clausura del diplomado en formación de educadores en sexualidad humana. ITESO, Mexico.

Schmidt, S. (2003). *Los grandes problemas nacionales: Versión siglo XXI*. Mexico City, Mexico: Aguilar.

Sistema educativo de los Estados Unidos Mexicanos. (2004). *Principales cifras ciclo escolar 2003–2004*. Mexico City, Mexico: SEP. Retrieved from www.sep.gob.mx

Stern, C., Fuentes-Zurita, C., Lozano-Trevinòo, L. R., & Reynoso, F. (2003). Masculinidad y salud sexual y reproductiva: un estudio de caso con adolescentes de la Ciudad de México. *Salud Pública de México, 45*, 34–43.

Stern, C., & Medina, G. (2000). Adolescencia y Salud en México. In M. C. Oliveira (Ed.), *Cultura, adolescencia e saude: Argentina, Brasil, e Mexico* (pp. 98–160). Campinas, Brazil: Consorcio de programas em Saude Reprodutiva e Sexualidade na America latina.

Stern, C., Rodriguez, G., & Pick, S. (1994). *Jóvenes, sexualidad, salud y embarazo adolescente*. Mexico City, Mexico: El Colegio de México.

Tello, C. (1998). *Reportes de investigacion de la práctica de la Educación Sexual*. Unpublished manuscript, Instituto Tecnológico y de Estudios Superiores de Occidente, Guadalajara, Jalisco, México.

Urteaga, M. (2004). Imágenes juveniles del México moderno. In J. A. Perez Islas & M. Urteaga (Eds.), *Historias de los jóvenes en México* (pp. 33–89). Mexico City, Mexico: Instituto Nacional de la Juventud.

Valdez Medina, J. L. (2003). Los valores éticos en adolescentes mexicanos (Ethical values in Mexican adolescents). *Enseñanza e investigación en psicología, 8*, 245–255.

Villaseñor Farías, M. (2003). *¿Qué sabemos de la perspectiva que las y los adolescentes tienen sobre la sexualidad y sobre la educación sexual que reciben?* Ponencia presentada en el seminario Adolescentes en México: estrategias para mejorar su salud sexual y reproductiva, El Colegio de México.

Villaseñor Farías, M., & Castañeda, T. J. (2002). Significados de la violencia sexual en adolescentes, zona metropolitana de Guadalajara. In C. B. Rasmussen & A. Hidalgo (Eds.), *Investigaciones en salud de adolescentes* (pp. 79–84). Guadalajara, Mexico: UIESSA-IMSS/OPSOMSM.

Villaseñor Farias, M., & Martinez, R. A. (2002). Analisis de texto de la autopercepción de adolescentes sobre sus cualidades y defectos. In C. B. Rasmussen & A. Hidalgo (Eds.), *Investigaciones en salud de adolescentes* (pp. 169–174). Guadalajara, Mexico: UIESSA-IMSS/OPS-OMS.

Welti, C. (2003). ¡Quiero contigo! Las generaciones de jóvenes y el sexo. In J. A. Perez Islas et al. (Eds.), *Nuevas miradas sobre los jóvenes*. Mexico City, Mexico: INJ.

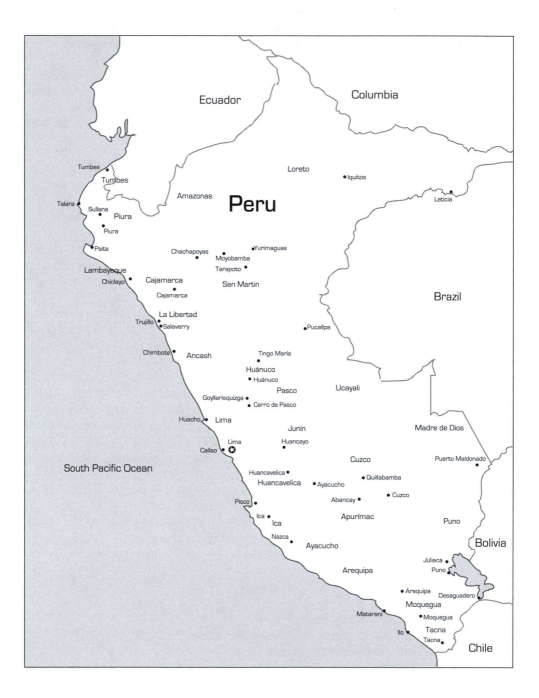

Chapter 15
Peru
Juana Pinzas

Background Information

Peru is the third largest nation in South America, with territory of over a million square kilometers including 200 miles of territorial sea in the Pacific Ocean. Geography divides the country into three land regions: the long and narrow coastline of deserts and valleys, the highlands (the Andes Mountains), and the tropical rainforest of the Amazon River basin. Eighty climates, nine ecological regions, and numerous unidentified fauna and flora illustrate Peru's unique biological diversity.

Census figures from 2007 show that over 28 million inhabitants are distributed among the coast (55%), highlands (32%), and jungle (13%). The capital city, Lima, has 31% of the country's population. Official languages are Spanish and Quechua. Aymara and numerous dialects are also spoken, for example in the jungle, where there are 65 ethnic groups.

A democratic republic, Peru is governed by a president and 120 congress members. Since the 1990s it has had a free-market economy which has shown impressive annual growth: It grew 9% in the years 2007 and 2008. In 2009 there was a decline of 1% in the economy in association with the world economic recession (www.bcrp.gob.pe). However, the expected economic growth for the coming years is 5% to 6%. Mining, services, and agro-industry render a per-capita annual income of USD19,150; 35% of Peruvians live in poverty, and 12% in extreme poverty.

The center of the Inca Empire (c. 1230), Peru was conquered by Spain and dominated by the Spaniards for almost 300 years. It became independent in 1821. From the early 1980s until 1995, two terrorist groups were active initially in the Andes, then spreading to the jungle and coastal towns and cities. The larger of these was a Maoist terrorist group known as *Sendero Luminoso* (Shining Path). The actions of these groups were geared towards destroying the democratic government and starting a communist regime. Their activities, especially those of Shining Path, seriously affected the life of all Peruvians, and especially children and adolescents. After incursions and battles in which whole towns were destroyed and their inhabitants were killed, large areas of Andean territories were declared "freed" and became Shining Path settlements, outside the scope of military intervention. On the coast, especially in Lima, numerous bombs exploded every night in different places, including large car bombs.

Months of blackouts, lack of energy and minimal water supply, and strong-armed military surveillance on the streets made daily life a difficult and even dangerous enterprise. Curfews and regulations, as well as fear of Shining Path's actions, made it almost impossible for young people to socialize, work, gather, or stay out. There was overall scarcity of almost everything, especially food. As a result of Shining Path and the military battle against it, an estimated 75,000 people were killed (Comisión de la Verdad y la Reconciliación, www.cverdad.org.pe), hundreds of villages were destroyed, large numbers of children and adolescents fled from the Andes to the coast, escaping Shining Path s forceful recruitment, and numerous Andean children were left orphans after witnessing the massive killing of kin and villagers.

Period of Adolescence

Recognition of adolescence as a separate life stage varies markedly with geographic location, socio-economic status, ethnic group, and whether the region is rural or urban. Westernized urban areas along the coastline clearly recognize an adolescent stage, while in the native communities (highlands) there is no recognized transition period between childhood and adulthood.

In the cities, the perception of adolescence is influenced by Western views. Public opinion, parents, and teachers consider adolescence as a difficult transition from childhood to adulthood, a stage of potential crisis and rebelliousness, a period of turbulence, and a time of struggle to become independent from parents. Adolescents socialize in the neighborhoods, malls, or small shopping areas; they show a need for privacy; and more hours are spent with friends and fewer with the family.

In the Westernized urban culture, adolescence starts around the age of 12 and extends until 18 or 20. The beginning of adulthood has also changed significantly. Youngsters are constantly looking for jobs, or they are working hard to keep their jobs. The last high school years (around the ages of 14 to 17) are a period of great pressure. At that early age, urban Peruvian adolescents have to choose their future career, choose the higher education institution to apply to (if they will be continuing their education), and find a job to pay for their expenses. Higher education is costly, unemployment is high, and adolescents struggle with the pressures of family traditions, their own professional interests, and the marketplace for employment.

Urban Peruvian adolescents do not have much time to invest in reflecting about themselves, systematically practicing sports, traveling, or developing hobbies—all of the experiences that would help them learn about who they are and what they would like to do with their lives. Most of them work and study. Upper-class urban adolescents live in a different situation and often go to study abroad.

In the Andes, adolescence does not exist as a separate stage of life. Children start working with their parents when they are around five, taking care of cattle and helping during planting and harvesting seasons. They learn to weave, fish, carry water, and help in many chores. Instead of developing from childhood into adolescence, there is a passage from childhood to adulthood. This passage happens around the age of 15 for girls and around the age of 17 for boys. At this time, they are expected to find a wife or husband and establish life as a couple. Hence, the rites of passage from childhood to adulthood are almost always linked to choosing a partner (Norma Fuller, personal communication). The highlands' carnivals are rituals of choosing a partner. Boys demonstrate skills, courage, and strength by dancing, while girls dance around flirting and watching.

In the jungle areas, both urban and rural, there is a short period of adolescence. It starts and ends earlier than in other regions of the country. Jungle female adolescents develop physically faster and are regarded as sexually much more active than highlanders and coastal inhabitants. They have their first child quite early: expectations are that by the age of 18 they will have at least one child.

Beliefs

Peru is mostly a Catholic country. However, in recent years, a number of smaller religious groups have proliferated, especially among the poor.

The Andean culture, based on community work and collectivism, has resisted the impact of external forces. In the Andean areas, ancestral traditions inherited from Inca times have gone through a process of synthesis with religious rites brought by the Spaniards in the sixteenth century. Young people participate in communal activities such as planting and harvesting and school or road building. They are also actively involved in religious processions, communal fiestas, carnivals, and celebrations. These are so deeply rooted in the youngsters that when they migrate to the capital or coastal cities, they go back to their homeland to join their communities in times of celebration.

Much of this was disrupted by Shining Path. Its communist ideology did not allow religious celebrations; young boys were taken away from their families and communities and forced to join the terrorist movement. Though cohesiveness and self-protection (self-defense groups) in these communities grew stronger, there was an increase in adolescents migrating to cities, fleeing from terrorism. Large groups of adolescents in southern Peru lost parents and kin who were killed by terrorists during "cleaning" operations, revenge missions, or night attacks.

Gender

In the traditional Peruvian view of gender, men and women are seen as inherently different. Male and female roles are taught from very early childhood and educational systems may discriminate against female children and adolescents. In a context of extremely poor schooling that yields youngsters who exhibit reading comprehension levels below the level expected, girls have even less educational opportunity than boys, especially in the extremely poor groups. Many more boys attend school in the highlands, because girls are in charge of household chores and younger siblings. Urban and rural working-class fathers may decide to stop sending their daughters to school because they have started to menstruate and there is fear of rape on the way to or from school. Or they anticipate a possible love relationship with a classmate that could lead to pregnancy. Menstruation may become an embarrassment for female adolescents when schools have no bathrooms, or bathrooms for both boys and girls, or bathrooms that are lacking doors. These girls do not find a place to wash the cloth towels they use or to throw away sanitary pads, and may be absent during menstruation periods. Peruvian women account for 70% of all illiterates in the country.

A Peruvian peasant male learns that he should be the provider and the head of the family. He will represent the family in public and will be responsible for its social behavior. Thus, he learns to be in charge of the economic, social, political, and moral order in his family and in the community in general. To fulfill these obligations, he is taught to be strong and independent. His wife is taught to respectfully listen to her husband, the family authority. She learns that her main function in life is to become a wife and a mother. Her goal is serving others: her husband, her children, her parents, and the community. She learns to be dependent, obedient, and available at all times. She also learns that her husband will often be violent with her, and this a sign that she is not his equal.

In urban middle-class and upper-class traditional families, when preparing for the baby's arrival, pink and flowers are for baby girls, light blue and cars are for baby boys. Extended families will celebrate the delivery of a baby boy, especially if he is the first one. In nursery and elementary schools, trucks, airplanes, and dinosaurs are toys for boys. Dolls, ponies, pretend kitchen utensils and pretend food are for girls. Rangers and firefighters are costumes for boys; brides and princesses are costumes for girls. Children's books and school texts portray a nuclear family in which the father works outside the house while mother stays home taking care of children and chores. The male partner is the breadwinner. The mother is responsible for supervising appropriate schooling, cleanliness, and healthy food.

However, the socioeconomic situation of middle-class and working-class Peruvians has forced men and women to change their views about gender roles. Many female adolescents, young adults, and mothers now work outside the house or at home. Working mothers on an eight-hour day are now common. Working-class women also do productive activities which generate additional income, such as working in the informal or black market as street vendors, in small booths or informal shops. Since men rarely assume domestic responsibilities with their babies and children, women have a larger workload. This is expressed as a "double" or "triple" working day. The load for women has lately increased as a result of the increased male migration, family disintegration, the increasing number of girls attending schools, and the longer lives of the elderly, who need someone to take care of them.

Professional women, who work as lawyers, architects, psychologists, or business entrepreneurs, face a number of stressors related to satisfying family, job, and marriage demands, as well as personal needs. However, an important change is noticeable in young couples having children in the early twenty-first century. Husbands are beginning to assume responsibilities in taking care of newborns or small children. Older male adolescents and young adults are beginning to work in jobs in which they take care of or teach small children in play groups, after-school activities, and sports.

The Self

In general, urban upper-class and middle-class Peruvian adolescents take longer to mature and become independent compared to many other cultures. This may be largely due to the type of upbringing and education they receive. Parents tend to regard childhood as a period in which children are to play, attend school, and study, while relatives or maids clean up after them and take care of their needs for food, clothing, and personal things.

Prejudice is a strong component of Peruvian society, and there are barriers to friendships that cut across social class or ethnic differences. Among men, this may be lessened due to the kinds of friendships that arise from sports such as football (soccer), the nation's passion, which may bring diverse people together. Music, cuisine, and art are channels of communication across ethnic and socioeconomic differences.

Urban youth culture is very distinct. The influence of Western society shows in the popular clothing of jeans, t-shirts, and sneakers, as well as the popular hairstyles. Tattooing and piercing have a strong presence, especially among working-class and migrant youth, who search for ways of adjusting to and adopting urban styles from North America and the UK. Perhaps adolescent language is the most outstanding component of youth culture for traditional Peru. Slang includes foul language and numerous aggressive terms, which are used quite casually.

Indigenous adolescents do not exhibit these traits. They continue to speak mostly Quechua or dialects, and they are initiated in Spanish due to Spanish-speaking demands in their communities and then later in their schools. However, one sees a tendency to combine their regional outfits with Western dress, including polleras (several large and wide skirts one on top of the other), t-shirts, and rubber sandals.

Family Relationships

In the middle and working classes, Peruvian youngsters, both male and female, highly value family life, and Sundays may be sacred days in which lunch with the extended family is a pleasant obligation. Male and female youngsters live with their extended family or parents until they get married—and sometimes even afterwards—and their whole life if they do not marry. It is quite normal to find 30-year-old men and women living in the parents' household, often contributing to the family's income. The high cost of living has made this even more common. It is uncommon for an older adolescent or young adult to leave the parents' house and live independently alone or with friends. In the upper class and upper middle class, however, these views of family life and daily closeness are slowly changing. Some people aged 21 and over may move out to live with peers, friends, or a boyfriend or girlfriend. These choices are seen as a desire for independence, a desire to live a different style of life, or "modern deviations" from the normal course of events and are not easily accepted.

Andean and migrant families are mostly patriarchal and develop around an older person, usually the grandfather. Weekend gatherings with the grandparents are a family ritual in which adolescents are expected to participate. Parents show up proudly with their sons and also with their daughters.

In the jungle, families are immersed in the native community; one could say all families in a town or community make one large family, and adolescents have specific roles every day. They are prepared for and taught fishing, agriculture, cooking, and weaving. Leisure and entertainment are minimal.

In the coastal urban areas, the patriarchal and "macho" family culture is still present, even among educated Peruvians. The father is the main authority in the house and the last word in decision-making. He will choose rewards and punishments, and the wife will be his adviser, or the family's emotional/affective support. However, the behavior of families and adolescents has been changing radically. The change shows in three aspects: (1) There may be a role-reversal (caused by the large number of middle-aged men who have lost their jobs or are called to early retirement), so men stay home taking care of the house and children, while the wife continues or starts to work outside the home and becomes the breadwinner; (2) in order to make a living according to their needs or lifestyle expectations, both parents work outside the home on demanding full-time jobs, leaving the house chores and care of the children to older children, grandparents or, quite often, maids (usually semi-literate); (3) in association with parental absence, peer pressure and strong Western influences, adolescent participation in family life, responsibilities and chores is in the process of decreasing notably in some groups and may tend to be limited to joining in celebrating family events, anniversaries, birthdays, or religious holidays.

Generational conflicts usually arise in relatively poor urban areas since opportunities to socialize and have a good time with peers or new friends (concerts, malls, discotheques, clubs, computer games, bars, and entertainment shops) stimulate adolescent curiosity and experimentation. This means extending the number of hours spent outside the home, learning slang, changing their looks and habits, and spending a large part of the night out. The "neighborhood" as a safe socialization space is in the process of disappearing. Internet use is widespread through "booths" rented for USD0.30 per hour. If the adolescents' friends and their backgrounds (especially if they are virtual) are new or unknown to the family, this leads to tension with parents who fear the experimentation and its consequences (i.e., drugs, sex, pregnancy, alcohol, coping with gangs) and would rather have their adolescent son or daughter socialize with peers from families they know or who appear to have less risky habits.

Even considering these changing patterns in some parts of the country, family is a very important social institution for all social classes in Peru. Most social institutions in Peru are weak; they do not fulfill their roles or may even be somewhat dysfunctional. This is the case with the police system, the justice system, and the public health system; families make up the only nonreligious social institution that can be trusted; relatives and family friends are the only ones who will help out when a problem arises.

In general, adolescents are expected to respect and help their parents and elderly. It is expected that they will accompany parents to gatherings with kin and attend mass on Sundays or religious events with the family. It is expected that they will spend time with the family and participate in family life. By tradition, boys are raised to follow the father's professional path, technical skills, or business interests. Mothers are more the affective component in the family and regard daughters as future company who, when married, will pull their husbands into the family, while fathers are the stronger authority figures. In working-class families the father can be an absent figure, while the mother is in charge. She may have several relationships in her life and children from different men. Many couples cohabit, even having several children. Divorce is much more accepted than before, so divorced women do not carry the stigma they used to.

Friends and Peers/Youth Culture

The time adolescents spend with their peers varies greatly among social classes in Peru. In the families in "new neighborhoods" surrounding coastal cities (in the past called shantytowns or slum areas), both parents struggle daily to earn a living by working from very early in the morning until late at night. Adolescents, children, and babies are left under the care of a young relative or neighbor. Adolescents in these peripheral districts spend a large number of hours with peers, unsupervised and with not much to do. Institutions that may provide healthy leisure opportunities or hobbies, such as sports areas or training, music classes, libraries, film clubs, artisanship, and so forth, are practically non-existent. They have developed a local adolescent culture different from all other cultures in the country. Already confident about their identity as urban inhabitants and able to speak Spanish and slang fluently, descendants from migrating families (second or third generation) mix their urban learning with the parental culture.

Adolescent music preferences and bands from these neighborhoods show the influence of their parents' homeland and the Western culture they have found in the city. Massive weekend concerts in these new urban areas play "chicha," salsa, and tropical music. Alcohol use is a must; drinking is considerable. Discotheques are numerous and usually crowded. In some districts, adolescents may also actively participate in gatherings that are not always for music and drinking; violent gangs develop. Drug use has been detected in these groups, especially cheap and highly toxic substances in combination with alcoholic drinks. This situation generates a complex combination of vandalism, public display of violence, fights between gangs and crime. Some districts are well known as dangerous areas where gangs may rob or assault individuals, so families live in fear and lock themselves up in the early evening.

Adolescents and youngsters from new neighborhoods also join the *barras bravas*—groups of fanatical followers of the most popular football teams. Usually, around five hours prior to a game, they gather in special meeting points and move together toward the stadium. At the end of the game, these *barras* walk back to their neighborhoods, committing acts of vandalism. Their extreme behaviors may be regarded as an expression of social psychopathology in a context of severe poverty, lack of educational and recreational opportunities and facilities, and unemployment.

Urban middle-class adolescents may display a very different behavior. A few may get together in marginal groups and display their differences in terms of hairstyles, tattoos, piercings, or clothing (i.e., black). They develop their own music and music groups, usually rock, heavy rock, or Latin-American. There are other groups which have an intense university life and spend the day outside their home with peers, attending classes, studying in the university's library or in study groups, going to the movies, theater, parties, and bars or discotheques. These older groups of adolescents also exhibit use of alcoholic drinks (namely beer). If there is drug use, it is mostly marijuana; hard drugs are less common but may also be present.

Urban upper-class adolescents have many more opportunities to interact with members of their social group than with adolescents from a different social status, since their parents are close friends, come from the same private schools in Lima, work in the same or similar companies/banks or are part of a network of extended kin. Groups of adolescents in this closed socioeconomic group normally gather in their summer beach houses or winter houses in very small neighborhoods, have specific interests (i.e., bullfights, polo, snow and water skiing, yachting, horse-back-riding, tennis), attend parties with high surveillance, move around to clubs and exclusive discotheques with drivers/chauffeurs and/or bodyguards. "Raves" (tech music) are very popular among them: alcohol, marijuana, and Ecstasy may be common in these events. These adolescents share a taste for North American and European music more than for Peruvian music, and it is common for boys and girls to develop Western-style friendships/romantic relationships.

Love and Sexuality

While the age of reaching puberty is decreasing in Westernized urban areas, the median marriage age is increasing in association with a desire for higher education or higher living standards. Thus, a number of adolescents are sexually active before marriage and are at risk for undesired pregnancy. It is estimated that 8% of women have their first sexual intercourse before the age of 15. Virginity is less valued than in prior times, and for many women it may no longer be an important component of their attractiveness,

Affectionate and lively, the fast-paced, coastal adolescents from the north love flirting, singing, and dancing (marinera, waltzes, and local romantic music). In the jungle, adolescents have a relaxed, easy-going, slow-paced lifestyle; flirting involves a sense of humor with sexual connotations, jovial heterosexual friendships, and plenty of loud tropical music. There is a higher rate of girls with early sexual initiation in the jungle, especially in its rural areas (José Carlos Vera, personal communication). It is a common assumption in Peru that jungle women are jovial, more open, very attractive, take initiatives and relate to men as equals. In south and southeastern Peru, the situation is different: Adolescents interact less than in other parts of the country. However, during communal activities, community events, or when participating in religious celebrations, there is intense social interaction between genders while dancing continually over several consecutive days, wearing elaborate costumes. It is well known that these are days of heavy drinking for all, and that sexual initiation or choice of a partner may take place. In these activities flute, harp, guitars, charangos (small guitars), and zampoñas (several flutes attached together) play music. Depending on the part of the highlands, bands and musicians render happy, sad, or deeply moving music that reflects the earthly loneliness of quiet and isolated peasant communities in the Andes.

Consensual cohabitation is a common and well accepted practice in the Andes. In Peru, poverty, education and/or culture seem to be the main factors that determine consensual cohabitation instead of marriage.

The meaning of adolescent pregnancy varies with each culture. In some regions it is socially accepted and may happen within cohabitation or marriage. However, in other regions it is perceived as a social and personal problem or stigma, since motherhood interferes with an adolescent's plans for the future (education, economic prosperity) and being a single mother is not widely accepted.

In Peru, 16% of women become mothers before turning 20 years old. Most adolescent pregnancies happen during the last years of adolescence: Pregnancy rates at 18 to 19 years of age are twice as high as the rates among 15- to 17-year-olds (ENAHO, 1998). In rural areas, one in every four women becomes a mother between 15 and 19 years of age, compared to one in 10 in urban areas. Jungle and highland adolescents have a higher probability of having a child before turning 20 compared to adolescents from urban Lima and the rest of the coast. Across all geographical, cultural, and ethnic differences, poorer adolescents have a higher probability of becoming pregnant.

The prevalence of sexually transmitted diseases is high in adolescent females. In a study carried out by the Ministry of Health in the Program for Control of Sexually Transmitted Diseases and AIDS (2000, unpublished data) it was found that prevalence of cervical infection by chlamydia in sexually active women younger than 20 was 26%, while it was 9% in women older than 20.

Depending on where they live, adolescent females may have more or less access to knowledge of and options for birth control. Limited or lacking access is largely due to social and religious beliefs that consider birth control a form of abortion, as well as economic and geographical barriers that make it difficult to reach certain distant areas. In general, there is poor knowledge on contraceptive methods as well as where to get them (Population Reference Bureau, 1996).

According to the 2004 Encuesta Demografica y de Salud Familiar, in the age group 15–19, 57% of females use some type of contraceptive method, 41% of them preferring modern methods. The pill is used by 12%, intra-uterine contraceptives are used by 2%, 19% use injections, and 7% use condoms. Fifteen percent use traditional methods such as periodic abstinence (12%), penis withdrawal (2.9%), and folkloric or herbal methods. Among females aged 20–24, 71% use contraceptives; 51% prefer the modern ones and 19% choose traditional methods. Interestingly, 14% use periodic abstinence, and 5% use penis withdrawal. (www.comunidadsaludable.org).

Health Risk Behavior

The context in which Peruvian urban adolescents socialize and entertain after the age of 15 frequently includes some use of drugs: tobacco, beer, and alcoholic drinks in general. Very recently laws have been passed regarding age requirements to buy or use alcoholic drinks. However, these drinks are sold to buyers of any age, usually in the belief (or excuse) that they are not buying for themselves. In fact, some parents may not see any problem in sending their children or adolescent sons or daughters to buy alcoholic drinks, and the children do not see it as something unusual or wrong. Only recently, with the large numbers of adolescents who have started beer drinking and smoking at the early age of 12, has public opinion started voicing alarm and forced authorities to take a stand.

From 15 years onwards, adolescents in urban Lima often use alcoholic drinks, and parties may include them as a norm. Smoking is common, and marijuana has become acceptable almost everywhere, especially after 15 or 16 years of age. Marijuana is privately shared by groups at parties of young adults and older adolescents and at concerts, but not all adolescents try or experiment with it. Cocaine use has grown, perhaps in association with the increase in drug dealing and cocaine production in the country. Use of psychoactive drugs has become part of the habit of large segments of Peruvian society. Many adolescents experiment with and are occasional users of such substances.

In association with very poor reading and writing, extreme poverty, continued unemployment, limited access to educational opportunities, and lack of sports or recreational facilities, inexpensive and highly toxic drugs are used in marginal new neighborhoods. Gangs use drugs in combination with alcoholic drinks and exhibit alarmingly aggressive behaviors. They go to nearby neighborhoods to steal from shops and houses and attack people they meet. According to the Direccion Nacional de Policia there are 410 gangs involving youngsters aged 13 to 21. These gangs have become a serious national problem and are growing in the degree of their delinquent behaviors, even having contacts with foreign gangs.

Education

The public secondary school system in Peru is coeducational and offers six years of compulsory education. Students tend to be rather young, starting around the age of 11 and finishing when 16 or 17. Part of the curriculum is national and mandatory, and part is to be designed and determined by regional authorities in accordance with their communities' characteristics and needs.

Considerable attention has been given to improving the quality of the educational system. Results have not been as positive as expected, in large part due to the complexity of a country as diverse as Peru, with enormous geographical barriers, mostly emergent bilingualism, functional literacy, and a budget assigned to education that remains lower than the Latin-American average. These are some relevant findings that illustrate the problems to be faced: One in five adolescents leaves school before completing elementary education, and one in five adolescents is still in elementary school because she or he enrolled late or failed one or more grades (UNICEF, 2003). Among all students entering high school, only about 20% graduate (Pinzás, 2003).

High-school students show very poor reading comprehension and math skills. Cross-national achievement tests for tenth grade in these areas show performance below basic standards. This means the students do not exhibit minimal achievement in knowledge and skills required according to objectives set in the national curriculum. Reading comprehension tests in public high schools yield results showing that only 20% of the population is at a sufficient performance level, while this level is 50% in private schools. More than 60% of students in public high schools and 25% in private high schools—after ten years of schooling—are unable to achieve reading comprehension or basic standards.

In both public and private schools, the level of achievement in math of a majority of students is below the basic standards; 80% in the public schools and 50% in the private ones (Unidad de Medición de la Calidad, 2002). These students cannot find a strategy to solve contextualized problems. At the extreme end, there are students unable to solve simple word problems even when the math content is evident.

Education continues to be highly valued by Peruvian parents, even though it remains of a lower quality than the Latin-American average (UNICEF, 2003). UNICEF lists the following conditions as clearly describing the situation: (1) The national rate of completion of elementary school is 60%, but in some Andean regions and the jungle it can fall below 30%. (2) Some urban schools teach less than 500 hours annually, and most rural schools limit the hours to as few as 250 (1,000 hours is the official requirement). (3) Costs to poor families for clothing, leather shoes, and all school supplies (textbooks, books, notebooks, paper, pencils, pens, etc.) prevent many children from going to school. (4) Schools located very far away from home make it difficult for small undernourished children and girls to attend. (5) Many families choose to send their sons to school rather than their daughters, who are kept home to look after cattle, take care of siblings or do domestic work.

Work

Throughout Peru, skilled and unskilled adolescents and young adults face the problem of finding a job. An unstable job market associated with global, national, and regional economic conditions creates occupational uncertainty. In a national survey on employment, 17% of male adolescents and 21% of female adolescents were working in 2003. Their jobs were informal, and pay was usually the national minimal wage. Informal employment, however, was estimated at 70% among youngsters in factories, small enterprises, as microbus ticket operators, and especially as street vendors.

Working adolescents mostly belong to families of low income, and they have to contribute to pay family expenses. Frequently, their informal jobs are poorly paid, but there is no choice, since they have not received enough education to establish a productive job or work in services. A number of female adolescents and youngsters do domestic work as part-time or full-time cooks, maids, or nannies; these jobs have the advantage of including food, housing, water, and electricity. Often they also include clothing and medical insurance. With the considerable economic growth in the country in recent years, new and better-paid jobs and opportunities have opened for them in hotels, hostels, restaurants, bars, travel agencies, and so forth.

A significant number of middle-class adolescents work part-time as English teachers, in tutoring, or in making and selling artisan jewelry, t-shirts, and Peruvian crafts. Their earnings mostly go to cover part of or the total cost of their higher education studies and personal expenses. Upper-class adolescents rarely work, and when they do it is usually when they are initiated in the family business.

Media

Peruvian adolescents scarcely read, even newspapers and magazines (an estimated 5% do so). In contrast, radio is used almost all over the country and is a common companion of adolescents, youngsters, and the whole family. Adolescents listen to music, news, and political satire programs (which are national favorites). Only the very isolated Andean communities and the self-segregated natives in the rural jungle have little access to radio.

Use of television is extensive: most homes—even in the very poor areas—have at least one TV set; upper-class and some middle-class homes may have five to seven sets. The programs mostly watched vary with social class. American series are favorites of upper- and upper-middle-class adolescents who have access to cable TV, PCs, and laptops; they can burn CDs and download music and films. As with most adolescents, they are music lovers, but their preferred bands and singers are foreign, so they may travel to concerts in bordering countries. Middle-class adolescents tend to watch foreign (series) and national TV programs (soap operas), but mainly sports. They prefer music from Latin-American singers and bands from bordering countries, mainly Colombia and Argentina.

Working-class adolescents watch national TV (soap operas, and highly popular humorous shows) and listen to a very different kind of music. Since they belong to the second or third generation of migrants but have developed an urban identity, their preferred music is usually new tropical music, such as *chicha*, salsa, and other types that include elements from their parents' or grandparents' place of birth in the Andes. Their music is a mixture of indigenous and tropical music. This may be strong, happy, lively music for dancing. But it can also be music about the problems and sufferings of the daily life of migrants and poor. Their musical idols are of indigenous descent.

Movies are extremely popular in Lima. Many older adolescents go to the movies at least once a week or watch them on TV or buy film DVDs. The black market of film DVDs is very large and is everywhere, and often movies that have not yet entered commercial cinemas can be bought at 10% of the cost of an original. Adolescents can buy all kinds of films, including pornography, without censorship. The most popular movies are from the United States, including situation comedies, love soap operas, and movies with considerable violent and sexual content.

Politics and Military

Citizenship is achieved at the age of 18, when youngsters can start participating formally in democratic national and local elections, since in Peru voting is a legal obligation and there is a fine for those who do not vote. However, among the young there is a strong tendency to move away from politics, almost to a point of excluding it from their lives. "There are more interesting things to do" seems to be their thinking, while they concentrate on personal needs and worries apart from issues related to life in a community. "Politics is dirty, and most politicians have their own interest as their main interest; politics is corrupt," they believe.

Military service was compulsory until 2003, but upper-class and many middle-class adolescents rarely participated and found health or study excuses to evade service. Working-class adolescents, especially in the Andes, served for at least two years. For them, however, it was an important way of making a living or even finding a job, given their parents' poverty and the scarce opportunities. It was also a way of learning technical skills that increased their chances of later finding a job. The compulsory military service has not been reinstated, but there is a system of recruitment of working-class youngsters. The laws establishes that youngsters who wish to be in the military service can do it if they fulfill certain requirements through a selection process.

Unique Issues

Beliefs, values, and behavior of Peruvian adolescents have been seriously impacted by two factors: the cruel terrorism of Shining Path and several consecutive government periods with unprecedented levels of corruption. These have influenced their view of the political system, contaminating their perception of adulthood by creating distrust and disbelief regarding adults' honesty, truthfulness, and respect for others' life and human rights. Many older adolescents and young adults focus on material goods and choose professions or occupations in which they can earn significant amounts of money in the short term and achieve high standards of living. Others may not see anything wrong in bribery and similar behaviors to ease their way around the social system, its rules, and the justice system. Yet another group has developed a compromise with respect for human rights and respect for differences.

Urban upper-class adolescents have a completely different lifestyle but tend to share the same views regarding adulthood and politics; their value system and beliefs have changed as well. During the elementary- and high-school years, many travel to the United States and also to Europe. Under the vigilant eyes of maids or bodyguards, and accompanied by their chauffeurs, they take on Western tastes and habits while remaining in a closed social circle.

References and Further Reading

Castillo, M. (Ed.). (2002). Sociedad civil, juventud y participación política. Lima, Peru: APOYO.

Comisión de lucha contra las drogas (Contradrogas). (2000a). *Experiencias sobre actuaciones con menores en situación de riesgo social y drogas. Revista de información serie niño y adolescencia 1*. Lima, Peru: Unidad de Prevención.

Comisión de lucha contra las drogas (Contradrogas). (2000b). *Comportamiento de Riesgo Adolescente. Revista de información serie niños y adolescencia 2*. Lima, Peru: Unidad de Prevención.

Comisión de lucha contra las drogas (Contradrogas). (2002). *¿Por qué debemos invertir en el Adolescente? En Revista de información serie niños y adolescencia 3*. Lima, Peru: Unidad de Prevención.

Comisión Nacíonal para el Desarrollo y Vida sin Drogas (DEVIDA). (2002). *Estudio epidemiológico sobre consumo de drogas en la población escolar de secundaria*. Lima, Peru: DEVIDA.

Comisión Nacíonal para el Desarrollo y Vida sin Drogas (DEVIDA). (2002–2007), *Encuesta Nacional de hogares sobre consumo de drogas*. Lima: DEVIDA.

Comisión Nacíonal para el Desarrollo y Vida sin Drogas (DEVIDA). (2004a). *Estrategia Nacional de Lucha contra las drogas*. Lima, Peru: DEVIDA.

Comisión Nacíonal para el Desarrollo y Vida sin Drogas (DEVIDA). (2004b). *Consumo de drogas y factores de riesgo y protección en escolares de educación secundaria*. Lima, Peru: DEVIDA.

Comisión Nacíonal para el Desarrollo y Vida sin Drogas (DEVIDA). (2004c). *Guía para el facilitador de grupos adolescentes*. Lima, Peru: DEVIDA.

Estudio epidemiológico sobre el consumo de drogas en la población escolar de secundaria de menores – 2002. Lima, Peru: Ministerio de Educación, DEVIDA, and United Nations.

Encuesta Demográfico y de Salud Familiar, 1986, 1991/92, 1996 y 2000. Lima, Peru: Instituto Nacional de Estadística e Informática.

Encuesta Nacional de Hogares. (2004). *IV trimestre*. Lima, Peru: Instituto Nacional de Estadística e Informática.

Escobar Hurtado, L. J. (1995). *El adolescente y su medio ambiente y actitudes*. Lima, Peru: Fondo Editorial de la Pontificia Universidad Católica del Perú.

Instituto Nacional de Estadística e Informática. (2004). *Congreso de la República*. Lima, Peru: INEI.

Manzanera, R., Torralba, L., & Martín, L. (2002). Música y drogas en la movida del fin de semana. *Adolescencia Latinoamericana, 3*(1), 14–20.

Pinzás, A. (1996). Éxitos y fracasos en la comunicación intercultural. *Plural, 3*, 105–128.

Pinzás, A. (1998). Representaciones corporales y jóvenes de clase media. *Plural, 6/7*, 13–42.

Pinzás, A. (2004). Estrategias argumentativas en discursos ordinarios. *Plural, 10*, 99–110.

Pinzás, A., & Kogan, L. (2001). *Entre el amor y la amistad: Los jóvenes limeños*. Lima, Peru: Informe interno de investigación, Universidad de Lima.

Pinzás, A., & Kogan, L. (2002). *Imagen de la corrupción entre los jóvenes universitarios*. Lima, Peru: Informe interno de investigación, Universidad de Lima.

Pinzás, J. (2003). High school education in Peru: Perspectives from the Third World. In F. Pajares & T. Urdan (Eds.), *International perspectives on adolescence* (p. 256). Greenwich, CT: Information Age Publishing.

Proyecto de Ley. (2004). *Consumo de drogas y factores de riesgo y protección en escolares de educación secundaria*. Lima, Peru: Ministerio de Salud, Dirección General de Salud de las Personas, Dirección Ejecutiva de Gestión Sanitaria.

Rodríguez, J., & Cueto, S. (2001). *El informe de resultados de la Evaluación Nacional 2001: Producción de Textos*. Lima, Peru: Ministerio de Educación.

Una evaluación del estado de conservación de las ecoregiones terrestres de América Latina y El Caribe. Lima: Universidad Nacional Agraria La Molina—Centro de Datos para la Conservación.

Unidad de Medición de la Calidad (UMC) del Ministerio de Educación del Peru (MED). (2001). *Reportes preparados a partir de los resultados de la Evaluación Nacional 2001 (EN 2001)*. Lima, Peru: Ministerio de Educación.

Rojas, M. (1999). *Factores de riesgo y de protección en el abuso de drogas ilegales en adolescentes jóvenes de Lima Metropolitana*. Lima, Peru: CEDRO.

UNICEF. (2003). *A review of UNICEF country programs based on human rights: The case of Peru*. New York, NY: UNICEF.

Unidad de Medición de la Calidad. (2002). Segundo informe de resultados por niveles de desempeño. Lima, Peru: Unidad de Medición de la Calidad. Retrieved from www.minedu.gob.pe

Visión del trabajo infantil y adolescente en el Perú. (2001). Lima, Peru: Instituto Nacional de Estadística e Informática–Organización Internacional del Trabajo.

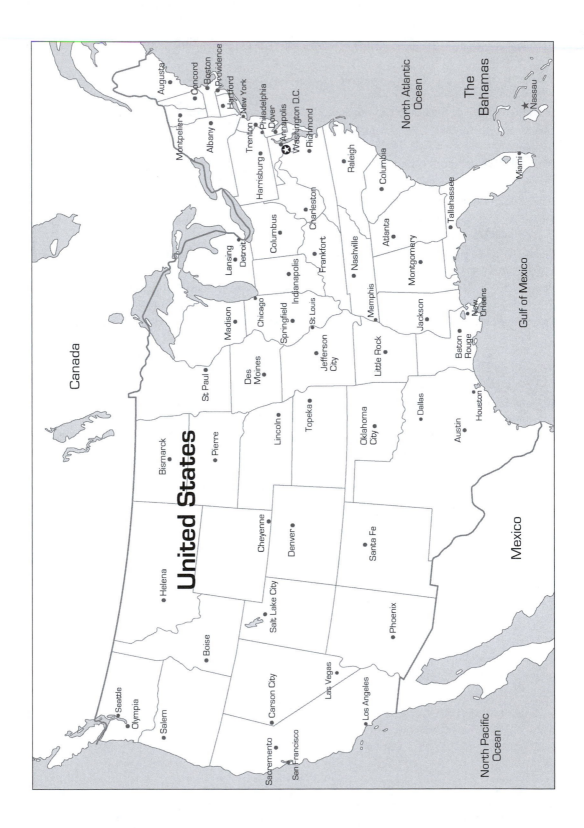

Chapter 16
United States of America
Angela de Dios

Background Information

The United States of America has more than 309 million people (US Bureau of the Census, 2010), and many of its citizens have immigrated to the United States from around the world. The majority identify themselves as European American (60%), but there is also a rapidly growing Latino population (15%), people of African descent (12%), people of Asian descent (4%), Native American or Native Alaskan people (1%), Native Hawaiians or Pacific Islanders (0.1%), and persons who are identified as mixed race (2.4%).

The United States is a federal constitutional republic with a two-party system (consisting of the Democratic and Republican parties). There are three branches in the federal government (legislative, executive, and judicial), which allows for checks and balances among the branches. American history has been shaped by the war of independence from England in the late eighteenth century and the Civil War fought between the Union and Confederate armies in the mid-nineteenth century. Today, although there are many opportunities for young people, they are not evenly distributed. Young people from ethnic minority groups are often disadvantaged because of lower levels of education as well as prejudice and discrimination.

Period of Adolescence

In the United States, adolescence is recognized as a distinct period of the life cycle that usually spans from age 10 to age 18. The beginning of adolescence is typically marked by the initial changes of puberty, and ends with high-school graduation since nearly all American adolescents attend high school (Arnett & Taber, 1994). Eighteen is also the age for attaining the legal status of adulthood in most respects, such as being able to vote and sign contracts.

After adolescence there is an important and related period of the life span: emerging adulthood. Emerging adulthood takes place between the ages of 18 and about 25 (Arnett, 1998). It is marked by five characteristics: the age of identity explorations, the age of instability, the self-focused age, the age of feeling in between, and the age of possibilities (Arnett, 2004). Emerging adulthood typically ends when individuals attain adulthood status, which tends to be gradual and mostly intangible. In the United States, the top three criteria for adulthood are individualistic traits: accepting responsibility for oneself, making independent decisions, and becoming financially independent (Arnett, 1998).

In the United States, there is no official rite of passage for the transitions to adulthood, but many ethnic groups have rites of their own that signify a more mature status in their culture. For example, Latino girls have *quinceñeras* at the age of fifteen, a kind of coming-of-age ball. Many religious groups also have ceremonies to celebrate the maturity of their members such as the confirmation in the Roman Catholic church, the Bar or Bat Mitzvah for Jewish adolescents, or doing missionary work for emerging adults in the Church of Jesus Christ of Latter-day Saints.

Beliefs

Generally speaking, the United States is considered to have values of independence and individualism (Arnett, 1995). Immigrants have unique experiences in socialization when they move to the United States, especially if they come from a culture that stresses interdependence (Arnett, 1995). Many studies have shown that American minority groups tend to have less individualistic and more collectivistic cultural beliefs than European Americans. For example, researchers have found that Latino adolescents have a strong sense of obligation to their families (e.g., Suárez-Orozco & Suárez-Orozco, 1996), Asian American adolescents have a duty to their families (Fuligni, Tseng, & Lam, 1999), and African Americans are less individualistic than European Americans but more individualistic than individuals in other minority groups (Phinney, Ong, & Madden, 2000).

Religion is another important influence on adolescent socialization and cultural values. In the United States, the largest religion is Protestantism, followed by Catholicism, Judaism, Islam, Buddhism, and Unitarian Universalism (Kosmin & Mayer, 2001). There is also a portion of American adolescents that are secular and report no religious affiliation (about 13%). According to the National Survey of Youth and Religion (NSYR), 84% of American adolescents believe in God or a universal spirit, 51% say that religion is important in their everyday life, and 52% attend religious services at least twice a month (Smith & Denton, 2005). However, religion is often considered a lower priority than other aspects of adolescent lives such as friends, school, and mass media (Smith & Denton, 2005). Furthermore, religiosity declines in the course of adolescence and continues to decline into emerging adulthood (e.g., Wallace & Williams, 1997).

Gender

The Women's Movement in the 1960s was important in challenging American ideas of masculinity and femininity. Though females today are less restricted by gender roles and enjoy more opportunities in education and the work force, the United States still has different expectations for men and women. The General Social Survey shows a rise in egalitarian gender attitudes in recent decades, but one fourth to over one third of Americans still believe in traditional gender roles: for example, that men should work while women should focus on the household and children (Cotter, Hermsen, Kendig, & Vanneman, 2006).

There is gender intensification during adolescence, when there is more social pressure for adolescents to conform to gender roles (Lynch, 1991). Peers also reinforce gender norms; they often ridicule adolescents that deviate from gender expectations (e.g., Eder, 1995). Because of the differential gender socialization received at school, many adolescents pursue occupations that are considered "traditional" for their gender, such as nursing and teaching for women and engineering and sciences for men. However, fields such as business, law, and medicine are more gender-equal now than in the past (Dey & Hurtado, 1999).

Gender socialization can be a source of problems for adolescents. In particular, girls are more likely than boys to have negative body images (e.g., Grabe, Ward, & Hyde, 2008), and some girls develop eating disorders that can have detrimental affects on their health and interpersonal relationships (Striegel-Moore & Franko, 2006). For boys, aggression is highly emphasized in adolescence, and boys who are more aggressive often exhibit higher levels of delinquent behavior such as vandalism, crime, and fighting (e.g., Arnett, 1992). Lower-status boys often suffer insults and humiliation from more aggressive boys (e.g., Pascoe, 2007).

Different ethnic groups in the United States have different patterns of gender roles than discussed above. African American adolescent girls often have higher self esteem and less concern with physical appearance than their European American counterparts (e.g., Basow & Rubin, 1999), and African American adolescent boys often adopt an extremely masculine character that displays toughness and aggressiveness (Majors, 1989). Latinos have highly traditional gender roles where girls model themselves after the Virgin Mary, while boys practice *machismo* that emphasizes male dominance of women (Arciniega, Anderson, Tovar-Black, & Tracey, 2008). Recently, Latinas have begun to navigate a compromise between traditional gender values and greater independence (Denner & Dunbar, 2004). Asian American adolescents receive similarly traditional gender socialization (Chao, 1994). Asian American girls are often portrayed in the media as exotic and submissive while boys are seen as less masculine than other men (Qin, 2009).

The Self

The United States generally promotes an independent self where it is valuable to reflect on who you are and to have a high self-esteem (Green, Deschamps, & Páez, 2005). Studies have shown that the self-esteem of Americans generally decreases in early adolescence and rises through late adolescence and emerging adulthood (e.g., Harter, 2006). Perceived physical appearance, in particular, is linked to levels of self-esteem in adolescence, and since girls are more critical of their physical appearance than boys, girls generally have lower levels of self-esteem (e.g., Shapka & Keating, 2005). In addition to fluctuations in self-esteem, there are also more fluctuations in emotionality in American adolescents. Adolescents are likely to feel more self-conscious and lonely than their parents, and when compared to preadolescents they are less likely to feel very happy or proud (Larson & Richards, 1994).

For Americans, identity development takes longer and is more complex than in past decades. Research shows that less than half of adolescents can be said to have reached identity achievement, where they have explored and made a commitment to their identity (Waterman, 1999). The United States is home to many immigrant groups whose adolescents must sort out an additional aspect of identity, their ethnic identity. Research has found that higher levels of ethnic identity are related to academic achievement, high self-esteem, and higher overall wellbeing (e.g., Yip & Fuligni, 2002). However, a strong sense of ethnic identity in addition to engaging with the dominant culture can contribute to better psychological adjustment (Phinney & Alipuria, 1990).

Family Relationships

In the United States, interactions with family change from preadolescence to adolescence. Adolescents spend less time with family members than they did in preadolescence (Larson, Richards, Moneta, Holmbeck, & Duckett, 1996). In addition, conflict between parents and adolescents sharply increases; conflict increases dramatically from childhood to adolescence, and by midadolescence the frequency decreases but conflicts increase in intensity (Laursen, Coy, & Collins, 1998). Nevertheless, high levels of serious conflict between parents and adolescents are actually not common and are experienced by less than 10% of families (Collins & Laursen, 2004). Adolescents typically have a lot of respect and love for their parents, and arguments stem from minor issues such as choice of friends, curfews, and clothing that adolescents see as a matter of personal preference but parents perceive as issues of parental authority (e.g., Smetana, 2005).

Levels of conflict with parents are lower in Asian American and Latino families (e.g., Harwood, Leyendecker, Carlson, Ascencio, & Miller, 2002). However, they have an additional source of conflict that non-immigrant families may not have. Immigrant adolescents can acculturate to American culture more quickly than their parents, which may create a discrepancy between what parents expect and what their adolescent desires. This discrepancy can create a cultural generation gap that can be a source of conflict between parents and their adolescents (Phinney et al., 2000).

About 80% of American adolescents have at least one sibling (US Bureau of the Census, 2010). Though adolescents typically have higher rates of conflict with their siblings than with parents, grandparents, teachers, or friends (e.g., Noller, 2005), conflict with their siblings is lower in adolescence than at younger ages (Brody, 2004) because they generally spend less time with their siblings (Hetherington, Henderson, & Reiss, 1999). Adolescent siblings who are experiencing their parents' divorce often have more conflict as well as more warmth in their relationships (e.g., Noller, 2005). In minority families, older siblings often have authority over their younger siblings and are responsible for caring for them (Zukow-Goldring, 2002).

In the United States, adolescents have infrequent contact with extended family members, and closeness with them declines from childhood to adolescence (Levitt, Guacci-Franco, & Levitt, 1993). However, ethnic minority groups often maintain closer relationships with their extended family than European Americans (Fuligni et al., 1999). African Americans, in particular, have a tradition of extended family households (Wilson, 1989). Research shows positive outcomes for adolescents who have relationships with their extended family members.

The divorce rate in the United States is one of the highest in the world, with over 40% of the current generation experiencing their parents' divorce before they graduate from high school. Research shows that adolescents who experience their parents' divorce are at risk for negative outcomes such as psychological distress, higher rates of risk behavior, and less academic success (Kelly, 2003). However, those who experience their parents' divorce in adolescence often have fewer negative outcomes than those who experience it in childhood (Klaff, 2007). It is also important to note that conflict between parents is especially damaging to children and adolescents, not solely the act of getting a divorce (e.g., Buchanan, 2000).

Of persons that experience divorce, about 75% remarry, resulting in 25% of young people living with stepfamilies before the age of 18 (Hernandez, 1997). In contrast to divorce, adolescents often have more problems adjusting to a stepparent/stepfamily than children do (e.g., Hetherington & Stanley-Hagan, 2000).

Friends and Peers/Youth Culture

As American adolescents spend less time with their parents, they spend more time with friends in their leisure time outside of school. They tend to feel more comfortable with their friends and depend on them—more than on their parents—for companionship and support. Though adolescents still prefer to discuss school and career goals with parents, they prefer to talk to their friends regarding romantic and sexual issues (Youniss & Smollar, 1985). Adolescents have greater intimacy in their friendships than children do. Children often stress shared activities as important aspects of their friendships, whereas adolescents mention intimacy through emotional support, advice, and talking more often (Savin-Williams & Berndt, 1990).

Adolescents often choose their friends based on proximity and similarity; they tend to have similar educational goals, preferences for media, leisure activities, and ethnic backgrounds. Most adolescents tend to have friends from the same race or ethnic group (Way and Chen, 2000). This pattern of choosing ethnically similar friends reflects ethnic segregation in schools and neighborhoods as well as the patterns of ethnic segregation in America as a whole (Mouw & Entwisle, 2008).

Adolescents have two types of social groups in the United States: cliques and crowds. Cliques are a small group of friends that know each other well and often have common interests and characteristics (Brown & Klute, 2003). Crowds are larger groups perceived by their peers to share certain characteristics, but the adolescents in a crowd may not all know each other or interact with each other. Crowds provide a social structure in which adolescents can situate themselves and their peers. In multiethnic high schools, cliques and crowds tend to form around racial lines. For example, there can be an Asian crowd and within the crowd there are different cliques—the Asian "populars," Asian "nerds," or Asian "burnouts."

Love and Sexuality

Involvement in romantic relationships increases with age during adolescence, and by the eleventh grade 80% of adolescents have been in at least one romantic relationship (Furman & Hand, 2006). Though dating in the United States is less formal now than it has been in the past, in general males still follow a proactive script where they initiate the relationship, plans, and sexual contact, whereas females follow the reactive script (Furman & Hand, 2006). Adolescent relationships usually lack long-term commitment, and only half of their relationships have lasted for eleven months or longer (Carver Joyner, & Udry, 2003).

For most adolescents, sexual activity proceeds through a progression of stages: masturbation, necking and petting, sexual intercourse, and oral sex (Carver et al., 2003). About 90% of boys masturbate by age 19 (Halpern, Udry, Suchindran, & Campbell, 2000), but only about 60%–75% of girls masturbate by age 20 (Masters, Johnson, & Kolodny, 1994). The average age of first intercourse in the United States is 17 (Avery & Lazdane, 2008). However, experiences of sexual intercourse vary by racial group. The Centers for Disease Control and Prevention (1997) have found that for high-school students, 44% of European American adolescents had experienced sexual intercourse, compared to 53% of Latinos and 67% of African Americans. Research has shown that Asian Americans are less likely to engage in sexual activity in adolescence (Connolly, Craig, Goldberg, & Pepler, 2004).

Adolescence is an important time for individuals who engage in same-sex behavior to develop a lesbian, gay, or bisexual (LGB) identity. Awareness of an LGB sexual identity usually begins in early adolescence and the average age of coming out—telling friends and family about one's sexual identity—is 16 (Savin-Williams, 2006). LGB adolescents often face ridicule and ostracism from peers because of their sexual identity, and this may be the basis of higher levels of substance abuse, suicide attempts, and difficulties at school (D'Augelli & Patterson, 2002). Though homophobia is still common in the United States, there has been a cultural shift toward a more tolerant perspective of LGB persons in recent years (Savin-Williams, 2006).

Because of the time lapse between first sexual encounter and marriage, most American adolescents have a long interval where they must use contraception in order to avoid pregnancy or sexually transmitted diseases. American adolescents often do not use contraception responsibly or consistently (Manlove, Franzetta, Ryan, & Moore, 2006), and the United States has the highest rate of teen pregnancy among industrialized countries (Teitler, 2002). Adolescent girls who have unplanned pregnancies are often from families with lower incomes, and they are twice as likely as other girls to drop out of school, less likely to get married, and more likely to get divorced (Moore & Brooks-Gunn, 2002). Adolescent fathers are unlikely to be heavily involved in their child's life, and they are also prone to more problems such as lower levels of education, use of drugs and alcohol, and feelings of depression (Buchanan & Robbins, 1990).

In addition to unwanted pregnancies, inconsistent contraception usage results in sexually transmitted infections (STIs). By age 24, one third of all sexually active Americans will have contracted an STI (Boyer et al., 1999). Adolescent girls and adolescents from minority groups (African Americans and Latinos in urban areas in particular) are at especially high risk to contract an STI (Centers for Disease Control and Prevention, 2007).

In the United States, 70% of adolescents who attend public school receive sex education (Landry, Singh, & Darroch, 2000). However, the type of sex education differs greatly from school to school. In general, there are two approaches to sex education in the United States: "abstinence-only" or "abstinence-plus." In abstinence-only curricula, adolescents are encouraged to wait until marriage to have sex, but this approach has been found to be ineffective in decreasing rates of sexual intercourse among adolescents (Kohler, Manhart, & Lafferty, 2008). Abstinence-plus programs promote abstinence, but still provide adolescents with information about STIs and contraception, and this has been more effective than the abstinence-only approach in preventing teenage pregnancy and STIs.

Health Risk Behavior

American adolescents are able to become licensed drivers at age 16 in nearly all American states. The National Highway Traffic Safety Administration (2008) has found that people between the ages of 16 and 24 have higher rates of car accidents, injuries, and fatalities than any other age group. In addition, boys are more likely to get into automobile accidents than girls. Younger drivers have less experience than older drivers, take more risks while driving, are more likely to violate traffic laws, more likely to drive under the influence of alcohol, and less likely to wear seat belts (Williams & Ferguson, 2002).

With regard to substance use, by age 18 more than half of adolescents have tried a cigarette and 25% have become regular smokers (Johnston, O'Malley, Bachman, & Schulenberg, 2004). In 2008, 43% of American high school seniors drank alcohol and 28% engaged in binge drinking (drinking 5 or more drinks in a row) in the past month (MTF, 2008). Most types of substance use in adolescence have been decreasing in recent decades. For example, alcohol use declined from 70% in 1975 to 43% in 2008. The peak of substance use actually comes later, in emerging adulthood (Schulenberg & Maggs, 2000).

The majority of crimes are committed by those (mostly males) between the ages of 12 and 25 (Eisner, 2002). In worldwide comparisons the United States ranks within the top quartile for juvenile homicide rates and property crimes (Eisner, 2002). However, crime rates have been dropping among adolescents in the past two decades.

Depressed mood is a common problem in adolescence, and researchers have found that adolescents often have higher rates of depressed mood than children or adults (e.g., Saluja, Iachan, & Scheidt, 2004). Depression can lead to suicide in some adolescents; which is the third most common cause of death in American adolescents (Mazza, 2006). Though suicide rates have declined since 1990, America still has a higher rate than it did in the 1950s and a higher rate than most other industrialized countries (CDC, 2007). Though females are four times more likely to attempt suicide, males are four times more likely to kill themselves (Oltmanns & Emery, 2001).

Education

American children begin school in primary school, transition to either middle school (grades six through eight) or junior high (grades seven through nine), go to high school, and many go on to college. The United States has a comprehensive high school system where students take classes in general education, college preparation, and sometimes vocational training. The United States has a lot of diversity in the education system because the federal government does not control schools. Instead, decisions about schooling are made by local and state governments because these agencies fund the schools in their state or district.

Compared to other countries around the world, the United States tends to be around the average in terms of adolescents' academic performance. American eighth graders generally have higher reading, math, and science scores than eighth graders in developing countries but lower than those in most industrialized countries (NCES, 2006). The National Assessment of Education Progress has found that student performance had increased during the 1990s, and though reading and science scores have stayed stable since then, math scores continue to rise (NCES, 2008).

Although high schools are comprehensive and include students of different backgrounds and abilities, many schools in the United States practice a tracking system where students are placed into different groups based on their abilities, and they take classes based on the track they are assigned to. Typically, there is a college preparatory track, a general education track, a remedial track, and sometimes a vocational track.

Since schools must accommodate students with different skill levels, special programs have been developed for some groups. For example, programs for gifted students have become more common. Many high schools offer advanced placement classes where students learn higher-level material and gain college credit if they pass the national advanced placement exam. In addition, schools must accommodate students with disabilities. About 10% of American adolescents have been diagnosed as having a disability and about half of those are learning disabilities. Some common disabilities are speech handicaps, mental retardation (special needs), emotional disorders, and attention-deficit hyperactivity disorder (Hallahan & Kauffman, 2003).

Most American students earn a high school degree, but some students drop out before then. By 2002, 90% of 24-year-old Americans had earned a high-school diploma (NCES, 2005). Although 30% actually drop out of school, some earn a General Education Development (GED) certificate later. Rates of dropping out are different for different ethnic groups (NCES, 2008): 23% of Latinos, 12% of African Americans, 10% of Asian Americans, and 7% of European Americans drop out.

Different factors, such as ethnicity and gender, are related to different levels of educational attainment. It is well established that Asian American adolescents have the best academic achievement of all ethnic groups. European Americans have the next highest achievement, followed by African Americans and Latinos (Qin, Way, & Mukherjee, 2008). Asian Americans may achieve more because their parents emphasize education and have high expectations, and they may have positive influences from their friends (Lee & Larson, 2000). On average, American girls earn higher grades than boys at every grade level, and they are more likely to attend college (Sommers, 2000).

Work

Work is an important aspect of life for adolescents in the United States. The most common first job in early adolescence for American girls is babysitting, and yard work (e.g., mowing lawns) is the most common first job for American boys (Mortimer, 2003). Beyond early adolescence, most adolescents work in retail or in food service (Staff, Mortimer, & Uggen, 2004). By the time they are seniors over 80% of adolescents will have had at least one part-time job (Barling & Kelloway, 1999). On average, high school seniors work 20 hours a week (Barling & Kelloway, 1999). Adolescent jobs are typically routine and monotonous, and they often do not relate to anything adolescents have learned in school. Moreover, such jobs do not usually prepare them for the kind of work they will be doing as adults (Mortimer, Vuolo, Staff, Wakefield, & Xie, 2008).

Since jobs in adolescence do not provide a basis for future careers, adolescents have different reasons for working. Most adolescents do not have to work to help their families financially; most work in order to have extra spending money for leisure (clothes, CDs, car-related costs, movies, eating out) (Mortimer & Staff, 2004). However, adolescents from racial minority groups may work because of perceived economic need of the family (Chaves et al., 2004).

When adolescents choose to work in formal employment, there are positive and negative consequences. Working can provide adolescents with good work habits, time management skills, a sense of responsibility, and better social skills. However, adolescents who work more than 10 hours a week are more prone to anxiety and depression (Lee & Staff, 2007); they tend to get less sleep and exercise (Bachman & Schulenberg, 1993); they are more likely to use alcohol, cigarettes and drugs (Longest & Shanahan, 2007); and they are more likely to have lower grades and have lower educational achievements and aspirations (Marsh & Kleitman, 2005).

Media

Media are a significant part of American adolescents' daily lives. They consume a variety of media: music, television, movies, magazines, and the Internet. The average American adolescent listens to music for two hours a day, and watches television for two hours a day (Roberts, Foehr, & Rideout, 2005). In addition, adolescents watch more movies than any other age group in the United States (Brown, Steele, & Walsh-Childers, 2002). Magazines are also popular among adolescent girls, and 70% of them read magazines regularly (Walsh-Childers, Gotthoffer, & Lepre, 2002). Furthermore, 90% of American adolescents have access to computers at home and at school (Roberts et al., 2005).

American adolescents typically spend a total of about 6.5 hours per day using media (Roberts Foehr, Rideout, & Brodie, 1999). Many adolescents use multiple forms of media simultaneously; for example, checking email while having music on. Though watching movies and chatting online can be social activities, much of adolescent media usage happens alone.

The Internet is a relatively new form of media that has become an essential part of adolescents' lives. Adolescents prefer using the computer to any other media source (Hellenga, 2002). American adolescents use the computer for school purposes, news updates, chat rooms, and email. Many adolescents also use social networking websites such as Facebook or Myspace, where they can keep in contact with "friends" from all over the world (Ellison, Steinfield, & Lampe, 2007), or keep blogs where they can write about their personal feelings and experiences. Cellular telephones have also become popular with American adolescents. About half of late adolescents and emerging adults have a cell phone (Roberts et al., 2005), but most of them use it for text messaging more than talking. This allows adolescents to stay in contact with their friends throughout the day.

Politics and Military

The legal voting age in the United States is 18 years, so adolescents cannot fully participate in the political system until then. However, some participate in student governments at school and are members of politically oriented clubs such as Model Senate, Model United Nations, the Young Democrats of America, or Young Republicans. Levine and Lopez (2004) have found that half of Americans between the ages of 15 and 20 feel that voting is important, and more than half grew up discussing political issues with their parents.

In the 2008 presidential election, the percentage of emerging adults that participated in voting increased from the 2004 election (Kirby & Kawashima-Ginsberg, 2009). This may be due to voter outreach programs, as well as interest in the election generated by the prospect of a close race. Youth voter turnout in 2008 was one of the highest since the United States made 18 years the legal voting age.

The United States does not require adolescents or emerging adults to serve any time in the military. However, adolescents can sign up for military service at age 17 with parental permission, and 18-year-olds can sign up on their own. The United States military branches have several ways to recruit members. They have recruitment offices all over the United States. Reserve Officers Training Corps (ROTC) programs train high-school and college students for military careers. Those who complete the ROTC programs can become commissioned officers in the military and get scholarships for their college tuition and expenses.

Unique Issues

Obesity is an important problem for adolescents in the United States. Obesity is defined as weighing 20% or more above the healthy weight for height in males, and 25% or more in females (Davies &

Fitzgerald, 2008). Research shows that 16% of American adolescents (ages 12 to 19) are overweight, far higher than other industrialized countries (Ogden, Flegal, Carroll, & Johnson, 2002). Furthermore, obesity rates are 50% higher in African American and Latino American adolescents than in European American adolescents (Fleming & Towery, 2003).

Patterns of overeating and under-exercising in the United States can cause obesity. Almost one third of American adolescents eat at least one fast-food meal every day (Bowman, 2004), and almost 100% of high schools have soft drink and junk food machines available on campus (Fleming & Towery, 2003). The United States is more automobile-oriented than other industrialized countries; adolescents ride cars more while walking and biking less, and exercise less than medical experts recommend (Fleming & Towery, 2003). Obesity is linked with later health problems, such as type II diabetes, high blood pressure, and high cholesterol (McConnaughey, 2004), and 80% of obese adolescents remain obese in adulthood (Engeland, Bjorge, Tverdal, & Sogaard, 2004).

References and Further Reading

Akos, P., Lambie, G. W., Milsom, A., & Gilbert, K. (2007). Early adolescents' aspirations and academic tracking: An exploratory investigation. *Professional School Counseling, 11*(1), 57–64.

Arciniega, G. M., Anderson, T. C., Tovar-Black, Z. G., & Tracey, T. J. G. (2008). Toward a fuller conception of machismo: Development of a traditional machismo and caballerismo scale. *Journal of Counseling Psychology, 55*(1), 19–33.

Arnett, J. J. (1992). Reckless behavior in adolescence: A developmental perspective. *Developmental Review, 12*, 339–373.

Arnett, J. J. (1995). Broad and narrow socialization: The family in the context of a cultural theory. *Journal of Marriage and the Family, 57*, 617–628.

Arnett, J. J. (1998). Learning to stand alone: The contemporary American transition to adulthood in cultural and historical context. *Human Development, 41*, 295–315.

Arnett, J. J. (2004). *Emerging adulthood: The winding road from the late teens through the twenties*. New York, NY: Oxford University Press.

Arnett, J. J., & Balle-Jensen, L. (1993). Cultural bases of risk behavior: Danish adolescents. *Child Development, 64*, 1842–1855.

Arnett, J. J., & Taber, S. (1994). Adolescence terminable and interminable: When does adolescence end? *Journal of Youth & Adolescence, 23*, 517–537.

Avery, L., & Lazdane, G. (2008). What do we know about sexual and reproductive health among adolescents in Europe? *European Journal of Contraception and Reproductive Health, 13*, 58–70.

Bachman, J. G., & Schulenberg, J. (1993). How part-time work intensity relates to drug use, problem behavior, time use, and safisfaction among high school seniors: Are these consequences or just correlates? *Developmental Psychology, 29*, 220–235.

Barling, J., & Kelloway, E. K. (1999). *Young workers: Varieties of experience*. Washington, DC: American Psychological Association.

Basow, S. A., & Rubin, L. R. (1999). Gender influences on adolescent development. In N. B. Johnson, M. C. Roberts, & J. Worell (Eds.), *Beyond appearance: A new look at adolescent girls* (pp. 25–52). Washington, DC: American Psychological Association.

Blum, V. L. (2003). *Flesh wounds: The culture of cosmetic surgery*. Berkeley, CA: University of California Press.

Bowman, S. (2004). Effects of fast-food consumption on energy intake and diet quality among children in a national household survey. *Pediatrics, 113*(1), 112–118.

Boyer, C. B., Shafer, M. A., Teitle, E., Wibbelsman, C. J., Seeberg, F., & Schacter, J. (1999). Sexually-transmitted diseases in a health maintenance organization teen clinic. *Archives of Pediatrics and Adolescent Medicine, 153*, 838–844.

Breivik, K., & Olweus, D. (2006). Adolescents' adjustment in four post-divorce family structures: Single mother, stepfather, joint physical custody and single father families. *Journal of Divorce & Remarriage, 44*(3–4), 99–124.

Brody, G. H. (2004). Siblings' direct and indirect contributions to child development. *Current Directions in Psychological Science, 13*(3), 124–126.

Brown, B. B., & Klute, C. (2003). Friendships, cliques, and crowds. In R. G. Adams & D. M. Berzonsky (Eds.), *Blackwell handbook of adolescence* (pp. 330–348). Malden, MA: Blackwell.

Brown, J. D., Steele, J. R., & Walsh-Childers, K. (2002). Introduction and overview. In J. D. Brown, J. R. Steele, & K. Walsh-Childers (Eds.), *Sexual teens, sexual media: Investigating media's influence on adolescent sexuality* (pp. 1–24). Mahwah, NJ: Lawrence Erlbaum Associates.

Buchanan, C. M. (2000). The impact of divorce on adjustment during adolescence. In R. D. Taylor & M. Weng (Eds.), *Resilience across contexts: Family, work, culture, and community*. Mahwah, NJ: Lawrence Erlbaum Associates.

Buchanan, M., & Robbins, C. (1990). Early adult psychological consequences for males of adolescent pregnancy and its resolution. *Journal of Youth and Adolescence, 19*, 413–424.

Bureau of Labor Statistics. (2010, July 2). Employment situation summary. Washington, DC: BLS. Retrieved from www.bls.gov

Carver, K., Joyner, K., & Udry, J. R. (2003). National estimates of adolescent romantic relationships. In P. Florsheim (Ed.), *Adolescent romantic relations and sexual behavior: Theory, research, and practical implications*. Mahwah, NJ: Lawrence Erlbaum Associates.

Centers for Disease Control and Prevention. (1997). *Sexually transmitted disease surveillance*. Hyattsville, MD: US Department of Health and Human Services.

Centers for Disease Control and Prevention. (2005, November 8). *STD Surveillance 2004: Special Focus Profiles*. Hyattsville, MD: US Department of Health and Human Services. Retrieved from www.cdc.gov

Centers for Disease Control and Prevention. (2007). Suicide trends among youths and young adults ages 10–24 years – United States, 1990–2004. *Morbidity and Mortality Weekly Report, 56*(35), 905–908.

Chao, R. (1994). Beyond parental control and authoritarian parenting style: Understanding Chinese parenting through the cultural notion of training. *Child Development, 65*, 1111–1119.

Chaves, A. P., Diemer, M. A., Blustein, D. L., Gallagher, L. A., DeVoy, J. E., Casares, M. T., et al. (2004). Conceptions of work: The view from urban youth. *Journal of Counseling Psychology, 51*(3), 275–286.

Clingempeel, W., Colyar, J., Brand, E., & Hetherington, E. (1992). Children's relationships with maternal grandparents: A longitudinal study of family structure and pubertal status effects. *Child Development, 63*, 1404–1422.

Collins, W. A., & Laursen, B. (2004). Parent–adolescent relationships and influences. In R. M. Lerner & L. Steinberg (Eds.), *Handbook of adolescent psychology* (2nd ed.). Hoboken, NJ: Wiley.

Connolly, J., Craig, W., Goldberg, A., & Pepler, D. (2004). Mixed-gender groups, dating, and romantic relationships in early adolescence. *Journal of Research on Adolescence, 14*, 185–207.

Cotter, D. A., Hermsen, J. M., Kendig, S. M., & Vanneman, R. (2006). *The end of the U.S. gender revolution: Changing attitudes from 1974 to 2004*. Paper presented at the annual meeting of the American Sociological Association, Montreal, Canada. Retrieved from www.allacademic.com

Cusumano, D. O., & Thompson, J. K. (2001). Media influence and body image in 8–11-year old boys and girls: A preliminary report on the Multidimensional Media Influence Scale. *International Journal of Eating Disorders, 29*, 37–44.

D'Augelli, A. R., & Patterson, C. J. (2002). *Lesbian, gay, and bisexual identities and youth: Psychological perspectives* (pp. 126–152). New York, NY: Oxford University Press.

Davies, H. D., & Fitzgerald, H. E. (Eds.). (2008). *Obesity in childhood and adolescence, Vol. 1: Medical, biological, and social issues*. New York, NY: Praeger.

Denner, J., & Dunbar, N. (2004). Negotiating femininity: Power and strategies of Mexican American girls. *Sex Roles, 50*, 301–314.

Dey, E. L., & Hurtado, S. (1999). Students, colleges, and society: Considering the interconnections. In P. G. Altbach, R. O. Berdahl, & P. J. Gumport (Eds.), *American higher education in the 21st century: Social, political, and economic challenges*. Baltimore, MD: Johns Hopkins University Press.

Eccles, J. S., & Roeser, R. W. (2003). Schools as developmental contexts. In G. Adams & M. Berzonsky (Eds.), *Blackwell handbook of adolescence* (pp. 129–148). Malden, MA: Blackwell.

Eder, D. (1995). *School talk: Gender and adolescent culture*. New Brunswick, NJ: Rutgers University Press.

Eisner, M. (2002). Crime, problem drinking, and drug use: Patterns of problem behavior in cross-national perspective. *Annals of the American Academy of Political and Social Science, 580*, 201–225.

Ellison, N. C., Steinfield, C., & Lampe, C. (2007). The benefits of Facebook "friends": Social capital and college students' use of online social network sites. *Journal of Computer-Mediated Communication, 12*(4), 1143–1168.

Engeland, A., Bjorge, T., Tverdal, A., & Sogaard, A. J. (2004). Obesity in adolescence and adulthood and the risk of adult mortality. *Epidemiology, 15*, 79–85.

Evans, E. D., Rutberg, J., Sather, C., & Turner, C. (1991). Content analysis of contemporary teen magazines for adolescent females. *Youth & Society, 23*, 99–120.

Fleming, M., & Towery, K. (Eds.). (2003). *Educational forum on adolescent health: Obesity, nutrition, and physical activity*. Chicago, IL: American Medical Association.

Fuligni, A. J., Tseng, V., & Lam, M. (1999). Attitudes toward family obligations among American adolescents with Asian, Latin American, and European backgrounds. *Child Development, 70*, 1030–1044.

Furman, W., & Hand, L. S. (2006). The slippery nature of romantic relationships: Issues in definition and differentiation. In A. C. Crouter & A. Booth (Eds.), *Romance and sex in adolescence and emerging adulthood: Risks and opportunities* (pp. 171–178). Mahwah, NJ: Lawrence Erlbaum Associates.

Grabe, S., Ward, L. M., & Hyde, J. S. (2008). The role of the media in body image concerns among women: A meta-analysis of experimental and correlational studies. *Psychological Bulletin, 134*(3), 460–476.

Green, E. G. T., Deschamps, J.-C., & Páez, D. (2005). Variation of individualism and collectivism within and between 20 countries: A typological analysis. *Journal of cross-cultural psychology, 36*, 321–339.

Hallahan, D. P., & Kauffman, J. M. (2003). *Exceptional learners*. Boston, MA: Allyn & Bacon.

Hallinan, M. (1992). The organization of students for instruction in the middle school. *Sociology of Education, 65*(2), 114–127.

Halpern, C. J. T., Udry, J. R., Suchindran, C., & Campbell, B. (2000). Adolescent males' willingness to report masturbation. *Journal of Sex Research, 37*, 327–332.

Harter, S. (1997). The development of self-representations. In N. Eisenberg (Ed.), *Handbook of child psychology* (5th ed., Vol. 3). New York, NY: Wiley.

Harter, S. (2006). The development of self-esteem. In M. H. Kernis (Ed.), *Self-esteem issues and answers: A sourcebook of current perspectives* (pp. 144–150). New York, NY: Psychology Press.

Harwood, R., Leyendecker, B., Carlson, V., Ascencio, M., & Miller, A. (2002). Parenting among Latino families in the U.S. In M. H. Bornstein (Ed.), *Handbook of parenting, Vol. 4: Social conditions and applied parenting* (2nd ed., pp. 21–46). Mahwah, NJ: Lawrence Erlbaum Associates.

Hellenga, K. (2002). Social space, the final frontier: Adolescents on the internet. In J. T. Mortimer & R. W. Larson (Eds.), *The changing adolescent experience: Societal trends and the transition to adulthood* (pp. 208–249). New York, NY: Cambridge University Press.

Hernandez, D. J. (1997). Child development and the social demography of childhood. *Child Development, 68,* 149–169.

Hetherington, E. M., Henderson, S., & Reiss, D. (1999). *Adolescent siblings in stepfamilies: Family functioning and adolescent adjustment.* Monographs of the Society for Research in Child Development (Vol. 64). New York, NY: Wiley.

Hetherington, E. M., & Kelly, J. (2002). *For better or worse: Divorce reconsidered.* New York, NY: Norton.

Hetherington, E. M., & Stanley-Hagan, M. (2000). Diversity among stepfamilies. In D. H. Demo & K. R. Allen (Eds.), *Handbook of family diversity* (pp. 173–196). New York, NY: Oxford University Press.

Hetherington, E. M., & Stanley-Hagan, M. (2002). Parenting in divorced and remarried families. In M. H. Bornstein (Ed.), *Handbook of parenting: Vol. 3: Being and becoming a parent* (2nd ed., pp. 287–315). Mahwah, NJ: Lawrence Erlbaum Associates.

Johnston, L. D., O'Malley, P. M., Bachman, J. G., & Schulenberg, J. E. (2004). *Monitoring the future national results on adolescent drug use: Overview of key findings, 2003.* NIH Publication 04–5506. Bethesda, MD: National Institute on Drug Abuse.

Kelly, J. B. (2003). Changing perspectives on children's adjustment following divorce: A view from the United States. *Childhood, 10,* 237–254.

Kirby, E. H., & Kawashima-Ginsberg, K. (2009, August 17). *The youth vote in 2008.* Meford, MA: The Center for Information & Research on Civic Learning and Engagement. Retrieved from www.civicyouth.org

Klaff, F. R. (2007). Children of divorce. In F. Shapiro et al. (Eds.), *Handbook of EMDR and family therapy processes* (pp. 284–305). Hoboken, NJ: Wiley.

Kohler, P. K., Manhart, L. E., & Lafferty, W. E. (2008). Abstinence-only and comprehensive sex education and the initiation of sexual activity and teen pregnancy. *Journal of Adolescent Health, 42*(4), 344–351.

Kosmin, B. A., & Mayer, E. (2001). *American religious identification survey.* New York, NY: City University of New York. Retrieved from www.gc.cuny.edu

Kroger, J. (2003). Identity development during adolescence. In G. Adams & M. Berzonsky (Eds.), *Blackwell handbook of adolescence* (pp. 205–225). Malden, MA: Blackwell.

Landry, D. J., Singh, S., & Darroch, J. E. (2000). Sexuality education in fifth and sixth grades in U.S. public schools. *Family Planning Perspectives, 32,* 212–219.

Larson, R. W. (1997). The emergence of solitude as a constructive domain of experience in early adolescence. *Child Development, 68,* 80–93.

Larson, R., & Richards, M. H. (1994). *Divergent realities: The emotional lives of mothers, fathers, and adolescents.* New York, NY: Basic Books.

Larson, R., Richards, M. H., Moneta, G., Holmbeck, G., & Duckett, E. (1996). Changes in adolescents' daily interactions with their families from ages 10 to 18: Disengagement and transformation. *Child Development, 32,* 744–754.

Laursen, B., Coy, K. C., & Collins, W. A. (1998). Reconsidering changes in parent–child conflict across adolescence: A meta-analysis. *Child Development, 69,* 817–832.

Lee, J. C., & Staff, J. (2007). When work matters: The varying impact of work intensity on high school dropouts. *Sociology of Education, 80*(2), 158–178.

Lee, M., & Larson, R. (2000). The Korean "examination hell": Long hours of studying, distress, and depression. *Journal of Youth & Adolescence, 29,* 249–271.

Levine, P., & Lopez, M. H. (2004). Young people and political campaigning on the Internet (CIRCLE Fact Sheet). College Park, MD: Center for Information and Research on Civic Learning and Engagement.

Levitt, M. J., Guacci-Franco, N., & Levitt, J. L. (1993). Convoys of social support in childhood and early adolescence: Structure and function. *Developmental Psychology*, *29*, 811–818.

Longest, K. C., & Shanahan, M. J. (2007). Adolescent work intensity and substance use: The mediational and moderational roles of parenting. *Journal of Marriage & Family*, *69*(3), 703–720.

Lynch, M. E. (1991). Gender intensification. In R. M. Lerner, A. C. Petersen, & J. Brooks-Gunn (Eds.), *Encyclopedia of adolescence* (Vol. 1). New York, NY: Garland.

Majors, R. (1989). Cool pose: The proud signature of black survival. In M. S. Kimmel & M. A. Messner (Eds.) *Men's lives* (pp. 83–87). New York, NY: Macmillan.

Manlove, J., Franzetta, K., Ryan, S., & Moore, K. (2006). Adolescent sexual relationships, contraceptive consistency, and pregnancy prevention approaches. In A. C. Croutter & A. Booth (Eds.), *Romance and sex in adolescence and emerging adulthood: Risks and opportunities* (pp. 181–212). Mahwah, NJ: Lawrence Erlbaum Associates.

Marsh, H. W., & Kleiman, S. (2005). Consequences of employment during High School: Character building, subversion of academic goals, or a threshold? *American Educational Research Journal*, *42*, 331–369.

Martin, N. C. (1997, April). *Adolescents' possible selves and the transition to adulthood*. Paper presented at the meeting of the Society for Research in Child Development, Washington, DC.

Masters, W. H., Johnson, V. E., & Kolodny, R. C. (1994). *Heterosexuality*. New York, NY: Harper Collins.

Matyas, M. L. (1987). Keeping undergraduate women in science and engineering: Contributing factors and recommendations for action. In J. Z. Daniels & J. B. Kahle (Eds.), *Contributions to the fourth GASAT conference* (Vol. 3, pp. 112–122). Washington, DC: National Science Foundation.

Mazza, J. J. (2006). Youth suicidal behavior: A crisis in need of attention. In F. A. Villarruel & T. Luster (Eds.), *The crisis in youth mental health: Critical issues and effective programs, Vol. 2: Disorders in adolescence* (pp. 155–177). Westport, CT: Praeger/Greenwood.

McConnaughey, J. (2004). *CDC issues diabetes warning for children*. New York, NY: Associated Press.

Monitoring the Future. (2011). Retrieved from www.monitoringthefuture.org

Moore, M., & Brooks-Gunn, J. (2002). Adolescent parenthood. In M. H. Bornstein (Ed.), *Handbook of parenting, Vol. 3: Being and becoming a parent* (2nd ed., pp. 173–214). Mahwah, NJ: Lawrence Erlbaum Associates.

Mortimer, J. T. (2003). *Working and growing up in America*. Cambridge, MA: Harvard University Press.

Mortimer, J. T., & Staff, J. (2004). Early work as a source of developmental discontinuity during the transition to adulthood. *Development & Psychopathology*, *16*, 1047–1070.

Mortimer, J. T., Vuolo, M., Staff, J., Wakefield, S., & Xie, W. (2008). Tracing the timing of "career" acquisition in a contemporary youth cohort. *Work and Occupations*, *35*(1), 44–84.

Mouw, T., & Entwisle, B. (2006). Residential segregation and interracial friendship in schools. *American Journal of Sociology*, *112*(2), 394–441.

Murnen, S. K., & Levine, M. P. (2007). *Do fashion magazines promote body dissatisfaction in girls and women?* Paper presented at the annual meeting of the American Psychological Association, San Francisco, CA.

National Center for Education Statistics (NCES). (2005, June 1). *The condition of education 2005*. Retrieved from http://nces.ed.gov

National Center for Education Statistics (NCES). (2006, June 1). *The condition of education 2006*. Retrieved from http://nces.ed.gov

National Center for Education Statistics (NCES). (2008, May 29). *The condition of education 2008*. Retrieved from http://nces.ed.gov

National Highway Traffic Safety Administration. (2008). *Traffic safety facts*. Washington, DC: US Department of Transportation.

Noller, P. (2005). Sibling relationships in adolescence: Learning and growing together. *Personal Relationships, 12*, 1–22.

Ogden, C. L., Flegal, K. M., Carroll, M. D., & Johnson, C. L. (2002). Prevalence and trends in overweight among U.S. children and adolescents, 1999–2000. *Journal of the American Medical Association, 288*, 1728–1732.

Oltmanns, T. F., & Emery, R. E. (2001). *Abnormal psychology* (3rd ed.). Upper Saddle River, NJ: Prentice Hall.

Pascoe, C. J. (2007). *Dude, you're a fag: Masculinity and sexuality in high school*. Berkeley, CA: University of California Press.

Paul, E. L., & White, K. M. (1990). The development of intimate relationships in late adolescence. *Adolescence, 25*, 375–400.

Phinney, J. S., & Alipuria, L. L. (1990). Ethnic identity in college students from four ethnic groups. *Journal of Adolescence, 13*, 171–183.

Phinney, J. S., Ong, A., & Madden, T. (2000). Cultural values and intergenerational value discrepancies in immigrant and nonimmigrant families. *Child Development, 71*, 528–539.

Qin, D. B. (2009). Being "good" or being "popular": Gender and ethnic identity negotiations of Chinese immigrant adolescents. *Journal of Adolescent Research, 24*(1), 37–66.

Qin, D. B., Way, N., & Mukherjee, P. (2008). The other side of the model minority story: The familial and peer challenges faced by Chinese American adolescents. *Youth and Society, 39*(4), 480–506.

Roberts, D. F., Foehr, U. G., Rideout, V. J., & Brodie, M. (1999). *Kids & media @ the new millennium: A comprehensive national analysis of children's media use*. New York, NY: Henry J. Kaiser Family Foundation.

Roberts, D. F., Foehr, U. G., & Rideout, V. (2005). *Generation M: Media in the lives of 8–18 year-olds*. Washington, DC: The Henry J. Kaiser Family Foundation.

Saluja, G., Iachan, R., & Scheidt, P. (2004). Prevalence and risk factors for depressive symptoms among young adolescents. *Archives of Pediatrics and Adolescent Medicine, 158*, 760–765.

Savin-Williams, R. C. (2006). *The new gay teenager*. New York, NY: Trilateral.

Savin-Williams, R., & Berndt, T. (1990). Friendship and peer relations. In S. Feldman & G. Elliott (Eds.), *At the threshold: The developing adolescent* (pp. 277–307). Cambridge, MA: Harvard University Press.

Schulenberg, J., & Maggs, J. L. (2000). *A developmental perspective on alcohol use and heavy drinking during adolescence and the transition to adulthood*. Washington, DC: National Institute on Alcohol Abuse and Alcoholism.

Shapka, J. D., & Keating, D. P. (2005). Structure and change in self-concept during adolescence. *Canadian Journal of Behavioral Science, 37*, 83–96.

Smetana, J. G. (2005). Adolescent–parent conflict: Resistance and subversion as developmental process. In L. Nucci (Ed.), *Conflict, contradiction, and contrarian elements in moral development and education* (pp. 69–91). Mahwah, NJ: Lawrence Erlbaum Associates.

Smith, C., & Denton, M. L. (2005). *Soul searching: The religious and spiritual lives of American teenagers*. New York, NY: Oxford University Press.

Sommers, C. H. (2000, May). The war against boys. *Atlantic Monthly*, pp. 59–74.

Staff, J., Mortimer, J. T., & Uggen, C. (2004). Work and leisure in adolescence. In R. M. Lerner & L. Steinberg (Eds.), *Handbook of adolescent psychology* (2nd ed., pp. 429–450). Hoboken, NJ: Wiley.

Striegel-Moore, R. H., & Franko, D. L. (2006). Adolescent eating disorders. In C. A. Essau (Ed.), *Child and adolescent psychopathology: Theoretical and clinical implications*. (pp. 160–183). New York, NY: Routledge/Taylor & Francis.

Suárez-Orozco, C., & Suárez-Orozco, M. (1996). *Transformations: Migration, family life and achievement motivation among Latino adolescents*. Palo Alto, CA: Stanford University Press.

Teitler, J. O. (2002). Trends in youth sexual initiation and fertility in developed countries: 1960–1995. *Annals of the American Academy of Political Science Studies*, *580*, 134–152.

US Bureau of the Census. (2010). *US and world population clocks*. Washington, DC: US Bureau of the Census. Retrieved from www.census.gov

Vandello, J. A., & Cohen, D. (1999). Patterns of individualism and collectivism across the United States. *Journal of Personality and Social Psychology*, *77*, 279–292.

Vazsonyi, A. T., Pickering, L. E., Belliston, L. M., Hessing, D., & Junger, M. (2002). Routine activities and deviant behaviors: American, Dutch, Hungarian, and Swiss youth. *Journal of Quantitative Criminology*, *18*, 397–422.

Wallace, J. M., & Williams, D. R. (1997). Religion and adolescent health-compromising behavior. In J. Schulenberg, J. L. Maggs, & K. Hurrelmann (Eds.), *Health risks and developmental transitions during adolescence* (pp. 444–468). New York, NY: Cambridge University Press.

Walsh-Childers, K., Gotthoffer, A., & Lepre, C. R. (2002). From "just the facts" to "downright salacious": Teens' and women's magazine coverage of sex and sexual health. In J. D. Brown, J. R. Steele, & K. Walsh-Childers (Eds.), *Sexual teens, sexual media: Investigating media's influence on adolescent sexuality* (pp. 153–171). Mahwah, NJ: Lawrence Erlbaum Associates.

Waterman, A. S. (1999). Issues of identity formation revisited: United States and the Netherlands. *Developmental Review*, *19*, 462–479.

Way, N., & Chen, L. (2000). Close and general friendships among African American, Latino, and Asian American adolescents. *Journal of Adolescent Research*, *15*, 247–301.

Williams, A. F., & Ferguson, S. A. (2002). Rationale for graduated licensing and the risks it should address. *Injury Prevention*, *8*,(Suppl. 2), ii9–ii16.

Wilson, M. N. (1989). Child development in the context of the black extended family. *American Psychologist*, *44*, 380–383.

Yip, T., & Fuligni, A. J. (2002). Daily variation in ethnic identity, ethnic behaviors, and psychological well-being among American adolescents of Chinese descent. *Child Development*, *73*, 1557–1572.

Youniss, J., & Smollar, J. (1985). *Adolescent relations with mothers, fathers, and friends*. Chicago, IL: University of Chicago Press.

Zukow-Goldring, P. (2002). Sibling caregiving. In M. H. Bornstein (Ed.), *Handbook of parenting: Being and becoming a parent* (Vol. 3). Mahwah, NJ: Laurence Erlbaum Associates.

SECTION IV
Europe

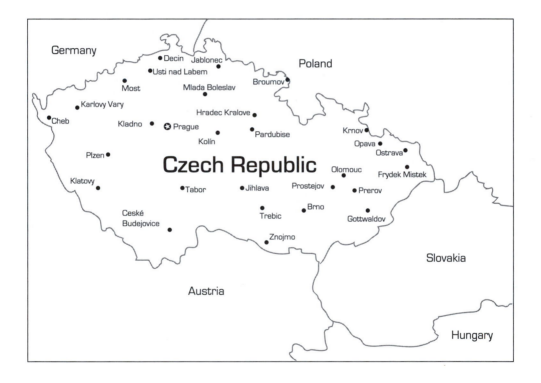

Germany

Poland

•Decin Jablonec
•Usti nad Labem
Most •   Mlada Boleslav   Broumov•

Karlovy Vary •
                        Hradec Kralove •
•Cheb   Krnov•
        Kladno • ✪ Prague   Opava•
                                  Pardubise •   Ostrava•
                Kolín •

Plzen •   Frydek Mistek•

                Czech Republic   Olomouc•

Klatovy •   Prostejov •   Prerov•
                Tabor •   Jihlava •
                                              Brno •
Ceské   Gottwaldov•
Budejovice •   Trebic •

                          Znojmo •

                                                          Slovakia

Austria

                                                          Hungary

Chapter 17
Czech Republic
Petr Macek, Lenka Lacinová, and Eva Polášková

Background Information

The Czech Republic is located in the Central European region. The Czech language belongs to the family of Slavic languages, but the Czech culture and lifestyle are deeply rooted in Western European culture. The Czech Republic was founded in January 1993 as a result of the peaceful split of the former Czechoslovakia into two independent states (the Czech Republic and Slovakia). The Czech Republic joined the European Union (EU) in May 2004.

Czechoslovakia (established in October 1918) was an industrial and democratic European country until 1939. After the Second World War Czechoslovakia became a Communist country dominated by the Soviet Union. However, this situation changed at the end of the 1980s, as democratic tendencies swelled in Central and Eastern Europe. Czech students initiated the "Velvet Revolution" in November 1989. This initiated a new era of political pluralism and democracy in Czech society.

The total population of the Czech Republic is about 10 million people. The Czech Republic is an ethnically homogeneous country. The majority of adolescents are Czechs (94% of the total population); Slovaks represent the largest minority (2%). There are other ethnic groups (Germans, Poles, Roma people, Ukrainians), but these minorities include less than 1% of the total population.

Period of Adolescence

As in other industrialized European countries, adolescence in Czech society has been recognized as a separate life stage since the 1850s. The recognition of this period was closely related to the establishment of a compulsory school system. It brought not only new institutions but also a new understanding of the rights and duties of young people, their cognitive competence and emotional nature, their values, and the normative steps of their transition to adulthood (Chisholm & Hurrelman, 1995).

The beginning of the period of adolescence is usually related to pubertal changes. In Czech adolescents, these changes have wide variation in both timing and tempo. The acceleration of physical growth (an increase in height and weight) appears usually at age 10 in girls and 12 in boys. The mean age of menarche for Czech girls is comparable to Western European countries and is slightly less than 13 years.

As in other advanced Euro-American countries, the adolescent period tends to be extended and the transition criteria into adulthood are rather vague. However, if adolescence is conceptualized as a gradual progress through specific stages on the path from childhood into adulthood, there are several important milestones marking this path. Among these important milestones and rites of passage are the following. (1) Age 15: This is the end of obligatory school education. It enables the adolescent to be employed, with certain limitations. This age is also when sexual contact and intercourse with another person becomes legal. (2) Age 18: This is the age of adulthood and full legal responsibility. Young people at this age have the right to vote, get married, obtain a driver's license, be fully employed with no limitations, and buy and consume alcoholic beverages.

It is important to note that full legal responsibility is not necessarily identical to one's subjective feeling of being an adult. Many young people connect their adulthood with economic independence from their parents and living separately from them. On the other hand, particularly among university and college students, there is a tendency to rely on financial support from parents. The developmental stage of emerging adulthood (Arnett, 2004) accurately describes young Czechs from ages 18 to 25. One of the characteristics of this period is a postponement of some of the goals and roles traditionally connected with adulthood. The time of study and career preparation has lengthened, the value of leisure time is enhanced, and the range of options of how to spend life as an adult is widened. The most striking changes can be seen upon entering married life and becoming a parent. Since the early 1990s, the mean age at marriage as well as the mean age of parents at birth of first child has risen significantly (for more details, see section on love and sexuality below).

Beliefs

Historically, the Czech Republic is one of a number of countries sharing a European Christian cultural heritage. The 40-year period of the Communist regime left indisputable traces in the beliefs and values of the country. The official ideology between 1948 and 1989 was based on an atheistic worldview and on the Marxist notion of collectivism. However, this form of collectivism was anonymous, disregarding the interests of individual people.

The political, social, and cultural changes at the beginning of the 1990s signified for many people important changes in their personal lives and destinies. More personal freedom brought a greater emphasis on personal responsibility and the value of the individual. Trends towards individualism gained in force and led to the gradual initiation of class differentiation and stratification. The post-totalitarian generation of Czech adolescents at the beginning of the 1990s perceived social changes extremely positively, since those changes represented personal opportunities and challenges (getting a good education, the possibility to travel and live abroad, and political and ideological freedom). On the other hand, the more recent generation of adolescents is apt to view the same conditions as ordinary attributes of everyday life.

Data from the year 2001 revealed that Czech youth at the turn of the twenty-first century were more similar to their Western European peers than to the former post-totalitarian Czech generation. These Czech youth experience personal freedom, but at the same time have more uncertainty and unpredictability in regard to their future. They also must take more responsibility for themselves. The value of education, money, success, social prestige, emancipation, free time, and entertainment has grown considerably (Macek, 2003).

The sense of community, which emphasizes the subordination of personal goals to group goals, does not prevail among young Czechs. On the other hand, there is a moderate growth of interest in public life, activities concerning the protection of the environment, solidarity or empathy with people in difficult life situations, and an increasing participation in volunteer and nonprofit activities.

Most Czech adolescents report very liberal and tolerant attitudes regarding drugs, abortion, and sexual freedom. According to Czech Statistical Office data from 2008, only about 18% of contemporary Czech adolescents consider themselves religious. The majority of these are Christian (77% Roman Catholic, 14% Protestant). Other denominations are rare. About 10% of adolescents declare themselves to be believers with no particular denomination.

Gender

During the Communist regime, Czech society underwent a process concerning gender roles that differed somewhat from that of Western European countries. The image of the "socially realistic" woman represented a typical example of the Czech woman (and those from other East European countries). According to this ideal she was politically involved, had her own income, and was a perfect housewife. This ideal corresponded to the image of the emancipated woman, who in Czech society was somewhat influenced by the paternalism of the Communist regime as well as the ideals for which Western feminists had fought.

However, only recently did the notion of gender become an important subject for discussion by those in the social sciences in the Czech Republic. Findings that outline the contemporary reality were disclosed in a study that focused on the conceptions of masculinity and femininity and the perception of gender role stereotypes among Czech adolescents and emerging adults (Wyrobková, 2007). The results show that young Czechs (aged 17 to 26) embody, to a great extent, both masculine and feminine characteristics and tend to blur gender differences and thus approximate the androgynous type of personality. However, men generally manifested typical masculine characteristics (ambitiousness, self-assertion, interest in sex) rather than feminine ones, and similarly, women proved to be more feminine. The situation was similar to the evaluation of the concepts of an ideal man and woman. In contrast to men, young women perceived as desirable a higher degree of masculinity in an ideal woman and a higher degree of femininity in an ideal man.

Since Western European cultural trends and ideals filtered into the Czech milieu at the beginning of the 1990s, the significance of the body—and body image—has been undergoing a gradual change. The Czech Republic has been experiencing an enormous expansion of the diet industry; body care facilities are also widespread. The ideal body type is becoming increasingly thin and is strongly supported by the mass media's propaganda of slimness being equal to success. Unhealthy media images and the pressure to be successful inevitably affect the values and lifestyle of Czech adolescents and influence their attitudes towards food and eating habits.

Data from a survey conducted with young people showed that men in the sample reflected more strongly the traditional views of masculine and feminine appearance than did young women (Brimová, 2004). Men struggled for a firm, adequately muscled body without excessive fat, and often wished to be taller. The women's concept of a female ideal ranged from tenderness to emphasizing muscles, but by no means did all women sampled view the image presented by the media (the extremely slim and tall model look) as their ideal. Nevertheless, the majority of them stressed the importance of a firm, slim body and had an aversion to being fat.

Body image and related matters have become issues in connection with the almost epidemic increase in eating disorders among Czech adolescent girls and young women. Research results show that up to 6% of Czech adolescent girls and young women suffer from eating disorders, and a third of them are underweight. Specialists' estimates are even higher—they estimate that about 10% of adolescent girls experience chronic problems with anorexia or bulimia (Možný, 2002). Most of them go undiagnosed until their illness causes secondary health problems.

The Self

Compared to previous generations, the self-system of contemporary adolescents appears to be more autonomous. The influence and importance of adult authorities (parents, teachers, and others) on self-definition has decreased. It is interesting to note that contemporary Czech adolescent girls presented higher self-esteem than the former generation of girls, and now there is no difference in relation to self-esteem between boys and girls (Macek, 2003).

Undoubtedly, the identity formation and self-definition processes of Czech adolescents are also shaped by historical and cultural contexts. The theme of identity and self-reflection of the Czech people gained specific prominence throughout the 1990s, during the period of major political, economic, and cultural changes. As there is an overall low mobility among the Czech population and most adolescents have spent their lives in one place, regional identity is important. At the same time, in connection with the admittance of the Czech Republic to the European Union, the issue of Europeanism has been accentuated. It is obvious that European identity is not opposed to national identity in the majority of young people, but is more likely to be the opposite: Those who think highly of their Czech identity also proclaim their Europeanism. National identity and pride have their historic roots; however, research among the young generation (the age group of 15 to 30) has proved that the success of popular and universally known personalities—above all of Czech sports athletes and some celebrities—forms part of the cultural sphere and is equally important in the formation of national pride (Sak & Saková, 2004).

Overall, democratization of Czech society has led to the reinforcement of individual freedom and dignity, the right to express individual opinions, and respect for the opinions and attitudes of others. The drawback of the democratization process is that there is a high degree of uncertainty in the sphere of values, standards, and unwritten rules of conduct among people. A view has developed that people can only find the basis for any moral decision in themselves (Baumeister, 1997), or in some cases in a moral discourse of negotiation with others in general and specific situations. This also helps us explain an increasing emphasis on the immediate and intensive consumption of pleasure in Czech adolescents and their tendency to reject long-term commitments in various spheres of life.

Family Relationships

A traditional model of parent and adolescent relationships that takes parental authority for granted still prevails. A spectrum of parenting styles and practices has been widening due to the liberalization of society and due to stress on the development of the individual. Parents' personal experiences and the values connected to their own childhood values and education all play a significant role in the style in which they choose to bring up their children. Parents with less education and those who grew up in the country usually favor a traditional division of roles in the family (the woman is primarily responsible for the household and the rearing of children, and the man is the breadwinner). Parents with a higher degree of education who live in the city prefer an equal division of roles, including in rearing their children.

The interaction between children and parents at the beginning and end of adolescence differs remarkably in Czech culture. An apparent asymmetry of the relationships between child and parent can be observed during the early adolescent stage. On one hand, the adolescent wants to have his or her way at all costs; on the other, the parents are often unable to refrain from their demands. The matter-of-fact nature of the conflicts is often banal. Quite naturally, the arguments pivot around household chores, pocket money, school duties, and free time. Several surveys have demonstrated that although the majority of adolescents admit to having arguments and conflicts with their parents, they get on well with them most of the time (Macek, 2003).

Girls in particular bear the brunt of parental restrictions in early adolescence. They are given a greater responsibility than boys for household chores. Also, parents exert more control over them; the parents' message is "be careful nothing bad happens to you." The change of status from child to emerging adult brings more advantages than disadvantages for boys. If parents exert any pressure on boys, it is usually about their behavior and their need to be more determined and assertive with their peers (in other words, the parents' message in this case is "show what you can do").

There is still an asymmetry in the relationship of child and parent that continues throughout mid-adolescence; however, interaction between the two is more open and constructive than it was before. There is an intense drive for adolescents to establish their right to freedom, whereas for the parents it is still immensely difficult to give up control of their child. A parent's control of their child's behavior rapidly decreases in emerging adulthood. The age of 18 represents a crucial landmark in the child–parent relationship. At this age adolescents reach adulthood in the Czech Republic and so gain all the elementary rights and responsibilities of an adult citizen. However, a surviving economical dependency of adolescents on their parents complicates the reaching of mutual acceptance and an equal, symmetrical relationship, especially for university students.

The divorce rate in the Czech Republic has been steady during recent decades; more than one third of all marriages end in divorce. Most adolescents who have experienced divorce describe it as a difficult time, but they do not perceive it as a stigmatizing event that negatively influences their personal development. Surveys suggest that adolescents whose parents divorce are more skeptical about their own future marriage or their ability to have lasting relationships than those adolescents whose parents stay together. On the other hand, unlike their peers who do not have this experience, they are able to view divorce as less destructive and their expectations for relationships as more realistic. They are often able to establish distance between their own relationship and that of their parents (Plaňava, 1999).

Friends and Peers/Youth Culture

From the ages of 10 to 18, the time spent at school and in the classroom forms the basic peer environment for Czech adolescents. Various types of interaction and relationships are established here: comradeship, deeper friendships, and their first intimate relationships. Moreover, the school organizes numerous after-school activities (such as sports, music, acting, and excursions).

Leisure centers also organize similar activities for children and young adolescents. The Scouts Union constitutes the widest membership among those official organizations that recruit children and adolescents. Its task is to encourage the mental, spiritual, social, and physical development of its members. The overwhelming majority of sports clubs have youth teams. At present, groups with environmental interests have lower memberships than two decades ago. Peer cliques have the same importance in early adolescence as do structured and organized peer activities. They are mainly formed by boys who share common interests and activities (sports activities, game playing, visiting of music clubs, music festivals, paintball, etc.).

There are no obvious class or social barriers to the bonds between adolescents' peers and friends. However, ethnic and racial barriers are more likely to determine the initiation of new relationships. Although Czech society has made some progress in this respect, it remains somewhat

xenophobic. Trust, or the lack of it, is unfortunately not based on following certain rules but on shared experiences. Often when Czechs confront unfamiliar people or things ("the other"), they are a priori distrustful and rejecting. The basis of the mainstream perception of "the other" relies on a dependence on the opinion of another kind of authority. Some Czechs among the older generation look down on such ethnic minorities as the Roma community or immigrants from Eastern Europe and Asia, and their opinion certainly has a negative influence on potential peer friendships or relationships among adolescents of different backgrounds.

The mainstream Czech adolescent culture has been increasingly tolerated in the Czech Republic and does not stand in direct opposition to the adult world. Czech adolescents are influenced by globalization and other mainstream trends that are typical for the lifestyle of adolescents in the cultural milieu of Euro-America. As in other countries, manufacturers in the Czech Republic target this particular age group (in fashion, music, and the sports industry). As it is, they incorporate the most up-to-date trends, such as hairstyles, clothing, as well as other aspects of fashion such as tattoos and piercing. Some attributes of this adolescent lifestyle and culture (fashion and music) are also attractive to adults.

It is indisputable that Czech adolescent culture also contains subcultures that are in opposition not only to the surrounding cultural milieu, but to each other as well. The subcultures are characterized by their unique outer attributes (slang, clothing, hairstyle) but also by their behavior and values. Very often their origination is inspired by a particular musical style and is demonstrated by participation at live performances, concerts, and such gatherings as techno parties, house parties, folk or rock festivals, clubs where different types of music can be heard (hip-hop can alternate with drum'n'bass, funk, or jazz). Attitudes to music and communication about it work as a quick indicator that defines peer attitudes, opinions, and values (in other words, "tell me what you listen to and I'll know who you are"). Sports club fans or groups centered around playing fantasy games also constitute an important element in the Czech subculture, as do groups with extreme political orientations, such as the skinheads and anarchists.

Love and Sexuality

Czech society can be characterized as being very liberal in respect to attitudes to love and sexuality. Traditionally, tolerance towards premarital sex has always been quite high (42% of men and 62% of women consider premarital sex admissible if practiced within a lasting relationship, and 49% of men and 29% of women think the same of engaging in random sexual contacts). There is a similar attitude to unfaithfulness in partner relationships (unconditionally rejected by 31% of Czech women and 25% of men). Only about 5% of the population is strictly against the use of contraception, and only 4% oppose abortions (Weiss & Zvěřina, 2001).

Parents are usually not very restrictive with their adolescent children in regard to their romantic relationships. Parents quite commonly tolerate their children's first dating at age 14 to 15 (more often girls than boys). Expressions of semi-intimate behavior (holding hands, kissing) are also common and tolerated in public and in secondary schools. Adolescents usually describe their romantic relationships mostly by affiliative characteristics such as shared leisure activities, humor, fun (Lacinová, Michalčáková, & Masopustová, 2008).

However, it is usually not the parents that provide effective sex education; there is a strong reliance on the schools to take on the role. School sex education targets boys and girls aged 11 to 14. The time devoted to dealing with sexual issues in sex education classes is quite limited (about four lessons for 11- to 12-year-olds and up to 15 lessons for 13- to 14-year-olds per school year) and in addition, teachers often fail to address important topics such as homosexuality. Many schools still do not provide effective sex education. Media, particularly the Internet, become the crucial source for information concerning sexual matters.

The legal age limit for having sexual intercourse in the Czech Republic is 15 years. This applies equally to heterosexual and homosexual behavior. Data regarding the sexual maturity and the initiation of sexual life for Czech adolescents does not differ much from those of youth in Western European countries. A gradual decrease in age for a first sexual encounter, recorded in the 1990s, has stopped and the age has remained steady during the past two decades. One quarter of 15-year-olds and almost half of 16-year-olds have experienced at least one sexual encounter. The rate for 17-year-old teenagers having their first sexual encounter is 64% and the figures grow to 75% of 18-year-old respondents. One third of boys and 12% of girls have their first sexual experience with a casual partner (Weiss & Zvěřina, 2001).

Concerning the use of birth control, over 50% of adolescents do not use any kind of contraception, nor do they practice safe sex during their first sexual encounter. Condoms are not very popular among Czech teenagers, On the other hand, the number of teenagers who use the birth control pill is steadily rising. This trend is closely connected to the substantial decrease in abortions during the past two decades.

Czech society has undergone significant changes in the family and in associated reproductive and sexual behavior during the past two decades. First marriages are often postponed until the late twenties/early thirties (the mean age of brides was 29.2 in 2009 compared to 21.8 in 1989, and for grooms it has risen from 24.6 to 31.9). The mean age of the birth of the first child has also risen demonstrably, and today almost 50% of children are born to mothers over 27 years of age.

At the same time, the number of children born to single mothers increased dramatically (39% in 2009). Overall, fertility has declined and childless couples are on the rise. The Czech Republic now has one of the lowest birth rates in Europe (1.49 children per woman in 2009). For the younger generations, the significance of marriage as a formal institution is declining. Unmarried partnerships and couples opting for a child-free life are on the increase and represent a discernible trend, especially for people with university degrees. Choosing a single lifestyle is another new phenomenon in Czech society and has become a distinct alternative to traditional partner relationships (Czech Statistical Office, 2010).

Czech society can be considered to be quite tolerant of homosexuality. According to data from a regular public opinion poll, there is a steady increase in social recognition and acceptance of same-sex couples, although this trend does not apply to child adoption and fostering rights for gays and lesbians. There still exists a certain fear of "coming out" among gay and lesbian youth, but most decide to disclose their sexuality quite soon after recognizing they are gay or lesbian. Among the first people they share this new knowledge with are usually their close heterosexual friends, but their parents are among the last to be told, if at all. Teenagers questioning their sexual orientation mainly seek information on the Internet (from specialized websites and chat rooms) where they usually find their first information.

Health Risk Behavior

Social problems became more visible in connection with the democratization of Czech society. State and institutional control over citizens' lives decreased, whereas the individual had to become more responsible for his or her own life. Not only did negative social phenomena become more visible, but their frequency and quantity also increased. This trend has affected Czech adolescents.

Alcohol consumption in the Czech Republic is the highest in Europe due to the fact that Czech society is exceptionally liberal in this respect. Although serving alcohol to those under 18 years of age is illegal, reality shows that the legal age restriction does not constitute any hindrance. The majority of adolescents have their first experience with alcohol between the ages of 9 and 11. Although most adolescents admit alcohol use can lead to obnoxious behavior and to the danger of excessive drinking, they still perceive alcohol as a natural part of their social life. Adolescents' underage alcohol consumption is a phenomenon that in itself is not harshly condemned. Among 15- to 18-year-olds, more than 50% occasionally drink alcohol, and fewer than 5% abstain completely. After coming of age at 18, nearly everyone is familiar with alcohol; among the 19- to 23-year-olds nearly 13% become regular drinkers (at least once a week) and 78% drink alcohol occasionally (Macek, 2003; Sak & Saková, 2004).

Smoking represents another major health risk. The majority of adolescents experience their first cigarette by the age of 15. According to data collected in 2000, about 13% of adolescents aged 15 to 18 smoke; the figure rises to 27% among the 19- to 23-year-olds (Sak & Saková, 2004). Unlike some Western European countries, the number of adolescent smokers in the Czech Republic is not decreasing.

The use of soft drugs, especially of cannabis, has increased a great deal, but recently this trend has begun to decrease. For most adolescents we can speak of experimentation, not addiction. By the age of 18, about a third of adolescents have experimented with soft drugs and about 16% admit repeated usage. As with smoking and consumption of alcohol, the first use of soft drugs (cannabis, Ecstasy) is regarded by adolescents as a social event (Macek, 2003).

Concerning hard drugs, Pervitin, a notorious Czech specialty, is the most common drug abused in the Czech Republic. Homemade and concocted from available medications, it is a substance whose effects are similar to heroin. It is difficult to determine the overall number of drug abusers in the adolescent population; estimates refer to 1% of adolescents.

Disorders of identity and depression (loss of reason for living, feelings of inferiority, loss of prospects for the future) have become increasingly frequent in recent years (although this is by no means a mass phenomenon). This may be due to the fact that contemporary society values a person according to his or her output and also emphasizes personal responsibility, decision-making, and self-control. On the other hand, the number of suicides has considerably decreased. Among youths aged 20 to 24 years, per population of 100,000, there were 11 suicides, while in the age group of 15 to 19 years this number was even lower.

If we focus on risks in the social behavior of adolescents, criminality is clearly the most serious. Trends in the growth of juvenile delinquency are relative to trends in the whole society. In the Czech Republic there was a considerable rise in criminality during the 1990s, though it has been steadily decreasing in the past few years. In 90% of cases, it is males that commit crimes.

Property crimes constitute about a third of adolescent crimes; thefts are the most frequent crimes in this respect (money, alcohol, cigarettes, bicycles, and cars stolen or broken into). These kinds of crime are seldom committed individually; in most cases adolescent gangs, sometimes controlled by adults, are responsible for them. Juvenile prostitution, the pornography trade, and violent crimes with racist and xenophobic motivations, though quite rare during the Communist regime, have been gaining prominence.

Education

The system of education in the Czech Republic has changed considerably since 1990. Schools ceased to be controlled by the state and became more autonomous. Apart from the state schools, private and church schools have also been introduced and represent about one-fifth of all secondary schools, which resulted in the provision of a wider educational spectrum. Thanks to the increasingly lower number of adolescents in the upcoming generations, two trends have recently become apparent: On one hand, there is an increase in schools that are not particularly appealing to students and that try to recruit new students with little success (due to their low quality or lack of prestige and success in teaching specialized subjects); on the other hand, there are prestigious schools that are unable to accept all the applicants.

Since 1774 school attendance has been compulsory in the Czech Republic. Children usually start attending school at the age of six and complete their primary education when they are 15. Consequently, all Czech adolescents are completely literate and attain a comprehensive level of elementary education, except for those who are seriously physically handicapped. All schools are coeducational, and girls and boys have equal access to education.

Secondary schools prepare students either for future professions or for further studies. There are three major types of secondary school in the Czech Republic: comprehensive secondary schools, secondary technical schools, and secondary vocational and apprentice schools. In the Czech Republic, the term "gymnasium" is used for a comprehensive secondary school. On average about 50% of applicants succeed in entrance exams to gymnasium, although acceptance might be lower for the most prestigious schools. At present they constitute about 20% of the total number of secondary schools in the Czech Republic. Their aim is to prepare students for further academic education, mainly university. Three subtypes of gymnasium exist in the Czech Republic according to the length of study, which is four years (from age 15 to 19), six years (from 13 to 19), or eight years (from 11 to 19). All students take the final *maturita* (graduation) exam at the age of 19. After passing the exam the student obtains a General Certificate of Secondary Education (GCSE), which entitles her or him to go to university.

Specialized secondary technical schools provide students with a four-year vocational education that concludes with a final graduation exam. This type of school accounts for 38% of all secondary schools. They prepare students for technical and other specialized practical activities, as well as for college and university. About 40% of the syllabus comprises general subjects, and 60% is specific vocational subjects. Vocational school types include specialties in engineering; chemistry; mechanical engineering; agriculture; construction; accounting and secretarial; teaching; nursing; arts, crafts, and design; and music, dramatic arts, and dancing. As with grammar schools, applicants do not always succeed in getting accepted by the school they desire.

Secondary vocational schools account for about 41% of all secondary schools. They offer two- or three-year apprenticeship courses concluded by a final exam, after which the apprenticeship certificate is granted. Practical training comprises about one-half of teaching time and aims at the acquisition of manual skills in a trade. The number of specializations amounts to 280. Four-year courses are also provided by secondary vocational schools, which conclude with a final exam. These courses are for training highly skilled manual workers.

State policy is also oriented toward children and youth with special educational needs. A fairly efficient network of special schools, classes, and other facilities has been established for children and youth with mental or physical handicaps, with impairment of hearing, vision, and/or speech, as well as for those with developmental and behavioral disorders. Nevertheless, the desire is to fully integrate these children into mainstream education, which is a process that has only recently been introduced. In the past, handicapped children tended to be secluded from the rest of society, so their integration into ordinary life was more difficult.

Integration of Roma children and youth into Czech society is still not very successful, although the situation has improved considerably in the recent years. A high proportion of Roma children are still perceived as being mentally disabled and are placed in special schools. However, even though disadvantaged socially, these children and adolescents have no mental handicaps.

According to education statistics and indicators from the OECD (2009), the Czech Republic ranks among those countries with high standards in secondary education. Czech secondary students (aged 15 years) have traditionally been good at mathematics, science, and reading literacy. Foreign languages, on the other hand, still seem to be a weak point for both Czech students and teachers (Možný, 2002).

Work

The transition from school to work represents a significant transitory stage and is often perceived as the transition from adolescence to adulthood. The age of transition from school to an economically active life is slightly below 20. However, the range in the age at which young people start working has been widening. The number of people who combine their studies with work has also increased recently (OECD, 2009). Although exact figures are not known, it has become evident that in recent years the number of university students who work part-time during their studies has increased.

Laws in the Czech Republic prevent employers from exploiting adolescents as cheap labor. The minimum working age for young Czechs is 15 years. In addition, legal protection guarantees that the employer must not give adolescents any overtime work or any night work. Adolescents under the age of 18 may not be employed in work that is dangerous or damages their health.

In early adolescence, work is often limited to household chores. According to daily activity surveys of 14- to 16-year-olds, they spend about a half an hour a day working in activities such as cleaning the house and shopping (Macek, 2003). Only a very small number of adolescents work part-time during the academic year. However, they often hold jobs during the summer holidays. The situation changes for 20- to 24-year-olds. In 2003, 56% of this age group worked, 25% were students, 4% were on parental leave, and 8% were unemployed.

As far as wages are concerned, employees aged 20 to 24 usually receive two-thirds of an average adult salary in the Czech Republic. Again, there are strong differences according to the level of education. Whether they are highly educated or not, most people in this age group are not satisfied with the overall amount of their income.

People aged 20 to 24 still clearly depend economically to a great extent on their primary family. About half of this age group still live with their parents. This dependence is not only of an economic character; the young also use or take advantage of their parents' social milieu, including their social network and informal influence. From a 2003 survey it could be inferred that more than half of the respondents relied on the help of their parents and friends when looking for a job (Burda, Festová, Úlovcová, & Vojtěch, 2003). Other results of this survey reflect that adolescents' transition from school to work is usually smooth. About 42% had no difficulty in finding a job, and more than a quarter of respondents were able to find one even while they were still studying.

The academic and labor opportunities for young people are likely to increase now that the Czech Republic has joined the European Union. It is difficult to assess the situation yet, but it is evident that people are interested in working and studying in EU countries. In 2001, more than 60% of adolescents aged 19 to 23 showed an interest in availing themselves of this opportunity (Sak & Saková, 2004).

Media

Mass media and information technologies strongly determine Czech lifestyles, including those of adolescents. Television and Internet are the most influential and most widespread. The Internet is used by 93% in the age group 12–18 years. Czech adolescents spend weekly on average approximately 12 hours online (older adolescents spend more time than younger) and 14 hours watching TV (Šmahel & Konečný, 2006; Subrahmanyam & Šmahel, 2010). Compared with TV, the influence of radio is far less significant and listening (weekly approximately 10 hours) often takes place with other activities (Macek, 2003).

Concerning adolescents' activities on the Internet, email usage and instant messengers are the applications most often used. Communication is probably the main purpose of Internet use for Czech adolescents (Subrahmanyam & Šmahel, 2010). But Czech adolescents also often download and listen to music online, download videos, and play online games. Online gaming is most widespread among younger adolescents—77% aged 12 to 14 years reported playing. School-related activities are also reported, but the communication and entertainment activities predominate. Online blogging (writing and reading diaries on the Internet) is one way some Czech adolescents express themselves online. About 62% of Czech adolescents are reading online blogs and 31% are writing their own blogs, presenting personal information (Blinka & Šmahel, 2009).

According to current data, about 99% of young Czechs are using mobile phones. For Czech adolescents, especially for those aged 14–20, a mobile phone is a highly personal object that is often worn like a piece of clothing. It can be adapted to the individual "look" or "expression" by changing the ring tone, the interface, the color of the shield, or by adding logos and/or stickers.

Politics and Military

Political participation was not easy for the generation of Czech adolescents living in the previous few decades. During the Communist era, political participation was explicitly associated with support of the Communist regime. In the second half of the 1990s the situation changed dramatically. Czech people became increasingly dissatisfied with the imperfect rule of law, the functioning of the political system, and representative and executive state institutions. Economic conditions deteriorated, unemployment rose rapidly, and much corruption was exposed. The interest of young people in homeland affairs and their active participation dropped markedly; people ceased to be interested, especially in local politics. Compared with the previous period, young people became more skeptical.

By no means do these findings show that young people succumbed to nihilism or despair. Their attitude to the current political situation is quite realistic and corresponds to the overall atmosphere in Czech society. As a 2002 survey shows, the overwhelming majority of young people aged 15 to 26 are content with the fact that they live in the Czech Republic. On the whole, distrust and skepticism still prevail on both local and national levels. In international comparisons, young Czechs' assessment of institutions does not differ markedly from the opinions of their counterparts in some Western European countries, such as France or Great Britain (Macek & Marková, 2004).

During the past two decades Czech youth became more trustful of the army and the police. As far as the army was concerned, this attitude was undoubtedly related to the Czech Republic joining NATO in 1999 and to the fact that the army gradually became more professional. After more than 80 years, the draft for all men aged 19 was abolished in 2004.

Young people over 18 have the right to vote for legislative and representative delegates, ranging from local municipal councils to members of parliament. Citizens over the age of 21 can run for a post in any representative body. On the whole, it could be said that young people are not very interested in politics. Lack of freedom during the Communist regime left significant memories; it is thus believed that changes are only important at the highest level of state administration, and people are suspicious of local politics (Možný, 2002).

Unique Issues

The use of information technologies such as the Internet and mobile phones cannot be seen as an issue unique to Czech adolescents. However, Czech adolescents are unusual in that 15 years ago almost none of them owned a mobile phone and today nearly all of them do.

Seven years ago, text messaging represented the main use of mobile phones by Czech youth, who were the most active users of this form of communication in the world. The reasons may be mainly financial, but text messaging has other advantages as well. It is not the mere transmission of information. Unlike phone calls, text messaging is only interactive in an indirect way and like emails it gives a greater sense of autonomy in communication with other teenagers.

Czech adolescents seem to be unique today in usage of online calling (e.g., Skype). Compared to other Western countries, online calling is more widespread in the Czech Republic. For example, about 43% of Czech adolescents use the Internet for calling, against 15% of adolescents in the US (Subrahmanyam & Šmahel, 2010). The reason for this difference is mainly economic; so-called "flat rates" on mobile phones (paying a certain amount of money for unlimited calls) are very expensive in the Czech Republic and adolescents cannot afford them, but online calling is free.

References and Further Reading

Arnett, J. J. (2004). *Emerging adulthood*. Oxford, UK: Oxford University Press.

Baumeister, R. F. (1997). "The self and society: Changes, problems, and opportunities." In R. D. Ashmore & L. Jussim (Eds.), *Self and identity*. New York, NY: Oxford University Press.

Blinka, L., & Šmahel, D. (2009). Fourteen is fourteen and a girl is a girl: Validating the identity of adolescent bloggers. *Cyberpsychology & Behavior*, *12*, 735–739.

Brimová, E. (2004). Ideál krásy: Štíhlí a svalnatí. *Psychologie Dnes*, *10*, 14–16.

Burda, V., Festová, J., Úlovcová, H., & Vojtěch, J. (2003). *Přístup mladých lidí ke vzdělávání a jejich profesní uplatnění*. Prague, Czech Republic: Národní ústav odborného vzdělávání.

Chisholm, L. Ch., & Hurrelman, K. (1995). Adolescence in modern Europe: Pluralized transition patterns and their implications for personal and social risks. *Journal of Adolescence*, *18*, 129–158.

Czech Statistical Office (2010). Data retrieved from www.czso.cz

Eurobarometr ČR (2002). Prague, Czech Republic: Institut dětí a mládeže MŠMT ČR. Retrieved from www.idm-msmt.cz

Lacinová, L., Michalčáková, R., & Masopustová, Z. (2008). Láska je láska: Představy a zkušenosti patnáctiletých adolescentů. *E-psychologie*, 2, 16–29. Retrieved from http://epsycholog.eu

Macek, P. (2003). *Adolescence*. Prague, Czech Republic: Portál.

Macek, P., & Marková, I. (2004). Trust and distrust in old and new democracies. In I. Marková (Ed.), *Trust and democratic transition in post-Communist Europe*. Oxford, UK: Oxford University Press.

Možný, I. (2002). *Česká společnost. Nejdůležitější fakta o kvalitě našeho života*. Prague, Czech Republic: Portál.

OECD (2009). *Education at a glance: OECD indicators – 2009 edition*. Paris, France: OECD. Retrieved from www.oecd.org

Plaňava, I. (1999). *Manželství a rodiny: Struktura, dynamika, komunikace*. Brno, Czech Republic: Doplněk.

Rabušic, L., & Hamanová, J. (2009). *Hodnoty a postoje v ČR 1991–2008*. Brno, Czech Republic: Masarykova Univerzita.

Sak, P., & Saková, K. (2004). *Mládež na křižovatce*. Prague, Czech Republic: Svoboda Servis.

Šmahel, D., & Konečný, Š. (2006). Vztahy na internetu: fantazie a zklamání. In P. Macek & L. Lacinová (Eds.), *Vztahy v dospívání*. Brno, Czech Republic: Barrister & Principal.

Statistical Yearbook of the Czech Republic (2003). Prague, Czech Republic: Czech Statistical Office. Retrieved from: www.czso.cz

Statistical Yearbook of the Czech Republic (2009). Prague, Czech Republic: Czech Statistical Office. Retrieved from: www.czso.cz

Subrahmanyam, K., & Šmahel, D. (2010). *Digital youth: The role of media in development*. New York, NY: Springer.

Weiss, P., & Zvěřina, J. (2001). *Sexuální chování v ČR – situace a trendy* [Sexual behavior in the Czech Republic: Situation and trends]. Prague, Czech Republic: Portál.

Wyrobková, A. (2007). *Reprezentace a hodnocení genderových kategorií*. PhD dissertation, Masarykova Univerzita, Brno, Czech Republic.

Chapter 18
France

Lyda Lannegrand-Willems, Colette Sabatier, and Camille Brisset

Background Information

With 64 million inhabitants, France is an established, prosperous, urbanized, powerful, officially monolingual, democratic, and secular country. In 2007 the country ranked eighth on the Human Development Index, which is provided by the United Nations Development Program in order to reflect the level of development for all in terms of education, access to health services, and equality. Economically, it is one of the wealthiest nations in Europe, with comprehensive policies on education, health, family support, and the distribution of wealth. Geographically, France provides a diversity of temperate weather and a variety of landscapes.

French demography is characterized by low rates of birth and long life expectancies with a very small positive migration balance. However, in comparison to other European Union (EU) countries, France has among the highest levels of both life expectancy (78 for men and 84 for women in 2008) and birth rate (2.01 children per woman in 2006). People live mostly in urban areas (74%).

France has experienced several waves of migration since the early period of its history and has been the subject of multiple invasions. A strong tradition of conquering territories between the 16th and 19th centuries and a liberal policy regarding immigration during the twentieth century are two other sources of the diversity of its modern population. Although the French government does not keep statistics about ethnicity and ethnic origin, it is estimated that 24% of the general population is a first-, second-, or third-generation immigrant, and 6% are not French citizens. Mainly a Catholic region, France also has the largest Jewish and Islamic populations in the European Union.

Period of Adolescence

The period of adolescence is recognized as beginning upon entrance into junior high school (age 12) and ending at the legal majority age of 18. In the 19th century, the term "adolescence" was narrowly applied to boys, especially those of the bourgeoisie. Other adolescents—boys of lower socioeconomic groups and girls—were not considered as a special population. They either were subject to strict parental control, in the case of girls, or were already contributing to the workforce, in the case of boys who were peasants or working class (Thiercé, 1999). It is only since 1890 that the concept of "adolescence" has been extended progressively to all without consideration of social class.

Puberty begins, like in most Western countries, for boys around 11.5 to 12 years of age, with testicular growth. First ejaculations appear on average around 14 years old and precede by about six months the presence of sperm. For girls, mammary development, which is the first outward sign, appears around 11 years. The mean age for menarche is between 12.5 and 13 years.

The first psychological study on French adolescents was conducted by Mendousse in 1907 for boys (1910 for girls). However, Debesse's influential work on identity and on the balance between conformism and anti-conformism (1936, 1937, 1942) is considered the foundation of the field in France. Translated into several languages, his monograph of 1942 is still in print.

At the economic and societal levels, the 1960s and early 1970s present three significant turning points: first, the economic boom and the prolongation of the mandatory school age until 16 years of age; second, the university student uprising of May 1968, joined by the majority of high-school youth and a large segment of the French society with demands for more freedom and fewer social conventions; and later, in 1974 and 1975, reforms and laws for modernization such as easy access to contraception, the legalization of abortion, democratization of studies, and the lowering of the majority age. These evolutions discharged adolescents from the constraints of early entrance into the labor market, from hierarchical relationships, and from extended dependency on parents. During this period, radio stations and magazines specially devoted to the adolescent subculture emerged.

Given the transformation of the society and the new economic demands since the 1960s and 1970s, individuals leave adolescence later. For example, the French live with their parents until the median age of 23 for men and 21 for women, with variations according to a conjunction of factors such as the area (Parisian area versus other regions), the availability of an allowance, the socioeconomic level of the parents, and the status of the family (intact versus divorced) (Driant, Casteran, & O'Prey, 2007/2008). Median age of leaving home has been relatively stable for the past 40 years.

The way young people become adults is intrinsically connected to the intervention of the State, the school and the family, in the country. As a unique French issue, to become an adult, young people in France have to *position themselves* in the society through their schooling and a "race" to diplomas, which comes with a prolonged dependence on the family (van de Velde, 2008). As a consequence, two main factors explain the later commitment to adult roles in France: the extension of school attendance, which is longer in France and Belgium than in other European countries, and the difficulties of gaining employment (Galland, 2004). "Emerging adulthood" affects almost all individuals, whatever their origin or social class, but two subtypes are observed. The first concerns those who have ended their studies and live with their parents, awaiting a favorable professional situation (50% without a diploma live with parents at least six years after the end of school, and 25% more than 10 years; Driant et al., 2007/2008).The second concerns postsecondary students who, by contrast, leave their parents' home earlier but remain financially dependent on them.

Beliefs

The European Values Study indicates that French values stand between northern and southern European ways of thinking, with some ambivalence or ambiguity (Bréchon, 2000). Being a Latin and mainly Catholic region (in terms of cultural history), France conceives the links between the state and the individual in a hierarchical model. Nonetheless, people want to master their own life and choose their ethical norms. They no longer accept imposed societal rules, but beyond their private lives, for which they do not accept societal control, many French people—including young people—seek collective rules and social order.

Since 1905, there has been a strict separation of church and state in France. Religion is considered a matter of private rights. Freedom of faith is guaranteed as an individual right. The main religions are part of the school curriculum as cultural heritage (faith, values, arts, customs, etc.). The religious communities collaborate with high schools and are allowed to organize teaching of religion. The main Christian, Jewish, and Muslim holy days are respected or accommodated. However, compared to some other European countries, religious values are less endorsed. Some declare to have no religion or faith, but others claim to be heathen, agnostic or laic; in other words, to have an axiological anchorage: 41% of people between 15 and 24 years of age (27% for all adults) declare to have no faith while 9% (13% for all adults) declare to have a regular practice (Bréchon, 2000; Roudet & Galland, 2005).

Gender

The laws structuring the equality of gender are relatively recent. Women obtained the right to vote in 1944, and it was not until 1965 that married women were allowed to open a bank account without a husband's authorization. School became mandatory for boys and girls in 1882, but in separate establishments. Coeducation became mandatory for all public schools in 1975. After this date, higher education institutions became, one after the other, accessible to both genders. There also exists a policy to encourage women to enroll in professions such as firefighting or policing.

In spite of the law guaranteeing gender equality, inequalities persist in the practices and representation of differential competencies. Unequal treatment is noticeable in terms of professional choices, more women working in services, and salaries. In 2006, women's salaries were equivalent to 73% of men's (DARES, 2008). Inequalities are obvious in the case of promotion and for political representation, especially in elected positions. In 2007, women filled 18% of parliamentary positions (Union Interparlementaire, 2008).

In the French academic curriculum, which is selective and competitive, math is perceived as masculine. Girls are underrepresented in scientific domains, and generally in all prestigious and selective fields, although they are on average schooled longer than boys. Several information campaigns and government texts try to convince girls to choose training in areas where there is currently a majority of boys. However, girls' professional goals are more often a compromise between professional and family life (Duru-Bellat, 1999).

Although the pressure for gender role conformity is generally strong, the hierarchical gender role is in favor of masculine behavior. The adoption of the other gender role is better accepted for girls than for boys (Mosconi, 1999). Gender stereotypes shape self-concept and self-presentation of adolescents. When girls describe themselves, they give greater importance to emotions and interpersonal relationships than do boys (Boyer, 1999). Preoccupied by their bodies and sensitive to the regard from others, they are more subject to diffuse somatic complaints, are more often depressive, and are more nervous than boys, who look for self-affirmation in sports activities (Choquet & Ledoux, 1994).

The Self

French adolescents' self-esteem varies according to gender and age. Girls have a lower global, emotional, and physical self-esteem than boys, while their future self-esteem is higher. Older adolescents (between 17 and 20 years) have a higher social self-esteem than younger ones (from 13 to 16 years). Nonetheless, as a whole, French adolescents' global and specific scores indicate a positive self-image (Sordes-Ader, Lévêque, Oubrayrie, & Safont-Mottay, 1998).

A study on the definition of the ideal self by French adolescents between 16 and 18 years indicates that references to external criteria such as social achievement (academic performance, appreciation from others) decrease with age, while references to self and self-realization (coherence with one's principles, openness to the world, to be oneself) increase. It seems that, among developmental tasks, adolescents first build an ideal image of themselves based on external criteria and, with age, they try to accomplish it (Bariaud & Bourcet, 1998).

Their professional paths get more precise as they grow up. Adolescents from the lower social class choose their way earlier than those from the upper social class, who pursue their studies to a higher education level. The last degree of the junior high school (*troisième*— ninth grade) is a turning point for school or professional orientation. Grade 9, called "vocational cycle" in France, constitutes the first vocational level characterized by a separation between high-school, technical, and vocational trainings. This becomes a crucial moment for identity and self-esteem, since pupils have to take one of three vocational paths (Lannegrand-Willems, 2008; Lannegrand-Willems & Bosma, 2006).

Family Relationships

French family members are generally close and maintain good relationships (Crenner, 1998, 1999). Members of the same family tend to live in nearby areas (30 kilometers on average). Adolescents participate in this familial solidarity (INSEE, 2000); they often meet with older members of their family (parents, siblings, uncles and aunts, cousins). Family networks are composed of 27 persons on average.

Family life is important for all generations—grandparents, parents, and adolescents. In a three-generations study, a correlation was observed between solidarity and interdependence as family values and life satisfaction for each generation (Sabatier & Lannegrand-Willems, 2005). The family includes typically two (married or not) adults and two or three children. One-child families make up 10% of families with children, and two out of 10 children are from a family of four or more children (Toulemon, 2003). As a result of high life expectancy, numerous children and adolescents know at least two of their grandparents and even one of their great-grandparents, who live independently for the most part (Kerjosse, 2000).

Family relationships, including relationships with grandparents, are important for French adolescents, who endorse the desire for children and family more than any other Western European adolescents (Nurmi, Liiceanu, & Liberska, 1999). Compared to Italians and Belgians, French adolescents visit their grandparents less often, but have a greater degree of attachment and more significant bonds (Claes, Lacourse, Bouchard, & Luckow, 2001).

Values that parents want to transmit are mainly tolerance, respect for others, and a sense of responsibility (Bréchon, 2000). Independence is ranked ninth, just after obedience. This indicates that French society is neither individualist nor collectivist, but is looking for a way for all to live together, with each individual assuming the appropriate amount of personal responsibility.

During late adolescence, parent–adolescent relationships in France are less warm but also less conflictual than those in Italy and Quebec, and parents monitor less but are less tolerant of misbehavior (Claes, Lacourse, Bouchard, & Perucchini, 2003). According to the adolescents' view, French parents offer less choice and more constraints than German ones (Schleyer-Lindenmann, 1997).

Fifty percent of children are born to unmarried couples, but only 17% of children live in a single-parent family, and 6% of families are stepfamilies (Vivas, 2009). Research studies on how French adolescents respond to the divorce or separation of their parents are very few. Parents' separation is associated with low school achievement (Archambault, 2002), and family changes have connections with adolescents' drug use (Mucchielli, 2000, 2002). Nevertheless, these adolescents do not have particular psychopathologies compared to adolescents whose parents are not separated (Messerschmitt, Legrain, & Hamasaki, 1998).

Friends and Peers/Youth Culture

Social interactions with peers are important in the adolescent world. More than 60% of adolescents go outside their family, invite each other out, and organize parties with friends. Their extracurricular activities are in close relation with a desire to meet friends; they plan to go out in groups, and choose clubs or associations in order to get together. Listening to music is usually an occasion for socialization with peers: Musical preferences are an important aspect of group distinctiveness (Boyer, 1999).

Friendship is a dominant aspect of the social life of adolescents, and they rarely say that they do not have a single friend (less than 1%). However, 23% of adolescents do not interact with their peers, 23% never go out with other adolescents, and 28% never go to a friend's home. In one case out of five, this social isolation is explained by parental restrictions, and in one case out of two, by

a lack of desire. Boys and girls from early adolescence choose different activities; girls are more attracted by home activities and boys by outside activities (Boyer, 1999).

As is generally observed with Western adolescents, French adolescents value intimacy between friends more in early adolescence than in middle childhood, especially with same-gender friends (Mallet, 1993). It is only around the age of 16 to 17 years that intimacy with the opposite gender is as high as with same-gender peers (Mallet, 1997). However, the intimacy between same-gender friends is highly valued. Less than one adolescent in four between 15 and 19 years old reports having other-gender friends and, among those who have a love relationship, 69% of them report to be more attached to their same-gender friends than to their romantic partner (Garcia-Werebe, 1988).

French adolescents spend more time leaning against, stroking, kissing, and hugging their friends than do American adolescents, who show more aggressive verbal and physical behavior (Field, 1999). The stability of friendship with same-gender peers, while love relationships gain in intimacy, according to Mallet (1997), suggests that friendship between same-gender peers supports the establishment of love relationships.

The opportunity for activities such as sports or cultural activities with friends is high and well organized everywhere in France. However, activities such as sports cost money and, in consequence, participation is related to the family income and the level of education of mothers.

Gatherings in public areas are the only way to socialize for adolescents and emerging adults who live in unprivileged suburban areas, as they cannot afford most leisure activities. These gatherings are considered a new phenomenon and a nuisance by the authorities, who fear acts of delinquency. In a process of stigmatization of suburban youth, a law was introduced in 2003 intended to reduce youth meetings under stairwells and in building entrances. The term "suburbs youth" has been created to point out and to stigmatize the specific population who live in areas called "sensitive," characterized by a high rate of social housing with the result of segregation (Bordet, 1998). These areas count more than 80% of their populace as working class, and more than 40% of persons are under the age of 20 years old. The unemployment rate is very high and the presence of immigrants in the population is three times higher than in other areas.

The suburbs youth constitute a microsociety organized around survival and defense against social exclusion. They feel themselves dominant inside their area but rejected by society. They invest in and control some spaces of their housing area (stairwells, caves, entrances) but consider inaccessible or "foreign" all spaces outside of their living area (Bordet, 1998). This microsociety is an inclusive place that is difficult to leave. However, it protects adolescents from the risk of roaming and identity loss, and offers an anchorage within a social network of relationships.

Love and Sexuality

Sexuality and love behaviors visible in France are similar to those in other Western countries. Adolescence and emerging adulthood are tolerated and even expected periods of exploration. The beginning of sexual life is clearly independent of the beginning of couple life, and it is neither hidden nor illegitimate. Parents agree with this dissociation between love relationships and couple formation, and for 25 years, the majority of the French have agreed with the access to oral contraception for girls before age 18 (Galland, 2004).

Since the late 20th century, the rate of sexual precocity has been generally stable, but involvement in a lasting relationship and parenthood are delayed. Among 14-year-olds, 50% have exchanged their first French kiss. The first sexual intercourse appears on average three and a half years later, at the age of 17. It occurs in two cases out of three either at the parents' or partner's parents' residence, indicating parental acceptance of adolescents' sexuality (Galland, 2004; INSEE, 2000).

Involvement in a lasting relationship occurs several years later. Marriage is delayed, and a period of cohabitation precedes marriage in 70% of cases. The median couple formation age is 25 years for women and 27 for men. The median age for marriage was 26 for women and 28 for men in 1990, and is now 30 for women and 32 for men, and the mean age for a woman at the first birth is 30 years (it was 24 years in 1975) (Pla & Beaumel, 2009). From the first kiss to cohabitation and marriage, experimentation with different partners is typical.

Patterns of family building among immigrants are in general more or less identical to the French one, but they vary according to the length of stay of the groups. People from older immigrant groups (Italian, Spanish, Portuguese, and Algerian) follow globally the same pattern of marriage and fertility as the French, except that cohabitation before marriage is less frequent among Algerian immigrants. In the two main more recent groups (Moroccans and Turks), women marry earlier and men later. They also have more children, and at a younger age (INSEE, 2005, 2006). The arranged marriage of minors is an issue with some African and Turkish immigrants, but there are no reliable data to evaluate its extent.

Because of the AIDS issue, one could have expected a rapid transformation of sexual practices, but sexual behaviors of French adolescents have not basically changed. The only exception is the usage of condoms, worn today by 90% of youth during their first intercourse (INSERM-INED-ANRS, 2007). Adolescents and young adults who say they have homosexual relations are rare—about 3% (Bajos & Bozon, 2008).

Sexual education is organized, especially within the school system. Children and adolescents are informed at school about body transformations during adolescence, sexuality, and birth control. The curriculum is planned to give information in several stages and to adjust the information according to the cognitive and sexual development of children. In addition to the transmission of information and knowledge, sexual education focuses on communication and relationships (Michaud, 1997). The approaches are interactively centered on adolescents' expectancies and questions on both sexual and romantic topics. A new goal is to educate young men on sexuality in a context of relationship and not as a demonstration of strength.

Since 1974, contraceptives have been offered to adolescent girls without parental authorization. Family planning centers, anonymous and free for minors, inform on contraceptive methods and provide contraceptives. In 2002, 63% of women between 18 and 19 years old used a contraceptive (80% between 20 and 24 years), usually birth control pills. Since 1990, these centers afford for minors, on a free and anonymous basis, testing for and treatment of sexually transmitted diseases.

The voluntary termination of pregnancy is legal since 1975 until 10 weeks, and after this period the only solution is an abortion for medical reasons. To have access to abortion, minors should have the authorization of at least one legal responsible adult, but in case of opposition, one can refer to a judge. Nonetheless, parents cannot oblige an adolescent to abort. Since 1999, school nurses and social workers are allowed to give the morning-after pill (RU86) without parental consent.

France is characterized by a very low rate of adolescent pregnancy. According to UNICEF (2001), it is among the lowest rates in the world. Nine women in one thousand between the ages of 15 and 19 years have a child, mainly Gypsies. As a basis of comparison, the US mean is 53 in 1,000, and the Canadian mean is 16.

Health Risk Behavior

The main health risk behaviors indulged in by adolescents are substance use (tobacco, alcohol, legal and illegal drugs), driving at high speeds, driving without a license, drug dealing, and crime (violence and thefts). The European School Survey Project on Alcohol and Other Drugs (ESPAD; Hibell et al.,

2009) indicates that, compared to the European mean, French youth smoke and consume cannabis more frequently, drink and are drunk less often, and have the same level of illegal drug consumption.

Cigarette smoking is a public health issue. Sixty percent of 16-year-olds have smoked once in their life, and 17% smoke on a daily basis. While a decrease in these trends has been observed in the past decade (they were respectively 80% and 31% in 1999), adolescents experience smoking earlier and earlier. Nine percent of 9–10-year-olds and 36% of 11–15-year-olds have already tried smoking (INPES, 2007; INSERM, 2009).

Concerning alcohol consumption and drunkenness, 90% of 16-year-olds have experienced alcohol intake and 13% have drunk alcohol at least 10 times during the past 30 days. Drunkenness is rare: 50% of 16-year-olds have been drunk once in their life, 33% in the last year, and only 3% at least 10 times during the past 30 days (INSERM, 2009). On the other hand, cannabis is a problem but its consumption among teenagers has been decreasing over the past few years. In 1999, France became the top European country for trying and consuming cannabis in adolescence. In 2007, 31% of 16-year-olds had used cannabis (compared to 35% in 1999). The proportion of regular users has dropped from 6% in 2003 to 3% in 2007 (INSERM, 2009). Five percent of adolescents have also tried other illegal drugs. Experimentation is more frequent among boys than among girls.

Suicide in adolescence among 15- to 24-year-olds is the second highest cause of death (15%), after road accidents (30%), and among 25- to 34-year-olds it is the most frequent cause. However, adolescents between 15 and 19 years seldom commit suicide as compared to emerging adults aged 20–24. In comparison with 17 European countries, the French suicide rate in adolescence is around the mean for boys and girls. There is, however, an unequal distribution within France, with an overrepresentation in rural areas (Brittany, Normandy, and Center) and in all really disadvantageous situations such as school dropouts and very low sociocultural levels (Pommereau, 2001). Concerning suicide attempts, the rate is higher for females than for males. Among people younger than 25 years, there is one death for 22 suicide attempts among boys and one death for 160 suicide attempts among girls (Mallet, 2004).

Education

Free schooling is a right (and duty) for every child from six to 16 years living in the French territory, even for illegal immigrant children. Since Jules Ferry's law in 1882, school (which is mandatory and free) has been seen as a "republican" instrument to educate peasants, the working class, and immigrants, and as a means of integration. Public school is considered as good as private school, and 70% of children attend public school, with little disparity between regions.

The typical school day lasts six hours on three days a week, with an additional half day. There is a rest day in the middle of the week where different leisure activities are offered and where children can attend catechism class. The number of school days a year as compared to other countries is small (177). Besides the two-month summer vacation and the two weeks for Christmas break, there are three other school breaks, one in each term.

The French school system is globally divided into four independent levels of institutions. The first one, preschool, is part of the public education system, and 98% of three-year-olds attend school at least half a day. The second level is the primary school with five grades. The third level is "college" (first level of secondary school) with basically four grades. The program is the same for everybody, with no speciality for the two first levels (sixth and seventh grades), and the only possible diversification is the choice of the second language. At the level *quatrième* (eighth grade), some different paths are possible.

At the fourth level, *lycée*, with three grades, a real diversification is possible. Students can enter vocational training, which ends with a professional diploma and opens the door for a job. However, school absenteeism is overrepresented in vocational training. Preventing school absenteeism and school dropout has become a priority for the French Government (Lannegrand-Willems, Cosnefroy & Lecigne, in press). Students can also choose a general education path either with theoretical and intellectual subjects or with an introduction to work-related activities and courses more oriented toward practical topics. The last year of *lycée*, called *terminale*, ends with a national examination, the *baccalauréat* or *le bac*. This highly valued diploma gives the right to enter university and many professional schools. In 1984, the government planned that 80% of youth should obtain the *baccalauréat* with the argument that a modern and competitive society needs people with a high-level qualification and good flexibility. In fact, in 2007, the proportion of *bacheliers* was 64% (70% of girls and 58% of boys).

Low grades are a source of anxiety and represent one of the major causes of depression for adolescents between 12 and 18 years (Bariaud and Oliveri 1989, Rodriguez-Tomé & Bariaud, 1990). The *baccalauréat* exam is another source of stress for almost all students, even those who succeed at school.

Work

Adolescents are not encouraged to work. There is little in the way of paid jobs, even for small amounts, with very few exceptions such as babysitting from the age of 14 years for girls. Apprentices are the main group among adolescents under 18 years old that work.

For more than 150 years, children's and adolescents' work has been progressively controlled. The first law, in 1841, prohibited work by children younger than eight years old in companies with more than 20 employees. In 1926, specific jobs were prohibited for children, and in 1933 the minimum age for paid employment was fixed at 14 years. Today, work by youth under 14 years old is strictly controlled and is possible for youth between 16 and 18 years old but under numerous conditions. New labor regulations in 2001 set the minimum age for paid work at 16 years (15 years for apprentices), with a limit of seven hours a day and 35 hours a week. Night work is prohibited from 8 p.m. to 6 a.m. (with very few controlled exceptions).

Emerging adults are the main target for employment policies because of the problems they face to find and keep a job. In 2007, the participation of emerging adults in the labor market concerned 12% of the 15–19-year-olds and 51% of the 20–24-year-olds. The rate of unemployment of young people has reached 26% for 15–19-year-olds and 17% for 20–24-year-olds, compared to 8% in the general population (DARES, 2009). The level of unemployment is higher for visible minorities with two immigrant parents.

Among the youth without the *baccalauréat*, more than half (more girls than boys) ask for help from special centers created to combat unemployment. Contracts of block-release training allow vocational training in business. Under 18 years of age, adolescents have the possibility to sign an apprenticeship contract, which is specially organized for those who do not obtain a diploma or who desire a training ending in a better recognized diploma. To get an occupation in which they have some interest is the main worry of French adolescents, and they are more attracted by the activity in itself than by its reputation or its earning power (Nurmi et al., 1999).

In spite of the absence of incentives to work, adolescents and children do have pocket money at their disposal. Parents meet the needs of their children as long as they do not work and do not earn enough money to live. In addition, 40% of parents provide help to their children older than 18 years living outside the family home, and they continue to do so when their children have become students, who get 73% of their income from parental help.

Participation of adolescents in household work is lower than in other European countries even when families value familial solidarity and family investment. This fact can be explained by less free time outside the academic workload (Alsaker & Flammer, 1999). Household work is seldom carried out as an exchange to obtain pocket money. Moreover, French parents and teachers consider that household work subtracts time from academic work, which is confirmed by French studies (Ferrand, Imbert, & Marry, 1996).

Media

The adolescent cultural world is heterogeneous, including rap culture, graffiti, piercing and tattooing, but also adolescents who read *Le Monde* and avoid TV in order to devote their time seriously to culture or sports, as well as some girls who, in an identity quest, attempt to wear the Islamic scarf even at school, where it was previously barely tolerated and has recently been forbidden (Bruno, 2000). This world is clearly distinct from that of their elders and includes media such as books, magazines, TV channels that address themselves specifically to adolescents, the numerous radio networks that have a real influence on their lifestyles and preferences, and mobile phones with texting.

All French adolescents have access to media, either through the radio—they all own one, usually in their bedroom—or through TV (97% of households own a TV and 83% a video/DVD player). Most adolescents have access to a computer: 93% of them have used one mainly at school, and 83% have used the Internet. However, 59% of families own a computer, and 48% are connected to the Internet (TEF, 2010). This creates a gap between those who have access to this resource and those who do not.

Mobile phone use is more democratic: 91% of 15–24-year-olds own one (TEF, 2010). Parents justify their purchase mainly by the facility of remaining in contact at all times, particularly when they are working and their children are not at school. The use of mobile phones and the Internet is embedded in multiple networks of rather positive sociability (friends, family, associations, etc.). Surveys indicate that, in spite of parents' initial fears, adolescent use of the Internet is above all for socialization purposes with friends, often involving games, even if the risk of delinquent behavior cannot be completely avoided.

All in all, French adolescents have access to culture. Only 20% of French adolescents have not participated, during the past 12 months, in a cultural activity such as book reading, movie viewing, or museum visiting (Tavan, 2003). However, because of the school schedule, with long hours and a heavy academic workload, French adolescents have less free time during an ordinary day than other European adolescents. As a result, because their time for TV or Internet use is considerably reduced compared to other Western European countries and North America, they have less experience with the Internet. They spend a smaller proportion of their free time in TV watching and Internet activities than adolescents in other countries (Alsaker & Flammer, 1999).

Politics and Military

In 1996, obligatory military duty disappeared and the army became professional and voluntary. The only obligation for military purposes is a six-day practicum preparing for defense. Girls and boys must register at the local townhouse for this practicum at the age of 16.

The construction of the European Union, promoting economic exchanges as well as establishing peace with neighbors, is highly valued by the French. It is taught in curriculum from the elementary school all through the school years. France is, with Germany, one of the leaders in the construction of the European Union and is among the four countries that really pride themselves on being European (Eurobarometer, 2000). In 2003, the French were less numerous than others in feeling a sense of belonging to their national group (34% compared to the European mean of 40% and the UK mean of 64%), but they were more numerous in endorsing double belonging (58% feel both European and French). Children and adolescents endorse the national and European identities in the same proportion as adults. Compared to other Europeans, they are more open to people from other countries but they value their own country less (Flanagan & Botcheva, 1999).

Adolescents and emerging adults are concerned by social life, but with a distance from political issues. More than 75% of adolescents are concerned with AIDS, poverty and hunger in the world, racism, and the environment, but they are reluctant to situate themselves along the right–left axis. Only 37% of young people between 18 and 30 years old declare to feel close to a political party, compared to 50% of the general French population (Galland, 2008). Their civic participation is only occasional: 1% are members of a political party and 5% of a political association (Muxel, 2010). They prefer to vote for broader national issues, such as in presidential elections, than on complex local issues. Their participation in voting is relatively high at age 18 but declines between 20 and 30 years old. In 2007, when election of parliamentary deputies followed immediately the Presidential election, only 30% of youth younger than 30 years voted in all elections compared to 65% of people older than 60 years (Galland 2002, 2008; Jugnot, 2007).

Unique Issues

A unique French issue is the tradition of collective mobilization. Fifty percent of young people have already participated in a street demonstration. Even if the rate of young people's participation in elections is usually at least 10 percentage points below that of other age groups, they are not depoliticized. In fact, their interest in politics tends to strengthen. In 1978, 48% of 18–30-year-olds were very or somewhat interested in politics, 52% in 2002, and 67% in 2007 (Muxel, 2010). Young people are politicized, but differently from the adults: less interested in the ideology and the organization, and more in the expressiveness and the emotion. This trend toward collective protest is also changing in the overall French population. In 2009, 60% of the French, and 75% of the 18–24-year-olds, declared themselves ready to protest to defend their interests.

Given decreasing participation in elections at all levels (national, regional, and local), the issue of citizenship has become a subject of concern. The objective of citizenship awareness programs is to make sure that adolescents know and understand the modern democratic structures and ways of life; that they understand the notion of social contract and take collective responsibilities, at school for example. The curriculum is enriched with class discussions on a regular basis to initiate adolescents about the collective life's social organization at their level of interest (TV, daily newspapers, racism, etc.). The electoral system is first experienced in junior high school with the student representatives' election in the class committee. In *lycée*, some members of the national school system are elected by students, and committees on high-school life chaired by the school director and a student as co-president have been instituted in order to make suggestions to enhance the quality of daily school life.

References and Further Reading

Alsaker, F., & Flammer, A. (1999). *The adolescent experience: European and American adolescents in the 1990s.* Mahwah, NJ: Lawrence Erlbaum Associates.

Archambault, P. (2002). Séparation et divorce: Quelles conséquences sur la réussite scolaire des enfants? [Separation and divorce: What consequences on children's success at school?]. *Population et Sociétés, 5,* 379.

Bajos, N., & Bozon, M. (2008). *Enquête sur la sexualité en France: Pratiques, genre et santé* [Study on sexuality in France). Paris, France: La découverte.

Bariaud, F., & Bourcet, C. (1998). L'estime de soi à l'adolescence [Self-esteem at adolescence]. In M. Bolognini and Y. Prêteur (Eds.), *Estime de soi: Perspectives développementales* [Self-esteem: Developmental perspectives] (pp. 125–146). Lausanne, Switzerland: Delachaux et Niestlé.

Bariaud, F., & Oliveri, L. (1989). Les états dépressifs dans le développement normal de l'adolescent [Depressive states in the normal development of the adolescent]. *L'Orientation Scolaire et Professionnelle, 18*(4), 315–335.

Bordet, J. (1998). *Les jeunes de la cité* [Youth of the city]. Paris, France: PUF.

Boyer, R. (1999). Le temps libre des collégiens et des lycéens [Free time of secondary students]. In Y. Lemel & B. Roudet (Eds.), *Filles et garçons jusqu'à l'adolescence: Socialisations différentielles* [Girls and boys till adolescence: Differential socialization] (pp. 249–268). Paris, France: L'Harmattan.

Bréchon, P. (Ed.). (2000). *Les valeurs des Français: Evolutions de 1980 à 2000* [Values of French people: Evolution from 1980 to 2000]. Paris, France: Armand Colin.

Bruno, P. (2000). *Existe-t-il une culture adolescente?* [Is there an adolescent culture?]. Paris, France: In Press.

Choquet, M., & Ledoux, S. (1994). *Adolescents: Enquête nationale* [Adolescents: A national survey]. Paris, France: Les Éditions INSERM.

Claes, M., Lacourse, E., Bouchard, C., & Luckow, D. (2001). Adolescents' relationships with members of the extended family and non-related adults in four countries: Canada, France, Belgium and Italy. *International Journal of Adolescence and Youth, 18*(2–3), 207–225.

Claes, M., Lacourse, E., Bouchard, C., & Perucchini, P. (2003). Parental practices in late adolescence, a comparison of three countries: Canada, France and Italy. *Journal of Adolescence, 18*(4), 387–399.

Crenner, E. (1998). *La parenté un réseau de sociabilité actif mais concentré* [Kinship, an active but condensed network for sociability]. Paris, France: INSEE Première 600.

Crenner, E. (1999). *Famille je vous aide* [Family, I help you]. Paris, France: INSEE Première 631.

DARES. (2008). *Les écarts de salaire entre les hommes et les femmes en 2006: Disparités persistantes* [Differences in salary between men and women in 2006: persistent disparities]. Paris, France: Premières synthèses, 44.5. Retrieved from www.travail-solidarite.gouv.fr

DARES. (2009). *Emploi et chômage des 15–29 ans en 2007* [Employment and unemployment of 15–29-year-olds in 2007]. Paris, France: Premières synthèses, 12.1. Retrieved from www.minefe.gouv.fr

Debesse, M. (1936). *La crise d'originalité juvénile* [The adolescent identity crisis]. Paris, France: Alcan.

Debesse, M. (1937). *Comment étudier les adolescents, examen critique des confidences juvéniles* [How to study adolescents: A critical examination of adolescent confidences]. Paris, France: PUF.

Debesse, M. (1942). *L'adolescence* [Adolescence]. Paris, France: PUF.

Driant, J.-C., Casteran, B., & O'Prey, S. (2007/2008). Les conditions de logement des ménages jeunes [Housing conditions of the young households]. Les travaux de l'Observatoire, 2007/2008(2), 253–288.

Duru-Bellat, M. (1999). Les choix d'orientation: Des conditionnements sociaux à l'anticipation de l'avenir [Career decision making: From social learning to future anticipation]. In Y. Lemel & B. Roudet (Eds.), *Filles et garçons jusqu'à l'adolescence: Socialisations différentielles* [Girls and boys till adolescence: Differential socialization] (pp. 117–150). Paris, France: L'Harmattan.

Eurobarometer. (2000). *Report 53*, May. Brussels, Belgium: European Commission. Retrieved from http://europa.eu.int

Ferrand, M., Imbert, F., & Marry, C. (1996). *L'excellence scolaire: Une affaire de famille. Le cas des normaliennes et normaliens scientifiques* [Academic excellence: A family matter. The case of women and men selected in National Scientific College]. Paris, France: CNRS/Ministère de l'Education Nationale.

Field, T. (1999). American adolescents touch each other less and are more aggressive toward their peers as compared with French adolescents. *Adolescence, 18*(136), 753–758.

Flanagan, C., & Botcheva, L. (1999). Adolescents' preferences for their homeland and other countries. In F. Alsaker & A. Flammer (Eds.) *The adolescent experience: European and American adolescents in the 1990s* (pp. 131–145). Mahwah, NJ: Lawrence Erlbaum Associates.

Fuligni, A. J. (Ed.). (2001). *Family obligation and assistance during adolescence: Contextual variations and developmental implications*. San Francisco, CA: Jossey-Bass.

Galland, O. (2002). *Les jeunes* [Youth] (6th ed.). Paris, France: Editions La Découverte.

Galland, O. (2004). *Sociologie de la jeunesse* [Sociology of youth]. (3rd ed.). Paris, France: Armand Colin.

Galland, O. (2008). Les jeunes et la société: Des visions contrastées de l'avenir [Young people and society: Constrasting views of the future]. In A. Stellinger & R. Wintrebert (Eds.), *Les jeunes face à leur avenir: Une enquête internationale* [Young people facing their future: An international survey]. Paris, France: Fondation pour l'innovation politique.

Garcia-Werebe, M. J. (1988). Relations amicales et amoureuses entre adolescents français [Friendly and love relationships between French adolescents]. *Neuropsychiatrie de l'enfant*, *18*, 193–200.

Hibell, B., Guttormsson, U., Ahlström, S., Balakireva, O., Bjarnason, T., Kokkevi, A., et al. (2009). *The 2007 ESPAD Report—Substance use among students in 35 European countries*. Stockholm, Sweden: The Swedish Council for Information on Alcohol and Other Drugs (CAN). Retrieved from www.espad.org

INPES. (2007). Tabac [Tobacco]. *Actualités*, *18*. Retrieved from www.inpes.sante.fr

INSEE. (2000). *Les jeunes* [Youth]. Paris, France: Institut national de la statistique et des études économiques.

INSEE. (2005). *Les immigrés en France* [Immigrants in France]. INSEE-références, édition 2005. Paris, France: Institut national de la statistique et des études économiques.

INSEE. (2006). *Populations étrangères et immigrées* [Foreign and immigrant populations]. RP 2006 exploitation principale. Paris, France: Institut national de la statistique et des études économiques.

INSERM. (2009). Usages d'alcool, de tabac et de cannabis des élèves français à 16 ans (Alcohol, tobacco and cannabis consumption of the 16 years old French pupils). Paris, France: INSERM. Retrieved from www.inserm.fr

INSERM-INED-ANRS. (2007). Contexte de la Sexualité en France (The Context of Sexuality in France). Communiqué et dossier de presse. Paris, France: INSERM-INED-ANRS. Retrieved from www.previh-anrs.fr

Jugnot, S. (2007). *La participation électorale en 2007: La mémoire de 2002* [Electoral participation in 2007. The memory of 2002]. Insee première 1169. Paris, France: Institut national de la statistique et des études économiques.

Kerjosse, R. (2000). *Bilan démographique 1999: Hausse de la fécondité et recul de la mortalité* [Demographic current state assessment in 1999. Increase of fertility and decline of mortality]. INSEE première 698. Paris, France: Institut national de la statistique et des études économiques.

Lannegrand-Willems, L. (2008). La question de la construction identitaire à l'adolescence à deux paliers de l'orientation: La troisième et la terminale. [Identity construction in adolescence at two transitional points of the French school system: 9th and 12th grades]. *L'Orientation Scolaire et Professionnelle*, *18*(4), 527–544.

Lannegrand-Willems, L., & Bosma, H. (2006). Identity development-in-context: The school as an important context for identity development. *Identity*, *18*(1), 85–113.

Lannegrand-Willems, L., Cosnefroy, O., & Lecigne, A. (2011 accepted). Prediction of various degrees of vocational secondary school absenteeism: Importance of the organization of the education system. *School Psychology International*.

Mallet, P. (1993). L'intimité émotionnelle entre primes adolescents: Aspects socio-cognitifs, sociaux et conatifs [Emotional intimacy between early adolescents: Sociocognitive, social and conative factors]. *L'Orientation Scolaire et Professionnelle*, *18*(1), 43–63.

Mallet, P. (1997). Se découvrir entre amis, s'affirmer parmi ses pairs. Les relations entre pairs au cours de l'adolescence [Discovering among friends, affirmation among peers in adolescence]. In H. Rodriguez-Tomé, S. Jackson, & F. Bariaud (Eds.), *Regards actuels sur l'adolescence* [Present views on adolescence] (pp. 109–146). Paris, France: PUF.

Mallet, P. (2004). L'idéation suicidaire à l'adolescence: Quelles relations avec la perception du milieu familial et les modes de faire face? [Suicidal ideation in adolescence: Which relations with perceived family system and coping?]. *L'Orientation Scolaire et Professionnelle*, *18*(2), 315–336.

Mendousse, P. (1907). *L'âme de l'adolescent* [The soul of adolescent boys]. Paris, France: Alcan.

Mendousse, P. (1910). *L'âme de l'adolescente* [The soul of adolescent girls]. Paris, France: Alcan.

Messerschmitt, P., Legrain, D., & Hamasaki, Y. (1998). Influence de la situation conjugale des parents sur la psychologie des adolescents [Influence of the conjugal status of parents on psychology of adolescents]. *Annales de pédiatrie*, *18*(10), 681–693.

Michaud, P. 1997. L'éducation sexuelle [Sexual education]. In P. A. Michaud & P. Alvin (Eds.), *La santé des adolescents: Approches, soins, prévention* [Adolescents' health: Approaches, care, and prevention] (pp. 324–334). Paris, France: Doin éditeurs.

Mosconi, N. (1999). Les recherches sur la socialisation différentielle des sexes à l'école [Studies on differential socialization according to gender at school]. In Y. Lemel & B. Roudet (Eds.), *Filles et garçons jusqu'à l'adolescence: Socialisations différentielles* [Girls and boys till adolescence: Differential socialization] (pp. 85–116). Paris, France: L'Harmattan.

Mucchielli, L. (2000). La dissociation familiale favorise-t-elle la délinquance? Arguments pour une réfutation empirique [Does family dissociation increase delinquency? Arguments based on empirical facts against]. *Recherches et prévisions*, *18*, 35–50.

Mucchielli, L. (2002). La dissociation familiale favorise t-elle la délinquance? [Does family dissociation increase delinquency?]. *Medecine & Enfance*, *18*, 581–595.

Muxel, A. (2010). *Avoir 20 ans en politique* [Being 20 years old in politics]. Paris, France: Seuil.

Nurmi, J.-E., Liiceanu, A., & Liberska, H. (1999). Future-oriented interests. In F. Alsaker & A. Flammer (Eds.), *The adolescent experience: European and American adolescents in the 1990s* (pp. 85–98). Mahwah, NJ: Lawrence Erlbaum Associates.

Pla, A., & Beaumel, C. (2009). *Bilan démographique 2009* [Demographic assessment 2009]. Paris, France: Division Enquêtes et études démographiques. INSEE Références. Retrieved from www.insee.fr

Pommereau, X. (2001). *L'adolescent suicidaire* [The suicidal adolescent]. Paris, France: Dunod.

Rodriguez-Tomé, H., & Bariaud, F. (1990). Anxiety in adolescence: Sources and reactions. In H. Bosma & S. Jackson (Eds.), *Coping and self-concept in adolescence* (pp. 167–186). Berlin, Germany: Springer-Verlag.

Roudet, B., & Galland, O. (2005). *Les jeunes Européens et leurs valeurs: Europe occidentale, Europe centrale et orientale* [Young European and their values: Western Europe, Central and Eastern Europe). Paris, France: La Découverte.

Sabatier, C., & Lannegrand-Willems, L. (2005). Transmission of family values and attachment: A French three-generation study. *Applied Psychology*, *18*(3), 378–395.

Schleyer-Lindenmann, A. (1997). *Influence du contexte culturel et familial sur les tâches de développement et l'investissement de l'espace urbain à l'adolescence. Etude sur les jeunes d'origine nationale ou étrangère à Marseille et à Francfort sur le Main* [Influence of cultural and familial context on developmental tasks and investment of urban areas at adolescence: Study with foreign and national adolescents at Marseille and Frankfurt-on-Main]. Unpublished doctoral thesis, Université de Provence Aix Marseille 1, Aix en Provence, France.

Sordes-Ader, F., Lévêque, G., Oubrayrie, N., & Safont-Mottay, C. (1998). Présentation de l'échelle toulousaine d'estime de soi [Presentation of Toulousean self-esteem scale]. In M. Bolognini & Y. Prêteur (Eds.),

Estime de soi: Perspectives développementales [Self-esteem: Developmental perspectives] (pp. 167–182). Lausanne, Switzerland: Delachaux et Niestlé.

Tavan, C. (2003). *Les pratiques culturelles: Le rôle des habitudes prises dans l'enfance* [Cultural practices: Role of childhood habits]. INSEE première 883. Paris, France: Institut national de la statistique et des études économiques.

TEF. (2010). Equipement des ménages [Households equipment]. INSEE Références. Paris, France: Institut national de la statistique et des études économiques. Retrieved from www.insee.fr

Thiercé, A. (1999). *Histoire de l'adolescence (1850–1914)* [History of adolescence (1850–1914)]. Paris, France: Belin.

Toulemon, L. (2003). *La fécondité en France depuis 25 ans* [Fecundity in France in the last 25 years]. Paris, France: Haut Conseil de la population et de la famille.

UNICEF. (2001). *A league table of teenage births in rich nations.* Innocenti Report Card No. 3. Florence, Italy: UNICEF Innocenti Research Centre. Retrieved from www.unicef-irc.org

Union Interparlementaire. (2008). *Les femmes au parlement en 2007: regard sur l'année écoulée* [Women in parliament in 2007: A glance at the past year]. Geneva, Switzerland: Union Interparlementaire. Retrieved from http://www.ipu.org/pdf/publications/wmn07-f.pdf

Van de Velde, C. (2008). *Devenir adulte: Sociologie comparée de la jeunesse en Europe* [Becoming adult: Youth sociology in Europe compared]. Collection « Le Lien social ». Paris, France: PUF.

Vivas, É. (2009). *1,2 million d'enfants de moins de 18 ans vivent dans une famille recomposée* [1.2 million children below 18 years old live in a reconstituted family]. Insee première, 1259. Paris, France: Institut national de la statistique et des études économiques.

Chapter 19
Germany
Eva Dreher, Ulrike Sirsch, and Sabine Strobl

Background Information

The Federal Republic of Germany lies in Central Europe. After losing the Second World War, Germany was divided in 1945 into four zones of occupation. With the advent of the Cold War, two German states were formed in 1949: From three zones (US, UK, France) the Federal Republic of Germany (FRG, West Germany) was developed, and from the earlier USSR zone, the German Democratic Republic (GDR, East Germany) was created. With the fall of the USSR and the end of the Cold War, West and East Germany were reunified on 3 October 1990 (now a national holiday).

Germany is an affluent and technologically powerful economy (the fourth largest national economy in the world). However, the modernization and integration of the eastern German economy continues to be a costly long-term process.

The general cost budget for unified Germany can be stated only approximately; rising annually about €100 million, it roughly lies between €1.3 and €1.6 billion (up to 2009) (Greive & Müller, 2009). Debts resulting from the unification process were taken over by the German Federal Republic budget in 2005 and the resulting burden of debt due to unification processes was no longer designated explicitly (Zinsmeister, 2009).

Germany's government type is a federal republic (capital: Berlin), with 16 states as administrative divisions. There is a bicameral legislature and the head of state, the president, is elected for a five-year term.

Germany is an ageing society with (as of 2008) 82 million inhabitants (Statistisches Bundesamt Deutschland, 2010). There is a very low birth rate, with a total fertility rate of 1.6 in 2009. Ethnic groups include: German 80%, Turkish and former Soviet Union each with 3%, other 14% (mainly European) (Statistisches Bundesamt Deutschland, 2010).

Period of Adolescence

Today's conception of youth/adolescence in Germany was determined with lasting effect by the civically characterized "youth movement" founded in 1895. Following the First World War, in line with the Weimar constitution of 1919, young people were given a better legal and social standing in terms of labor laws and the establishment of compulsory schooling (of 12 years' duration). The humanistic pedagogy and psychology of the time also made a contribution in this respect. In the Third Reich (1933–1945), a high proportion of young people became socially integrated outside of the family affiliation in the so-called *Hitler Youth*, whereby the groups that had emerged in the youth movement were politicized.

In the period following the Second World War, this procedure of assimilating youth to the state in East Germany (GDR) was seamlessly continued (Free German Youth). In the rebuilding and postwar period in West Germany, the youth were predominantly individualistic, but nevertheless adaptable and prepared to integrate, helped also by a commercially driven consumer society.

Today a temporal demarcation of the duration of adolescence is difficult, as biological puberty is beginning increasingly earlier (11 to 14 years), but the extension of professional training means that the entry to the job market is taking place increasingly later (17 to 30 years, depending on educational path). Investigations into life course changes of children and young people over the past 120 years show that some marks of status (e.g., school entry, participation in youth culture, entering into long-term partnership/marriage) are nowadays reached earlier than they were in 1890, while others (e.g., completion of mandatory school education, entry into the job market) begin later (Chisholm & Hurrelmann, 1995).

Beliefs

Essential knowledge about the value orientation of adolescents in Germany is based on comprehensive empirical cross-sectional studies, known as the Shell Youth Studies. Results can be compared over various measurement time points, which enable statements to be made about differences, but not about developments in the proper sense—which would be the case with longitudinal studies. The thirteenth Shell study (Deutsche Shell, 2000) investigated eight value dimensions that are important for adolescents, with autonomy (creativity and ability to deal with conflict), career orientation (good education/training and interesting job) and family orientation (partner, home, and children) occupying the top three rankings. Following these are humanity (tolerance/helpfulness), attractiveness (pleasant appearance and material success), authenticity (personal freedom of thought and action), self-management (discipline and ability to fit in), and modernity (participation in politics and technological progress). In part, there are differences between male and female adolescents with regard to the level of importance of these factors. Family orientation and humanity are preferred above all by female adolescents, while modernity appears to be more important to males (Fritsche, 2000).

The sixteenth Shell study (Shell Deutschland Holding, 2010) describes developments over recent years. Family, partnership, and friends remain central to the value orientation: friendship (very important: 2002, 87%; 2010, 94%), to have a trusting partnership (very important: 2002, 82%; 2010, 90%) and to lead a decent family life (important: 2002, 85%; 2010, 92%).

A further value orientation category with increasing significance incorporates "to take personal responsibility for one's own life and actions" (important: 2002, 84%; 2010, 90%). Between 2002 and 2010 an interesting increase of significance can be found within the opposing categories of "diligence/ambition" (important: 2002, 72%; 2010, 78%) vs. "hedonistic orientation/enjoyment of life" (important: 2002, 72%; 2010, 78%) (Gensicke, 2010).

The characteristics of a pragmatic generation—highlighted in the Shell study of 2003 and affirmed in that of 2006—can also be found within the present Shell study of 2010. Adolescents try to approach their lives with pragmatic principles. The analysis of life organization within the pragmatic generation shows some problems related to prospects and success. The concern about a good education or a positive occupational position and anxiety over unemployment or poverty are indications of such problems.

Gender

Uncertainty about the future and life planning results in insecurity that is found to a greater degree among male adolescents than among females. The relevance of gender differences in relation to occupational orientation can no longer be confirmed (Hagemann-White, 2006). For male adolescents this results in an increase of uncertainty concerning a stable gender identity. While girls and women can take on typical male occupational positions or roles without a decline in status, boys and men usually do not experience an increase in social recognition—but rather a decrease in prestige—when taking on typical female occupational positions and roles (e.g. positions in nursing or childrearing) (Leven, Quenzel, & Hurrelmann, 2010). In those strata of society marked by lower education, in which young women demonstrate high competences in regard to dealing with occupational challenges (self-management, self-discipline, high motivation, well-directed study and work habits), a need for action is noticeable in regard to male adolescents with a low commitment to education (Albert, Hurrelmann, & Quenzel, 2010b).

Female adolescents show greater dissatisfaction with their body image than males do. The contrast between the socially imparted ideal of beauty and the body development in puberty has so far been seen as the dominant explanation for a multitude of measures for weight reduction. An alternative perspective is provided by the fact that apart from dissatisfaction and internalized body images, weight manipulation represents a salient possibility to exert control over one's own body, be it as compensation for the perceived loss of control through the bodily experiences of puberty or as an expression of self-induced autonomy (Oerter & Dreher, 2008). The importance attached to body-related control is also testified by the rising number of adolescents who wish for or indeed carry out cosmetic surgery to "correct" their appearance or figure. The more positive picture among male adolescents in terms of the evaluation of the body image is based, among other things, on the greater correspondence between biological change and psychological effects; thus the muscle growth strengthens the rise in internal locus of control and both contribute to a perception of the body as more active and capable (Weichold & Silbereisen, 2008).

In regard to body image, it is increasingly noticeable that both young males and females take part in competitive drawing of attention to their bodies. Strategies of gaining attention are tattooing, piercing, hair styling and cosmetic changes. Piercing is at present understood as a general phenomenon in fashion culture (Abendroth, 2009). Findings of the Shell study 2010 show that 16% of adolescents between the ages of 12 and 25 state that they have (one) piercing. Piercing is especially popular among female adolescents (26%; male adolescents 6%). With an increase in age the contentment with one's body weight decreases: roughly one-third of adolescents are of the opinion that they are too fat—young females, 44%; young males, 27% (Leven et al., 2010). Health awareness is valued more highly by female adolescents than by male adolescents. The value orientation 'healthy lifestyle' has risen from 2002: 71% to 2010: 78% (Gensicke, 2010).

The Self

In an individualistic culture such as in Germany, dealing with one's own identity is deemed to be a relevant developmental process. "Identity formation" takes on an important status among the developmental tasks of adolescence. The development of one's own viewpoint, which encompasses self-awareness and value orientations for one's actions, is a partial aim in this regard. While the formation of one's "own" viewpoint is still seen as an important developmental step in early adolescence, the weighting of the identity contribution increasingly changes in emphasis toward the ability to examine one's own viewpoints through new information and experience and, where necessary, to revise them.

In contrast to their parents' generation, adolescents in Germany experience, in addition to far-reaching economic changes, a sociocultural change that is based on the one hand on immigration and reunification, and on the other on courses of internationalization within Europe and beyond our continent. In this regard, "globalization" and "localization" can be distinguished as two opposing trends that are relevant for parallel forms of ethnic identity formation and demand complex orientation accomplishments from adolescents—with and without experience of migration. The real *Lebenswelt* (life-world) that can be experienced offers a wealth of cultural dimensions of influence in the form of "styles" (e.g., music, language, eating habits, value preferences), the emergence and passing of which occur at such a great speed that children and youth are not only recipients, but also help to actively fashion cross-cultural "trends". While in Germany roughly 20% of the youth are an active part of and engage in youth cultures, 70% only orient themselves at youth cultures. "Hip-hop" represents the largest youth culture, yet youth cultures revolving more around sports also enjoy great popularity (Farin, 2010).

Family Relationships

Youth studies so far have shown that, these days, adolescents remain longer in their parental homes due to the extended years of education and begin later with starting their own family. A result of this is a "double relation" to parents and friends. The desire to establish oneself professionally delays the starting of a family, as does the uncertainty of the future, which is heightened through economic crises and structural constraints in the job market.

The desirability of a lifestyle model "family" has not, despite the change of family models, subsided. According to the Shell youth study the present youth generation is definitely family-oriented. The majority of adolescents would like to have their own family at some point. They want to raise their own children in the same or in a similar manner to how they themselves were raised (Albert, Hurrelmann, & Quenzel, 2010a). Two of the Shell studies (Deutsche Shell, 2003; Shell Deutschland Holding, 2006) show that the majority of adolescents model their life conduct on that of their own parents; they consider them to be the most important mentors and role models in regard to coping with life problems. The Shell study 2006 documents that adolescents also have a fundamentally positive relation to the generation of their grandparents.

In contrast to the earlier traditional family form, nowadays large changes have emerged due to the changed role of women (employment, a different role of the mother), the changed family size (drop in the birth rate from 2.2 children per woman in 1930 to 1.8 in 1969, and 1.4 in 2008; Statistisches Bundesamt Deutschland, 2010), the family composition (see below), and the prevailing value of pluralism in German society. Today's family is defined more ambiguously, and different family forms can be distinguished, although the nuclear family, in which the two persons of the older generation are the biological mother and father and only biological children of these parents are living with them, continues to be the dominant family form.

Investigations show (Fuhrer, 2005) that over the past 30 years, a change has occurred in parents' attitudes to goals of upbringing and values that they wish to impart to their children. Nowadays, independence and personality development of children are given greater emphasis than traditional goals such as diligence, orderliness, and obedience. The parent–child relationship in adolescence has therefore changed significantly in comparison to its traditional form. The authority of the parents is characterized less strongly than in the past, and adolescents no longer have to "push their parents away" in order to be able to go their own way. The "commando family" (normative regulation by cross-individual standards) has been replaced by the "negotiation family," in which rules are less fixed and are instead more frequently also explained and discussed (though this does not apply to the traditional Muslim immigrant families).

In this process of reorganization of relationships, parents remain important sources of support and persons to whom adolescents feel emotionally tied. However, this does not always occur without conflict—rather, the negotiating of everyday problems is a part of everyday life. In general, an increase in conflict with parents occurs for both genders between the ages of 12 and 15 years. For the 13-year-olds, "clothes" and "shopping" were the most frequently cited sources of conflict, while for the 15-year-olds, the focus was on political differences of opinion and negotiating the evening curfew ("going out") (Fend, 2000).

In the representative Shell survey (Shell Deutschland Holding, 2010), the desire to have one's own children later in life has clearly risen: 2006, 62%; 2010, 69%. Interesting changes appear within the statements on the desire to have children. This desire increased for male youths within the age group of 15–17 from 56% in 2006 to 65% in 2010; for female youths this figure was 73%. Comparing the different parts of the country shows that during 2002–2010 the trend increased in western states (from 64% to 68%), while in East Germany it decreased (from 76% to 72%) (Leven et al., 2010).

Friends and Peers/Youth Culture

For German adolescents, the peer group is a source for psychosocial wellbeing (recognition, protection), support (in terms of burdens and problems), and fostering development with regard to social behavior, competencies, and moral concepts. Peer relationships are, moreover, an important source of self-experience and consequently of self-definition for the adolescents. Adolescents of the same age have a different, namely more egalitarian position, and provide different feedback from different areas than the parents or other adults. This is important for the development of self-concept and identity formation, as well as for the acquisition of social skills (Oerter & Dreher, 2008).

The amount of time that is spent with peers corresponds roughly to that spent with the family. Peers mainly fulfill the task of organization of leisure time, while the family brings with it obligations and duties. A decisive difference also exists in terms of relationships of power and influence: With friends, the power relations are more or less equal, while the parents exert influence and control. Thirty-six percent of all young Germans are members of a youth organization, a youth club, or the youth section of an association or other type of organization. Among the adolescents and young adults who are members of youth organizations, there are clearly more males than females. In the west, 45% of 14- to 27-year-old males are members, and only 31% of females. In the east, these figures are, today, 35% of men and 24% of women. Youth organizations and associations are most sought after by the younger groups surveyed: For instance, 48% of the 14- to 17-year-olds in western Germany indicated belonging to a youth organization while this figure was only 31% among the 25- to 27-year-olds. In the east, the same picture is apparent, with 38% in the youngest group and 23% in the oldest group.

The majority of young Germans are members of sports clubs (west, 64%; east, 62%), followed in the west with a large gap by churches (12%), the fire brigade/Technisches Hilfswerk (THW; relief organization) (8%), *Freizeit und Geselligkeit* (a type of youth club) (8%), music clubs (7%), and trade organizations (1%). In the east, the fire brigade/THW is at second place (9%), followed by *Freizeit und Geselligkeit* and churches (8% each), music clubs (7%), and trade organizations (4%) (Institut für praxisorientierte Sozialforschung, 2003).

Since the 1960s, various different dominant youth cultures, occurring one after the other, have been observable in Germany. At the end of the 1960s and beginning of the 1970s, hippies and rebellious students spread across Federal German society; 10 years later punks and squatters caused a stir, marked by political impetus and staged generational conflict. This was followed by the techno scene, which was nonpolitical in nature and accompanied by a consumer-oriented fun ethos. The turn of the new millennium, by contrast, emerged without the development of a new youth culture. It was observable that each new youth culture was at some point taken over by commerce and strayed into the mainstream—anything authentically new has become rare, and not implicitly recognizable as such (Rink, 2002).

Love and Sexuality

Due to secular acceleration (e.g., decline in the age at menarche), social changes (e.g., coeducation, increasing distance from church and religion), and medical advances (e.g., contraceptive pill, intra-uterine contraception), from the 1960s onwards, a liberalization in sexual matters and a dramatic change of sexual morality took place in Germany; for example, the attitude to premarital intercourse changed from nearly 80% rejection in the mid-1960s to almost 90% assent at the beginning of the 1990s (Fend, 2000). Nevertheless, among young people today, sexuality is not marked by liberality and lack of restraint, but rather the management of sexuality is integrated in the emergence of intimate social relationships, for which responsibility, social ties, authenticity, acceptance, and self-worth are objects of a reciprocal negotiation process.

In Germany, the choice of a partner, which is based strongly on attractiveness and "personal chemistry," is nowadays generally the responsibility of the young people themselves. This does not apply, however, to an unlimited extent to foreigners living in Germany (e.g., Muslim minorities), as in this case the establishment of partnerships is often a matter for the parents to decide, and male and female adolescents are often kept separate from one another.

The time point of the first romantic relationship varies strongly from person to person and is influenced by sociocultural, family, and peer-group norms as well as psycho-biological maturity. The coming together of the sexes in Germany mostly takes place through "dates," although this does not correspond precisely to the US understanding of the term "dating." In Germany, male and female adolescents can agree to meet up in groups. One does not require a particular date with only two people in order to go to nightclubs or parties. Often, however, adolescents go along in order to find somebody for a short-term or long-term (steady boyfriend/girlfriend) romantic relationship (Furman & Wehner, 1997).

Once hormonal changes have occurred in puberty and it is possible for an adolescent to be sexually active, then, in interaction with socially imparted models, a motivational readiness for sexuality results, whose implementation is culturally determined. In the life period from 13 to 16 years, we find the first serious entry into sexual behavior, which in Germany follows an almost ritualized sequence: kissing, stroking, closer touching, petting (breasts, genitalia), sexual intercourse. Today, 79% of 14- to 17-year-old girls and 76% of boys in Germany are sexually experienced. However, there is a large group (34% of girls and 35% of boys) who have not yet had sexual intercourse at the age of 17 years. Only 5% of girls and 14% of boys state that they have had their first intercourse with either persons they "casually/barely know" or "strangers/persons" they do not know (BZgA, 2010b).

The average age of the "first time" was 15.4 years for the age group of 14- to 17-year-olds in 2009 (modal value for girls and boys 16 years). For the majority of adolescents, the first sexual intercourse is unplanned: Only 29% of girls and 28% of boys knew in advance that "it" would happen; 17% of the girls and 16% of the boys did not expect it. Contraceptives were used during the first intercourse by 92% of girls and 92% of boys between 14 and 17 years (of this, condom: 76% and/or pill: 40%) (BZgA, 2010b).

Parents are taking on an increasing responsibility for sexual education in terms of the contraceptive behavior of adolescents; since 1980, advice imparted within the family has doubled. A steadily growing group (in 2009 69% of girls and 58% of boys) stated that they had been advised by their parents (usually the mother) about contraception; the boys are recommended condoms (71%), and the girls the pill (46%) and additionally the condom (19%). Boyfriend/girlfriend and mainly sexual education in school, as well as doctors, continue to play a role. However, 8% of girls and as many as 18% of boys stated that they currently had nobody with whom they could speak about sexual matters. Furthermore, many adolescents overestimate their knowledge about contraception (BZgA, 2010b).

The dangers of sexual transmitted diseases are not taken seriously enough by youths, and awareness of such diseases is not very evident. The proportion of youths that do not or only partially use contraceptives is declining (BZgA, 2006). A great deal of information on unprotected sex is provided; 88% of the 14- to 17-year-olds stated that sexually transmitted diseases are covered in sex education class. Nevertheless a subjective informational deficit regarding this topic exists among 42% of the girls and 33% of the boys (BZgA, 2010b). Girls and young women under the age of 25 can get tested by a gynecologist once a year for early recognition of chlamydia, which is paid for by state insurance (BZgA, 2010c).

Health Risk Behavior

For Germany, the following picture emerges with regard to adolesents' health risk behavior (BZgA, 2001, 2009a, 2009b, 2010a).

1. The health situation of German adolescents is generally good from an international comparative perspective.
2. Since 2007 the percentage of underage smokers has decreased immensely due to new legal regulations (sales of tobacco products are only permitted to persons of or over 18 years of age, and a non-smoking policy for children and adolescents in public) (Leven et al., 2010). In a representative survey (BZgA, 2009b), 32% of 12- to 25-year-olds stated that they were frequent or occasional smokers, with no considerable difference in terms of gender. Among 12- to 17-year-olds, the proportion of smokers (only legally permitted from the age of 16 years) increased from 20% in 1993 to 28% in 2001 (BZgA, 2001) but decreased to 10% in 2009 (BZgA, 2009b). Today, 6% of 12- to 17-year-old boys and girls are daily consumers of tobacco. The proportion of heavy smokers among adolescents, though, has on the whole notably decreased: 1993, 34%; 2001, 19% (BZgA, 2001); and 2008, 13% (BZgA, 2009b). Furthermore, the proportion of those who have never smoked almost tripled between 1973 and 2001 (data for West Germany) (BZgA, 2001) and in 2009 60% of 12- to 17-year-olds had never smoked (BZgA, 2009b). A new trend of shisha (flavored tobacco) smoking can be traced: The lifetime prevalence of 12- to 17-year-olds is 38% and the 30-day prevalence 10%. Especially critical is that 91% of this age group consider smoking harmful, but only 38% also consider shisha smoking a health hazard (BZgA, 2007). According to the current law, shisha smoking is included in the smoking ban.
3. According to surveys, almost all adolescents (93%) had already used alcohol in their lives; 7% stated that they were completely abstinent (BZgA, 2009a). In 2008, 17% of adolescents between 12 and 17 years of age stated that they regularly drink alcohol (at least once a week), with males drinking more beer and females more wine. Of the 12- to 15-year-olds, only 6% regularly drink alcohol, and of the 16- to 17-year-olds 36%; 35% of the 12- to 15-year-olds and only 6% of the 16- to 17-year-olds were abstinent, and there are no gender differences (BZgA, 2009a). Due to the extraordinary tax on alcoholic "alcopops," the monthly consumption has dropped since 2004 (2004, 28%; 2005, 16%; 2007, 10%; 2008, 10%). Eight percent of adolescents between 12 and 17 years old maintain a high consumption of alcohol (binge-drinking: five glasses or more per day). Considered over the span of a whole week, the rate of male adolescents (8%) is double that of female adolescents (4%) (BZgA, 2009a).
4. In 2009, 11% of the adolescents and emerging adults between 12 and 25 years of age had tried an illegal drug at least once, with 4% in the past 30 days. Cannabis is the most frequently consumed substance with 28%; 2.3% of the 12- to 25-year-olds indicated that they had consumed cannabis more often than once a week. On the whole, there are only small gender differences (BZgA, 2010a).
5. In Germany, approximately 18% (based on the definition) of 11- to 17-year-old adolescents are classified as overweight and 8% as obese, with a strong upward trend especially for youth in families with lower income (Kurth & Schaffrath Rosario, 2007). There is a very high rate of 12- to 17-year-olds who are dissatisfied with their bodies (43%) because they see themselves as being too fat (44% of the girls, 27% of the boys), and the dissatisfaction increases continuously with age (Leven et al., 2010). In addition, 29% of 11- to 17-year-old girls and 17% of the boys describe symptoms of an eating disorder (Hölling & Schlack, 2007).

6. The most frequent psychological disorders of the 11- to 17-year-old adolescents are emotional disorders including social withdrawal (approximately 7%) as well as anxiety/ depression (approximately 13%) (Hölling, Erhart, Ravens-Sieberer, & Schlack, 2007). In the age group of 15- to 20-year-olds, suicide is the second most frequent external cause of death after accidents, with the proportion of male adolescents predominating (43%, girls 33%). Furthermore, boys attempt suicide more often (17%) than girls do (13%) (Statistisches Bundesamt Deutschland, 2010).

Education

The school system in the Federal Republic of Germany is very heterogeneous and comprises a large number of different school types (Deutscher Bildungsserver, 2010). Almost all elementary and secondary schools and about 90% of higher education institutions are public (Autorengruppe Bildungsberichterstattung, 2010). The literacy rate (definition: those aged 15 and over who can read and write) in Germany is 99%. School attendance is mandatory for a minimum of nine years, beginning at age six. A student who starts vocational training as an apprentice must attend a part-time vocational school until the age of 18. The system of different types of secondary schools in Germany requires that adolescents must decide at a relatively early age which direction to pursue for their education and occupation. Later, changing school directions is possible, but difficult.

Secondary education is divided into two levels, junior (Level I: age 10 to 16) and senior (Level II: age 16 to 19). Level I starts with two years (grades five and six) of orientation courses during which students explore a variety of educational career paths open to them.

Secondary Education Level I

Upon completion of the Grundschule, students between the ages of 10 and 16 attend one of the following types of secondary school: *Hauptschule, Realschule, Gymnasium, Gesamtschule*, or *Sonderschule* (the last of these being for children with special educational needs). Students who complete this level of education receive an intermediate school certificate. About one-third of students completing primary school continue in secondary general schools (Hauptschule). The curriculum of the Hauptschule stresses preparation for a vocation as well as mathematics, history, geography, German, and one foreign language. After receiving their diploma, graduates either become apprentices in shops or factories while taking compulsory part-time courses or attend some form of full-time vocational school until the age of 18.

Another one-third of primary school leavers attend the Realschule. These intermediate schools include grades five through 10 for students seeking access to middle levels of civil service, industry, and business. The curriculum is the same as that of the Hauptschule, but students take an additional foreign language, shorthand, word-processing, and bookkeeping, and they also learn computer skills. Graduation from the Realschule enables students to enter a higher technical school (Fachoberschule), a specialized high school or grammar school (Fachgymnasium), or (for a few students) a Gymnasium for the next stage of secondary education.

The Gymnasium begins upon completion of the Grundschule or the orientation grades, and includes grades five through 12 (in some regions 13). The number of students attending the Gymnasium has increased dramatically in recent decades; by the mid-1990s, about one-third (36% in 2008) of all primary school leavers completed a course of study at the Gymnasium (Autorengruppe Bildungsberichterstattung, 2010), which gives them the right to study at university level. Up to the present day, the Gymnasium continues to be the primary educational route into the universities, although other routes have been created.

The Gesamtschule originated in the late 1960s to provide a broader range of educational opportunities for students than the traditional Gymnasium. The Gesamtschule has an all-inclusive curriculum for students aged 10 to 18 and a good deal of freedom to choose coursework. The popularity of the Gesamtschule has been mixed; their presence is marginal when compared with the Gymnasium (9% attend Gesamtschule; Autorengruppe Bildungsberichterstattung, 2010).

Secondary Education Level II

The variety of educational programs, tracks, and opportunities available to students increases at Level II. The largest single student group (65%; Autorengruppe Bildungsberichterstattung, 2010) attends the senior level of the Gymnasium (*Gymnasiale Oberstufe*). This level includes the traditional academically oriented Gymnasium, the vocational Gymnasium, the occupation-specific Fachgymnasium, and the Gesamtschule. Graduation from these schools requires passing the *Abitur*, the qualifying examination for studying at university level.

Vocational Education and Training:

The German education system has been praised for its ability to provide good-quality general education combined with excellent specific training for a profession. In 2008, about 66% of the country's total workforce had been trained through vocational education. There are a variety of types of vocational school. The method of teaching used in vocational schools is called the dual system (*Duales System*) because it combines classroom study with a work-related apprenticeship system. The length of schooling/training depends on prior vocational experience and may entail one year of full-time instruction or up to three years of part-time training.

Tertiary or Higher Education

In the 2010/11 academic year, higher education was available at 371 institutions of higher learning (of which 122 are universities) (Deutscher Bildungsserver, 2010). In 2008, 45% of students were qualified to enter higher education, but only 75% of these started higher education (Autorengruppe Bildungsberichterstattung, 2010). German university students can complete their first degree in about five years, but on average university studies last for seven years. Advanced degrees require further study. The proportion of female students amounts to approximately 50% (Autorengruppe Bildungsberichterstattung, 2010), which corresponds to the proportion of women in the population.

The percentage of first-year students has risen in recent years. This is due to a prolonged attendance in education (obtaining a necessary certification required for access to higher education). With a percentile of 40%, this figure nevertheless remains 10 percentage points below the OECD average. In the course of the reformation of the educational structure (Bologna proceedings), 80% of colleges of higher education and 55% of universities have already been converted to Bachelor–Master programs in recent years. As key points of the reform induce critique during the process of implementation, further developments are expected (Autorengruppe Bildungsberichterstattung, 2010).

In a study carried out by the OECD (2001) in 32 industrialized nations (PISA: Programs for International Student Assessment) with 15-year-old pupils, German adolescents performed very poorly. The "PISA shock," which was a direct result of this, triggered a controversial education discussion, in the wake of which reforms were introduced, including the introduction of binding national educational standards for all schools, Abitur after 8 years, and more all-day schools. The PISA data of 2006 document an improvement in ranking: reading literacy, rank 10-17 (within OECD average); mathematical literacy, rank 11–17 (within OECD average); scientific literacy, rank 7–13 (significantly higher than OECD average) (OECD, 2006).

Work

In Germany, children and adolescents (under 18 years) are prohibited by the Young Persons Employment Act from pursuing employment. With parental approval, however, from the age of 14 they are allowed to take on a minor job with temporal restrictions (e.g., delivering newspapers, babysitting, after-school tutoring, messenger work, and gardening) (Flammer, Alsaker, & Noack, 1999). A steadily growing group of adolescents have a job outside of school: 15% of the 12- to 14-year-olds but 33% of the older adolescents; furthermore, more youth in the East of Germany have jobs outside of school (Leven et al., 2010). Their earnings are rarely expected to contribute to the domestic budget of the parents; generally speaking, the money serves to supplement their pocket money. As school and vocational education in Germany is very differentiated, nowadays it often reaches far into adulthood. The multitude of different paths brings with it a broad variation in the ages at which adolescents enter into the world of work.

Many students take a "gap year" after completing the Abitur, during which they either work or travel. Many also interrupt their degree course for general educational or social experiences. In addition, the option of a so-called "voluntary social or ecological year" offers young people between the ages of 16 and 26 the opportunity, before commencing further education or training, to gain an insight into social work, care work, or ecological professions, and to try them out under the guidance of professionals. The framework conditions for this are regulated by law (12 months' full-time employment; pedagogical support; pocket money; free insurance, board, and lodgings). The number of young people graduating from this scheme in 2009 was approximately 40,000 (Autorengruppe Bildungsberichterstattung, 2010).

So-called broken-off education in the secondary or tertiary area often results in unskilled labor. In order to facilitate the transition for the adolescents from school into the world of work, in Germany all school-leavers are offered individual career advice by the Federal Employment Agency, which consists of the following elements: preparation of job selection, clarification of abilities and interests, provision of information about careers (including offers of work experience and "taster" programs), help with career decisions, and help in the search for apprenticeships and job placements.

In an international comparison, youth unemployment is rather low: The unemployment rate among 15- to 24-year-olds has over the past 10 years remained constant at approximately 10% in Germany. In comparison, the rate in the OECD countries amounted to an average of 12.4% (Hoeckel & Schwartz, 2010). According to an analysis of all EU states, responsible for these favorable values is Germany's dual vocational training, which on average pushes down youth unemployment by 5%. The success of this state-controlled market model can be gauged from the number of people in Germany who achieve a higher degree: In 2008 about 61% of 30- to 35-year-olds had completed a vocational training (apprenticeship, advanced technical college) and 21% a university degree (18% had no educational achievement) (Autorengruppe Bildungsberichterstattung, 2010).

Media

Since 1998 the pedagogical media research association Südwest (Medienpädagogischer Forschungsverbund Südwest) has mapped the media-related behavior of 12- to 19-year-olds in

Germany with its representative serial study "JIM." The JIM study 2009 (Medienpädagogischer Forschungsverbund Südwest, 2009) shows that families with adolescents between the ages of 12 and 19 are equipped with media devices significantly above the federal average (100% with mobile phones and computers/laptops; 98% with access to the Internet and TV; about 90% DVD, MP3-player and iPod).

Youths of 12–19 years predominantly spend their free time in non-media-related pursuits: 88% meet with friends, 70% do sports, and 67% rest or do nothing. Boys prefer sports and playing music themselves; girls prefer to rest or do creative activities. The outward orientation rises with increasing age, while sporting activities and family ventures decrease.

In everyday life the Internet is of highest importance to adolescents (88%); the significance of television is cited by 65%. On average adolescents state a daily usage of the Internet of 134 minutes, and 137 minutes of watching television. The Internet is mostly used for communication (47%), but also for entertainment (22%), for games (18%) and for informational research (14%). The mandatory labeling of age ranges, which exist in Germany for the protection of youths, is not adhered to by adolescents; thus 82% of the boys and 38% of the girls play games for which they are too young. The "isolated permanent player," frequently cited in the media, is not the usual behavior of adolescent players (Leven et al., 2010). An age trend can be seen in Internet usage: The older the adolescents, the more they search for information and the less they play games. Most adolescents use the computer and/or the Internet for homework or their studies for school at home (Medienpädagogischer Forschungsverbund Südwest, 2009).

Listening to music is also highly valued. Over the past few years, besides listening to the radio, the technical possibilities for listening to music (e.g. the Internet as a music platform, listening to music via mobile phones) have increased significantly. Fifty-eight percent use the radio daily. While girls prefer to listen to music (via radio, CDs) and read, it is notable that boys use computer games/ console games and watch DVDs and videos much more frequently. With age, the usage of online newspapers and magazines rises, while playing computer/console games and watching television decreases. Despite the rapid developments within the media, 40% regularly read books during their spare time (Medienpädagogischer Forschungsverbund Südwest, 2009).

For some years now the mobile phone has belonged to the basic equipment of adolescents: 95% of adolescents have their own mobile phone (85% with an integrated MP3-player, 73% with radio, 94% with a camera, 86% with Bluetooth interface, 80% with Internet access, 50% with information interface, 28% with GPS, 12% with TV). Apart from the main functions (text messages and speaking via telephone), the mobile phone is used daily/several times during the week by about 50% of adolescents to listen to music, by 40% to take pictures or movies; about 30% send data via Bluetooth (music and photos/videos), 15% use it for games, 9% as a radio, and 6% receive news services (Medienpädagogischer Forschungsverbund Südwest, 2009).

Politics and Military

Up until the 1980s (55%) and early 1990s (57%), being politically interested was part of young people's (between 15 and 24 years of age) attitude. The value placed on politics dropped in 2002 to a low of 34%. The sixteenth German Shell Youth Study (2010) showed that political interest and engagement of adolescents in Germany is becoming increasingly important: 40% of today's adolescents between the age of 12 and 24 years describe themselves as "politically interested." The most noticeable increases are found in the age groups of 12- to 14-year-olds (2002, 11%; 2010, 21%) and 15- to 17-year-olds (2002, 20%; 2010: 33%). Male youths are more interested in politics than females (2001, 23%; 2010, 31%). Besides age and gender, the level of education plays an important role in this regard: The education and mindset of the family background are crucial, i.e. the political interest of the parents (69% of students with politically highly interested parents were themselves interested) (Schneekloth, 2010). In 2009, 18- and 19-year-olds were allowed for the first time to cast their vote for the federal parliament. Sixty-seven percent of young male voters and 56% of young female voters showed interest in the Bundestag elections (Medienpädagogischer Forschungsverbund Südwest, 2009).

In contrast to the population as a whole, adolescents continue to categorize themselves politically as slightly left of center. Political extremism is strongly rejected. Between 2006 and 2010 no significant changes in regard to political positioning occurred. The following distribution shows the current political landscape (Schneekloth, 2010): left (9%) and tending towards left (29%); middle (29%); tending towards right (15%) and right (3%); without positioning (14%).

The overwhelming majority of adolescents see democracy as a good form of government. This is demonstrated through the rise in acceptance of the democratic form of government between 2002 and 2010: in East Germany (2002, 64%; 2010, 70%) and in West Germany (2002, 81%; 2010, 86%). However, a considerable "political abstinence" remains; especially an increasing distance from political and economic institutions (parties and banks) is visible. By contrast, party-independent state organizations (police/justice), but also human rights and environmental protection groups, are seen as trustworthy.

In spite of the moderate level of political interest, many adolescents are socially active in their own living environment. In this regard, they orient themselves toward concrete and practical questions, which are linked for them with personal opportunities and use (own interests, leisure activities). Although adolescents do lend their support to other people or environmental and animal protection, the popularity of citizen action initiatives, aid organizations such as Greenpeace or Amnesty International, parties, and trade unions is significantly lower than that of local organizations, educational institutions, and self-organized groups. Higher participation in political activities correlates with interests in politics, the political positioning (tending towards the left), the sex (female) and a higher education. Forty percent of adolescents show a high willingness to be politically active, 23% show no or low willingness (Schneekloth, 2010).

The German army is a conscript army, with a strength in 2010 of 248,700 soldiers (of these, more than 17,000 are female). Male citizens (from 18 to 45 years) have been required to do general military service for nine months; since 2001, women too have been able to undergo military service voluntarily, but are not obligated to do so. Those who refuse military service through conscientious objection (approximately 20% of those recorded as liable for military service) have had to take part in an alternative community service (also nine months). In the general consciousness of adolescents, and due to the handling of obligatory service in practice, there has been more or less freedom of choice between military service and alternative community service. A transition to the model of an army of volunteers no longer is out of the question (Bundeswehr, 2010); since the amendment, compulsory military service may be discontinued at some point.

Unique Issues

The reunification of Germany took place in 1990, through the "accession" of the GDR to the old Federal Republic; it was linked with an abrupt change and a seamless adoption of the complete West German societal system in East Germany. The question of how, against the background of the same cultural traditions, these new, different political–social relations affect the development and socialization of children and adolescents, and how such an exceptionally abrupt political, social, and ideological change makes itself felt in adolescents, has been examined in many longitudinal studies. In all, this social change has had less of a dramatic effect on the social behavior and the personality development of children and adolescents than was originally expected (Silbereisen, 2005).

Roughly every second respondent in the East and West (46%) is pleased about the unification of Germany. However, 20 years after the reunification the Germans are of the opinion that it will take another 20 years until "inner" unification is also accomplished (Brähler & Mohr, 2010). The younger East Germans between 14 and 24 years, who have not at all or not consciously experienced the GDR, view this historic event as especially positive. Here the joy over the reunification is highest, at 64%. Also in the West, 49% of the so-called children's generation are pleased about the unity, which is more than the average of West Germans. Clear differences can be seen when asking whether there are more commonalities between East and West than differences. Roughly two-thirds of the West Germans (66%) see more commonalities than differences, but less than half of the East Germans (47%) share this view. Discrepancies are also found across generations. The older the respondent, the fewer commonalities are perceived. The reunification is viewed the most skeptically by the East Germans over 75 years of age. Persons who fully experienced and substantially helped build up the GDR system are those who still identify with it. Nevertheless, fears of contact between East and West also remain within the younger generations; these are visible in for example the reluctance of West Germans to take on their studies in East German cities, despite the fact that the conditions for studying are often better there than in West German universities (Zick, 2010).

References and Further Reading

Abendroth, A. (2009). *Body modification. Tattoos, Piercings, Scarifications. Körpermodifikation im Wandel der Zeit*. Diedorf, Germany: Ubooks.

Albert, M., Hurrelmann, K., & Quenzel, G. (2010a). Jugend 2010: Selbstbehauptung trotz Verunsicherung. In Shell Deutschland Holding (Ed.), *16. Shell Jugendstudie: Jugend 2010. Eine pragmatische Generation behauptet sich* (pp. 37–51). Frankfurt-on-Main: Fischer Taschenbuch Verlag.

Albert, M., Hurrelmann, K., & Quenzel, G. (2010b). Jugendliche in Deutschland – Optionen für Politik, Wirtschaft und Pädagogik. In Shell Deutschland Holding (Ed.), *16. Shell Jugendstudie: Jugend 2010. Eine pragmatische Generation behauptet sich* (pp. 343–360). Frankfurt-on-Main: Fischer Taschenbuch Verlag.

Arnett, J. J. (2004). *Emerging adulthood: The winding road from late teens through the twenties*. New York, NY: Oxford University Press.

Arnett, J. J. (2007). Emerging adulthood: What is it, and what is it good for? *Child Development Perspectives, 1*, 68–73.

Autorengruppe Bildungsberichterstattung. (2010). *Bildung in Deutschland 2010*. Bonn, Germany: Bundesministerium für Bildung und Forschung. Retrieved from www.bildungsbericht.de

Blossfeld, H. P., Klijzing, E., Kurz, K., & Mills, M. (Eds.). (2005). *Globalization, uncertainty, and youth in society*. New York, NY: Routledge.

Brähler, E., & Mohr, I. (Eds.). (2010). *20 Jahre deutsche Einheit – Facetten einer geteilten Wirklichkeit*. Gießen, Germany: Psychosozial-Verlag.

Bundesministerium für Familie, Senioren, Frauen und Jugend (BMFSFJ) (2010). *Kompass Erziehung: Mediennutzung*. Berlin, Germany: BMFSFJ. Retrieved from www.bmfsfj.de

Bundeswehr (2010). *Die Stärke der Streitkräfte*. Bonn, Germany: Bundeswehr. Retrieved from www.bundeswehr.de

Bundeszentrale für gesundheitliche Aufklärung (BZgA) (2001). *Jugendsexualität*. Cologne, Germany: BZgA. Retrieved from www.bzga.de

Bundeszentrale für gesundheitliche Aufklärung (BZgA) (2006). *Jugendsexualität*. Cologne, Germany: BZgA. Retrieved from www.bzga.de

Bundeszentrale für gesundheitliche Aufklärung (BZgA) (2007). *Förderung des Nichtrauchens bei Jugendlichen*. Cologne, Germany: BZgA. Retrieved from www.bzga.de

Bundeszentrale für gesundheitliche Aufklärung (BZgA) (2009a). *Die Drogenaffinität Jugendlicher in der Bundesrepublik Deutschland 2008. Verbreitung des Alkoholkonsums bei Jugendlichen und jungen Erwachsenen*. Cologne, Germany: BZgA. Retrieved from www.bzga.de

Bundeszentrale für gesundheitliche Aufklärung (BZgA) (2009b). *Die Drogenaffinität Jugendlicher in der Bundesrepublik Deutschland 2008. Verbreitung des Tabakkonsums bei Jugendlichen und jungen Erwachsenen*. Cologne, Germany: BZgA. Retrieved from www.bzga.de

Bundeszentrale für gesundheitliche Aufklärung (BZgA) (2010a). *Die Drogenaffinität Jugendlicher in der Bundesrepublik Deutschland 2008. Verbreitung des Konsums illegaler Drogen bei Jugendlichen und jungen Erwachsenen*. Cologne, Germany: BZgA. Retrieved from www.bzga.de

Bundeszentrale für gesundheitliche Aufklärung (BZgA) (2010b). *Jugendsexualität 2010. Repräsentative Wiederholungsbefragung von 14- bis 17-Jährigen und ihren Eltern – Aktueller Schwerpunkt Migration*. Cologne, Germany: BZgA. Retrieved from www.bzga.de

Bundeszentrale für gesundheitliche Aufklärung (BZgA) (2010c). *Begriffserklärung. Chlamydien-Infektion*. Cologne, Germany: BZgA. Retrieved from www.bzga.de

Chisholm, L., & Hurrelmann, K. (1995). Adolescence in modern Europe: Pluralized transition patterns and their implications for personal and social risks. *Journal of Adolescence, 1*, 129–158.

Deutsche Shell (2000). *Jugend 2000, 13. Shell Jugendstudie, Band 1*. Opladen, Germany: Leske und Budrich.

Deutsche Shell (2003). *Jugend 2002, 14. Shell Jugendstudie. Zwischen pragmatischen Idealismus und robustem Materialismus* (4. Auflage). Frankfurt-on-Main, Germany: Fischer TB Verlag.

Deutscher Bildungsserver (2010). *Hochschulbildung*. Frankfurt-on-Main, Germany: Deutscher Bildungsserver. Retrieved from www.bildungsserver.de

Farin, K. (2010). Jugendkulturen heute. *Aus Politik und Zeitgeschichte, 1*, 3–8.

Fend, H. (2000). *Entwicklungspsychologie des Jugendalters*. Opladen, Germany: Leske and Budrich.

Flammer, A., Alsaker, F., & Noack, P. (1999). Time-use by adolescents in an international perspective. In F. Alsaker & A. Flammer (Eds.), *The adolescent experience: European and American adolescents in the 1990s* (pp. 33–60). Hillsdale, NJ: Lawrence Erlbaum Associates.

Fritsche, Y. (2000). Moderne Orientierungsmuster: Inflation am Wertehimmel. In Deutsche Shell, *Jugend 2000, 13. Shell Jugendstudie, Band 1* (pp. 93–157). Opladen, Germany: Leske und Budrich.

Fuhrer, U. (2005). *Lehrbuch Erziehungspsychologie*. Berne, Switzerland: Huber.

Furman, W., & Wehner, E. (1997). Adolescent romantic relationships: A developmental perspective. *New Directions for Child and Adolescent Development, 1*, 21–36.

Gensicke, T. (2010). Wertorientierungen, Befinden und Problembewältigung. In Shell Deutschland Holding, *16. Shell Jugendstudie: Jugend 2010. Eine pragmatische Generation behauptet sich* (pp. 187–242). Frankfurt-on-Main, Germany: Fischer Verlag.

Greive, M., & Müller, U. (2009). Seit Mauerfall flossen 1,3 Billionen Euro gen Osten. *Welt Online*. Retrieved November 2, 2010 from www.welt.de

Hagemann-White, C. (2006). Sozialisation – zur Wiedergewinnung des Sozialen im Gestrüpp individualisierter Geschlechterbeziehungen. In H. Bilden & B. Dausien (Eds.), *Sozialisation und Geschlecht: Theoretische und methodologische Aspekte* (pp. 71–88). Opladen, Germany: Budrich.

Haid, M.-L., Seiffge-Krenke, I., Molinar, R., Ciairano, C., Karaman, N. G., & Cok, F. (2010). Identity and future concerns among adolescents from Italy, Turkey and Germany: Intra- and between-cultural comparisons. *Journal of Youth Studies, 1*, 369–389.

Hoeckel, K., & Schwartz, R. (2010). *Lernen für die Arbeitswelt. OECD Studien zur Berufsbildung. Deutschland.* Paris: OECD. Retrieved from www.oecd.org

Hölling, H., Erhart, M., Ravens-Sieberer, U., & Schlack, R. (2007). Verhaltensauffälligkeiten bei Kindern und Jugendlichen. Erste Ergebnisse aus dem Kinder- und Jugendgesundheitssurvey (KiGGS). *Bundesgesundheitsblatt – Gesundheitsforschung – Gesundheitsschutz, 1*, 784–793.

Hölling, H., & Schlack, R. (2007). Essstörungen im Kindes- und Jugendalter. Erste Ergebnisse aus dem Kinder- und Jugendgesundheitssurvey (KiGGS). *Bundesgesundheitsblatt – Gesundheitsforschung – Gesundheitsschutz, 1*, 794–799. Retrieved from www.kiggs.de

Institut für praxisorientierte Sozialforschung (IPOS) (2003). *Jugendliche und junge Erwachsene in Deutschland 2002.* Mannheim, Germany: IPOS. Retrieved from www.bmfsfj.de

Kurth, B.-M., & Schaffrath Rosario, A. (2007). Die Verbreitung von Übergewicht und Adipositas bei Kindern und Jugendlichen in Deutschland. Ergebnisse des bundesweiten Kinder- und Jugendgesundheitssurveys (KiGGS). *Bundesgesundheitsblatt – Gesundheitsforschung – Gesundheitsschutz, 1*, 736–743.

Leven, I., Quenzel, G., & Hurrelmann, K. (2010). Familie, Schule, Freizeit: Kontinuitäten im Wandel. In Shell Deutschland Holding, *16. Shell Jugendstudie: Jugend 2010. Eine pragmatische Generation behauptet sich* (pp. 53–128). Frankfurt-on-Main, Germany: Fischer Taschenbuch Verlag.

Medienpädagogischer Forschungsverbund Südwest (mpfs) (2009). *JIM-Studie 2009. Jugend, Information, (Multi-)Media. Basisstudie zum Medienumgang 12- bis 19-Jähriger in Deutschland.* Stuttgart, Germany: Medienpädagogischer Forschungsverbund Südwest.

OECD (2001). *Knowledge and skills for life: First results from PISA 2000.* Paris, France: OECD. Retrieved from www.mpib-berlin.mpg.de

OECD (2006). *Education at a glance.* Paris, France: OECD. Retrieved from www.oecd.org

OECD (2010). *Education at a glance.* Paris, France: OECD. Retrieved from www.oecd.org

Oerter, R., & Dreher, E. (2008). Jugendalter. In R. Oerter & L. Montada (Eds.), *Entwicklungspsychologie* (6, vollständig überarbeitete Auflage, pp. 271–332). Weinheim, Germany: Beltz PVU.

Pinquart, M., & Silbereisen, R. K. (2008). Jugendliche im sozialen Wandel. In R. K. Silbereisen & M. Hasselhorn (Eds.), *Entwicklungspsychologie des Jugendalters. Enzyklopädie für Psychologie, Themenbereich C: Theorie und Forschung, Serie V: Entwicklungspsychologie* (Vol. 5, pp. 835–888). Göttingen, Germany: Hogrefe.

Rink, D. (2002). Beunruhigende Normalisierung: Zum Wandel von Jugendkulturen in der Bundesrepublik Deutschland. *Aus Politik und Zeitgeschichte, B5*, 3–6.

Schlack, R., & Hölling, H. (2007). Gewalterfahrungen von Kindern und Jugendlichen im subjektiven Selbstbericht. Erste Ergebnisse aus dem Kinder- und Jugendgesundheitssurvey (KiGGS). *Bundesgesundheitsblatt – Gesundheitsforschung – Gesundheitsschutz, 1*, 819–826.

Schneekloth, U. (2010). Jugend und Politik: Aktuelle Entwicklungstrends und Perspektiven. In Shell Deutschland Holding, *16. Shell Jugendstudie: Jugend 2010. Eine pragmatische Generation behauptet sich* (pp. 129–164). Frankfurt-on-Main, Germany: Fischer Taschenbuch Verlag.

Schneekloth, U., & Albert, M. (2010). Entwicklungen bei den "großen Themen": Generationengerechtigkeit, Globalisierung, Klimawandel. In Shell Deutschland Holding (Hrsg.), *16. Shell Jugendstudie: Jugend 2010. Eine pragmatische Generation behauptet sich* (S. 165–185). Frankfurt-on-Main, Germany: Fischer Taschenbuch Verlag.

Seiffge-Krenke, I., Bosma, H., Chau, C., Cok, F., Gillespie, C., Loncaric, D., et al. (2010). All they need is love? Placing romantic stress in the context of other stressors: A 17-nation study. *International Journal of Behavioral Development, 1*, 106–112.

Shell Deutschland Holding (2006). *15. Shell Jugendstudie: Jugend 2010. Eine pragmatische Generation behauptet sich.* Frankfurt-on-Main, Germany: Fischer Taschenbuch Verlag.

Shell Deutschland Holding (2010). *16. Shell Jugendstudie: Jugend 2010. Eine pragmatische Generation behauptet sich.* Frankfurt-on-Main, Germany: Fischer Taschenbuch Verlag.

Sirsch, U., Dreher, E., Mayr, E., & Willinger, U. (2009). What does it take to be an adult in Austria? Views of adulthood in Austrian adolescents, emerging adults and adults. *Journal of Adolescent Research, 1*, 275–292.

Silbereisen, R. K. (2005). Social change and human development: Experiences from German unification. *International Journal of Behavioral Development, 1*, 2–13.

Statistisches Bundesamt Deutschland (2010). Retrieved from www.destatis.de

Steinberg, L. (2008). *Adolescence* (8th ed.). New York, NY: McGraw-Hill.

Weichold, K., & Silbereisen, R. K. (2008). Pubertät und psychosoziale Anpassung. In R. K. Silbereisen & M. Hasselhorn (Eds.), *Entwicklungspsychologie des Jugendalters.* Enzyklopädie der Psychologie, Themenbereich C, Serie V, Vol. 5 (pp. 3–53). Göttingen, Germany: Hogrefe.

Zick, A. (2010). *Die Vorurteile bleiben – Soziologe: Kontakt zwischen Ost und West fehlt.* Retrieved from www.3sat.de/nano

Zinsmeister, F. (2009). Die Finanzierung der deutschen Einheit – Zum Umgang mit den Schuldlasten der Wiedervereinigung. *Vierteljahrshefte zur Wirtschaftsforschung, 1*, 146–160.

Chapter 20
Italy
Silvia Bonino and Elena Cattelino

Background Information

Italy is a peninsula in the center of the Mediterranean Sea, comprising many different kinds of territory: coasts, islands, plains, and even high mountains. The number of inhabitants is around 60.5 million (ISTAT, 2011; all the statistics reported come from ISTAT, National Institute of Statistics, if no other reference is indicated), making Italy one of the most densely populated countries in Europe. The inhabitants are not distributed evenly; nearly two-thirds live in urban zones.

There are significant differences among the various regions. The main industries of the country are concentrated in the north, while the south accounts for the lower range of income. Despite the post-Second World War economic boom, which made Italy one of the 10 most industrialized countries in the world, the unemployment rate remains high (about 9%, reaching 29% in young people between 15 and 24) and it varies from area to area, with a higher concentration in the south. Emigration has been a reality since the end of the nineteenth century; after the Second World War and up to the end of the 1960s there was an important internal migration from the agrarian south to the industrialized north. Today Italy is a country of immigration, especially from Eastern Europe and the Mediterranean basin. There are almost 4,500,000 immigrants; illegal immigrants are estimated at 750,000 (http://stats.oecd.org).

Italy has been a unified nation since 1861. Since 1946 it has been a parliamentary democratic republic. Italy is part of the European Union and its currency is the euro.

Period of Adolescence

As in other postindustrial European societies, adolescence is socially recognized as a period of socialization and preparation for entrance into adulthood. The extension of such a period for all adolescents, and not only for those of a higher social class, took place in the decades immediately after the 1950s; this was in relation to the minimum school leaving age being raised, and to the growing industrialization and increased welfare of society.

The first signs of physical maturation are visible in girls between 9 and 12 years, and for boys between 11 and 14 years. Menarche begins between 11 and 14 years, the average age being 12.3 years (Centro Studi Auxologici, 2005). From a legal point of view, the coming of age is 18, but this does not correspond to an emotional and economic independence or to the assuming of adult responsibilities. In Italy there is a long period of emerging adulthood—longer than in other European countries. Economic and social differences existing among various Italian regions and social classes, related to the continuation of studies and the beginning of working life, are also reflected in the duration of adolescence and in the period of emerging adulthood. In some groups, emerging adulthood is accompanied by unemployment, under-employment, and temporary work, while in other groups it leads to a longer education in regard to preparation for a more advanced career.

Nevertheless, there is a common tendency to continue living in the parental home. Ninety percent of young people between 18 and 24 years of age live with their family, and 43% of those between 25 and 34 years of age. The percentage is higher for boys, even when they work, and it is found to be higher in the south and in the islands than in the north. Therefore, there is a generation for whom entering adulthood does not necessarily mean leaving the family—a family in which relationships are based primarily on compromise and negotiation and not on conflict (Scabini, Marta, & Lanz, 2006). At the root of this phenomenon are various interacting causes: unemployment, difficulty in finding a stable and adequately paid job, lack of services and policies for youth, and also a cultural tradition of family support and closeness.

On a social level, representation of adolescents, especially teenagers, is quite negative, and does not correspond to reality. Mass media greatly emphasize negative events (for example, suicides and acts of aggression) in spite of statistical evidence to the contrary. There are no recognized rites of passage that specify the transition from adolescence to adulthood, although it is thought that some adolescent risk behavior can subjectively have the role of visibly marking this passage (Bonino, Cattelino, & Ciairano, 2005).

Beliefs

As with the majority of other European Union countries, Italy has a set of individualistic as opposed to collectivistic values. However, some studies group the south of Italy in a particular collectivistic area, more common to other countries of southern Europe, that privileges the family as a group. In Italian society, family still carries great importance also for adolescents. For the future, having a family is a significant goal that most adolescents aspire to, immediately followed by a rewarding job.

The dominant religion in the country is Catholicism and nearly 86% of children are baptized. The number of confirmed adolescents is lower, and both percentages have decreased in recent years. In 2004, 68% of young people between 15 and 20 declared themselves to be Catholic (Grassi, 2006), whereas in 2000 this percentage was 81% (Buzzi, Cavalli, & de Lillo, 2007). Adolescents attend church more than adults but the number of those who go at least once a week decreases strongly as they get older: from about 65% when they are under 13 years of age to about 20% when they are between 15 and 20 (Grassi, 2006); just 10% of adolescents have a stable involvement in religious groups (Garelli, Palmonari, & Sciolla, 2006). At the same time, the number of adolescents who never go to church increases. At 18 to 19 this is around 15% and it tends to increase in the following years. The majority of adolescents do not follow Catholic moral dictates regarding premarital sexual relations.

As in other Western countries, communication media mainly promote consumer-led values that privilege appearances and possession of status symbols, such as mobile telephones. One can in fact affirm that adolescents live in a society where points of reference for values are very different—

often contradictory and opposite. This multitude of possibilities leaves space for a lot of individual choices but it can also create difficulty in choosing.

Research has shown that adolescents mostly place themselves as conservative toward traditional values: They prize family, friends, school, work, and health. A minority of around 10% place themselves in a position of opposition and defiance toward dominant values, but without proposing a precise alternative (Sgritta, 2000). As for social values, adolescents prove to be particularly sensitive to the protection of family and of human life, and the defense of freedom of opinion and peace (Buzzi, Cavalli, & de Lillo, 2007; Garelli et al., 2006).

Gender

Italian society presents a particularly complex and contradictory situation regarding women's role in society. Basically, girls are offered two roles: the traditional role of motherhood, offered to girls from childhood, or a career outside the home. The fact that the latter possibility is seriously considered by girls and by their families is shown by the high level of attendance in secondary school and also at university, where there are more females than males, and by their commitment in school, which leads to results generally superior to those of males.

In reality, not only are the two roles difficult to integrate, but they are both also difficult to obtain. Fulfillment in a family and maternal role is first of all postponed, because of the generalized condition of prolonged emerging adulthood. The average age of women at first childbirth is the highest in Europe. First-time mothers are on average 29 to 32 years old, and 34% of Italian women conceive their first child after 35; 6% of women give birth to their first child after 40. Furthermore, the average number of children is very low: Italy has one of the lowest birth rates in Western Europe at 1.42 children per woman. This phenomenon is the subject of great discussion. According to some social scientists it is strongly tied to the lack of adequate policies supporting motherhood and family: For this reason it is particularly difficult for women to reconcile the role of mother with that of worker.

Outside the family, a good education and good academic results achieved by girls in secondary school and during university do not lead to an adequate and easy insertion into a job. The rate of unemployment for women, although differing markedly among the various Italian regions, is always higher than the rate of unemployment for men, and in some cases is nearly double. Furthermore, the kind of job women receive is often of an inferior level and for lower pay, compared to the school qualifications obtained. Jobs in education, health, and personal care generally continue to be more available to them.

To this we must add that, as in many other Western countries, the media offer girls a strong and sexually active female role, based primarily on physical appearance. In this situation the body becomes an object of attention, and adolescents mostly manifest dissatisfaction toward their physical appearance, which is considered inadequate compared to the unobtainable models of thinness, beauty, and physical perfection offered by the media. For this reason, the body becomes the main target of discomfort for a lot of adolescents. Girls are significantly more prone to eating disorders than boys. Disturbed diet (comfort eating, diets, elimination behavior) is a mainly female phenomenon that shows itself in the first period of adolescence but tends to last even into emerging adulthood. This is accompanied by an excess of attention to one's body and to one's physical image. Girls are unhappier with their appearance and their weight and mostly judge themselves as too fat even when they are within the normal weight range. More generally, girls set themselves higher targets of realization at a social and academic level; their levels of self-esteem and self-efficacy are lower than those of males of the same age, despite better school results.

For boys, the conflict of roles is not centered as much around family and work as around the model of masculinity. On one side is the role of the strong aggressive male, sure of himself and powerful, while on the other side there are ever-increasing requests for a greater emotional involvement toward the partner and children. In this situation many males carry out, especially during the first stages of adolescence, behaviors that could lead to "externalizing" deviance: dangerous behavior, sexual risk behavior, and dangerous driving (Bonino et al., 2005; Cattelino 2010). These behaviors are thought to have the function of expressing, in a visible and exaggerated way, a strong masculinity in a condition of psychological uncertainty.

The Self

As in other Western societies, the construction of identity in Italian adolescents does not occur in a single way. Rather, the construction of the different components of identity is a long and differentiated process, depending on the different life areas (Bosma & Kunnen 2001). This means that the exploration and the commitments in significant life areas are diverse, and they can happen at different times, with different solutions. As a result of this, in adolescence one can find a development of identities that have been defined as "imperfect" (Palmonari, 1997), with a non-homogeneous identity status in the various areas. In recent years, in a context socially definable as postmodern, characterized by very different and rapidly changing models, exploration and diffusion without commitments have shown the tendency of increasing and lengthening through emerging adulthood, and according to some, also into adult age (Oliverio Ferraris, 2007).

The development of identity is strongly tied to the opportunities offered by family, school, groups, and economic context, giving different possibilities of exploration and achievement (Aleni Sestito, 2004). The development of identity is also tied to regional belonging, because of the dissimilar history, traditions and values of the various regions of Italy. We note regarding this that the different regional dialects continue to be used by Italian families and young people.

It is thought that the diffused involvement in numerous risk behaviors has functions for the development of identity (Jessor, 1998; Jessor, Donovan, & Costa, 1991; Silbereisen & Noack, 1988; Silbereisen, Eiferth & Rudinger, 1986). Risk behaviors serve for adolescents the purpose of reaching personally and socially meaningful objectives in the process of construction of an autonomous adult identity, especially for those Italian adolescents who have fewer personal and contextual resources, in family, school, and community of origin (Bonino et al., 2005). These behaviors are different according to gender and type of school attended.

In their free time Italian girls spend more time alone than boys do (nearly 25% of girls' free time versus 17% for boys). The time spent on their own is mostly taken up by activities such as reading, hobbies, and going to libraries.

Family Relationships

Family in Italy plays a central role in social organization and in individual life for adolescents, who find in their family a valid source of support and see the building of a future family of their own as a main value for their own fulfillment. During the past century, family structure has undergone important transformations and, especially in urban centers, there has been a change from an extended family, characterized by the presence of multiple generations, to a more limited family nucleus made up of the parents and one or two children. The main family types, apart from 26% single people, are about 20% childless couples, 38% couples with children, 8% single-parent families with children, and 8% other. Families in a free union, lacking a publicly recognized bond such as marriage, are 5% of couples, whereas couples reconstituted after a divorce are 6%; these family forms are constantly growing. Adolescents generally live with both parents, and nearly two-thirds have at least one brother or sister. The presence of grandparents in the family household is from 10% to 16%, depending on the area, with a greater proportion of grandmothers.

Family relationships between adolescents and parents are mostly characterized by an open attitude to dialogue, confrontation, and support (Marta, 1997; Scabini et al., 2006). The prominent educational style is authoritative, characterized by high levels of control and support (Cicognani & Zani, 1998). By 16 to 17 years of age, the authoritative style tends to become for both genders a supportive one, characterized by lower levels of supervision and control and higher levels of support (Cattelino, Calandri, & Bonino, 2001). Relationships between mother and daughter are generally characterized by greater closeness but also by greater conflict (Cicognani & Zani, 2010).

The good quality of relationships represents a resource, helping adolescents to face, with minor anxiety, certain roles of development, in particular those tied to school and working experiences (Graziano, Bonino, & Cattelino, 2009); but it also contributes to rendering the eventual break more difficult, creating obstacles for the acquisition processes of emotional independence (Scabini, 1995; Lo Coco & Pace, 2009).

Though conflict is present in families with adolescent children, in most cases it is neither heated nor frequent, and concentrates mostly on exterior aspects (such as hairstyles and clothes styles) or on behavioral autonomy (hours outside the home, friends, proper behavior). However, especially in some southern areas, there seems to be greater conflict and interference from parents toward daughters, especially in the context of a more traditional family, where greater dependence on parents and less freedom of choice is required of daughters.

Both from the children's and the parents' side, the style of the conflict is mainly oriented toward compromise. So we are not talking about conflicts that create a fracture between generations, but of conflicts that tend to create new balances and consolidate deep existing ties (Honess et al., 1997). Therefore, conflict does not seem to favor a break, but is helpful in building a new balance inside the family.

The tendency for a low birth rate has led to a reduction in the presence of siblings, and one-third of adolescents are an only child, while the rest mostly have only one brother or sister. The presence of siblings of different gender makes the execution of family rules more difficult: In fact, in Italy males generally have greater freedom outside the domestic walls and they have to tolerate fewer demands concerning participation in housework. So when there are adolescents of different genders there is the possibility of numerous conflicts among both siblings and parents. Siblings in general, apart from being a model, are a source of support as well as conflict.

The number of separations and divorces is increasing (separations were 16% in 1995 and 30% in 2009; divorces were 8% in 1995 and 18% in 2009), and these generally have a negative impact on the feelings of wellbeing of adolescent children. Italian law tends to give custody to the mother (over 90% of the cases) and often the relationships with the father are relegated to some weekends and half of the summer holidays.

For custody of children under 18, the progressive application of a law in 2006 caused a strong increase in joint custody, determining 72% of joint custody of children after separation (only 39% in 2006) and 50% of joint custody after divorce (28% in 2006). In 2007, sole custody to mothers—which used to be the most frequent type of custody—decreased, becoming 26% of custody after separation and 46% after divorce (respectively 58% and 67% in the previous year).

Friends and Peers/Youth Culture

During adolescence, friends and peers become very important for Italian boys and girls, as in other Western countries. The amount of time spent with peers increases during adolescence and is greater for boys (40% of boys go out with their friends every day compared to 20% of girls of the same age). Nevertheless, in Italy the family still has a relevant influence (Scabini, Lanz, & Marta, 1999; Scabini et al., 2006; Kirchler, Palmonari, & Pombeni, 1993). Adolescents are likely to select friends whose opinions on important issues in life are quite similar to the opinions of their parents.

During a normal school week adolescents usually spend more time at home (studying, reading, and listening to music) than outside of it (e.g., in pubs and discos) and they are more likely to have dinner at home with the family than to eat out with friends. Meeting friends, going out and sharing meals with them (a pizzeria is more likely than a fast-food restaurant) is more frequent during the weekend, and especially on Saturday evenings. Nevertheless, time spent outside the home varies greatly based on gender, age, and place of residence. Family rules about what time to come home at night and the people the adolescent is allowed to spend time with are stricter for girls, even older ones, especially in small towns and in the south. However, staying at home with friends (watching TV programs or videos, playing with the computer, and also eating with friends' parents) is common and generally approved of by the parents. Throughout Italy, sharing meals is part of the normal process of maintaining friendships and building new ones, during adolescence and beyond.

Peer crowds are usually formed on the basis of common interests in sports, music, school, or sharing other types of activities. Generally, there are great similarities between the behaviors of the adolescents and those of their friends (Buzzi, Cavalli, & de Lillo, 2002).

Generally speaking, adolescents are more involved in sports groups (around 35%) than in other types of organizations. In Italy the most popular sport is football (soccer), but adolescents mainly play team sports such as five-a-side football and volleyball. Belonging to a sports group is more common for boys and in the north or center of Italy. Nevertheless, belonging to a sports group does not imply exercising regularly, since watching sports matches or using the sports group as a recreational place is also widespread. Sports groups are followed in importance by church groups and scout groups, which are more attended at younger ages and by girls, and by volunteer and political groups, which are more attended by older adolescents and emerging adults (Marta, Rossi, & Bocaccin, 1998; Marta & Pozzi, 2006; Ufficio Nazionale Servizio Civile, 2010).

The Italian church group has some peculiarities, such as the fact that not only very religious people belong to it and that recreational activities are also offered. In many small towns it is one of the few social outlets for adolescents. In addition, the church group has been shown to fulfill a protective role against involvement in risk behaviors, as it offers the opportunity to participate in organized and long-term planned activities (Bonino et al., 2005).

The tendency to move from more person-centered needs (such as those expressed by participating in sports) to more socially oriented values (such as participating in volunteer work or political activities) is characteristic of the transition from adolescence to emerging adulthood. However, while adolescent involvement in volunteer work is basically stable in Italy (11% of young people in Italy between 14 and 19 years of age declared having carried out volunteer work for associations, with a similar rate of participation between boys and girls; Eurispes, 2010), only a small percentage belong to political groups (around 5%) and generally they have extreme (left- or right-wing) political views. Nevertheless, interest in major issues such as peace, equality, and pollution has increased in the past few years, especially among older adolescents and emerging adults, though it is not related to a particular group.

A distinct youth culture exists to the same extent as in other Western countries. This culture is influenced by both Americanization and globalization and is marked off from adult culture by dress, music, piercing, and tattoos. Italian adolescents, especially girls, attribute great value to the freedom of choosing their clothes, and generally parents are likely to accept their choices. The clothes and hairstyles worn by adolescents and emerging adults vary in relation to the type of music they listen to (such as disco and pop, rap, and metal) and the value attributed to physical appearance (in terms of clothes as well as body image). However, clothes and hairstyles change very rapidly, making it impossible to distinguish stable, specific groups.

Love and Sexuality

In Italy, as well as in all of Western society, learning to be involved in dating, romantic, and sexual relationships may be considered one of the main adolescent developmental tasks (Ciairano, Kliewer, Bonino, Miceli, & Jackson, 2006; Zani, 1993). Italian adolescents are increasingly engaged in love and sex: At older ages, having a boyfriend/girlfriend becomes more common (from about 30% at 15 years to 60% at 19 years), and engaging in sex increases. According to the data of the Italian Society of Pediatrics, 62% of boys and 59% of girls between 15 and 19 years of age have had sexual intercourse. The average age for first intercourse is 17 years of age.

Marriage before 20 years old is very rare (around 2%), and even at 29 years old only 30% are married (currently, first-time grooms are about 32 years of age and first-time brides are almost 30). The percentage of cohabitation is low (around 5% of couples) and leaving home usually does not occur until marriage.

Birth control is commonly used. The most widely used contraceptive methods are condoms (around 75%), the pill, and withdrawal (about 20% each, although use of the pill increases after 20 years of age). About one-third of the adolescents do not always use safe prevention methods. The majority of adolescents always use some contraceptive method and a low percentage (less than 10%) never use contraceptives. In fact, the incidence of teen pregnancy is one of the lowest in Europe (around 5% of total birth and abortion rates) and births to teenage mothers are constantly decreasing (from 1995 to 2006 they diminished by over 24%). Only 1% of women have a child before they are 18 years old, around 11% before 24 years, and 30% between 25 and 29 years. However, births to mothers over 40 are increasing.

Attitudes to sex are still different for boys and girls. In continuity with the traditional model, the image of male sexuality is strong and aggressive. Pornography and sexual harassment toward peers are both higher among boys (Bonino et al., 2006). Boys who have already had sex are likely to have higher status than others in their peer group. Attitudes to female sexuality are more ambivalent. Nowadays willingness to have sex is normally expected of girls, but a negative attitude to women who have sex with a series of partners is still common.

In general, attitudes to sex are rapidly becoming more liberal and a matter of individual choice (Buzzi et al., 2002). Nevertheless, there are varying degrees of approval for gender, age, and level of education. Older adolescents and emerging adults and better-educated people are more likely to approve. Parental attitudes to adolescent sex are in line with the general attitude. Generally speaking, mothers talk more with their children (especially daughters) about sex than fathers do. More precisely, mothers talk with their daughters in terms of postponement and contraception. Boys are less likely to talk of sex with their parents and more with friends.

In Italy, contraception and abortion became legal only at the end of the 1970s. Minors are required to have the consent of parents or permission from a juvenile judge in order to have an abortion. The rate of minors' abortion is less than 3% of all abortions.

Sex education in the school and social policies for safe sex were uncommon until the 1990s, when AIDS started to become a problem of worldwide relevance. The first campaigns against AIDS and the other STDs were managed by a number of different public and private organizations, and only later was an institutional policy organized. This policy was more focused on limiting the damages than on a positive and psychological approach, such as the enjoyment of sex and gaining a greater confidence with one's own body. The programs of sexual education are often still very limited in duration; most of them are confined to one or two lessons by medical experts coming to the classroom, or addressed to the whole student population of a school during a general meeting. Also, the contents are often limited to the physical aspects of risk.

Homosexuality is present in low percentages of male and female adolescents (from 1% to 6%). The attitude toward homosexuality is becoming more liberal among Italian adolescents, though attitudes vary greatly based on cultural and educational contexts.

Health Risk Behavior

In Italy, as in other European countries, adolescence is a crucial period for experimentation with most behaviors that put people's health and wellbeing at risk (Currie et al., 2008; Hibell et al., 2009). Furthermore, a lot of these behaviors diminish over time, some after the ages of 16 to 17 (e.g., marijuana use) and some after the age of 24 (e.g., deviance), while others stabilize in time (e.g., risky driving).

In Italy the consumption of alcohol, particularly wine, is deeply rooted in the national economy and culture. However, beer and certain other alcoholic beverages (spritz, cocktails, etc.) are the most common among young people (18% of 11- to 15-year-olds and 53% of 16- to 17-year-olds drink alcoholic beverages all year). Consumption is usually occasional, generally tied to going out at the weekend. Habitual beer drinkers and those who drink more than half a liter a day represent a low percentage but they are increasing among the young. It is generally a moderate consumption and abuse is quite rare. Twenty percent of boys and 15% of girls between 11 and 15 years of age drink alcoholic beverages at least once a year. Among 16- to 17-year-olds, 11% of the boys and 4% of the girls indulge in binge drinking. Young people between 18 and 24 years of age represent the segment of population at the highest risk of drinking alcoholic beverages to excess. In particular, 22% of males and 7% of females indulge in binge drinking.

Early initiation generally happens in the family, and for this reason it is associated with a moderate consumption and tied to participation in special occasions. In contrast, initiation during adolescence, which is less common, happens mostly in a peer context, which also favors less control and a greater consumption.

European statistics (European Union, 2010) underline that in recent years in southern European countries (in particular Italy) there has been a gradual decrease in the overall consumption of alcohol and in the problems associated with this. There has been a progressive and more evident change in alcohol consumption models in young people between 18 and 24. It may be that even in Italy the "Mediterranean" style, characterized by mainly drinking wine during meals or on special occasions, is in the process of being replaced by a "Northern" style, which is characterized by a high consumption of beer and the consumption of spirits.

Cigarette smoking among adolescents aged between 14 and 24 varies from 20% to 25%, depending on gender, age, and region. Males smoke more and are generally more prone to a heavy and habitual consumption (15% of males and 9% of females between 14 and 19 years of age habitually smoke). Furthermore, young people who live in metropolitan and central areas smoke more. Most young people start smoking between the ages of 14 and 18. An early start (before 14) represents a low percentage, with girls making up a larger proportion.

The most-used drug is cannabis: Its use ranges from 12% to 30% depending on the gender, age range, type of school attended, and place of residence. Marijuana is a drug that in Italy is defined and perceived as "soft" and not dangerous. The most hallucinogenic drug used is Ecstasy, which has a much lower consumption. Even less used are the so-called "hard" drugs, used by only about 2% of the young population. However, in Italy 3.2% of the population between 15 and 34 years of age have used cocaine in the past 12 months. This is the highest percentage in Europe. The initiation age for cannabis-derived products is between 15 and 17 years, while for heroin, cocaine, and other hard drugs it is usually between 18 and 25.

Juvenile delinquency is not particularly high, but there are great differences connected to gender (with a greater implication for boys), age, and geographical area (Cattelino, 2010). Theft is the crime mostly committed by young people, in particular underage people. The phenomenon of criminal gangs is limited.

Even if the number of deaths is progressively decreasing, road accidents remain the main cause of death among adolescents and young people between 14 and 24 years old. For the younger ones (14 to 17) accidents mainly occur with a motorcycle, while between the ages of 18 and 24, nearly half of the accidents involve young people driving a car. Road accidents that mainly involve adolescents and emerging adults happen in the night hours of the weekend, frequently while they are coming back from a disco. The causes can be mostly found in a lack of respect toward the traffic code, while the seriousness of the effects is increased by the lack of attention given to safety: In fact, although crash helmets on motorbikes and seatbelts in cars are legally required to be used, they are regularly used by only a very low percentage of youngsters.

The number of suicides and depressions among adolescents of 15 to 24 years old is very limited. In fact, among European countries Italy has one of the lowest suicide rates (about 7.5 out of 100,000 youngsters). Furthermore, the number of suicides and attempted suicides is slightly but continually decreasing. There are some differences in gender: Suicide is most common among boys, especially underage (under 18), and attempted suicide is more common among girls. In both cases, the motivations are mainly of an emotional kind.

Education

The minimum school-leaving age in Italy was one of the lowest in Europe until recently; in 2000 it was raised from 14 to 16 years and in 2005 to 18 years. Even when the legal leaving age was 14, about 85% of young people continued their studies, with big differences connected to the geographic area: For example, the percentage increased to over 90% in the northwest and decreased in certain regions, especially in the south of the country.

Adolescents with a regular school path enter secondary school at 14 years; this lasts from three to five years. Five-year courses (lyceums, technical and professional institutes, art institutes) finish with a State examination which allows admission to university studies. Professional and art institutes offer three-year courses as well as five-year courses at the end of which a professional qualification diploma or an art teacher's diploma is achieved. So there are different paths for secondary school with diverse specializations. Generally, they can be divided into lyceums (classical, scientific, linguistic, psycho-pedagogic, artistic schools), technical institutes (for accountants, surveyors, industrial technicians) and professional institutes (with specializations ranging from artisan or secretarial and tourism to social care). The lyceums offer a wider general cultural education, giving more space to Italian and foreign literature, history, and philosophy; the technical and professional institutes mostly teach practical subjects and give a preparation that aims for a faster insertion into the workforce.

Choice among the different types of secondary school is influenced by the previous scholastic career of the adolescent, the level of education of the parents, and their expectations about the educational outcome of their child. The consequence is that the more gifted and motivated students generally enroll in a lyceum while the students who previously encountered some problems in their studies and who think that they do not want to continue with a university path tend to choose a technical institute. Students whose career has been particularly troubled, and who have had one or more failures of the scholastic year, generally enroll in a professional institute. Some of these pupils reach the legal school-leaving age and then abandon school without any qualifications.

At the end of the school path, regardless of the kind of school attended, all students have access to a university path, and generally around 56% of young people continue to study after secondary school. A lot of differences have been noted regarding university specialization connected to gender. Boys are more numerous in the scientific and engineering degree group, while girls mostly choose a literary, linguistic, psychological, or education degree group. No differences emerge for the medical, biological, law, economic, and architectural degree group. The high percentage of enrollment to university degrees is due to the fact that alternatives to the traditional forms of higher qualifications are limited and professional advanced training is not very developed.

Levels of irregular careers and dropping out before obtaining a university degree are high. Undergraduates who obtain the best results are the ones coming from a lyceum (55% manage to get a degree), while the biggest problems are met by young people coming from professional and technical institutes (with success rates respectively of 23% and 31%). Girls commit themselves more and have a greater success compared with boys at university.

High school provides differentiated programs for disabled adolescents, called individualized educational programs (PEI). Furthermore, for young people with physical or sensory disabilities or with slight cognitive difficulties, classes have fewer students and there is the presence, at least for some hours per week, of a support teacher. Adolescents with severe handicaps are mostly placed in educational structures alternative to school, funded by public territorial structures (regional, provincial, or town council). There are no specific programs for gifted students.

Work

Three age periods may be distinguished in adolescent work. First, there is the work of adolescents younger than 15 years (or those who have not yet finished the period of compulsory education), which is not allowed by Italian law. Second, there is the work of adolescents from 15 to 19 years old, though school continues to be their main activity. Third, there is work in emerging adulthood after completion of high-school or university education.

It is very difficult to estimate the extent of work by adolescents under age 15, which is illegal. However, official statistics indicate that around 3% of young adolescents work (this percentage is higher for boys and increases sharply at 14 years) and that around 1% are exploited. Most work by young adolescents is seasonal, although intensive. The activities may be divided into two types. The first is more similar to adult work, such as working in a garage, a construction site, or a factory (more common for boys and more at risk of exploitation). The second consists of supporting the work of the family (more common when the parents are farmers, or own a shop, restaurant, or small business). In the second case, the work by young adolescents represents the attribution of some responsibility within a specific family culture; generally the young adolescents do not perceive their work as tiring or dangerous and they like it, sometimes even more than going to school. The link between school failure, dropping out, and work is greater for the adult-like work than for family work. Besides, competition between work and school is greater, especially when the parental level of education is low, in two opposite conditions: where the employment rate is high (such as in the northeast of the country; in this case school may not seem too important for gaining economic wellbeing) and where it is low (in this case work by young adolescents may be an important source of earning for the family).

The work of immigrant adolescents under age 15 is even more difficult to investigate than that of native Italian adolescents of the same age. Two elements have to be taken into consideration:

continuity with the original culture (whose representation of adolescence may be different from the Italian one) and the novelty of the new cultural context (whose moral values may be different). A third element consists of the difficulty in distinguishing between legal and illegal activities, such as when young adolescents beg for money, wash car windows, or sell something in the streets. The likelihood of being obliged to work in slavery conditions and to be sexually exploited is higher when the young adolescents are clandestine or alone. Nevertheless, the majority of immigrant young adolescents combine work and school (MIUR, 2009). The original culture fulfills an important role. Two different cases have been investigated the most: the case of Chinese young adolescents, who generally work with their parents in family activities, and the case of North African young adolescents, who are more likely to have come to Italy alone to work and to send money to the family in their country of origin.

Some experience with work also involves about 30% of adolescents between 15 and 19 years, who are normally attending high school. However, the large majority of this work is related more to the desire to gain some economic independence than to the need to contribute to the family economy or to the obligation to work. In fact, most of these adolescents work during the summer school holiday or on the weekend. They work in public places (such as pubs, restaurants, and shops), or do some type of apprenticeship (more or less related to their studies, though this is more likely for boys) or care-work (e.g., babysitting or helping younger children with their homework, though this is more likely for girls).

In general the work by adolescents is paid "under the table"—that is, it is not registered officially and the owners do not pay taxes and health contributions to the national institutions. Adolescents generally like to work, although work may negatively influence their interest in academic achievement and performance. Moreover, the availability of money, often outside the control of the family, may offer these adolescents more chances than their peers to be involved in emerging adult-like activities, such as going to pubs and discos or buying legal and illegal substances.

The situation is different when the apprenticeship is part of a structured vocational course and is regularly and officially registered. Although there are some difficulties in organizing these courses effectively and in motivating pupils to participate, a regular apprenticeship may fulfill an important protective function for adolescents with a history of school failures who do not want to continue studying. Sometimes it may also promote a desire to return to high school. Recently, school-work alternation has been introduced; it involves periods of classroom training and periods of learning through work experience for young people between 15 and 18 years of age. These pathways take place under the responsibility of the school institution, which plans and implements the short training period under agreement with the training organizations willing to take on the student.

The percentage of emerging adults who work regularly differs greatly according to the type of high school attended: In fact, in 2009 high-school graduates whose sole occupation was to work were not very common among young people who had attended the lyceum (4%), compared to high-school graduates from a technical school (35%) or a professional school (51%). Lyceum graduates were mainly devoted to their university studies (79%), compared to technical school graduates (34%) or professional graduates (15.5%).

The job market is probably more open now to emerging adults than it was a few years ago because of a more flexible job market. However, most of these jobs are precarious, temporary, and part-time. This condition of uncertainty is likely to be one of the reasons for the continuing postponement of further steps toward adulthood (e.g., independent living and marriage).

A lack of job orientation and of communication between school and the job market is still common in Italy, despite the recent introduction of orientation programs in schools and of private agencies for temporary work. Most emerging adults are still more likely to find a job within their family or friendship networks than in other more structured ways.

Adolescents are significantly involved with voluntary work, especially in local organizations, in various fields (health, education, environment, church, etc.). The percentages of involvement are estimated for emerging adults to be between 8% and 14%, but they vary a lot depending on the field.

Media

Children and youngsters use technology more and more frequently. The use of mobile phones is increasing foremost: Between 2000 and 2008, use among 11- to 17-year-olds increased from 56% to 92%. The largest increase was among younger children. The percentage of children between 11 and 13 who use a mobile phone—and usually own it—has gone from 35% to 84%, while the percentage of youngsters between 14 and 17 has risen from 70% to 98%. Mobile phones are not used only for calling. The main uses are calling (94%) and text messaging (81%). More than half of the teenagers play with their phone, 47% change their ringtones and 43% use their mobile directory. Among other uses are taking or receiving photos (39%), listening to music (33%), filming movie clips (15%), taping conversations (10%), using the calendar (11%) and connecting to the Internet (4%). The average number of functions used by 11- to 13-year-olds is five; it rises to 5.3 between 14 and 17 years of age.

The number of adolescents using a PC and connecting to the Internet is increasing (82%). The development of new technologies has caused a decrease in time spent in front of the TV. TV programs, just like films, are both local productions and imported, especially from the United States.

The radio audience is very high, especially among very young people. Adolescent readership of newspapers is quite low; only 20% of adolescents read them more than five times a week. On the other hand, comics and magazines specially printed for teenagers are widespread among this age group. Furthermore, the readership of books is not very high—about 57% read one to three books a year—even if there are great extremes among the different social classes and the types of schools. In the past decade, the number of adolescents going to theaters (30%), the movies (87%), concerts (28%), art galleries, museums (42%), and monuments (27%) has increased.

Politics and Military

In Italy the voting age corresponds to the legal age, which is 18. At 18, people vote for the European Parliament, for one of the two Houses of the Italian Parliament (it is possible to vote for the Senate only after the age of 21), and for the local administrations (municipality, province, and region). Moreover, they can vote in referenda (special votes on specific subjects, which take place after being proposed by 500,000 citizens). From the foundation of the Republic in 1946, men and women have had the same voting rights.

Generally speaking, Italian adolescents do not participate much in the political life of the country, at least not through institutionalized political groups or other political organizations, from which the majority seem to be detached. Most youths value peace, environmental protection, and justice, but only a minority actively participate in demonstrations against war and globalization (e.g., anti-World Trade Organization).

The rules concerning military service were changed in 2005, transforming it into a voluntary service. The change from a one-year period of compulsory military service for all young men aged from 18 to 26 years to a voluntary system was made to guarantee a more qualified presence of Italians in international peacekeeping initiatives, in cooperation with other European and Western countries.

The current voluntary military service is better paid and more flexible than the previous one: Volunteers have the opportunity to choose the duration of their military service and are offered positions in public administration upon finishing. For all these reasons voluntary military service is likely to become an important source of work for emerging adults. It is now open also to women, although very few women choose it (www.esercito.difesa.it).

Unique Issues

A characteristic trait that distinguishes Italian society from the rest of the countries of the European Union, even Mediterranean ones, is the very low birth rate, a phenomenon that has been happening since the 1960s. The birth rate had decreased in 1995 to a minimum of 1.19 children per woman, and it is now at 1.42 (1.32 considering only Italian women and not immigrants). This does not guarantee a generational renewal and the maintenance of the current size of the population. Together with this low birth rate, there is a constant growth in the population of the elder generation due to increased longevity, which is one of the highest in the world: The lifespan in Italy is 79 years for men and 84 for women. Italy was the first nation where people over 65 outnumbered minors under 14 (in 1993).

This imbalance between the older generation, the adolescents, and the younger generation is creating heated debates on the future of the retirement system, on the welfare system, on the social politics of the family, and also on immigration. The phenomenon reflects on adolescence; in fact, the decrease in the number of adolescents and the parallel augmentation of the number of older people contribute to the intensification in negative and erroneous prejudice toward adolescents and young people: a minority group with interests, life styles and experiences that are very different and separate from those of the elderly. Furthermore, there is a negative impression in adolescents and young people of having to take responsibility in the future, for a large part of the life cycle, for an enlarged older population that is no longer productive, and of having to continue to work well into old age to guarantee an adequate welfare system.

References and Further Reading

Aleni Sestito, A. (2004). *Processi di formazione dell'identità in adolescenza* [Processes of identity formation in adolescence]. Naples, Italy: Liguori.

Bonino, S., Cattelino, E., & Ciairano, S. (2005). Adolescents and risk: Behaviors, functions and protective factors. Berlin, Germany: Springer-Verlag.

Bonino, S., Ciairano, S., Rabaglietti, E., & Cattelino, E. (2006). Use of pornography and self-reported engagement in sexual violence among adolescents. *European Journal of Developmental Psychology, 3*(3), 265–288.

Bosma, H., & Kunnen, S. (Eds.). (2001). *Identity and emotion: Development through self-organization.* Cambridge, UK: Cambridge University Press.

Buzzi, C., Cavalli, A., & de Lillo, A. (Eds.). (2002). *Giovani del nuovo secolo. Quinto rapporto IARD sulla condizione giovanile in Italia* [Youths of the new century: Fifth report of IARD on the juvenile condition in Italy]. Bologna, Italy: Il Mulino.

Buzzi, C., Cavalli, A., & de Lillo, A. (Eds.). (2007). *Rapporto giovani. Sesta indagine dell'Istituto Iard sulla condizione giovanile in Italia* [Report of IARD on the juvenile condition in Italy]. Bologna, Italy: Il Mulino.

Cattelino, E. (Ed.). (2010). *Rischi in adolescenza* [Risks in adolescence]. Rome, Italy: Carrocci.

Cattelino, E., Calandri, E., & Bonino, S. (2001). Il contributo della struttura e del funzionamento della famiglia nella promozione del benessere di adolescenti di diverse fasce di età [The role of family structure and family functioning in the promotion of wellbeing in adolescents of different ages]. *Età Evolutiva, 69,* 49–60.

Centro Studi Auxologici. (2005). *Growth and development of the baby and adolescent.* Florence, Italy: Centro Studi Auxologici. Retrieved from www.auxologia.it

Ciairano, S., Kliewer, W., Bonino, S., Miceli, R., & Jackson, S. (2006). Dating, sexual activity, and well-being in Italian adolescents. *Journal of Clinical Child and Adolescent Psychology, 35,* 275–282.

Cicognani, E., & Zani, B. (1998). Parents' educational styles and adolescent autonomy. *European Journal of Psychology of Education, 13*(4), 485–502.

Cicognani, E., & Zani, B. (2010). An instrument for measuring parents' perception of conflict styles with adolescents: The "When We Disagree" scales. *European Journal of Developmental Psychology, 7*(3), 390–400.

Currie, C., Nic Gabhainn, S., Godeau, E., Roberts, C., Smith, R., Currie, D., et al. (2008). *Health policy for children and adolescents, No. 5. Inequalities in young people's health.* Report from the Health Behaviour in School-Aged Children 2005/06 survey in 41 countries. Copenhagen, Denmark: WHO. Retrieved from www.hbsc.org

Eurispes. (2010). *10° rapporto nazionale sulla condizione dell'infanzia e dell'adolescenza* [10th national report on the condition of childhood and adolescence]. Rome, Italy: Eurispes. Retrieved from www.eurispes.it

European Union. (2010). *Health EU Portal. Public Health Europe.* Brussels, Belgium: European Commission. Retrieved from www.health.europa.eu

Garelli, F., Palmonari, A., & Sciolla, L. (2006). *La socializzazione flessibile* [Flexible socialization]. Bologna, Italy: Il Mulino.

Grassi, R. (Ed.). (2006). *Giovani, religione e vita quotidiana.* [Youth, religion and everyday life]. Bologna, Italy: Il Mulino.

Graziano, F., Bonino, S., Cattelino, E. (2009). Links between maternal and paternal support, depressive feelings and social and academic self-efficacy in adolescence. *European Journal of Developmental Psychology*, 6(2), 241–257.

Hibell, B., Guttormsson, U., Ahlström, S., Balakireva, O., Bjarnason, T., Kokkevi, A., et al. (2009). *The 2007 ESPAD report*. Stockholm, Sweden: CAN. Retrieved from www.espad.org

Honess, T. M., Charman, E. A., Zani, B., Cicognani, E., Xerri, M. L., et al. (1997). Conflict between parents and adolescents: Variation by family constitution. *British Journal of Developmental Psychology*, 15(3), 367–385.

ISTAT. (2011). Roma, Italy: ISTAT. Retrieved from www.istat.it

Jessor, R. (Ed.). (1998). *New perspectives on adolescent risk behavior*. Cambridge, UK: Cambridge University Press.

Jessor, R., Donovan, J. E., & Costa, F. M. (1991). *Beyond adolescence: Problem behavior and young adult development*. Cambridge, UK: Cambridge University Press.

Kirchler, E., Palmonari, A., & Pombeni, M. L. (1993). Developmental tasks and adolescents' relationships with their peers and their family. In. S. Jackson & H. Rodriguez-Tomé (Eds.), *Adolescence and its social world*. Berlin, Germany: De Gruyter.

Lo Coco, A., & Pace, U. (2009). L'autonomia emotiva in adolescenza [Emotional autonomy in adolescence]. Bologna, Italy: IL Mulino.

Marta, E. (1997). Parent–adolescent interactions and psychosocial risk in adolescents: An analysis of communication, support and gender. *Journal of Adolescence*, 20, 473–487.

Marta, E., Rossi, G., & Boccacin, L. (1998). Youth, solidarity and civic commitment in Italy: An analysis of the personal and social characteristics of volunteers and their organizations. In J. Youniss & M. Yates (Eds.), *Community service and civic engagement in youth: International perspectives* (pp. 73–96). Cambridge, UK: Cambridge University Press.

Marta, E., & Pozzi, M. (2006). Young volunteers, family and social capital: From the care of family bonds to the care of community bonds. In M. Hofer, A. Sliwka, & M. Diedrich (Eds.), *Citizenship education: Youth theory, research and practice*. Münster, Germany: Waxmann.

MIUR. (2009). *Gli alunni stranieri nel sistema scolastico italiano* [Foreign pupils in the Italian school system]. Rome, Italy: MIUR. Retrieved from www.istruzione.it

Oliverio Ferraris, A. (2007). *La ricerca dell'identità* [The search for identity]. Florence, Italy: Giunti.

Palmonari, A. (Ed.). (1997). *Psicologia dell'adolescenza* [Psychology of adolescence]. Bologna, Italy: Il Mulino.

Scabini, E. (1995). *Psicologia sociale della famiglia* [Social psychology of the family]. Turin, Italy: Bollati Boringhieri.

Scabini, E., Lanz, M., & Marta, E. (1999). Psychosocial adjustment and family relationships: A typology of Italian families with a late adolescent. *Journal of Youth and Adolescence*, 28, 633–644.

Scabini, E., Marta, E., & Lanz, M. (2006). *The transition to adulthood and family relations: An intergenerational approach*. Hove, UK: Psychology Press.

Sgritta, G. B. (2000). Adolescenza: La transizione difficile. [Adolescence: The difficult transition]. In G. V. Caprara & A. Fonzi (Eds.), *L'età sospesa* [The suspended age] (pp. 3–26). Florence, Italy: Giunti.

Silbereisen, R. K., & Noack, P. (1988). On the constructive role of problem behavior in adolecence. In A. Bolger et al. (Eds.), *Person in context: Development process* (pp. 152–180). Cambridge, UK: Cambridge University Press.

Silbereisen, R. K., Eyferth, K., & Rudinger, E. (1986). *Development as action in context: Problem behaviour and normal youth development*. Berlin, Germany: Springer-Verlag.

Ufficio Nazionale Servizio Civile. (2010). Retrieved from www.serviziocivile.it

Zani, B. (1993). Dating and interpersonal relationships in adolescence. In S. Jackson & H. Rodriguez-Tomé (Eds.), *Adolescence and its social world*. Berlin, Germany: De Gruyter.

Chapter 21
The Netherlands
Wim Meeus

Background Information

The Netherlands is one of the smallest countries in Europe. Its origins as a state date from the year 1579, when it was founded as the Republic of the Seven United Provinces. By the beginning of the twenty-first century, slightly more than 16 million people were living in The Netherlands. The 12 to 24 age group accounted for 2.5 million persons. About 15% of the individuals in this age group were of non-Dutch and non-Western origin (most of them originate from Surinam, Morocco, and Turkey). In 2009 the gross national income was about €527,000 million (CBS 2010b), approximately 62 times larger than in the late 1940s (CBS, 2001b).

Period of Adolescence

The best-documented fact concerning the beginning of puberty in The Netherlands is the age of menarche (a girl's first menstrual period). In 1997 the median age of menarche was 12.65 years; in 1955 it was 13.15 years (Fredriks, 2004). Since gonadarche, the process leading to menarche, starts at least two years earlier, puberty in Dutch girls begins nowadays at about 11 years of age. Thus, in many girls the start of puberty can be observed in the last year of primary education. Menarche in Turkish and Moroccan girls starts about five months earlier than in Dutch girls. No Dutch data are available on spermarche (a boy's first ejaculation of semen).

Dutch boys and girls are the tallest in the world (Hauspie, Vercauteren, & Susanne, 1996; TNO, 2010); in 2010 the mean height in boys and girls was about 184 and 171 cm respectively. Turkish and Moroccan boys and girls reached in 2010 a mean length that was 6 and 8 cm smaller as compared to Dutch youngsters, respectively.

Mainly due to sustained economic growth, adolescence has become institutionalized as a prolonged life phase in The Netherlands since the Second World War (Du Bois-Reymond & van der Zande, 1994; Social and Cultural Planning Office (SCP), 1985). The average prolongation of full-time education between 1950 and 2000 can be estimated at five years at least. Consequently, adolescence can be defined as an educational moratorium. Young people have a substantial period in life to pursue a school career and can choose from a wide variety of educational options. Psychologically, this means that adolescents have the sexual and relational opportunities of adults relatively early in life, while formal adult obligations, such as an occupational career, financial independence, and responsibility for a family, are relocated to a later stage in life. This discrepancy between relational and sexual independence and financial and economic dependence constitutes one of the problematic aspects in the lives of modern Dutch adolescents. They have to be able to cope with this ambiguity.

Due to this prolongation, Dutch researchers nowadays divide adolescence into four subphases: early adolescence, from 12 to 14 years; middle adolescence, from 15 to 17; late adolescence, from 18 to 20; and post-adolescence, from 21 to 23 (Meeus and 't Hart, 1993) Early adolescence begins when children make the transition from primary to secondary education, middle adolescence is marked by the beginning of first intimate relationships, late adolescence by the transition from secondary to tertiary education or for the lower educated (about 25%) to work (CBS, 2003), and post-adolescence by the transition from school to work. Post-adolescence could also be described as "emerging adulthood" (Arnett, 2000). In post-adolescence, young people acquire full sexual and relational independence, while most of them are economically dependent and not committed to the adult roles of being married and having children.

Beliefs

Dutch citizens endorse individualistic values very strongly. In the European Values Studies (EVS), a periodically repeated survey in 19 European countries and the United States and Canada, The Netherlands stands out as one of the most individualistic countries (Ester, Halman, & de Moor, 1993). Dutch citizens have among the highest scores in calling marriage an outdated institution, in acceptance of divorce, in denying the importance of the family, in accepting women's choice of not having children, in egalitarian parent–child relationships, on homosexuality, and on adultery. A trend toward individualizing and liberal attitudes and values in family and relationship issues as well as economic issues has been observed since the late 1960s. The attitude best summarized as "live and let live" is strong in The Netherlands, also pertaining to socioeconomic issues. Although the majority of Dutch citizens embrace the welfare state with its social provisions, in recent decades there has been a growing recognition that citizens should be responsible for their own economic position. In general Dutch youngsters are more liberal in family and relationship issues than the older generations (Vollebergh, Iedema, & Meeus, 1999).

This individualistic trend can also be observed in the life goals Dutch parents want to transmit to their children. Deković, Groenendaal, and Gerrits (1996) report that Dutch parents want to teach their children first and foremost to be autonomous, then to be social, then to be conformist, and only in last place to be achievement-oriented. This last finding concurs with the observation made in the EVS that The Netherlands is among the least self-centered achievement societies in Europe, despite its individualism.

In 2006–2008, 22% of Dutch youngsters between 12 and 24 defined themselves as Catholic, 14% as Protestant, and 8% as belonging to another denomination (including Islam) (CBS, 2009a). About 20% of the Dutch youngsters attend church and other religious meetings on a regular basis. Church membership has been on the decline in The Netherlands since the late 1950s (Becker & de Wit, 2000). In 1958 about 76% of the Dutch population belonged to a church; in 2006–2008 the percentage fell below 55. Nowadays there is a strong difference in church membership between Dutch youngsters on one hand and Turkish and Moroccan youngsters on the other: About 51% of Dutch youngsters define themselves as church members (CBS, 2009a), while about 95% of the Turkish and Moroccans do so (Phalet & Haker, 2004). Both Dutch and nonindigenous youngsters are less often church members and show a lower level of religious participation than the older generations. For instance, while in 2006–2008 51% of young people in The Netherlands were church members, more than 60% of the older generations were.

Gender

Since the feminist revolution in the early 1970s, acceptance for egalitarian gender roles has grown substantially in The Netherlands. On the other hand, total equality between boys and girls has not been achieved.

In 1999 the majority of Dutch adolescents wanted a future division of tasks between men and women in which both partners had a paid job and did work in the household as well (SCP, 2000). Ninety percent held the opinion that both partners should contribute to the rearing of children. Closer inspection of the findings, however, shows some important distinctions between boys and girls. Seventy percent of the girls prefer that both partners have a paid job, while only 50% of the boys do; 89% of the girls have the opinion that taking care of children is a task of both parents; while only 79% of the boys do; and only 30% of the girls have the opinion that cooking and house-hold chores are female tasks, while 50% of the boys do.

Changes in the Dutch educational system since the 1970s have contributed strongly to a growing equality between genders. In 1970 girls were lagging behind boys in educational participation: 50% of the 16- to 18-year-old males were in full-time education, while only 34% of the 16 -to 18-year-old females were. In 2004/2005 the picture looked totally different: Educational participation of boys and girls was the same and girls achieved a higher mean educational level than boys did: More than 45% of the girls graduated at the two highest levels of secondary education, whereas only 40% of the boys did (CBS, 2007). On the other hand, there are still strong differences in the preferences of boys and girls for certain educational tracks. Boys choose technical and economic educational tracks at least twice as often as girls, while girls choose educational tracks in teaching and care at least twice as often as boys. These differences in boys' and girls' choices of educational tracks illustrate the persistence of gender differences in future orientation and role expectations. Girls' choices for education in care and teaching parallel classic female roles of parent and teacher within the parental home, while boys' choices reflect a long-standing orientation toward managing general economical and technical issues in society.

In general, girls have more negative body images than boys. The ideal of thinness plays a role here. The prevalence of anorexia nervosa and bulimia nervosa among female adolescents and young adults is at least 10 times higher in girls than in boys (Van Son, Van Hoeken, Bartelds, Van Furth, & Hoek, 2006).

The Self

The Netherlands is one of the few countries in which the identity formation of adolescents has been studied in a nationally representative sample (Meeus, Iedema, Helsen, & Vollebergh, 1999). In their study Meeus et al. (1999) generally found that the number of identity diffusers decreases with age and the number of identity achievers increases. Meeus et al. also found this pattern for the longitu-dinal change in diffusion and achieving commitment. A recent study (Meeus, van de Schoot, Keijsers, Schwartz, & Branje, 2010) confirmed these findings.

Second-generation ethnic minority adolescents in The Netherlands face the formidable task of having to combine Dutch liberal and individualistic values with traditional and collectivist values of the parental home. It is evident that this burden can pose a threat to the development of self and identity of ethnic minority adolescents. However, findings of Dutch studies on this issue are

inconclusive. For instance, while the SCP (1994) reported lower levels of self-esteem in Turkish and Moroccan adolescents as compared to Dutch adolescents, Verkuyten (1992) did not find differences in self-concept and self-concept stability.

Recently, a limited number of studies have suggested that acculturation might be a key factor here. Vollebergh and Huiberts (1997) reported that ethnic minority adolescents who combine a negative attitude to their own ethnic group with a negative attitude to the Dutch have the highest level of psychological stress. Stevens, Vollebergh, Pels, and Crijnen (2007) showed that Moroccan girls with an ambivalent acculturation pattern had the highest level of internalizing and externalizing problems. Recent studies also show that behavioral autonomy (making own decisions in various issues) of Moroccan adolescents is smaller than that of Dutch adolescents (Huiberts, Oosterwegel, Vandervalk, Vollebergh, & Meeus 2006), and that internalizing and externalizing problems are more prevalent in ethnic minority group adolescents than in Dutch adolescents (Hale, Raaijmakers, Muris, & Meeus, 2005; SCP, 1994; Stevens et al., 2003).

Family Relationships

Relations between Dutch adolescents and their parents became more egalitarian in the second half of the twentieth century. For example, in 1965 only 31% of Dutch children were allowed to call their parents by their first name, but in 1997 65% were allowed to do so; in 1965 48% of 18-year-olds were allowed to read everything, but in 1997 the percentage had risen to 86; and in 1965 only 17% of daughters were allowed to decide for themselves at what time to come home after a party, but in 1997 the percentage was 47 (SCP, 2000). Findings from the beginning of the present century confirm the continuation of this trend (CBS, 2003).

Dutch parents experience puberty and middle adolescence as the most difficult period in the upbringing of their children. Twenty-eight percent see early adolescence as the most difficult period, while 38% see middle adolescence as most difficult (Deković et al., 1996). This is a huge difference from parental views on other developmental periods: For instance, only 5.3% see the child's first year as most difficult and only 14% the toddler period.

Parents' perceptions of adolescence as a difficult time may be due to relatively high levels of conflict. As has been repeatedly shown in international studies (Laursen, Coy, & Collins, 1998), also in The Netherlands prevalence of conflict with parents is highest in early adolescence. Most conflicts are about daily issues: watching TV, using the phone, homework for school, household chores, cleaning their room, etc. A study among about 2,300 early and middle adolescents (Meeus et al., 2002) showed that youngsters had 1.9 conflicts with their father in the previous week, 2.3 with their mother, and 1.6 with their best friend. Interestingly, adolescents had the most conflicts with their mothers, while they also indicated that they considered their mother as the most supportive family member. At the beginning of the twenty-first century, Moroccan girls in particular showed a high level of conflict with their parents (Huiberts, 2002). Stevens, Volleverbergh, Pels, and Crijnen (2007) showed that parent–adolescent conflict is especially high in ambivalently acculturated Moroccan girls.

The typical Dutch family consists of two parents with two children (CBS, 2001a). More than 50% of Dutch women with an intimate partner have two children or expect to have them. About 30% of women currently have one child or no children. About 20% have three children or more. Most Dutch adolescents have one sibling. Siblings are expected to be friendly, supportive, and helpful to each other. However, recent studies show that adolescents experience less support from their siblings than from both parents (Branje, van Aken, & van Lieshout, 2003). Also, attachment to siblings is lower than attachment to parents, although attachment of girls to sisters is much higher than attachment of girls to brothers and of boys to brothers and sisters (Buist, Deković, Meeus, & van Aken, 2002).

In The Netherlands the extended family does not exist on a large scale. Grandparents typically do not live in the same home as parents and children (CBS, 2001a).

Regarding divorce, although exact figures are not available, a reliable estimate is that about 25% of adolescents have personal experience with divorce (Clement, van Egten, & de Hoog, 2008). Eighty-five percent of post-divorce children stay with the mother, while about 10% stay with the father. There is a visiting arrangement by law for the nonresident parent. Recent studies show that parental divorce has lasting negative impact on adolescent wellbeing. For instance, Vandervalk (2004) reports that post-divorce adolescents and young adults in the age range 12 to 29 show higher prevalence of internalizing and externalizing problem behavior.

Friends and Peers/Youth Culture

Friends are very important for Dutch adolescents. As many as 82% of them named spending free time with friends as their favorite activity in 1997 (SCP, 2000). On the other hand, recent studies show that friends' support is not of more importance for adolescents than parental support (Helsen, Volleverbergh, & Meeus, 2000; Meeus, 1994b). In early adolescence youngsters receive more support from parents than from friends, while from middle adolescence on they receive about equal support from parents and friends. In general, it has been consistently found that in early and middle adolescence parental support is more predictive of adolescent emotional adjustment than friend support (Helsen et al., 2000) or peer support is (Meeus, 1994b).

In The Netherlands there are no formal restrictions on friendships that are based on gender, social class, or ethnicity. On the other hand, studies show that most of the friendships are same-sex, within the same social class, and intra-ethnic. Most studies also show that female friendships are more supportive than male friendships (Baerveldt, van Duijn, Vermeij, & van Hemert, 2004; Meeus, 1994b). As for ethnicity, intra-ethnic support in peer relations has been found to be substantially stronger as compared to inter-ethnic support; for instance, a study showed that Dutch adolescents received 79% of their support from Dutch peers, and Turkish adolescents received 59% of their support from Turkish peers (Baerveldt et al., 2004). Also, it has been found that immigrant adolescents indicate that they have more problems in making friends and more often miss a good friend as compared to Dutch adolescents (SCP, 2000).

A study showed that the 10 most frequent peer crowds in The Netherlands can be grouped in four categories: alternative (punks, metal heads, and Goths), conventional (rural youth, Christian youth, and normals), urban (hip-hoppers and rastas), and achievement-oriented (elite and brains) (Delsing, ter Bogt, Engels, & Meeus 2007). Since most of the adolescents indicate that they identify with more than one of these four peer crowd categories, it is difficult to give percentages of peer crowd membership. The study by Delsing et al. (2007) also reported that the urban category had somewhat more internalizing problems, while the achievement category had fewer externalizing problems. The achievement group came more often from the higher social classes and did best at school.

As in most Western societies, there is a huge youth cultural market in The Netherlands. Apart from the 10 peer crowds mentioned above, we can distinguish about 15 musical preference styles nowadays, ranging from classical music to trance, from reggae to gospel, and from r&b to hard rock. Overall, preferences for black music (soul, r&b, reggae, hip-hop, and rap) and dance (trance, techno, clubhouse) seem to be strongest. Since all the mentioned styles and cultures have their own dress code, party scene, and free time activities, the youth cultural scene is diversified in The Netherlands. Most of the styles are based on Western youth cultures, although many of them mix elements from various cultures.

Dutch youth organizations can be grouped into four categories. In 1999 11% of Dutch adolescents were members of youth associations and clubs, another 11% of music or other art-oriented associations, 6% of hobby clubs, and 52% of sports clubs; 60% of the adolescent population were members of at least one of these youth organizations (SCP, 2000).

Love and Sexuality

In the 1990s, Dutch adolescents had their first intimate relationship at a mean age of 15.6 years (SCP, 2000; Spruijt, 1993). Deković, Noom, and Meeus (1997) reported that Dutch parents find it acceptable for their children to go steady at the age of 16.2 years. Sexual activity in adolescence starts much earlier; for example, the mean age of the French kiss was 12.7 in 1994 (Brugman, Goedhart, Vogels, & Van Zessen, 1995). The mean age of first sexual intercourse declined more than five years in the late twentieth century, from 22.5 in 1950 to 17.2 in 1995 (Brugman et al., 1995).

In 1950 the mean age of first marriage was close to 27 years; 50 years later the mean age had risen to 28.5 years (SCP, 1997; CBS, 2003). This relatively slight difference is due to a curvilinear trend. From 1950 to 1975 mean age of first marriage declined to 22.9 years, followed by a sharp rise (CBS,

1987). The rise from 1975 onward can be explained mainly by the increased popularity of cohabitation. Cohabitation is a common practice today: At least 80% of Dutch adolescents cohabit before marriage (CBS, 2001a). This also means that almost all Dutch adolescents and young adults are sexually experienced before marriage. Acceptance of sexual experience before marriage is general: Dutch parents find it acceptable for their children to have sexual contacts at the mean age of 17.7 years (Deković et al., 1997). Premarital pregnancy is also widely accepted; 22% of Dutch mothers nowadays give birth to children while in a premarital relationship (CBS, 2009c). Most of these premarital births (more than 98%) are not to single mothers on their own but to women who are cohabiting.

Sex education is common in The Netherlands. Lessons on sexuality are given in all secondary education schools, contraceptives are available to almost all adolescents, and a study in the early 1990s showed that about 25% of adolescents discuss sexual issues with their parents (Ravesloot, 1997). Compared to international standards, the prevalence of abortion is very low in The Netherlands (CBS, 1999). As for other sexual risks: About 9% of Dutch adolescents had unsafe sex in the mid-1990s (Brugman et al., 1995).

The majority of Dutch adolescents accept homosexuality. A national survey conducted in 2005 showed that homosexuality was acceptable to 75% of adolescents (de Graaf, Meijer, Poelman, and Vanwesenbeeck, 2005). Acceptance was lower among boys and lower-educated adolescents.

Health Risk Behavior

In 2003, the lifetime prevalence in adolescents aged 12 to 18 of smoking, alcohol use, cannabis use, and cocaine use was 39%, 79%, 17%, and 2% respectively (Monshouwer et al., 2008). The lifetime prevalence of smoking decreased since 1988, while the prevalence of cannabis use rose substantially between 1988 and 1996 and then decreased, although the prevalence of 2007 is still higher than that of 1988. The lifetime prevalence of cocaine use also rose substantially between 1988 and 1999 and decreased between 1999 and 2007.

Adolescents are allowed to buy alcohol at shops and bars at the age of 16. Although the use of soft drugs (marijuana and hash) has not been legalized, adolescents are allowed to buy soft drugs at coffee shops at the age of 18. Dutch soft drug policy has been the target of much international debate, especially the fact that Dutch adolescents are allowed to buy soft drugs freely at coffee shops even though the use of soft drugs is formally prohibited. International comparisons, however, show that Dutch drug policy does not have strong negative effects: In 2007 15% of Dutch adolescents used cannabis, while the figures for Spain, Switzerland, and France were higher (Van Laar, Cruts, van Ooyen-Hoeben, Meijer, and Brunt, 2009).

In 2007, the self-reported prevalence of participation in violent crime in adolescents aged 12 to 18 was 15% or lower for various offenses (fighting, beating someone up, etc.), the prevalence of various property offenses was 12% or lower, and the prevalence of vandalism offenses was 10% or lower (Van der Laan, Blom, & Bogaerts, 2007). In 2005 about 5% were ticketed by the police. Police statistics also systematically show that prevalence of crime in youngsters is substantially higher than in adults, while self-report studies show that prevalence of crime is at least twice as high in ethnic minority adolescents as in indigenous adolescents (Junger, Wittebrood, & Timman, 2001). Dutch criminologists agree that the general level of youth delinquency has risen since the 1960s, but disagree as to how much of the increase can be attributed to changes in police activities and registration systems. In general, adolescents are tried as adults in court from the age of 18.

A recent study showed that last-year prevalence of depression and anxiety disorders was 7% and 12%, respectively, in late adolescents and early adults (De Graaf, ten Have, and van Dorsselaer, 2010). These findings fit in with those of earlier studies among adolescents aged 12–18 reporting prevalence rates of depression and anxiety disorders of 5%–6% and 11%–12%, respectively (Junger, Mesman, & Meeus, 2003) The rate of first suicide ideation and first suicide attempt in late adolescents and early adults aged 18 to 24 was 3% and 0.3% across a three-year period, respectively (ten Have et al., 2009).

Risk factors for adolescent psychopathology in The Netherlands are the same as reported in the international literature: vulnerable personality, poor relations with parents and peers, low level of school achievement, and poor living conditions. Also, as is the case in international studies, in The Netherlands systematic gender differences in psychopathology are found. Females show higher levels of depression, anxiety, and other internalizing problems, while males show higher levels of delinquency and other externalizing problems.

Education

All adolescents in The Netherlands attend secondary school. Between 55% and 60% attend schools preparing for lower- and medium-level blue- and white-collar jobs, while 40%–45% attend schools preparing for higher education (CBS, 2007). Dutch government is aiming to raise the latter percentage to 50.

There is no difference between males and females in their access to secondary school or higher education. For instance, in 2007–2008 47% of students at Dutch polytechnics and at universities were female (CBS, 2009a). Educational achievement of ethnic minority groups rose substantially between 1988 and 2002 (SCP, 2003b). While in 1988 less than 15% finished medium level tertiary education, in 2002 more than 30% did, and whereas in 2003 about 73% achieved the educational starting qualification, in 2008 about 83% did (CBS, 2009a). On the other hand, differences between indigenous and ethnic minority adolescents are still very big: In 2006/7 the ratio of indigenous adolescents and ethnic minority adolescents graduating at polytechnics or universities was about 10 to 1 (CBS, 2009b). Internationally, academic achievement of Dutch adolescents seems to be very good. A report by OESO (2003, cited in CBS, 2003) showed reading skills of Dutch middle adolescent girls to be better than those of pupils in most EU countries. Reading skills of Dutch middle adolescent boys were better than those of boys in most other EU countries. Dutch middle adolescents also showed better mathematical skills as compared with pupils of most EU countries.

Work

The vast majority of Dutch adolescents are not expected to work to contribute financially to their families. Most of the adolescents that work in a family business (mainly shops or farmhouses) get paid by their parents. In 2001 about 50% of school-going adolescents held a part-time job; most of these jobs took less than 12 hours per week and did not require more than basic education.

In some respects, work conditions of adolescents are worse than those of adults, while in other respects they are the same. Adolescents more often have physically demanding jobs that require significant physical power and have a repetitive and monotonous character. Adolescents also work more often during the weekends. In terms of noise, stench, danger, and working in shifts or during the night, there are no differences between adolescent and adult jobs (SCP, 2000).

In 2008 42% of the 15- to 24-year-olds did voluntary work. Most voluntary work was done in youth work organizations and sports clubs (CBS, 2010a).

In almost all years, youth unemployment figures are higher than adult unemployment figures. Here we can speak of a "reversed generation gap" (Meeus, 1994a). Unemployment figures of indigenous adolescents and ethnic minority adolescents show wide differences. In 2008, 80% of the indigenous adolescents and early adults available for the labor market had a job, whereas only 56% of ethnic minority adolescents and early adults did (CBS, 2009b) On the other hand, statistics show a systematic improvement of employment figures of ethnic minority adolescents: Between 1997 and 2007 unemployment rates decreased from 27% to about 15% (CBS, 2008).

Media

In recent decades, among Dutch adolescents aged 12 to 24, time spent reading newspapers, magazines, and books fell substantially: from 4.7 hours per week in 1975 to 1.38 hours per week in 2000. Time allocated to electronic media (TV, video/DVD, and PC), sports, and free time mobility rose. Most remarkable here is the increase of electronic media time: from 11.1 hours in 1975 to 15.3 hours in 2000 (SCP, 2000, 2003a). Hidden within the electronic media data is another change during the 1990s: watching TV decreased substantially, while use of personal computers rose strongly (SCP, 2000). Between 2005 and 2008 the percentage of daily Internet users increased from about 75 to about 86 (CBS, 2010a).

Since adolescents are one of the most targeted age groups by advertisers, TV programs, DVDs, videos, and CDs carry an obligatory age indication. The age indications 12 and 16 make clear that children younger than 12 and 16 respectively should not watch the program or use the video, DVD, or CD (SCP, 2003a).

Politics and Military

The Netherlands is a constitutional monarchy, which means that the country is ruled by a government that holds the majority in parliament, while the queen acts as a primarily ceremonial head of state. Elections for national parliament are held once in four years and citizens aged 18 or older are entitled to vote.

Interest in politics is relatively low among emerging adults. In 2006, 71% of them voted in the national elections, whereas 80% of other adults did. About 33% participated in political activities (discussions, demonstrations, etc.) (CBS, 2009b). In 2003 only 1% were members of a political party. Males expressed a stronger interest in politics than females: 34% were interested in political issues, while 27% of the females were. The same differences were found for political discussions and political party preference (CBS, 2003).

Although Dutch youth express a relatively low interest in politics, this does not mean that they are not politically active. In 2006 the prevalence of conventional political participation (seeking contact with local government, a political party, or any other way) was about 8%, while that of nonconventional political participation (participating in demonstrations, protest meetings, or being a member of an action group) was 11% (CBS, 2009a).

Since 1996, The Netherlands has had a professional army, and military service is no longer legally required. Since the late 1950s, Dutch youth have not had substantial experience with military conflicts. The last military mission Dutch youngsters were engaged in on a large scale took place in the late 1940s in Indonesia, when they had to wage war with the revolutionary forces fighting for the independence of Indonesia. In this conflict about 5,000 Dutch soldiers were killed.

Unique Issues

In this overview a series of inter-ethnic comparisons have been presented. We typically compared indigenous Dutch adolescents and ethnic minority adolescents of non-Western descent, originating mainly from Morocco, Turkey, Surinam and The Netherlands Antilles. Together they made up 14% and 16% of Dutch youth in 2000 and 2009, respectively (CBS 2009a). Indigenous adolescents are taller than ethnic minority adolescents, are less religious, do better at school and in the labor market, and are less delinquent. In general, these findings show that ethnic minority adolescents have a less privileged position in Dutch society as compared with their Dutch counterparts. On the other hand, educational achievement figures and employment rates of ethnic minority adolescents show systematic improvements since the late 1980s.

Since the attacks on the World Trade Center in New York and the assassinations of the rising Dutch politician Pim Fortuyn in 2002 and the well-known filmmaker Theo van Gogh in 2004, public opinion polls show growing inter-ethnic tensions in The Netherlands. These tensions mainly exist between indigenous Dutch citizens and ethnic minority groups originating from the Muslim countries Morocco and Turkey. The tensions arise from gang-like behavior of especially Moroccan youngsters and also pertain to differences in worldview of Muslims and the majority of secular Dutch citizens. Two issues are critical here: (1) Division of religion and state: should religion dictate politics or not? (2) Equality between men and women. Muslims tend to accept religion-dictated politics and gender inequality more.

In general, two positions on integration of non-Western youth exist in The Netherlands. The optimistic position points at the improvement of educational achievement figures and employment rates of ethnic minority adolescents and predicts a growing integration in Dutch society. The pessimistic position points at growing international tensions and religious-inspired conflicts and predicts that these conflicts will become a dominant problem in Dutch society and consequently will hamper the integration of ethnic minority adolescents.

Demographic data show that the proportion of adolescents in the total Dutch population will decrease substantially. While in 2002 children and adolescents aged 0 to 24 made up 31% of the population (CBS, 2003), demographers predict that they will make up only 25% of the population in 2050 (CBS, 1999). For the elderly a reversed picture emerges. While people older than 65 years made up 13% of the population in 2000, they will make up 25% in 2040 (SCP, 2000). Another demographic change has to do with the growing proportion of non-Dutch, non-Western adolescents. In 2002 they made up 15% of the youth population; in 2050 they will make up at least 20% of that population.

These demographic trends make clear what kind of challenges Dutch adolescents will have to face in the coming decades. Society will have to bear the financial burden of the pensions of a steadily growing elderly population, and consequently will have less money available for young people. Young people will have to learn to adapt to a more and more multicultural society. The current rise of tension and antagonism between secular Dutch attitudes and Islamic views shows that religious struggles are not over.

Two other trends that are likely to affect Dutch adolescents in the coming decades are the internationalization of the workplace and the use of new cosmetic medical interventions to change the body. Since the European Union now offers the possibility to Dutch citizens to work in any European country, Dutch adolescents are entitled to apply for any job across Europe. The trend to design and change the body is due to the development of medical technology. Since adolescents worry more than any other age group about their bodies they may be heavy users of these new cosmetic medical technologies.

References and Further Reading

Arnett, J. J. (2000). Emerging adulthood: A theory of development from the late teens through the twenties. *American Psychologist, 55,* 469–480.

Baerveldt, C., van Duijn, M., Vermeij, L., & van Hemert, D. (2004). Ethnic boundaries and personal choice: Assessing the influence of individual inclinations to choose intra-ethnic relationships on pupils' networks. *Social Networks*, *26*, 55–74.

Becker, J. W., & de Wit, J. S. J. (2000). *Secularisatie in de jaren negentig* [Secularisation in the nineties]. The Hague, The Netherlands: SCP.

Branje, S., van Aken, M., & van Lieshout, C. (2003). Relational support in families with adolescents. *Journal of Family Psychology*, *16*, 351–362.

Brugman, E., Goedhart, H. Vogels, T., & Van Zessen, G. (1995). *Jeugd en seks 1995* [Youth and sexuality 1995]. Utrecht, The Netherlands: SWP.

Buist, K. L., Deković, M., Meeus, W., & Van Aken, M. (2002). Developmental patterns in adolescent attachment to mother, father and sibling. *Journal of Youth and Adolescence*, *31*, 167–76.

CBS. (1987). *Maandstatistiek van de bevolking*, *1* [Monthly population statistics]. Voorburg, The Netherlands: CBS.

CBS. (1999). *Vademecum gezondheidsstatistiek Nederland* [Handbook of health statistics of The Netherlands]. Voorburg, The Netherlands: CBS.

CBS. (2001a). *Samenleven* [Living together]. Voorburg, The Netherlands: CBS.

CBS. (2001b). *Tweehonderd jaar statistiek in tijdreeksen 1800–1999* [Two hundred years of statistics in time series]. Voorburg, The Netherlands: CBS.

CBS. (2003). *Jeugd 2003* [Youth 2003]. Voorburg, The Netherlands: CBS.

CBS. (2007). *Landelijke jeugdmonitor. Rapportage 2e kwartaal 2007.* [National youth monitor: Second three-monthly report]. The Hague/Heerlen, The Netherlands: CBS.

CBS. (2008). *Jaarrapport integratie 2008* [Annual report on integration 2008]. The Hague/Heerlen, The Netherlands: CBS.

CBS. (2009a). Jaarrapport 2009. Landelijke jeugdmonitor. [Annual report 2009: National youth monitor]. The Hague/Heerlen, The Netherlands: CBS

CBS. (2009b). *Landelijke jeugdmonitor. Jeugd en integratie* [National youth monitor: Youth and integration]. The Hague/Heerlen, The Netherlands: CBS.

CBS. (2009c). *Relatie en gezin aan het begin van de 21ste eeuw.* [Relationships and family at the beginning of the 21st century]. The Hague/Heerlen, The Netherlands: CBS.

CBS. (2010a). *Landelijke jeugdmonitor. Vrijetijdsbesteding en maatschappelijke participatie van jongeren* [National youth monitor: Free time and social participation of youth]. The Hague/Heerlen, The Netherlands: CBS.

CBS. (2010b). *Nationale rekeningen 2009* [National economic figures 2009]. The Hague/Heerlen, The Netherlands: CBS.

Clement, C., van Egten, C., & de Hoog, S. (2008). *Nieuwe gezinnen* [New families]. The Hague, The Netherlands: E-Quality.

De Graaf, H., Meijer, S., Poelman, J., & Vanwesenbeeck, I. (2005). *Sex onder je 25e* [Sexuality below 25]. Delft, The Netherlands: Eburon.

De Graaf, R., ten Have, M., & van Dorsselaer, S. (2010). *Nemesis 2: De Psychische gezondheid van de Nederlandse bevolking* [Nemesis 2: Mental health of the Dutch population]. Utrecht, The Netherlands: Trimbos Instituut.

Deković, M., Groenendaal, H., & Gerrits, L. (1996). Opvoederkenmerken [Parental characteristics]. In J. Rispens, J. Hermanns, & W. Meeus (Eds.), *Opvoeden in Nederland* (pp. 70–94). Assen, The Netherlands: Van Gorcum.

Deković, M., Noom, M., & Meeus, W. (1997). Verwachtingen van jongeren en ouders over ontwikkelingstaken in de adolescentiefase. *Kind & Adolescent*, *18*, 114–125.

Delsing, M., ter Bogt, T., Engels, R., & Meeus, W. (2007). Adolescents' peer crowd identification in the Netherlands: Structure and associations with problem behaviors. *Journal of Research on Adolescence, 18,* 467–479.

Du Bois-Reymond, M., & Van der Zande, I. (1994). The Netherlands. In K. Hurrelmann (Ed.), *International handbook of adolescence* (pp. 270–286). Westport, CT: Greenwood Press.

Ester, P., Halman, L., & de Moor, R. (Eds.). (1993). *The individualizing society.* Tilburg, The Netherlands: Tilburg University Press.

Fredriks, M. (2004). *Growth diagrams. Fourth Dutch nation-wide survey 1997.* Unpublished doctoral dissertation, Rijksuniversiteit Leiden, The Netherlands.

Hale, W., Raaijmakers, Q., Muris, P., & Meeus, W. (2005). Psychometric properties of the screen for child anxiety related emotional disorders (SCARED) in the general adolescent population. *Journal of the American Academy of Child and Adolescent Psychiatry, 44,* 283–290.

Hauspie, R. C., Vercauteren, M., & Susanne, C. (1996). Secular changes in growth. *Hormone Research, 45* (Suppl. 2), 8–17.

Helsen, M., Vollebergh, W., & Meeus, W. (2000). Social support from parents and friends and emotional problems in adolescence. *Journal of Youth and Adolescence, 29,* 319–335.

Huiberts, A. (2002). *Individualisme en collectivisme in de adolescentie* [Individualism and collectivism in adolescence]. Unpublished doctoral dissertation, Utrecht University, The Netherlands.

Huiberts, A., Oosterwegel, A., Vandervalk, I., Vollebergh, W., & Meeus, W. (2006). Connectedness with parents and behavioural autonomy among Dutch and Moroccan adolescents. *Ethnic and Racial Studies, 29,* 315–330.

Junger, M., Mesman, J., & Meeus, W. (2003). *Psychosociale problemen bij adolescenten* [Psychosocial problems in adolescents]. Assen, The Netherlands: Van Gorcum.

Junger, M., Wittebrood, K. & Timman, R. (2001). Etniciteit en ernstig en gewelddadig crimineel gedrag [Ethnicity and serious and violent delinquency]. In R. Loeber, W. Slot, & J. Sergeant (Eds.), *Ernstige en gewelddadige jeugddelinquentie* (pp. 97–127). Houten/Diegem, The Netherlands: BSVL.

Laursen, B., Coy, K., & Collins, A. (1998). Reconsidering changes in parent–adolescent conflict across adolescence: A meta-analysis. *Child Development, 69,* 817–832.

Meeus, W. (Ed.). (1994a). *Adolescentie* [Adolescence]. Groningen, The Netherlands: Wolters Noordhof.

Meeus, W. (1994b). Psychosocial problems and social support in adolescence. In K. Hurrelmann & F. Nestman (Eds.), *Social networks and social support in childhood and adolescence* (pp. 241–255). New York, NY: W. de Gruyter.

Meeus, W., Akse, J., Branje, S., Ter Bogt, T., Engels, R., Finkenauer, C., et al. (2002). *CONAMORE: CONflict And Management Of RElationships, Wave 1.* Unpublished raw data.

Meeus, W., Iedema, J., Helsen, M., & Vollebergh, W. (1999). Patterns of adolescent identity development: Review of literature and longitudinal analysis. *Developmental Review, 19,* 419–461.

Meeus, W. & 't Hart, H. (1993). *Jongeren in Nederland* [Young people in the Netherlands]. Amersfoort, The Netherlands: Academische uitgeverij.

Meeus, W., van de Schoot, R., Keijsers, L., Schwartz, S., & Branje, S. (2010). On the progression and stability of adolescent identity formation: A five-wave longitudinal study in early-to-middle and middle-to-late adolescence. *Child Development, 81,* 1565–1581.

Monshouwer, K., Verdurmen, J., van Dorsselaer, S., Smit, E., Gorter, A., & Vollebergh, W. (2008). *Jeugd en riskant gedrag 2007* [Youth and risky behavior 2007]. Utrecht, The Netherlands: Trimbos Instituut.

Phalet, K., & Haker, F. (2004). *Moslim in Nederland. Diversiteit en verandering in religieuze betrokkenheid: Turken en Marokkanen in Nederland 1998–2002* [Muslim in the Netherlands: Diversity and change in religious involvement: Turks and Moroccans in the Netherlands 1998–2002]. The Hague, The Netherlands: SCP.

Ravesloot, J. (1997). *Seksualiteit in de jeugdfase vroeger en nu* [Sexuality in adolescence in earlier times and nowadays]. Amsterdam, The Netherlands: Het Spinhuis.

Rispens, J., Hermanns, J., & Meeus, W. (Eds.). (1996). *Opvoeden in Nederland* [Parenting in the Netherlands]. Assen, The Netherlands: Van Gorcum.

SCP. (1985). *Jongeren in de jaren tachtig* [Young people in the eighties]. Rijswijk, The Netherlands: SCP.

SCP. (1994). *Rapportage jeugd 1994* [Youth Report 1994]. Rijswijk, The Netherlands: SCP.

SCP. (1997). *Het gezinsrapport* [The family report]. Rijswijk, The Netherlands: SCP.

SCP. (2000). *Emancipatiemonitor 2000* [Emancipation monitor 2000]. The Hague, The Netherlands: SCP.

SCP. (2002). *Jeugd 2002* [Youth 2002]. The Hague, The Netherlands: SCP.

SCP. (2003a). *Rapportage jeugd 2002* [Youth report 2002]. The Hague, The Netherlands: SCP.

SCP. (2003b). *Rapportage minderheden 2003* [Minority report 2003]. The Hague, The Netherlands: SCP.

Spruijt, E. (1993). Relaties: feiten, opvattingen en problemen. In W. Meeus & H. 't Hart (Eds.), *Jongeren in Nederland* [Youth in the Netherlands] (pp. 56–79). Amersfoort, The Netherlands: Academische Uitgeverij.

Stevens, G., Pels, T., Bengi-Arslan, L., Verhulst, F. C., Vollebergh, W. A., & Crijnen, A. A. (2003). Parent, teacher, and self reported problem behavior in the Netherlands: Comparing Moroccan immigrant with Dutch and with Turkish immigrant children and adolescents. *Social Psychiatry and Psychiatric Epidemiology*, *38*, 576–585.

Stevens, G., Vollebergh, W., Pels, T., & Crijnen, A. (2007). Problem behavior and acculturation in Moroccan immigrant adolescents in the Netherlands: Effects of gender and parent–child conflict. *Journal of Cross-Cultural Psychology*, *38*, 310–317.

Ten Have, M., de Graaf, R., van Dorsselaer, S., Verdurmen, J., van 't Land, H., Vollebergh, W., et al. (2009). Incidence and course of suicidal ideation and suicide attempts in the general population. *Canadian Journal of Psychiatry*, *54*, 824–833.

TNO (2010, June). *Factsheet resultaten vijfde landelijke groeistudie TNO 10 juni 2010* [Factsheet results fifth national growth study TNO June 10th 2010]. Retrieved from www.tno.nl

Van der Laan, A., Blom, M., & Bogaerts, S. (2007). *Zelf gerapporteerde jeugdcriminaliteit* [Self-reported youth delinquency]. The Hague, The Netherlands: WODC.

Vandervalk, I. (2004). *Family matters*. Unpublished doctoral dissertation, Utrecht University, The Netherlands.

Van Laar, M., Cruts, A., Van Ooyen-Hoeben, M., Meijer, R., & Brunt, T. (2009). *Nationale Drug Monitor 2009* [National drugs monitor 2009]. Utrecht, The Netherlands: Trimbos Instituut.

Van Son, G., Van Hoeken, D., Bartelds, A., Van Furth, E., & Hoek, H. (2006). Time trends in the prevalence of eating disorders: A primary care study in the Netherlands. *International Journal of Eating Disorders*, *39*, 565–569.

Verkuyten, M. (1992). *Zelfbeleving van jeugdige allochtonen* [Self-concept of immigrant adolescents]. Amsterdam, The Netherlands: Swets & Zeitlinger.

Vollebergh, W., & Huiberts, A. (1997). Stress and ethnic identity in ethnic minority youth in the Netherlands. *Social Behavior and Personality*, *25*, 249–258.

Vollebergh, W., Iedema, J., & Meeus, W. (1999). The emerging gender gap: Cultural and economic conservatism in the Netherlands 1970–1992. *Political Psychology*, *20*, 291–321.

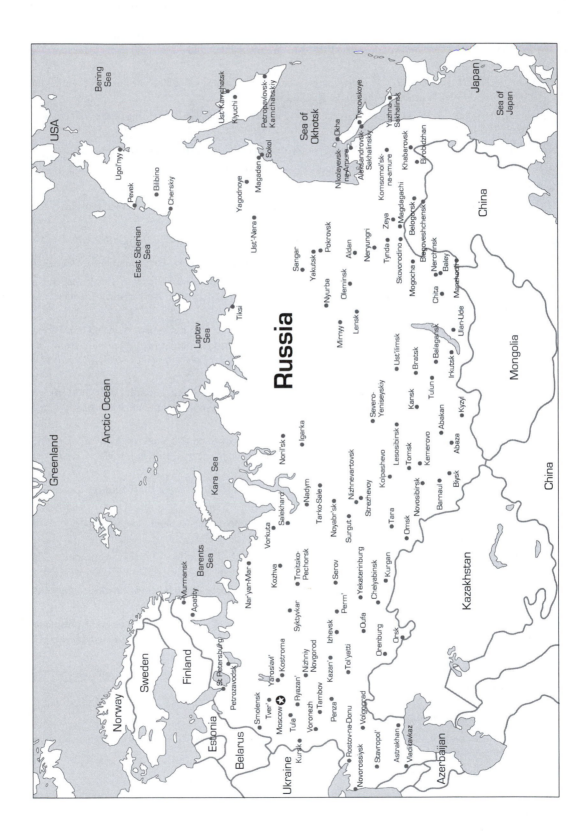

Chapter 22
Russia
Andrei Podolskij

Background Information

The Russian Federation (Russia) covers one-eighth of the earth's surface, stretching from Europe to Asia, and is easily the world's largest country. The country has a tremendous wealth of natural resources, producing 17% of the world's crude oil, 25–30% of its natural gas, and 10–20% of all nonferrous, rare, and noble metals mined across the globe. It contains some 130 nations and ethnic groups, including the following: Russian 82%, Tatar 4%, Ukrainian 3%, Chuvash 1%, Bashkir 1%, Byelorussian 1%, Moldavian 1%, and other 8%. The total population is approximately 145 million. At birth the life expectancy is 59 years for males, and 73 years for women (2009).

Russia is a democratic state with a republican form of government. The head of state is the president, who determines the main direction of domestic and foreign policy and represents the country in its foreign relations. The president is elected for a five-year term and cannot be elected for more than two consecutive terms. The parliament of Russia, the Federal Assembly, is the nation's highest representative and legislative body. It consists of two chambers, the Federation Council and the State Duma. Two deputies from each of the 89 federation members are elected to the Federation Council. The 450 deputies of the State Duma are elected from parties and public movements, or as individual candidates.

Period of Adolescence

Adolescence certainly exists as a recognized life stage in Russia, both in public opinion and in many scientific works of psychologists, sociologists, and educationalists. In accordance with a psychological periodization of the human life span by D. B. Elkonin (1977), adolescence occupies a period roughly between 11 and 16 years of age. Its beginning corresponds with a transition from primary to secondary school (fifth grade, 11 to 12 years old), and it finishes with the end of compulsory school education (ninth grade, 15 to 16 years old). At the same time, an alternative, more extended representation of adolescence has become more popular among Russian experts, where adolescence is considered to cover almost one and a half decades from 11 until 22 to 25 years of age.

There certainly exists a period of "emerging adulthood" in contemporary Russian society. There is a large divergence with regard to the indicators of reaching adulthood. For instance, adolescents may become more independent of their parents psychologically and remain dependent economically, or vice versa. Young people may be committed to several adult roles (e.g., marriage, parenthood) and at the same time share a home with their parents and continue to be fully dependent on them financially. Such heterogeneity in the process of emerging adulthood is a characteristic of different social strata of current Russian society and is not a selective feature of the elite only.

The main civil identification document, the Russian civil passport, is given at the age of 16 years; this is also the age of full criminal responsibility. At 18 Russians gain the right to vote and to be elected to government. It is possible to get a driving license and marry at that age as well. Another important rite of passage is graduation from secondary school, which is traditionally finalized by the graduation ball (taking place in all secondary schools every year, usually on the 21st to 23rd of June). Entering university or another higher education institution may also be considered as a serious step in the direction of reaching adulthood.

Beliefs

During the period between 1991 and 2002 there were a number of essential changes in religious orientations of teenagers (Sobkin, 2003). The basic tendency is a steady increase in the share of teenagers who consider themselves to be Orthodox and a reduction in the share of adolescents "not professing any religion." Alongside this, there has been an increase in the share of senior adolescents professing Islam (see Figure 22.1).

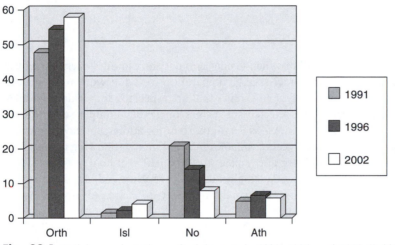

Fig. 22.1 Religious orientations of adolescents in 1991, 1996, and 2002 (Sobkin, 2003) (Orth = Orthodox Christianity, Isl = Islam, No = not professing any religion, Ath = atheist).

It is necessary to note that among the teenagers professing Orthodoxy, the share of those who do not recognize other religions as having any right to existence is high. Such an approach suggests that Orthodox Christianity is a dominating religion in Russia. Muslims are inclined to adhere to a position of a minority, which is characterized by a tolerant attitude to other religions. The majority of adolescents adopt a tolerant position in relation to religion in general and religions other than their own, and for girls such a position is more characteristic than for boys.

One more researched parameter of tolerance of teenagers is their estimation of their own likelihood to marry a person professing a religion other than their own. About half of the interviewed adolescents claimed that the religious beliefs of their future spouse "has no value for them" (49%). About a quarter of teenagers can imagine as possible for themselves a marriage with a person professing another religion, but they note that "it is possible only with representatives of certain faiths." Those who follow Orthodoxy and Islam are more likely to agree to this distinction. More than half (53%) among Muslims take this position, and 24% among Orthodox.

Traditionally, Russian and Soviet society has been considered a collectivist one. Indeed, the very existence of multimillion-strong children and youth unions such as the Pioneers (10- to 14-year-old children) and Komsomol (Young Communist League) (15- to 25-year-old adolescents and emerging adults) organizations mostly provided a collectivist orientation. Komsomol had little direct influence on the Communist Party, and on the government of the Soviet Union, but it played an important role as a mechanism for teaching the values of the Communist Party in the young, and as an organ for introducing the young to the political domain. Along with these purposes, the organization served as a highly mobile pool of labor and political activism, with the ability to move to areas of high priority at short notice. Active members received privileges and preferences in promotion. Many Komsomol committees in industrial enterprises, scientific-research and educational institutions have held Komsomol meetings and activist sessions, during which both professional and ideological issues were under discussion. Collectivistic vs. individualistic values were always considered to be primary and most activities—sport, volunteer activity, music, etc.—were considered through the prism of the collective activity and its success. Avoidance of such activities might be evaluated as a negative feature of the youngster. Collectivism was also a declared basis of mutual relations of Pioneers.

Gender

Certainly there is a long list of issues within which gender comparisons in adolescence might be made, such as gender role expectations; gender-specific preparation for adult work roles; gender-specific physical ideals; any gender and body image issues that are especially important in adolescence (for example, eating disorders). We selected three lines of gender comparison—tobacco smoking, alcohol drinking, and sexual behavior—as very important for adolescent development.

In terms of tobacco smoking, the most recent available data contain the following figures: 7.1% of 7th-grade male students and 8.7% of 7th-grade female students (~13 years old) smoke; 31% of 9th-grade male students and 27.4% of 9th-grade female students (~15 years old) smoke; 35.1% of 11th-grade male students and 37.8% of 11th-grade female students (~17 years old) smoke. As one can see, there is a strong increase in the number of smokers of both genders between 7th and 9th grades (between 13 and 15 years of age) (Sobkin, Abrosimova, Adamchuk, & Baranova, 2005).

In terms of drinking alcohol, data show that 9% of 7th-grade male students and 5.8% of 7th-grade female students regularly (at least once a week) drink beer; in 9th grade the figures increase (28.4% and 17.9% respectively); a further increase takes place among 11th graders (39.2 and 22.6%). It's not difficult to see both similar and different trends in tobacco smoking and alcohol drinking: in both cases there is a strong increase in the number of students commencing unhealthy behavior between 7th and 9th grades. There are always more alcohol drinkers among male students, and there are more female smokers in two of three age ranges (Sobkin, et al., 2005).

In terms of sexual behavior of adolescents, only one aspect of this highly important issue will be presented here, namely adolescent attitudes to age-restrictive regulations. Students of 7th, 9th, and 11th grades (the following figures are calculated for all three together) were asked if they evaluate sexual contacts at their age as inadmissible or admissible. Of male students, 29.6% and of female students, 41.9% believe that sexual contacts are inadmissible at their age, and they don't have sexual contacts. In contrast, 16.1% of male students and 8.8% of female students believe that sexual contacts are completely admissible at their age, and they do have sexual contacts; 37.3% of male students and 36.9% of female students believe that sexual contacts are admissible in their age, but they don't have sexual contacts. Finally, 4.5% of male students and 3.0% of female students answered that they they were too young, but they did have sexual contacts. Only unambiguous answers ("I behave as I believe") demonstrated highly significant gender differences ($p = .00001$). Gender differences between those male and female students who found difficulty in answering the questions (12.5% and 9.5%, respectively) were also significant ($p = .01$) (Baranova, 2006).

The Self

The concept of identity or self-identity includes many aspects. Here, we emphasize only one such aspect: the emotional acceptance or rejection of the adolescent's own ethnic group. Scholars from the Centre of Sociology of Education (Russian Academy of Education) believe that adolescents' attitudes regarding their own ethnicity are mostly positive. The respondents (Moscow secondary school adolescents) were asked to assess their relation to their own ethnicity, by offering them different modalities such as "pride," "indifference," and "shame." A distribution of the answers of differently aged adolescents is presented in Table 22.1.

Table 22.1   Attitudes of Russian Adolescents to Their Own Ethnicity (%) (Sobkin, 2003)

Answer	7th Grade		8th Grade		9th Grade	
	Boys	Girls	Boys	Girls	Boys	Girls
I feel pride	68	65	74	63	77	63
I am indifferent	23	30	21	35	18	35
I feel discomfort	2	2	1	0	0	0
I often feel shame	3	0	2	1	1	1
I'd prefer to belong to another ethnicity	3	2	1	1	2	1

As the table shows, the majority of adolescents feel pride concerning their ethnicity. At the same time, about one-quarter of the interviewed students answered "I am indifferent" (Sobkin, 2003). According to data gathered by the same center, 55% of adolescents define an ethnicity by a shared language. A similar percentage of respondents define an ethnicity by appearance (54%). The third position is occupied by the answer "to define an ethnicity by first name or family name" (47%). An ethnicity is defined by the ethnicity of parents by 36% of adolescent respondents, by place of birth by 27%, by religion by 20%, and by national traits of character by 10% (more than one answer could be given).

Family Relationships

According to the Conception of Demographic Development of the Russian Federation for the period until 2015, the demographic situation is characterized by families restricting themselves to few children, only one or two in total (Koncepciya demografichescko razvitiya Rossiyskoy Federacii na period do 2015 goda, 2001). There is a higher birth rate in the Muslim regions of the Northern Caucasus and in some other regions of the Russian Federation.

One large-scale research study, where the subjects were students in the seventh through eleventh grades, demonstrates how much parents take into account and respect the position and opinions of adolescents. The data showed that the majority of the respondents (76%) noticed and appreciated that their parents valued their opinions. Adolescents' opinions are usually ignored in only 13% of cases, and the rest (12%) stated that they generally prefer not to express their opinion. The subjects were also asked what they usually discuss with parents. Almost one in two of the interviewed students mentioned school and achievements at school as the most frequently discussed topics. Another popular topic of discussion is other school issues such as the administration, teachers, and classmates.

Gender is the essential factor determining the contents of parent–adolescent dialogue. Girls more frequently discuss classmates with parents than boys do. In contrast, boys are more inclined to discuss nonschool topics with parents: politics, economics, and ethnic relations. The analysis of age dynamics shows that from ninth to eleventh grade the share of the teenagers interested in discussing politics with their parents increases (respectively, 21% and 33%), as does interest in discussing the economy (19% and 21%), and the acts of state leaders (13% and 21%) (Sobkin, 2003).

Five areas of conflict between parents and adolescents have been found (*Materialy Vserossiyskoy nauchnoy konferencii "Semya I semeinye otnosheniya"*, 2003), as follows.

1. Social life and habits (a choice of friends, leisure activities, appearance, fashion).
2. Responsibility (performance of duties in the house, care of personal things and family property, earnings and expenditure of money).
3. Schooling (progress, school behavior, relations with teachers, attendance of classes, performance of homework).
4. Mutual relations in the family (disrespectful relations with parents and other members of family, quarrels and confrontations with siblings).
5. Following moral standards and social rules (smoking, use of alcohol and drugs, obscene expressions, early sexual life of teenagers, lying, nonobservance of laws).

Grandmothers play an important role in the daily lives of many adolescents (*Materialy Vserossiyskoy nauchnoy konferencii "Semya I semeinye otnosheniya"*, 2003). More than 50% of children lived with grandmothers, and more than 45% were in constant contact—no less than once a week. Thus, the greater part of the modern young generation was brought up with a direct participation of grandmothers. According to the research results, the grandmother: prepares meals; goes to shops for products; looks after the grandchildren when they are sick; tells fairy tales; never punishes; consoles in troubled times; forgives all insults; always sympathizes and understands children's problems.

There are 600 divorces for every 1,000 marriages in contemporary Russia—one of the highest divorce rates in the world. The number of divorces after a subsequent marriage is higher than after the first one (1.75 times). It is necessary to note that many divorced fathers do not keep any contact with the children, and remain only biological. The statistics show that 4% of children under 18 years live with only fathers, 56% live with mothers, and only 40% live in full families. (Koncepciya demografichescko razvitiya Rossiyskoy Federacii na period do 2015 goda, 2001.)

Extramarital childbirth has long ceased to be a social aberration for a greater part of the population and has become a normal part of social behavior, one of the alternative styles of family formation. Deliberate formation of a one-parent family is a phenomenon that has spread recently as one of the consequences of social and economic independence of modern women, who make such decisions quite consciously in order to avoid loneliness in maturity and old age (*Materialy Vserossiyskoy nauchnoy konferencii "Semya I semeinye otnosheniya"*, 2003).

Friends and Peers/Youth Culture

T. N. Malkovskaja, who surveyed 1,500 randomly selected St Petersburg senior secondary school students (15 to 17 years old), has found that the overwhelming majority prefer to spend leisure time outside of school (99%) and outside of the house (93%). They spend most of their leisure time with peers and friends (79%) (cited by Volkov, 2001). According to data collected by L. N. Zhilina and N. T. Frolova, the consumerist orientations of Moscow adolescents are most strongly influenced by friends. However, adolescents rely on their parents more than peers when they encounter problems. In one study, adolescents were asked to fill in questionnaires about with whom they would prefer to spend their free time: parents, friends, peers of the same gender, mixed company, and so on (cited by Volkov, 2001). Parents appeared in the boys' answers in the last (sixth) place, and among the girls in fourth place; the company of peers appeared to be obviously preferable to that of parents. But, answering the question: "Who would you consult in a difficult everyday situation?" both girls and boys placed "mother" first. Boys put "father" second, while "female friend" occupied the second position in the girls' answers. In other words, findings indicated that friendships are important, but in difficult situations, family becomes more important (Volkov, 2001).

The most popular types of adolescent peer crowds are: "extremals," engaged in extreme kinds of sports, 10%; football fans, 8%; and rappers, 8%. Age structure is as follows: A group of rappers is formed mostly by seventh-graders (48%), while the majority among football fans is of ninth-graders (45%). It is interesting that membership in a peer crowd is not the determining factor of a choice of friends for most of the adolescents (70%), even for those who belong to a crowd (Bashkatov, 2001).

There exists a clearly distinguished youth culture in contemporary Russia, marked off from adult culture by many indicators: dress, hairstyle, tattooing/piercing, music, slang, and so on. This youth culture has a mostly international view in the style of globalization, and it would be difficult to distinguish Russian adolescents from their Western European or American peers.

After the disbanding of the Pioneers and Komsomol, the two main youth organizations under the Communist regime, Russian adolescents mostly were left to their own resources. Thus, at the beginning of the 1990s about 20% of adolescents attended sports, musical, and art schools, while another 20% attended programs in the Children and Youth Palaces, and the rest were not engaged in organized leisure activities. By the mid-1990s, about 50% of adolescents spent their free and leisure time in the company of friends, while about 10% spent that time with their families, and only 2% to 3% were involved in various military, sports, ethnic, art, religious, or labor clubs.

Love and Sexuality

Absence of data precludes the presentation of a full picture of sexual behavior of teenagers in Russia. Nevertheless, the available data make two tendencies clear. First, since the mid-1990s, the number of adolescents engaging in sexual behavior has increased. For example, according to the regional research, more than 70% of randomly selected women aged 20 to 24 years had had sexual relations before the age of 20, whereas among women between the ages of 40 and 44, this percentage was less than 50%. Second, adolescents initiate sexual relations at increasingly early ages. Twelve percent of sexually active students in St Petersburg began sexual relations before the age of 16, whereas only 5% of adolescents younger than 16 were sexually active in 1965 (Table 22.2). The increased sexual activity among teenagers is connected to several kinds of risks, among which are abortions, STDs, and increased maternal death rate.

Table 22.2 Prevalence of Premarital Sexual Contacts and Age of Sexual Debut among High-School and University Students in St Petersburg (1965–1995)

Time of research	Percentage of persons having premarital sexual contacts		Age of sexual debut (percentage of those who have had a sexual experience)			
	Males	Females	Before 16	16–18	19–23	24 and older
1965	80	38	5	33	40	22
1995	80	80	12	53	31	4

Though the average age of first marriage in Russia remains rather low—24.4 years for men and 22.2 for women—Russians apparently depart from a traditional model of early marriage more and more. Thus, though the sexual life of youth begins earlier, the age for the first marriage increases. Also, public opinion has begun to consider unregistered marriages as more tolerable. Their number has begun to increase, superseding a part of the registered marriages. Earlier beginning of a sexual life is not accompanied by a growth of the number of births, but the percentage of children who were born outside of registered marriage has risen among Russian teenagers: 30% to 40% of children born to 15- to 19-year-old mothers are born outside of registered marriage (Denisenko & Dalla Zuanna, 2001).

Data presented confirm that there is no effective adolescent sexual education in Russia, and adolescents pick up most information by communication with each other (Rezner, 2003). The official data on use of contraception among the Russian population are rather poor and are usually presented without breakdown on age groups. Available evidence indicates that the extent of using contraception in Russia is much lower than in the Western countries, especially with regard to the first sexual contact. According to the report *Reproductive Health of Russian Women* (1998), only 44% of randomly selected female respondents in the age group of 15 to 24 years used any contraception at the first sexual contact. In The Netherlands, where the level of teenage pregnancies is one of the lowest in the world, the share of the teenagers using contraception at a sexual debut is 85%, and in the United States it is 75%.

The 1990s in Russia were marked by a sharp rise in sexually transmitted diseases (STDs). This is connected, apparently, to a new stage of sexual revolution and the lack of corresponding preventive programs. The country appeared unprepared for liberalization in the sexual sphere.

As medical statistics show, the growth of STDs has concerned younger age groups to the greatest degree. The most serious STD is, certainly, HIV/AIDS. The youth from 15 to 29 years old account for about 75% of new cases of HIV infection (Baranova & Sannikov, 2002).

Health Risk Behavior

The data on smoking indicate that almost 40% of teenagers smoke. The peak is in 13- to 15-year-olds. The tendency toward decrease in the age of smoking initiation means that now 10- to 11-year-olds more often begin to smoke. Alcoholism is a serious problem. In the year 2004 the number of teenagers suffering from alcoholism exceeded the number of drug-addicted teenagers. It appears that the level of drug use among teenagers is almost twice as high as among the whole population, and glue sniffing is higher by eight times. Such kinds of drugs as "tranquilizers," LSD, and Ecstasy are used at least once a month by every tenth teenager. Lower percentages of teenagers have used heroin (6%) and cocaine (4%) (Rean, 2004). The basic motives for using psychoactive substances include: curiosity, 80%; because friends have offered, 9%; because of troubles, 9%.

In the 1990s, more and more adolescents began to use alcohol and drugs. Rates of adolescent prostitution increased. There was also a large increase in adolescent crime. These destructive processes occurred and continue to occur against a background of the decreasing prestige and authority of teachers, parents, political and public figures, scientists, and artists.

The most typical crimes of the teenager are, in descending order: thefts of personal and state property, hooliganism, robbery, physical injuries, armed assaults, rapes, and other crimes. The three top reasons for deaths of teenage children are murders (51%), suicides (13%), and poisonings (31%) (Rean, 2004).

Education

The system of general education and vocational training in Russia affects all Russian youth. Completing general secondary education takes 11 years and includes technical school, higher school, and postgraduate courses. Approximately 13% of students, on leaving the ninth grade, enter vocational school, which combines general education training with a mixture of general technical and theoretical and practical skills and knowledge. There are two main types of vocational school, according to vocational sector: technical schools (industrial, transport, and building trades) and specialized schools (medical, pedagogical, cultural, etc.).

Institutions of higher education—universities, academies, and institutes—only accept those who have graduated from a secondary school of general education or secondary specialized school. A survey of school graduates has shown that about half intend to enter higher schools immediately on leaving secondary school. Of those leaving technical and vocational schools, only one-fifth will continue higher education.

The overall level of literacy has traditionally been considered to be very high among Russian students, considerably exceeding that of other highly developed countries. Russia also performs well in international comparisons of secondary school performance.

Russian adolescents on average spend two to three hours daily on their homework, including approximately one hour on mathematics and less than one hour on science subjects. This schedule leaves them ample time for other activities. Thirteen-year-old students watch television for three hours per day, talk with their friends for three hours, and play sports for about one hour. Besides those activities, Russian adolescents play computer games for one hour per day (more than in other countries), and more than one hour each day is devoted to reading for pleasure (also more than in other countries). One and a half hours per day are devoted to helping parents (Sobkin & Evstigne-eva, 2001). Children can combine playing sports or playing computer games with dialogue with friends.

Work

Despite increasing economic growth in the past decade, poverty persists and unemployment is high. In these conditions, the temporary employment of teenagers from poor families is a necessary contribution to the family income. Adolescents who work also avoid the harmful influence of the streets and familiarize themselves with the working world. At the same time, in the past decade teenagers' share of the official labor market was rather insignificant: no more than 3% of the employed population. As a rule, the following kinds of work are offered to adolescents: gardening and care of public spaces; agricultural work based around harvests; restoration and preservation of historic and architectural monuments and parks, memorials, and cemeteries; book repair; house cleaning; mail delivery; and posting of flyers (Kuleshov, 2003). According to the Labor Code of the Russian Federation, the amount of daily work by employees aged 15 to 18 cannot exceed five hours. If the adolescent is combining study with work, he or she can work no more than 2.5 hours per week if he or she is 14 to 16 years old, or no more than 3.5 hours if he or she is older than 16. Approximately 45% of adolescents worked in 2008 (full-time or part-time) (www.jobsmarket.ru)

One of the reasons for adolescent unemployment is that teenagers do not possess sufficient knowledge and qualifications. Their professional opportunities are limited to work that does not require extensive qualifications, or that can be done in a part-time capacity. Graduates of secondary schools have more chances in the labor market than their peers who do not finish school. Many employers demand a certain educational level for performance of the given work. Therefore teenagers who have not finished secondary education are frequently refused a job, not because they are not capable of performing it, but because they cannot present the required educational documents (www.jobsmarket.ru).

Media

Media are a big part of the daily lives of Russian adolescents. Table 22.3 shows young men's and women's preferences regarding mass-media information. The sample was drawn from randomly selected 15- to 17-year-old Moscow secondary school students.

Table 22.3   Mass-Media Information Considered to Be of the Most Interest by Russian Adolescents

Rank	Male	Female
TV-programs		
1	Music	Music
2	News	Entertainment programs
3	Sports	News
4	Popular science programs	Travel
5	Entertainment programs	Programs about animals
6	Programs about animals	Popular science programs
7	Travel	Political shows
8	Erotic shows	Erotic shows
9	Ecological shows	Sports
Movie and video		
1	Comedies	Comedies
2	Fantasy	Melodramas
3	Insurgents	Fantasy
4	Adventures	Adventures
5	Thrillers	Thrillers
6	Westerns	Insurgents
7	Animated	Animated
8	Erotic	Westerns
9	Melodramas	Erotic

Source: Sobkin, 2003.

Teenagers turn to mass media not to acquire new knowledge, but primarily to be entertained. This conclusion is supported by research carried out in 1997 by the Center of Sociology of Education of the Russian Academy of Education. To study the motives of adolescents when watching TV, the target group of adolescents was offered questionnaires. They could offer the following as reasons for watching TV: a desire to have a good time, a desire to keep abreast of events, a desire to increase one's cultural and educational level, a need for dialogue. About 70% of teenagers marked that they turned to television for entertainment.

Teenagers find information received from the mass media more attractive than that received from educational institutions. It is more emotionally accessible, the media speak in their own language, and the mass media are perceived as a choice—one that is not intellectually taxing. Most mass media consumed by adolescents involve slightly modified Western programs, movies, and videos (mostly made in the United States). At the same time, since 2000, relatively old Russian (Soviet) movies from the 1970s and 1980s have attracted more of the attention of adolescents. Modern Russian movies are also increasingly interesting to adolescents, given that the heroes act and conduct themselves in a manner well known to and accepted by adolescents (Sobkin, 2003).

Politics and Military

Although some teenagers participate in pre-election coverage as "live advertising" (for money), there is no data on the serious participation of teenagers in the political life of the country. Interest in politics is basically pragmatic (Hrapenko, 2004). There are various public organizations for teenagers at most schools, and also youth associations based on various political parties, such as the Liberal-Democratic Party, the Communist Party of the Russian Federation, and Unity.

Adolescents who live in the "hot" areas of political and military tension (such as the Northern Caucasus, and especially Chechnya) are forced to take part in armed combat or undergo the effects of such warfare. Little to no quantitative data is available on this subject. The compulsory military service of male adolescents has become a controversial and important topic of political discourse. By law, all males over the age of 18 are obliged to take part in such a service. However, approximately 90% of them are either released from duty due to health problems, or use a postponement provided by their study in an institution of higher education. Accordingly, there exists a tension in the society: Adolescents and their parents try to do their best to avoid compulsory service, and military officials act in the opposite direction. The Russian Parliament is now considering several suggestions concerning both a reduction in the releases and postponements and concerning alternative service.

Unique Issues

The fall of the communist government, the dissolution of the Soviet Union, and the transition from a socialist economy to a market economy have been highly challenging for all Russians, including adolescents. There is a lack of scientific information on how contemporary Russian adolescents are able to adapt themselves to these rapid socioeconomic changes, and how those changes influence their psychological wellbeing. Until the mid-1990s, there was no systematic research on depression among Russian adolescents from non-clinical samples. A collaborative Russian–Dutch study sponsored by the European Union on adolescent development in Russia was started in 1994, and this and later studies provided information on adolescent depression in Russia (Figure 22.2; Podolskij, Idobaeva, & Heymans, 2004).

The following key factors that affected an adolescent's high level of depressed mood and anxiety were found.

Adolescents
  1. Misunderstandings by parents.
  2. Problems in communication with peers.
  3. Lack of self-regulation, emotional instability.
  4. Lack of moral self and self-positioning among others (peers and adults).

Parents
  1. Lack of adequate understanding about adolescent emotional (and general) development.

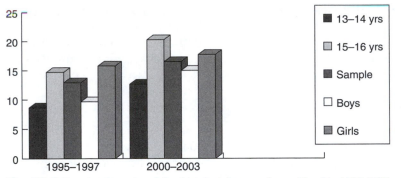

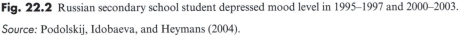

Fig. 22.2 Russian secondary school student depressed mood level in 1995–1997 and 2000–2003.

Source: Podolskij, Idobaeva, and Heymans (2004).

2. Dominance of disparate parenting styles resulting in hostility and, especially, inconsistency, as perceived by adolescents.
3. Mutual misunderstanding of parents and adolescents with regard to the core problems of adolescent values, goals, and intentions.

Teachers
1. Lack of adequate understanding about adolescent emotional (and general) developmental.
2. Lack of understanding or misunderstanding of the extent and paths by which a teacher's emotional state and mood influence a student's.
3. Emotional instability, lack of self-regulation (Podolskij et al., 2004).

The data show that adolescent psychoemotional non-wellbeing reflects a complex variety of factors related to both adolescents' own characteristics and the characteristics of their parents and teachers. This means that to uncover the mechanism of such psychoemotional non-wellbeing is to deal with the full scope of the social content of adolescents' development—their interrelations with close and social adults and peers, development of self-concept, etc. (Vygotsky, 1998; Podolskij et al., 2004).

References and Further Reading

Baranova, E. V. (2006). Social construction of sexual scenarios in adolescence. In V. S. Sobkin (Ed.), *Sociocultural transformation of adolescent subculture* (pp. 150–164). Moscow, Russia: Centre of Sociology of Education [In Russian].

Baranova, A., & Sannikov, A. (2002). Polovoe vospitanie podrostkov i zabolevaniya, peredavaemye polovym putem [Sexual education of adolescents and sexually transmitted diseases]. *Sociologicheskie issledovaniya*, *11*, 118–122.

Bashkatov, I. V. (2001). *Psichologija neformalnyh podrostkovyh grupp* [Psychology of informal adolescent groups]. Moscow, Russia: Sfera Publishing House.

Denisenko, M. B., & Dalla Zuanna, Z.-P. (2001). Seksual'noe povedenie rossiyskoy molodezhi [Sexual behavior of Russian youth]. *Sociologicheskie issledovaniya*, *2*, 85–90.

Dubrovina, I. V. (1995). *Rabochaya kniga shkol'nogo psichologa* [Working book of the school psychologist]. Moscow, Russia: Academia Publishing House.

Elkonin, D. B. (1977). Toward the problem of stages in the mental development of the child. In M. Cole (Ed.), *Soviet Developmental Psychology*. New York, NY: M. E. Sharpe.

Golod, S. I. (1996). *XX vek I seksual'nye otnosheniya v Rossii* [XX century and trends in sexual relations in Russia]. St. Petersburg, Russia: Accent Publishing House.

Heymans, P. (1996). *Depression among Vidnoe adolescents: Report on the Vidnoe project*. Utrecht, The Netherlands: Utrecht University.

Hrapenko, I. B. (2004). *Politicheskie predstavlenia v detskom I podrostkovom vozraste* [Political representations among children and adolescents]. PhD dissertation, Moscow City Pedagogical University, Moscow, Russia.

Koncepciya demografichescko razvitiya Rossiyskoy Federacii na period do 2015 goda [Conception of demographic development of Russian Federation till 2015]. (2001). *Bulleten' Ministerstva truda I social'nogo razvitiya Rossiyskoy Federacii, 10,* 17–24.

Kuleshov, E. (2003). Ob organizacii sezonnoy zaniatosti podrostkov [On the organization of seasonal adolescent employment]. *Sluzhba zaniatosti, 10,* 27–36.

Leonov, R. (2004). Vazhnaya forma social'noy zashity podrostkov [Important forms of adolescent social protection]. *Social'noe obespechenie, 1,* 24–30.

Materialy Vserossiyskoy nauchnoy konferencii "Semya I semeinye otnosheniya" [Proceedings of the All-Russia scientific conference "Family and family relations"]. (2003). Moscow, Russia.

Podolskij, A. (1994). Russia. In K. Hurrelman (Ed.), *International handbook of adolescence*. Westport, CT: Greenwood Press.

Podolskij, A., Idobaeva, O., & Heymans, P. (2004). *Diagnostika podrostkovoy depressivnosti* [Diagnostics of adolescent depressivity]. St Petersburg, Russia: Piter Publishing House.

Priazhnikov, N. S. (2004). *Professional'naya orientaciya* [Professional orientation]. Moscow, Russia: Academia Publishing House.

Rean, A. (2004). Psichologiya podrostka [Psychology of adolescents]. St Petersburg, Russia: Piter Publishing House.

Renewal of Education in Russia (Regional Level). (2000). Report 18666-RU (pp. 3–24). Washington, DC: The World Bank.

Reproductive health of Russian women. Final report. (1998). Washington, DC: Centers for Disease Control and USAID.

Rezner, T. (2003). Mediko-social'nye podhody k organizacii seksual'nogo obrazovaniya [Medical and social approaches to the organization of sexual education]. *Sociologicheskie issledovaniya, 1,* 102–108.

Sobkin, V. S. (1997). *Starsheklassnik v mire politiki* [Secondary school students in the world of politics]. Moscow, Russia: CSO RAO.

Sobkin, V. S (Ed.). (2000). *Televidenie I obrazovanie. Sociologicheskie aspekty* [Television and education: Sociological aspects]. Moscow, Russia: CSO RAO.

Sobkin, V. (Ed.). (2003). *Problemy tolerantnosti v podrostkovoy subculture* [Problems of tolerance in the adolescent subculture]. Moscow, Russia: CSO RAO.

Sobkin, V., & Evstigneeva, Y. (2001). *Podrostok: virtual'nost' I social'naya real'nost'* [The teenager: Virtuality and social reality]. Moscow, Russia: CSO RAO.

Sobkin, V. S., Abrosimova, Z. B., Adamchuk, D. V., & Baranova, E. V. (2005). *Teenager: Norms, risks, deviations*. Moscow, Russia: Centre of Sociology of Education [In Russian].

Volkov, B. S. (2001). *Psichologiya podrostka* [Psychology of adolescents]. Moscow, Russia: Academia Publishing House.

Vygotsky, L. S. (1998). *The collected works of L. S. Vygotsky, Vol. 5: Child psychology*. New York: Plenum Press.

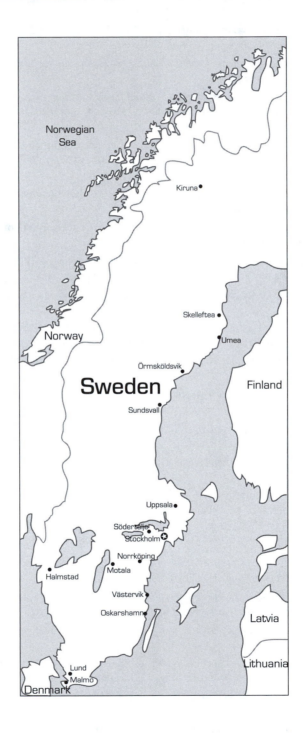

Chapter 23
Sweden
Kari Trost

Background Information

Sweden, the fifth largest country in Europe, is surrounded by the Baltic Sea, Norway, and Finland. The terrain is mostly flat, with mountains in the northwestern regions. The climate in the south is temperate with cold and cloudy winters, but in the north it is sub-arctic during winter. Summers are mild in both areas, although shorter in the north.

Sweden is a parliamentary monarchy with a prime minister, who is proposed to the parliament by the speaker of the parliament and, in turn, approved by the majority of the parliament, as well as a head of state, who is the king or queen at the time. Although it was a military power in the 1700s, Sweden has not been to war in several decades and remained neutral during both world wars of the twentieth century. Sweden became a member of the European Union in 1995 but voted in 2003 not to adopt the euro as its currency.

At present, the population of Sweden is slightly over 9 million (Statistics Sweden, 2010a) and the majority live in the southern regions of the country. In 1980, Sweden had one of the highest fertility rates in Europe at 2.1, but this dropped to 1.5 in the late 1990s, and in 2009, the rate at 1.9 was comparable to that of other Nordic countries (Andersson, 2004; Statistics Sweden, 2010a).

Until 1950, Sweden was ethnically a homogeneous society for the most part. In recent decades large numbers of labor immigrants from other European countries, particularly from Finland but also from the former Yugoslavia, Greece, Germany, Turkey, Poland, and Italy, have immigrated to Sweden. Today, the majority of immigrants are political refugees (Statistics Sweden, 2003b). A gap still remains among the native and foreign-born population that is particularly evident in the employment rates between the two groups (Wiesbrock, 2011).

Period of Adolescence

Sweden recognizes a clear life stage called adolescence (Swedish Academy, 2003). During adolescence, many social rights and duties come into effect. At the age of 15, one has criminal responsibility, legally can consent to sex, and legally can see adult-rated films. At the age of 18, one can vote. At the age of 20, one can purchase alcohol at the Swedish Alcohol Retail Monopoly (Systembolaget) and enroll, if accepted, at the police academy. During middle to late adolescence, many governmental and parental obligations cease. For example, all parents receive a child allowance until their child is 16 years of age, parents' obligation to support their child ceases at the age of 21 (at age 18 if the child is not in school), and entitlement to free dentistry ceases when one reaches the age of 19.

Like many other countries, the period of adolescence has become longer in Sweden. This may be partly due to earlier pubertal maturation, longer years in school, the tendency to live in their childhood home longer, and the later age of full-time employment. In Europe, there has been a secular trend in adolescent growth toward increased height and, although to a lesser extent, there is also a secular trend toward earlier puberty in Sweden (Karlberg, 2002). In Sweden in 1920 the mean age of menarche was approximately 13.7 years, in 1954 it was 13.25 years, and in the early 1970s girls reached their menarche at 13 years approximately (Ljung, Bergsten-Brucefors, & Lindgren, 1974; Onland-Moret et al., 2005). Today, normal maturation usually means reaching menarche at age 12 to 13 (WHO, 2004).

After pubertal maturation, the next important age during adolescence is age 15. At this time, the adolescent can continue to upper secondary education and choose between the national and a specialized study program, which usually last for three years. The entry to emerging adulthood is usually marked by one's completion of upper secondary education, usually around age 19, when individuals are viewed as independent from their parents but not committed fully to adult roles of, for example, marriage, parenthood, home ownership, or employment.

Approximately 25% of Swedish adolescents are vegetarians, vegans, or food exclusive in some way (Larsson Klock, Astrøm, Haugejorden, & Johansson, 2001). Of the young Swedish vegetarians and vegans, more tend to be girls. This may be due to the tendency for girls to be concerned with diet and weight (Kenyon & Barker, 1998; Neumark-Sztainer, Story, Perry, & Casey, 1999).

Beliefs

As in other Scandinavian countries, personal autonomy is valued and conformity is common. Being shy is not necessarily considered a negative characteristic. Verbal passivity is associated with traits such as reflection and modesty, and modesty is highly appreciated. Those who gesticulate intensively and speak loudly are likely to be viewed negatively. Although the term originated from the Danish-Norwegian author, Aksel Sandemose, Swedes commonly refer to *Jante's law*, which basically means that no one should believe he is better than anyone else. In addition, being prompt, honest, and fair are important virtues in Sweden. The Swedish mentality as elucidated by a Swedish ethnologist (Daun, 1996) contains four distinct parts: conformity, conflict avoidance, modernity, and equality. Although these qualities are not specific to Swedes, many value these characteristics, and they may be more prevalent in Sweden than in other places in the world.

Religion no longer plays a major role in the lives of Swedish citizens. In 2000, the church and the state separated and the (Lutheran) Church of Sweden became an open national church and no longer a part of the public sector (Government Office of Sweden, 2000). Most Swedes are not regularly active in the church and usually only come into contact with the church for occasions such as baptisms, confirmations, weddings, and funerals. More specifically, confirmations have declined sharply; 38% of Swedish adolescents were confirmed in 2003, as opposed to 80% in 1970 (Church of Sweden, 2005).

Gender

Although the belief in equality is commonplace for most in Sweden, there are gender differences in various areas. In education, more women than men both apply to and attend colleges and universities, but only 14% of all full professors are women (National Agency for Higher Education, 2005). Women, however, are well represented in humanities and social sciences and men are well represented in technology-related subjects.

In the family domain, most fathers take advantage of the paid 10-day leave immediately after their child is born, but they usually return to work full-time and mothers usually care for their children full- or part-time. It is important to note that this trend is changing for some cohorts of fathers. Swedish men take more parental leave than any of their Nordic country counterparts with the exception of Iceland (Statistics Sweden, 2009).

In the workplace, more women are temporary, part-time, or project employees and are paid less than men. In 2008, 30 of the most common occupations in Sweden continued to be sex-segregated, with the exception of four: university/higher education teachers, chefs/cooks, administrators in the public sector, and physicians, which were represented by 45%, 57%, 50%, and 47% women respectively (Statistics Sweden, 2010c).

These gender differences across various domains are likely making an impression on the youth. Adolescents in Sweden also admit that there are activities that are stereotypically perceived as masculine or feminine. Among the various activities, working on cars, watching a hockey game, lifting weights, and fishing were considered highly masculine; horseback riding, aerobics, writing poetry or in a diary, and babysitting were considered highly feminine; and golf, looking at art, watching movies, competing, and working with social issues were considered gender-neutral (Swedish National Board of Youth Affairs, 2005).

Although the labor market and higher education continue generally to be sex-segregated and salary differences remain, comparatively to other countries Sweden has come far in achieving equal rights for men and women. As early as 1921, women gained national suffrage and had the right to hold office at the national level, and in 1980 a law was established against sex discrimination in employment. Young people in Sweden do not associate successful careers and employment with men only. In 2003, the proportion of women between the ages of 20 and 64 in the workforce was 79% and the corresponding proportion of men was 84% (Statistics Sweden, 2004c). Besides having their working mothers as role models, girls in Sweden have many role models in the public sector. In 2002 the parliament members were 45% women and 55% men and the eventual successor to the throne and head of state was Crown Princess Victoria Bernadotte.

The Self

As in other countries, the development of self-identity and self-esteem is important to Swedish youth. Body image seems to be an important aspect of self-worth. In recent Swedish adolescent population-based studies, it was reported that 40% of girls between 13 and 15 believed they were obese, 15% of girls between 13 and 15 were trying to actively lose weight, 84% of girls between 15 and 16 desired to change their body in some way, and 20% of the boys between 13 and 15 believed they were too thin. In turn, low self-esteem was linked with higher BMI and high self-esteem was linked with satisfaction with one's body size (National Board of Health and Welfare 2005; Swedish National Institute of Public Health, 2010). These findings are similar to those in other European countries.

A major task for adolescents is the development of identity. Increasingly in Sweden, this includes ethnic identity. Of youth between the ages of 13 and 24 in Sweden, approximately 14%

have a foreign background. Approximately 25% of youths in school feel they have experienced racism at school and 20% of the teachers believe there is racism at school (Swedish National Agency for Education, 2009). An aspect of identity that is important to adolescents with foreign backgrounds is to reconcile "ethnic minority identity" and "majority identity," the latter referring to the identification with, not rejection of, the majority or host society (see Phinney, 1999). This can be difficult for some immigrant youth, particularly if they perceive their environment as highly prejudiced.

Family Relationships

Most adolescents get along well with their parents, and conflicts are usually not serious. Extreme familial discord during adolescence is likely to be linked with other family characteristics such as family problems long before adolescence (Collins, 1991) or a family history of punitive disciplinary practices (Stattin & Trost, 2000). Swedish parents do not tend to be authoritarian and most have moderate levels of control and high levels of warmth and communication (Trost, 2002).

Since it is illegal for parents, teachers, or caregivers to abuse a child mentally or physically in any way, which includes spanking and slapping, parental styles in Sweden use alternative forms of discipline rather than negative punishment. In fact, in 1979, Sweden was unique in the industrialized world for having passed the first explicit ban on corporal punishment. Most adolescents and parents would agree that their relationships are a combination of respect for autonomy and parental involvement/supervision. In a study looking at over 1,000 Swedish 16-year-olds, the vast majority (72%) of the adolescents reported that their parents used a democratic style of negotiations in their families and only 12% reported a dictatorship pattern in their homes (Trost, 2002).

The vast majority of youths have parents who work outside the home. Seventy percent of mothers and 94% of fathers with a child between the ages of 11 and 17 are employed full-time (Statistics Sweden, 2004b). Swedish adolescents spend far less time with their parents today than ever before. Much of the time spent together is while a parent is doing housework, and the most common activity with either parent is eating meals together and watching TV. Although Swedish adolescents spend little time with their parents daily, most find it easy to talk to their parents (WHO, 2004).

When it is time to move out of their parental home, most do not move directly to live with a partner or spouse. Usually, the first move from the parental home is to a rented apartment or a student dormitory-type apartment (Statistics Sweden, 2004b). Today, since housing is expensive, many may stay in their parental home into their twenties. This is particularly the case for youth living in metropolitan areas of Sweden or youth of immigrant parents. Moreover, youth with two immigrant parents and living in suburbs of large cities in Sweden are on average 23 to 24 years of age when they move out of their childhood home for the first time (Statistics Sweden, 2006).

Emerging adults with divorced or separated parents leave their parental homes earlier than other emerging adults (Bernhardt, Gahler, & Goldscheider, 2005). This is likely due not to divorce or separation *per se* but rather task overload (Weiss, 1979), possible conflicts in the home (Bernhardt et al., 2005), or it could simply be a logical step toward independence for a well-adjusted adolescent who is spending less time with parents (Grossmann, Grossmann, & Zimmermann, 1999).

Most adolescents have siblings. In 2003, 69% of adolescents had one or two siblings living at home, 11% had three to five siblings living at home, and 19% were the only child living at home (Statistics Sweden, 2005a). It is rare in Sweden to find multiple generations in one household. Although grandparents usually have a role in the family, it is not one of primary caregiver. Grandparents usually have independent lives from their children and grandchildren.

By the age of 17 at least 25% of adolescents have experienced their parents' separation/divorce. Compared to the 15% rate of 15 to 25 years ago, this is an increase. Although the divorce rate is high, 63% of adolescents between 13 and 17 live with both of their parents, 7% live with their mother and stepfather, 1% live with their father and stepmother, 22% live with their mother only, and 5% with their father only (Statistics Sweden, 2003b).

Friends and Peers/Youth Culture

In an international survey comparing 35 countries of the Americas and Europe, Swedish adolescents between the ages of 11 and 15 spend the least amount of time with their friends after school (WHO, 2004). It is also relevant to mention that, in order of importance, many Swedes between the ages of 16 and 19 believe that friends, family, and their free time are the most meaningful parts of their lives (Swedish National Board of Youth Affairs, 2005).

Considering that spending time with peers is important, it is not surprising to find that young people in Sweden have opportunities to meet in diverse ways. It may be through school, sports, or political organizations, to name a few. In Sweden, about 11% of 16-year-olds belong to a film club and about 7% belong to a choir or music club (Swedish National Board for Youth Affairs, 2005). Many Swedish adolescents also enjoy sports. Adolescents are well represented among sports organizations throughout the country (Swedish Sports Federation, 2004). Football/soccer, horseback riding, golf, and ice hockey remain the most popular activities (Statistics Sweden, 2010b).

Adolescent peer groups are usually in the form of small, closely knit groups or cliques of two to six friends who share values, interests, and activities. The exclusive clique provides security, acceptance, and a feeling of importance, all of which are important for developing self-identity. Cliques usually form or are formed from a large group or network of both boys and girls. Couples usually develop from these large groups and new cliques based on couples can develop or the old clique can be altered. Like their European counterparts, some common activities that Swedish adolescents do with their friends are going to cafés, going to concerts, shopping, playing games or musical instruments, singing, playing sports, or listening to music.

Bullying in Sweden has been a concern, although the prevalence is low. In a recent study comparing 35 countries, Swedish adolescents bullied and were victims of bullying the least (WHO, 2004). This may be due to the public awareness about bullying. Most schools and youth organizations have a program to prevent bullying and other offensive behavior. There is also a national organization, Children's Rights in Society, that focuses on helping those under 18 who are exposed to physical, mental, or sexual abuse, bullying, loneliness, or suicide. Another reason why bullying may have low prevalence in Sweden could be that youths are quite tolerant in terms of ethnicity, religion, and homosexuality. Furthermore, the government supports volunteer groups that oppose racism and xenophobia.

There are many organizations, including the Swedish National Board for Youth Affairs, set up for youth specifically. The National Council of Swedish Youth Organizations is a coordinating body and network for almost 100 Swedish and international youth organizations. Sports-affiliated organizations have the largest number of members (Swedish Sports Federation, 2004). A wide range of sports are offered, from horseback riding, running, soccer, baseball, and martial arts to kayaking, golf, and aerobics, to name just a few.

Since the 1960s, nationally sponsored youth reaction centers have been a meeting place for teenagers in Sweden. These centers were initially started to reduce youth crime and to keep teenagers off the streets during the evenings, weekends, and summers. Although these centers vary in structure, education of workers, resources, and supervision level, many host special events such as dances or field trips. Not until fairly recently have these centers been looked at critically. After studying a representative Swedish sample of teenagers and reaction center activity, Mahoney and Stattin (2000) concluded that low structured participation at centers was linked to antisocial teenage behavior and highly structured activity participation was linked to low antisocial teenage behavior, for both boys and girls.

Love and Sexuality

The age of consent for sexual activity is 15 years. The general view in Sweden is that one should wait for parenthood until one is an adult; however, it is accepted that youths have sex as long as they are monogamous and in love (Danielsson, Rogala, & Sundstrom, 2003). Abstinence before marriage is not expected and it is socially acceptable to have sex before marriage. The average age for first sexual intercourse is about 16 years (slightly earlier for girls than for boys), and it has remained so for the past 40 years (Forsberg, 2006; Lewin, Fugl-Meyer, Helmius, Lalos, & Månsson, 2000). Today, if an older adolescent has a boyfriend or girlfriend, it is acceptable and common to have them stay overnight, with parental knowledge. Although the views on sexuality are liberal, parents do not usually discuss sex freely in the home.

Although sex is an acceptable part of adolescent behavior, there is not an exceedingly high rate of sex-related problems in Sweden. This could be due to the widespread, free, youth gynecological clinics. Since 1975 the Swedish government has invested in the health promotion of teenagers, which includes issues involving drugs, alcohol, and reproductive health. At the youth clinics, contraception, reproductive health care, counseling, screening for disease/infections, and abortions up to 18 weeks are available (Edgardh, 2002). Despite advances in prevention and treatment of sexually transmitted diseases, there are more people living with HIV in Sweden than ever before and chlamydia has increased over 200% since 1997 (Swedish National Institute of Public Health, 2010).

Attitudes to contraceptive use are positive (Oddens & Milsom, 1996). Sweden was one of the first countries to provide government assistance for birth control, which it did as early as the 1930s. Over the past few decades, condom use has been increasing for those between the ages of 16 and 17 in Sweden (Herlitz, 2001). In general, however, youths are reporting other risky behaviors. In 2003 approximately one in four between the ages of 16 and 19 had experienced a one-night-stand sexual experience in the past 12 months, and 18% did so without using a condom (Herlitz, 2004). In a study by the Swedish National Institute of Health, approximately 35% of those between the ages of 18 to 25 had multiple sex partners in the past year (2001). It has also been reported that sexual risk behaviors seem to increase between the ages of 16 and 24, especially for young Swedish women (Herlitz & Forsberg, 2009).

In Sweden, there appears to be a strong and universal perception that having a child during adolescence is undesirable, and abortion is not discouraged. Teenage pregnancies are far less prevalent than in other Western countries (WHO, 2004). Although relatively low compared to other countries, the induced abortion rate in Sweden is increasing in all age groups except among teenagers (Swedish National Institute of Public Health, 2010). However, the incidence of unplanned pregnancies is higher in youth compared with the adult population in Sweden. The emergency contraception pill has been available for many years by prescription in Sweden, and in 2001 it became available over the counter.

For those youth who choose to give birth, social, economic, and educational support is available. Teen mothers usually receive help from their parents when it comes to early childcare, but daycare is also available. Due to the government and familial support, it is rare for a teenage mother to choose to put her child up for adoption. Even with subsidized daycare, schooling, and previous socioeconomic status, however, Swedish teen mothers risk a disadvantaged future. Olausson, Haglund, Ringback, Weitoft, and Cnattingius (2001) reported that, in a study of all women born in Sweden from 1941 to 1970 who were younger than age 30 when they first gave birth ($N = 888{,}044$), teenage mothers fared far worse in respect to welfare dependency and low education than mothers who gave birth in their twenties. In fact, women and men tend to have their first child later in Sweden than in other countries (Andersson, 1999). In 2003 the mean age for first-time parents was 29 years for women and 31 years for men (Statistics Sweden, 2004c).

Sexually transmitted diseases and infections are a high priority in public health education programs. Sweden has one of the lowest incidences of HIV in the world (Swedish Institute for Infectious Disease Control, 2004). This is likely due to the nationwide AIDS campaign in the late 1980s. Although there are few incidences of gonorrhea annually in Sweden, chlamydia incidence has increased for teenagers and the young adult population particularly (Swedish Institute for Infectious Disease Control, 2004).

Many young Swedes tend to meet potential romantic partners through friends, family, or at school (Trost, 1993; Trost & Levin, 2005). Most youths have a considerable amount of freedom when it comes to where, when, and how they will meet their present or future boyfriend or girlfriend. With the increased use of the Internet, Internet dating and chatting has become more popular with adolescents than in previous decades and one of the most visited websites in Sweden is a site for teenagers and young adults to chat, meet, and surf (Nielsen/Net Ratings, 2005).

Sweden has one of the most tolerant views of homosexuality. Many Swedes, especially women and young people, feel that gay people should be allowed to legally marry. For a decade now in Sweden, homosexual registered partnerships have had the same rights as married couples in the eyes of the law. Furthermore, many Swedes refer to gays who have civil union ceremonies as married couples. Although most young people would consider themselves accepting of homosexuality, many homosexual young people report discrimination.

Health Risk Behavior

Like most adolescents, Swedish youth engage in various risky behaviors. During adolescence, the majority try smoking, alcohol, and *snus* (moist Swedish chewing tobacco placed in upper lip). The government attempts to delay such behaviors since those under the age of 18 may not purchase beer, alcohol, or tobacco products. In principle, tobacco and alcohol advertising is banned. More 15–16 year olds are abstaining from alcohol than in the previous three decades (CAN, 2009). In the past few years, younger adolescents have shown a decrease in alcohol consumption but older adolescents have shown an increase. Compared to a decade ago, more youth are being treated today for alcohol poisoning and more young men have had alcohol-related deaths (National Board of Health and Welfare, 2005).

In terms of other drug habits, Swedish adolescents tend to use less than their counterparts from other countries. In a recent study comparing 30 countries ($N > 2{,}400$ per country) by the European School Survey Project on Alcohol and Other Drugs (ESPAD), Swedish teenagers consistently reported lower drug use, particularly for marijuana and hashish (7% compared to 21% for other countries). Furthermore, adolescents in Sweden reported less smoking in the past 30 days (23% compared to 35% for other countries).

Another risk behavior during adolescence seems to be driving a car. Since the legal minimum driving age is 18 years, many attempt to get their driver's license in their late teens or during their early twenties. In 2001, 57% of all 18- to 24-year-olds had a driver's license. Although this group makes up only 7% of those with a driver's license in Sweden, they—particularly men of this age group—are overrepresented in traffic accidents and fatal car accidents (Gustafson & Magnusson, 2004). Of the 511 fatal car accidents in 2001, nearly 20% involved a driver between the ages of 18 and 24. The vast majority of these fatal accidents were due to excessive speed, being under the influence of drugs or alcohol, or lack of seat belt usage (Gustafson & Magnusson, 2004; Engstrom, Gregersen, Hernetkoski, Keskinen, & Nyberg, 2003).

Since most adolescents are not of legal age to drive and getting a driver's license is considered fairly costly, bicycling is a popular alternative form of transportation as well as a sporting activity, and every cyclist under the age of 15 must legally wear a helmet. Helmets must also be worn when driving any type of moped. Mopeds are quite popular with teenagers in Sweden since they are inexpensive, no practical test is required, and one must only be 15 to drive one.

The other most common problem behaviors for adolescents are theft, truancy, and fare dodging. Based on anonymous self-report questionnaires from 5,300 to 8,200 adolescents during 1995 to 2003, over half of the adolescents reported a theft-related act within the past year and approximately 40% reported being truant (Ring, 2005). More serious thefts and acts involving violence are far less common. Only 1 in 10 have been involved with drugs or involved in a violent act toward another person.

Education

Like other countries in Northern Europe, Swedes value education. Their near 100% literacy rate is evidence of early learning. Compulsory schooling has been in practice for over 150 years. Today, nine years of compulsory schooling from the age of seven apply, and all education throughout the public school system is cost-free including meals, transport, health services, and educational materials.

When youths reach approximately age 15 to 16, the vast majority attend upper secondary school education. At present, there are 17 national three-year upper secondary education programs and most include workplace training. Grades are on a four-point basis of fail, pass, pass with distinction, and pass with special distinction.

For those who have difficulty with schoolwork and are attending regular classes in compulsory or upper secondary schools, special support is given. There are many special programs and special schools for those in need of additional assistance based on cognitive challenges. There are special remedial classes for students with functional cognitive disabilities as well as for students with social and emotional problems. If a student is having difficulty with schoolwork, he or she is entitled to additional help from a special education teacher inside and outside of class.

University education is free in Sweden at all levels. Anyone up to the age of 54 can receive study aid for university studies in Sweden for a maximum of 240 weeks. Students are also given a weekly allowance from the state for living expenses.

Work

Most adolescents are involved in school and organizations and are not employed in the traditional sense of the word. Common types of adolescent employment are usually part-time, service, or manual labor types of jobs. Summer jobs are common for Swedish adolescents. During 2002–2003,

of the youth between the ages of 13 and 15, approximately 19% had a summer job and of the youth between 16 and 18, approximately 61% had a summer job (Statistics Sweden, 2005a). Today, the figures remain about the same although youth may report having difficulty finding summer or seasonal work (Statistics Sweden, 2010d). Youth between the ages of 14 and 18 may work legally up to 35 to 40 hours a week, with no night work. Youth under the age of 13 may not work legally.

In a study of a representative cohort of 584 Swedish 16- to 19-year-olds commissioned by the Swedish National Board of Youth Affairs (2005), it was reported that studying at a university for at least three years, traveling internationally for a year or more, and trying out various jobs were what many expected to be doing in the coming years. Since Swedes tend to value and enjoy travel, many older adolescents try to combine travel and working internationally as au pairs, sport instructors, manual laborers, or service personnel, among others. Moreover, approximately 20% of all new university students in Sweden under the age of 26 have studied abroad for at least one semester (National Agency for Higher Education, 2005).

Media

Compared to other countries within and outside the European Union, Sweden is advanced in the use of the Internet, computers, and mobile telephones. In 2009 most of the compulsory schools in Sweden had access to the Internet (Swedish National Agency for Education, 2009). It is not uncommon to have several computers in the home. Like other Scandinavian countries, the broadband infrastructure is widely used in Sweden, where only 7% of the population has never used the Internet and 89% of the population between 16 and 74 have access to Internet in their private homes (Statistics Sweden, 2009). On average, half of those between the ages of 15 and 24 use the Internet daily. When using the computer, adolescent girls spend time surfing, emailing, seeking specific information, and doing homework and boys tend to surf, email, play games, and download games/music (Swedish Media Council, 2010; Swedish National Board of Youth Affairs, 2005).

In the 1970s only a few channels were broadcast on TV. Today, the youth have access to a plethora of national and international programs and the majority have their own television in their room (Statistics Sweden, 2009). Adolescents get a lot of exposure to many different cultures and languages, particularly English. Unlike some countries, foreign TV programs broadcast in Sweden have subtitles rather than dubbing. Adolescents spend approximately two hours per day watching TV or movies in Sweden.

Cellular or mobile phones are common in Sweden. In fact, there are more registered cellular telephones than land-line telephones. Of youth between ages 10 and 18, 95% of the girls and 92% of the boys have their own cell phones (Statistics Sweden, 2009). Cell phones are used to make phone calls, access the Internet, and for texting messages.

Although Swedish youth are not unique in listening to and enjoying music, the importance of music has a history and is instilled early in life. Free government-subsidized public concerts have been held at the outdoor parks for decades and they are a unique tradition where both new and internationally and nationally well-established performers take part. The Swedish dedication to music, recorded or live, is also evident in the educational system, where all students are encouraged to take at least one year in music composition and given an opportunity to gain training in any of the hundreds of music schools across the country. This early music education can make a young Swedish listener a very sophisticated listener. Thus, it is no surprise that although a small country, Sweden has become the world's third largest exporter of popular music after the United States and the United Kingdom, with revenues exceeding two billion SEK (Forss, 1999).

Politics and Military

Voting participation in general elections has been slowly decreasing during the past 30 years (Bennulf & Hedberg, 1999). According to a national survey conducted from 1980 to 2004, young people between the ages of 16 and 24 have consistently not been active in political parties (Statistics Sweden, 2005c). However, there was a substantial increase in voter participation for those between the ages of 18 and 29 from 12% at the 2004 European parliamentary election to 40% at the 2009 European parliamentary election (Statistics Sweden, 2010e). It is important to note that compared to adolescents in Europe, the Baltic nations, and the United States, Swedish adolescents and emerging adults tend to report more trust in politicians' willingness to listen and find out about what the public wants (Amna & Munck, 2003).

Based on large-cohort studies of young people in Sweden, 80% report that they plan to vote (Swedish National Board of Youth Affairs, 2003). At the 2002 national election, those who were eligible to vote for the first time and were between the ages of 18 and 22 had a participation rate of 70% (Statistics Sweden, 2003a).

Military service is voluntary in Sweden during times of peace. One can apply if one wants to, take admissions tests, and if accepted, can choose whether to take part in military service or not. In the event of crisis, however, everyone living in Sweden as well as Swedish citizens living abroad between the ages of 16 and 70 will be expected to give service in some form.

Unique Issues

Generally, Swedish adolescents are physically, mentally, and socially healthy, particularly when compared with other nations. For many observers, Swedish adolescents seem to be growing up in an ideal and unique country. A country with four seasons, easy access to the Internet and outdoors, free education where one is given an allowance for existing, an allowance for studying, an allowance to live properly if needed as well as paid parental leave of 480 days which can be used any time before the child turns eight years old. Moreover, Sweden is among the first countries to view spanking as a criminal offense, prohibit smoking in restaurants, cafes, and bars, provide early sex education and legalize same-sex marriages.

Swedish adolescents however do have a growing number of expectations set upon them by society and themselves. Although Swedish youth generally do not have to concern themselves with basic needs, those of today report more emotional problems than their counterparts from previous decades. Why this is the trend is unclear, but one underlying explanation could be that they have fewer demands on their time than in the past. For example, regarding the possibility of having a full-time job after high school/gymnasium compared to 20 years ago, many may study further although they would prefer to have employment. More youth today than in the previous decades report doing nothing and having no obligations such as military service, work in the home or outside the home, or studies. Every generation of young people in every country has obstacles from various domains that they must tackle in order to emerge as adults on the other side.

References and Further Reading

Amna, E., & Munck, I. (2003). Forskarreflektion [Researchers' reflections]. In I Bohlin (Ed.), *De kallar oss unga* [They call us young] (pp. 188–215). Stockholm, Sweden: National Board of Youth.

Andersson, B., Hansagi, H., Damstrom, T. K., & Hibell, B. (2002). Long-term trends in drinking habits among Swedish teenagers: National School Surveys 1971–1999. *Drug Alcohol Review, 21,* 252–260.

Andersson, G. (1999). Childbearing trends in Sweden 1961–1995. *European Journal of Population,* 15, 1–24.

Andersson, G. (2004). Demographic trends in Sweden: An update of childbearing and nuptiality up to 2002. *Demographic Research,* 11, 95–110.

Bennulf, M., & Hedberg, P. (1999). Utanfor demokratin. Om det minskade valdeltagandets sociale och politiska rotter [Outside of democracy. On the social and political roots of declining voter participation]. In E. Amna (Ed.), *Valdeltagande i forandring* [Changes in voter participation]. Stockholm, Sweden: Demokratiutredningens Forskarvolym.

Bernhardt, E., Gahler, M., & Goldscheider, F. (2005). Childhood family structure and routes out of the parental home in Sweden. *Acta Sociologica, 48,* 99–115.

Billari, F. C., & Kohler, H. P. (2004). Patterns of low and lowest fertility. *Population Studies, 58,* 161–176.

Bjorklund, A., Ginther, D. K., & Sundstrom, M. (2004). *Family structure and child outcomes in the United States and Sweden: Provisional working paper.* Discussion paper series. Bonn, Germany: Institute for the Study of Labor.

Boulton, M., Bucci, E., & Hawker, D. (1999). Swedish and English secondary school pupils' attitudes towards, and concepts of, bullying: Concurrent links with bully/victim involvement. *Scandinavian Journal of Psychology, 40,* 277–284.

Bygdeman, M., & Lindahl, K. (1994). *Sex education and reproductive health in Sweden in the 20th century.* Report for the International Conference on Population Development in Cairo. Stockholm, Sweden: Swedish Government Official Reports.

CAN. (2009). *Skolelevers drogvanor 2009* [Students drug behaviors 2009]. Stockholm, Sweden: CAN.

Carlberg, G. (1989). *Dynamisk utvecklingspsykologi* [Dynamic developmental psychology]. Stockholm, Sweden: Natur och Kultur.

Carlsson, U. (Ed.). (2005). *Sweden Mediebarometer 2004*. Stockholm, Sweden: Nordicom Sweden.

Church of Sweden. (2005). *Kyrkostatistik* [Church statistics]. Retrieved from www.svenskakyrkan.se

Collins, W. A. (1991). Shared views and parent–adolescent relationships. *New Directions for Child Development, 51*, 103–110.

Council of Europe. (2001). *Recent demographic development in Europe*. Strasbourg, France: Council of Europe Publishing.

Daun, A. (1996). *Swedish mentality*. University Park, PA: Pennsylvania University Press.

Danielsson, M., Rogala, C., & Sundstrom, K. (2003). *Fa tonarsgraviditeter I Sverige—jamforelse mellan fem bast lander* [Few teenage pregnancies in Sweden—Comparison between five of the best countries]. *Lakartidningen, 100*, 2003–2006.

Diener, E., Diener, M., & Diener, C. (1995). Factors predicting the subjective well-being of nations. *Journal of Personality and Social Psychology, 69*, 851–864.

Donnellan, D. M., Ge, X., & Wenk, E. (2000). Cognitive abilities in adolescence-limited and life-course persistent criminal offenders. *Journal of Abnormal Psychology*, 109, 396–402.

Edgardh, K. (2002). Adolescent sexual health in Sweden. *Sexually Transmitted Infection*, 78, 352–356.

Ekman, J., & Todosijevic, S. (2003). *Unga demokrater—En översikt av den aktuella forskningen om ungdom, politik och skolans demokrativärden* [Young democrats—An overview of youth, politics and school democracy research]. Stockholm, Sweden: Swedish National Agency for School Improvement.

Engstrom, I., Gregersen, N. P., Hernetkoski, K., Keskinen, E., & Nyberg, A. (2003). *Young novice drivers, driver education and training: Literature review*. Linkoping, Sweden: Swedish National Road and Transport Research Institute.

Engstrom, L. M. (1996). Sweden. In P. De Knop et al. (Eds.), *Worldwide trends in youth sports*. Champaign, IL: Human Kinetics.

Erikson, E. (1968). *Identity: Youth and crisis*. London, UK: Faber and Faber.

European School Survey Project on Alcohol and Other Drugs. (2005). Retrieved from www.espad.org

Forsberg, M. (2006). *Unga och sexualitet* [The young and sexuality]. Stockholm, Sweden: National Board of Health.

Forss, K. (1999). *Tuning in—A summary about the Swedish music export successes*. Expert Group for Studies in Public Economic Report. Stockholm, Sweden: Ministry of Finance.

Government Office of Sweden. (2000). *Changed relations between the state and the Church of Sweden*. Fact sheet. Stockholm, Sweden: Ministry of Culture.

Grossmann, K. E., Grossmann, K., & Zimmermann, P. (1999). A wider view of attachment and exploration: Stability and change during the years of immaturity. In J. Cassidy & P. R. Shaver (Eds.), *Handbook of attachment: Theory, research, and clinical applications* (pp. 760–786). New York, NY: Guilford Press.

Gustafson, A., & Magnusson, P. (2004). *18–24 ariga personbilsforare inblandade i dodsolyckor ar 2001—Analys av Vagverkets djupstudiematerial* [18-to 24-year-old licensed drivers in fatal accidents during the year 2001: An intensive study by the Swedish Road Administration]. Stockholm, Sweden: Swedish Road Administration (SRA).

Guttormsson, U., Andersson, B., & Hibell, B. (2004). *Ungdomars drogvanor* [Youth drug use]. 1994–2003. Report 75. Stockholm, Sweden: Center for Information on Alcohol and Other Drugs.

Haggstrom-Nordin, E., Hanson, U., & Tydén, T. (2002). Sex behavior among high school students in Sweden: Improvement in contraceptive use over time. *Journal of Adolescent Health*, 30, 288–295.

Herlitz, C. (2001). *Allmanheten och HIV/AIDS kunskaper, attityder och beteenden 1989–2000* [The public and HIV/AIDS knowledge, attitudes, and behavior 1989– 2000]. Stockholm, Sweden: National Institute of Public Health.

Herlitz, C. (2004). *Allmanheten och HIV/AIDS kunskaper, attityder och beteenden 1987–2003* [The public and HIV/AIDS knowledge, attitudes, and behavior 1987–2003]. Stockholm, Sweden: National Institute of Public Health.

Herlitz, C. A., & Forsberg, M. (2009). Sexual behaviour and risk assessment in different age cohorts in the general population of Sweden (1989–2007). *Scandinavian Journal of Public Health, 38*, 32–39.

Institute of Higher Education. (2005). *Academic ranking of world universities—2005*. Shanghai, China: Shanghai Jiao Tong University. Retrieved from http://ed.sjtu.edu.cn

Karlberg, J. (2002). Secular trends in pubertal development. *Hormone Research, 57*, 19–30.

Kenyon P., & Barker, M. (1998). Attitudes towards meat-eating in vegetarian and non-vegetarian teenage girls in England: An ethnographic approach. *Appetite, 30*, 185–198.

Kriminalstatistik 2004 [Crime statistics 2004). Official Statistics of Sweden. Stockholm, Sweden: National Council for Crime Prevention.

Lange, L., Loow, H., Bruchfeld, S., & Hedlund, E. (1997). *Utsatthet for etniskt och politiskt relaterat hot m.m., spridning av rasistiskt och antirasistisk propaganda samt attityder till demokrati m.m. bland skolelever* [Vulnerability for ethnically and politically related threats, etc., spreading of racist and antisemitic propaganda as well as attitudes to democracy, etc., among school students]. Stockholm, Sweden: Stockholm University Centrum for Immigrant Research and Swedish National Council for Crime Prevention.

Larsson, C. L., Klock, K. S., Astrøm, A. N., Haugejorden, O., & Johansson, G. (2001). Food habits of young Swedish and Norwegian vegetarians and omnivores. *Public Health Nutrition, 4*, 1004–1014.

Larsson, C., Ronnlund, U., Johansson, G., & Dahlgren, L. (2003). Veganism as status passage: The process of becoming a vegan among youths in Sweden. *Appetite, 41*, 61–67.

Lewin, B., Fugl-Meyer, K., Helmius, G., Lalos, A., & Månsson, S. A. (Eds.). (2000). *Sex in Sweden*. Stockholm, Sweden: National Institute of Health.

Ljung, B. O., Bergsten-Brucefors, A., & Lindgren, G. (1974). The secular trend in physical growth in Sweden. *Annals of Human Biology, 1*, 245–256.

Lund, G. (2003, December 9). Swedish Minister for International Economy and Finance. *The Swedish vision of 24-hour public administration and e-government*. Cisco Public Services Summit. Stockholm, Sweden.

Lundgren, E., Heimer, G., Westerstrand, J., & Kalliokoski, A. (2000). Captured queen: Men's violence against women in "equal" Sweden—A prevalence study. Report for the The Crime Victim Compensation and Support Authority. Stockholm, Sweden: Fritzes Offentliga Publikationer.

Mahoney, J., & Stattin, H. (2000). Leisure activities and adolescent antisocial behavior: The role of structure and social context. *Journal of Adolescence, 23*, 113–127.

Moffitt, T. (1993). Adolecence-limited and life-course persistent antisocial behavior: A developmental taxonomy. *Psychological Review, 100*, 674–701.

National Agency for Higher Education. (2005). *Swedish universities and university colleges*. Annual report 2005. Stockholm, Sweden: National Agency for Higher Education Report Series.

National Board of Health and Welfare, The. (2005). *Ungdomars behov av samhallets stod* [Youth's need for social support]. Stockholm, Sweden: National Board of Health and Welfare.

Neumark-Sztainer, D., Story, M., Perry, C., & Casey, M. A. (1999). Factors influencing food choices of adolescents: Findings from focus-group discussions with adolescents. *Journal of the American Dietary Association, 99*, 929–937.

Nielsen/Net Ratings. (2005, May 26). *Svenskar tillbringade 53 miljoner timmar pa webben I april. Plus 6 miljoner pa ett ar* [Swedes spend 53 million hours on the Internet in April, and 6 million hours on the Internet in one year]. Press release.

Nobel Foundation. (2001). *The Nobel Prize: The first 100 years.* A. Wallin Levinovitz & N. Ringertz (Eds.). London, UK: Imperial College Press.

Nordstrom, B. J. (2000). *Scandinavia since 1500.* Minneapolis, MN: University of Minnesota Press.

Norstedts. (2003). *Nordstedts Engelska ordbok* [English dictionary]. Stockholm, Sweden: Norstedts Academic Publishers.

Oddens, B., & Milsom, I. (1996). Contraceptive practices and attitudes in Sweden 1994. *Acta Obstetricia Gynecologica Scandinavica, 75,* 932–940.

Olausson, P. O., Haglund, B., Ringback Weitoft, G., & Cnattingius, S. (2001). Teenage childbearing and long-term socioeconomic consequences: A case study in Sweden. *Family Planning Perspectives, 33,* 70–74.

Olsson, G. I., & von Knorring, A. L. (1999). Adolescent depression: Prevalence in Swedish high school students. *Acta Psychiatrica Scandinavica, 99,* 324–331.

Onland-Moret, N. C., Peeters, P. H., van Gils, C. H., Clavel-Chapelon, F., Key, T., Tjønneland, A., et al. (2005). Age at menarche in relation to adult height: The EPIC study. *American Journal of Epidemiology, 162,* 1–10.

Osterman, K., Bjorkqvist, K. Lagerspetz, K., with Kaukiainen, A., Landau, S. F., Fraczek, A., et al. (1998). Cross-cultural evidence of female indirect aggression. *Aggressive Behavior, 24,* 1–8.

Phinney, J. S. (1999). Ethnic identity and self-esteem: Review and integration of literature. *Hispanic Journal of Behavioral Sciences, 13,* 193–203.

Ring, J. (2005). *Theft, drugs and violence among ninth grade youth. Results from five self-report surveys.* Stockholm, Sweden: National Council for Crime Prevention.

Ring, J., & Morgentau, S. (2005). *Intolerance: Antisemitic, homophobic, Islamophobic, and anti-immigrant tendencies among young people.* Stockholm, Sweden: Swedish National Council for Crime Prevention.

Ringback Weitoft, G., & Rosén, M. (2005). Is perceived nervousness and anxiety a predictor of premature mortality and severe morbidity? A longitudinal follow-up of the Swedish survey of living conditions. *Journal of Epidemiology and Community Health, 59,* 794–798.

Romelsjo, A. (1987). Decline in alcohol-related problems in Sweden greatest among young people. *British Journal of Addiction, 82,* 1111–11124.

Schoon, C. (2004). *Traffic legislation and safety in Europe concerning the moped and the A1 category (125 cc) motorcycle. A literature and questionnaire study commissioned by the Swedish National Road Administration.* Leidschendam, The Netherlands: Institute for Road Safety Research.

Scott, F. D. (1989). *Sweden: The nation's history.* Carbondale, IL: Southern Illinois University Press.

Standar, R. (Ed.). *Official criminal statistics of Sweden 2004.* Stockholm, Sweden: National Council for Crime Prevention.

Statistics Sweden. (2003a). *Allmanna valen 2002* [General elections in 2002]. Stockholm, Sweden: Statistics Sweden.

Statistics Sweden. (2003b). *Befolkningsstatistik 2002* [Population statistics 2002]. Stockholm, Sweden: Statistics Sweden.

Statistics Sweden. (2003c). *Levnadsforhallanden. Offer for vald och hotelser bland kvinnor och man* [Life circumstances. Victims of violence and threats among women and men]. Stockholm, Sweden: Statistics Sweden.

Statistics Sweden. (2004a). *Sveriges befolkning efter kon och alder 2003* [Sweden's population based on sex and age]. Stockholm, Sweden: Statistics Sweden.

Statistics Sweden. (2004b). *Time children spend with their parents.* Demographic Reports [In Swedish]. Stockholm, Sweden: Statistics Sweden.

Statistics Sweden. (2004c). *Women and men in Sweden: Facts and figures.* Orebro, Sweden: Statistics Sweden.

Statistics Sweden. (2005a). *Barnens villkor* [Children's living conditions]. Life Conditions Report 110. Stockholm, Sweden: Statistics Sweden.

Statistics Sweden. (2005b). *Befolkningsstatistik i Sammandrag 1960–2004* [Summary of population statistics]. Stockholm, Sweden: Statistics Sweden.

Statistics Sweden. (2005c). *Participation in the European Parliament election in 2004.* Stockholm, Sweden: Statistics Sweden.

Statistics Sweden. (2006). *Boendeort avgör när man flyttar hemifrån.* Välfärdsrapport, 3. [Where you live reveals when one moves out of the childhood home]. Stockholm. Sweden.

Statistics Sweden. (2009). *Social protection in the Nordic countries 2006/07.* Stockholm Sweden.

Statistics Sweden. (2010a). *Population statistics.* Stockholm, Sweden: Statistics Sweden.

Statistics Sweden. (2010b). *Källa SCB tidning, 1* [Source SCB journal]. Stockholm, Sweden: Statistics Sweden.

Statistics Sweden. (2010c). *Women and men in 2010: Facts and figures.* Stockholm, Sweden: Statistics Sweden.

Statistics Sweden. (2010d). *Arbetskraftsundersökningen kvartal 1 och 2 i 2010* [Labor force survey quarter 1 and 2 in 2010]. Stockholm, Sweden: Statistics Sweden.

Statistics Sweden. (2010e). *European Parliament election 2009.* Stockholm, Sweden: Statistics Sweden.

Stattin, H., & Trost, K. (2000). When do preschool conduct problems link to future social adjustment problems and when do they not? In L. Bergman et al. (Eds.), *Developmental science and the holistic approach.* Mahwah, NJ: Lawrence Erlbaum Associates.

Swedish Academy. (2003). *Svenska Akademiens ordlista over svenska* [Swedish Academy's dictionary]. Stockholm, Sweden: Norstedts Academic Publishers.

Swedish Armed Forces. (2005). *Facts and figures.* Stockholm, Sweden: Swedish Armed Forces.

Swedish Institute for Infectious Disease Control. (2004). *Infectious diseases 2004.* Annual report of the epidemiological unit. Solna, Sweden: Swedish Institute for Infectious Disease Control.

Swedish Media Council. (2010). *Ungar och medier 2010: Fakta om barns och ungas användning och upplevelser av medier.* [Youth and Media 2010: Facts about children and youths' use and experiences of media]. Stockholm: Swedish Media Council.

Swedish National Agency for Education. (2009). *Facts and figures 2009: Pre-school activities, school-age childcare, schools and adult education in Sweden.* Stockholm, Sweden: National Agency for Education.

Swedish National Board of Youth Affairs. (2003). *Unga medborgare* [Young citizens]. Stockholm, Sweden: DocuSys Press.

Swedish National Board of Youth Affairs. (2005). *Arenor for Alla. En studie om ungas kultur och fritidsvanor* [An arena for all. A study about youth culture and free time activities]. Stockholm, Sweden: Bodoni Press.

Swedish National Institute of Public Health. (2010). *Samtal om sexualitet* [Conversation on sexuality]. Ostersund, Sweden: Swedish National Institute of Public Health.

Swedish Sports Federation. (2004). *Idrotten i siffror* [Sports in numbers]. Stockholm, Sweden: Swedish Sports Federation.

Trost, J. (1979). *Unmarried cohabitation.* Vasteras, Sweden: International Library.

Trost, J. (1993). *Famlijen i Sverige* [The family in Sweden]. Stockholm, Sweden: Liber.

Trost, J., & Levin, I. (2005). Scandinavian families. In B. N. Adams & J. Trost (Eds.), *Handbook of world families.* London, UK: Sage.

Trost, K. (2002). *A new look at parenting during adolescence: Reciprocal interactions in everyday life*. Orebro, Sweden: Orebro University Library Press.

Tydén, T., Olsson, S. E., & Haggstrom-Nordin, E. (2001). Improved use of contraceptives, attitudes to pornography, and sexual harassment among female university students. *Women's Health Issues, 11*, 87–94.

Virta, E., Sam, D., & Westin, C. (2004). Adolescents with Turkish background in Norway and Sweden: A comparative study of their psychological adaptation. *Scandinavian Journal of Psychology, 45*, 15–25.

Virta, E., & Westin, C. (1999). *Psychosocial adjustment of adolescents with immigrant background in Sweden*. Stockholm, Sweden: Centre for Research on International Migration and Ethnic Relations.

Wangby, M., Magnusson, D., & Stattin, H. (2005). Time trends in the adjustment of Swedish teenage girls: A 26-year comparison of 15-year-olds. *Scandinavian Journal of Psychology, 46*, 145–156.

Weiss, R. S. (1979). *Going it alone: The family life and social situation of the parent*. New York, NY: Basic Books.

Wiesbrock, A. (2011). The integration of immigrants in Sweden: A model for the European Union? *International Migration, 49*.

World Health Organization (WHO). (2004). *Young people's health in context: Health Behavior in School-aged Children (HBSC) study: International report from the 2002/2002 survey*. Copenhagen, Denmark: WHO.

Chapter 24
United Kingdom
John Coleman and Debi Roker

Background Information

The United Kingdom is located off the coast of mainland Europe. It consists of four countries: England, Scotland, Wales, and Northern Ireland. The UK has a monarch, Queen Elizabeth II, but in effect is a parliamentary democracy. Scotland, Wales, and Northern Ireland have some devolved powers, and there are legal as well as social, cultural, and historical differences between the countries. The legal relationship between the four countries is a topic of regular political and public debate. The UK is a member of the European Union, but has opted out of the eurozone, and therefore has retained its own currency. The country has a population of approximately 61 million.

The UK has a long history as a colonial power, an era that could be said to have come to an end with the granting of independence to India in 1947. Queen Elizabeth II remains the titular head of the Commonwealth, a body having a membership of 53 countries. As a result of Britain's colonial past, a significant proportion of its population today comes from ethnic minorities, representing African, African-Caribbean, Asian, and Chinese cultures. Minority cultures account for approximately 7.9% according to the last census, held in 2001. In terms of family, the UK has a relatively high divorce rate, and approximately 25% of all children grow up in families headed by a single parent. The UK is well known for its welfare system, and its national health service has been copied the world over. However, in recent years it has become more difficult to fund both education and health services, and these public services are now operated by a mixture of public and private finance.

Note that in the rest of this chapter, information and trends that are generally applicable across all four countries of the UK will be referred to, where findings for each country are not available. However, there are still clear legal or social differences on some issues. Readers are therefore referred to the references at the end of the chapter for further information about these issues.

Period of Adolescence

Adolescence has been recognized as a separate stage of development in the UK for at least 150 years, since Victorian times (Coleman & Hendry, 1999). Indeed, some of the earliest recorded measurements of growth around puberty were taken in Britain at the famous private school, Rugby, in the middle of the nineteenth century, and are still used as a baseline in the twenty-first century. In more recent times, during the 1950s and 1960s, the physician James Tanner worked at London's Institute of Child Health and established the Tanner guidelines of pubertal status, used across the globe to this day.

The current age of menarche in Britain is usually considered to be 11.8 years. This has changed hardly at all since Tanner's work in the 1960s (Tanner, 1978). However, it is clear that various social indicators of puberty are to be seen in children at very much younger ages, and evidence suggests that 25% of girls will have started their periods before their eleventh birthday (Coleman & Hendry, 1999).

The ending of adolescence is certainly something that has shown major change over the past 20 years, and adolescence now continues longer than it did a generation ago. This can be judged as much by social factors as by physical and emotional ones. For example, in the twenty-first century very few young people in the UK go to work at age 16, and most will go on to some form of further education or training until the age of 18. Furthermore, approximately 46% of British pupils now go to university (Coleman & Brooks, 2009). In addition to this prolongation of education, more young people stay on in the family home until their mid-twenties, and in this respect Britain is becoming more like some southern European countries (Bradley & Hickman, 2004; Coleman & Schofield, 2005).

Britain is not a country where traditional rites of passage are in use, apart from those seen in religious ceremonies such as confirmation. The entry to adolescence can be marked in many different ways, but is often seen by young people and parents as being the beginning of the teenage years, that is, at age 13. Most children in state education transfer to secondary school at age 11, so this also marks an important transition. As far as definitions of adulthood are concerned, this is a subject fraught with uncertainty in the UK. In relation to sexual behavior, the age of consent is 16. At this age young people can also join the army, with their parents' consent. A young person can drive a car and get married at 17, and yet he or she cannot vote until the age of 18 (Roche & Tucker, 2004).

However, many of these indicators of adulthood are contradicted by the state of continuing financial dependence experienced by almost all young people, often until their early twenties. While the concept of "emerging adulthood" is not one that is current in the UK, nonetheless it is certainly the case that most young people from the age of 16 onward experience an "in-between" stage before reaching adulthood proper.

Beliefs

It is difficult to be specific about the "beliefs" of all young people in the UK. However, it is possible to make some observations and cite some research findings about belief systems and religion. Although no firm figures are available, anecdotal evidence suggests that the majority of young people do not identify with a specific religion and thus do not attend or follow religious events or ceremonies. However, a minority of young people follow formal faiths, broadly reflecting the cultural makeup of the UK (Garratt, 2004). The most common formal religious beliefs are Anglican, Hindu, Sikh, Judaism, and Islam. Many young people describe themselves as having spiritual beliefs; that is, a belief in a greater being or entity.

In terms of broader beliefs, most research has demonstrated generally liberal attitudes among young people. Thus, for example, the majority of young people are tolerant and accepting toward those with different political or religious views, those growing up in a range of family types, and those people who are gay or lesbian. This said, however, there is a minority of young people who hold very illiberal views. There is some evidence of a growing support among some young people for far right and anti-immigration policies. This is a pattern repeated among young people in a number of European countries, and is most common in socially deprived areas. In all the surveys undertaken into this topic among UK youth, higher levels of education have been found to be correlated with more open and tolerant attitudes (see, for example, Eden & Roker, 2002; Rogers, Rogers, Vyrost, & Lovas, 2004; Wilkinson & Mulgan, 1995).

Gender

Over the course of the past century the UK, along with most other Western countries, has moved toward equality of opportunity for girls and boys in education. In most cases, boys and girls attend the same schools, do the same lessons, and take the same examinations. In spite of this, there are obvious social differences; this is seen especially in play among pre-teens and in the choice of games and activities in the older groups. For most of the time from age seven or eight onward, boys and girls play in same-sex groups, and it is not until the age of 13 or 14 that this begins to shift, with the two genders starting to come together in their after-school activities.

In terms of educational choice, boys and girls in Britain tend to study very similar subjects until the age of 16, when the first major examination, the GCSE, takes place. However, at this stage it is apparent that girls outperform boys, especially in arts subjects, and there has been much discussion about why this should be so. It seems most likely that more boys than girls, especially those of lower ability, are disaffected with school, and therefore less motivated toward schoolwork at this age.

Turning now to the stage from 16 onward, here again young women continue to outperform young men in examinations. However, gendered subject choice becomes more apparent at this stage, and it is striking that boys are much more likely to choose science subjects, while girls opt for the arts and humanities. Already at this point, the two genders can be seen moving toward very different career options.

A growing range of vocational education courses is available to young people in the UK. However, these too are heavily gendered, with the majority of young women doing certain courses (such as hairdressing and child care) and young men doing others (car maintenance, engineering). This pattern is much less noticeable in single-sex schools, where there is evidence of less gender stereotyping around subject areas. Considerable effort is under way, particularly in schools and colleges, to challenge some of these gender stereotypes. However, the stereotypes are still pervasive and have considerable influence on many young people's future jobs and careers (Coleman & Roker, 1998).

One area where gender differences are especially apparent is that of physical development. Young people in Britain are no different from others across the globe in that girls begin their pubertal development at an earlier stage than boys. There is approximately an 18-month disparity between the genders in this respect (Tanner, 1978). Another difference is that girls are generally more sensitive to issues about body image and more affected by images of the "ideal" body shape. This leads to a greater dissatisfaction with the body among early adolescent girls and more anxiety for them about their growth and development at this stage. This is seen to be associated with the higher incidence of such things as eating disorders among girls of this age, and may be linked to some extent with the role of the media (Graham, 2004).

The Self

Young people in the UK, like those in most similar countries, have complex and many-sided views of themselves. There are many theories about the self and identity, and different views of

how best to understand the development of the self-concept. Turning first to the physical self, girls in particular show less satisfaction with their bodies, as we have seen, and this leads to an overall lowering of self-esteem during early adolescence. Studies show that in this stage around puberty girls have lower self-esteem than boys, but the disparity disappears with increasing age.

What factors affect the way young people see themselves? We know that the views of parents are paramount. Children and teenagers are strongly influenced by their parents and by the degree to which parents are able to place a positive value on their sons and daughters. However, as adolescence begins, the views of the peer group also become important, and young people are very much influenced in their perceptions of themselves by how they believe their peers see them. This is particularly the case in the early years of adolescence. As young people grow older and more confi-dent in themselves, they are able to develop a more rounded self-concept, one that is not so depen-dent on the views of others (Coleman & Roker, 1998).

There has been a great deal of interest in the notion of self-esteem in the UK, and in this the nation has been very much influenced by the importance placed on the concept in the United States. In schools and in community settings, programs have been developed that aim to enhance self-esteem, and it has become a key element in work with socially excluded or marginalized young people. We also know from research that many factors affect the trajectory of self-esteem during adolescence. Of course, some young people show no change in levels of self-esteem during these years. Others, however, experience enhanced self-esteem because of success in such things as sports or schoolwork, while some may experience a reduction in their level of self-esteem because of difficult family circumstances, bullying at school, or other negative influences.

The relation between race, culture, and the self has been prominent in the UK since the late twentieth century. Various writers have identified differential outcomes for the UK's cultural and ethnic groups, in terms of such things as identity and self-esteem, and education, employment, and crime (see Bhattacharyya & Gabriel 2004, for a useful review). Negative outcomes in many of these respects are more common among black young people, and among black young men in particular. However, there are many cultures in Britain, and self-concept development for Asian or Chinese young people is very different from that of black young people (who have been the primary focus of research to date). There has also been some interest in mixed race (or "dual heritage") adoles-cents, with research showing that many such young people have a positive view of themselves. However, there remains a minority for whom their mixed-race background has a powerful and not always positive impact on their self-concept. This is often linked to racism and discrimination within a predominantly white country (Bhattacharyya & Gabriel, 2004).

Family Relationships

There has been an increased amount of research in recent years into parenting and family relation-ships in the UK. A number of conclusions can be drawn from this, particularly in relation to family structures, parent–adolescent relationships, leaving home, and the experiences of young people who do not live with their families. Young people in the UK today grow up in a range of family structures. These include single-parent households, step-families, two-parent families, and, increas-ingly, families headed by gay and lesbian individuals or couples. There has been a particular increase in the number of single-parent families over recent decades. Single-parent households now account for 23% of all families, the majority headed by mothers (Coleman & Brooks, 2009).

This change in family structures and family life has become a significant political issue. Many commentators accept that a society based on two-parent couples, marriage, and stability in family relationships is a thing of the past. For others, particularly on the political right, a wide range of social ills are blamed on the demise of "traditional" family life. It should also be noted that poverty is closely linked to family type in Britain, with lone-parent families experiencing much higher levels of economic hardship than couple families (Roker & Coleman, 2000). While the evidence is mixed in relation to outcomes for children of lone-parent families, there are some indicators showing poorer outcomes, as in, for example, higher rates of smoking and lower levels of education attain-ment (Coleman & Hendry, 1999).

A key question in parenting and family relationships in the UK at present concerns the level of responsibility that parents have for their children and young people (Jones, 2005). In many respects, young people are now much freer from parental control than they have been in the past; for example, they can receive confidential advice about their health without parents being told. However, in other respects parents are considered to be responsible for the actions of the children. A good example of this has been the introduction of Parenting Orders. These legal sanctions can be applied to parents by the courts, where children have been involved in offending and antisocial behavior, and/or have not been attending school. When a Parenting Order is imposed on a parent, they are required to receive "guidance and support" in relation to their parenting on a regular basis for a period of up to 12 weeks. The courts can also now impose fines on parents for their child's nonattendance at school.

There is an image in much of the popular press in the UK that most families containing young people are characterized by conflict and disagreement. This is not borne out by research. Clearly, a small proportion of families function in this way, or have times when relationships are difficult and contentious. However, numerous research studies show that there are generally good and positive relationships between parents and their teenage children in the UK In two-parent families it is notable that there are gender differences in this respect, with more young people feeling able to discuss and disclose issues with mothers rather than fathers. A consistent finding from the research is that there are gender differences (among both young people and adults) in family communication (Catan, Dennison, & Coleman, 1996). Girls are able to share more with their parents and seek out parents, especially mothers, as confidantes.

As has also been noted already in this chapter, young people in the UK are now leaving home at an older age compared to previous generations. Thirty years ago, it was not uncommon for young people to move out of the family home at the age of 17 or 18. In the twenty-first century this is very rare, and in 2008, for example, 52% of young males and 37% of young females aged 20 to 24 were living in the family home (Office for National Statistics, 2009). While this represents a considerable change for the UK, it is of note that this figure is still lower than the numbers of young adults living at home in Spain, Italy, and Portugal.

Finally, it is important to mention the experiences of those young people who do not live with their families. There are 60,000 children and young people in England alone who live "in care," that is, they are "parented" by the state. Some of these children and young people spend most of their early life in care, while other do so for a short period of time only. Research has consistently shown that this group has significantly worse outcomes in terms of their rates of educational achievement and health risks (Bradshaw, 2005). There are now a wide range of government and practice initiatives focused on the needs of this group, but the figures (in terms of less positive outcomes) remain worryingly stable.

Friends and Peers/Youth Culture

There are some consistent patterns among children and young people in the UK in relation to friendships and peer relationships. Up until the preadolescent years (age 9 or 10), most children spend time with same-sex peers. Most also spend a considerable amount of time in or near the family home. Once young people start secondary school (at age 11 or 12), there are changes in their social lives and friendships. Most young people start to have more freedom and autonomy in relation to how they spend their time. They also start to spend time in mixed-sex groups, and many enter into relationships.

As in many Western countries, social relationships during adolescence are both positive and negative. It is clear from research that young people come to depend on their friends for support and intimacy as they move into the adolescent years. There are clear gender differences here, with girls more inclined to share emotions and feelings and to talk about relationships with their friends, while boys are more likely to engage in activities, particularly sports, with their friends. However, there are some less positive aspects of friendship. For girls, jealousies and rivalries can become problematic, and feeling excluded from the group or losing a best friend can be a difficult experience to handle, especially in the early years of adolescence. This is less of a problem for boys, primarily because there is less intimacy in their friendship relationships.

The UK has traditionally had an extensive youth service, which funded youth workers and a range of social and educational activities for young people. Since the mid-1990s or so, however, funding for the youth service has been reduced, and the range of such activities is now much less. Increasingly, research has demonstrated the importance of out-of-school provisions for young people's social and emotional development. In addition, "diversionary" activities for children and young people have been shown to be positively correlated with lower rates of crime, antisocial behavior, and risk-taking.

There is no single style of youth dress or culture in the UK. Rather, there are a range of trends and styles, reflecting differing identifications with music, sports, and lifestyles. There is a growing interest among many young people (from a range of backgrounds) in black culture, including in particular language and music (Robinson, 2004). Commercial pressures play a major part in transmitting values and codes of behavior where dress, music, and lifestyle choices are concerned. As with most other Western countries, the UK is also affected by global norms and attitudes, so that what is happening in North America or in Africa can be as important for youth culture as what is happening in London.

Love and Sexuality

In Britain the sexual health of young people is a matter of intense public interest and concern. Much publicity has been given to the fact that Britain has the highest rate of teenage pregnancy in the European Union. In addition, reports show that there are increasing rates of sexually transmitted infections among the population in the UK, with this increase being most notable among those under the age of 21 (Coleman & Brooks, 2009).

The issue of young people's sexuality has been regularly discussed, resulting in the age of consent for gay and lesbian youth being reduced from 18 to 16 years, the same as that for heterosexual young people. However, many gay and lesbian young people continue to experience bullying and discrimination and are at particular risk of mental distress and suicide. There is now a wide range of information and support services specifically aimed at this group and for those who are unsure about their sexuality.

There are many contradictory features of the situation regarding teenage sexuality in Britain. While on one hand it is accepted that young people are becoming sexually active at an earlier age than in previous generations, there is intense debate among politicians, policymakers, and the media about how to regulate this activity. The question of sex education in school has continued to provoke intense controversy, and the subject is still not a mandatory element of the school curriculum. Furthermore, the role of parents in relation to young people's health is a controversial one. There are regular media stories and court cases in which parents say their child has received sexual advice or treatment without their knowing.

While the subject of teenage sexuality is clearly important and controversial, there have been very few good research studies to guide policy in this area. Only one good study of the sexual behavior of those under 16 has been carried out, and this shows that about 40% of 14-year-olds have been involved in various types of sexual exploration, without full intercourse having occurred. Among this age group, 18% of boys and 16% of girls reported that they had engaged in full intercourse

(Henderson, 2002). Other studies have looked at a slightly older group, with the most recent results here reporting that 38% of boys and 31% of girls aged 15 have had sexual intercourse (Currie, 2004).

A key element of the overall picture relating to sexual activity concerns the rate of abortions. Among the 13- to 15-year-olds, 55% of conceptions lead to abortion, while among the 16- to 19-year-olds, only 39% of conceptions lead to abortion. This means that among those aged 15 and below, 45% of conceptions lead to a live birth. The situation is more complicated by the fact that there are marked regional variations as well as variations due to social background. In particular, it is notable that young women from families with professional or managerial backgrounds are much more likely to have an abortion than those from less affluent or less educated backgrounds. It is often said that educational or employment opportunity is the best contraceptive, and this is certainly borne out in the UK (Coleman & Schofield, 2005).

At present one of the worrying features of sexual behavior among young people is the increasing rates of sexually transmitted diseases. All infections have shown rising levels of occurrence, with the most striking increases being seen for chlamydia, gonorrhea, and genital herpes. To give an example, numbers of chlamydia cases being seen in clinics increased among young women from 5,000 per annum in 1995 to 22,000 per annum in 2009 (Coleman & Brooks, 2009). Although rates are lower in young men, there has been a similar proportional increase. There is still no clear explanation of such changes in evidence of risk behavior, but there is no doubt that increasing sexual activity must be one reason. Other factors may include a higher level of public awareness of such conditions and gradually improving health services available to treat them.

Regarding contraception, since the advent of HIV/AIDS in the late 1980s there has been a marked change in attitudes concerning the use of condoms. Condoms have become much more widely available for young people in Britain, and many services provide free condoms for younger and more vulnerable groups. As far as the oral contraceptive is concerned, research shows that 34% of young women under 16 who are sexually active report using the pill, while this figure rises to 51% among those aged between 16 and 19 (Coleman & Schofield, 2005). There has been much debate about what is known as "emergency" contraception, also known as the "morning-after" pill. Many health service professionals believe that such contraception should be available to young people, no matter what their age or status is. However, this is not accepted by all, and as a result the availability of this method of contraception is patchy and determined by locality.

Health Risk Behavior

The UK is a country where the young have high rates of substance misuse and where levels of binge drinking are among the highest in Europe. Looking first at alcohol, there has been much concern over the increased levels of drinking among teenagers. On almost all indices relating to drinking, British teenagers come either at the top or within the three countries having the highest levels of alcohol use. Fifty-two percent of British 15-year-olds report drinking alcohol at least weekly, compared with 40% in Germany and 25% in France (Coleman & Brooks, 2009).

The picture is similar when one looks at illegal substances. The use of particular drugs, such as Ecstasy and crack cocaine, has increased over the past decade, although the use of cannabis has not shown any obvious increase during this period. Approximately 35% of those under the age of 16 have used cannabis during the previous year. If the UK is compared with similar European countries, again young people in England, Scotland, and Wales come close to the top on any criterion assessing the level of drug use (Parker, Aldridge, & Measham, 1998).

What are the reasons for this? It is generally agreed that availability of substances, whether alcohol or illegal drugs, must play a key part here. Many people believe that the UK could do more to restrict the availability of drugs and alcohol. There is also the question of disposable income. All these substances require some form of finance, and one of the conclusions about alcohol is that more disposable income, particularly among vulnerable groups, has led to an increase in alcohol consumption. Lastly, the educational system and the changing nature of the job market may also play a part. Alcohol and substance abuse go hand in hand with deprivation and poor educational and economic opportunities.

Crime among the young is a further cause of public anxiety in Britain. In the media it appears to be a common assumption that offending among adolescents is on the increase, and that this is linked with a generally deteriorating situation for young people. The facts are rather different. The most recent crime statistics, those looking at recorded crime, show that this is going down rather than up. For example, the number of males between the ages of 15 and 17 found guilty of, or cautioned for, a crime in the UK fell from 7,000 cases in 1993 to 4,200 cases in 2008 (Coleman & Brooks, 2009). Similar falls in numbers can be seen among other age groups. The gap between public perception and reality is striking, and no doubt reflects the way in which enduring and powerful stereotypes of young people continue to operate in our society.

Finally, some mention should be made of gender differences in crime. As with most other Western countries, young men account for much more criminal activity than young women. The ratio in Britain is approximately 4:1 in all adolescent groups. There has been some discussion as to whether crime among young women has increased since the mid-1990s or so, but there is little evidence to support this notion. The level of recorded crime among young women has fallen in much the same way as it has for young men.

We can now turn to issues surrounding mental health. Since 1990, in Britain there has been a very high degree of public interest in this subject, especially because the suicide rate for young men showed a marked increase during the 1980s. Looking back, it seems probable that this was closely associated with changing economic circumstances, since Britain, in common with many other European countries, saw a marked deterioration in the job market. Young people were affected by this situation more than other age groups and were exposed to very high levels of unemployment during this period.

Suicide rates, while still far too high, have fallen slowly since 1990. Young men between the ages of 15 and 24 show a suicide rate of 11 per 100,000, down from 19 per 100,000 in 1990 (Coleman & Brooks, 2009). Gender is important here, too. As with other similar countries, young men are four times more likely to take their lives through suicide than young women. However, where attempted suicide is concerned, the gender ratio is reversed. Approximately three times more young women than young men engage in self-poisoning or other forms of self-injury.

Looking now at other forms of mental disorder, research has shown that approximately 10% of young people in the UK can be shown to have a mental health problem. Such problems include depression, anxiety, and conduct disorders. Overall, more males than females appear to have mental disorders; while anxiety and depression are higher among young women, conduct disorders are higher in young men. Those in prison and those looked after by the state are likely to have very much higher levels of mental disorders than the general population.

Education

There are differences in educational structures and practices in the four countries of the UK. However, there are common themes. In general, children attend primary schools from age five until the age of 10 or 11. At that point they transfer to secondary schools. A few parts of the UK have a slightly different system, where children attend middle or junior schools between the ages of seven and 11, prior to going to secondary school.

The vast majority of children and young people attend state-funded primary and secondary schools. Around 8% of those under 16 attend fee-paying private schools. In addition, an increasing number of religious-based schools are being established, for example, for Jewish or Muslim young people. Education is compulsory for both girls/young women and boys/young men, from ages five to 16.

There is a national curriculum for UK schools, specifying a core range of subjects that all children and young people must study. Again, there are differences in educational policies and practices across the four countries. At the age of 16 or 17, all young people take common examinations in a range of subjects. At age 16, most young people take GCSEs. A widely used "marker" of achievement at this point is that a young person has achieved five GCSEs at grades A through C. Approximately 50% of young people achieve this level of passes.

There has been a considerable amount of change in post-16 destinations over the past 25 years. In the 1970s, most young people went into employment at the age of 16. As the world of work and education changed, more young people came to stay on in education at this age. Most young people now stay on in education or training at age 16, undertaking academic or vocational subjects, or a combination of the two. For example, there were 1.7 million young people in higher education in 1970/71 compared with 3.6 million in 2007 (Devitt, Knighton, & Lowe, 2009).

There was also a rapid increase in these years in the number of young people who went on to university at age 18. In total, 44% of young adults were at university at the turn of the century (Coleman, 2000; Graham, 2004). It is of note that the government target in this respect is 50%, but the most recent figures for 2008 show that 46% were in fact attending university (Department of Children, Schools and Families, 2009). Although this increase in numbers at university may be positive in terms of general rates of educational participation, there is a growing level of graduate unemployment in the UK as a result of the recent economic recession.

There has been a longstanding debate about the best way to educate and support young people with disabilities and/or special needs in the UK. An integrationist policy has been pursued since the 1980s, which has aimed to educate the majority of young people, with and without disabilities, in state schools. However, this has been controversial, with some parents (and specialists) claiming that those with special needs should be educated separately from those with more mainstream needs. There has been no resolution to this issue, and in 2005 only those children and young people with very complex needs were educated separately.

Finally, there is an increased interest among practitioners and policymakers in the education of gifted children. Many professionals consider that, within the secondary school system, very able young people are not sufficiently stretched. As a result, a variety of structures have been set up to help support schools in teaching gifted individuals. In particular, the government has set up the National Academy for Gifted and Talented Youth to help develop policies and practices in this area. This is an area of education policy that has received little attention.

Work

While at school, most young people in the UK undertake some sort of part-time work. The types of work undertaken by young people are very broad but include, in particular, work in shops, cafés and restaurants, and the hotel industry (Bradshaw & Mayhew, 2005). There is a debate about the impact on young people of working while at school; some policymakers and practitioners believe that it damages young people's education and progress, while others feel it is an essential preparation for the world of work.

As stated above, hardly any young people now enter full-time employment at age 16, with approximately 50% entering full employment at age 18. Those entering employment at this age tend to continue their training in some way, often undertaking on-the-job training or a day-release to a college. Many young people now do not start work until their early twenties, after attending university. However, it is important to note that rates of graduate unemployment are increasing. In addition, many young people with degrees are working in jobs that do not require their high level of qualifications. This is prompting an ongoing debate about the future for young people in terms of education, training, and employment.

It is notable, also, that the world of work is very different for young people in the twenty-first century compared to that of their parents and grandparents. Few young people now expect to start a particular job, or work in a particular sector, and stay with that for the rest of their working lives. Most young people expect to experience a considerable amount of change and development in their working lives, between different jobs and careers, between part-time and full-time work, and in terms of where in the country they work. Few young people today will have a concept of a "job for life."

There are now a number of apprenticeships and vocational training courses available to young people in the UK. However, the past few years have seen continual debate over the most appropriate way to offer vocational training, and there are at present at least four different options for those leaving school at 16. In 2009 the Government of the day made a commitment to the extension of the school leaving age from 16 to 18 for all young people. This is to be introduced in stages, with 17-year-olds being required to remain in education from 2013, with a similar provision for 18-year-olds by 2015.

There is a minimum wage in the UK. In 2010, it stood at £4.83 per hour for workers aged 18–21, and £3.57 for those of 16 and 17 years of age. Since the inception of the minimum wage, there has been a bitter political debate about the different levels for those aged under and over 21. Despite these arguments, however, having a minimum wage does protect many young people from very low wage levels.

This section has focused so far on information in relation to young people and work. It is also important to note that there is a significant level of unemployment among young people in the UK (Bynner & Parsons, 2002). Figures for 2009, for example, show that 17.3% of 18–24-year-olds were unemployed at this time (Devitt et al., 2009). It is important to note that these figures vary considerably in terms of region and are also two to three times higher for many black and minority ethnic groups.

The significant proportion of young people who are not in education, training, or employment is a key social and political issue in the UK. Figures for England show that in 2008, 185,000 16- to 18-year-olds (8.4% of the age group in England) were not in work, training, or education (Coleman & Brooks, 2009).

Media

There is no doubt that for young people in Britain the media play an important role in a variety of ways. Teenagers watch on average between two and three hours of TV a day, and some watch considerably more. Teenage magazines are widely read, especially by the younger age groups. Many of the things that are important to young people, such as sports, the latest music, styles of clothing, celebrity lifestyles, and information about love, romance, and sexuality are promoted through the media. In addition to this, adolescents are a key market for many large commercial companies, and therefore the media provide an extremely important channel for the advertising of products aimed at the young.

A TV is present in almost every household, and in many homes young people will have their own TV in their bedrooms. Figures show that approximately half of all young people have their own TV set, on which they can watch videos and DVDs as well as a wide variety of TV channels. There has been much debate about censorship and about ways to prevent young people seeing material that is deemed to be harmful. The TV channels operate a "watershed" system, so that what are considered to be "adult" programs are not shown before 9:00 p.m. Whether this works is open to debate, since very few teenagers, even in the early stages of adolescence, will be going to bed before nine o'clock. Videos and DVDs are classified according to their suitability for young people, but again such a system is extremely hard to police, and in practice it is relatively easy for teenagers to watch material that is classified as appropriate for those over 18.

The media can play a positive role, particularly as a channel through which health education material can be communicated to young people. However, commercial pressures are always present, and that means that teenagers are more likely to see sex and violence than sensible messages about drugs or alcohol. The question of regulation is fraught with difficulty, and while in Britain there are a variety of agencies charged with attempting to restrict the impact of adult material on young people, one cannot help but feel that they are fighting a losing battle.

Politics and Military

There is no compulsory military service for young people in the UK. The armed forces are made up of those who apply to join. It is noted that this is a significant source of employment for many young men and young women, who generally join at age 16 or 17. Many join in order to learn a particular trade or craft, such as engineering.

There are some interesting trends to report in terms of young people's engagement in formal politics, such as in terms of political parties and voting behaviors. There is increasing evidence that many young people are uninterested in and disengaged from formal politics (Office for National Statistics, 2002). As an example of this, a fifth of all young people are not registered to vote. Rates of voting in elections are lower for young people, who are eligible to vote from the age of 18, than for any other age group (Eden & Roker, 2002). Only 37% of 18- to 24-year-olds voted in the 2005 general election; this represented the lowest percentage turnout (Devitt et al., 2009). Successive governments have attempted to address the issue of political apathy and disengagement in formal politics among UK youth.

Young people in the UK are more likely to be involved in specialized groups than in conventional politics. There are now a wide range of groups and activities designed to promote environmental issues, and young people are at the heart of these. Organizations such as Friends of the Earth and Greenpeace have large numbers of youth members. In addition, issues around fair trade are a topic of heated debate for many young people. It is notable that during the G8 summits and meetings of the World Bank in 2005, which were characterized by protests around the world, many UK youth walked out of their schools and/or took part in demonstrations. There is clear evidence that relationships between different parts of the world, particularly in terms of food, health, and welfare, are a key issue for many young people today.

There is a long tradition of volunteering by young people in the UK. Research by the authors has shown that much of this is unknown by the general public, and that it has not received widespread publicity, particularly in comparison to publicity regarding antisocial behavior or negative images of youth (Eden & Roker, 2002). The authors' research showed that a wide range of young people are involved in activities that benefit others, including helping out at youth groups and other organizations, and campaigning in relation to the environment or equality issues. For example, in 2003, 64% of young adults polled in the Populus survey revealed that they had at some point signed a petition, 57% had donated to a cause, and nearly 20% had participated in a march or demonstration (Devitt et al., 2009). In addition, more formal volunteering activities are undertaken by young people in the UK, including via youth organizations such as Scouts and Guides, and through campaigning and social action groups.

Unique Issues

In some senses growing up in the UK is much the same as in many other European countries. There is a similar population demographic, similar educational provision, a welfare state, and similar levels of aspiration and life chances for adolescents as they move to adulthood. However, if one takes a more detailed look at the situation in the UK, it becomes apparent that there are some important differences between this country and other countries in Western Europe.

Considering demographic issues first, the UK comprises four different individual countries, and while political relationships between the four are benign, with a degree of devolution experienced by each country, the circumstances for adolescents in each of the countries are somewhat different. Scotland has the greatest degree of political autonomy, with a particularly strong educational sector, excellent universities, and arguably the greatest focus on the health of young people. This is possibly because some of the greatest health inequalities are evident in Scotland, with especially high levels of alcohol and substance misuse. As far as Wales is concerned, this is the most rural of the four countries, with higher levels of unemployment and greater problems of access to services than other countries.

Growing up in Northern Ireland has been dominated by the political tensions and sectarian violence of the past 50 years. Since the Good Friday agreement of 1998, the political situation has stabilized, yet young people are still very much affected by their history and by the divisions between religious groups. Catholic communities in Northern Ireland have been disadvantaged for almost a century, and this inequality has affected all aspects of young people's lives, including health, education, and employment opportunities. Perhaps not surprisingly, evidence shows high levels of mental health problems among adolescents in Northern Ireland, and suicide rates for young men are the highest among the four countries of the UK (Coleman & Brooks, 2009).

Turning now to cross-European comparisons, on a number of indicators it appears that young people in the UK do worse than many of their contemporaries in similar countries. Looking first at poverty, it is striking that in the UK there are a greater proportion of children and young people living in workless households or households below the poverty line than in other European countries. Although comparisons are difficult, using the most commonly accepted definition of household poverty it is the case that the UK does remarkably poorly in this respect. Latest figures show approximately 17% of those under 16 growing up in poverty in the UK (Coleman, 2010).

As far as health is concerned, much is made of the UK's poor record in respect of teenage pregnancy. Again comparisons are difficult, especially as many European countries do not collect data that can be compared with that of the UK. However, from the most recent statistics in the UK, it would appear that the rate of 38 conceptions per 1,000 young women between the ages of 15 and 17 (NHS Information Centre, 2009) is among the highest in Europe. The British Government has made considerable efforts to tackle this problem, with the establishment of the Teenage Pregnancy Unit in London, and it should be noted that the rates have come down steadily since 1998 when the unit was first set up. The figure quoted above is the lowest in the UK for 30 years. This is encouraging news, but there is still a long way to go before the UK has similar teenage pregnancy rates to other European countries. Another worrying trend is that young people in the four UK countries appear to be drinking more, and indulging in binge drinking more, than those in most other countries apart from those in Scandanavia (Currie, Morgan, & Patchett, 2008).

Let us turn now to the educational situation in the UK, and particularly to the situation for those over the age of 16. If comparisons are drawn between Great Britain and other European countries, two salient facts become apparent. First, Britain has among the lowest numbers of young people between the ages of 16 and 18 in full-time education. This is because in most European countries the school-leaving age is 18, as it is in the USA. However this is not the case in the UK, although the Government has signalled its intention to raise the school-leaving age to 18 by 2015. Currently the UK has approximately 70% of this age group in some form of education or training, significantly lower than most other European countries (Coleman & Brooks, 2009). On the other hand, when we turn to higher education, Britain has among the highest number of young adults between the ages of 18 and 24 at university or technical college. Current figures show 46% of this age group to be in higher education, significantly higher than in other countries. Tony Blair, Prime Minister from 1997 to 2008, famously promised to get 50% of the age group to university by 2020, but today this looks like a promise that is unlikely to be fulfilled (Coleman, 2010).

Finally a word should be said about ethnicity and the cultural context of adolescence in the UK. While all European countries have experienced considerable immigration in recent decades, each country has a unique blend of circumstances to which it has to adapt. Thus France has had immigration from North Africa, Germany from the Middle East, and for Britain the major flow of immigration has been from the Caribbean and from South Asia. This has created a range of special circumstances for young people growing up in the UK, with the particular mix of talents and capabilities of these cultures in such fields as music and sport blending in to the indigenous culture. This has led to a particularly rich multicultural environment for adolescents in the UK today.

References and Further Reading

Bhattacharyya, G., & Gabriel, J. (2004). Racial formations of youth in late twentieth century England. In J. Roche et al. (Eds.), *Youth in society*. London, UK: Sage/Open University.

Bradshaw, J., & Mayhew, E. (Eds.). 2005. *The well-being of children in the U.K.* London, UK: Save the Children.

Bynner, J., & Joshi, H. (2002). Equality and opportunity in education: Evidence from the 1958 and 1970 birth cohort studies. *Oxford Review of Education*, 28, 405–425.

Bynner, J., & Parsons, S. (2002). Social exclusion and the transition from school to work: The case of young people not in education, employment or training. *Journal of Vocational Behaviour*, 60, 289–309.

Catan, L., Dennison, C., & Coleman, J. (1996). *Getting through: Effective communication in the teenage years*. London, UK: BT Forum.

Coleman, J. (2000). Young people in Britain at the beginning of a new century. *Children and Society, 14*, 230–242.

Coleman, J. (2010) *The nature of adolescence* (4th ed.). London, UK: Routledge.

Coleman, J., & Brooks, F. (2009) *Key data on adolescence* (7th ed.). Brighton, UK: Young People in Focus.

Coleman, J., & Cater, S. (2005). *Underage "risky" drinking: Motivations and outcomes*. York, UK: Joseph Rowntree Foundation.

Coleman, J., & Hendry, L. (1999). *The nature of adolescence* (3rd ed.). London, UK: Routledge.

Coleman, J., & Roker, D. (1998). Adolescence: A review. *Psychologist, 11*, 593–596.

Coleman, J., & Roker, D. (2001). *Supporting the parents of teenagers: A handbook for professionals*. London, UK: Jessica Kingsley.

Currie, C. (Ed.). (2004). *Health behaviour in school-age children study: International report from the 2001/2002 survey*. Geneva, Switzerland: World Health Organization.

Currie, C., Morgan, D., & Patchett, R. (2008). *Health behaviour in school-aged children: international report from the WHO*. Edinburgh, UK: Centre for Adolescent Health Research, University of Edinburgh.

Department of Children, Schools and Families. (2009). *NEET Statistics Quarterly Briefing*. London, UK: HM Government.

Devitt, K., Knighton, L., & Lowe, K. (2009). *Young adults today*. Brighton, UK. Young People in Focus.

Eden, K., & Roker, D. (2002). *Youth and social action in the UK*. Leicester, UK: Youth Work Press.

Garratt, D. (2004). Youth cultures and sub-cultures. In J. Roche & S. Tucker (Eds.), *Youth in society* (2nd ed.), London, UK: Sage/Open University.

Graham, P. (2004). *The end of adolescence*. Oxford, UK: Oxford University Press.

Green, H., Green, H., McGinnity, A., Meltzer, H., Ford, T., & Goodman, R. (2005). *Mental health of children and young people in Britain, 2004*. London, UK: Office for National Statistics.

Helve, H., & Wallace, C. (Eds.). (2001). *Youth, citizenship, and empowerment*. Aldershot, UK: Ashgate.

Henderson, M., et al. (2002). Heterosexual risk behaviour among young people in Scotland. *Journal of Adolescence, 25*, 483–494.

Jones, G. (2005). *Young adults and the extension of economic dependence in youth*. London, UK: National Family and Parenting Institute.

Neale, J. (2005). Children, crime, and illegal drug use. In J. Bradshaw & E Mayhew (Eds.), *The well-being of children in the UK. London*. London, UK: Save the Children.

NHS Information Centre (2009). *Sexual health statistics for the UK – 2008/2009*. London, UK: National Health Information Centre, Department of Health,.

Office for National Statistics. (2002). *Social trends*. London, UK: HMSO.

Office for National Statistics. (2008). *General Lifestyle Survey*. London, UK: HMSO.

Office for National Statistics. (2009). *Social trends*, No. 39. London, UK: HMSO.

Parker, H., Aldridge, J., & Measham, F. (1998). *Illegal leisure: The normalization of adolescent recreational drug use*. London, UK: Routledge.

Robinson, L. (2004). Black adolescent identity. In J. Roche & S. Tucker (Eds.), *Youth in society* (2nd ed.). London, UK: Sage/Open University.

Roche, J., & Tucker, S. (Eds.). (2004). *Youth in society* (2nd ed.). London, UK: Sage/Open University.

Rogers, W., Rogers, R., Vyrost, J., & Lovas, L. (2004). Worlds apart: Young people's aspirations in a changing Europe. In J. Roche & S. Tucker (Eds.), *Youth in society* (2nd ed.). London, UK: Sage/Open University Press.

Roker, D., & Coleman, J. (2000). The invisible poor: Young people growing up in family poverty. In. J. Bradshaw & D. Sainsbury (Eds.), *Experiencing poverty*. Andover, UK: Ashgate.

Roker, D., Player, K., & Coleman, J. (1999). Participation in voluntary and campaigning activities as sources of political education. *Oxford Review of Education, 25*, 185–198.

Schoon, I., & Bynner, J. (2003). Risk and resilience in the life course: Implications for interventions and social policy. *Journal of Youth Studies, 6*, 1–31.

Stace, S., & Roker, D. (2005). *Monitoring and supervision in "ordinary" families*. London, UK: National Children's Bureau.

Tanner, J. (1978). *From foetus into man*. London, UK: Open Books Publishing.

Wilkinson, H., & Mulgan, G. (1995). *Freedom's children: Work, relationships and politics for 18–34 year olds in Britain today*. London, UK: Demos.

Author index

Subject index

subcultures in, 249
unique issues in, 254–255
Velvet Revolution in, 243
work in, 252–253
xenophobia in, 247–248, 251
youth culture in, 247–249
Czechoslovakia, 243

D

Dafur, Sudan, 74, 78, 83
Dance
  in Argentina, 155–156
  in Cameroon, 5–6, 8
  in India, 105
  in Mexico, 196
  in the Netherlands, 312
  in Nigeria, 65
  in Peru, 212, 218, 221
  in Sweden, 340
Dangdut (Indonesian music), 126
Dating
  in Argentina, 156
  in Germany, 279
  in Indonesia, 126
  in Mexico, 198, 200
  in the Philippines, 138–139
  public, 20, 49
  taboo, 53
  in the USA, 229
Daughters, unmarried, 108
Death, 7, 104, 134, 143, 166, 327
  adolescent, 110, 142, 171–172, 202, 230,
    264, 281
  causes of, 142, 299, 328, 341
  in conflicts, 25, 74
  rites, 5, 105, 121
Delhi, India, 110, 112
Delinquency
  in Cameroon, 10–11
  in Canada, 168–169, 172
  in China, 94
  in the Czech Republic, 251
  in Italy, 299
  in Morocco, 54
  in Peru, 219
  in the USA, 227
Democracy
  in Argentina, 160–161
  in Cameroon, 3
  in Canada, 165

in Chile, 181–183, 189
in the Czech Republic, 243, 246, 250
in France, 257, 267
in Germany, 285
in Indonesia, 121, 129
in Israel, 29
in Italy, 291
in Mexico, 195, 205
in Nigeria, 62, 69
in Peru, 211, 221
in Russia, 321
in the UK, 353
Depression
  in Cameroon, 10
  in Canada, 172
  in China, 95, 98
  in the Czech Republic, 251
  in Ethiopia, 21
  in France, 265
  in Germany, 281
  in Italy, 299
  in the Netherlands, 313–314
  in Russia, 331–332
  in the UK, 361
  in the USA, 230, 232
Deviant behaviors, in Ethiopia, 21
Dinka group, Sudan, 73, 74, 76–77
Discotheques, 52, 127, 216–217, 296, 299, 301
Discrimination
  in Argentina, 155
  in Canada, 174
  in Chile, 189
  in China, 98
  condemnation of, 189
  in the Czech Republic, 247–248
  in Ethiopia, 17
  due to gender, 17, 106, 123, 337
  illegal, 155
  in India, 106
  in Indonesia, 123, 130
  in Israel, 34
  due to race, 130, 174, 225, 247, 357
  due to sexual orientation, 34, 341, 359
  due to social class, 98, 155, 247
  in Sweden, 337, 341
  in the UK, 357, 359
  in the USA, 225
Disease
  in China, 87
  in India, 104, 110
  in the Philippines, 142